UNDERSTANDING EDUCATIONAL RESEARCH

AN INTRODUCTION

FOURTH EDITION

DEOBOLD B. VAN DALEN, Ph.D.
University of California, Berkeley

D0068880

McGRAW-HILL BOOK COMPANY

New York St. Louis San Francisco Auckland Bogotá Düsseldorf
Johannesburg London Madrid Mexico Montreal New Delhi
Panama Paris São Paulo Singapore Sydney Tokyo Toronto

This book was set in Melior by Black Dot, Inc. (ECU).
The editors were Eric M. Munson and James R. Belser;
the designer was Joan E. O'Connor;
the production supervisor was Dominick Petrellese.
New drawings were done by Fine Line Illustrations, Inc.
Fairfield Graphics was printer and binder.

UNDERSTANDING EDUCATIONAL RESEARCH: AN INTRODUCTION

1 2 3 4 5 6 7 8 9 0 F G R F G R 7 8 3 2 1 0 9 8

Library of Congress Cataloging in Publication Data

Van Dalen, Deobold B., date
  Understanding educational research.

  Bibliography: p.
  Includes indexes.
  1. Educational research. I. Title.
LB1028.V3 1978   370'.78   78-9077
ISBN 0-07-066883-3

CONTENTS

PREFACE

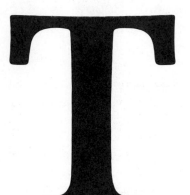he objective of this book is to help students understand the research process and to imbue them with a respect for the scientific spirit of inquiry. The discussion is designed to make readers appreciate the complexity of social phenomena, the difficulties investigators encounter, and the importance of promoting sound research projects. The text strives to encourage and enable teachers to locate, read, and evaluate research reports in their field. Perhaps this volume will give some of them the confidence and impetus to undertake modest investigations, to broaden and deepen their knowledge in this field, and eventually to prepare themselves for professional research work.

In this text the viewpoint of the readers who are approaching the systematic study of research for the first time is constantly kept in mind. To aid the students who have a limited background in psychology, logic, and mathematics, the text links scientific terminology and tactics to their everyday experiences. Through illustrations of commonplace activities in classroom and life situations, the text explores techniques that people have devised to solve problems. With a minimum of technical jargon and some carefully constructed stepping-stones of understanding, the text introduces students to the psychological and logical foundations of scientific investigation. Readers gradually become acquainted with the goals, basic assumptions, limitations, and language of scientists—(with the way researchers talk and how their minds work in getting results.) The text imparts what James Conant calls for in *Science and Common Sense*: some knowledge of "tactics and strategy" and of "what science can and cannot accomplish."

The text then gives some insight into how scholars tackle investigations; how they locate problems; the methods, procedures, and tools that they employ; the general sequence of events that occurs during an investigation; the skills and kinds of knowledge required to undertake various types or studies; the library and research tools that are available; and the study habits and attitudes that are conducive to fruitful work.

The reader has the right to know what changes the author has made in the revision of the book. The general format and purpose of the book remain the same as in the earlier editions, but some changes have been made in the organization of the text and some content has been selectively omitted or extensively revised to permit the introduction of new content. Many of these changes have been made in response to the suggestions and criticisms of students and professors who have corresponded with the publisher and the author about these matters.

Items of reorganization worthy of mention include the reordering of the experimental, descriptive, and historical research chapters and moving the chapter on tools of research to Chapter 6 in this edition. The major addition to the text is the new chapter on the nature of measurement, which defines measurement and gives a simple explanation of the function, analysis, and the fallibility of measurement and an intensive treatment of nominal, ordinal, interval, and ratio scales. Other additions or revisions include: ethics of conducting research (formerly in Chapter 10 now expanded in Chapter 2); causal-comparative and path-analysis research (Chapter 10); the expanded discussion of reliability and the inclusion of cumulative and sematic differential scales and Q-sort technique (Chapter 6); constitutive definitions and their relation to theory (Chapter 7); updating and incorporating new documentary source materials (Chapter 4); and a discussion on the life of facts (Chapter 3).

To help the reader surmount the inherent difficulties of some topics, the author has introduced new figures, tables, hypothetical examples, and examples taken from published research. The author also made an effort to avoid a sexist vocabulary without resorting to awkward constructions or sacrificing the clarity of the discussion.

The production of the text is not an individual enterprise. The author is indebted to many other individuals whose names appear in the bibliography and to the publishers who generously gave permission to quote or use materials from their publications. I am deeply grateful to my wife, Marcella, whose numerous contributions are significant. She, as in the past, has contributed equally to all phases of the revision— from the collection of the materials, to the rewriting of the content, to the typing of the manuscript. Without her efforts, this work would be far less perfect.

As you know, introduction-to-research texts have a high mortality rate; few of them survive to a second edition. Obviously, I am deeply grateful to the many professors who have adopted this text over the past seventeen years as suitable for their classes. I hope that this fourth edition will be as well received as its predecessors.

Deobold B. Van Dalen

1 METHODS OF ACQUIRING KNOWLEDGE

Knowledge, broadly speaking, consists of facts and theories that enable one to understand phenomena and to solve problems. Knowledge can be obtained from direct personal experience or from many secondhand sources that inundate us constantly with rival claims of useful information. Knowledge claims—facts, generalizations, hypotheses, theories—may range from those that are highly reliable to those that are completely unreliable. The flickering motion pictures recorded on our consciousness may trick us into making inaccurate observations of phenomena. The secondhand authority upon whom we rely for information may not know what he or she is talking about. To be certified as reliable, knowledge must pass successfully certain tests: it must be supported by facts—observable evidence. What evidence is required? How much evidence is required? At what point does one really know one knows? The degree of reliability required of knowledge depends on the use that is to be made of it.

Scientists have developed exacting methods of observation and specific criteria for validating facts and theories. Moreover, they have not merely discovered knowledge, presented supporting evidence, and stored it forevermore in a knowledge warehouse. Our scientists' work is never done. The discovery of new evidence, the imaginative reordering of old evidence, and the intellectual insights of gifted investigators have repeatedly upset the knowledge warehouse. Acquiring reliable knowledge is not a one-shot, finished business; it is a complex, challenging, continuous adventure.

We are all somewhat scientific in nature; we are curious, exploratory animals who want to understand our environment and to solve problems. In many instances, however, acting without accurate knowledge does not deeply disturb us. We accept alleged knowledge without testing it, settle for ad hoc solutions, improvise something that works in the immediate situation even though in the long run the consequences may be undesirable. Indeed, we may not only refrain from exerting the self-discipline to obtain reliable knowledge ourselves but also may ruthlessly repress others who construct theories or develop inventions that would make us change our behavior or beliefs. The adventure of coping with new ideas and adopting new life-styles may excite us or frighten us. Not uncommonly, we fear change. We fear that it may adversely affect our economic or social status, may require us to reeducate ourselves, or may force us to alter our customary life patterns. We feel safer sticking with the status quo. The acquisition and expansion of reliable knowledge is not an automatic, self-perpetuating process. It rests on our willingness to develop critical thinking skills and the moral fiber necessary to accept change as a constant.

Centuries of effort were required for our predecessors to improve their capacity and readiness to obtain reliable knowledge. To gain some insight into the tortuous pathway they traversed, the following discussion briefly examines various sources of knowledge they have drawn upon to solve problems: (1) authority, (2) personal experience, (3) deductive reasoning, (4) inductive reasoning, and (5) the scientific method.

OLDER METHODS OF ACQUIRING KNOWLEDGE

When their habitual method of dealing with situations produced discouraging results, our predecessors resorted to crude trial-and-error methods of seeking solutions. Through considerable experience with problem solving, they were gradually able to refine their knowledge-seeking methods. Periods of complacency and retardation periodically halted cultural progress, but exciting leaps forward also occurred, and the long-term trend was characterized by an extension of knowledge.

Authority

Seeking and accepting the explanations of authorities were a well-established method of solving problems encountered in the environment in the earliest civilizations. Today we also often turn to authorities for explanations of phenomena. In many instances, we do not evaluate the truth or falsity of our beliefs any more than our forefathers did.

TRADITION   In any society, a member unconsciously or unquestioningly accepts many traditions of his culture, such as the customary modes of dress, speech, food, worship, and etiquette. In the world of practical affairs this automatic acceptance of approved patterns of behavior is often necessary, for one cannot question *all* things. But one should not make the mistake of assuming that everything that has customarily been done is right or that an appeal to the accumulated wisdom of the ages will always lead to the truth.

Historical records reveal that our predecessors not only solved many problems and accumulated much wisdom but also formulated many erroneous explantions of phenomena. Many long-revered educational, medical, and scientific theories have been proved false. For instance, people once believed that children differed from adults only in size and dignity, that asafetida bags warded off disease, and that the planets revolved around the earth. Truth is not a guaranteed product of a popularity contest: a statement is not true merely because "everyone knows it" or "everybody has always believed it." Age, alone, is not sufficient to establish the truth or falsity of a belief.

CHURCH, STATE, AND ANCIENT SCHOLARS   Preliterate man turned to tribal leaders when seeking knowledge. When floods, famine, lightning, or leprosy terrified them, they blindly accepted the ancestral explanations that their elders imparted. In medieval times, people believed that ancient scholars and churchmen had discovered the truth for all time and that their pronouncements could not be questioned. The Scholastics, for example, accepted Aristotle's conjecture that women have more teeth than men as absolutely true, even though simple observation and enumeration would have provided evidence to the contrary. When invited by Galileo to view the newly discovered moons of Jupiter, one scholar refused to look through the telescope. He was convinced that the moons could not possibly be seen because Aristotle had not mentioned them in his discussions on astronomy. Like most scholars of that era, the man who declined Galileo's invitation clung blindly to faulty Grecian theories and attacked any new idea that contradicted the accepted authorities. With the rise of strong secular states, after the Middle Ages, man began to turn to kings, legislatures, and courts as sources of information. Today, many citizens also expect government officials and legal authorities to solve problems for them.

People often prefer to rely on the judgment of outstanding authorities whose beliefs have withstood the test of time, because they fear that if they themselves searched for answers to difficult questions, they might make errors. But if they can make errors when searching for knowledge, their ancestors must have been subject to the same weakness. If tradition, the church, and the state are to be the source of all reliable information, what happens when these institutions render opinions that conflict with one another? The authorities in different churches and states do not always agree, and traditions of cultures vary. People may encounter perplexing problems when they turn to the multiplicity of existing authorities in a search for answers to their questions. Ignoring the cultural cumulations of the centuries is imprudent, for little progress will occur if each generation rejects the judgment of the ages and starts from scratch to accumulate knowledge. On the other hand, refusing ever to question any accepted belief—total reliance on dogmatic authority—will result in social stagnation.

EXPERT OPINION   Rather than attempting to determine truth independently, people often seek the advice of experts who, because of their intellect, training, experience, or aptitudes, are better informed than other people. A trial lawyer may ask a psychiatrist to testify concerning the sanity of the defendant, a ballistics expert to give opinions concerning weapons, and a handwriting expert to compare signatures. Experts are necessary in a complicated culture such as ours. An effort must be made, however, to find out whether the experts are recognized by other authorities in the field and whether they are in a position to know the facts about the particular problem under consideration. One should check not only the credentials of experts but also the arguments and evidence upon which they base their claims to knowledge.

Accepting experts' opinions unconditionally and for all time is a dubious if not a dangerous practice.

Personal Experience

When confronted with a problem, people often try to recall or to seek a personal experience that will help them reach a solution. When searching for food, ancient nomads probably remembered that certain berries always made them ill, that fish were more plentiful in some streams than others, and that grains ripened at particular times of the year. When trying to determine the quickest route to work, modern man may time himself on different roads. When given a handful of coins to divide with his brother, a small boy may recall that selecting the biggest piece of candy on a plate is usually a wise choice; because of his previous experience with candy, he may decide to keep the big nickels and give his brother the little dimes.

Appealing to personal experiences is a useful and common method of seeking knowledge. An uncritical use of personal experience, however, may lead to incorrect conclusions, as the boy who selected the nickels with his "candy measuring stick" discovered. People may make errors when observing or when reporting what they have seen or done. They may (1) omit evidence that does not agree with their opinion, (2) use measuring instruments that require many subjective estimates, (3) establish a belief on insufficient evidence, (4) fail to observe significant factors relating to a specific situation, or (5) draw improper conclusions or inferences owing to personal prejudices. To avoid dangerous pitfalls, modern research workers exercise many precautions when they turn to experience in their search for reliable knowledge.

Deduction

To obtain more reliable knowledge, Aristotle developed the *syllogism*, a deductive argument which provides a means of testing the validity of a particular conclusion. A syllogism consists of three statements or propositions. The first two statements are called *premises*, since they furnish the evidence or grounds for the *conclusion*, which is the statement standing last. Aristotle defined the syllogism as "a discourse in which certain things being posited, something else than what is posited necessarily follows from them." The categorical syllogism analyzed below is an example of such a discourse. Note that if the premises "all mammals are mortal" and "all men are mammals" are true, then we must conclude that "all men are mortal."

(Major premise)	All mammals are mortal. (middle) M (major) P	If all M are P, and
(Minor premise)	All men are mammals. (minor) S (middle) M	all S are M, then
(Conclusion)	All men are mortal. (minor) S (major) P	all S are P.

A valid syllogism contains terms referring to three and only three classes[1] of things. In the above argument the classes are mortals, mammals, and men. Each statement in the *categorical syllogism* contains two terms. Each term appears twice in the syllogism. The subject term S of the conclusion (men), which is called the *minor term,* also appears in the minor premise. (See above.) The predicate term P of the conclusion (mortal), which is known as the *major term,* is also found in the major premise. The third or middle term M (mammals) occurs once in each premise and *does not* appear in the conclusion. The function of the middle term is to establish the relationship between the minor term and major term which is asserted in the conclusion.

In the argument above, "mammals" is the middle term, or mediating factor, which brings the minor term "men" in the conclusion into the asserted relation with the major term "mortal." The function of the middle term will become clearer if you examine Figure 1.1 as you read the following review of the argument. If the class of mammals M is included in the large class of mortals P as the major premise stipulates, and the class of men S is included in the class of mammals M as the minor premise stipulates, then it follows logically that the class of men S is included in the class of mortals P. Thus, this argument is valid, for the premises are related to the conclusion in such a way that the conclusion must be true if the premises are true. If readers accept the premises, they must agree to the conclusion that follows, because the conclusion merely states explicitly or reformulates information which is already implicit in the premises.

---

[1] A logical class is a collection of particulars—things, persons, qualities—which are all alike in some defining respect. Consequently, one can infer with confidence knowledge about members of the class from knowledge of the class. Whatever can be asserted or denied of a whole class can be asserted or denied of any member of that class.

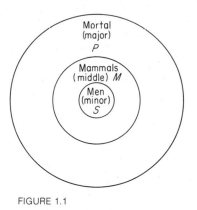

FIGURE 1.1

A schematic representation of a valid argument.

A syllogism does not have to be composed exclusively of categorical statements. As the examples below reveal, arguments may involve *hypothetical, alternative,* or *disjunctive* propositions.

Hypothetical.
If the school is on fire, then the children are in danger.
The school is on fire.
Therefore, the children are in danger.

Alternative.
Either I will get a passing mark on this test, or I will flunk the course.
I will not get a passing mark on this test.
Therefore, I will flunk the course.

Disjunctive.
It is not the case that it is both a rainy day and a good day to present the school pageant outdoors.
It is a rainy day.
Therefore, it is not a good day to present the school pageant outdoors.

As you note in the examples, each syllogism is labeled according to the type of proposition occurring in the major premise. Each type of syllogism is used in different stages of assurance concerning knowledge. Let us examine when the various types of syllogisms are used.

Categorical propositions represent a certain settled stage of our knowledge, and conclusions validly drawn from categorical syllogisms are unconditional. Hypothetical or conditional propositions, however, represent an unsettled stage in thinking and knowing. Hypothetical thinking proceeds on various levels, from the solution of simple problems of daily life, and the detection of crime, to the technique of identification and classification in science, and the search after scientific laws by means of the statement and testing of hypotheses. Likewise alternative arguments represent an unsettled state of knowledge, but within limits; the alternative often being quite well within the possibility of progressive elimination or verification. The disjunctive syllogism is a combination of knowledge and ignorance, like the alternative, but is an advance upon the alternative in the direction of more definite knowledge, and reaches a conclusion by means of what is known and can be asserted in the minor premise [91:114–115].[2]

In personal and professional life, you use deductive reasoning when solving problems. The lawyer, doctor, soldier, and detective often resort to deductive argument. In investigating a murder case, a prosecuting attorney may search through piles of evidence—existing knowledge—select previously unconnected facts, and combine them in such a way that they logically imply a hitherto unsuspected conclusion. Deductive reasoning enables an attorney to organize premises into patterns that provide conclusive evidence for the validity of a particular conclusion.

Modern research workers also utilize deductive reasoning to carry out certain phases of their work. Some people scoff at the role of reason in research and contend that investigators are concerned only with facts they can obtain through observation and experiment. But collecting facts is not sufficient. Without deduction "most of our preoccupation with facts would be fruitless, since we could not fit them into the increasingly deductive systems which we call sciences. The latter are man's most economical instruments" (65:113). Scientists frequently try to pigeonhole a particular instance under an already established principle from which the instance can be deduced. Through the use of the tools of deduction, they hypothetically manipulate and explore possibilities that may open up new areas of inquiry.

In daily discourse many assertions are deductive in nature and may be logically correct without appearing in a syllogistic form. Outside of logic texts one rarely finds arguments set off in the middle of the page and explicitly labeled. The premises may or may not precede the conclusion, and some premises may be missing. The conclusion may come first, last, or even in the middle of the argument. One must be

[2]Numbers in brackets refer to the numbered bibliography on pages 531–537.

able to recognize arguments that appear in prose or discourse; locate the premises and conclusion; supply the missing premises, if necessary; restate the argument in a complete and explicit form; and then apply logical standards to determine whether the argument is logically correct or fallacious.

When analyzing a deductive argument, one must pay close attention to language. Words may have more than one meaning; consequently, language may play tricks that lead thinking astray. A syllogistic argument is not valid unless each term is used in the same sense throughout the argument. A shift in the meaning of any term leads to an error in reasoning. Examine the following syllogism:

Only man can talk.
No woman is a man.
All women cannot talk.

The above argument would be valid if the term "man" had the same meaning in each premise; but in the major premise the term "man" means "human being," and in the minor premise it means "human male." Since the meaning of the middle term "man" has been changed during the course of the argument, there is no mediating term which links the two premises together so that they yield a logical conclusion.

The categorical syllogism has severe limitations. The content of the conclusion of the syllogism cannot exceed the content of the premises. A categorical syllogism deduces the consequences of preexisting knowledge; it does not enable scholars to gain new knowledge or to make new discoveries. A second weakness of deductive reasoning lies in the possibility that one or more of the premises are not materially true. When the validity of a deductive argument is checked, questions are raised not about the content (truth or falsity) of the statements but about the forms of the arguments. One asks: Are these premises related to the conclusion in such a way that a person cannot accept the premises and reject the conclusion? The formal reasoning in an argument may be sound even if the argument is based on false premises. Consider the following as an example:

All professors of education hold doctoral degrees.
All men in this meeting are professors of education.
Hence, all men in this meeting hold doctoral degrees.

The conclusion "all men in this meeting hold doctoral degrees" is valid, for it necessarily follows from the premises given. But the conclusion is not true in fact, for some professors in the meeting hold only master's degrees. In this instance the major premise was not true in fact. The conclusion reached by a deductive argument produces reliable knowledge only if it is deduced from true premises and the premises are properly related to the conclusion. Deductive logic, therefore, cannot be relied upon exclusively in searching for the truth, because it is not a self-sufficient means of securing dependable knowledge.

Induction

If the conclusions reached by deductive reasoning are true only if derived from true premises, some way must be found of determining whether the premises are true. Consequently, inductive reasoning has been devised to complement deductive reasoning as a means of searching for knowledge. In inductive reasoning, an inquiry is initiated by observing particular instances (concrete facts). From an examination of these facts, a general conclusion is established about the whole class to which these particular instances belong. General conclusions that are arrived at through induction may be used as major premises for deductive inferences.

PERFECT INDUCTION   One form of induction is complete enumeration. In this form of induction, one simply counts *all* the instances in a given class and announces the results in a general conclusion. In other words, a conclusion about all instances of a class is drawn from premises which refer to the observed instances of the class. For example, to determine the occupations of the members of a club, one questions each member, tabulates the results, and announces the conclusion: All twenty-five members of this club are teachers. Perfect induction obtains reliable information. But how often does one have an opportunity to examine all the instances to which a conclusion refers? This type of enumeration cannot be employed as a method of investigation in the solution of most problems.

IMPERFECT INDUCTION   Whereas perfect induction establishes a conclusion by an exhaustive enumeration of all instances that are subsumable under it, imperfect induction arrives at a generalization by observing only *some* instances that make up the class. The research worker utilizes imperfect induction more often than perfect induction, for in most investigations it is not possible to examine all the instances to which a conclusion refers. From observing some instances, however, one can draw a general conclusion regarding all similar instances, some of which one has not observed.

When examining all the instances of a class under consideration is not practical, one does the next best thing: arrive at a generalization by observing an adequate and representative sample from the entire class. To check on the purity of the water in a swimming pool, for instance, a health officer may take a single sample of water, test it, and draw a conclusion about the purity of the water in the entire swimming pool. Perhaps on the same day, a restaurant owner purchases 500 steaks. To ascertain whether they are of choice quality without examining each steak, the owner selects at random a few steaks and finds that they are choice grade. From these selective observations the owner draws the conclusion that all the steaks are probably of choice quality.

Drawing an inference about a whole class of things after sampling a few of its members does not necessarily yield absolutely certain knowledge. The size and representativeness of the instances observed determine whether one arrives at a sound conclusion. If the material observed is homogeneous, one or a few samples may be adequate for arriving at a reliable generalization. If the material is not homogeneous, the same number of samples probably will yield a less reliable generalization. The conclusion drawn from one sample of water, for example, may be more satisfactory than one drawn from several samples of steak. Previous knowledge of the composition of water gives the health officer greater assurance (that all the water in the pool is like the small sample) than the restaurant owner can expect from a larger number of instances taken from cattle of different breeds and environments.

Both deductive and inductive arguments have advantages and disadvantages. A deductive argument does not guarantee that the conclusion is true, but if the two premises are true, the deductive argument arrives at a conclusion that is necessarily true. The conclusion of the deductive argument, however, does not probe beyond that which is already known—already present, at least implicitly, in the premises. In an imperfect inductive argument, the conclusion does contain information that is not present, even implicitly, in one of the premises (the observed instances). This type of argument is absolutely necessary if scholars are to extend knowledge. Through imperfect induction, however, an investigator merely arrives at conclusions of varying degrees of probability. If all the premises (observed instances) are true, the conclusion is probably but not necessarily true. The possibility always exists that some unexamined instance of the class does not agree with the conclusion. To summarize, the inductive argument expands the content of the premises at the expense of achieving absolutely certain knowledge; the deductive argument arrives at absolutely certain knowledge (if the premises are true) by sacrificing any expansion of the content (88:15).

MODERN METHOD OF ACQUIRING KNOWLEDGE

Francis Bacon (1561–1626) planted the seeds of the modern scientific method of acquiring knowledge when he attacked the medieval practice of deducing conclusions from self-evident or authoritative premises. He held that investigators should not enslave themselves to the thoughts of ancient authorities and recommended that they reach conclusions on the basis of observed facts. But the exhaustive system Bacon recommended for searching for facts, without any principle—hypothesis—to determine what was relevant or irrelevant did not win many converts. To construct a more practical method of attaining reliable knowledge, such men as Newton, Galileo, and their successors eventually combined the inductive and the deductive thought processes. This synthesis of reason and observation produced the modern scientific method of research.

Steps in the Scientific Method

In the scientific method, purposeful fact gathering replaces unsystematic fact gathering, and premises are tested probabilities rather than assumed truths. When using the scientific method, one shuttles back and forth between deduction and induction; one engages in reflective thinking. In 1910, John Dewey in *How We Think* analyzed the stages of activity involved in the act of reflective thinking. The following discussion distinguishes five stages in the act of problem solving:

1   A felt difficulty.
    One encounters a puzzling obstacle, experience, or problem.
    a.   One lacks the *means* to get to the *end* desired.
    b.   One has difficulty in identifying the character of an object.
    c.   One cannot explain an unexpected event.

2 Location and definition of the difficulty.
   One makes observations—gathers facts—to define the difficulty more precisely.
3 Suggested solutions of the problem—hypotheses.
   After a preliminary study of the facts one makes intelligent guesses about possible solutions of the problem. The conjectural statements—generalizations one offers to explain the facts that are causing the difficulty—are called hypotheses.
4 Deductively reasoning out the consequences of the suggested solutions.
   One deductively reasons that if each hypothesis is true, certain consequences should follow.
5 Testing the hypotheses by action.
   One tests each hypothesis by searching for observable evidence that will confirm whether or not the consequences that should follow actually occur. By this process, one finds out which hypothesis is in harmony with observable facts and thus offers the most reliable solution to the problem.

These steps in the act of reflective thinking reveal how induction and deduction serve as opposing blades of the scientific shears that cut out segments of truth. "Induction provides the groundwork for hypotheses, and deduction explores the logical consequences of the hypotheses, in order to eliminate those that are inconsistent with the facts, while induction again contributes to the verification of the remaining hypothesis" (91:4). In an investigation, one continually shifts among collecting facts, making generalizations (hypotheses) to explain facts, deducing the consequences of one's hypotheses, and seeking additional facts to test the hypotheses. By employing both induction and deduction, one is able to arrive at reliable knowledge.

The scientific method of thinking presented above gives an insight into the procedures that are involved in conducting an investigation. Listing these steps separately and distinctly, however, may give an inaccurate impression of the research process. These steps do not provide a rigid pattern into which scientists must force their thinking, for thinking simply cannot be scheduled. Investigators rarely follow a prescribed sequence of procedures. Research is often a confused, floundering process rather than a logical, orderly one. In an investigation, one does not tackle one step at a time, complete that process, and then move on to the next step. One may tackle the steps out of order, shuffle back and forth between steps, or work on two steps more or less simultaneously. Some steps may require little effort; other steps may absorb a disproportionate amount of time and effort. When research findings are reported to the scientific community, however, they are presented in a precise and logically arranged form which closely parallels the steps of the scientific method listed above.

Illustration of the Scientific Method

The five steps or processes in reflective thinking will be discussed in greater detail in later chapters. For the time being, the following homely illustration may give you a better insight into the scientific method of securing knowledge.

A man returns from his vacation and discovers that his garden is destroyed (felt difficulty—step 1). He examines the garden and finds a twisted fence, flattened flowers, and uprooted stakes (concrete facts that enable him to define the precise nature of the difficulty—step 2). While searching for an explanation of these facts, he considers whether the neighbors' children may have deliberately destroyed the garden (hypothesis or generalization explaining the facts—step 3). His hypothesis goes beyond existing knowledge, for he did not see the children perform the act. He also thinks of a second hypothesis which may explain the facts—a bad storm may have wrecked the garden. Consequently, he suspends judgment and searches for proof.

By deduction, the man reasons out the consequences of his first hypothesis (step 4): If the children wrecked the garden, they had to have been at home during the time he was on his vacation. To test his hypothesis (step 5), he questions the neighbors and learns that the children were away at camp while he was on vacation. Thus, he must reject his first hypothesis, for it is not in harmony with the verifiable facts. He then reasons out deductively the consequences of his second hypothesis (step 4): If a severe storm destroyed the garden, it probably wrecked other nearby gardens. To test this hypothesis (step 5), he observes other gardens and finds they have also been destroyed. He checks in newspapers and finds an account of a storm which destroyed many gardens in his section of the city. A neighbor tells him he watched the hail and wind uproot the garden. The man concludes that his second hypothesis is a reasonable explanation of the facts.

Thus, by reflective thinking, one moves from particular facts to general statements of explanation about these facts and from one's general statements of explanation to a search for facts that will support them. One continues to shuttle between inductive and deductive approaches to the problem until a defensible explanation of the facts has been established.

Progress Made in Acquiring Knowledge

Human beings have made considerable progress in developing better methods of seeking knowledge through the ages and, in so doing, have learned to approach the unknown with greater humility. Authorities in various fields once believed that they possessed a store of absolutely reliable knowledge which enabled them to give authoritative answers to questions. Modern research workers are less dogmatic, for they know that the revolutionary advances made by science within the past century have overthrown some long-standing theories. Their awareness of the tentative, evolutionary status of knowledge makes them more willing to challenge accepted theories when they become suspicious about their validity. After carrying out investigations, they make no claim that their conclusions are infallible; rather, they invite others to confirm, modify, or refute them. If their hypothesis is found to be incompatible with reliable evidence produced in later experiments, they know that the scientific community will abandon or alter it. Modern researchers are cognizant of the notorious fallibility of knowledge. They expose their ideas to critical examination, because they know that only through testing, rechecking, and refining our concepts concerning the nature of phenomena will uncertainity be reduced and knowledge become cumulative.

The scientific method does not lead to absolute certainties, but Cohen and Nagel point out that this method of obtaining knowledge is more reliable than some methods that claim they do.

> The other methods . . . are all inflexible, that is, none of them can admit that it will lead us into error. Hence, none of them can make provision for correcting its own results. What is called *scientific method* differs radically from these by encouraging and developing the utmost possible doubt, so that what is left after such doubt is always supported by the best available evidence. As new evidence or new doubts arise, it is the essence of scientific method to incorporate them—to make them an integral part of the body of knowledge so far attained. Its method, then, makes science progressive because it is never too certain about its results [22:195].

The scientific method is a powerful and practical torchlight for investigators to use in lighting the way to the discovery of new knowledge. Searching for knowledge in this manner is a slow process, but the tentative solutions to problems that are found may be accepted with greater confidence than definitive answers that are based on arbitrary assumptions and pontifical pronouncements which preclude any further investigation.

Despite the improvements people have made in searching for knowledge, they have not yet arrived at a perfect method for seeking answers to their questions. Authority, experience, and both inductive and deductive reasoning have certain limitations as research tools. The scientific method has proved to be an especially useful means of seeking knowledge in the natural sciences, and it has also helped educators to probe into problems. But the scientific method is not a suitable instrument for seeking answers to certain types of questions.

Some critics question whether the scientific method follows a *single* method of investigation. They believe that no rigid set of logical rules can be established for physical scientists, archaeologists, mathematicians, psychologists, sociologists, educators, and historians to follow in their respective undertakings. These critics argue that since sciences differ from one another, each science requires a different method. When questioned about the existence of a general scientific method, other scholars note the numerous common features in scientific inquiries conducted in different fields and suggest that

> . . . on a highly conceptual level science may be considered a general method. When scientists study specific problems, however, this general method is modified in numerous ways, and many of these adaptations are of sufficient importance and sufficiently general in nature to be considered methods within themselves. Science, then, is a very general method, modified in various ways into many less general methods that are utilized in the study of specific problems [13:5].

Controversy exists concerning the scientific method, but most scholars regard this intellectual tool as one of the most promising instruments that society possesses for pushing back the frontiers of human understanding and increasing the accumulation of tested and verified knowledge. Thus, you will want to become better acquainted with this disciplined and scholarly method of investigation, particularly as it relates to the solution of educational problems.

2 CONCEPTS CONCERNING THE SCIENTIFIC METHOD

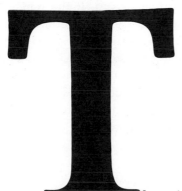he scientific method has evolved down through the years out of the various methods scientists have devised for solving problems. Particularly since the beginning of this century, scholars have critically examined the scientific method, and the steps listed in the last chapter summarize one well-known analysis that materialized. This simplified account provides a thumbnail sketch of the activities involved in scientific investigations. But to comprehend the conceptual framework upon which the scientific method is founded, one must also examine the goals that scientists hope to achieve and the assumptions they make about the universe that enable them to hope for success in their ventures.

ASSUMPTIONS UNDERLYING THE SCIENTIFIC METHOD

The scientific method rests upon certain fundamental assumptions about nature and the psychological processes. These assumptions directly influence all research activity: they form the basis for the research procedures, influence the methods of executing them, and affect the interpretation of the findings. Probing the validity of these assumptions falls within the domain of the philosophy of science. The researcher merely accepts them on a commonsense basis because one cannot proceed in a quest for scientific knowledge without assuming that they are valid.

Assumption of the Nature of Reality

Scientists assume that we live in a knowable, real world. They do not necessarily agree on the nature of the reality that exists "out there" awaiting discovery, but they assume there is an objective reality which is not the creation of the individual human mind. If the real world exists only in the human mind, if it consists only of orderly mental constructs without objective referents, scientists could present no empirical evidence to support their facts and theories. Logical consistency would be the only possible test of the truth value of scientific statements. Scientists justify their assumption that there is an objective reality on the pragmatic grounds that this assumption is more fruitful for inquiry than any alternative explanation of reality.

Assumption of the Uniformity of Nature

The principal of the uniformity of nature means that "there are such things in nature as parallel cases; that what happens once, will, under sufficient degree of similarity of circumstances, happen again, and not only again, but always" (73:184). The scientist must accept the assumption that nature is so constituted that whatever is true with any one case is probably true in all cases of a similar description, that what has been found to be true in many instances in the past will probably continue to hold true in the future. In other words, nature is orderly; events in nature are not purely random or unrelated occurrences. Assuming that nature is absolutely uniform in all respects is not necessary; but science is only possible to the extent that nature is reasonably uniform.

If the assumption of the uniformity of nature is divided into individual postulates, each can be examined in greater detail. Thus, the following paragraphs discuss the postulates of (1) natural kinds, (2) constancy, and (3) determinism.

POSTULATE OF NATURAL KINDS   When people observe natural phenomena, they notice that some objects and events possess a number of striking likenesses. Consequently, they examine phenomena to determine their essential properties, functions, or structures. After finding several objects or events that have common characteristics, they place them in a group; give them a class name; divide the class into categories, each characterized by object resemblances and distinguishable from other categories; and, if possible, order the categories according to quantity or amount. The resemblances they note may be of color, size, shape, function, structures, occurrences, or varied combinations of relationships between these resemblances. Thus, investigators may group people by color of hair; or they may observe structural resemblances, such as a relationship between blond hair and delicate skin, or functional relationships, such as poor muscular coordination and poor mechanical skills; or they may correlate structural and functional resemblances, such as cleft palate and difficulty in pronunciation.

People have always turned to pigeonholing like events and objects when trying to understand phenomena and to solve problems. In the interest of survival, members of cultures in early times classified berries as edible or poisonous, animals as dangerous or harmless, neighbors as friendly or unfriendly. Classification is also characteristic of the early developmental stage of any science. Researchers must have some knowledge of the resemblances and regularities in nature before they can discover and formulate scientific laws.

By classifying phenomena in accordance with their resemblances, scientists organize masses of information into a coherent and unified structure that is useful. The organization of plant and animal life into species, genus, and order and the periodic table of chemical elements worked out by Mendeleev have proved invaluable to investigators in those fields. Classification schemes help workers in a discipline to (1) identify and deal with individual cases, (2) communicate with colleagues more efficiently and accurately about phenomena in their fields, (3) search for additional resemblances that members of categories may have in common, and (4) formulate hypotheses that suggest why differences between categories exist.

By looking for resemblance between things, classifying the things into groups, and summarizing information about the entities in categories, scientists gain a better understanding of phenomena, but they also lose some information—some of the richness and variety of individual differences. Any classification scheme magnifies some differences and ignores others. Observations must be placed on one side or the other of the classificatory line. Classification has drawbacks as a scientific tool, but to avoid any classification or generalization makes science impossible. Scientists, therefore, assume that although no two things or people are exactly alike, they may be similar enough to make classification fruitful for their purpose.

If importance is attributed to resemblances that are of no significance, a classification scheme is of little value. If several girls flunk chemistry in a given class, the professor may observe that they all wear the same shade of lipstick, but this resemblance is not the key factor causing their failure. If an alcoholic notes that he always adds soda to his bourbon, gin, or scotch, he has recognized a resemblance among his drinks, but giving up soda will not cure his drunkenness. Classification schemes that prove most useful penetrate to the underlying key characteristics of phenomena. These characteristics are not usually the most obvious ones; they are discovered through intensive and devious examination rather than casual and superficial observation.

POSTULATE OF CONSTANCY   The postulate of constancy assumes that relatively constant conditions exist in nature; that is, some phenomena do not appreciably change their basic characteristics over time. The postulate of constancy does not demand absolute conditions of fixity, persistency, or permanency, nor does the postulate deny that rates of change vary for different phenomena. Some phenomena remain substantially unchanged over the years; other phenomena exhibit relatively marked rates of change. The sun, planets, and diamonds display exceptionally enduring qualities down through the millennia; fruit flies, blooming flowers, and chicken eggs do not. In some respects, John and Mary remain more or less the same throughout grade school; in other respects, they change rapidly. Their peripheral personality traits may change considerably as they react to certain kinds of experiences, but their central core of personality traits will not vary appreciably.

The postulate of constancy is a prerequisite for scientific advancement. Absolute constancy is not required, but changes must take place slowly enough for scientists to draw valid generalizations concerning phenomena that will hold true for a given period of time. The period must be long enough for other men to confirm the findings and for society to apply the knowledge before subsequent events render it useless. If phenomena were capricious, all inquiries into the innermost secrets of nature would be fleeting, fruitless historical accounts. The knowledge gained in one study could never be applied when dealing with the same phenomena in the future. Without some permanence of phenomena, science cannot carry out its primary function, the accumulation of verified and predictable knowledge. If science denies the postulate of constancy, its predictions possess little value, for they merely rest on blind speculations and chance occurrences.

POSTULATE OF DETERMINISM   The postulate of determinism denies that the occurrence of an event is the result of chance or an accidental situation, or that it is purely a spontaneous incident. Rather, the postulate affirms that natural phenomena are determined by antecedent events. If water is to boil, a definite set of conditions must exist before the event will take place. If an explosion occurs, one is certain that sufficient and necessary circumstances existed before this event happened, and whenever these conditions occur one can be certain that an explosion will follow. The postulate of determinism assumes that the occurrence of a given phenomenon is invariably preceded by the occurrence of other events or conditions.

Human beings have been aware of orderliness in nature since earliest times. They noticed regularities in nature: day followed night and seasons came in a regular order. To understand nature, they also searched for antecedent conditions that appeared to be related to events, but they often concluded that supernatural forces or whatever immediately preceded an event was the cause of it. Hence, they reasoned that the floods were caused by the thunder of angered gods and that a good day of hunting was the result of finding a rare flower at dawn. By attacking problems more systematically and searching more deeply to find functional relationships, modern research workers have been able to discover regularities in nature that are not detected through casual observation.

Determinism is a necessary and fundamental concept that underlies all scientific enterprises. Yet, rigidly interpreted determinism, belief in eternal natural stability and absolute certainty of uniformity, is questioned as a result of modern developments in physics. Scientists no longer assume that they deal with absolute certainty, but only with levels of probability. This revised version of determinism continues to play a role in research, for the scientist requires lawfulness in the events of nature. If any phenomena fall outside the postulate of determination, they are also outside the realm of scientific investigation.

If scientists must consider each phenomenon as a capricious rather than a determined event, they are deprived of a means of attacking problems that enables them to formulate laws capable of explaining large bodies of phenomena. No pattern or scheme for setting up and controlling an experiment can be established and no predictions about what will happen in the future can be made if the assumption that what has happened in the past will happen again is false. The best that scientists can do in an indetermined situation is to describe the character of an isolated incident.

Assumptions Concerning the Psychological Process

Research workers accept the assumption that they can gain knowledge of the world through the psychological processes of perceiving, remembering, and reasoning. The scientific method cannot operate without utilizing these processes. Perceiving, remembering, and reasoning, however, are subject to error. If inaccurate processes are at work, they subsequently reflect their unreliability in the results of the investigation and invalidate it. Research workers, therefore, must acquaint themselves with the nature of these psychological processes and must take the necessary steps to obtain the highest possible degree of accuracy when employing them.

POSTULATE OF THE RELIABILITY OF PERCEIVING   In their laboratories, investigators routinely record information they have experienced through their senses. Yet they know that the human sense organs are limited in range and in fineness in discrimination. A dog can hear the high tones of a whistle that are inaudible to them. Their colleagues may be able to hear a greater range of sounds than they can. Their sense perceptions may differ not only from those of their friends but also in successive observations they make themselves. Because their senses are subject to fatigue and adaptation, they may experience varied perceptions when exposed repeatedly to the same sound, taste, or odor.

Errors in visual perception are as commonplace as errors in auditory perception. Through illusions and shifts of attention, a chic dress designer, a deft magician, a war camouflage expert, a football strategist, or a clever advertiser can lead people to make false judgments and inferences. For example, twenty subjects in a psychological experiment were shown a line drawing of a man's expressionless face on a screen. After seeing the word "happy" intermittently flashed beneath the picture, they thought the face gradually became happier even though it had not changed.

Everyone experiences visual deceptions. On her annual August vacation, an elementary school teacher may encounter several perceptual puzzles. At the railroad station, she may have the illusion that her train is pulling out, when it actually is standing still but the train on the next track is beginning to move in the opposite direction. At the beach, she may notice that her vertically striped swimming suit makes her appear thinner than the one with horizontal stripes. When she looks down the road, her eyes will tell her that it converges at a point in the distance.

Scientists have no more natural immunity to faulty perception than the elementary school teacher. When working on a problem, they may make inaccurate observations because of momentary distractions, strong intellectual biases, personal prejudices, emotional sets, and inaccurate discriminations. Sometimes they may see what they expect to see whether it is there or not, or they may fail to perceive relevant factors. History is studded with stories of scientists who failed to track the trail of truth because they were guilty of making perceptual blunders. Despite the untrustworthiness of the perceptual processes, scientists assume that they can obtain reliable knowledge through their sense organs. But they familiarize themselves with the common errors made in observation and take the necessary precautions to prevent such errors from creeping into their work.

POSTULATE OF THE RELIABILITY OF REMEMBERING   Remembering, like the activity of perceiving, is subject to error. Everyday experiences indicate the frailties of our mental processes. A teacher may be unable to recall where she parked her car or the name of a former student. We often recall only those things we want to recall: A boy may remember that his mother promised to take him to the circus but forget that she asked him to mow the lawn. Scientists may remember things that support their beliefs rather than those that do not.

Despite the weaknesses of the human memory, the research worker accepts the assumption that one can obtain fundamentally reliable knowledge from this source. An investigator must accept this assumption, for progress would terminate if one questioned the accuracy of every single fact. But since forgetting information or recalling it inaccurately is easy, a scientist develops systematic methods of recording information; periodically reviews these data; and sometimes takes photographs, movies, recordings, or x-rays of conditions or events for future reference. Adopting such practices enables one to improve the range, accuracy, and completeness of one's memory.

POSTULATE OF THE RELIABILITY OF REASONING   Reasoning, even by exceptionally intelligent individuals, is beset by many potential pitfalls. Mistakes in reasoning occur because of use of false premises, violation of the rules of logic, presence of intellectual biases, failure to grasp the exact meanings of words, and the making of faulty judgments regarding the suitability and use of statistical and experimental techniques.

Despite the limitations of the reasoning process, scientists recognize its value as an implement of research. Any attempt to order a mass of data into a coherent and intelligible narrative, with accompanying interpretation, calls for the constant exercise of reasoning powers. More specifically, researchers resort to reasoning when selecting and defining their problems, when framing solutions, when deciding what observations to make, when devising techniques for obtaining data, when interpreting their data, and when determining whether to accept, modify, or reject their hypotheses. Without mentally manipulating ideas, scientists cannot make much progress in any investigation. Therefore, they accept reasoning as a generally reliable tool of research. They take many precautions, however, to detect and to check errors in their thought processes. They examine the premises on which their reasoning is based to determine whether these premises are true, and they subject their arguments to the rules of logic that govern correct reasoning. Since confused reasoning can stem from the slovenly use of language, they endeavor to assign clear, correct, consistent, and specific meanings to words, phrases, and terms. Because personal prejudices and wishes may cause them to ignore facts and to reason illogically, they deliberately search for and give fair consideration to evidence that does not conform to their hypotheses.

GOALS OF SCIENTISTS

The goals of scientists are not unlike those of other human beings as evidenced down through the ages. Centuries ago people were led by a craving for knowledge of the world about them to construct crude explanations for phenomena. A deep desire was to acquire knowledge that would enable them to control floods, famine, diseases, and other forces impinging upon their lives. With more refined methods, modern scientists also seek to understand the phenomena they observe. Discovering order in the universe, comprehending the laws of nature, and learning how to harness the forces of nature are their objectives. The goal of scientists is to improve their ability and success in explaining, predicting, and controlling conditions and events.

Explanation as a Goal of Scientists

The essential purpose of research is to go beyond mere description of phenomena and provide an explanation for them. Scientists are not completely satisfied with naming, classifying, or describing phenomena. Rather than terminating their investigations with simple observations, such as that apples fall down, balloons rise, some children stutter, or certain diseases kill, they probe more deeply to find reasons for the occurrence of these events. Going behind casually observed factors to search for some underlying pattern that explains them is their objective. After discovering a possible relationship between antecedent factors and the particular event or condition, they frame a verifiable generalization that explains how the variables involved in the situation behave. Explanation—not mere description—is the product of their effort.

Scientists do not want to know only *what* phenomena are, but also *how* phenomena act as they do. A person may notice, for example, that on a hot summer day a steel cable expands, as do metal beams. From one's observation of these particular incidents, one may propose the generalization that heat expands metal. This low-level explanation is useful information for it describes what happens to heated metals, but it does not reveal how metals expand when heated.

When scientists tried to find some underlying principle to account for the fact that heat expands metal, they framed the following explanation: all heat is caused by the motion of molecules of matter: the greater the motion of the molecules, the greater is the heat of a body. The agitation of the molecules makes them jostle one another apart; hence, they take up more space. Thus, an increase in temperature results in expansion. This generalization gave scientists a better understanding of the phenomena observed, for it revealed the causes of the expansion of metal.

Once investigators understood and confirmed this scientific principle, they were able to apply it to other facts. Thereafter, upon encountering any phenomena involving expansion, they looked for heat as a possible cause; whenever heat was present, they considered expansion as a possible effect. Thus, the principle not only helped them to understand a particular phenomenon, but it also enlarged their capacity to explain a large range of natural events. Basically, scientific knowledge explains phenomena by locating their place in a larger body of systematic coherent relations.

Formulating generalizations—conceptual schemes—that explain phenomena is a major goal of scientists. A generalization which explains a limited body of phenomena is useful, but scientists aim to develop ever more far-reaching conceptual schemes. Their ultimate goal is to seek laws of the highest generality—laws of the utmost comprehensiveness. Newton's theory of gravitation is an example of a comprehensive explanation. Before Newton was born, Galileo formulated his law of falling bodies, which explained the motion of bodies on the surface of the earth. About the same time that Galileo proposed his explanation for terrestrial motion, Kepler formulated the laws of celestial motion. When Newton came upon the scene, he devised a more comprehensive generalization that applied to all massive bodies, whether terrestrial or celestial. His new theory performed the work of the two generalizations it replaced. Thus, Newton helped scientific knowledge take a giant stride forward. Since his time, a procession of creative geniuses has been endlessly "lifting science from problem to problem and adequate theory to more adequate theory with greater and greater generality" (77:29). Their successively more comprehensive theoretical explanations have given humankind important keys to understanding the universe.

Prediction as a Goal of Scientists

An explanation that does not increase our power over natural events may be useful, but it is not as valuable as one that enables us to predict events. Scientists, therefore, are not satisfied merely with formulating generalizations that explain phenomena; they also want to make predictions concerning the way a generalization will operate in new situations. Their objective is to take known data and accepted generalizations and from them to predict some future event or hitherto unobserved phenomenon. By noting gaps in the periodic table that classified the known chemical elements, Mendeleev was able to predict in 1871 the existence of a new element, germanium, fifteen years before it was discovered. By studying the data, theories, and laws available in their fields, modern research workers also make rather accurate forecasts concerning the coming of an eclipse, future weather conditions, or the probable scholastic success individual members of the freshman class will attain in college.

The natural scientist has been able to make predictions in many fields, and some of these predictions possess such a high degree of probability that they are almost absolutely certain. Making predictions has been much more difficult for social scientists, and the predictions they have proposed are of an approximate character or are confined to relatively simple problems. Because of the difficulty of the feat, making an accurate prediction is a satisfying and spectacular achievement.

Control as a Goal of Scientists

Scientists dig deeply into the nature of phenomena to discover the specific factors and relationships that cause a particular condition to exist. They strive to attain such a thorough understanding of the laws of nature that they are able not only to predict but also to control an increasing range of events. "Control" refers to the process of manipulating certain of the essential conditions that determine an event so as to make the event happen or prevent if from occurring. Doctors, for example, know that if the pancreas fails to secrete insulin, the body is unable to utilize properly the carbohydrates in the body. Doctors can predict what will happen to patients when this condition, diabetes, exists, and they can control diabetes by giving the patients injections of insulin. When doctors predict and control a diabetic condition, they are actually demonstrating their understanding of the nature of the disease.

Psychologists and educators have long been investigating the skills and aptitudes that lead to success in particular vocations. They hope that sufficient understanding of the conditions necessary to become a superior dentist, teacher, doctor, or electrician will enable them to construct aptitude tests that will predict the caliber of work an individual will do in a given field. If such knowledge is obtained and predictions are made with a sufficiently high degree of accuracy, these vocational guidance instruments will prevent square pegs from trying to force themselves into round holes. If the selection of students trained in each field is controlled through an aptitude testing program, the nation will be assured of a more effective utilization of the human potentialities in our society.

One of the goals of scientists is to control natural events, but this objective is difficult to achieve. Scientists can predict but cannot control many events. Qualified individuals are able to predict, with varying degrees of success, the weather, the coming of a comet, or the course of cancer, but they are unable to control the conditions causing these phenomena. Scientists can neither predict nor control some events. They cannot yet predict precisely, for example, when and where earthquakes will take place, nor can they control them. In general, scientists have made greater progress in learning to control natural than social phenomena. One of the desperate demands of society today is to discover means of controlling phenomena such as destructive wars, juvenile delinquency, human oppression, and intergroup tensions that weaken our social structure.

DIFFERENCES BETWEEN THE SOCIAL SCIENCES AND THE NATURAL SCIENCES

As we have noted, the natural scientists have made considerable progress in achieving some of their aims. Progress in the social sciences, such as history, economics, and education, has lagged far behind. A few leaders believe that our approach to the social sciences never can become "scientific." Some authorities contend that progress will gradually be made, but our knowledge of the social sciences will not reach the high level of that of the natural sciences. Other authorities admit that our understanding of the social sciences is on an immature level, but they claim that research in these areas eventually will become as "scientific" as in the natural sciences. A number of obstacles, however, will prevent the ready realization of this objective. In the endeavor to obtain a better understanding of the fundamental factors underlying human behavior so that they can explain, predict, and control social phenomena, the social scientists encounter many difficulties. The following paragraphs discuss some of their problems.

Complexity of Subject Matter

Natural scientists are concerned with phenomena on the gross physical level. Their studies involve a comparatively small number of variables (the set of conditions required for an event) that can be measured quite precisely. Because social scientists are concerned with people as individuals and as members of groups, they must disentangle much more complex systems of interaction. Social problems may involve such a large number of variables that they overwhelm investigators with the possibilities to consider.

When a natural scientist investigates a chemical explosion, *relatively few physical factors* will account for the event. When a social scientist investigates a social explosion—a riot or a crime— *innumerable factors,* some of them not physical, may be involved: a switchblade knife, the force and direction of the blow, blood vessels severed, the intoxicated condition of the murderer, the strength of the adversary, biological heredity, gang social pressures, the lack of police protection, the hot and humid evening, rejection by parents, poverty, and strained race relations.

A number of physical explanations may be given for a crime or any other social phenomenon. Moreover, social phenomena may be observed not only on the physical level but also from the sociological or psychological point of view, or from any combination of these. They can be explained in patterns of—just to mention a few—growth, time, type, place, activities, motivation, or trends. This state of affairs creates many difficulties. One is always plagued with the problem of what points of view and what variables to select to explain phenomena satisfactorily.

Observability of Subject Matter

Direct observation of phenomena is more difficult in some respects for the social scientist than for the physical scientist. A social scientist cannot see, hear, touch, smell, or taste phenomena that existed in the past. An educator studying colonial schools cannot personally view the children, teachers, and instructional procedures of that early era in American history. A chemist or physicist can set up the same desired conditions again and again and directly observe what takes place, but a psychologist cannot put ingredients into a test tube and conjure up the exact events of an adult's childhood. The nature of past social phenomena precludes direct and repeated observation.

Social scientists can observe some present social phenomena directly, but they cannot bring others into the open for scrutiny. In a child study laboratory, investigators may observe whether Johnny Jurk slaps his companions, how many words he reads in a minute, and what range of sounds he can hear. But some social factors, such as his preferences, motives, and dreams, are matters of inner consciousness and are not accessible to direct public examination. Investigators must either (1) interpret that "inner state" themselves, which they can do only in light of their own life experience, a process that leaves room for error, or (2) accept their subject's description of his inner state, which may be inaccurate.

Social facts are more variable than physical facts. For most purposes in chemistry, an observation of any cubic centimeter of sulfuric acid will be as good as another. But observations of 30 seventh-grade pupils in one city will not necessarily coincide with the observations of a like number and age of pupils in another city. The height, weight, size of vocabulary, play participation, and arithmetic achievement of one ten-year-old may vary widely from those of his age-mates. In some situations a social scientist may treat all individuals alike, such as in the tabulation of births. But because of the wide range of differences in humans, attributing to a whole class what is true of selected samples is dangerous.

Non-repeatability of Subject Matter

Social phenomena are less repeatable than natural phenomena. Many phenomena of the natural sciences are highly uniform and recurrent; they lend themselves to abstraction and the precise, quantitative formulation of generalizations. Social problems usually deal with specific historical happenings; they are concerned with singularities, with events that occur but never recur in exactly the same way. Some generalizations may be made about social life and human behavior. Generalizations may be formulated, for example, about certain features that wars, raids, and revolutions or adults, adolescents, and infants have in common. Yet a social phenomenon has its unique and non-repeatable character that needs to be comprehended in its entirety if it is to be understood. Thus, abstracting factors that are common to several social events so as to formulate a generalization cannot be carried too far without falsifying the material. Because social phenomena are less uniform and recurrent than natural phenomena, it is more difficult to establish and verify social laws.

Relationship of Scientists to Their Subject Matter

Physical phenomena such as chemical elements are impersonal. Natural scientists do not have to consider the purposes or motives of planets or oceans. But social science phenomena are concerned with human beings, who are purposeful creatures. People seek certain desirable ends and possess the capacity to make choices, which enables them to modify their conduct. Human free will is the "incalculable element" in social phenomena. Because people are subject to certain geographical, historical, physiological, and social-economic forces, they may ordinarily operate in a rather uniform way in a given space and time context. But such uniformity is relative, for human free will enables people to make themselves exceptions to laws in some instances. Since social science subject matter is strongly influenced by human decisions, social phenomena are constantly changing as a result of action taken by human beings.

Natural scientists inquire into nature's processes and formulate general laws governing these processes. They do not expect to alter nature or to approve or disapprove of its processes. They merely hope their knowledge of physical phenomena will enable them to make better use of nature's processes. When natural scientists construct a hypothesis to explain a physical phenomenon, they know that their generalizations will not cause the phenomenon to modify its character.

If an astronomer formulates a generalization to explain the orbits of planets, he does not expect the planets to react to his theory in any way. The celestial bodies will remain unchanged by his pronouncements. They will not call a celestial congress to campaign for the adoption of new patterns of movement.

Because the social sciences are integrally interwoven with the social fabric, they present a different situation. Generalizations made to explain social phenomena may affect social events and conditions. If people accept an explanation of social phenomena, they may decide to readjust social patterns in view of this knowledge and thereby create conditions which make the generalization invalid. Consequently, accurate prediction is more difficult in economics and education than in astronomy or physics.

Predictions about population growth and the accompanying problems may cause young people to limit the size of their families. A prediction that a school board candidate will lose an election may cause his partisans to rise to the emergency and help him win. A prediction about the number of people who will be killed in highway accidents over the Memorial Day weekend may alarm citizens and cause them to conduct nationwide safety campaigns that reduce the anticipated highway slaughter. The findings in natural science lose their strength only when they are replaced by better insight into the phenomena. But findings in the social sciences may lose their value if the knowledge they provide causes humans to change the social conditions.

Social scientists are not impartial observers who stand outside society to watch its processes. They are an integral part of the subject matter they observe. People may impartially observe physical phenomena such as the structure of protoplasm, but their own interests, values, preferences, and purposes influence their judgments when they observe social phenomena. People are much less capable of remaining objective about human reactions in school segregation incidents than about chemical reactions in test tubes, about social stress in slum areas than about physical stress in physics, about a communist system of government than about the solar system in nature. Emotional attachments to particular systems of values tend to make social scientists approve or disapprove of particular social processes. Eliminating personal biases when observing social science phenomena is difficult.

Natural scientists are concerned with problems of fact; they confine their investigations to the conditions that exist in nature. Social scientists are also interested in problems of fact. To ascertain what conditions exist in society, they study the characteristics and causes of poverty, juvenile delinquency, reading failure, or a similar problem. But social scientists are interested not only in understanding society as it is but also in developing theories to designate what ought to be—what is socially desirable. Some social scientists contend they are not concerned with social ends, but they may unconsciously accept the prevailing order as the ideal. Some researchers may ignore social ends, but the findings of their studies may cause others to seek the development of an ideal social order. Because social science subject matter is intimately related to human beings, who are purposeful, value-seeking creatures, it presents types of problems that the natural sciences do not present.

ETHICS OF CONDUCTING RESEARCH

The scientific method is concerned with finding facts to test hypotheses and does not involve judging whether the facts obtained are morally good or bad, but researchers cannot live in a moral vacuum. Society holds them accountable for their conduct in obtaining, interpreting, and reporting their findings. Ethical norms that have been established by law or tradition stipulate what researchers' obligations are to their human subjects, their scientific colleagues, and society.

Ethical Obligations to Human Subjects

Because of concern about the value judgments made in some experiments with human subjects in the recent past, an aroused public has challenged the authority of experts to make such decisions unilaterally. More rigorous systems for protecting the rights, dignity, and welfare of subjects are being established by researchers because (1) some subjects have taken legal action against investigators, their institutions, or sponsoring agencies, (2) legislation[1] has been passed that requires institutions seeking Department of Health, Education, and Welfare (DHEW) funds to establish boards to review research proposals and certify that proper provisions have been made for the protection of human subjects, (3) some institutions have extended the DHEW policies to all investigations involving human subjects whether they are supported by the government or not, and (4) professional organizations have revised their codes of ethics to make explicit investigators' responsibilities toward human subjects (2).

The local human-subjects review committee, which may consist of peer representatives from various disciplines within the institution and informed outsiders, requires an investigator to submit a protocol

[1]National Research Act, July 12, 1974, *United States Statutes at Large*, 88:342.

describing a proposed study and the plans for protecting subjects from any potential physical, psychological, or social stress or harm which goes beyond the ordinary risks of living. If considerable concern or disagreement exists about the amount of risk to the subjects, the investigation may have to be abandoned, but the fact that risk exists does not necessarily mean it must be abandoned. If the importance of the knowledge to be gained or the potential benefits to the subjects outweighs the possible adverse effects on the subjects, the review committee may (1) approve of the study, (2) suggest modifications or an alternative approach that will minimize the danger to or discomfort of the subjects, (3) require that the investigator obtain additional training in a specific research technique or call in an expert to perform the work, or (4) require additional checks to be made at intervals. The concepts discussed below may be considered by human-subject review committees on the local level and within DHEW or other agencies.

CONCEPT OF PRIVACY   Human subjects have the right to privacy: the right to choose the extent to which and manner in which they will share or withhold information about their behavior, attitudes, or opinions. Some people may not wish to make disclosures about their home life, religious beliefs, or aggressive behavior. If information about them is obtained without their knowledge through the use of informants, institutional records, one-way mirrors, sophisticated personality tests, or concealed microphones, cameras, or recording devices, their right to privacy is violated. But answers to some research questions can be found only by probing deeply into the feelings, attitudes, and behavior that people normally conceal. When the goal of an investigation is important and can be reached in no other way, permission may be obtained to enter the private domain of the subjects, but only if (1) the value of the data to be obtained outweighs the possible adverse effects on the subjects, (2) the invasion of privacy is limited to the narrowest extent possible, (3) the procedures to be employed will minimize the possibility of embarrassing or degrading individuals, making them subject to public censure or ridicule, or endangering their social, economic, or physical well-being, (4) the subjects are free to consent or to refuse to participate in the study, and (5) the data are obtained from the subjects and are used by the researcher and his assistants under conditions of complete anonymity or strict confidentiality.

CONCEPT OF ANONYMITY   The identity of the participants in an investigation is divorced as fully and effectively as possible from the information they furnish. Whenever possible, a promise of complete anonymity is given to subjects. Data of value can sometimes be obtained from unsigned questionnaires, but promising the subjects anonymity and secretly marking the questionnaires in a way that enables the investigator to identify them is unethical. If the legitimate needs of the study require some knowledge of the identity of the subjects, such as the need to link up data on diverse records with a particular individual, a researcher can take some of the following precautions to protect the privacy of the subjects: (1) remove their names from data and identify their responses only by a code number, keep the code in a locked file, make it accessible only to responsible assistants, destroy the code as soon as it is practical to do so, (2) report research results in terms of group averages so the individual responses cannot be identified, and (3) refrain from reporting any aggregate data that permit others to identify a subject, such as when the number of subjects in a subgroup of an investigation is small.

CONCEPT OF CONFIDENTIALITY   Human subjects have the right to know that access to their private data will be limited to the people and purposes they agree upon. An agreement to reveal data about political beliefs, sexual life, or drug usage to a researcher is not a license to give this information to others. To protect the confidentiality of data obtained from subjects, a researcher (1) refuses requests for information about a particular subject received from parents, school administrators, employers, data bank managers, or other people unless the subject gives his consent to such disclosure, (2) informs subjects in studies of criminal or other deviant behavior of the steps that will be taken to protect them if required by law to reveal data, such as not using a written consent form or any means of linking the subject to his data, (3) destroys any data—including films, videotapes, or sound recordings— that can be linked with an individual as soon as it is practical to do so unless the subject gives his consent to preserve the data for future use by the researcher or other people.

CONCEPT OF INFORMED CONSENT   Ethical practice in research utilizing human subjects requires an investigator to obtain a legally effective, informed consent from each subject or his parent or legally authorized representative and to carry out all promises made in the agreement. Human subjects include the unborn and dead to the extent that their rights can be exercised by the next of kin. The person granting the consent must be in a position to exercise free power of choice without improper or undue inducement or any subtle or obvious form of constraint or coercion. If a child or a mentally retarded or disturbed person is capable of making a responsible decision, a consent statement from him as well as his parents may be required. If data are obtained from school, hospital, or other institutional records, consent is obtained from the individual as well as the institution. A promise of anonymity is not a complete substitute for consent. The consent agreement, oral or written, must not include exculpatory language through which the subject is made to waive any of his legal rights. The elements that may be incorporated into the agreement are as follows:

1   An accurate, understandable explanation of the nature and purposes of the research.
2   An understandable description of the procedures to be employed, including an identification of those which are experimental, and the attendant emotional or physical stresses, discomforts, or risks, as well as any benefits that are reasonably to be expected.
3   An explanation of how and why the subjects were selected to participate.
4   An explanation of the possible uses to which the data will be put, and whether the use and analysis of the data will be limited to the researcher or will be shared at some future time with other scholars or data banks.
5   An offer to answer any questions concerning the study or the procedures.
6   An assurance that the subjects are completely free to decline or to withdraw their consent and discontinue participation in the study at any time without prejudice to the subjects.
7   A statement regarding the sponsorship and sources of financial support, if any, of the project.
8   An explanation of the procedures the subjects should follow in event of injury resulting directly from participation in the project.

In some extremely valuable research studies, if the subjects had prior knowledge of the fact they were being observed, of the hypothesis under investigation, of the sponsor, or of the procedures used, they might alter their behavior or answers; hence, valid data could not be obtained. If the subjects knew, for example, that a questionnaire was designed to measure prejudice, they might be careful to check the "least prejudiced" answers. In some such instances, subjects are provided with incomplete information or misinformation about a study to elicit their normal reaction to the factor under investigation. In this type of study and in some studies of deviant behavior, waiver of the prior-consent principle may be permitted by a review committee, but only under carefully justified circumstances. Such circumstances are as follows:

1   Members of the committee must agree that the risk to the subjects would be minimal.
2   Research objectives of considerable importance would be invalidated by obtaining prior-consent statements.
3   Any alternative means for attaining these objectives would be less advantageous to the subjects.
4   The risks to the subjects inherent in obtaining a written consent, usually psychological or legal risks associated with deviant behavior, would be greater than the risks that originally caused such signatures to be sought.
5   A debriefing session is held immediately following the completion of the activity in which the subjects receive a full explanation of the nature of the research, the procedures employed, and the reasons why any concealment, manipulation, or other deception was used.
6   After the debriefing, the subjects give their consent to use the data they have provided or request that their data be withdrawn. In instances such as item 4 above, neither a pre- nor a post-experimental consent statement may be required.

Accountability to Colleagues and Society

In addition to providing for the protection of human subjects, researchers are held accountable for special ethical responsibilities in their relationships with colleagues and society. These principles are formulated by scientific consensus expressed in professional codes of ethics or more informal codes of tradition.

INTEGRITY OF INVESTIGATORS   Researchers are expected to give proper credit to their colleagues and students who assist them in conducting investigations or to anyone from whom they borrow ideas no matter how much modified. They are also expected to refrain from quoting or paraphrasing out of context any written or verbal statements made by their colleagues and from misrepresenting any other source.

Society expects researchers to be dedicated to a search for the truth. But breaches in the integrity of scientific investigators do occur. Some researchers are made vulnerable to chicanery and deceit by direct or subtle pressures from financial supporters or authority figures, a strong desire to win scientific recognition in a highly competitive field, an opportunity for economic gain or professional advancement, or the amount of time and ego involved in formulating and testing a hypothesis. Researchers who rig an experiment, tamper with or fabricate data, ignore or suppress data that do not sustain their hypotheses, refrain from reporting the technical shortcoming of investigations, or encounter unexpected findings and construct post-experimental hypotheses to predict them are dishonest and weaken our social fabric. Their unethical practices may cause other scientists to spend considerable time and money checking false leads that otherwise could be spent on constructive work. They may cause parents, teachers, and other consumers of research to make changes in their practices that are unnecessary or harmful.

COMPETENCY OF THE INVESTIGATORS   Society has a right to expect nothing less than scientific expertise from researchers. The public will be reluctant to support investigations if the literature is proliferated with mostly worthless, poorly designed, and negligently performed studies. Investigators have no right to produce studies that (1) require background knowledges or data collection or processing skills they lack, (2) fail to produce some valuable information or to permit the widest applicability of the findings because of careless planning for the collection of the data, (3) do not incorporate the controls, statistical techniques, instruments, or procedures required to obtain valid findings, (4) present an inaccurate analysis of the data or conclusions drawn from insufficient, valid evidence, or (5) are not ultimately reported to the scientific community and made available for use.

   If researchers do not want to have their work hobbled by restrictive laws or lack of funds or to have promising areas of research closed off for future investigation, they must search for the truth in a manner that does not violate humanistic or scientific norms. Constructing scientifically sound, ethically acceptable research studies that are administratively feasible is difficult. But through individual inventiveness and collective critical appraisals, scholars engaged in educational research can find ways of achieving these goals which will improve the quality of their work and will win public support for research.

QUESTION OF ETHICS   Because educators often use youngsters rather than inanimate elements in their investigations, their freedom to manipulate experimental treatments and exercise experimental controls is somewhat limited. The methodological rigor required to obtain valid and generalizable data is often in conflict with the ethical principles governing the protection of human subjects. Good experimental design, for example, may require that the experimenter withhold beneficial treatment from subjects in the control group, but human concern for these deprived subjects argues the other way. The obvious presence of a camera in a classroom to collect data may cause students to alter their behavior, but hiding the camera violates the right students have to privacy. The ethical obligation to inform subjects that they can drop out of a study at any time conflicts with the scientific need to obtain data from a random sample of subjects assigned to treatment at random for the sake of statistical generalization.

The ethical obligation to obtain a voluntary informed consent statement from each subject at risk prior to participation in an experiment also presents a problem. The theories, hypotheses, and procedures involved may be too complex and technical for subjects to evaluate whether they want to participate. Even if the investigation is relatively simple, mentally retarded or disturbed subjects may be incapable of making responsible decisions. The degree of discomfort or stress that will be experienced by some subjects may not be ascertainable prior to participation.

The requirement that researchers obtain consent statements from subjects prior to administering the experimental treatment is waived in some investigations. When this is done, the study is fully explained in a debriefing session immediately after the administration of the experimental treatment, and subjects are asked to give or withhold their consent to use the data collected from them. This debriefing session may minimize any damaging aftereffects from participation, but the knowledge about the experiment obtained by the first group of subjects may invalidate the data obtained from them or other subjects in subsequent sessions of the experiment. If no great risk is involved in delaying the debriefing until the end of the experiment, relocating the subjects may present problems. In some instances, the information provided in the debriefing session, such as telling subjects they were selected for the study because of their unrecognized homosexual tendencies or bigoted behavior may make the subjects face aspects of themselves that will lower their self-esteem or cause them continuing personal distress.

3 NATURE OF OBSERVATION

Observation is fundamental in research, for it produces one of the basic elements of science: facts. Observing is an activity research workers engage in throughout the several stages of their investigations. By utilizing their senses of hearing, sight, touch, and taste, they gather facts—empirical data—that help them locate a problem, construct theoretical solutions for it, and determine whether there is evidence that will support their solution. From the inception of an inquiry to the final confirmation or rejection of their proposed problem solution, research workers rely on observation to keep them on the trail to truth.

Because observation, facts, and theories are closely related factors that play a significant role in scientific investigations, understanding their nature, function, and relationship is important. The layman is familiar with these terms, but his concept of their meaning is usually quite different from the definition a scientist would give. This chapter, therefore, will explore the following questions: What is the nature of scientific observation? What is the nature of a fact? What is the nature of theories? What is the relationship between theory and fact in research?

CONDITIONS NECESSARY FOR OBSERVATION

Since observation is essential in scientific inquiry, neophytes should learn how to establish the conditions within themselves and their working environment that will enable them to obtain reliable facts with maximum efficiency. Involved in observation are four psychological factors to which they must give due consideration: attention, sensation, perception, and conception.

Attention

Attention is a necessary condition for successful observation. This condition is characterized by a mental set or a state of alertness which an individual assumes so as to sense or perceive selected events, conditions, or things. Being bombarded constantly by a multiplicity of stimuli, the nervous network of the human organism cannot simultaneously channel all of them to the cortex for interpretation. Hence, an observer sifts out the specific ones from which he wants to receive messages. This process of selection is *attention.* Adequate attention is imperative if one is to acquire clear, concise and detailed information about phenomena. If thoughts about the attractive young woman or man across the aisle are flashing through your mind at the moment, you are probably receiving blurred messages from this printed page. Indeed, you may "read" the whole page without acquiring any knowledge of its contents, for your attention is elsewhere: you are not ready to receive the stimuli of the printed word.

Learning to "pay attention" is an important part of observational training. By cultivating a deep interest in a particular point of view when engaged in research you can motivate yourself to observe a specific segment of phenomena with an active, inquiring mind. By incorporating control procedures in your research design, you can fix your attention on the phenomenon you want to observe and can screen out competing stimuli. By exercising a high degree of self-control, you can keep strong and interesting extraneous stimuli from capturing your attention and can curb any natural restlessness that might permit your attention to wander.

Human beings cannot successfully fix their attention upon objects or events that are exceptionally unstable or elusive. Thus, phenomena too big, too small, too fleeting, or too chaotic to be perceived with the senses and special instruments are not suitable subjects for an investigation. When engaged in research, you will want to direct your attention toward phenomena that are small enough to be encompassed and are sufficiently stable, constant, and manageable that others can view them at the same time or check them at a later date.

Sensation

You become aware of the world about you through your senses or their extension by appropriate "sensing" apparatus. When changes occur in your internal or external environment, they stimulate your sense organs, which in turn excite your sensory nerves. When these sensory impulses reach your brain, you experience a *sensation*: a smell, a taste, a shape, or a sound.

Your sense organs can detect thousands of qualities, yet they have definite limitations. They are not reliable tools for making exact measurements of distance, speed, size, or intensity, and they are poor instruments for making comparisons. The observations you make can be distorted for a variety of reasons. Your sense organs may be too limited in scope to detect certain differences, or may be defective because of a congenital imperfection, such as color blindness, or may be temporarily impaired by fatigue, drugs, or emotional status, or may be deteriorating because of age or illness. Strong competing stimuli or a confusion of extraneous ones makes it difficult for your senses to isolate the significant stimuli. A foreign or distracting medium that comes between you and your subject matter can create many problems. A dirty test tube, for example, or undetected biases of subjects in an experiment may cause you to make startling but faulty observations. The mere presence of you and your research equipment and recording devices may affect the phenomena you wish to study and change the signals you receive from them. Social scientists, for example, have found that responses to interviews vary with the differences between the interviewer's and the respondent's sex, age, color, religion, and other background factors. If a sixty-year-old man is asked his opinions on some educational issue, he may respond quite differently if the interviewer is a barefoot, long-haired male than if it is an attractive young woman or a conservatively dressed middle-aged woman.

To obtain clear, undistorted, normal signals from phenomena, you can take the following precautions: Remove any cues that might cause subjects to alter their behavior, eliminate competing sensory stimuli, place yourself in the most favorable vantage point for observations, and employ specially devised instruments to extend the range and clarity of your observations.

Perception

Observation is more than experiencing sensations. Observation is sensation plus perception. Sensation is the immediate result of a stimulus to the sense organs: a sound, a smell, or a visual experience. This information is not useful unless it is interpreted. One can hear a sound, but it remains a mere noise until one learns to identify it as the ringing of the telephone, rumbling of thunder, or mewing of the cat. *Perception* is the art of linking what is sensed with some past experience to give the sensation meaning. When the Hontoon family is at the park, tiny baby Tim notices a moving object; his four-year-old brother Dale recognizes that it is a bird, for he has seen them in his storybooks; his mother explains that a recent magazine called these small yellow birds warblers; and his father, an ornithologist, identifies the bird as a Nashville warbler. Aside from the baby, each member of the family linked up what he had seen with his past experience; each engaged in perception.

Meanings are in people's minds rather than in the objects themselves. Hence, when looking at the same object, everyone does not "see" the same thing. A layman may view chairs as solid objects; a physicist may view them as unstable, moving clusters of atoms. One person, moreover, may see the same object in different ways at different times. One may look at a line drawing of a cube, for example, and see it as an open box at one moment, a solid cube of ice at another time, and a square wire frame at a later date. The drawing does not change, but the observer's organization of what he sees does.

Perceptions may be relatively simple or highly complex. They may involve a single sense organ, as when one identifies the color of an object. On the other hand, several senses, a wide background of experience, and prolonged training may be required for a person to give a detailed interpretation of the sensations contributing to a given experience. The perceptions of a novice in any field—science, education, music—are apt to be vague, meager, and uncritical. Those of an expert are more definite, detailed, and discriminate.

Conception

An investigator cannot rely exclusively on attention, sensation, and perception to observe and gain reliable knowledge about phenomena. On some occasions one encounters similarities in diverse phenomena for which one's current perceptions—storehouse of past experience—do not provide adequate meaning. If these similarities appear to give a meaningful insight into some differentiating characteristic of reality, a researcher may construct and define an imaginative concept—brain waves, genes, self-concept, attitude, social distance—to identify and explain this phenomenon that has not previously been stored in scientists' perceptual memory banks.

A *concept* is a symbol or term—a class name—that is invented to communicate with others about the similarities or relationships that one has noted. In a nonresearch environment, one can talk loosely about motivation, social cohesiveness, morale, or any other concept; but in a research situation, one defines concepts clearly and devises indexes that will enable another observer to identify the value of the concept in any particular occurrence. The definition states explicitly not only what to observe—what to include and exclude—but also how to observe and measure it.

Concepts are products of both abstracting and generalizing; they contain both more and less meaning than the empirical data from which they are derived. The concept of "liquidity," for example, can be derived from experiences with honey, water, milk, brandy, syrup, and oil. This concept makes one see what is common in objects that are quite different and enables one to identify and group similar entities under this unifying concept. The concept of liquidity is more meaningful than the observation of honey alone, since it summarizes a number of observations, yet it loses some of the uniqueness and concreteness of honey, such as its color and sweetness.

Concepts can range from simple similarities which are directly observable, such as liquidity, to complex relationships which are hidden from view but presumably exist. Through logical arguments one ties concepts to empirical referents—observable evidence. Knowledge, for example, is not an observed entity; it is merely inferred from using instruments which sample subject behavior. Motivation is inferred on the basis of observed relationships between entities and events. Reading readiness, cooperative attitudes, and conditioned reflexes cannot be observed directly; they are observable only indirectly as they manifest themselves in behavior.

After constructing a concept or conceptual scheme, one reobserves phenomena to see whether one can find facts—observable evidence—that fit into this framework. If support is available, the newfound concept feeds back into perception, giving scientists cores of knowledge that they can use and need not learn again. What one observes depends, in part, on one's conceptual equipment, one's ability to conceive of logical constructs that are meaningfully related to education but are not obvious to everyone.

Conditions That Impede or Improve Observation

Observations can be made by anyone, but accurate and fruitful observations are usually the product of considerable practice and training. The following discussion gives a brief survey of some of the conditions that impede or improve observation.

OBSTACLES TO ACCURATE OBSERVATION   People in all walks of life use their sensory capacities to become aware of phenomena in their environment and interpret these sensations in terms of their past experiences. All too frequently, they quickly associate a sensory signal with some previously acquired knowledge and jump to the conclusion that they have seen or heard something they really have not. When a small, dark object travels across a picnic table, you may immediately associate this occurrence with your storehouse of picnic information and conclude that the object is an ant when it actually is a crumb that has rolled off the chocolate cake. Anticipation of an event can also cause people to make a faulty inference. Newspaper stories concerning flying saucers usually bring a rash of reports from readers who have seen a moving object and have concluded that it is a spaceship. The possibility of perceptual error is always present when the observer makes inferences on the basis of scanty sensory cues.

Strong personal interests tend to make research workers see only those things they want to see. After having reviewed many scientific studies made of animal learning, Bertrand Russell noted that

> . . . all the animals have behaved so as to confirm the philosophy in which the observer believed before his observations began. Nay, more, they have all displayed the national characteristics of the observer. Animals studied by Americans rush about frantically, with an incredible display of hustle and pep, and at last achieve the desired result by chance. Animals observed by Germans sit still and think, and at last evolve the solution out of their inner consciousness [87:32–33].

Because human beings can choose to interpret or ignore stimuli impinging upon them, their private passions and preconceptions can often serve as stumbling blocks to impartial observation.

Perceptions are subject to distortions because of the observer's emotions, motivations, prejudices, mental sets, sense of values, physical condition, and errors of inference. Psychology professors often demonstrate the unreliability of human observation by staging a well-rehearsed mock shooting and asking students to write a description of what they have seen. The results are amazing! Not uncommonly students fail to agree on the size, age, dress, and number of participants in the incident, as well as the order of events and the type and number of weapons used. They not only miss seeing some important things but also report details that are pure fabrications.

A person tends to see what he knows. If a teacher, doctor, and architect inspect a school building, each will see the things that are of special interest to him or her and will tend to overlook other matters. The teacher will notice the instructional situations, the doctor the health conditions, and the architect the structure and design of the building. If one knows little about a particular subject, one usually does not "see too much" when observing it.

EFFORTS TO OBJECTIFY OBSERVATIONS   Everyone observes, but usually casually rather than systematically. To increase the range, richness, and accuracy of scientific observations, a researcher acquires a broad background of knowledge in the field wherein a problem lies. This knowledge helps one to determine what facts to look for and when and where one may find them and to perceive them when they are present. A scientist also studies the special observational instruments and procedures designed to gather facts, learns about their limitations, and becomes proficient in employing them and checking their operational performance for precision and accuracy. Movie cameras, mechanical counters, tape recorders, and similar devices are not subject to selective memory decay and may provide an investigator with firsthand knowledge that is more richly detailed and more reliable than a human observer can record. The evidence, moreover, can be studied immediately or as often as necessary in the future.

Because workers in a research project may fail to record significant data or may interpret what they observe in light of their own cultural experiences and biases, a scientist gives explicit directions for making measurements and observations and works out special devices and procedures to reduce the amount of variation that will occur in viewing phenomena or reporting data. Like a proofreader, piano tuner, tea-taster, or airplane spotter, a researcher trains the people who work with him to discriminate between similar stimuli that are encountered in the field. Alfred Kinsey required that his interviewers have a full year of training before he would accept their data.

To guard against becoming so obsessed with a hypothesis—so set on finding facts that support a proposed solution to a problem—that they fail to detect or ignore facts that do not conform to it, researchers make a serious study of competing hypotheses that is, of proposed explanations differing from their own. When making observations, they strive to notice all significant aspects of the situation—unanticipated as well as anticipated events and conditions—and deliberately search for unsuspected facts that disprove their hypothesis. Researchers always invite colleagues to check their findings. Whenever possible, they repeat experiments to see whether the results will be the same on each occasion.

To avoid errors in perception that arise because of faulty recall, researchers record their data in an exact system of notation as soon after making an observation as possible. Delaying the compilation of their notes may cause them to forget relevant data or to have blurred, distorted, or incorrect impressions of what happened. When recording data, they include every significant detail about the phenomena, equipment, procedures, and difficulties encountered. To avoid over-looking important facts, they may construct a list of items to be noted during each observation. A novice observer may err in keeping too few and too scanty notes. Experience teaches trained scientists to record comprehensive, complete notes and to make detailed drawings of all pertinent incidents that transpire during the investigation, for these items prove to be invaluable possessions when the time comes to analyze and interpret the data or to explain and defend their findings.

A research worker soon learns that words that seem to be specific may carry more than one meaning. As one man suggests, "age" of the subject may refer to present age, age at last birthday, or age at next birthday. Consequently, in scientific work investigators define their terms and check to make certain that each sentence describes exactly what they observe and that no other interpretation can be placed upon their words.

Whenever possible, investigators describe their data quantitative-ly: in terms of height, distance, duration, speed, or number of units. Rather than describing pupils as large boys, they give anthropometric measurements. Rather than recording that pupils look at television programs frequently, they record the number of minutes per day which the pupils spend viewing television. Rather than describing their subjects as "a group of students," they state the exact number of pupils of each sex in the group and the range of their ages. Numerical measures are more precise than word descriptions and may make possible further analysis of the problem by statistical procedures. Whenever scientists use questionnaires, ratings, or lists to gather data, they try to put them in a form that requires quantitative answers.

NATURE OF FACTS

Scientists make observations to get at facts. But what are facts? Facts are different things to different people. When laymen speak of wanting the facts, they may have a rather narrow concept of the nature of facts. They may believe that facts are precise, permanent, and self-evident in meaning. To scientists, facts are not things that are evident but, rather, data one discovers through purposeful probing.

Scientists are not dogmatic about the certainty of facts. They emphasize the usefulness of facts but are constantly critical of them. They do not expect all facts to be equally stable, precise, and accessible. Their prolonged pursuit of facts has taught them that some can be expressed quantitatively, others can be expressed only in words, and some do not readily lend themselves to either mathematical or verbal descriptions. To scientists, facts are events that occur and leave records. They may occur naturally or researchers may·make them occur. Since facts are records of occurrences, scientists devote considerable effort to developing techniques or devices for making records of events. Ultimately, facts are also statements in words or mathematical symbols that are based on records of events. To scientists, a fact is any experience, change, occurrence, or event that is sufficiently stable and supported by enough evidence to be counted on in an investigation.

Accessibility of Facts

Not all facts are equally accessible to the observer. Personal or private facts, such as dreams, fears, preferences, feelings, and revelations, lie hidden deep within the individual. They may be very real to the person concerned and pass that individual's personal tests of reliability, but they are not accessible for examination by others. Pink elephants are real to the alcoholic and horrible dreams are real to a child, but these specific facts cannot be verified empirically by someone else. One cannot observe these inner, personal phenomena directly to see whether one draws the same conclusions about them as other observers or the individual having the experience. If one relies on the individual's description of a personal experience, the observer may obtain inaccurate information. Tommy may tell the doctor that his stomach hurts when the pain is actually located in his chest or when he feels good but has an intense longing to stay home from school.

Research workers may infer that the private experience of an individual is like one they themselves had under similar circumstances, but this may not be true. In daily life people often make such errors. Joe Adams assumes that his wife gets as much pleasure out of witnessing a football game as he does. Investigators studying people of a culture, social status, or era different from their own may fall into error if they conclude that their subjects experience the same reaction to given stimuli as they do. Raw fish eyes served at a puberty rite feast may be a nauseous form of nourishment to an American anthropologist but a delightful delicacy to the natives. Watching a child being flogged will not arouse the same response in a modern educator as it did in a teacher of ancient Sparta. When seeking reliable information, it is always dangerous for a scientist to equate another person's inner experiences with his own.

Because of the hidden nature of personal facts, social scientists often have difficulty in interpreting a commonplace event. If a student takes the smallest piece of cake at a tea, for example, different observers may conclude that he is trying to be polite, doesn't like chocolate cake, or thinks the hostess is a poor cook. The student may report that his doctor has placed him on a diet to conceal the fact that he has just eaten two candy bars and is not hungry. Personal, inner facts are one person's knowledge, and that person may not be willing or able to analyze his experience accurately.

Public facts—those which can be observed and tested by everyone—constitute relatively impersonal knowledge. They do not depend on the peculiarities of a single individual for verification. Because they are open to inspection by everyone and are agreed upon by a number of independent observers, public facts are much more reliable than inner, personal facts. If one observer asserts that an object weighs ten pounds, for example, it is not necessary to take his word for it. Any normal person can test the validity of that statement by reference to evidence which is independent of the observers. If many people use their senses and special instruments to test the weight of the object and they all reach approximately the same conclusion, their findings can be accepted as being quite reliable. In time, public facts win common acceptance as the most trustworthy knowledge available.

Natural scientists deal primarily with public facts, but some of the most pressing problems demanding solution in the social sciences involve personal, inner facts or a mixture of public and personal facts. Natural scientists have devised a number of reliable instruments that enable workers to weigh, measure, and time phenomena in their field. When social scientists attempt to create similar instruments, they are confounded by the concealed, elusive nature of private facts.

Levels of Facts

Some facts are derived directly from the impact of stimuli upon the senses; others are reached by conceptual manipulations. For purposes of summarization, the following paragraphs discuss three levels of facts that range from (1) those that one becomes aware of through immediate sense experiences to (2) those that one identifies by describing or interpreting immediate personal experiences to (3) those one identifies by engaging in a highly abstract reasoning process.

Facts of immediate experience are pure sensations without any names or labels. They represent raw experiences because no attempt is made to identify, interpret, or assign meaning to them. These facts are known by immediate apprehension alone. It is doubtful that people other than babies can have such raw experiences, for human beings early in life begin to name or assign meaning to experiences. Even the most primitive type of "knowing" involves a slight degree of conceptualization.

The second level of facts, those describing or interpreting immediate experience, comprises not just raw experience. When you describe or interpret a sensation as a sound of a jet engine, you engage in perception or a low level of conceptualization. Through an intellectual process, you associate the raw sensation with your past experiences and identify it with that class of things you call "sounds from jet aircraft." Facts describing immediate experiences are relatively close to sensory experiences. They are not highly conceptualized. Some, however, are more conceptual than others. Facts which are primarily sensory in nature, such as sound or smell, are less conceptual than those derived from thought or reasoning experiences, such as memories or ideas.

The third level of facts includes those which are highly abstract

and conceptual in nature. These facts are remote from sensory experiences. They are derived primarily from human reasoning processes and
cannot be observed directly by the senses. Although they are highly
conceptual in nature, they are supported by enough empirical evidence
to prove they exist and, therefore, are acceptable as facts. Through an
involved reasoning process, for example, you construct the proposition: The world is "round."[1] You cannot see that it is round with your
naked eye, but you can provide sufficient evidence traceable to various
forms of sensory experience to confirm this proposition. You may point
out that a ship disappears over the horizon progressively—hull, cabins,
and finally smokestack. Another example of a fact derived from abstract
reasoning is one that shows the relationship between two concepts.
That reading ability is closely related to arithmetic ability is accepted
as a fact. This relationship cannot be observed directly by an individual;
it can be only experienced on the conceptual level. Since this concept
can be traced to empirical referents, it receives indirect substantiation
as a fact. Most people do not realize how little of what they accept as
facts is given by raw experience alone. Conceptualizing plays a major
role in obtaining facts.

Life of Facts

Scientists do not claim that facts possess everlasting validity; they
believe that facts are subject to reinterpretation or revision whenever
researchers gain a better insight into phenomena. Facts, especially
those that are highly conceptual in nature, can have careers. They are
born to satisfy a need; they survive and are used elsewhere. Some facts
experience a long life—what may appear to be an everlasting life. But,
as the years pass, other facts may gain new meanings—meanings that
may broaden, narrow, negate, or contradict the original functions of the
concepts. The term "good health" once conveyed the meaning of
physical well-being, but later was broadened to include mental and
emotional well-being. The meaning of "democracy" was once confined
to political aspects of life, but later broadened to include economic and
social aspects of life. Words have meanings that people give them.
Believing that concepts bearing the same label are the same functionally may lead a researcher into serious trouble. A fact may have validity
in one context, at one point of time, when measured by one type of
technology, but be invalid if any of these factors change. Researchers

[1]Studies of the orbital flight of Vanguard I show the earth to be slightly pear-shaped rather than a
bulging sphere.

are always wary of facts; they want to know how the observed facts were defined and what techniques were employed to measure them.

Functions of Facts

Human beings are forever searching for a better understanding of the world in which they live. Finding answers to their questions entails a persistent search for facts. The marriage of facts and theories produces many advances in science. The following paragraphs examine some of the functions facts play in this marriage.

STIMULATION OF THEORIZATION BY FACTS   The scientist does not theorize in a vacuum. The history of science is replete with instances of simple observation of facts that have led to the formulation of important theories. When Archimedes observed water overflowing while he was taking a bath, he grasped the principle of displacement. When Newton saw an apple fall, he developed the principle of gravitation. When Watt watched steam escape from a teakettle, he envisioned the principle of steam power. Facts are prods that stimulate the theorizing process.

Of course, not everyone is capable of leaping from a fact to a theory; many people made the same observations as Newton, Watt, and Archimedes without being intellectually stimulated. Several scientists noticed the inhibition of bacterial growth by molds before Fleming saw the significance in this fact that led to the discovery of penicillin. As Pasteur pointed out, when people make observations, "chance favors the prepared mind." One must have a broad background of knowledge if one is to recognize an unusual fact and utilize this sudden insight to structure an explanation for the nature of the phenomenon. Facts cannot initiate theorization unless an alert, disciplined, and imaginative mind observes them and mentally constructs a possible explanation for them.

CONFIRMATION OF THEORIES BY FACTS   Facts are essential for the establishment of a scientific theory: they determine whether a theory can be confirmed or should be rejected or reformulated. Facts may not be available immediately for the confirmation or rejection of a theory, but they are necessary for the eventual acceptance or abandonment of it. The discovery of pertinent facts that support a theory strengthen it. But, if facts are found that do not substantiate the theory, one must reject or reformulate the theory to fit the new evidence. Theories must be tailored to fit the facts and remodeled whenever new facts reveal the need for such action.

CLARIFICATION OF THEORIES BY FACTS   Theories are refined and clarified as knowledge accumulates. New theories in the social sciences are apt to be elusive and ill-defined; they often give a rather crude, general explanation of phenomena. Further observation and experimentation may reveal, however, facts that not only agree with the theory but also specify in detail and with precision what the theory states in a general way. For instance, modern psychologists have developed the so-called "field theories of learning" which contribute to our general understanding of the learning process. Yet, investigations conducted by Tolman, Lewin, Anderson, Murphy, and many others have added considerable substance and depth to these general theories of learning. Their work illustrates how additional facts can give greater specificity and breadth to a theory.

NATURE OF THEORIES

What are *theories?* They are statements that explain a particular segment of phenomena. These statements, which may be called "guesses," "hunches," "principles," "empirical generalizations," "models," "hypotheses," "theories," or "laws," differ in explicitness, scope, depth, and fertility of explanation. They range along a continuum from nonscientific to scientific, from the very crude to the quite refined. Some theories, for example, deal with practical classroom problems, such as methods of teaching addition. More sophisticated theories may seek to explain learning, retention, or transfer, which apply to all school subjects and to all ages of humans.

The average person thinks that the philosopher is concerned with theories and the scientist with facts. A scientist is envisaged as a disciplined, dedicated investigator who searches for the "true" facts, rather than as an unconventional intellectual adventurer who creates imaginative structures. Many people dismiss theories as mere speculations or daydreams, but they respect facts. They believe that facts are definite, real, and concrete, and that their meaning is self-evident.

Many educators also scoff at theories and demand that researchers provide them with "practical facts" that will help them in the classroom. But a mass of isolated concepts—some that have been verified as facts through observation and others that are suspected but as yet unverified facts—are not adequate tools for solving problems. To push back the frontiers of knowledge, concepts must be bound together into a testable theory. Consequently, researchers move back and forth between the operational, inductive activities of observing, defining, and accumulating facts and the conceptual, deductive activities of theorizing about facts and their relations to one another.

Construction of Theories

A scientific theory consists of statements which connect concepts in a logically unified way to provide an interpretation of a particular segment of phenomena. The theorist formulates and uses concepts that have a particular relevance for the phenomena under study. And, in addition to checking the substance and clarity of the concepts, he or she states explicitly the functional relationship between or among them. By the means of logical inference, the theorist ties the concepts together into an internally coherent framework that provides an explanation of events.

A scientific theory consists of concepts and their relations to one another. A theory is, ideally, a universal empirical statement which asserts a causal connection between two or more types of events. At its simplest, a theory states that whenever X occurs, then Y occurs. A scientific theory is universal because it states something about the conditions under which one class of phenomena will be connected with another class of phenomena so that an event occurs. Theories have universal applicability, assert general rules, and make statements about whole categories of events rather than particular events; but they are empirical in that consequences can be deduced from them which can be checked by observations of particular events.

Little scientific progress would be made if researchers rejected reasoning and accepted only those facts that the senses could immediately apprehend. Conceptual fertility—the capacity to structure bold and radical guesses about how facts are ordered—is the greatest gift a scientist can possess. Although science stresses objectivity, it is to a large degree concerned with the subjective act of theorizing. Theorizing is not an esoteric exercise that researchers practice in their "ivory towers," but rather a practical form of mental gymnastics that enables them to explore the underlying mechanisms of their phenomena. Theorizing provides the road maps for research; without it new knowledge cannot be discovered.

Types of Theories

The entities, events, or relationships that researchers choose to observe are dictated by some theory. They cannot proceed without a theory, but they may proceed without clearly identifying their theory. Their theory may be a vague hunch, an informed guess, a set of inconsistent assumptions, or a logically structured explanation. When structuring theories, not all scientists give equal emphasis to the fact-gathering inductive procedures and the theory-formulating deductive procedures, nor do they move from one procedure to the other in the same order (71:4–46).

HYPOTHETICAL-DEDUCTIVE THEORY   Deductive theories emphasize logical coherence. The knowledge systems developed by logicians and mathematicians, which may state nothing about the real world, are by their very nature deductive. That is, they consist of sets of axiomatic statements which are true by definition, and then by logical argument other statements are derived. All well-developed scientific theories have this form of logical-deductive character, but scientific theories cannot rest solely on logic. The logical claims must be verified by actual observation of what happens in the real world of experience.

Some researchers emphasize the explicit and logical formulation of explanatory propositions even when the observational evidence is known to be inadequate. Their motto is: Theorize first and then make empirical checks to correct the theory. The hypothetical-deductive theory consists of (1) a set of definitions of the critical terms, (2) a set of hypothetical statements concerning the presumptive relationships among the phenomena represented by the critical terms, and (3) a series of deduced consequences that are logically derived from the hypothetical statements.[2] These elements are tied together in the form of a conditional "if-then" statement which stipulates: If such and such antecedent condition exists, then such and such consequences will be observable (see Appendix E). The validity of a hypothetical-deductive theory is dependent upon the extent of the agreement between the deduced consequences, on the one hand, and the observation of phenomena to which it refers, on the other.

FUNCTIONAL THEORY   Some theories are evolved in a less formal manner. Many investigators believe that an undue, premature concern with ordering facts and structuring highly formalized theories may cause

---

[2]Hypothetical statements may be referred to as "postulates" or "axioms," and deduced consequences may be called "theorems."

them to terminate their exploratory activities too soon and may blind them to other facts and ordering possibilities. To them, a theory is a provisional tool. They place less emphasis on elegant conceptualizations and logical-deductive procedures and more explicit emphasis upon observation and data-oriented explanations. They believe that the interaction of observational and conceptual processes is necessary for scientific progress and that, therefore, the two processes should proceed simultaneously and should be given more or less equal emphasis.

INDUCTIVE THEORY   The inductive theory emphasizes after-the-fact explanation. Facts are established first, and theory emerges from a careful consideration of these facts. Factual acquisition is maximized and the hypothetical-deductive process is minimized. The theory is no more than a summarizing statement about specific, concrete observations. Some highly imaginative and productive researchers claim that this is the procedure that they follow. But their claims are exaggerated, for they do not merely make chance observations. Their minds are not virgin receptacles and their observations are not completely unbiased. They start out with some expectations; some informal theory governs the choices they make. They cannot keep these hunches private forever; eventually, they must communicate them effectively. Critics of the radical empiricists also believe that a reluctance to utilize deductive procedures makes it more difficult to deal with the intricacies of complex phenomena.

MODEL   The term *model* (paradigm) has become quite fashionable in the literature, and a bewildering array of models have been developed. Essentially, models are simplified or familiar structures which are used to gain insights into phenomena that scientists want to explain. (See Appendix F for an educational model.)

Models may be drawings or physical replicas that represent the real thing, or they may be more abstract. Mathematical equations, verbal statements, symbolic descriptions, graphic presentations, or electromechanical devices may be used to represent objects and relationships that are being modeled. Some investigators locate a structure about which much is known and use it to gain insight into a field about which little is known. A researcher who wishes to study how rumors spread, for example, may wonder whether they spread in the same way as diseases. In other words, the researcher may utilize the laws of epidemiology, about which much is known, as a model for a theory about rumor transmission.

Some scholars contend that models and theories are one and the same thing, but other scholars make the following distinction (71:104–129): Both theories and models are conceptual schemes that explain the relationships of the variables under consideration. But models are analogies (this thing is like that thing) and therefore can tolerate some facts that are not in accord with the real phenomena. A theory, on the other hand, is supposed to describe the facts and relationships that exist, and any facts that are not compatible with the theory invalidate the theory. In summary, some scholars argue that models are judged by their usefulness and theories by their truthfulness; models are not theories but tools that are used as a basis for formal and rigorous theory construction.

Functions of Theories

Theories serve as tools and goals, as means and ends. As goals, they provide explanations for specific phenomena with maximal probability and exactitude. As tools, they provide a guiding framework for observation and discovery. The following paragraphs explain how theories help researchers examine and explain phenomena and thereby contribute to the advancement of knowledge.

IDENTIFICATION OF RELEVANT FACTS Theories govern the kind of phenomena that investigators study. Theories provide frameworks within which and against which investigators observe, test, and interpret their observations. Scientists cannot collect facts about everything. They must narrow the area of their interest to limited segments of phenomena and give these segments their undivided attention. Investigators, for example, may study the game of baseball in the sociological framework of play, in the physical framework of stress and velocity, in the economic framework of supply and demand, or in many other ways. But a multiplicity of facts are associated with any one of these problem areas. Not until researchers construct theoretical solutions for their problems do they know precisely what facts to observe. After theorizing that there is a relationship between *A* and *B*, they know which specific facts to locate: those that will provide the empirical evidence necessary to confirm or disconfirm their theory. The theory determines the number and kinds of facts that are relevant to a study. Facts do not identify themselves as relevant; only a theory can tell an investigator what to observe and what to ignore.

FORMULATION OF LOGICAL CONSTRUCTS Reliable knowledge can be acquired through direct observation and measurement, but many factors that contribute to the educational phenomena are not observable directly. Consequently, investigators often create imaginative concepts, such as anxiety, dogmatism, or motor set, to account for behavior or effects that they observe. These concepts may be called *logical constructs, theoretical constructs,* or just *constructs.* A concept is a product of observing diverse entities, abstracting similarities from them, and making a generalization about them. Observation precedes the theoretical operation, but the intellectual process of abstracting and generalizing are necessary to produce a new core of meaning about some aspect of reality. Concept development and the precise description of the referent behavior are of utmost importance in research, for these shorthand symbols are the major elements of theories; they guide theoretical and experimental thinking. Concepts convey considerable compact information to scientists and make it easier for scientists to manipulate facts and to communicate findings.

CLASSIFICATION OF PHENOMENA   Scientists cannot work efficiently and effectively with masses of assorted facts; they need some scheme for ordering the data in their fields. Therefore, the first stage in any science consists in constructing theoretical frameworks for classifying facts. Classifying involves formulating hypotheses as to the nature of subject matter in a field. In the beginning, any arbitrary scheme of grouping phenomena may be temporarily adopted in the interest of mastering the subject matter. Phenomena in any field have many similarities that may be employed as a basis for classification. Using the more obvious ones is often the initial step taken in deriving a classification system. With more experience, scientists usually detect less obvious but more relevant and significant concepts or principles for grouping, dividing, and analyzing subject matter. Classifying substances in accordance with their color, for example, gives us some knowledge about them, but classifying them in accordance with their chemical composition gives us knowledge about all the known reactions that depend on that composition. Classification systems differ widely in their fruitfulness as principles for yielding and organizing knowledge. Some classification schemes serve very limited purposes; they are derived from concepts that do not provide a framework for systematizing all that is known or can be found out about phenomena. The objective in any science is to develop classification systems that will provide the most significant clues to the nature of phenomena in the field and that will allow the discovery of many more resemblances among like phenomena and many more hypotheses about the subject matter than were originally recognized.

The older sciences have been quite successful in devising such systematic conceptual schemes. Geologists have developed systems for classifying rocks, and botanists have developed systems for classifying plants. Educators have devised some classification schemes for phenomena in their field, but many of these schemes have been rather crude and of limited usefulness. But as more and more investigators describe the complex and diverse facts relating to their subject matter, note the similarities, differences, and relationships among them, and structure frameworks to categorize them, they should gain a deeper and clearer insight into teaching, learning, and the development of children.

SUMMARIZATION OF FACTS   Theorization is used to summarize knowledge with varying degrees of comprehensiveness and precision. These summaries may range from relatively simple generalizations to exceedingly complex theoretical relationships. A summarization may describe a limited range of events, such as when an educator makes a generalization about the practice of granting varsity letters to high school athletes. This low level of summarizing is not usually referred to as a "theory." But one might later note a relationship between varsity letters, honor societies, and certificates of achievement and construct the broader generalization that public recognition rewards are a means of motivating pupils. Summarization on a high scientific level, of course, involves integrating the major empirical generalizations into a more comprehensive theoretical framework.

PREDICTION OF FACTS   A generalization about data—a theory—enables one to predict the existence of unobserved instances conforming to it. For instance, if the generalization that a high rate of truancy is associated with slum areas has been confirmed, one can look for and expect to find this pattern in slum areas where no truancy statistics have been compiled. Theory enables one to predict what should be observable where data are not available. Theory serves as a powerful beacon that directs investigators in their search for facts.

REVELATION OF NEEDED RESEARCH   Because theories may lack some supporting evidence that is necessary to provide the maturity and vitality essential for their proper functioning, they are an excellent source to turn to when in search of research problems. Even a rather low level of theorization can point out the need for further research. Suppose, for example, that an investigator finds evidence supporting the following generalization: A rather high correlation exists between the physical endowments and proficiencies of students in a suburban junior high school and the frequency, duration, and nature of their play activities. This generalization suggests problems that other workers might explore: Does the general relationship above hold true for elementary and high school students? Does this pattern hold true for rural groups or youths in other countries? Does it hold equally true for both sexes? Does grouping the students in accordance with their body builds (ectomorphy, mesomorphy, and endomorphy) or their intelligence influence the general relationship in any way? Theorization on any level tends to open up new avenues of inquiry even as it did in this instance.

Interdependence of Components

Scientific investigations involve several components that are interdependent. The discussion below gives a simplified summary of their relationships.

INTERDEPENDENCE OF METHODS AND THEORIES   The methods employed to do the work in each stage of research are depicted within the circle in Figure 3.1. The various stages of research that are involved in formulating and testing theories are depicted on the rim of the circle. You will note that the methods of logical induction and deduction are employed to select or create relevant concepts (verified and unverified facts), trace possible relations between them, weave them into theories, and deduce the consequences that must be observable to confirm the theories. The methods of operationalization and instrumentation are employed to define what operations or testing instruments are to be used to ascertain whether the consequences are observable. The methods of scaling and measurement are employed to classify and quantify the data which provide the observable evidence required to confirm or disconfirm the theory. During an investigation, one may discover new concepts or relations or learn how to describe old ones more accurately. These new or reformulated concepts, in turn, may be woven into a new theory that can be tested.

Theory formulation and verification are not separated from method; the two processes are highly interdependent. The precision of the instruments available to make measurements, for example, can influence the facts that are obtained to test theories. When speed is measured by a stopwatch, the observed fact (two athletes were tied in a

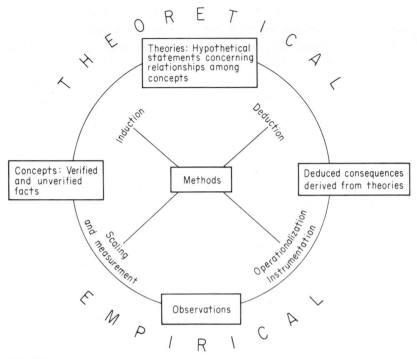

FIGURE 3.1

A simplified representation of the components and processes involved in scientific investigations.

footrace) may be a different perception of reality than when it is measured by an electronic device (one athlete won the race). What perception of reality is arrived at depends on the method employed to define the concepts that are woven into a theory. The theory that poverty and slums cause crime, for example, may be confirmed if crime is defined as "officially measured" crime, but it may not be confirmed if the definition of crime includes "white-collar" crimes committed in business, government, and professional circles. The methods employed to define concepts and test theories influence theories, and, in turn, theories suggest what types of instruments to use or operations to perform for the theory tests.

INTERDEPENDENCE OF FACTS AND THEORIES   Advances in knowledge in any field are dependent upon theorization, but theories cannot be constructed or confirmed without the aid of facts, that is, concepts that have been verified by observation or "guessed-at" or suspected facts that await verification. Facts supply the raw building materials; the investigator's imagination and intellect supply the theoretical framework—the blueprint that describes the known and unknown facts and relationships that presumably produce the phenomena under consideration. Facts alone are a rather useless pile of bricks, and theories must rely on facts as the building blocks for their construction. Facts contribute to both the conception and the confirmation of theories. In science, scholars put their trust "not in facts as such, but rather in the interaction of many minds observing similar facts, projecting these facts against different conceptual backgrounds, testing the divergent interpretations by means of further observation, and seeking explanations of any final differences" (89:34). Science rests on facts and on ideas; it is both objective and subjective; it is a product of empirical knowledge and imaginative mental constructs; it advances under the power of inductive and deductive thought processes.

4 DOCUMENTATION IN PROBLEM SOLVING

few centuries ago the scholar aspired to acquire an encyclopedic education that would acquaint him with all available knowledge. But keeping abreast of the vast and complex developments in one specialized field is difficult today. To aid the research worker in locating, selecting, and utilizing the references that appear in an ever-increasing variety of printed resources, this chapter provides a study guide for surveying (1) the types of available references, (2) the nature of information that each contains, and (3) how to use these references.

REFERENCE BOOKS

To facilitate the search for reference books, such as encyclopedias, dictionaries, yearbooks, and directories, one may consult the following carefully compiled volumes: *Guide to Reference Books,* by Constance

M. Winchell (114), which has biennial supplements to bring the information up-to-date and describes and evaluates about 7,500 references. *Guide to Reference Material*, by Albert J. Walford, is a three-volume work which covers (1) science and technology (1966), (2) philosophy and psychology, religion, social sciences, geography, bibliography, and history (1968), and (3) reference books, languages, arts, and literature (1970). Compared with Winchell's *Guide*, Walford's work is more comprehensive and more international in scope. *Publications of the United Nations System: A Reference Guide* gives information published by that organization. *A Reference Guide to Audiovisual Information* (1972) is a key to the books and periodicals relating to the media.

If you desire more detailed bibliographic information about the sources listed in this chapter, you may find them in the preceding guides. Even after becoming thoroughly familiar with various reference books, it is advisable to check Winchell or the other guides occasionally to discover whether any useful new references are available or whether any changes have been made in the author, editor, title, publisher, or scope of material covered by the older references. If you fail to take such precautions, you may continue to search for items in a periodical index long after the information that interests you has been dropped; moreover, you may never discover that materials that were once published in one journal or index are now being presented in another source or under a new title.

Encyclopedias

Encyclopedias may be used to check a fact or to obtain a brief overview of a topic. These storehouses of information usually contain well-rounded discussions and selected bibliographies that are prepared by specialists. Every educator finds the comprehensive *Encyclopedia of Educational Research*, Robert L. Ebel (ed.), 1969, an invaluable reference. This book is arranged alphabetically by subject, and for each field of research it (1) presents a critical evaluation and summary of the work that has been done, (2) suggests needed research, and (3) includes a selective bibliography. In addition, there are many special-field encyclopedias available, such as *The Encyclopedia of Sports, Encyclopedia of Human Behavior*, and *Encyclopedia of Education*.

The following list gives samples of other types of encyclopedias that educators might use: *International Encyclopedia of the Social*

Sciences, Van Nostrand's Scientific Encyclopedia, Encyclopedia of Sociology, Encyclopedia of Psychology, Encyclopaedia of World History, Encyclopedia of Philosophy, Encyclopedia of Mental Health, and *Encyclopedia of Associations.*

Dictionaries

Dictionaries are the constant companions of a researcher. Among the better-known general dictionaries are the *Oxford English Dictionary,* twelve volumes; *Dictionary of American English on Historical Principles,* four volumes; *Funk and Wagnalls New Standard Dictionary;* and *Webster's New International Dictionary of the English Language.* More specialized dictionaries are also needed at times, such as *Acronyms* and *Initialisms Dictionary,* which is a guide to alphabetic designations, contractions, and similar condensed appellations; and *Words and Phrases Index,* which is a guide to antedatings, new words, new compounds, and new meanings. Because a researcher must define educational terms with precision, a researcher in this field usually owns a copy of the *Dictionary of Education,* Carter V. Good (ed.), 1973. Some of the special-field dictionaries one may use are: *Dictionary of Sociology,* G. D. Mitchell (ed.); *Dictionary of Social Sciences,* Julius Gould and William Kolb (eds.); *Comprehensive Dictionary of Psychological and Psychoanalytical Terms,* H. B. English and Ava C. A. English; *Dictionary of Statistical Terms,* Maurice G. Kendall and William R. A. Buckland (eds.); and *Dictionary of Modern History, 1789–1945,* Alan W. Palmer (ed.).

Thesauri

A new type of reference, a thesaurus of descriptors, has been compiled in conjunction with the development of information-retrieval systems. A thesaurus of descriptors is a list of words and phrases that indexers use to describe a periodical article or research report so that it can be stored for future search and retrieval and that researchers can use to search for information that has been stored in the system. Four of the thesauri that provide indexers and researchers with a common communication system are *The New York Times Thesaurus of Descriptors: A Guide for Organizing, Indexing, and Searching Collections of Information on Current Events; The Thesaurus of ERIC Descriptors; Informational Retrieval Thesaurus of Educational Terms;* and the *UNESCO: IBE Education Thesaurus.*

Almanacs and Yearbooks

A wealth of current information may be found in almanacs and yearbooks. Up-to-date statistics and data concerning events, progress, and conditions in a wide variety of social, educational, industrial, political, financial, and religious fields appear in the *World Almanac, 1868–,*[1] *Information Please Almanac, 1947–,* and *The People's Almanac, 1975–.* The *Standard Education Almanac, 1968–,* provides a compendium of facts and statistics on virtually every aspect of education. *Negro Almanac, 1968–,* provides a compendium of information on the history and culture of Negroes, particularly in the United States. The *Almanacs of the United States* is a compilation of early almanacs and calendars (1639–1875) by states and also cites the depository of these materials.

EDUCATIONAL HANDBOOKS AND YEARBOOKS   The *Second Handbook of Research on Teaching,* R. M. W. Travers (ed.), contains scholarly materials concerning theoretical orientations, methodologies in research on teaching, and research on teaching various grade levels and subject matters. *The Yearbook of Higher Education* provides a national directory of higher education, statistics, and resource information relating to higher education, 1969–.

Recent statistics and discussions on educational problems, thought, and practices are found in several outstanding yearbooks. Some yearbooks cover a new topic of current interest each year; others give more general reviews of events. One of the most valuable yearbooks has been put out since 1902 by the National Society for the Study of Education. Each yearbook in this series is now issued in several parts; thus, a reference to this source must indicate the part as well as the year.

Many worthwhile yearbooks are also published in special fields. Educators may consult the *Mental Measurements Yearbook* (title and years of publication vary—1938, 1941, 1949, 1953, 1959, 1965, 1972), which is compiled by Oscar K. Buros. It lists all commercially available educational, psychological, and vocational tests published during the period covered by the volume and gives price, publisher, grade level, and evaluations. *The Yearbook of School Law,* edited by M. M. Chambers, 1932 to 1942, Lee O. Garber et al., 1950–1971, L. J. Peterson, 1972, and R. E. Phay, 1973–, presents abstracts of important court cases dealing with education as well as a few feature articles.

[1]Interpret references of this nature as follows: published from 1868 to the present.

Education Yearbook, 1972–73, is a comprehensive body of information reflecting the current educational scene from the local to a worldwide perspective. *Educational Media Yearbook*, 1973–, reviews and capsulizes significant aspects of the current status of educational media.

STATISTICAL INFORMATION   Statistics concerning public and private schools on all levels appear in the indispensable *Biennial Survey of Education in the United States* for the years 1916 to 1958. This work contains data on such things as personnel, enrollment, receipts, expenditures, salaries, attendance, buildings, and per-capita costs. The National Center for Education Statistics of DHEW publishes a compilation of significant statistical material in the *Digest of Educational Statistics*, 1962–, and *Projections of Educational Statistics*, 1967–. *Social Indicators*, 1973–, provides statistics on social conditions and trends in the United States in areas of health, public safety, education, employment, income, housing, leisure, recreation, and population. *Statistical Sources*, 1962–, is a source book for current statistical data. The NEA, Research Division, issues *Research Reports* and *Research Summaries*, which are excellent sources for recent statistics and discussions on topics such as salaries, working conditions, educational practices, and teacher supply and demand.

The United States Census Bureau's ten-year reports and its *Census Abstract* are reliable and detailed. The *Statistical Abstract of the United States*, 1878 –, is the annual authoritative summary of statistics on the political, social, industrial, and economic organization of the nation. *Historical Statistics of the United States*, a supplement to the *Statistical Abstract*, contains more than 8,200 time series, mostly annual, on American social and economic development covering the periods from 1610 to 1957. The *American Statistics Index* is a comprehensive guide and index to statistical publications of the United States government. Since 1947, UNESCO has published international economic statistics in the *Statistical Yearbook* and population and social statistics in the *Demographic Yearbook*.

INTERNATIONAL INFORMATION   International surveys and descriptions of educational systems in many countries are found in the *World Yearbook of Education*, 1965– (formerly the *Year Book of Education*, 1932 to 1940, 1948 to 1964). The early volumes reviewed educational developments in the major European and English-speaking nations. Since 1953, each annual edition has examined at length a particular aspect of education in many countries of the world. The theme of the 1972–1973 edition, for example, was "Issues in Education." Issued by

UNESCO is the five-volume *World Survey of Education*: vol. I, *Handbook of Educational Organization and Statistics*, 1955; vol. II, *Primary Education*, 1958; vol. III, *Secondary Education*, 1961; vol. IV, Higher Education, 1966; and vol. V, *Educational Policy, Legislation and Administration*, 1971.

Directories

Directories are as valuable in professional life as a personal address book is in private life. An educator uses them to locate the names and addresses of persons, periodicals, publishers, organizations, or firms. By consulting directories, you may find people or organizations who have similar professional interests or who are qualified to answer your questionnaires or help solve your problems. To locate an appropriate directory, you may use the *Guide to American Educational Directories*, which assembles in one volume over 3,000 educational and allied directories. The directories are listed alphabetically and are arranged under subject headings.

The Education Directory, published by the Office of Education, is a widely used reference. It has five parts and includes the following data: part I, state and territorial school officials; part II, public officials; part III, higher educational institutions—enrollment, curricula, officers, accrediting agency, and statistical tables; part IV, officers of educational associations, religious and international organizations, and educational foundations; part V, federal personnel in education. Similar information appears in *Patterson's American Education*. The *NEA Handbook* lists the NEA departments and affiliated associations and their officers. Many educational associations include membership lists in their yearbooks.

An educator might also have the occasion to consult specialized directories, such as *Research Centers Directory, Annual Register of Grant Support, Guide to American Educational Directories, Foundations Directory, The International Foundations Directory, Directory of Publishing Opportunities, Directory of Data Bases in the Social and Behavioral Sciences, National Faculty Directory*, and *Awards, Honors, and Prizes*.

Biographical Sources

When carrying out a research study, one may have to obtain a specific fact about a person, such as his birthdate, degrees, publications, present position, or professional affiliations. This type of information, as well as general information concerning the background, competency, prestige, or biases of a person, may be found in encyclopedias or in one of the following sources:

The *Biography Index*, 1947–, provides a comprehensive guide to biographical materials appearing in current books, periodicals, and *The New York Times*. This quarterly index, which has annual and three-year cumulations, indexes items by profession and occupation as well as by name. It includes persons both living and dead, lists obituaries, and indicates which articles include portraits. *The New York Times Obituaries Index*, 1858–1968, is an alphabetized listing of deceased individuals in issues of *The New York Times Index*, with entries giving complete information to locate the original news story.

Reference books that contain biographies of notable personalities both living and dead are *Webster's Biographical Dictionary*, which gives brief sketches, and the comprehensive *National Cyclopaedia of American Biography*. Deceased notables are found in the reliable and scholarly *Dictionary of American Biography* and in *Who Was Who in America*. Notable contemporaries are listed in sources such as *World Biography; Who's Who in America*, a biennial with monthly supplements; *Who's Who of American Women; Who's Who in the East* (volumes are also published for other sections of the United States); and similarly named publications in other countries. *Current Biography Yearbook* gives lively sketches of recent newsworthy names throughout the world. Some educators are included in the *Directory of American Scholars* and the *American Men of Science*, and many are listed in *Who's Who in American Education, Leaders in Education,* and *Who's Who in American College and University Administration*. Similar references have been compiled to cover art, music, government, industry, and many other fields.

Bibliographical Sources

Compiling a bibliography is one of the first and one of the last things you do in conducting a study. This essential task is less arduous and time-consuming if you are well acquainted with the various labor-saving devices at your disposal. You may find books and periodicals in the library that will help you locate bibliographies that have already been compiled. Of course, the bibliographies will vary in type and quality; some will be exhaustive and others selective or brief; some will be annotated and others not. If the bibliographies are compiled by experts in the field and give clues to the content, general value, scholarship, and significant features of the publications, they may save you weeks of searching time.

Since 1937, the excellent *Bibliographic Index* has provided a guide to bibliographies in all fields. Under subjects only, it lists bibliographies that are published as separate books or pamphlets as well as those appearing in books, pamphlets, and periodicals, both in English and foreign languages. This triannual subject index has annual and larger cumulations. For materials published earlier than 1937, an educator can consult Winchell (114) under the heading Bibliographies.

For locating educational bibliographies published since 1928, the best source is the *Education Index.* In this guide, bibliographies are listed as a subhead under a main head subject (i.e., main head Social Sciences, subhead Bibliography). Earlier bibliographies can be found in *Bibliographies and Summaries in Education to July 1, 1935*, by Walter S. Monroe and Louis Shores (eds.). Bibliographies also appear in the *Cumulative Book Index.*

Excellent educational bibliographies also may be found in the *Encyclopedia of Educational Research*, issues of the *Review of Educational Research*, and books, articles, or indexes in special fields. The United States government, particularly the Department of Health, Education, and Welfare, publishes a number of bibliographies, for example, *Poverty Studies in the Sixties*, 1970; *Mental Health and Social Change: An Annotated Bibliography*, 1972; and *Bibliography on Smoking and Health*, 1974.

BOOKS AND MONOGRAPHS

Books and monographs are major research resources. To ascertain what publications the local library has on a subject and to find the titles and locations of those that are available elsewhere, one must learn how to locate and interpret the information provided by the card catalog, book lists, and reviews.

Card Catalog

The card catalog is the key to the local library's collection of books and some other items. The "dictionary-type" catalog contains (1) author, (2) title, and (3) subject cards arranged alphabetically. Cross-reference cards which carry the notation "see" or "see also" are inserted in the catalog when the information sought can be located under other subject headings or when the author uses a pseudonym.

Libraries are now dividing their card catalog into two sections—one for authors and title cards and the other for subject cards. They also may have separate catalogs for dissertations, reserved books, large-type books, microforms, and other special collections.

Books Not in the Local Library

What do you do if you need information about a book that is not available in the local library? How can you determine whether a book has been published on a given subject? How can you get data to correct or complete a reference listed in your bibliography? How can you obtain information about a book that was published by an author in 1940? How can you find out which libraries have a copy of the book you want? By becoming familiar with some of the following guides, you usually can answer such questions.

BOOKS FROM OTHER LIBRARIES   If a book is not in the local library, it may be available in another institution. The *National Union Catalog* and other national and regional catalogs, which contain entries of works cataloged by many libraries, give such information. By consulting them, you can discover what institution has a particular book and request the local reference librarian to obtain it for you on an interlibrary loan.

GENERAL LISTS OF BOOKS   A number of sources may be consulted to find the title, author, or publisher of a book. Prepublication information is found in *Forthcoming Books* and *Subject Guide to Forthcoming Books*. The most recent books published in the United States are listed in *Publishers' Weekly*. Books published in the past months or years are indexed soon after their publication in monthly issues of *Choice*, 1964–; *American Book Publishers Record (BPR)*, 1960–; and the *Cumulative Book Index (CBI)*, 1928–. The *CBI* includes most English-language publications but omits pamphlets, government documents, and maps. Entries in the *Cumulative Book Index* are cataloged by author, title, and subject in one alphabetical list; the author entries give the complete bibliographical information (see Figure 4.1). Older books can be found in the *United States Catalog*, which lists books in print 1899 to 1928, and the *American Catalogue of Books*, which covers the 1876 to 1910 period.

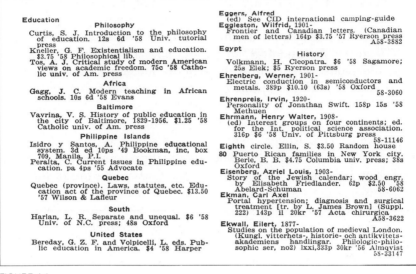

Education
Philosophy
Curtis, S. J. Introduction to the philosophy of education. 12s 6d '58 Univ. tutorial press
Kneller, G. F. Existentialism and education. $3.75 '58 Philosophical lib.
Tos, A. J. Critical study of modern American views on academic freedom. 75c '58 Catholic univ. of Am. press
Africa
Gagg, J. C. Modern teaching in African schools. 10s 6d '58 Evans
Baltimore
Vavrina, V. S. History of public education in the city of Baltimore, 1829-1956. $1.25 '58 Catholic univ. of Am. press
Philippine Islands
Isidro y Santos, A. Philippine educational system. 3d ed 10ps '49 Bookman, inc, box 709, Manila, P.I.
Peralta, C. Current issues in Philippine education. pa 4ps '55 Advocate
Quebec
Quebec (province). Laws, statutes, etc. Education act of the province of Quebec. $13.50 '57 Wilson & Lafleur
South
Harlan, L. R. Separate and unequal. $6 '58 Univ. of N.C. press; 48s Oxford
United States
Bereday, G. Z. F. and Volpicelli, L. eds. Public education in America. $4 '58 Harper

Eggers, Alfred
    (ed) See CID international camping-guide
Eggleston, Wilfrid, 1901-
    Frontier and Canadian letters. (Canadian men of letters) 164p $3.75 '57 Ryerson press
                                                        A58-3882
Egypt
                    History
Volkmann, H. Cleopatra. $6 '58 Sagamore; 25s Elek; $5 Ryerson press
Ehrenberg, Werner, 1901-
    Electric conduction in semiconductors and metals. 389p $10.10 (63s) '58 Oxford
                                                        58-3060
Ehrenpreis, Irvin, 1920-
    Personality of Jonathan Swift. 158p 15s '58 Methuen
Ehrmann, Henry Walter, 1908-
    (ed) Interest groups on four continents; ed. for the Int. political science association. 316p $6 '58 Univ. of Pittsburg press
                                                        58-11146
Eighth circle. Ellin, S. $3.50 Random house
80 Puerto Rican families in New York city. Berle, B. B. $4.75 Columbia univ. press; 38s Oxford
Eisenberg, Azriel Louis, 1903-
    Story of the Jewish calendar; wood engr. by Elisabeth Friedlander. 62p $2.50 '58 Abelard-Schuman
                                                        58-6062
Ekman, Carl Axel
    Portal hypertension; diagnosis and surgical treatment [tr. by L. James Brown] (Suppl. 222) 143p il 20kr '57 Acta chirurgica.
                                                        A58-3622
Ekwall, Eilert, 1877-
    Studies on the population of medieval London. (Kungl. vitterhets-, historie- och antikvitets-akademiens handlingar. Philologic-philosophic ser, no2) lxxi,333p 30kr '56 Almqvist
                                                        58-33147

FIGURE 4.1

Typical entries in the *Cumulative Book Index. (The H. W. Wilson Company.)*

BOOKS IN PRINT   Sometimes it is necessary to know whether a book is in print. If the author or title of the book is known, it may be found in *Books in Print*; otherwise, it may be found in *Subject Guide to Books in Print*. Paperbacks may be located in *Paperbound Books in Print*. Out-of-print books may sometimes be found through the columns of the weekly *Antiquarian Bookman*.

EDUCATIONAL PUBLICATIONS   Current textbooks are listed in *Books in Print, American Book Publishers Record*, and the *Cumulative Book Index*. Most educational organizations compile lists or catalogs of the publications that they produce or that may be obtained from other sources. Selective, annotated, interdisciplinary books and articles may be located in the *ABS Guide to Recent Publications in the Social and Behavioral Sciences*, 1965–.

GOVERNMENT PUBLICATIONS   Books, pamphlets, and other publications from various governmental agencies are a rich source of information, for they include statistical data, research studies, official reports, laws, and other materials that are not always available elsewhere. Locating government documents may be difficult, especially if one does not know that librarians index government publications under the name of the official body responsible for them rather than under the author's name.

The publications of the Office of Education are listed in the *Education Index* under the main heading United States. To find publications of government agencies, an educator may refer to the *Monthly Catalog of United States Government Publications*, which lists entries by departments and has a subject index; the *Monthly Checklist of State Publications* issued by the Library of Congress; the *Guide to U.S. Government Periodicals* (formerly the *Guide to U.S. Serials and Periodicals*, 1966–1972); the *Index to U.S. Government Periodicals*; and *Government Publications: A Guide to Bibliographic Tools*.

PERIODICALS AND OTHER SERIALS

Information about new ideas and developments often appears in periodicals long before it appears in books. Periodicals also publish articles of temporary, local, or limited interest that never appear in book form. Current periodicals are the best source for reports on recent research studies, and the older volumes provide a priceless record of past proposals, accomplishments, conflicts, attitudes, propaganda, ideas, and events.

Periodical Indexes

What a hopeless task you would face if you had to leaf through all the periodicals in the library to find the articles you needed! Fortunately, expertly compiled indexes are available that serve as guides to the contents of periodicals. These guides usually list the selected magazines they index on the inside covers or near the front of each issue. This list changes occasionally when new periodicals are added or old ones are dropped. You should always check whether a periodical guide indexes the magazines that are likely to answer your problems. Before writing out a call slip for a periodical, you should also check whether the local library has a copy of it. In the reference or periodical room, you may find a list or file which will provide you with the names and volume numbers of the periodicals that the library has available.

EDUCATIONAL INDEXES   One worksaving device created for educators is the *Education Index*. This valuable guide is a cumulative author-subject index to educational material that appears in over 200 periodicals and to some materials printed by the United States government (see Figure 4.2). Between September 1961 and September 1969 this guide was only a subject index. To locate articles that were published before the *Education Index* was established in 1929, one can examine a number of other guides: The *Record of Current Educational Publications* compiled by the Office of Education covers the period from

FIGURE 4.2

Typical entries in the *Education Index*. *(The H. W. Wilson Company.)*

ECHOLS, Frank H. jr. See Garbin, A. P. jt. auth. — Joint authors

ECKSTEIN, Max A. — Author heading
On teaching a scientific comparative education. Comp Ed R 14:279-82 O '70
Toward a strategy of urban-educational study. World Yr Bk Ed 1970:19-29

ECLIPSES, Solar
Eye injuries and the solar eclipse; results of a survey. E. M. Hatfield. Sight-Saving R 40;79-85 Sum '70

ECOLOGY
Ecology: rhetoric and reality. H. Gilliam. Ed Digest 36;35-6 N '70
See also — Cross reference
Biotic communities

Bibliography
Bibliography on environmental problems; comp. by C. M. Ury. Phi Delta Kappan 51: 570-2 Je '70 — Compiler

Field work — Subheadings
Exercise in winter ecology. J. Murphy. il Sci Teach 37:59-61 O '70
Mudhole ecology. F. Krall. il Am Biol Teach 32:351-3 S '70

Teacher education in service
Live and learn; Family camp workshops in natural science and ecology. J. Rosner and H. Rosner. il Sci & Child 8:24-5 S '70

Teaching
High schools
Mudhole ecology. F. Krall. il Am Biol Teach 32:351-3 S '70 — Illustration

Nursery schools
Ecology for the young. B. Persky. il Instr 80:122-3 Ag '70

ECOLOGY, Social — Subject heading
Biological and ecological influences on development at 12 months of age. T. E. Jordan and S. D. Spaner. bibliog Human Develop 13 no3:178-87 '70
Social environmental influences on individuals in sub-cultural and cross-cultural perspective. J. I. Roberts. bibliog Comp Ed R 14: 301-11 O '70 — Bibliography
See also
Man–Influence on nature

January 1912 to March 1932; indexes have also been compiled for the early NEA publications (114); and the *Ohio State University Periodical Index* (Ohio File) includes articles published between 1919 and 1929. Thereafter, it specializes in local and state journals. The *State Education Journal Index*, 1963–, is an annotated subject arrangement of more recent state journals.

The newest and most comprehensive cumulative index of the core periodical literature in the field of education is the *Current Index to Journals in Education (CIJE)*, 1969–. *CIJE* is organized to be compatible with the ERIC information retrieval system. The main sections of the *CIJE* are the main entry index, subject index, author index, and journal content index. The main entry section is arranged alphabetically and numerically by Clearinghouse accession numbers. A list of the ERIC clearinghouses and their identifying letter codes can be found on the inside cover of *CIJE*. The main entry lists several descriptive terms which characterize the contents of the article (see Figure 4.3). The *Thesaurus of ERIC Descriptors* (see page 64) is used by the indexer for assigning these terms. The terms preceded by an asterisk are the descriptors under which the article is listed in the subject index.

Social Sciences Citation Index, 1973–, is an international multi-disciplinary index to the literature in approximately 1,000 key journals in the social, behavioral, and related sciences. This work possesses a "Permutern® Subject Index" which involves the permutation of all significant words within the article to form all possible pairs of terms.

Information on education in foreign English-speaking countries is indexed. The *British Education Index*, 1954–; *Australian Education Index*, 1958–; and the *Canadian Education Index*, 1965–, all quarterly publications, index books, articles, reports, and pamphlets within their respective countries.

READERS' GUIDE   Since 1900, the *Readers' Guide to Periodical Literature* has served as a faithful servant to library patrons. This semimonthly (monthly in July and August) subject and author index lists general-interest articles in more than 150 magazines, but it rarely duplicates those that appear in the *Education Index*. For educational literature prior to 1929, it is one of the best indexes.

INTERNATIONAL AND EARLY INDEXES   When one is searching for technical articles concerning education prior to 1929, the *International Index to Periodicals* is the most helpful source to consult. Between 1965 and 1974, this excellent guide was known as the *Social Sciences*

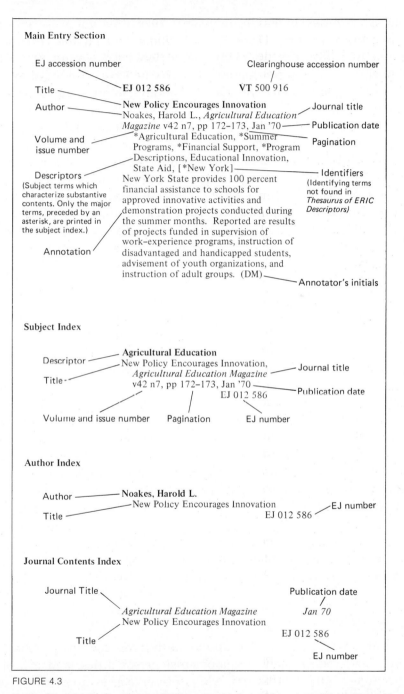

FIGURE 4.3

Typical entries in the *Current Index to Journals in Education*. (*Macmillan Information.*)

and Humanities Index. Beginning in 1974, this guide became two publications, (1) the *Social Sciences Index* and (2) the *Humanities Index.* In addition to indexing the periodical literature, these two publications now carry citations to book reviews. These indexes are published quarterly and cumulated annually. Before 1920, the *International Index* was called the *Readers' Guide Supplement.* The first volume of the series, 1907–1915, carried the index back to supplement the last volume of the pioneer guide—*Poole's Index to Periodical Literature,* 1802–1907, which is the traditional source to consult for the nineteenth century. Another guide to periodicals in the last century is the *Nineteenth Century Readers' Guide to Periodical Literature,* which covers the period from 1890 to 1899, with *Supplemental Indexing,* 1900–1922.

Periodicals Not Available Locally

Since the local library cannot subscribe to all periodicals that are printed each year, you sometimes must locate a publication elsewhere. The following work will advise you which libraries have what volumes of a given publication. *New Serial Titles 1950–70* is a four-volume reference work covering 220,000 serials issued throughout the world after 1949 and held by 800 United States and Canadian libraries. Entries in this work are arranged alphabetically by title. Supplements to the *New Serial Titles,* which are published periodically, list the new titles and additional locations. A companion two-volume *New Serial Titles 1950–1970: Subject Guide* is also available. For serials issued before 1950, the *Union List of Serials in Libraries of the United States and Canada* is the best source to use.

Regional catalogs which contain lists of periodical holdings are quite common. For example, there are the *Union List of Serials in the Washington* [D.C.] *Metropolitan Area, SUNY Union List of Serials, Union List of Serials in the Libraries in the Miami Valley* [Ohio], and *Intermountain Union List of Serials* [Arizona, Nevada].

Newspapers

Current newspapers provide up-to-date information on speeches, reports, conferences, new developments, personalities, and a host of other topics. Old newspapers, which preserve a record of past events and the evolution of movements and ideas, are particularly useful in historical inquiries. The larger metropolitan Sunday editions, such as *The New York Times,* have special sections devoted to weekly news reviews and to educational affairs. Current events and educational news are also reported in periodicals such as *Time, Newsweek, Current History,* and *Foreign Affairs.* The loose-leaf encyclopedia of current events, *Facts on File,* 1940–, which is usually found in the reference room of a library, gives a weekly digest of world news in a few pages. Keesing's *Contemporary Archives,* 1931–, provides similar information. *Editorials on File,* 1970–, carries the nation's editors' comments on matters of the day.

To locate articles in a newspaper, a reader can refer to *The New York Times Index,* a semimonthly publication with annual cumulations. Since 1913, it has classified all important items in the paper alphabetically by subject, personality, and organization. Since most news events of wide public interest are published immediately, *The New York Times Index* gives a reader clues concerning the dates when a particular item may have appeared in other newspapers. Other newspaper indexes which are available are the *Christian Science Monitor Index,* 1950–; *National Observer Index,* 1962–; and the *Newspaper Index,* 1972–, which covers the *Los Angeles Times, Chicago Tribune, New Orleans Times-Picayune,* and *Washington Post.*

Lists of early American newspapers and the location of existing files are found in Clarence S. Brigham's *History and Bibliography of American Newspapers, 1690–1820,* and Winifred Gregory's *American Newspapers, 1821–1936.* The *New York Daily Tribune Index,* 1875–1906, is useful for the dates it covers. Some libraries, state historical associations, and universities prepare lists of the newspapers and existing files in their local areas, such as the *Guide to Colorado Newspapers, 1859–1963;* the Consortium of Western Universities and Colleges' *Union List of Newspapers Currently Received by Member Libraries, December, 1968; Union List of Newspapers in the Libraries of the Fort Worth–Dallas Major Resource Centers,* 1969; *The Durham Morning Herald Index 1930–1969; Latin American Newspapers in the United States Libraries: A Union List;* and *Newspapers Currently Received and Permanently Retained in the Library of Congress.*

Two English indexes that cover a span of many years are *The Official Index to the Times* (London), 1906–, and *Times Index* (London), 1790–. Ayer's *Directory of Newspapers and Periodicals* has listed sectional or local American newspapers since 1880.

Directories to Periodicals, Newspapers, and Manuscripts

Sometimes you may have to find what publications are available in a particular field or geographical area. To proceed with some phases of your work, you may need the name, address, price, circulation figures, or date of origin of a periodical. To evaluate a magazine or newspaper, you may want to know the name of the publisher or editor, the political bias of a publication, or where it is indexed. By consulting one or more of the following directories, you can usually find answers to such questions.

America's Education Press: A Classified List of Educational Publications Issued in the United States and Canada is published in odd-numbered years in the yearbook of the Educational Press Association of America. This list classifies periodicals under a number of educational subject headings and indexes them alphabetically by title. *Ulrich's International Periodicals Directory* covers a list of about 57,000 in-print foreign and domestic periodicals in all fields. N. W. Ayer's annual *Directory of Newspapers and Periodicals* gives an extensive coverage for newspapers and periodicals. It contains several lists, such as agricultural; college; Negro; religious; and trade, technical, and class publications. The main catalog list of over 1,200 pages is arranged geographically, first by state, and then by city or town of publication. The *Standard Periodical Directory*, 1973, contains 62,583 titles covering every type of periodical with the exception of suburban, weekly, and small daily newspapers. *Newspaper Press Directory*, 1846–, is a guide to newspapers throughout the world. *The Working Press of the Nation* gives a listing of personnel of daily newspapers in the United States and Canada.

Historical research depends upon the availability of primary source materials. Locating the sources is sometimes a frustrating task. This burden has been eased considerably with the publication of the *National Union Catalog of Manuscript Collections*, 1959–. This *Catalog*, with cumulations, brings the total number of collections to 23,000 for the 723 reported American repositories that are regularly open to scholars. A similar work of manuscripts in Canadian repositories, 1968–, is also available.

Microforms

Through the means of microforms, the modern researcher can examine copies of the Bay Psalm Book[2] of 1640, a colonial or modern newspaper, an 1898 educational periodical, rare books in foreign libraries, or a recent doctoral dissertation. The local library may own some micro-

---

[2]The correct title is *The Whole Book of Psalms Faithfully Translated into English Metre.*

forms and may help patrons obtain copies from other institutions or agencies.

A few guides have been published to help locate microforms. *Newspapers in Microform: United States, 1948–1972*, and *Newspapers in Microform: Foreign Countries, 1948–1972*, are cumulations of earlier editions of *Newspapers on Microfilm,* 1948–1967. An annual supplement to the cumulations began in 1973. *Newspapers on Microfilm and Special Collections,* 1973/74, and *Times* [London] *on Microfilm,* 1785–, *Canadian Newspapers on Microfilm,* 1959–, are additional sources to examine.

Guide to Microforms in Print, 1961–, is an annual guide to microforms, except theses and dissertations, that can be obtained from United States publishers. *Subject Guide to Microforms in Print,* 1962–, a companion volume to the preceding entry, lists materials under subject classifications. *Serials in Microform,* 1975, contains the largest and most comprehensive selection of periodicals, documents, newspapers, and other serial literature available anywhere in microfilm. *American Periodicals: 1800–1850* and *American Periodicals: 1850–1900* are guides to microfilm collections.

Any student engaged in research will have occasion to refer to *Master's Abstracts,* 1962–, and *Dissertation Abstracts International,* 1970– (formerly *Dissertation Abstracts,* 1952–1970, and *Microfilm Abstracts,* 1938–1952), which are put out by the University of Microfilms International, Ann Arbor, Michigan.

EDUCATIONAL RESEARCH

You cannot engage in research successfully unless you become adept at locating theses, dissertations, and the reports of studies that embody the bulk of the work done in your field. You may begin searching for this literature in the previously discussed *Education Index, Current Index to Journals in Education, Review of Research in Education, Encyclopedia of Educational Research,* and *Second Handbook of Research on Teaching* (Travers). As soon as possible you should form the habit of examining the following sources regularly.

Review and Abstracting Journals

Review and abstracting journals which give brief summaries of research studies reported in a wide variety of periodicals are great timesavers. They enable you to keep abreast of the work being done in your own field and also in related fields. Some of these journals give brief summaries of individual studies, and others go into greater detail. Some summarize all the work being done in an area; in addition, they may trace trends, discuss new techniques, point out gaps in research, and present bibliographies. Abstracts of research reports naturally lag considerably behind the original publication of the studies.

The *Review of Educational Research* gives you an excellent overview of the work that has been done in the field and helps you keep up with recent developments. This publication, between 1931 and 1969, reviewed about every three years eleven subdivisions of education. Since June 1970, the *Review of Educational Research* has pursued a policy of publishing unsolicited reviews and research on topics of the contributor's choosing. The role played by this publication in the past has been assumed by an *Annual Review of Educational Research*.

The *Review of Research in Education*, 1971–, presents critical and synthesizing essays in the substantive problems and domains of education as well as assesses and evaluates technical and methodological developments. ERIC Clearinghouse on Early Childhood Education issues *Research Relating to Children*, 1948–. Another publication, *Review of Research in Visual Arts Education*, 1973–, carries reviews in the visual domain.

Resources in Education (RIE), 1966–, represents the most comprehensive publication of research materials today. *RIE* is published monthly by the Educational Resources Information Center (ERIC) and indexed annually. Each monthly issue contains three sections: (1) *Document* section with document résumés; (2) *Index* section with subject, author, and institution indexes and accession numbers which cross-reference the ERIC Clearinghouse number to the ERIC Document (ED) number for résumés published in each issue of *RIE*; and (3) *New Thesaurus Terms* section with terms that have been added to the *Thesaurus of ERIC Descriptors* (see sample entry, Figure 4.4). All documents cited in the *Document* section of the journal, except as noted, are available from the ERIC Document Reproduction Service. Availability, prices, and instructions on how to order ERIC documents are found in each publication.

Psychological Abstracts, 1927–, is a monthly work which contains abstracts of articles appearing in over 530 journals—many of them predominantly educational periodicals. The biannual issues (January–June, July–December) contain both an author and a subject index.

Perhaps there is no better way to become acquainted with research techniques and progress than by reading several periodicals devoted

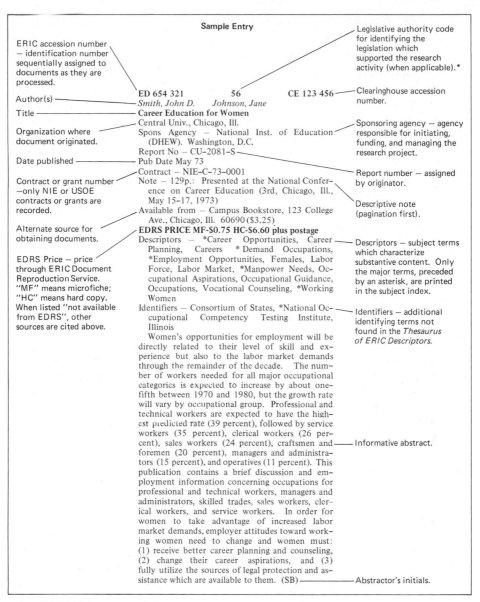

FIGURE 4.4

Typical entries in *Resources in Education. (Education Resources Information Center.)*

primarily to abstracts and reviews. In addition to the above periodicals, a student may examine some of the following publications: *Annual Review of Psychology*, 1950–; *Child Development Abstracts and Bibliography*, 1927–; *Psychological Bulletin*, 1904–; *Sociological Abstracts*,

1952–; *Educational Administration Abstracts,* 1966–; *Sociology of Education Abstracts,* 1965–; *Human Resources Abstracts, 1966–; DSH* [Deafness, Speech, and Hearing] *Abstracts,* 1961–; *College Student Personnel Abstracts,* 1966–; *Exceptional Child Education Abstracts,* 1969–; *Language and Language Behavior Abstracts,* 1967–; *Women's Studies Abstracts,* 1972–; *Mental Retardation and Developmental Disabilities Abstracts,* 1964–; *Abstracts of Research Materials in Vocational and Technical Education,* 1967–; and *Research into Higher Education Abstracts,* 1967–.

Many other professional periodicals and yearbooks include some reviews of research and scholarly discussions of educational problems in one or all of their issues. Some of the sources that an educator may profitably consult are as follows:

Educational research
Journal of Educational Research, Educational and Psychological Measurement, Journal of Experimental Education, Research Quarterly, Journal of Research in Music Education, American Educational Research Journal, Speech Monographs, and *Reading Research Quarterly.*

Psychology.
Journal of Educational Psychology, Journal of Psychology, Journal of Social Psychology, and *Journal of Applied Psychology.*

Sociology.
Sociology of Education, American Journal of Sociology, Sociology and Social Research, and *Sociometry.*

Dissertations and Theses

Theses and dissertations are usually housed by the institutions that award the authors their advanced degrees. Sometimes these studies are published in whole or in part in educational journals. Because many graduate studies are never published, a check of the following specialized guides is necessary for a thorough coverage of the research literature.

BIBLIOGRAPHICAL GUIDE   The entry "Dissertations, Academic" in each issue of the *Bibliographic Index* is a comprehensive listing of sources to theses, dissertations, research in progress, etc.

GENERAL GUIDES   Doctoral dissertations in all fields, including education, can be found in the *Comprehensive Dissertation Index 1861–1972*

(*CDI*). The *CDI* is an all-inclusive index to American and many Canadian doctoral dissertations. It consists of a five-volume author index, arranged alphabetically by author, and thirty-two subject volumes, divided by discipline and organized alphabetically by key words extracted from dissertation titles. Educational entries in the subject index are located in volumes 20 to 24 inclusive. The *CDI* is so exhaustive that it is practically the only reference you need to consult when looking for bibliographical information on doctoral dissertations. (See Figure 4.5 for the organization of the *CDI*.)

Dissertation Abstracts International, (*DAI*) May 1970, is published monthly in two parts: Section A, dissertations in the humanities and social sciences and Section B, dissertations in the physical sciences and engineering. For each dissertation there is a 600-word abstract, written by the doctoral candidate. By reading abstracts, you may often glean enough information to satisfy your needs. Moreover, you may quickly scan not only education theses but also those from related fields. If you want to read a complete study of a dissertation that is presented in *DAI*, you may purchase a microfilm or photocopy from University Microfilms International. The order number and price are given in the abstract. The ten-volume *Cumulative Subject and Author Index*, 1970, indexes the file of the earlier *Dissertation Abstracts* and the *DAI* dating back to 1938.

Masters Abstracts, 1962–, is the counterpart to *DAI* and is published quarterly by University Microfilms International. Prior to 1962, master's theses for many institutions are listed in the annual *Master's Theses in Education*, 1951–.

FIGURE 4.5

Typical entries in the *Comprehensive Dissertation Index*. (*University Microfilms International*.)

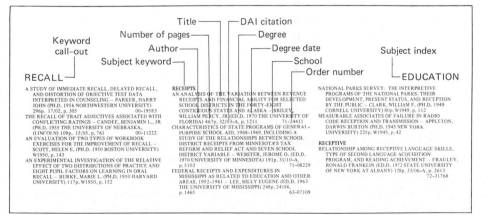

Monographs

Pertinent educational information sometimes appears in monograph form. *Monographic Series*, 1974–, lists all monographs which appear as parts of series, in any language, anywhere in the world. Both popular and scholarly series are included, with the exception of government documents and promotional materials. *Monograph Abstracts*, which uses the same format as *Masters Abstracts*, is a source for edited and approved, original, unpublished monographs.

LIBRARY SEARCHING PROCEDURES

When you engage in an investigation, the number of reading hours you log and the amount of notes you take do not provide a reliable gauge of your problem-solving productivity. Time and motion studies of your work may reveal an enormous waste of effort. Mastering the guides to the literature that are presented in this chapter may seem a time-consuming task, but an educator who remains ignorant of these professional tools encounters insurmountable obstacles when wading into the ever-expanding volume of literature. Locating the best available sources pertaining to a problem and extracting the essential information from them is of such importance in research that you should make every effort to improve your techniques. The following discussion suggests some worthwhile habits for you to form.

Traditional Searching Practices

Before using a new library, familiarize yourself with its layout, facilities, services, and regulations. Learn how to use the microform readers, photocopiers, and other mechanical aids. In the stacks and in the periodical, reference, reserved book, and rare books rooms, note where materials that you will use frequently are placed. If possible, schedule your work session in a library when you will encounter the least competition for resources and services. Make out call slips for all or most books needed in one session. Copy *all* the information that the librarian needs to obtain each reference for you, and before closing the periodical index or card catalog, *recheck* and *rectify* any errors or omissions. Arrange to spend a block of time in the library that is sufficient to accomplish a specific task. When little time is available, clear up questions that can be answered quickly in reference books that are readily accessible.

Before initiating a search for materials in a library, write down questions that pinpoint precisely what information you wish to locate and group the questions in accordance with the areas in the library where the answers may be found. You can zero in on information more quickly if you know what subject headings—key words and synonymous key words—to search under and how to broaden and narrow your search through larger and narrower area classification terms. Because technical terminology in education and the names of periodicals, professional organizations, and government agencies change over the years, you should have some knowledge of both past and present terminology. Also remain on the alert for recent changes in terminology that may require you to look under new subject headings for materials you have previously found elsewhere. To develop a set of suitable subject headings under which to begin a search, you might consult the *Thesaurus of ERIC Descriptors*, which has been discussed previously; *Sears List of Subject Headings*; *Library of Congress Subject Headings*; and dictionaries of education, statistical terms, psychological terms, or the social sciences.

Have you ever been frustrated because you did not know how a reference book was organized or how to interpret some of the symbols in it? Have you ever spent considerable time searching for information in an index, periodical, or book before you discovered that the desired information was purposely omitted from the work? To avoid such exasperating experiences, examine a reference before searching for information in it and ask pertinent questions about the scope, quality, and nature of the services and information it offers: Are any keys, codes, statements of explanation, pages of directions, or other conventions provided that interpret the abbreviations, symbols, and other data used in the reference? Does the list of periodicals that the index covers (which is usually found in the introductory pages) include those in which you are particularly interested? Are the delimitations of the reference stated in the subtitle, preface, introduction, or elsewhere (for example, "This bibliography includes United States but not foreign research reports.")? Is this periodical indexed in each issue, in an annual issue, or in a standard periodical index? Are certain features in this periodical covered monthly, annually, or at other stated intervals? Is the publication issued monthly, annually, or at other stated intervals? Are there supplements that bring the reference up-to-date? Does the publication date indicate that the reference is too old or too recent for your purposes? Does the number of pages reveal that the discussion is too comprehensive or too limited to serve your needs? Does the author, periodical, or publisher have a reputation for maintaining high scholarly standards?

New Bibliographical and Information-retrieval Systems

In 1850, a thousand scientific journals were published in the world; by the year 2000, over a million journals may be published. This explosive expansion of knowledge makes the traditional, time-consuming methods of searching for publications relevant to research interests totally inadequate. But recent computer and microform innovations promise to rescue the researcher from a life of library drudgery.

The more highly developed knowledge storage and retrieval systems require that a publication, title, abstract, or document be coded so that retrievable words or phrases can be stored on magnetic tape for use by an electronic computer. Coders index documents according to master formulas utilizing relevant descriptors. A thesaurus of descriptors is a term-association list (1) that indexers use to describe subject information of a document to a desired level of specificity at input and (2) that researchers use to describe in mutually precise terms the information they require at output from an indexing or information-retrieval service.

In some forms of key-word indexing, a computer is instructed to read the titles of books or articles which have previously been stored on tape or other media and to search for the appearance of predefined words. In KWIC indexing (Key Word in Context), the computer finds and arranges the key words in an alphabetical column surrounded by a few words of the title or context.

The library of tomorrow will be completely transformed by the information storage and retrieval revolution. Ultramicrofiche (UMF), which can reproduce 3,000 pages on a 4- by 6-inch transparency, will alleviate current library storage problems. More library space will be devoted to projection units and electronic aids. Someday the library may be connected with a high-speed automated system for storing and retrieving documents, such as the MICROCODE System.[3] This system stores documents on 16-millimeter microfilm and to each assigns an identifying code for retrieval. In milliseconds, the retrieval system reads these codes to answer a client's question, displays the document on a screen, and if the print button is pressed, produces a black-and-white photographic print.

[3]Microfilm Information Access CODE, designed and produced by Eastman Kodak Company.

In the past few years, a number of educational information retrieval services have been developed. DATRIX II offers a computerized service that provides access to most of the post-1861 doctoral dissertations in North America. To initiate the search for appropriate dissertations, you select one or more key words relating to your interests, and make out an order form asking that a computer search be made for all dissertations that contain a single key word, any one of alternative key words, or a combination of key words. In return, you will receive a computer printout which includes for each reference the title, author, degree, degree year, university, location in *Dissertation Abstracts International*, the price, and information for ordering a copy from University Microfilms International, Ann Arbor, Michigan.

A search service of the Library of Congress MARC data base is now available from the Cataloging Distribution Service on a fee basis to any requester. The MARC data base can produce bibliographic listings by accessing any data found on a catalog card since 1968, plus many additional elements which have been specifically coded in the machine record, such as bibliographies, translations, language of text, and directories. (Information on such coding may be found in *Books: A MARC Format*, 5th ed., 1972, which is for sale by the Superintendent of Documents.) Searching may be done on a one-time basis or on a monthly update basis.

ERIC, the Educational Resources Information Center, provides a systematic, comprehensive information-gathering service. ERIC clearinghouses, each specializing in a specific field of education, acquire, abstract, and index educational documents. The inputs from all clearinghouses are merged to produce the journals *Resources in Education* (*RIE*) and *Current Index to Journals in Education* (*CIJE*). In addition, ERIC prepares some special publications, and each clearinghouse responds to questions in its area of specialization. The ERIC Document Reproduction Service (EDRS) sells copies of reports cited in *RIE*, either in microfiche or paper copy. The ERIC publication, *Survey of ERIC Data Base Search Services*, lists other organizations that offer literature search services.

The *Psychological Abstracts* Search and Retrieval (PASAR) service searches for references in the psychological literature and charges for the computer time. Research and Information Services for Education (RISE)[4] was originally a local-regional operation in Pennsylvania and is now a statewide one. RISE makes literature searches for administrators

---

[4]198 Allendale Road, King of Prussia, Pa. 19406.

and teachers and assists school districts in conducting research. In the future, other state or regional centers may be developed. *Current Contents/Social and Behavioral Sciences*, a weekly publication service of the Institute for Scientific Information (ISI),[5] gives one a bird's-eye view of the current literature by reproducing the tables of contents of more than 700 journals. This publication also includes an Author Index and Address Directory for articles appearing in each issue. For a small fee, one can obtain an article from a journal listed in *Current Contents* by filling out the Original Article Tear Sheet (OATS) order form that appears in every copy of this publication. ISI also operates Automatic Subject Citation Alert, which for an annual fee provides a monthly computer printout with complete bibliographical data on information relating to the subscriber's previously specified interests.

Through terminals connected via telephone lines to a computer center, which houses *The New York Times Information Bank*, an educator has access to a broad range of subjects covered in newspapers and magazines. The terminal displays abstract summaries of articles with bibliographic references. Users can also have the abstracts printed—and in the case of *The New York Times* stories—view the full text, available on microfiche.

NOTE-TAKING TECHNIQUES

After locating source materials, you should read them and take notes in a manner that furthers the whole investigative process. Critical note taking is an exciting, challenging experience; passive note taking is a monotonous, boring activity. A nonselective, unsystematic method of recording notes usually piles up tangled masses of data that are a greater obstacle than aid to a researcher who is working on a problem. An effective note-taking system preserves the most significant ideas in a form that facilitates shifting, comparing, grouping, and ordering items. When you write a report, pertinent, precise, and flexible notes can be organized and synthesized into original thought patterns more easily than continuous pages of rambling, jumbled information. Any note-taking system that serves your needs is acceptable, but the following well-tested bibliographical and subject note procedures are worthy of consideration.

[5]325 Chestnut Street, Philadelphia, Pa. 19106.

Bibliographical Notes

Bibliographical notes are made for several purposes: (1) to have the complete bibliographical information available for each reference that may contribute to an investigation, (2) to facilitate the relocation of a reference in the local library, (3) to preserve a brief record of the general nature and value of a reference, and (4) to have the information necessary for constructing a formal bibliography.

INFORMATION ON BIBLIOGRAPHICAL NOTES   A bibliographical note carries all the data necessary for the writer, reader, or librarian to relocate the reference. The following information is the minimum needed for a book bibliographical card: (1) full name of the author (two initials if the first name is not given, or issuing agent if author is not given); (2) full title of the work, underlined;[6] (3) place, publisher, and the publication date of the book; (4) edition if given; (5) the total pages and/or the particular pages used may be included; and in some instances (6) the volume and part numbers may be needed to locate the reference. A bibliographical card for a periodical or newspaper article is somewhat different. It includes (1) the full name of the author; (2) the full title of the article in quotation marks; (3) the name of the publication, underlined; (4) the volume number; (5) date of issue; and (6) the number of the initial page or the range of the pages the article covers.

To help you relocate a reference quickly, place on the front or back of the bibliographical card, but always in the same place and set conspicuously apart from the other information, (1) the library call number; (2) the name of the library if you patronize more than one; and (3) the room, department, division, or section that houses the work (see Figure 4.6).

After using several references, an investigator may become confused about what information is in the various volumes. Writing brief notes on the back of the bibliographical card concerning the nature, scope, special features, or chief strengths and weaknesses of the book and the page numbers of the most pertinent topics (see Figure 4.7) will help you recall what contributions the reference may make to your study. When compiling an annotated bibliography for the final research report, these notes will provide you with much useful information.

---

[6]In a typewritten manuscript, underlining indicates the material is to be italicized.

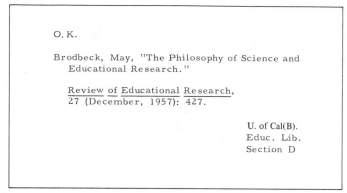

O. K.

Brodbeck, May, "The Philosophy of Science and
  Educational Research."

Review of Educational Research,
27 (December, 1957): 427.

U. of Cal(B).
Educ. Lib.
Section D

FIGURE 4.6

Front of a bibliographical card for a periodical.

HOW TO TAKE NOTES   To economize on time and effort, establish efficient bibliographical note-taking habits. Screen references before copying a single item so as to avoid accumulating many useless cards. Refrain from scribbling partial bibliographical information on any available scrap of paper. Scattered, fragmentary notes that are written on assorted sizes of paper are easy to lose, difficult to relocate and file, and hard to interpret.

Copying each reference in full, once and for all, on a *separate* standard-size card or sheet of paper is a prudent practice. Cards are more durable and easier to handle, to sort, and to file than lists of sources on sheets of paper. A 3- by 5-inch card is convenient to carry,

FIGURE 4.7

Back of the same bibliographical card.

Excellent review of literature (1948-1957) on:

Operationalism	427
Nomological Network	429
Causation	433
Theories	435
Models	439

Gives appropriate examples and implications
  for education.
Cites pertinent bibliography.
Points out criticisms of operationalism.
Draws attention to the form of operational
  definition—conditional or "if-then" sentence.

but some researchers prefer larger cards. If you keep a few blank cards in your purse or pocket at all times, recopying bibliographical information will not be necessary.

Before compiling your bibliography, investigate the form and content of the entries that you will be required to use in the final report. Different professors, institutions, and publishers establish style standards that vary slightly. If they do not have their own style manual, they require that scholars conform to some other recognized style manual (18, 34, 111).

If you form the habit of recording bibliographical notes in conformity with a recommended style manual, you can type the final bibliography directly from these cards without reorganizing the data. This practice eliminates the tedious task of shifting items on cards and avoids the errors that may creep into a bibliography during the recopying process. Always carry sample style cards for a book, periodical, and newspaper with you and refer to these samples when you write bibliographical notes. To save time and to eliminate errors, you may prefer to purchase printed bibliographical cards or to mimeograph cards that provide blanks for required items.

If you keep a style manual accessible while working, you can check the correct bibliographical form when special problems arise, such as how to write up the entry when an organization is the author; when a pseudonym is used; when a translator or editor is noted; or when the article comes from an encyclopedia, a chapter of a yearbook, or a newspaper. When you do not have a style manual available, copy all the essential information from the reference; reorganize these items in accordance with the approved style before you include them in the formal report.

Before taking a single note from a reference, make out a bibliographical card neatly and legibly in ink. Procure the information for books from the title page rather than from the cover of the book. After completing the task, check carefully whether you have omitted any necessary data—an item, word, letter, punctuation mark, or number—and check the correctness of the spelling, punctuation marks, and call number. When you are finished, make an "OK' notation on the card so that no doubts concerning its accuracy will arise later. The extra minutes expended in recording bibliographical information accurately is time well invested, for careless errors may later cause you to spend hours searching for missing items, recopying cards, and retyping entire bibliographies. Merely omitting the pages covered by an article on an entry may force you to make a special trip to the library, and if the volume is out, a return trip and more wearisome waiting at the circulation desk will be necessary.

HOW TO FILE NOTES After collecting a number of bibliographical notes, one must organize them into some meaningful order. An alphabetical arrangement by authors' surnames—or the first important word of the title if there is no author given—proves satisfactory in most studies. Some workers file their bibliographical cards under subject headings and then alphabetize them by authors' surnames. They make out duplicate or cross-reference cards for a work that is used in more than one section of the report, annotating its usefulness for each section. In some studies, researchers classify cards under primary and secondary sources; under types of references, such as books, periodicals, and pamphlets; or under a chronological arrangement. Because elaborate filing systems are cumbersome, experienced writers employ simple systems.

Subject Notes

Subject and bibliographical notes serve different purposes. Each type of note possesses its individual characteristics. From a practical standpoint, mongrel notes (part bibliographical and part subject) are useless. Copying full bibliographical data on each subject note would be excessively time-consuming; failing to put full data on mongrel notes would cause difficulties; therefore, keeping the two types of notes separate is advisable.

The information that you record on subject notes depends upon the nature of your problem and your experiental background. During an investigation, you may (1) copy many specific facts from references, such as dates, places, names, statistics, formulas, and definitions; (2) summarize or copy arguments, questions, explanations, illustrations, or descriptions; (3) write comments about your reactions to reference materials; (4) state relationships, conclusions, or interpretations that come to mind during the contemplative phases of your work; and (5) jot down items that require further checking.

Subject notes usually make up the bulk of the notes taken in any study; they form a reservoir of facts. When writing a report you may draw upon them to (1) support a particular position, (2) illustrate a point of view, (3) make comparisons, (4) weave a web of logical evidence, or (5) buttress arguments by passages from recognized authorities. Discriminatingly selected subject notes provide the building blocks that you need to solve a problem; haphazardly collected notes may cause your investigation to collapse.

TAKING NOTES AFTER EVALUATING ITEMS   Copying subject notes about every item that remotely relates to your problem is an unprofitable practice. To avoid wasting time writing, filing, reexamining, and culling many worthless subject cards, form the following habits: Before taking any notes, skim quickly through a few of the best references. Examine the table of contents, topical headlines, and summary paragraphs to ascertain the purpose, scope, biases, and distinctive features of the reference. Read only those sections that relate to your problem and record the location of important facts or passages. If you own the book, underline these items; if not, list the location of them on a card in an abbreviated form, such as "198:2, 4–6" (page 198: paragraph 2, lines 4 to 6). Photocopying some materials may save considerable time. After you have skimmed the references, reevaluate the underlined, listed, or photocopied passages and copy or paraphrase the most pertinent ones.

TAKING FLEXIBLE, DURABLE NOTES   A system of note taking that produces permanent, easy-to-handle notes lessens the labor involved in assembling the final report. Writing notes consecutively in bound books or on pages of paper is an unwise practice, for the items will later have to be relocated, reclassified, and either recopied or indexed elaborately. A note is of the greatest value if it is a complete unit that can be found quickly in a sheaf of notes, traced readily to the original source, and transferred easily from one position in your outline to another.

If each item is placed on a separate card or page, you can run through notes taken from many sources and at different times, slip out those cards that pertain to the same subject, and reorganize them quickly in a logical sequence for your report. When several items of information are placed on one card, problems arise. If the items fall logically into different sections of the report, the process of shuffling cards and ordering them into the proper report sequence is a confusing and arduous task. You may overlook important information that is buried among other data on a card, or you may combine unrelated facts in a report merely because they were on the same card.

WRITING INTELLIGIBLE NOTES   Since smeared penciled notes or illegible pen scratchings that are crammed with complicated abbreviations will impede your progress, always type notes or write them in ink.

Make an effort to form each letter and figure perfectly and to use a simple abbreviation system consistently. After taking a note, check to make certain that you or a secretary can decipher each word accurately now and in the future.

USING UNIFORM-SIZE NOTE SHEETS   Because assorted shapes of note sheets are clumsy to organize and easy to lose, write all subject notes on paper or cards of the same size. Some workers prefer to use notepaper because it is not as bulky as cards, provides more space for writing, and is more convenient to use when typing; others prefer cards because they are more durable and easier to sort and arrange. The nature of the study and the idiosyncrasies of the writer determine what size card or paper is most serviceable. Subject notes may require a larger card than bibliographical notes.

USING ONE SIDE OF PAPER   Writing notes on both sides of a paper is a mistake. If you must flip papers constantly when organizing notes into a logical order, you may become confused and overlook items. Have you ever searched desperately for a note, only to find it much later tucked away on the back of a page you assumed was blank? If an entire note cannot be placed on one side of a card, complete it on a second card. Write "to be continued" on the first card and "continued from card one" on the second card, and staple them together.

USING TOPIC HEADINGS THAT CONFORM WITH THE REPORT OUTLINE To give clues concerning the content of the notes on cards, place suitable topic headings, or slugs, consistently at the top left- or right-hand side of the subject cards. If these slugs are the same as the topics and subtopics in your tentative report outline, they will facilitate the locating, sorting, and classifying of the cards and the writing of the report. If you encounter materials in a reference that suggest a new or more effective topic heading, use it and revise your outline accordingly. When you cannot decide where to file a note, study its relationship to the subject and determine whether your outline contains overlapping, vague, or insufficient subject headings. Your initial outline and the headings you assign to topics will not be perfect. You will discover weaknesses in them and ways to improve them as you work.

NOTING LOCATION IN REFERENCE   On each subject card place the source from which the information was obtained, either on the bottom of the card or opposite the topic heading at the top of the card. Since bibliographical cards carry the complete data for references, the subject card may merely identify the source by author or by author and an abbreviated title, but it must indicate the exact page or pages from which the note is derived (see Figure 4.8). Since each footnote in your final report will have to state the complete bibliographical information for the reference, forgetting to record the source and page of a note may cause discouraging delays when you are ready to write up the study. Days may be spent in obtaining a reference again and rereading it to locate a quotation—and the search may not always culminate in success!

QUOTING REFERENCES PROPERLY   After locating pertinent material in a reference, you may decide to copy it verbatim, paraphrase it, or summarize it. Your decision will determine the type and form of the note you make. Never copy a statement word for word unless it is especially significant and vitally important to your study. Enclose a copied statement in quotation marks at once so that you will not later assume these are your own words and commit an act of plagiarism unwittingly. Copy quoted passages exactly as they appear in the original. Permit errors to stand, but call attention to them by adding the notation "[*sic*]" immediately after their occurrence in a passage. If you insert a word or phrase to clarify a quotation, enclose the addition in brackets. For example, "A former department head [James Damber] wrote the report." To inform the reader that words have been omitted, insert ellipses—three periods with alternating spaces. For example,

FIGURE 4.8

A summary subject note with comments.

```
Brodbeck, Phil. of Sci.,                Operationalism, Nature of

     Concept formation in science is operational:  The mean-
ings of terms are not defined by listing the observable attri-
butes of objects — shape of chair — but by reference to more
abstract properties — IQ — obtainable by dividing M.A. by
C.A.  Operationalism holds that concepts derive their mean-
ings from the techniques employed in observation or investi-
gation —their operations.  427-428

   *Check: Bridgman, P.W., Logic of Modern Physics for his ex-
planation.
    **Sometimes called operationism, why?
   ***Does this definition have application to historical research?
```

"Professor Thomas Wood . . . first outlined the program in 1910." If you omit something from the end of a sentence or delete more than one sentence, add an additional period—making four periods in all. After copying a quotation, recheck each word, punctuation mark, and capital letter to make certain that you have not made a mistake or omitted anything.

LEARNING TO PARAPHRASE   Refrain from copying pages of direct quotations. Get the full meaning out of the author's ideas and then paraphrase these ideas into notes that can be woven into the first draft of your report with little or no recasting. Stringing quotations together to form a research report is an indication of sloppy, superficial thinking; such compilations make dull reading and no significant contribution to the advancement of knowledge. A worthwhile report is a product of critical thinking: it presents the investigator's own ideas and is written in the investigator's own words. Copying notes verbatim merely postpones the time when you must analyze and synthesize the source materials.

Paraphrasing and summarizing are skills that require practice. Copying phrases, words, or partial sentences usually produces unsatisfactory notes, for after a lapse of time these isolated items may not convey significant meanings and the partial quotes may be mistaken for one's own words or may be easily distorted. You cannot assimilate an author's ideas if you merely copy fragments of sentences or change a word or two. Assimilation requires effort: you must concentrate on passages until you eliminate unessential details, single out the significant ones, and recast these ideas into sharply coined, original sentences that reproduce the exact intent of the author. A few carefully drafted notes are invaluable; an abundance of inaccurate, ambiguously stated notes is useless.

RECORDING REACTIONS TO REFERENCES   Accepting and copying unquestioningly the words on a printed page is a dangerous and unfruitful practice. Reference materials vary in reliability; consequently you must become a skillful detective who makes comparisons, notes discrepancies, sees relationships, analyzes arguments, and evaluates data. During this process, disturbing doubts and challenging questions may seep into your mind. You may ask: Did the author actually observe these conditions? Did the author borrow these ideas from someone else? Does this statement contradict what the same author wrote earlier or what some other authority reported? From what source were these statistics obtained? How were they derived? Is the definition given for this new term different than that given by other authorities? Does this new term refer to the same concept that other authorities identify with other terms? Do the statements presented as supporting evidence justify the author's conclusions?

Critical reading will produce many questions such as these. Keeping a record of them and seeking answers to them will prod your investigation toward a successful solution. Personal reactions to reference materials may be written on separate notes or below a summary or quotation note. If you register a personal reaction to a source material directly on a subject note, distinguish your words from those of the author by enclosing them in brackets or by placing an asterisk or some similar symbol beside them (see Figure 4.8).

RECORD TEMPORARY NOTES   Brief notes may be made of items that vie for your attention when you are trying to concentrate on something else. While reading, note-taking, or engaging in some other pursuit, you may encounter a worthwhile reference, see a desirable method of classifying some facts, question a point, or become concerned about a personal problem. To avoid becoming sidetracked and to prevent worthwhile ideas from escaping you, jot down quickly in abbreviated form to preserve them for later consideration. For example, "Good bibliography on Russian education, Staley, p. 322. How long did Mr. Sach observe Russian schools? What is Tom's unlisted phone number? What are Professor Jack's office hours?" Once recorded, these thoughts are less likely to keep intruding on your train of thought and interrupting the work at hand. At some later time you can pursue these questions and cross them off your list when answers are found.

FILING NOTES   To prevent materials from getting lost during the collection of data, file your notes regularly in a convenient depository. Use vertical files, letter files, accordion files, work organizers, or large manila folders and a cardboard box of the proper size. To speed the filing of notes and to order them in a manner that will facilitate writing the final report, label the file guide cards with the main topics and subtopics in your report outline. Keep your filing system up-to-date. If a category that was once important is no longer useful, place the notes under other topics or place them in an inactive file until the study is completed. When you must add new topics, fit them properly into the organizational scheme of the report.

5 NATURE OF MEASUREMENT

ducation students are often somewhat appre-
hensive or skeptical about taking research courses because they know
that measurement, mathematics, and statistics are employed in collecting and analyzing data. Perhaps you have some fears about the
difficulty or doubts about the usefulness of measurement. To allay such
concerns, this chapter presents a simple explanation of what measurement is, why it is valuable, and how it is related to mathematics and
statistics.

FUNCTION OF MEASUREMENT

Measurement is not an end itself. It is an efficient tool that enables you
to obtain knowledge about phenomena. Throughout your career you
will seek answers to many questions: "How much progress have my
students made in reading this year?" "Is there a relationship between
this new teaching method and reading comprehension?" "How do our
mathematics teachers rate with respect to teaching efficiency?" Both in

the classroom and in the research laboratory you will repeatedly employ measurement to answer questions about problems that are of concern to you. Have you ever thought of how difficult it would be to make decisions in a world without measurement? What progress could be made in education if everyone relied solely on subjective appraisals, personal judgments, and intuitive processes?

Specification of What to Measure

One advantage of measurement is that it takes the guesswork out of observation and the interpretation of data. Measurement involves specifying or defining exactly what is to be measured, the operations to be employed in making measurements, and the conditions under which the observations are to be made. With agreed-upon, unambiguous, specifications of what to observe and what to record, disagreements about the observations of events and the meaning and application of the findings are greatly minimized.

Description of What Is Measured

The data collection process involves making subtle discriminations between phenomena and describing unequivocally the differences. A description may be a *qualitative* statement—"this entity is different from that entity" (a purely classificatory concept)—or a *quantitative* statement—"this entity is different from that entity in [some degree or amount]" (a numerical concept).

Upon first entering the research field, some students argue that for educators the bare abstractions presented by quantitative data are not as informative and useful as qualitative data. They forget that both number and word descriptions are arrived at by abstracting some concept, such as intelligence, from entities and omitting information about other characteristics of the entities. The qualitative description "she is exceptionally intelligent" describes an abstract property in commonplace language that is easy to understand, but the boundaries of "exceptionally intelligent" are unknown. The quantitative description "she has an IQ of 150" is more precise.

Some researchers argue that if something cannot be quantified, knowledge about it has not advanced to the stage of science. They are not fully aware of the interdependence of qualitative and quantitative measurement. A logical continuity exists in each discipline from the formulation of qualitative classifications (based on unaided, individual judgments) to simple levels of measurement (such as rating scales) to the most rigorous and precise levels of quantitative measurement. With respect to their roles in the scientific quest, qualitative data identify the significant factors that researchers might profitably measure quantitatively, whereas quantitative data extend and solidify knowledge.

Language of Communication

To communicate information efficiently and effectively, a language must be used that is understandable and unmistakable in its meaning. The words used in qualitative descriptions—"very aggressive," "average intelligence," "middle class," "very anxious"—are quickly and easily translated, but they do not hold the same meaning for all people. Students who are classified as "very aggressive" by a football coach and by a music teacher might differ; what is classified as a "cold day" by a teacher in Fairbanks, Alaska, might not be the same temperature as one so classified by a teacher in Palm Springs, California.

Investigators who report that a particular experimental treatment made the subjects "appear very anxious" give us some concept of what they have observed. But the vagueness of the term "appears very anxious" invites disagreements both about the meaning and about the boundaries of what is being described. Owing to these ambiguities, other investigators seeking to build upon the knowledge produced by this study or to replicate it to verify the results would likely be ineffective in their efforts. If standardized measures of anxiety were available and the subjects could be assigned the precise number that represents their level of anxiety, better communication could be achieved. When qualitative description gives way to quantitative description, unambiguous classification is possible and "calculation replaces debate."

Quantitative descriptions often require a different language from that which is normally used in daily discourse. The use of numbers and abstract symbols, which convey blocks of meaning about measurement operations and the relations of data, simplifies, standardizes, and speeds up the communication process. Translating the message, however, is often difficult for a novice. Learning how to cross the language barrier requires effort, but the reward is great, for the power of mathematics will be at your disposal. You will be able to make precise, refined description of phenomena that are unmistakable in their meaning. Without further ado, resolve not to be a "measurement mute." If you have learned the English language, you can master the measurement language.

Standardization of Measurement Instruments

Communication about the observations that are made in an investigation is much easier when standardized measuring instruments are available. A measure is considered to be "well standardized" if different users of the instrument obtain the same results. Much work is required to develop a standardized measure that is easy to use and has a wide applicability, such as a thermometer, a yardstick, the Consumers Price Index, or an intelligence test, but once developed, the use of it is much more economical of time and money than subjective evaluations.

Without a standardized measurement instrument available, a researcher might observe a group of youngsters for months and take voluminous notes before arriving at judgments and writing qualitative descriptions of their intelligence. By administering a standardized group intelligence test, one could make a more precise appraisal in a relatively short time. The IQ scores obtained could be used, immediately or later, to make meaningful comparisons of the children in this group or of this group and other groups of children.

If advances in obtaining knowledge are to be made, researchers must be able to compare their findings with those they have obtained in the past or will obtain in the future and with the findings of other researchers working on similar problems. Once a standardized measure has been established, all data reports can be adjusted to them. Standardized measures simplify the amount of reporting required, permit meaningful comparisons to be made, and facilitate efficient communication between researchers.

Elaboration of Theories

The primary goal of research is to establish theoretical structures by means of which observable phenomena can be described, explained, predicted, or controlled. To carry out this work, researchers formulate hypotheses and collect and compare data to ascertain whether the hypotheses they have formulated can be verified. Until they can count, weigh, time, or in some way quantify the phenomena under investigation, researchers are seriously handicapped in carrying out their work. The abstract nature of mathematics offers a variety of possibilities for logical manipulation and analysis. Researchers can operate on the numbers obtained in an investigation in all permissible ways. By this process, they can emerge with conclusions about the relations of the data that apply back to the observed phenomena and provide a web of evidence that either does or does not support their hypotheses.

In summary, if a property is measurable quantitatively,

> . . . it makes for greater descriptive flexibility. . . . It also gives information about the relations between various quantities of the property. In terms of explanation, it allows for more precise formulation of general laws relating different constructs, and it enables the paraphernalia of mathematics to be extensively applied to science. Functional relations between constructs can be expressed in terms of mathematical functions. Theories and laws can be formulated in terms of mathematical equations [109:12].

Because measurement can make significant contributions to the scientific enterprise, this chapter will focus on the procedures and pitfalls in using this tool.

DEFINITION OF MEASUREMENT

In popular usage, the term "measure" has many different meanings and applications. In one study of its occurrences in a large sample of words, measure was used in forty different ways. The term may refer to the act of, the result of, the instrument for, or the graduated units used in measuring. In the scientific community, the definition is restricted to permit more effective communication. In this chapter, *measurement* refers to the procedures employed to establish rather than to use a measuring device. Making measurements with a yardstick, attitude scale, or some other established instrument is a relatively simple procedure to carry out, but developing a new and suitable scale of measurement, which is often necessary in an investigation, may not be.

Researchers work basically with groups. Each group is a logical collection of particulars which are alike in some defining respect. Researchers refer to a group as a *set* or *class* and to like members of a group as a *subset, subclass,* or *category.* In general, *measurement involves* (1) *assigning a set of numerals* (2) *to a set of entities* (3) *in accordance with some logically acceptable rule.* The following discussion explains each of the above factors that are involved in measurement.

Set of Numerals

The choice of the word *numeral* in the definition of measurement is deliberate. A numeral is a symbol of the type 1, 2, 3 . . . or A, B,

C . . . or I, II, III. . . . This symbol has no inherent quantitative or qualitative meaning unless such a property is assigned to it. Numerals become numbers if they are assigned one or more of the following properties: identity, order, additivity. The three types of numbers are nominal, ordinal, and cardinal, and each type has different properties.

NOMINAL NUMBERS A nominal number is a numeral that has been assigned the meaning of *identity*; it is unique in that it is not exactly the same as any other number, but a nominal number has no further property—no quantitative meaning. Nominal numbers may be assigned to entities that are unique from other entities, such as telephones, bank accounts, or subjects in an investigation. In Figure 5.1, which presents some data about a footrace, you will note that John is assigned number 3 to wear on his back as a distinguishing label to help observers keep track of him.

ORDINAL NUMBERS An ordinal number is a numeral that has been assigned the meaning of *rank order*; one ordinal number is greater than or less than another on some underlying continuum. Ordinal numbers may be assigned to entities that are orderable on the dimension being assessed. In Figure 5.1, John is assigned number 1, Joe number 2, etc., to provide information about the order in which the footrace contestants crossed the finish line. Ordinal numbers possess the properties of identity and order, but they do not possess additivity.

CARDINAL NUMBERS A cardinal number represents an absolute magnitude (size, amount), and, hence, possesses the property of *additivity*. By adding together two cardinal numbers, a new unique number is obtained; by adding negative numbers, one can subtract; by adding the same number to itself a specified number of times, one can multiply; by making successive subtractions, one can divide. The ability to add, subtract, multiply, and divide gives the researcher a versatile tool for analyzing data. From the data in Figure 5.1, for example, one could find out by how many seconds the winner of the race, John, beat Joe or any other contestant.

Set of Entities

The purpose of measurement is to acquire information about a set of entities with respect to their possession of a property. A set or class of entities is a well-defined collection of similar particulars: organisms (such as students, teachers, voters, or rats), objects (such as books,

	RESULTS FROM 100-METER DASH					MEANING OF NUMBERS	TYPE OF NUMBERS
Participant's number	3 (John)	10 (Joe)	7 (Tom)	14 (Bob)	2 (Tim)	Identity	Nominal
Place in event	1	2	3	4	5	Rank-order	Ordinal
Elapse time of dash (in seconds)	10.4	10.5	10.7	10.8	10.10	Absolute time	Cardinal

FIGURE 5.1

Comparison of nominal, ordinal, and cardinal numbers.

typewriters, or desks), or events (such as fire drills, field trips, or football games).

PROPERTY OF ENTITIES   What is measured is not a set of entities—fifty students—but indicants of some property of the entities. A student cannot be measured, but indicants of his weight, intellectual capacity, achievement in arithmetic, punctuality, or other properties can be. Explanations of the terms *property* and *indicants* are given below.

1   A *property* is a concept or logical construct that describes a particular characteristic which is common to all members of a set, such as punctuality or IQ, but on which members of the set vary.[1]
2   An *indicant* is something that points to the property and helps define it. Indicants of the property punctuality might be "is never tardy to class," "hands in term papers on or before the due date," and "is among the first people to arrive for meetings."

TYPES OF VARIABLES   In a scientific investigation, the term *property*, is synonymous with the term *variable*. In a research report, a variable may be represented by a symbol, such as X. If the variable in an investigation is the IQ score that students possess, the value of X will vary for different entities: 110 IQ for Jane; 105 IQ for Mona; and 100 IQ for Lisa.

There are two types of variables (properties), continuous and discrete. When constructing a measurement instrument or selecting a statistical technique to analyze the data, one must first decide what kind of variable (property) is under consideration. The kind of variable

[1] In the literature, the term *phenomenon, attribute, characteristic, dimension,* or *variable* is often used instead of *property*.

determines the amount of information that can be obtained and the type of statistical analysis that can be legitimately employed.

1 A *continuous variable*, such as height, weight, or intelligence, represents a continuous progression from the smallest possible amount to the largest possible amount, with measurement theoretically possible at any point along the continuum. It is a variable with graduated measures that may differ by infinitely small amounts. Precise measurement is possible because both whole and fractional units are used. The values of a continuous variable reflect at least rank order, for 100.5 pounds is greater than 98.6 pounds, 98.6 pounds is greater than 95.3 pounds, etc.

2 A *discrete* (or *discontinuous*) *variable* is one for which measurement and classification are possible only in whole units, for example, size of family, number of schools attended. A discrete variable, which belongs to the kind of measurement called nominal, can be either of the following:

a A *two-category variable (dichotomous),* such as life status (living or dead, for example)

b *Multiple-category variable,* such as the country in which a person is born (Norway, England, or Spain, etc.)

A true discrete variable, such as life status (living or dead) cannot be converted into a continuous variable, for one cannot be 20, 40, or 60 percent alive or dead. A true discrete variable is measured only by a nominal scale which can distinguish differences between entities but not degrees of difference.

A continuous variable, on the other hand, can be converted into a two-category (dichotomized) or a multicategory variable. Weight, for example, is a continuous variable with graduated measures that may differ by infinitely small amounts, but it can be converted into a three-category variable: light, average, and heavy weight. If this is done, one can ascertain relative differences in weight, but information about the exact weights will be lost; the researcher must decide whether the findings will be sufficiently precise to accomplish the purpose of the investigation.

Rules for Assigning Numerals to Entities

In an investigation, the objective is to seek knowledge not about mere particulars, but rather about relationships: (1) about how entities in a set may stand in relation to one another with respect to their possession of a property and (2) about how their positions on one property are related to their positions on other properties. Researchers learn about a high level of arithmetic achievement, aggression, anxiety, or athletic ability only as they study it in relation to other levels of the property and in relation to other properties. Scientific facts are knowledge about relations. A measurement procedure establishes a relation.

Researchers establish a relation by assigning a set of symbols, usually numbers, to a set of entities in accordance with a logical rule. The rule, which may be called a *rule of correspondence*, an *assignment rule*, or a *mapping rule*, stipulates exactly what operations one performs to map the members of a set of numbers onto members of a set of entities.[2] Each entity is assigned one and only one number or symbol which shows its position on the property in relation to the position of other entities.

An investigator assigns to entities numbers that have the property or combination of properties—identity, order, additivity—that parallels the properties of the entities. Ordinal numbers can be assigned to represent the heights of students, for example, because the students possess the property of order and succession with respect to height. But ordinal numbers cannot be assigned to represent the students' religious affiliations because the categories of affiliation—Jewish, Catholic, Protestant—cannot be rank-ordered; each category has a unique religious identity, but one category is not greater or lesser than the other. The rule of correspondence, stated more formally, requires that (1) the relation between the numbers assigned to entities must correspond with (2) the relation between the entities themselves with respect to their possession of the property.

EXAMPLES OF THE ASSIGNMENT OF NUMBERS In Figure 5.2, observe how the mapping, or assignment operation, in the three examples establishes the relation between the buildings on a campus with respect to the properties (A) identity, (B) height, and (C) size. Example B establishes the relation of the buildings with respect to the property height. The rule of correspondence in this instance might read: Assign the numbers 1–4 to the buildings to identify their position with respect to height with number 1 corresponding to the highest building and number 4 corresponding to the lowest building. The arrows drawn from the numbers (range) to the entities (domain) depict which

---

[2]Usually, when numbers are assigned to entities, the entities are said to be mapped onto an abstract numerical space of some known property. To make the mapping concept consistent with the definition of measurement and the procedures easier to understand, the direction of mapping has been reversed in this chapter.

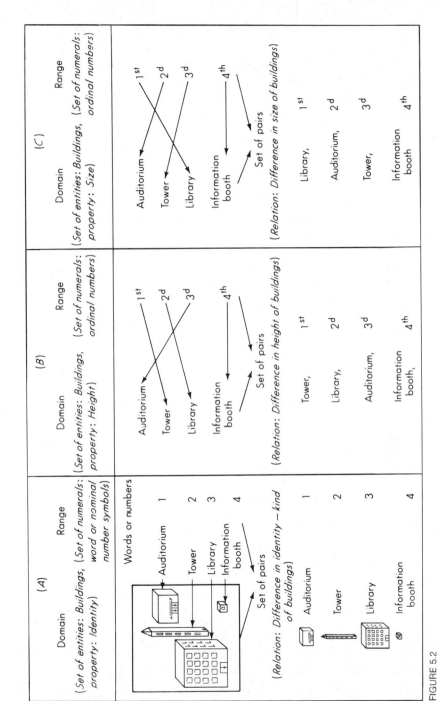

FIGURE 5.2

Examples of mapping to show relations of entities.

numbers correspond with the buildings with respect to height. When completed, the mapping procedure creates a new set, a set of ordered pairs. The first member of each pair is the entity measured, and the second member is the number assigned to the entity (tower—1, library—2, auditorium—3, information booth—4). This set of ordered pairs establishes the relation of the buildings with respect to the property height; it ties the theoretical concept of height, which is represented by numbers, to observable, real entities.

QUALITY OF RULES OF CORRESPONDENCE   The effectiveness of a measurement instrument, such as a questionnaire, attitude scale, anxiety scale, or public opinion survey, depends on how good or poor the rules of assignment are. The rules clarify what the numbers mean. The numbers do not know what they mean or what they measure. In Figure 5.2, number 1 is assigned a different meaning in each example: in example A, it identifies the auditorium on a map; in example B, it identifies the rank order of the tower with respect to height; and in example C, it identifies the rank order of the library with respect to size. Numbers do not know what they mean; likewise, entities do not have numbers embedded in them that represent them in every way. In Figure 5.2, the auditorium is assigned number 1 to identify it on the map, number 3 to identify its position with respect to height, and number 2 to identify its position with respect to size. A number means what the investigator says it means in the rule of assignment. The quality of any measurement procedure, therefore, depends on how unambiguous the rules of correspondence are. Developing a set of explicit rules for assigning entities numerals that represent their positions with respect to a quantity of some differentiating property is a challenging task.

The "goodness" of a mapping (correspondence) rule is determined by how well it links up (1) a conceptualized property (a theoretical construct) with (2) an observable, real entity (empirical data). A good rule of correspondence makes statements about the indicants of a property that can be empirically tested. The statements communicate what is observable by human senses or by mechanical devices that extend the senses. The assignment rule makes clear what observable indicants of the property correspond with what numeral.

The indicants of physical properties, such as sex, height, weight, color of eyes are closely tied to direct observation. But many complex properties invented by investigators, logical constructs, such as motivation, self-concept, mechanical ability, cannot be seen directly and are not as clearly quantifiable as weight and height. Their existence is inferred from observations of presumed indicants of the property.

These "invented properties" or logical constructs can be observed only indirectly. Through logical arguments they are tied to observable data.

Writing an unambiguous rule of assignment for a property that is closely related to direct observation is easier than for an "invented property" that can be observed only quite indirectly. For example, writing an unambiguous definition of what observable indicants to look for to assign the number 1 to a female entity and number 2 to a male entity is not difficult, but defining what observable indicants to look for to assign the number 1 to a student with a high level of motivation and number 0 to a student with a low level of motivation is a more demanding task.

SCALES OF MEASUREMENT

The rules of correspondence that are used to assign numbers to entities clarify what the numerals mean—what they represent; they give directions for classifying members of a set into subsets; they define the

FIGURE 5.3

Rule of correspondence links theoretical concepts or constructs to observable data.

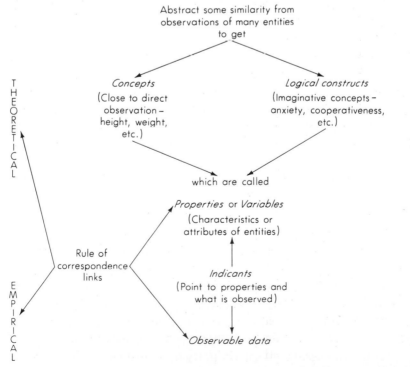

nature of the measuring instrument and the level of strength of the measurement. The four general levels of measurement, ordered in accordance with the amount of information the numerals on the scales represent, are nominal, ordinal, interval, and ratio.

To provide a better understanding of the four levels of measurement, some of the relations that can exist between entities are described below. The symbols employed have the following meanings:

= equal or alike	> greater than, older than, etc.	
≠ unequal or different	≯ not greater than, not older than, etc.	

TYPE OF RELATION	DEFINITION	EXAMPLE
Symmetry	Relation holds between entities in both directions.	If $a = b$, then $b = a$. If a is the same height as b, then b is the same height as a.
Asymmetry	Relation holds between entities in one direction but not in the other.	If $a>b$, then $b>a$ and $a \neq b$. If a is taller than b, then b is not taller than a, and a and b are not equal in height.
Transitivity	If a relation holds between two entities, the second of which has the same relation to the third, then the first must also stand in that relation to the third.	If $a>b$ and $b>c$, then $a>c$. If a is taller than b, and b is taller than c, then a is taller than c. or: If $a = b$ and $b = c$, then $a = c$. If a is as tall as b and b is as tall as c, then a is as tall as c.

Nominal Scales

The most primitive level of measurement is a nominal scale in which the only function of the numerals is (1) to identify (label) individual entities or (2) to classify a set of entities in accordance with their similarities and differences with respect to some property.

A nominal scale has the property of identity and nothing more; it is capable only of distinguishing differences in kind. If number 12 is assigned to an individual football player or a male subject in an experiment, it enables us to identify him, to distinguish him from other players or subjects. If numbers are assigned to students to classify them into distinct subsets, number 1 to black students and number 2 to white students, the numbers serve only as racial identification labels.

A nominal scale can be constructed if the relationships exist among the entities that are required for classification. The classification system must be mutually exclusive and exhaustive. The rule of correspondence assigns each entity one and only one number (to one and only one subset). An appropriate subset is available for every entity. The subsets bear a logical relationship to the property under consideration and to each other. A logical classification of hair color could include "golden," "brown," "black," "white," and "red" subsets, but not a "curly" subset because "curly" is related to the property hair texture rather than hair color. In a nominal scale, all entities assigned the same numeral (to the same subset) are equal or alike with respect to the possession of the property, and all entities assigned different numerals (to different subsets) are different, not equal. In the illustration below, for example, the female students were assigned to subset A and the male students were assigned to subset B. Symbol A identifies a group of like or equal students with respect to sex identification; they are all females. The students in subset A and subset B differ with respect to sex identification.

The formal requirements for establishing a nominal scale involve the two types of relationships that are necessary for classification, as shown in the accompanying illustration.

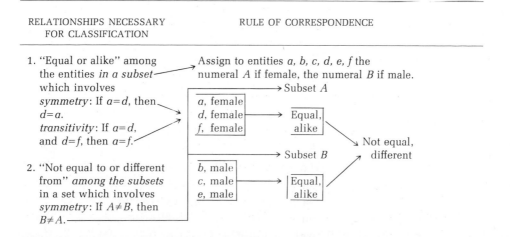

RELATIONSHIPS NECESSARY FOR CLASSIFICATION	RULE OF CORRESPONDENCE

1. "Equal or alike" among the entities *in a subset* which involves *symmetry*: If $a=d$, then $d=a$. *transitivity*: If $a=d$, and $d=f$, then $a=f$.

Assign to entities a, b, c, d, e, f the numeral A if female, the numeral B if male.
→ Subset A

a, female
d, female
f, female
→ Equal, alike
↘ Not equal, different

2. "Not equal to or different from" *among the subsets* in a set which involves *symmetry*: If $A \neq B$, then $B \neq A$.

→ Subset B
b, male
c, male
e, male
→ Equal, alike

Nominal scales do not provide much information, but they do enable significant spadework in research. All sciences begin to seek knowledge of their subject matter by classifying phenomena in their field. Each of the higher-level scales of measurement involves classification as a minimal operation. But nominal scales have limited strength, because the numbers on the scales are merely distinguishing identification labels that represent differences in kind with respect to a property without an apparent underlying continuum. Numbers on a nominal scale are qualitative; they have no quantitative implications; they do not represent a quantity, size, amount, or degree of a property. The assignment of numbers is almost purely arbitrary; hence, the structure of the scale would not be altered if the numbers were interchanged or new numbers were assigned to the series. The only requirement is that each subset is assigned a different number.

Because nominal numbers do not represent a quantity, no meaningful information can be obtained by adding, subtracting, multiplying, or dividing them. No one assumes that a football player who wears number 40 on his uniform is twice as anything as his teammate who wears number 20. No meaningful information can be obtained by applying arithmetical operations to the scale numbers, but some useful information can be obtained by counting the entities in each labeled subset, comparing the frequency with which entities appear in each subset, and computing the percentage or proportion of entities in each subset.

Ordinal Scales

The numbers on an ordinal scale provide information not only about (1) the individual identity or classificatory category of entities but also about (2) their rank order on some underlying property continuum. Ordinal scales yield more information than nominal scales because they distinguish not only differences in kind but also the relative degree of the difference. But a rank-order number represents a relative quantity of the property and nothing more; it does not represent an absolute quantity.

The order and the succession on the ordinal scale may be from "greatest to least," "fastest to slowest," "highest to lowest," etc., or vice versa, on some property. The relation among the numbers in a set assigned to the entities must reflect the order or relation of the entities on the scale property. Any numerical assignment is permissible which parallels that order. Hence, "light-, average-, and heavy-weight" entities may be assigned the numbers 1, 2, 3, respectively; 7, 8, 9, respectively; or 5, 10, 15, respectively; but not 2, 1, 3, respectively; for the last set of numbers does not correspond to and preserve the "light-, average-, heavy-weight" relation among the entities.

To establish an ordinal scale, the same relationships must hold among the entities in a subset (equal to or alike—symmetry and transitivity) and among the subsets (not equal to, different from— symmetry), as hold in a nominal scale. In addition, in an ordinal scale, a "greater than" relationship must hold among the subsets which involves the following:

RELATIONSHIPS NECESSARY TO ESTABLISH RANK ORDER	EXAMPLES
Asymmetry: If $A>B$, then $B \not> A$.	If entities in subset A are greater in weight than those in subset B, then it cannot be true that entities in subset B are greater in weight than those in subset A.
Transitivity: If $A>B$ and $B>C$, then $A>C$.	If entities in subset A are greater in weight than those in subset B, and entities in subset B are greater in weight than those in subset C, then entities in subset A are greater in weight than those in subset C.

If asymmetry and transitivity relationships hold among the subsets, they possess the property of rank order, and subsets A, B, C can justifiably be placed along a single continuum.

Difficulties can be encountered when one attempts to rank-order entities on some properties. Observers can recognize the differences in relative height, weight, and many other properties rather easily, but in many instances a property is a complex resultant of several properties. Sometimes a comparison can be made but a ranking cannot. Success at tennis, for example, depends on many factors. If a coach observes that Al defeats Bob ($a>b$), and Bob defeats Carl ($b>c$), but Carl defeats Al ($a \not> c$), he can compare but cannot rank the players. Carl's rude court behavior may have upset Al but not upset Bob. The fact that Carl defeats Al violates the transitivity condition of perfect order: If $a>b$ and $b>c$, then $a>c$.

When using an ordinal scale, it is important to recognize that the *distance or interval between the numbers is unknown and not necessarily equal.* Because the interval is unknown, the property of additivity is not present: one cannot legitimately add, subtract, multiply, or divide ordinal numbers. Educational researchers, however, often do apply arithmetic operations to ordinal data. If they do so without evaluating the risks involved, they may make claims about their findings that are grossly in error.

The problems that can arise when arithmetic operations are applied to ordinal numbers is illustrated in Figure 5.4 which depicts (1) the *relative* quantities of weight that three subjects possess on an ordinal scale and (2) the *absolute* quantities of weight they possess on a "true" value scale. On the ordinal scale, the entities *a, b, c,* were assigned the rank values for the property weight of 15, 10, 5, respectively. These ordinal numbers provide information about differences in relative magnitude: *a* weighs more than *b*, and *b* weighs more than *c*. They do not, however, tell us how much more or the absolute quantity of weight. The assumption cannot be made that because the ordinal numbers, 15, 10, 5, are equally spaced (by 5 units), the underlying property, the weights they represent, is equally spaced. The claim cannot be made that *a* (rank value 15) equals the weight of *b* plus *c* (rank values 10 + 5) or that *a* is as much heavier than *b* as *b* is heavier than *c* (interval 15–10 is equal to interval 10–5). The true or absolute weights of *a, b,* and *c* may be as depicted on the "true" value scale: 140, 130, and 100 pounds, respectively. On the "true" value scale, the interval, or distance, between *a* and *b* (10 pounds) and between *b* and *c* (30 pounds) are not equal.

Interval Scales

Interval scales are sometimes called equal-interval scales, because the distance, or difference, between the numbers on the scale is known and always equal. Because a *constant difference* (one inch, for example) exists between every pair of adjacent categories (0–1, 1–2, 2–3), interval scales indicate how far apart entities are from one another with respect

FIGURE 5.4

Comparison of intervals on an ordinal scale and on a "true" value scale.

Ordinal scale			
Entities	*a*	*b*	*c*
Relative quantity of weight	15	10	5
"True" value scale			
Entities	*a*	*b*	*c*
Absolute quantity (pounds) of weight	140	130	100

to the property. The numbers on an interval scale provide information not only about (1) identity and (2) rank order of the entities (Bob is taller or shorter than Allan), but also about (3) *differences in magnitude from an arbitrary point of origin* (Bob is 4 inches taller or shorter than Allan, who was chosen as the arbitrary starting point for measurement). But an interval scale does not stipulate the absolute magnitude of a property for any particular entity (how tall Bob and Allan are remains unknown).

On an interval scale, one begins to count or add successively not from an absolute zero point that represents total absence of a property, but from an arbitrary or artificial zero point. Many properties are measured from arbitrary zero points. Different cultures, for example, have chosen different zero points from which to start numbering years: the birth of Christ on the Christian calendar, the flight of Mohammed from Mecca to Medina (A.D. 62) on the Islamic calendar, and the reign of the "Yellow Emperor," Huang Ti (2697 B.C.), on the Chinese calendar. On a centigrade thermometer, the zero point, 0°C, is placed at the freezing point of water, which is equal to 32° Fahrenheit, and 0°F is the same as -17.8°C. Thus, the zero point is arbitrary; it is located at different points on the two scales. In neither instance does it indicate complete absence of temperature. Only the kelvin scale, which physicists use, has an absolute zero which represents the absence of any heat at all. The kelvin zero point is the equivalent of -273.15°C and -459.67°F.

The key requirement for constructing an interval scale is establishing the size of a *common unit of measurement*; one unit that can be agreed upon as possessing the same quantitative meaning at any point on the scale. An inch, for example, represents the same difference in distance between 1 and 2 inches as between 22 and 23 inches. Weight in pounds, temperature in degrees Fahrenheit or centigrade, and income in dollars are other examples of common units of measurement. The unit chosen must always have a relation to the property under consideration. The dollar, for example, is a suitable unit to employ if the property under investigation is the amount of money a person earns. But if income is conceived in terms of quality of living permitted, the dollar unit of measurement does not have the same quantitative meaning at any point on the scale. An increase in salary from $5,000 to $10,000 a year may mean the difference between an impoverished and a modestly comfortable standard of living, but an increase in salary from $45,000 to $50,000 a year may represent a negligible improvement in the quality of life.

The common unit of measurement in interval scales produces

cardinal numbers which represent an absolute magnitude and have the property of additivity. Arithmetic and statistical operations, therefore, may be applied to interval data which enable one to obtain more information than from either nominal or ordinal data. Addition and subtraction of interval-scale values are permissible operations because of the equal unit of measurement. But because the numbering on the scale begins at an arbitrary rather than an absolute, or "true," zero point, multiplication and division are permissible only with respect to the intervals and not with respect to the scale values. Figure 5.5 and the following discussion explain why this limitation exists.

The difference in the absolute magnitude that may exist if different arbitrary zeros are used is illustrated in Figure 5.5, which depicts the body height measurements of four students, a, b, c, d. The subjects were measured not directly but rather from an arbitrary zero point, a, the shortest subject. The scale shows how many common units of measurement (inches) $b, c,$ and d are, respectively, from a, the arbitrary zero point, and from one another. It informs us that d is 12 units taller than a $(12-0=12)$ and 4 units taller than c $(12-8=4)$. But because measurement on this scale begins with an arbitrary zero, d's scale value does not inform us how tall d is. Student d may be 84 inches tall if a, the arbitrary zero point, is a 72-inch-tall basketball player $(72+12=84)$ and 48 inches tall if a is a 36-inch-tall dwarf $(36+12=48)$.

Knowledge of equal units of measurement permits us to find the *ratio between any two intervals*—pairs of scale values on an interval scale: the difference in height between a and c is twice the difference in height between a and b $(8-0=8, 4-0=4, 8 \div 4=2)$. But because mea-

FIGURE 5.5

Comparison of interval scales with different arbitrary starting points.

		Interval scale		
Common unit, inch Arbitrary zero, shortest boy	0	4	8	12
Position of subjects on scale	a	b	c	d
		"True" value scales		
If basketball player is the arbitrary zero, the actual height of the subjects is	72	76	80	84
If a dwarf is the arbitrary zero, the actual height of the subject is	36	40	44	48

surement begins from an arbitrary zero, we cannot legitimately compare scale values by finding the *ratio between any two scale values*. We cannot say that one scale value, *c*, is twice as great as another scale value, *b* (8÷4=2). If *c* is actually 80 inches tall and *b* is actually 76 inches tall, the ratio of their actual height values 80÷76 does not equal 2.

In summary, interval scales have the properties of identity, order, and additivity. Knowledge of equal units permits one to employ some arithmetic operations to obtain information that cannot be obtained with nominal or ordinal scales. Indeed, because nominal and ordinal scales do not have the property of additivity, the procedures employed to obtain data by these methods are sometimes called scaling rather than measurement. The property of additivity gives the interval scale considerable strength; on the other hand, measuring from an arbitrary zero point limits the amount of information that it can obtain.

Ratio Scales

A ratio scale, the highest level of measurement, possesses all the properties of an interval scale: (1) identity, (2) rank order, and (3) additivity—equal units of measurement. In addition, (4) it begins measurement from an absolute ("true," or natural) zero point signifying the total absence of the property; it offers a consistent rather than an arbitrary starting point for measurement. Hence, numbers on a ratio scale, unlike those on an interval scale, indicate the actual quantity of the property being measured.

Because the zero point is fixed on a ratio scale, at absolute zero, all fundamental arithmetic operations are possible. One can compare scale values by finding the ratio between two scale values. If the subjects in Figure 5.5 had been measured from an absolute zero, rather than from an arbitrary zero, *a*, the shortest subject, one could say that a subject with a height of 72 inches was twice as tall as one with the height of 36 inches.

ANALYSIS OF MEASUREMENT

After making all the measurements needed in an investigation, one can seldom look at the mass of raw data—perhaps hundreds or thousands of scores—and perceive clearly the significant relations between the properties studied. The data must be organized and reduced into a convenient and meaningful form so that the findings can be analyzed

LEVEL OF SCALE	RELATION WITHIN EACH SUBSET	RELATION WITHIN SERIES OF SUBSETS	MEASUREMENT PROPERTIES	DETERMINATION OF OPERATIONS	EXAMPLES
Nominal	Equal–alike	Not equal–different	Identity	Likeness and differences	"Numbering" of football players
Ordinal	Equal–alike	Not equal–"greater or less than" relationship	Identity		
			Order	Differences in relative magnitude	Rank ordering of handwriting specimens
Interval	Equal–alike	Not equal–"greater or less than" relationship	Identity Order	Differences in magnitude from arbitrary zero	Calendar dates, temperature
			Additivity	Common unit of measurement–equal intervals	
				Ratio between any two intervals–pairs of scale values	
Ratio	Equal–alike	Not equal–"greater or less than" relationship	Identity Order	Differences in magnitude from absolute zero	Weight, length
			Additivity	Common unit of measurement	
				Ratio between any two intervals	
				Ratio between any two scale values	

FIGURE 5.6

Classification of scales of measurement.

and interpreted in terms of the original research hypothesis or question.

To summarize and analyze raw data, a researcher applies logical sets of arithmetic operations to them. Each set of arithmetic operations is called a *statistical measure*. Different statistical measures are used for different purposes. The two broad categories of purpose are *descriptive* and *inferential*.

Descriptive Statistics

As the name indicates, a descriptive statistic can give one a snapshot picture of all the scores in a set of data. Descriptive statistics make it possible to obtain a single numerical value that describes a whole set of data with respect to some distributional property or the relationship between two sets of data.

TYPES OF MEASUREMENT   The major types of descriptive statistics are measures of central tendency, measures of variability, and measures of relationship.

1   *Central tendency measures* (mode, median, mean) inform one about the average, or central, value of a distribution of scores, such as the IQ value that typifies all the cases in a distribution.
2   *Variability measures* inform one of the dispersion—the amount of clustering or spread of the scores around the measure of central tendency. The amount of dispersion will be greater for some distributions than for others. The most commonly used measures of variability are the variance (σ^2) and the standard deviation (σ) about the mean.[3]
3   A *correlation coefficient* describes the degree to which the scores of the same entities on different variables are related; for example, whether a high, a low, or no correlation exists between the amount of education obtained and the yearly income received by subjects. The correlation coefficient, symbolized as r, can range from a perfect positive relationship, $r = 1.00$, to a perfect negative relationship, $r = -1.00$.[4] Because most research consists of finding out what is and what is not related to what, being able to state relationships in a compact form is advantageous.

CURVES OF DISTRIBUTION   The data obtained in an investigation can be presented in the graphic form of a histogram or frequency polygon. The line drawn on the graph paper gives one a visual picture of the frequency of the occurrence of the scores in the distribution. This is an *empirical curve of distribution*; it is a picture derived from the

---

[3]You may wish to familiarize yourself with measures of central tendency and variability at this time in Appendix A.1.

[4]A discussion of correlation is presented in Chapter 10 and Appendix A.2.

observations of real entities. A normal curve of distribution, on the other hand, is a *theoretical curve of distribution* that is deductively arrived at from mathematical theory through the use of a formula rather than from observing real entities. You are undoubtedly familiar with the symmetrical, bell-shaped, normal curve in which most of the measurements are located in the center near the mean of the distribution, a very few at the extremes. Figure 5.7 shows the percentage of cases falling under portions of the normal curve.

The normal curve of distribution is a mathematical concept or model of great significance in statistical theory. The normal curve is often called a normal probability curve, for it is possible to predict from it how an infinitely large number of observations varying only by chance would be distributed. The mathematical definition of the normal curve would probably not mean much to you if you have not had advanced training in mathematics. But it is important to remember that the normal curve is a theoretical curve of distribution, a mathematical ideal.

The normal curve is useful because the scores on many properties of interest to educators, if a sufficient number of subjects are measured, tend to be distributed symmetrically about their mean scores in proportions which approximate those of the theoretical normal curve. Because of this fortunate relationship between the world of observation and the world of mathematical equations, the theoretical properties of the normal curve are of considerable value in describing data.

Inferential Statistics

Nearly all research studies in education involve making measurements of a limited number, or sample, of entities that are selected from a well-defined population. Inferential statistics involve the process of

FIGURE 5.7

Proportion of normal curve with ordinate erected both at the mean and at each standard deviation above and below the mean.

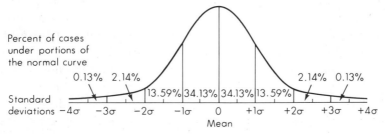

moving from knowledge obtained from a part (a sample) to a generalization about the whole (a population). One uses the data obtained from a limited group of observations to make a reasonable inference about the larger, unobserved population from which the smaller group was drawn. One may, for example, measure the height of 300 randomly selected female students at a state university, and, from the data obtained, draw a generalization about the height of the entire female student body at that university. By chance, of course, the females in the sample may be the tallest girls in the population. But inferential statistics enable one to estimate, within a specified degree of confidence, whether the sample data (the empirical distribution) are statistically significant, that is, represent a significant departure from what might be expected to occur by chance alone in a normal distribution. A number of tests are available that are appropriate for testing different sets of data. The most commonly used ones are the t test, analysis of variance (F test), and chi-square test (χ^2) of significance.

Selection of Statistical Measures

Before discussing the selection of statistical measures, the difference between measurement and mathematics should be noted. Both measurement and mathematics may involve the use of numbers but in different ways. Measurement is concerned with the real world, with the degree of or quantity of properties present in real entities. In measurement, the numbers represent some aspect of reality. Mathematics, on the other hand, is an abstract activity that makes no reference to observation and sensory experiences. Mathematics is concerned with deductive reasoning, with the process of going from a set of definitions, assumptions, and internally consistent rules for the manipulation of symbols to a set of conclusions by means of logical reasoning. In summary, measurement enables us to obtain empirical data; mathematics enables us to examine the relations of the data obtained by measurement.

Statistical measures can be obtained for any distribution of numbers. A statistic is unconcerned about the nature of measurement scales. Nothing prevents one from calculating the arithmetic mean of the numbers on the backs of a group of football players. Adding these nominal numbers and dividing them by the number of players would produce an arithmetic mean that would accurately represent the average value of the numbers, but the information would not help one interpret anything meaningful about the players observed.

Educators often face a frustrating task when they must select statistical techniques. Their objective is to select (1) those that are most appropriate for answering the questions raised by the investigation and (2) those that can be used legitimately with the level of measurement the data have obtained. But the educators cannot always establish the measurement conditions that will permit them to use the statistical techniques they want to employ. You will recall that cardinal numbers have the property of additivity. When cardinal numbers are assigned to entities, the measurement process attains the level of the interval or ratio scale. The property of additivity makes it legitimate to use more powerful statistical techniques than can be used with nominal or ordinal data.

Physicists can establish the conditions required to measure length, time, mass, heat, and several other properties with additivity-status scales. But educators cannot measure many properties of interest to them with interval or ratio scales, because they have difficulty establishing proof of absolute equality of intervals and absolute zero points to begin measurement. Educators can establish a difference in degree of anxiety, adjustment, or aptitude, but they cannot prove that the units of measurement on these scales are absolutely equal or that any living individuals can be said to have absolutely zero anxiety, adjustment, or aptitude.

Tests that measure many educational properties are ostensibly ordinal, they reflect rank-order positions of individuals on the property, but not the quantity of the property that they possess. In a strict sense, with ordinal scales, no fundamental operations of arithmetic may be applied, for it makes no sense to add, subtract, divide, and multiply ranks (intervals that may be unequal). When these operations cannot be applied to data, one cannot use the more powerful statistical methods of analysis, the methods that provide the most information.

Finding a rich set of meaningful relations among the variables under investigation is the objective of researchers. The nature of educational subject matter seems to prevent this dream from becoming a reality, but the situation is not as hopeless as it may appear. The distinction between some ordinal scales and interval scales is not sharp. Numerous educational measurement scales, although not strictly of interval strength, are only slightly distorted versions of interval scales. When educators employ ordinal scales that approximate interval equality fairly well, they treat these ordinal scales with considerable assurance that they are just as reliable and meaningful as though they were interval measurements. They apply statistics that call for interval equality to extract the most information from the data, but they always keep in mind the amount of inequality of intervals. They weigh the advantages and risks of employing statistical procedures that require interval strength when the data are not strictly of interval strength.

FALLIBILITY OF MEASUREMENT

When you make measurements and obtain numerical answers, what do the numbers mean? Why bother with measurement in an investigation? The discussion thus far in this chapter has challenged the argument that numbers are useless, impersonal abstractions that do not help one deal with the educational process. Knowledge about educational phenomena can be expressed more precisely with quantitative than with qualitative descriptions. Moreover, arithmetic operations can be applied to numerical data which make it possible to obtain more information about educational phenomena than would otherwise be possible.

On the other hand, numbers do not possess occult powers. They are not self-evident segments of truth that have universally understood, unalterable meanings. Numbers bear the imprint of all the operations by which they are obtained. The numbers themselves know nothing about their heredity, about the researcher's objectives, or about the reality they are expected to represent. Numbers are assigned meanings, are manipulated by and are interpreted by fallible human beings; hence, they are not infallible.

Meaning of Numbers

Numbers have a variety of meanings. A researcher or a consumer of research must recognize from the context of a report whether number 1, 2, or 3 refers to the identity of the entity, the order of the entity in a sequence, the sum of all the entities in a set, or the amount of the entity. Likewise, they must ascertain whether the level of measurement obtained in collecting the data—nominal, ordinal, interval, or ratio—permits the use of the statistical techniques that were employed in analyzing the data. To obtain meaningful measures, the data must have the property of additivity if many statistical techniques are to be employed. A highly sophisticated statistical analysis is useless if the numbers inserted into the analysis cannot be used legitimately for that purpose. Research findings are not accepted until the ancestry of the numbers is carefully checked.

Sources of Error

Errors can creep into measurement from the day that a researcher first conceptualizes a property. The question always has to be raised. Did the researcher conceive of a property that actually exists? The unsatisfactory results obtained when trying to measure the property "rigidity" in people, for example, makes it doubtful that the property exists. If a property does exist, the definition of it and the rules established for observing and making the measurements of it may be so poorly structured that the numerical findings are meaningless. Assigning numbers to entities is no difficult feat, but making numbers correspond with observable indicants of many properties is. The question that must always be raised is: Does this measurement procedure have some logical and observable correspondence with reality?

Two types of error in measurement are common:

1   *Systematic* (constant) *errors*—uniform inaccuracies—which affect the *validity* of measuring instruments. The following questions may be asked about the validity of an instrument: Does the instrument measure what it is supposed to measure? What evidence is there that the numbers obtained to represent intelligence, attitude, or aptitude actually do so? Did the questions asked on a test or questionnaire actually elicit responses that are indicants of the property being investigated?

2   *Random errors*—chance inaccuracies—which reflect the *reliability* of the instruments. The following questions may be asked about the reliability of an instrument: Is the instrument consistent in measuring whatever it measures? Will the same results be obtained if an entity is measured again and again with this instrument by the same person or by some other person under the same conditions?

To illustrate the difference between these two types of errors, let us assume that a person makes measurements with a one-foot ruler. This ruler is not properly calibrated; it is worn at the end, and, hence, is a quarter of an inch shorter than a foot. If repeated measurements are made with that ruler and the same results are obtained, the instrument is perfectly reliable. But the measurements are not valid, for the ruler does not measure what it is supposed to measure. Because the ruler does not conform to the standards agreed upon for one foot, a systematic error has been introduced. The data obtained are not accurate.

On the other hand, if the ruler were properly calibrated but a nearsighted investigator misread it while making measurements, random errors would occur and the measurements would not be reliable. Many factors can reduce the reliability of measuring instruments: mistakes in reading an instrument, in scoring a test, and in printing some of the tests, as well as differences in the conditions under which a test is taken by different subjects. Obviously, when interpreting the meaning of a test score, one must take into account the possibility that systematic and random errors may have been made in making the measurements.

Distribution of Errors

Investigators make every effort to minimize errors that can result from the fallibility of the observers, the technical inadequacies of the tests or apparatus, and the differences in conditions under which the measurements are made. But despite all the controls that are established, these factors will vary a little. No measurement, therefore, is perfectly reliable—entirely free from error. A measurement obtained in an investigation gives one the "probable value" on the property, but it must be considered to be only an approximation and not necessarily the "true value" that would be obtained if a perfect instrument and perfect measurement conditions existed.

Suppose a researcher measured a subject a number of times for a certain property, such as systolic blood pressure, reaction time, or intelligence. The observed scores on the various administrations of the test would vary somewhat because of chance errors. The observed scores would consist of the "true value" of the property plus or minus whatever error of measurement existed. If the frequency distribution of

FIGURE 5.8

A theoretical curve of normal distribution "fitted" to a simplified presentation of a distribution of auditory reaction times for one subject.

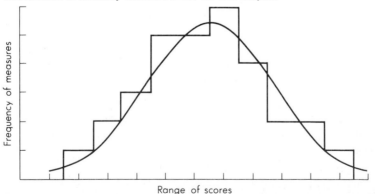

the observed scores of an auditory-reaction-time test were represented graphically by a histogram and if a theoretical normal curve were superimposed on it, the obtained data would closely resemble a normal curve (see Figure 5.8).

The results obtained in Figure 5.8 would closely resemble those obtained in similar investigations; the theoretical curve of normal distribution frequently provides a good fit to an empirical (observed) distribution of measurement errors. The question naturally arises: What is the best estimate of the "true value" on a property? Fortunately, statistical techniques are available which permit one to accept an observed score as the "true value" and to utilize the mathematical properties of the normal probability curve to estimate how accurate that assumption is. These techniques will be discussed in a later chapter.

6 TOOLS OF RESEARCH

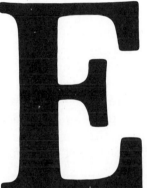arly in the planning stage of the research project, investigators weigh the merits of various procedures for collecting evidence. After determining which approach yields the form and kind of data necessary to test their hypothesis, they examine the available tools and choose the ones that are most appropriate for their purpose. If the existing instruments do not meet their specific needs, they supplement or modify them or construct their own.

Note that the inquiry starts with the problem and that the nature of the hypothesis governs the selection of the tools. One does not master a single method of obtaining data, such as the questionnaire, and apply it to every problem that arises. Each tool is appropriate for acquiring particular data, and sometimes several instruments must be employed to obtain the information required to solve a problem. Researchers, therefore, must possess considerable knowledge about a wide variety of techniques and instruments. They must be familiar with each one: the nature of the data it produces, its advantages and limitations; the assumptions upon which its use is based; and the extent of its reliability, validity, and objectivity.

No single method of obtaining data to test a hypothesis is perfect. Each one has certain inadequacies which leave the door open for the possibility of rival hypotheses explaining the findings. For this reason, collecting data by more than one method is often a prudent procedure. If a questionnaire is employed, one may bolster the self-reporting weak spot in this method by adding supplementary methods that have different methodological weaknesses, such as observing the subject and interviewing their parents. If a hypothesis can survive the onslaught of a series of imperfect measures (the questionnaire, observation, and interview) and provide consistent results, greater confidence can be placed in it than if it is tested by one method.

SAMPLING TECHNIQUES

Many problems in scientific research cannot be solved without employing sampling tools. Since most educational phenomena consist of a large number of units, an investigator cannot always interview, test, or observe each unit under controlled conditions. Sampling tools solve this dilemma, for they help researchers select representative units from a population. From the data gathered from these units, researchers draw inferences about the nature of the entire population. They generalize that what is true of the sample will be true of the population.

Construction of Samples

Sampling does not consist in collecting data casually from any conveniently located units. To obtain a representative sample, one systematically selects each unit in a specified way under controlled conditions. Several steps are involved in the process. A researcher must (1) define the population, (2) procure an accurate and complete list of the units in the population, (3) draw representative units from the list, and (4) obtain a sufficiently large sample to represent the characteristics of the population.

DEFINING THE POPULATION   A population is a well-defined group (set) of human beings or other entities. The size of populations can vary. Researchers might like to obtain data about all teachers in the United States, but the time and resources at their disposal may cause them to limit a study to a more accessible population, such as the teachers in one community. But they must recognize that the findings obtained for a randomly selected sample of teachers in one wealthy su~~bu~~ generalized to all teachers in that suburb but not to all teachers in the United States. The suburban teachers will probably differ in many respects from teachers in rural, industrial, and inner-city areas and in some respects from teachers in other suburbs.. Considerable thought must be given to choosing a population. The members must possess the property under consideration. The definition of the population must clearly identify what units are to be included and excluded. If a population is vaguely defined, one does not know what units to consider when selecting the sample. To obtain information about the average salary of university professors, for example, investigators must define the specific population about which they intend to draw generalizations. Do they want to include professors of all ranks, in all schools—medicine, liberal arts, law—and in administrative positions? Certainly a salary generalization drawn from a population that includes administrators will differ from one that is confined to the lower-paid liberal arts professors. People are repeatedly deceived by institutional, political, and advertisers' reports because they assume the generalizations presented were drawn from one population when they actually were drawn from another.

LISTING THE POPULATION   Once the population is clearly identified, the investigators obtain or construct a complete, accurate, and up-to-date list (called a frame) of all the units in the population. This task may consume considerable time, and obstacles may arise that will prevent them from obtaining the required data. Suppose that they wish to obtain information concerning the salaries of university professors in a specific geographical area. Institutions will have these records available, but they may be unwilling to reveal the information. In many instances the investigators may find that no tailor-made list of units in a population is available. Suppose that they want a list of the unemployed experienced teachers living in Ohio or the boys who committed crimes in New York last year. No one agency keeps a record of all unemployed teachers. The courts may have information about juveniles, but their records may include neglected as well as delinquent children, and of course, they would not list unidentified criminals.

Many investigators produce disappointing results because they use available population frames without investigating the methods that were used to compile them and without ascertaining whether all members of the population were included. Sometimes they select unit lists that are out-of-date, contain inaccuracies or duplications, or do not

adequately represent the population. A classic example of this occurred in 1936 when telephone directories and automobile registrations were used to obtain a sample of how people would vote in the
presidential election. On the basis of the data obtained from this
sample, the prediction was made that Alfred Landon would be elected.
What went wrong? Since the telephone directories and automobile
registrations did not include the great number of voters in the lower
economic brackets, a sample selected from these lists did not represent
all members of the voting population.

SELECTING A REPRESENTATIVE SAMPLE   After defining a population (a
set) and listing all the units, investigators select a sample of units (a
subset) from the list. Drawing a sample is a relatively simple task, but
fatal mistakes are frequently made. If units are selected that are
conveniently at hand—a group of ·volunteers, the first twenty-five
names on a list, the people who live in one block, or the parents who
attend a meeting—these units may differ from the remaining units;
hence, they may not be representative of the population. The slum
dwellers living in one New York block are units in this metropolitan
population, for example, but generalizations derived from data concerning their health, salaries, and dwellings certainly are not applicable to all citizens in the city. A "good" sample must be as nearly
representative of the entire population as possible.

OBTAINING AN ADEQUATE SAMPLE   Some samples are too small to
represent the characteristics of the population. The IQ scores of two
students selected as a sample from a population of 100 children, for
example, are not likely to represent the average IQ of that group. But
how large must a sample be to achieve an acceptable degree of
reliability? No specific rules on how to obtain an adequate sample have
been formulated, for each situation presents its own problems. If the
phenomena under study are homogeneous, a small sample is sufficient.
A few cubic centimeters from a 1,000-gallon container of a particular
chemical may be adequate. But, if the units under study are variable, as
height, intelligence, aptitudes, and many other educational phenomena
are, a much larger sample is necessary. The greater the variability of the
phenomena, the greater is the difficulty of obtaining an adequate
sample. Increasing the size of the sample is of little value, of course, if
units are not chosen in a way that ensures representativeness of the
sample. The safest procedure is to use as large a sample as possible. In
descriptive research, a sample of 10 to 20 percent of the population is

often used. In experimental research, a sample of thirty subjects permits the use of large sample statistics. In general, three factors determine the size of an adequate sample: the nature of the population, the type of investigation, and the degree of precision desired. Researchers give careful consideration to these factors and then select the sample design that will provide the desired precision at minimum cost.

Types of Sampling Designs

Several methods have been devised to select representative samples. The following discussion briefly describes random, stratified, double, systematic, and cluster sampling. Detailed explanations of these and other sampling techniques can be found in texts that are devoted to the subject.

RANDOM SAMPLING To many people, the words "random" and "chance" suggest guesswork. Randomization is not a haphazard method of assignment, however, but rather a carefully controlled process. In an investigation, researchers refrain from exercising direct control over the selection of subjects, for they may consciously or unconsciously select the subjects who are most likely to produce data that will confirm their hypothesis. To avoid the introduction of such sampling biases, researchers employ some randomization technique to ensure that each unit in the population has an equal or known chance to be included in the sample. They may number all 100 units in a population and place corresponding numbers on slips of paper. They put these slips in a container, mix them thoroughly, draw a slip, and record the number. They then throw the slip back into the container and continue drawing until the required size sample is selected. The slips must be thrown back into the container to ensure that every unit has the same chance of being chosen. If the same number is drawn twice, the second drawing is ignored.

Perhaps the best method of selecting a sample is to employ a table of random numbers containing columns of digits, such as those prepared by Fisher and Yates, Tippett, or Kendall and Babington-Smith. After assigning consecutive numbers to units of the population, one starts at any point on the table of random numbers and reads consecutive numbers in any direction (horizontally, vertically, or diagonally). When a number is read that corresponds with that written on a unit card, that unit is chosen for the sample. One continues to read until a sample of the desired size is obtained. If the number selected as

a starting point—10144—is in a column of five-digit numbers, researchers need to use only the last three digits—144—if their population
consists of 200 units and only the last two digits—44—if their population consists of 50 units.

After an adequate sample is selected, some invited units may
decline to participate in the experiment, and, during the experiment,
some units may drop out. A sampling bias will be introduced if these
units differ from the remaining participants in characteristics that are
known to be related to the phenomenon under study. An investigator,
therefore, should always report not only the size of his sample but also
the number of dropouts, the number of invited units that did not
participate, and, if possible, the variables relevant to the study in which
they differed from the remaining participants.

A randomly selected sample, even if all invited units participate,
does not necessarily represent the characteristics of the total population, but when the choice of subjects is left to chance the possibility of
bias entering the selection of the sample is reduced. By chance, of
course, one could randomly select a sample that did not accurately
represent the total population. The more heterogeneous—dissimilar—
the units are and the smaller the sample, the greater is the chance of
drawing a "poor" sample.

In describing the data obtained from a random sample, an investigator usually computes the M, mean (average score), as well as the σ,
standard deviation (measure of variability or spread of the scores
around the mean).[1] This sample mean is considered to be an unbiased
estimate of the population mean. In any such estimate, a certain degree
of error is involved. The mean IQ of a sample of students drawn from a
given population is likely to differ somewhat from sample to sample.
Through the use of inferential statistics, however, one can estimate,
within a specified degree of confidence, how far the sample mean is
likely to differ from the population mean. By dividing the standard
deviation of the sample by the square root of the sample size minus
one, the standard error of the mean is obtained: $SE_{mean} = \sigma/\sqrt{N-1}$. The
least amount of error will occur when the number of units in the
sample (N) is large and the standard deviation (σ) is small. After finding
the mean or the sample and the standard error of the mean, one can use
the areas of the normal probability curve of distribution to estimate the
limits within which the population mean is located.

---

[1]Appendix A.1 presents explanations of the mean and standard deviation.

STRATIFIED SAMPLING   Since a randomly selected sample, particularly a small sample, may by chance have an undue proportion of one type of unit in it, an investigator may use stratified random sampling to get a more representative sample. When employing this technique, one divides the population into strata by some characteristic which is known from previous research or theories to be related to the phenomenon under investigation, and from each of these smaller homogeneous groups one draws at random a predetermined number of units. To ascertain how people may vote on a public school issue, for example, one may subdivide a population into groups on the basis of known voting behavior—perhaps age, income, educational level, or religion. Stratified sampling, of course, is no better than simple random sampling unless one knows that a high correlation exists between certain groups of people and their voting behavior.

Proportional stratified sampling enables one to achieve even greater representativeness in the sample. This technique requires selection of units at random from each stratum in proportion to the actual size of the group in the total population. Hence, if 20 percent of the voting population are college graduates, 20 percent of the sample is taken from this stratum (see Figure 6.1). Because proportional sampling

FIGURE 6.1

Subject selection using proportional stratified random sampling technique.

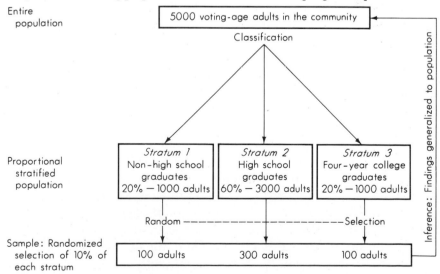

improves representativeness, a researcher may use a smaller sample and thereby reduce the cost.

DOUBLE SAMPLING   When employing a mailed questionnaire, double sampling is sometimes used to obtain a more representative sample. This precaution is taken when some randomly selected subjects do not return their questionnaires. The missing data will bias the results of the study if the people who fail to reply to the query differ in some fundamental way from the other subjects in respect to the phenomena being studied. To eliminate this bias an investigator may draw a second sample at random from the nonrespondents and interview these people. If their responses do not differ significantly in any way with those of the initial respondents, the investigator can assume that the data obtained from the initial response group represents an unbiased sample; hence, the data can be generalized to the population. Double or multistage sampling may also be used to "spot-check" data. After making a simple, inexpensive survey of a large sample, an investigator may select another sample from this group for a more comprehensive investigation.

SYSTEMATIC SAMPLING   When a frame of a given population is available, a sample is sometimes drawn from fixed intervals on the list. To select a sample of 50 names from a list of 500 schoolchildren, one first divides 50 into 500 to determine what size of interval to use (in this case, 10). Then, one picks a starting number at random from 1 to 10 (assume the number is 9) and selects each tenth name thereafter (thus, 9, 19, 29, . . .) until the desired 50 names have been drawn. If the names on the list are randomized at the beginning, this method is equivalent to the random-sampling technique.

But one must be wary of certain departures from randomness, such as a "trend." Suppose that children are listed by age in years and months and sample units are drawn at fixed intervals of 10. The estimated mean age of the group would vary from sample to sample, depending on the beginning number selected at random. A group selected from intervals beginning at 2 would have a different mean age from one beginning with unit 10 on the list, for in the latter sequence each child would be older than his counterpart in the other sequence by eight ranks. Cyclical fluctuations are another factor that one must be on the alert to detect. If a list is kept of the number of college students utilizing the library each day, a biased sample will probably be obtained if every seventh day is chosen as a sample unit, for fewer students probably study in the library on Sundays than on weekdays.

CLUSTER SAMPLING In cluster sampling the sample unit contains groups of elements (clusters) instead of individual members or items in the population. Rather than listing all elementary school children in a given city and randomly selecting 15 percent of these students for the sample, a researcher lists all the elementary schools in the city, selects at random 15 percent of these clusters of units, and either uses all the children in the selected schools as the sample or randomly selects the same number of children within each of these schools. Rather than listing all the dwellings in a city, an investigator may list all the blocks in the city, select at random 7 percent of these clusters of units, and include all the dwellings in the selected blocks in the sample. Observing clusters of units in a few schools is easier and less costly than observing randomly selected students scattered in many schools throughout the city. On the other hand, a cluster sample usually produces a larger sampling error than a simple random sample of the same size, for each cluster—such as a block in a given neighborhood—may be composed of units that are like one another, which reduces the representativeness of the sample.

INSTRUMENT EVALUATION

The research findings obtained from a sample of subjects can be no better than the instruments employed to collect the data. One of the most important tasks researchers perform, therefore, is to evaluate the validity, reliability, objectivity, and suitability of their data collection instruments and to explain and defend their evaluations in the written reports of their investigations.

Validity

An appraisal instrument that measures what it claims to measure is valid. A measuring instrument does not possess "all-purpose" validity. A test may be highly valid for one purpose or for one age or type of subject, but invalid in another situation. Because an invalid test can serve no useful purpose, a researcher must present some evidence which provides confidence that a test measures the precise characteristics for which it was designed. When appraising the validity of a test for a specific study, an investigator may check one or more of the following types of validity: content validity, criterion-related validity, and construct validity.

CONTENT VALIDITY Content validity, which is also known as *logical, sampling,* or *curricular* validity, is most widely used in achievement testing. To establish content validity, the test constructor analyzes the content of the area that the test is to appraise and structures a representative instrument to measure the various aspects of that content. To design a standardized algebra test, for example, one may examine many textbooks in the field and the courses of study and objectives prepared by the state departments of education and professional bodies. From these materials, one determines what content the test should cover and what proportion of it should be devoted to various aspects of algebra. One may ask qualified experts to rate test items as to their importance and devise some method of pooling their judgments. When checking content validity, the test constructor alone and with the aid of others judges the extent to which the test items present a representative sample of the universe of the content that the test is designed to measure. To determine whether a published test has content validity for the subjects in an investigation, one compares the content of the course that the subjects have taken with the content of the test.

CRITERION-RELATED VALIDITY Validity that is demonstrated by comparing test scores with one or more external variables, or criteria, considered to provide a direct measure of the behavior or attribute under study, is called *criterion-related validity* and consists of two subclasses: predictive and concurrent validity.

1 Predictive Validity Educators frequently are interested in using a test to predict some future outcome, such as success in school or in a job. A test that makes accurate forecasts concerning the future behavior for which it is designed possesses predictive validity. The basic procedure for determining predictive validity is (1) to administer the test, (2) to wait until the performance predicted by the test has occurred, and (3) to correlate the test scores and the actual performances the test is designed to predict. Suppose a scholastic aptitude test is designed to predict academic success in college during the freshman year. To determine the predictive validity of the test, one would

administer the test to a large randomly selected sample of first-semester senior high school students. After these students have completed their freshman year in college, one would correlate the predictions of the aptitude test with the academic grades the freshmen students received (criterion measure). The higher the correlation, the more effective the test would be as a predictor.

Two problems are associated with predictive validity. The prediction will hold true only in the situation in which it was validated or in a similar situation. If the previous scholastic aptitude test were validated for a sample of junior college students, the same test might not make satisfactory predictions for students who plan to attend Princeton University. When developing a test that is to be used for predictive purposes, one may also discover that establishing the criteria to measure an outcome such as vocational success may be difficult. Establishing an unambiguous and agreed-upon criterion for teacher effectiveness, for example, is a vexing problem.

2 Concurrent Validity   The procedure for establishing concurrent validity is the same as that for establishing predictive validity except that the outcome that is predicted is measured at approximately the same time as the predictor test is taken. If a new test is structured, for example, the scores that the students receive on the test may be correlated with the marks they recently received in the subject, ratings made by their teachers, or scores obtained on a similar test that has been validated which may be more expensive or more difficult to administer. Rather than waiting several years to ascertain whether a vocational interest test can predict success in a given occupation, an investigator may correlate the scores obtained on the test by people who are successful in a given occupation with those of people successful in other occupations to determine if the test discriminates between the groups. Concurrent validity provides some immediate evidence of the usefulness of a test, but the fact that a test has concurrent validity does not guarantee that it has predictive validity. Concurrent validity is often the initial step, however, for establishing predictive validity.

CONSTRUCT VALIDITY   Perhaps one of the most important types of validity to check is construct validity. A logical construct is a property that is hypothesized to explain some aspect of human behavior, such as mechanical ability, intelligence, or introversion. Each such construct refers to a highly complex concept which is composed of many interrelated factors. Each construct may be exhibited in a number of situations, but no one observation may be regarded as a criterion of the construct.

Construct validation begins with defining the meaning of the construct and deducing certain consequences, in a wide variety of situations, that should and should not be observable if the construct that has been hypothesized does exist. The investigator then ascertains whether a given test shows that all these relationships between the construct and the predicted outcomes do hold. Cronbach suggests, for example, that "an investigator might define 'flexibility' in terms of the following expectations, among others: artists will be more flexible than nonartists; flexible persons will relearn a maze rapidly when the goal is shifted to a new position; flexible persons exposed to propaganda will shift their attitudes more rapidly than will nonflexible persons. He can then determine whether a certain test measures flexibility, so conceived, by investigating whether high scorers on the test exhibit the expected behaviors" (26:1554).

Construct validation is not merely an appraisal of the test alone, but also an assessment of the theory behind the test. It determines to what extent a test taps what is implied by the theoretical definition. If the predictions of the theory are borne out by the evidence obtained from the samples, all is well—at least for the present. Evidence has been obtained that confirms the hypothesis and indicates that the test does measure the relationships predicted by the hypothesis. If the predictions are not confirmed, the investigator assumes that one of the following possibilities accounts for this lack of verification: the test does not measure the construct, the hypothesis is incorrect or needs to be revised to conform with the evidence, or the experimental design did not test the hypothesis properly (27:295).

Reliability

A test or scale is reliable if it consistently yields the same results when repeated measurements of a property are taken of the same entities under the same conditions. If a student receives a score of 110 on an intelligence test, for example, he should receive approximately the same score when an equivalent form of the test is given several weeks later. Four methods of estimating reliability are discussed below.

TEST-RETEST RELIABILITY   The test-retest method involves administering the same instrument twice to the same subjects under the same conditions and comparing (correlating) the paired scores to estimate the reliability of the instrument. The advantage of this method is that only one form of the test is needed. The possibility always exists, however, that the scores on the two administrations of the test will differ not because of the instability of the test, but because the retest scores were affected by the practice received on or recall from the first administration of the test, the maturation or experiences of subjects between test sessions, or variations in the subjects or environmental conditions during the two sessions. If the test-retest reliability method is used, sufficient time should elapse between the two administrations of the test to insure "forgetting," but not enough time for subjects to have experiences that would change their performances on the test. These conditions are difficult to establish unless one is dealing with rather stable properties; hence, the test-retest reliability is not appropriate in many situations.

PARALLEL-FORMS RELIABILITY To estimate reliability through the parallel-forms technique, which is sometimes called *equivalent,* or *alternate, forms* technique, two forms of the test are constructed. Form A and Form B are alike in every way except that the specific items that measure each indicant of the property are not the same, but they are similar in content and in level of difficulty. The two forms of the test are administered to the same subjects, and then the scores on the two tests are correlated to ascertain the degree of relationship between them. (See discussion on correlation on page 307.) The parallel-forms technique eliminates the recall effects that may be present when the same test is given twice. The principal disadvantage of this technique is the difficulty of writing two forms of the test that are meticulously equivalent.

SPLIT-HALF RELIABILITY A measure of reliability can also be obtained by determining whether the two halves of the test are measuring the same property. This method requires only one form and one administration of the test. The test is subsequently divided into two parts, presumably equivalent halves, usually odd-numbered items constitute one half and even-numbered items the other. Scores are obtained for each subject on each half of the test, and the two sets of scores are correlated.

If the correlation coefficient (r) computed between the two halves of the test is $r = .70$, this statistic represents the reliability of a test only half as long as the total test and will underestimate the reliability of the total test.[2] This problem arises because reliability is related to the length of a test: generally, the longer a test is, the more reliable it is, because the greater length permits a more stable sample of the subjects' possession of a property. Fortunately, the split-half reliability coefficient can be entered into the Spearman-Brown prophecy formula to obtain an estimate of the reliability of the whole test. This formula gives an estimate of what the reliability would be if each half of the test were twice as long. You will note below that if the split-half correlation coefficient were $r = .70$, the estimated reliability of the total test obtained by using the Spearman-Brown prophecy formula would be $r = .82$.

Estimated reliability of total test calculated by the Spearman-Brown prophecy formula

$$r = \frac{2 \times \text{correlation between halves of test}}{1 + \text{correlation between halves of test}}$$

$$r = \frac{2 \times .70}{1 + .70} = \frac{1.40}{1.70} = .82$$

One problem with the use of the Spearman-Brown prophecy formula is that it tends to give a higher estimate of reliability than would be obtained by the test-retest or parallel-forms techniques. When selecting a test for an investigation, this fact should be kept in mind when comparing the reliability coefficients of the various standardized tests that are available. When constructing a test for an investigation, the split-half technique should not be used for short tests or speed tests. With speed tests, spuriously high coefficients are obtained by this method. The scores of the subjects on speed tests usually vary widely, but the difference in their scores is a difference in speed. Most of the answers given by each subject will be accurate up to a point where time is called; hence, the correlations of each subject's odd and even scores will be high.

RATIONALE EQUIVALENCE RELIABILITY   Kuder and Richardson devised formulas 20 and 21 for estimating the internal consistency of a test without splitting the test into halves. These formulas estimate the extent to which all items in the test measure the same general factors of ability, personality, or interest. This technique determines how answers to each item on the test relate to answers on each other item and to the test as a whole.

[2]An interpretation of what constitutes an acceptable level of reliability may be found on page 325.

An example of the Kuder-Richardson formula 21 (KR_{21}) is given below, because it is easier to compute than formula KR_{20} and requires less time than any other method of measuring reliability. Formula KR_{21} requires only the test mean (M), the variance (σ^2), and the number of items on the test. The formula is

$$r_{KR_{21}} = \frac{N\sigma^2 - M(N - M)}{(N - 1)\sigma^2}$$

For example, on a 60-item test, if the mean score is 30 and the standard deviation (σ) is 10, the reliability estimate is

$$r_{KR21} = \frac{60(10^2) - 30(60 - 30)}{(60 - 1)(10^2)} = \frac{60(100) - 30(30)}{(59)(100)} = \frac{6000 - 900}{5900} = .864$$

The values of $r_{KR_{21}}$ are slightly less accurate than the values of r_{KR20}, but the differences are not usually great. The rationale equivalence formulas tend to give more conservative estimates of reliability than the other procedures. They have essentially the same advantages, disadvantages, and limitations as the split-half procedure.

Objectivity

An objective instrument is one that produces the same findings regardless of who administers it or records the findings. To attain this quality in a test-collection instrument, precautions are taken to prevent the examiner's behavior or any of the test instructions or examples from influencing the responses of the subjects and to eliminate the need for anyone to make subjective judgments in recording observations or scoring the test.

Suitability

When selecting a test, scale, or inventory, one must determine whether the instrument is suitable for one's purpose. Does it measure the particular property (variable) one is trying to measure? Will it produce measurements that are sufficiently precise to detect the differences required in the investigation? Will it be suitable for the age and type of subject and the time and locality in which one intends to use it? Does it require responses that subjects, parents, or school boards would find objectionable? Will it require more time, money, and trained assistance and more sophisticated techniques to interpret it than one can reasonably attain? If two tests are equally reliable and valid, the instrument that is the cheaper, more easily and quickly administered and scored, that is available in alternative forms, and that is accompanied by norms is usually preferable to its counterpart. Most publishers print manuals that give detailed information about the construction, administration, time requirements, and reliability and validity of standardized tests as well as the population upon which the norms are based. A prudent researcher carefully examines these explanations when searching for appropriate testing instruments.

APPRAISAL INSTRUMENTS

Where does one begin to search for data-collection instruments? An examination of research studies that are closely related to your investigation will acquaint you with the choices made and the problems encountered by your predecessors. Good guidance to a comprehensive list of published instruments is provided by Buros' *Mental Measurements Yearbooks* and *Tests in Print.* Some research journals also describe and evaluate tests. These sources usually give the name of the publisher, the price, a description of the test and the group for which it is designed, the number of forms, and the reliability and validity data. They may include a critical review of the special requirements and problems.

The types of instruments that are available are classified below on the basis of the characteristics they measure.

1   *Performance and potentialities of the subjects:* intelligence tests, information and achievement tests, and aptitude tests.
2   *Preferences and behavior of subjects:* inventories of interest in particular occupations or activities; assessments of attitudes and beliefs concerning issues, institutions, activities, or segments of society; measures of one or several personality traits; and value scales.
3   *Environmental and physical status of individuals and institutions:* home appraisals of socioeconomic status, parent-to-parent, child-to-child, or parent-to-child relationships; institution or community appraisals of facilities, finances, programs, practices, and leadership services; medical, sensory capacity, motor ability, and physical fitness tests.

Explanations of the techniques employed in constructing and evaluating appraisal instruments appear in several measurement and evaluation texts. Because of the extensive literature in the field, this chapter will give only brief descriptions of some types of instruments.

Tests

A variety of tests have been developed to appraise the performance and potentiality of subjects. (1) Intelligence tests, for example, measure general mental abilities, and certain specialized tests assess a limited range of abilities, such as those required in mechanical comprehension or in the judgment of spatial relations. (2) Information and achievement tests measure the present level of mastery in a subject or skill that a person has attained as a result of instruction. Some tests measure proficiency in a specific area, such as typing, spelling, reading, or arithmetic. Other tests present educational achievement batteries that measure performance in several areas. (3) Aptitude tests, which are more commonly used in guidance than research, test subjects in some areas in which they have not received specific training, such as medicine, music, or stenography, and from the data obtained predict their ability to improve with additional training.

Scales

You are probably more familiar with the standardized tests that measure the performance of subjects than with scales that "take stock" of one or more aspects of an entity's or social unit's present status or of a subject's typical behavior, attitudes, beliefs, preferences, or personality traits. Since the 1930s considerable progress has been made in finding scaling techniques to transform qualitative data about these aspects of entities into quantitative measures that are more amenable to analysis and interpretation. But much imaginative and disciplined work is involved in detecting the existence of a differentiating property, identifying indicants of the property, and assigning numbers to represent the position of entities with respect to the quantity of the property.

The effectiveness of a rating scale depends in part, of course, upon the qualifications of the raters. Some people may not have sufficient knowledge about a factor to make discriminating observations and judgments. Not uncommonly, individuals check scale choices—assign numbers—on the basis of inadequate evidence, or they merely guess if they have had little or no opportunity to observe the factor being evaluated. Raters often suffer from a halo effect—they carry over a general impression gained from rating one factor to all factors that they rate. Some people rate everyone too severely or too leniently or refrain from checking items at either extreme of the scale. Because each rater tends to make judgments upon the basis of a slightly different frame of reference, pooled ratings are sometimes preferred.

From the discussion in the previous chapter, you know there are four levels of scales: nominal, ordinal, interval, and ratio. Data about some properties—discrete variables, such as political party registration or church membership—are obtained by nominal-scale instruments that identify or classify entities. In some investigations, a simple nominal scale that discriminates likenesses and differences in position, such as identifying people who favor or oppose, like or dislike, agree or disagree with a policy may provide all the information that is needed. If a nominal scale does not meet one's needs, it may be possible to transform it into an ordinal scale by eliciting responses that can be rank-ordered, such as "strongly agree," "agree," "neutral," "disagree," "strongly disagree." By using an ordinal scale, more precise knowledge of the relative positions of the respondents can be obtained.

In an investigation one must consider not only what level of measurement to achieve but also what is the best technique to employ to attain that level. The following discussion gives a description of several types of scales.

RATING SCALE   A rating scale ascertains the degree, intensity, or frequency of a variable. To construct such a scale, an investigator identifies the factor to be measured, places units or categories on a scale to differentiate varying degrees of that factor, and describes these units in some manner. No established rule governs the number of units that should be placed on a scale, but having too few categories tends to produce crude measures that have little meaning, and having too many categories makes it difficult for the rater to discriminate between one step and the next on the scale.

The description of the scale units may consist of (1) points, (2) numbers, or (3) descriptive phrases placed along a line:

1.   ———————————————————————————————————

2.   _____1_____2_____3_____4_____5_____

3.   *almost always, frequently, occasionally, rarely, almost never*

Since these points, numerical symbols, and generalized terms do not necessarily carry the same measurement meaning to all people, more specific descriptive phrases may be presented to give the rater a clearer standard for judgment.

Sometimes specimens of work are used to describe units on a scale. Samples of handwriting that represent various levels of merit, for example, may be placed on a continuum according to values determined by a jury. To rate a product, one matches it with the scale specimen that the product most nearly resembles. Person-to-person scales are similar to product scales except that the bench marks on them are names of about three to five people. These people are known to the judges, and they possess varying degrees of a particular trait—say, leadership. Subjects are rated by matching them with the persons on the scale that they most nearly resemble.

SCORECARD   A scorecard, which is frequently called a numerical rating scale, provides for the appraisal of a large number of items that contribute to the status or quality of some complex entity. Scorecards have been developed, for example, to evaluate school facilities, institutional programs, communities, textbooks, and the socioeconomic status of families. Each item on a scorecard is assigned a predetermined numerical value, and ratings are made by awarding all the points or some fraction thereof for the amount of the factor judged to be present. By combining all the ratings, one obtains a total score that indicates the overall evaluation of the entity observed. This technique is rather satisfactory when used to appraise physical facilities but less effective when used to evaluate the program or quality of an institution. Certain intangibles in group activities seem to defy quantitative appraisal.

RANK-ORDER SCALE   Rather than rating subjects, objects, products, or attributes on an absolute scale, a rank-order scale compares them with one another. To rate twelve teachers in respect to leadership ability, for example, one assigns the teacher with the highest leadership qualities serial number 1; the next highest, serial number 2; and the lowest, serial number 12. Since more average teachers than extremely "good" or "poor" ones are found in most groups, detecting degrees of difference between the average teachers is often difficult. Rank-order scales, therefore, usually give a more reliable measure at the extremes of the scale than in the central portion.

PAIRED COMPARISONS In the method of paired comparisons, the subjects are presented with a list of items, such as different ethnic groups, occupations, or recreational activities, and are asked to judge each item in turn with every other item, indicating which they prefer. The subjects, for example, may be asked to underline which activity in each of the following pairs of activities they enjoy participating in more:

Football—tennis	Baseball—tennis
Baseball—checkers	Ping-Pong—football
Tennis—Ping-Pong	Tennis—checkers
Football—baseball	Ping-Pong—baseball
Checkers—Ping-Pong	Checkers—football

The judgments of the subjects can be manipulated so that each activity can be assigned a scale value. This method, which may give more accurate results than the rank-order approach, is satisfactory when a small number of items is compared, but the procedure is too time-consuming and laborious when a large number of comparisons is required.

EQUAL-APPEARING INTERVALS SCALE The technique of equal-appearing intervals, which Thurstone utilized to assign values to items on attitude scales has become widely employed. In this method a hundred or more separate statements expressing various degrees of intensity of feeling toward a group, institution, object, or issue may be given to between fifty and a hundred judges. Each judge is asked to arrange the statements as objectively as possible into piles (usually seven to eleven) that appear to him to be equally spaced psychologically and to order the piles so that statements in the first pile represent the most favorable attitude toward the factor being evaluated, those in the center pile represent a neutral attitude, and those in the last pile represent the most unfavorable attitude. Afterward, the number of times that each statement is included in the several piles is tabulated, and each statement is assigned a score value based on the median position given to it by the judges. Statements that are too broadly scattered by the judges are discarded as ambiguous or irrelevant. To construct the final scale, somewhere between fifteen and forty of the remaining statements are so selected that the intervals between them are equal. These items which represent the different intensities of the attitude in question are arranged in random order on the final test.

The following sample statements are taken from Thurstone and Chave's scale Attitude Toward the Church (108:60–63). The scale values do not appear on the subjects' tests.

I believe the church is the greatest institution in America today. (Scale value:0.2)

I believe in sincerity and goodness without any church ceremonies. (Scale value:6.7)

I think the church is a parasite on society. (Scale value:11.0)

This type of scale is scored by finding the mean scale value of all the statements with which the subject agrees.

METHOD OF SUMMATED RATINGS   The method of summated ratings, which was introduced by Likert, scales the subjects with respect to an attitude, but makes no attempt to scale the items as is done in the Thurstone scale. The summated rating method, which does not claim to be more than an ordinal scale, is as reliable as the Thurstone technique and somewhat simpler. The trial Likert test contains a large number of positive and negative statements regarding an attitude object. The subjects indicate their positions on each statement by checking one of several alternative answers, such as "strongly approve," "approve," "neutral," "disapprove," "strongly disapprove." The "arbitrary" or "sigma" methods may be used in scoring. The arbitrary method, which is sometimes preferred, will be explained because it is simpler. This method arbitrarily gives a weight of 1 to 5 to the alternative answers, and the same numerical values are always given to the responses that show the greatest favorableness toward the phenomena, for example:

"Exclude all blacks from the city." (Strongly disapprove—weight of 5)

"Appoint a black to the schoolboard." (Strongly approve—weight of 5)

Although the answers differ, they receive the same weight because they both reveal a favorable attitude toward blacks. The total score for each subject is the sum of the values assigned to each item that the individual checked. Before constructing the final test, the investigators apply techniques that help them identify weak items. They eliminate those items that do not exhibit a substantial correlation with the total score or do not possess the power to discriminate consistently between people who receive high and low scores on the scale. Statements about black people that all subjects strongly agree with are eliminated, for example, because they fail to discriminate between people whose attitudes toward black people differ.

CUMULATIVE SCALES   In the 1920s, the cumulative Bogardus social-distance scale was constructed to measure attitudes toward ethnic groups. To administer this type of scale, one asks subjects to check statements to indicate whether they would be willing to have an average member of the listed ethnic groups (1) as a visitor restricted to a limited area of this country, (2) as a visitor to all parts of this country, (3) as a citizen of this country, (4) as a fellow employee, (5) as a neighbor, (6) as a personal friend, or (7) as a mate. You will note that the items on a cumulative scale are related to each other in a way so that ideally the subjects who reply favorably to item 4 also reply favorably to items 3, 2, and 1; hence, there is a cumulative relation between the items and the total score. The scale provides a data-reduction device which maintains the original information. If one knows a subject's total score, one can tell what items he agreed with. The subjects can also be rank-ordered according to their score responses.

During the 1940s, interest in cumulative scales was revived by investigators interested in the development of unidimensional scales. Critics had questioned the Thurstone and Likert scales that contained statements referring to different aspects of the property being measured. The Peterson scale of attitude toward war, for example, contained statements about the ethics of war activities and the economic results of war which made it difficult to determine exactly what the scale was measuring and what the score was representing. Louis Guttman and others developed a technique for determining whether a set of items forms a unidimensional scale, a scale that measures only one variable. In the Guttman procedure, a series of items is considered unidimensional only if it yields a perfect, or a nearly perfect, cumulative scale—one in which an individual who agrees with a given statement will agree with all preceding statements. If the pattern of responses of a large number of subjects arrange themselves in the manner indicated below, then the items are said to be unidimensional and a given score always has the same meaning.

AGREE WITH ITEM 3 2 1	TOTAL SCORE	NUMBER OF SUBJECTS
x x x	3	110
o x x	2	140
o o x	1	90
o o o	0	45

Any departure from the illustrated pattern of responses, such as subjects who agree to item 3 but do not agree to items 2 and 1, would indicate that the items do not form a perfect Guttman scale.

SEMANTIC DIFFERENTIAL SCALES   Everyone knows what concepts like self, teacher, and school discipline mean, but different people and groups have different perceptions of the concepts. The semantic differential technique provides a method of measuring indirectly these perceptions by asking subjects to rate concepts such as superintendent or curriculum on several scales, usually seven-point scales with bipolar adjectives, such as "good" and "bad," located at each end. The three dimensions of meaning that these scales measure with examples of typical bipolar adjectives are as follows: (1) *evaluation:* good-bad, beautiful-ugly; (2) *potency:* large-small, strong-weak; and (3) *activity:* active-passive, sharp-dull. An investigator may need scales for only one dimension or scales for dimensions other than these three main ones. Each dimension is usually measured by at least three separate scales.

If the concept "teacher" were to be judged, a subject might check the first five scales on the instrument as shown in the accompanying illustration.

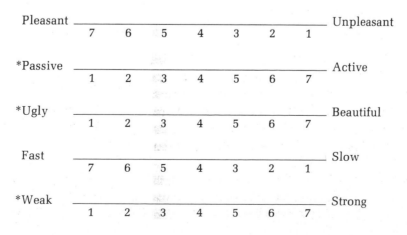

Pleasant	7	6	5	4	3	2	1	Unpleasant
*Passive	1	2	3	4	5	6	7	Active
*Ugly	1	2	3	4	5	6	7	Beautiful
Fast	7	6	5	4	3	2	1	Slow
*Weak	1	2	3	4	5	6	7	Strong

The asterisks indicate that the adjectives and score values have been reversed. The pairs of adjectives are reversed at random to counteract the tendency of subjects to check all scales at the same point. The score values, of course, would not appear on the instruments that the subjects are given. By obtaining ratings of five different concepts that are related to a problem under investigation, such as school environment—for example, principal, teachers, curriculum, discipline, building—it is possible to determine a subject's attitude toward the concepts and the likenesses and differences between a subject's concept ratings and between the ratings of different subjects and groups. The semantic differential scales are a simple, useful, and versatile tool for collecting data.

Q-SORT TECHNIQUE   The Q-sort technique, like the Thurstone method of equal-appearing intervals, involves a sorting process for the purpose of assigning scale values to items. Subjects are given a large number of cards (sixty to one hundred) containing drawings or descriptive words, phrases, or statements that are relevant to the topic under investigation. They are asked to sort the cards into piles, usually nine to eleven, according to their view of the relative standing of the descriptive items along a single continuum, such as "most like me–least like me," "most important–least important," "most prefer–least prefer." The number of cards that subjects are instructed to place in each pile is usually predetermined by the investigator to form a roughly normal frequency curve.

Below is a distribution of 65 statements. The numbers above the line represent the number of cards to be placed in each pile. The numbers below the line are the score values for the cards in the piles. The 2 cards in the "most-approved" pile, for example, are each assigned the score value 10 and the 13 cards in the center pile are each assigned the score value 5.

Most approved											Least approved
Frequency of cards	2	3	5	7	9	13	9	7	5	3	2
Score value	10	9	8	7	6	5	4	3	2	1	0

The Q-sort technique is used to assess attitudes, values, artistic judgments, and interests of subjects. It may be used to study intensively the characteristics of one individual or clusters of individuals. The subjects may be assigned one Q-sort or several related Q-sorts. They may be assigned the same Q-sort more than once, such as before and after a training program, to assess the changes that have taken place or to describe perceived self and ideal self in a study of adjustment. The Q-sort technique is used to identify clusters of subjects in a group with similar responses and to analyze how the various clusters differ. The Q-sort technique is particularly useful in the exploratory stage of research. It is, however, time-consuming to construct and to sort, it is not appropriate for studies using large numbers of subjects, and one cannot usually generalize the findings to a population from a Q-sort subject sample.

SELF-CONSTRUCTED INSTRUMENTS Before collecting any data, investigators must determine whether what they want to measure is an aptitude, intelligence, achievement, or attitude variable or some other kind of variable. If no suitable standardized measure exists for measuring what they want to measure, they may construct their own instrument. This, however, is an arduous task. Many steps are involved, including identifying the population for which the test or scale is intended, defining the precise property that is to be measured, analyzing the factors that contribute to the property, constructing appropriate tasks or items to cover each of these factors, establishing time limits for various phases of the test if needed, and developing a format that is easy to read and to answer and that gives results easy to tabulate.

After pretesting the preliminary draft by administering it to a small sample of subjects, many additional steps are taken. These include refining the content where it was not clear or where it elicited falsified or no responses, employing statistical techniques to eliminate weak items, revising directions that were confusing, correcting weaknesses in the format, improving and standardizing the method of scoring and administering the test or scale, and establishing reliability and validity data. In many instances, the revised test is pretested with another sample of subjects before it is used in an investigation. If the final revision of the test is administered to a large, clearly identified population and a table of norms is established, other investigators can use the test and refer to the table of norms to interpret the scores their subjects receive.

Sociometric Technique

In recent decades workers have been developing sociometric methods for obtaining data on social interaction among group members. In its simplest form, this technique involves asking each person in a group to select which other member he would prefer to associate with in a particular relationship or activity, for example, as a roommate or as a co-worker on a project. Sometimes subjects are asked to select second and third choices and to list the persons that they would reject. The choices may be plotted on a sociogram, which presents each student's name within a circle or triangle and utilizes connecting lines (solid for acceptance and broken for rejection) and arrows to show the flow of interpersonal relationships. This network of acceptances and rejections reveals the star and mutual attractions in the group as well as the fringers and isolates; the sociogram depicts social subgroupings, cleavages, and cohesiveness. Sociometric data may also be presented on a matrix chart upon which all pupils' names are listed horizontally and vertically; first, second, third, and rejection choices (given and received) are plotted in the proper squares or cells; and the total acceptances and rejections for each subject is tabulated below. Sociometric techniques have been employed by researchers to correlate leaders or isolates with various personality traits, to study the relations among ethnic groups, and to compare sociometric patterns before and after experimental treatments have been introduced to change them.

Projective Techniques

Projective techniques are used to probe areas that cannot be reached easily by other means or areas in which direct questions are apt to elicit distorted data. Instead of asking a subject for specific information, an investigator has him interpret or respond freely to ambiguous stimuli, such as inkblots, pictures, unfinished sentences, word associations, or lifelike dramatic roles. Through self-structured, spontaneous responses, the subject unconsciously reveals manifestations of his personality characteristics and organization. Only highly trained workers can interpret the implications of these responses, however, and scoring them is laborious. Projective techniques are difficult to validate, and many of the tools have not been standardized. Some weaknesses in them are being overcome, but much work remains to be done.

QUESTIONNAIRES

For some studies or certain phases of them, presenting respondents with carefully selected and ordered questions is the only practical way to obtain data. Isolating specific questions for consideration tends to objectify, intensify, and standardize the observations that respondents make. Some subjects may not supply accurate answers, however, for they may suffer from faulty perception or memory or may not be able to express their impressions and ideas adequately in words. Respondents who are not free, willing, or qualified to divulge information may ignore certain questions or falsify their answers. Many people do not give thoughtful consideration to questionnaires; they fill out the forms carelessly or report what they assumed took place. Not uncommonly, respondents tailor replies to conform with their biases, to protect their self-interests, to place themselves in a more favorable light, to please the researcher, or to conform with socially accepted patterns. To obtain reliable data, therefore, questionnaires must be carefully structured. If they are to be used to measure variables in an investigation, they must be pretested, refined, and subjected to the same evaluative criteria of validity, reliability, and objectivity as tests, scales, and other measurement instruments.

Methods of Presentation

Questionnaires may be presented to respondents in two ways: through the mails or in a face-to-face situation. In the latter case, a questionnaire is sometimes called a *schedule*, particularly if the interviewer rather than the subject fills out the query.

DIRECT CONTACT   Fewer partial responses and refusals to reply are obtained when the researcher personally presents the questionnaire, for the researcher can explain the purpose and significance of the study, clarify points, answer questions, and motivate respondents to answer questions carefully and truthfully. But bringing a group together to fill out a questionnaire is often difficult, and meeting members individually may be excessively costly and time-consuming; hence, questionnaires are usually sent through the mails.

MAILED QUESTIONNAIRES   Mailed questionnaires reach many people in widely scattered areas quickly and at a relatively low cost. The returns, unfortunately, do not bound back with equal celerity, and partial returns may introduce a bias that will render the obtained data useless. If nonrespondents are quite different from the respondents— less educated or less interested in the issue—they may not hold the same views as the respondents. If answers could be obtained from the nonrespondents, the findings of the study might be changed substantially.

To achieve an acceptable number of returns from a mailed questionnaire, a researcher first makes certain that the study is of sufficient importance to warrant asking busy individuals to answer the questions, that the information cannot be easily obtained elsewhere, and that the questionnaire has been made as short, clear, attractive and easy to fill out as possible. Before mailing a questionnaire, the investigator obtains permission to contact respondents from the highest authority in all units, such as both the principal and the parents, the school board and the teachers' union. Respondents are sent a covering letter that explains clearly the purpose and importance of the study, indicates that the investigation is sponsored by a reputable institution, arouses interest in contributing accurate information, promises to protect the confidentiality of the data, informs the respondents why they were chosen to participate, offers to provide them with a summary of the findings, sets a definite date for the return of the questionnaire, and includes a stamped, self-addressed envelope for the return of the questionnaire.

After the deadline for the return has passed, the researcher can present a polite, persuasive reminder to nonrespondents, by telephone or postcard, and, if necessary, follow up with a second mailing of the questionnaire. If the number of nonrespondents remains high after all these steps have been taken, a small random sample of them might be interviewed to check on the reliability of the data obtained from the initial respondents.

Forms of Questionnaires

A researcher may cast questions in a closed, an open, or a pictorial form, or any combination of these forms. The nature of the problem and the character of the respondents determine which form or forms will most likely supply the desired data.

CLOSED FORM Closed-form, or structured, questionnaires consist of a prepared list of concrete questions and a choice of possible answers. To indicate their replies, respondents mark "yes" or "no"; check, circle, or underscore one or more items from a list of answers; mark points or units on scales; or rank a series of statements in order of their importance (1, 2, 3 . . .). Sometimes they are asked to insert brief statements into blank spaces or on empty lines ("How old were you on your last birthday?＿＿＿").

Closed-form questionnaires are easy to administer to large numbers, help keep the respondents' minds riveted on the subject, and facilitate the process of tabulation and analysis. But they often fail to reveal the respondents' motives (why they answered as they did), do not always yield information of sufficient scope or depth, and may not discriminate between fine shades of meaning. Fixed alternatives responses may make respondents take a stand upon issues about which they have no crystallized opinion or may force them to give answers that do not accurately express their ideas. The listed alternative answers may be written in a way or placed in an order that encourages the respondent to reply in accordance with the researcher's wishes. If proper precautions are taken in constructing the questionnaire, these weaknesses can be somewhat overcome. To avoid biasing the results by placing the desired answers in the most conspicuous place, for example, items in a checklist may be randomized. Yes-no and true-false questions may be improved upon by inserting a third choice ("undecided," "don't know," or "no opinion"). When investigators cannot provide a full range of choices in a checklist, they may resolve the difficulty by adding the statement "None of the above descriptions apply," or by leaving a blank in which the respondents may clarify, amplify, or qualify their answers.

OPEN FORM   Rather than forcing respondents to choose between rigidly limited responses, the open-form questionnaire permits them to answer freely and fully in their own words and their own frame of reference. This method of collecting data gives the subjects an opportunity to reveal their motives or attitudes and to specify the background or provisional conditions upon which their answers are based. When subjects have no clues to guide their thinking, however, they may unintentionally omit important information or fail to note sufficient details. If subjects are not highly literate and willing to give considerable time and critical thought to questions, they cannot provide useful data. If they are capable of providing a wealth of pertinent information, the task of categorizing, tabulating, and summarizing their many different, detailed, and complex answers may be extremely difficult and time-consuming. Because open-form questionnaires achieve less uniformity of measurement than closed-form questionnaires, they achieve less reliability.

PICTORIAL FORM   Some questionnaires present respondents with drawings or photographs from which to choose answers, and the directions may be given orally. This form of questionnaire is a particular suitable tool for gathering data from children and adults with limited reading ability. Pictures often capture the attention of respondents more readily than printed words, lessen subjects' resistance to responding, and stimulate their interest in the questions. Pictures may depict clearly some situations that do not lend themselves readily to verbal descriptions or may enable one to detect attitudes or to gather information that could not be tapped by other procedures. Pictorial techniques, however, possess at least two limitations: (1) They can be used only in situations involving distinguishable and understandable visual characteristics. (2) They are difficult to standardize, particularly when the pictures are photographs of human beings.

Construction of Questionnaires

Questionnaires are a popular research tool because most investigators assume that they know how to ask questions. But asking questions that will obtain precise data required to test a hypothesis is no easy task. Researchers are often amazed when respondents draw many different meanings from questions that they thought were perfectly clear. And they may prickle with resentment when colleagues point out biases in the wording or structuring of their questionnaires which seem objective to them.

To obtain data about the income, marital status, or age of teachers, researchers must ask specific rather than "shotgun" questions. Do they want to know the respondent's age on his or her last birthday, or in years and months at the present time? Do they want to know total income from all sources or only from teaching? Do they want to obtain salary information for the regular school session or also for summer school and evening classes? A question that merely asks respondents to check whether or not they are married may need to be recast. To obtain more specific information, one might ask: "Are you at present: Married____Single____Widowed____Divorced____? Framing questions to obtain honest answers is an art. Note the difference between the following pairs of questions: "Do you believe in the communist policy of providing free college education for everyone?" versus "Should we provide everyone with a free college education?" "Did you exercise your American right to vote in the last school election?" versus "Did you vote in the last school election or for some reason were you unable to vote? Did____Did not____."

Questionnaires have been subject to severe criticism, but many common weaknesses in them can be avoided if they are structured carefully and administered effectively to qualified respondents. The following discussion raises some pertinent questions concerning the use of this research tool. (Also see questions in Chapter 14.)

FRAMING THE QUESTIONS Have the researchers thoroughly explored their hypotheses, experiences, the literature, and other questionnaires so as to frame questions that measure the precise variables under investigation and that probe the crucial issues in depth? Have they allocated the number of questions in accordance with the cruciality of the issue? Have they checked all questions for unnecessary repetition and redundancy? In determining the length of the questionnaire, have they given consideration to the amount of time that will be required to answer the questionnaire and the cost of preparing and mailing it? Are the questions stated in crystal-clear, simple language and focused sharply on specific points? Are subordinate questions asked or is an exhaustive list of alternative choices provided so as to explore various aspects of a decision and to probe beneath vague, stereotyped, "don't-know," or evasive answers? Are questions framed to elicit unambiguous answers (if possible, quantified answers—number of times per week rather than "sometimes," "often," or "always")? Are the questions framed in a moralistic or censuring language that will cause subjects to provide socially desirable rather than true responses?

ORDERING OF QUESTIONS Are items placed in a psychologically or logically sound sequence—simple, interesting, neutral questions preceding more difficult, crucial, or personal ones and those that establish a frame of reference or provide keys to recall before those asking for details? Is a smooth transition made from one group of questions to the next?

DESIGNING THE DIRECTIONS AND FORMAT Are clear, complete directions given concerning the type and scope of information wanted, the location for the responses, and the form in which the answers are to be given? Are the categories, format, and directions designed to elicit accurate, unambiguous answers, to require a minimum of the respondent's time, to facilitate the tabulation and interpretation of data, and if possible, to permit the quantification of results? Are the categories structured in accordance with the specific scaling and data-analysis schemes that are to be employed in reporting the findings?

ELICITING HONEST REPLIES Are directions and questions worded and ordered so as to allay any fears, suspicions, embarrassment, or hostility on the part of the respondent? If personal questions are asked, is a guarantee of anonymity given, or is there assurance that the responses will be held in strict confidence? Are any questions colored or phrased so as to elicit replies that will support the researcher's beliefs? Are respondents asked for information concerning subjects about which they have little or no knowledge? Are specific questions asked in order to check the truthfulness of answers to general questions? Are parallel questions asked in order to check consistency of answers?

INTERVIEWS

Many people are more willing to communicate orally than in writing and, therefore, will provide data more readily and fully in an interview than on a questionnaire. Indeed, several advantages accrue from the friendly interaction in an interview that cannot be obtained in limited, impersonal questionnaire contacts. In a face-to-face meeting, an investigator is able to encourage subjects and to help them probe more deeply into a problem, particularly an emotionally laden one. Through respondents' incidental comments, facial and bodily expressions, and tone of voice, an interviewer acquires information that would not be conveyed in written replies. These auditory and visual cues also help him key the tempo and tone of the private conversation so as to elicit personal and confidential information and to gain knowledge about motivations, feelings, attitudes, and beliefs. Presenting questions orally is a particularly appropriate means for gathering information from children and illiterates.

Interviews are useful tools, but more time, money, and energy are required to conduct interviews than to administer questionnaires and the interviewers may bias the responses. The race, age, sex, religion, vocabulary, accent, ethnic background, or social class of the interviewer may alter the responses of the respondents; hence, these factors must be considered in selecting interviewers. Several extraneous factors may, in part, account for the variations in a set of findings: an increase or decrease in the fatigue, boredom, or recording skill of the interviewers; their knowledge of the hypothesis being tested or of early data returns; and the subtle but often unconscious visual or vocal cues they give respondents. Interviewers' opinions and attitudes and their expectations of the respondents' opinions and attitudes may influence whether and what answers are given and whether and how they are recorded. Intensive training of interviewers and keeping them ignorant of both the hypotheses being tested and the data returns may minimize the influence of some of these effects.

Individual and Group Interviews

Most interviews are conducted only once, but some are repeated at intervals to trace the development of behavior, attitudes, or situations, such as the progressive reactions of parents toward a school bond issue or school desegregation. Most interviews are conducted in a private setting with one person at a time so that the subject feels free to express himself fully and truthfully. In some instances, however, group interviews produce more useful data. Varied viewpoints are obtained when qualified individuals with common or divergent backgrounds are brought together to explore a problem, to provide information about a subject in a case study, or to evaluate the merits of a proposition. The participants may not only present a wide range of information but also help one another recall, verify, or rectify items of information. Subjects may, however, refrain from expressing some points before a group that they might reveal in a private interview. One person (and not necessarily the best-informed one), moreover, may dominate the discussion, so that the viewpoints of the other participants are not explored thoroughly.

Structured Interviews

Some interviews are rigidly standardized and formal: the same questions are presented in the same manner and order to each subject and the choice of alternative answers is restricted to a predetermined list. Even the same introductory and concluding remarks are used. These structured interviews are more scientific in nature than unstructured ones, for the standardized approach introduces controls that permit the formulation of scientific generalizations. A standardized interview is not a rubber yardstick, but it has certain limitations: collecting quantified, comparable data from all subjects in a uniform manner introduces a rigidity into the investigative procedures that may prevent the investigator from probing in sufficient depth.

Unstructured Interviews

Unstructured interviews are flexible; few restrictions are placed on respondents' answers. If preplanned questions are asked, the queries, vocabulary, and order are altered to suit the situation and subjects. Sometimes subjects are encouraged to talk freely and fully concerning a particular issue, incident, or relationship. The interviewer then serves as a good listener who unobtrusively inserts a judicious "Hmm," "That is interesting," "Go on," or generalized question to stimulate the flow of conversation. When the interview is drawing to a close, the investigator may ask some direct questions to fill in the gaps and round out the discussion.

In an informal, unstructured interview, one can gain an insight into the character and intensity of a respondent's attitudes, motives, feelings, and beliefs and can detect underlying motivations and unacknowledged attitudes. One can penetrate behind initial answers, follow up unexpected clues, redirect the inquiry into more fruitful channels on the basis of emerging data, and modify categories to provide for a more meaningful analysis of data. Quantifying the accumulated qualitative data, however, may be difficult. Because of the nonuniform tactics that are employed in collecting the information, one usually cannot compare data from various interviews and derive generalizations that are universally applicable.

Nonstructured interviews are not ordinarily employed when one is testing and verifying hypotheses, but this informal approach is very helpful in the exploratory stage of research. The answers given by subjects under such conditions may help identify unanticipated variables and relations that relate to the area of the investigation and may lead to the formulation of fruitful hypotheses. The answers may also suggest items and frames of references to use in the construction of standardized measurement instruments. Nonstructured interviews are also used to follow up unexpected results in an investigation or a pretest of an instrument and to go deeper into the reasons for the responses.

Conduct of an Interview

A successful interview is a dynamic interpersonal experience that is carefully planned to accomplish a particular purpose. Creating a friendly, permissive atmosphere, directing the discourse into the desired channels, encouraging the respondent to reveal information, and motivating him to keep presenting useful facts require a high degree of technical skill and competence. Establishing rapport with informants may take considerable time. In conducting a case study of an elementary school principal, one investigator did not interview the teachers in the school until he had been there six months. One must be careful about establishing too close social relationships with the informants, however, for "overrapport" may make it difficult to ask sensitive questions. To evaluate the effectiveness of interviews, one must keep in mind many of the questions that were raised concerning questionnaires, as well as the following questions:

PREPARING FOR THE INTERVIEW Did the interviewers decide what areas of information to cover, and did they prepare appropriate questions to extract the desired data? Did they insert comments that made the respondents feel at ease and stimulated the flow of conversation? Did they find out as much as possible about the interests, beliefs, and backgrounds of the subjects so that they could gain their confidence, avoid antagonizing them, and "draw them out" about their experiences and special areas of knowledge? Did they obtain sufficient information to understand the respondents' frames of reference and interpret their replies as they were intended? Did they make a definite appointment for each interview at a time that was convenient for the subjects? Did they plan for interviews in an environment where the subjects would be at ease (usually in private) and in a setting where the most fruitful information could be obtained? Did they conduct a few preliminary interviews to detect weaknesses in their methods, questions, or recording system?

ESTABLISHING RAPPORT Were the interviewers pleasant, efficient, straightforward, and poised? Did they refrain from assuming an overly sentimental, solemn, or sympathetic attitude? Did they avoid adopting a superior, patronizing, clever, cunning, or "third-degree" manner? Did they dress appropriately and use a suitable vocabulary and approach for working with each respondent?

ELICITING INFORMATION Were the interviewers attentive, analytical listeners who discerned when they should repeat or explain a question? Did they detect when answers were vague, contradictory, evasive, or deceptive? Did they introduce alternative or more penetrating questions to help respondents recall information, amplify statements, clarify their thinking, rectify facts, or give more concrete evidence? Did they pace the questions at the proper speed for the respondents? Did they ask general questions first and then sharpen the focus of succeeding questions? Did they follow up crucial clues provided by responses and stay with fruitful lines of questioning until they had extracted all the useful information? Did they inject courteous comments to redirect interviews into channels that were more pertinent to the inquiry? Did they sense when it was best to approach delicate matters and to probe for "depth materials"? Did they plan carefully the wording of such questions? Did their tone of voice, facial expression, or phrasing and timing of questions imply what answers they preferred? Did they avoid blaming or censuring the respondents and refrain from revealing that an answer shocked, annoyed, or displeased them? Did they seek the same information in different ways during the interview to check the consistency of responses? Did they check some replies against official records or reports of the other witnesses to determine whether they were accurate? Did they terminate the interviews before the subjects became tired?

RECORDING DATA   Did the interviewers use a schedule, a structured format, or a system that enabled them to record notes quickly and accurately? Did they make a legible record of the exact (nonedited) words of the respondents during the interviews or immediately after-ward? Did they consider using tape recorders that would free them during the interviews, provide a means of verifying responses later, preserve the emotional and vocal character of replies, and help them avoid the omissions, distortions, modifications, and errors that some-times are made in written accounts of interviews? Did the interviewers make notes concerning any behavior or conditions that they observed which did not conform with the respondents' replies? Did they make a record of significant emotional displays, hesitations, stammering, sud-den silences or transitions, quickly corrected words, and obvious omissions?

OBSERVATION

In observational studies researchers collect data on the current status of entities by watching them and listening to them rather than asking questions about them. Observation may be controlled or uncontrolled, scheduled or unscheduled, visible or concealed, participant or nonpar-ticipant.

Under controlled laboratory conditions, investigators have some assurance that the experimental treatment rather than other experienc-es have caused the observed effect on subjects' performance. On the other hand, the findings about the effect of the experimental treatment may not be generalized to normal-life situations, where many experi-ences are interacting simultaneously.

Direct observation always raises the question of subject reactivity, that is, whether the subjects will alter their behavior when they know they are being observed. A more normal view of behavior may be obtained from uncontrolled, concealed, or unscheduled observations. But obtaining data by observing subjects through a one-way-vision glass, by assuming a role as an unidentified participant-observer in a group, by deceiving the subjects about the true purpose of the research, or by any other concealed method involves the difficult ethical question of invasion of privacy. By participating actively in a group, one may gain insights into a subculture and obtain sources of information that are not accessible in any other way, but by becoming emotionally involved one may lose objectivity. By revealing one's identity to a group and then giving the subjects an acceptable rationale for observing them and assurances of confidentiality, one may reduce anxiety or distrust. By remaining inconspicuous and allotting sufficient time for everyone to adjust to one's presence, an investigator may find that subjects will resume normal patterns of behavior.

Unstructured Observation

Methods of observation range from those that are relatively unstructured to those that are formally structured to test a hypothesis. The unstructured methods are employed in the initial stages of research when one is searching for relevant variables, refining the definition of the problem, and generating hypotheses and theories.

Unstructured studies may vary with respect to how many entities and properties are observed and for how long. Researchers may observe many subjects, social units or settings for an extended period of time and write richly detailed descriptions of many factors. On the other hand, they may observe only one or a few subjects for a relatively short period of time and keep a continuous detailed record of everything that takes place, such as a study by Barker and Wright (9) that required 420 pages to describe a boy's life during a single day.

To focus attention on a selected type of subject behavior, such as physical aggression or food consumption, an investigator may make *anecdotal records* of each incident that is observed over an extended period of time. As soon as possible after viewing an incident, a factual statement is written about what the key subject in the situation said and did; when, where, and under what conditions the incident took place; and how other people reacted. For this type of record an effort is made to record positive as well as negative data and to avoid vague generalizations and subjective interpretations. Whenever possible, direct quotations are used and precise nouns and verbs rather than adjectives and adverbs are chosen, for example, "she sucked her thumb" rather than "she felt very insecure."

After collecting the data in an unstructured observational study, researchers code each description into as many different categories as possible, examine the data that are in the categories, and search for likenesses and differences within and between categories which may lead to the formulation of hypotheses and to the identification of the variables that are critically related to them.

Structured Observation

When investigators know what variables are relevant in a study, they plan to observe subjects and to collect and record data in a very systematic way. They include checks and controls in their procedures to establish the reliability and validity of the data-collection techniques. In addition to the scorecards and rating scales that have been discussed previously, they may employ some of the following techniques.

CHECKLISTS AND SCHEDULES   Researchers often construct checklists or schedules to facilitate the recording of data. These instruments list items (carefully defined, observable factors) that are relevant to the problem and, if possible, group them into categories. After each item, a space is provided for the observer to write a few descriptive words or to indicate the presence, absence, or frequency of the occurrence of the phenomenon. These guides enable investigators to record many different observations rather quickly and to avoid overlooking relevant evidence. Checklists also tend to objectify the observations and provide for a uniform classification of data. Some lists are designed so that the researcher can arrive at a score enabling comparisons with other data or determination of the general condition of an object or facility.

Both in observation and interview studies, the clearer the definition of the units to be evaluated, the fewer the inferences required of the observer; and the more training that has been given especially in rating marginal or difficult units, the less variable and more reliable will be the ratings. If pilot studies are conducted to train observers, data can also be obtained that can be used to estimate the reliability and validity of the checklist or schedule. No research project should get underway until the observers have achieved a high percentage of agreement on their independent observations.

TIME SAMPLING   The time-sampling technique requires that one record the frequency of observable forms of occurrences during a number of definite time intervals that are systematically spaced. Let us consider an uncomplicated example to illustrate this technique. To ascertain the types of activity engaged in by John Adams, an investigator may record observable forms of behavior that this pupil exhibits during a specified five-minute interval in a history class each school day for a two-week period. Rather than record everything the boy does, a decision may be made to tabulate the occurrence or nonoccurrence of one objectively defined form of behavior, such as "the frequency of class participation." To obtain such data, the investigator observes John Adams during one class period each day for two weeks and records each time that John contributed to the class discussion. The length of the observation interval depends upon the nature of the problem and such practical considerations as the availability of the subjects for the duration of the observation period. Research reveals that, in general, several short, well-distributed observations provide a more typical picture of behavior than a few long periods of observation. Random sampling of time units permits control over the possibility of participation in different activities at different times of the day, month, or year. Time sampling is a valuable technique, because observable instances of behavior are quantified directly, and the scores obtained lend themselves readily to statistical treatment.

Instrument Hardware

When several observers describe the same incident, their reports may vary because of their personal biases, selective perceptions, emotional involvements, or capricious memories. Various types of instrument hardware which are unaffected by such factors often obtain a more accurate record of an event. Motion pictures, videotape recorders, and sound recordings preserve details in a reproducible form, so that the full account of an incident may be studied repeatedly and intensively by the investigator and also may be checked by other research workers. Films are used to analyze audience reactions, to make slow-motion analyses of complex activities that cannot be studied under normal conditions, and for many other purposes. Some mechanical and electrical instruments give a reliable account of what happened in a quantified form. Dynamometers, for example, measure the strength of the hand grip, electromyographs record the frequency, intensity, and duration of the activity of a muscle, ultrasonic motion detectors and voice tremor detectors can be used to study behavior of interest to some investigators, and telemetry permits the collection of heart activity data during an athletic contest by using miniaturized, battery-operated amplifiers and radio transmitters to pick up and transmit data to a compatible recorder. Rather than measuring the responses of subjects, some instruments control the stimulus source in an experiment. The episcotister, for example, regulates the intensity of light emanating from a source. Hundreds of instruments, such as timing and counter instruments, tape recorders and exposure apparatus, have been constructed, and the research worker should become familiar with those that are used in his field.

Although mechanical and electrical devices may produce more refined and reliable data than human observers, these instruments are subject to certain limitations. They can be employed more easily in controlled laboratory experiments than in studies conducted in a natural setting, such as a classroom. The presence of the instrument sometimes alters the behavior of the subjects and as a consequence the investigator does not get an accurate measure of their typical behavior. The money and time required to construct, utilize, or maintain an instrument may be prohibitive. Instrument hardware can yield useful data only if one operates it properly, controls outside phenomena to keep them from influencing the accuracy of the measurements, tests the reliability of the instruments by ascertaining whether the same value is obtained if the same entity is measured many times, calibrates the instruments to ascertain how closely the measurements made with them conform to measurements made on known standards, checks the accuracy of the instruments at different points on the scale range, and checks for differences in the responsiveness of the instruments throughout the range attributable to time lag, inertia, wear, or other factors.

7 ANALYSIS OF THE PROBLEM

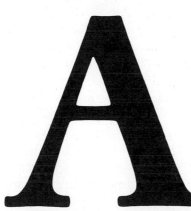n overview of the scientific method of
solving a problem was presented in Chapter 2. The next two chapters
will present a more detailed consideration of the processes involved in
(1) discovering and defining a problem and (2) constructing and testing
hypotheses. Planning an investigation is a fumbling, flexible process: In
the beginning, you may follow many false clues, pursue fruitless ideas,
collect irrelevant data, and try faulty techniques. The various steps in
problem solving are not necessarily well delineated one from another
or taken in order. During an investigation, you move back and forth
from one problem-solving task to another: searching, evaluating,
changing, and clarifying. You tackle a problem like an artist who works
constantly on his whole composition rather than first perfecting an eye,
then a nose, and then a mouth. Research work is inventive and
individualistic rather than routine and mechanical. No two investigators work alike. Research is not a completely haphazard undertaking,
however, for all creative work entails necessary disciplines and procedures.

Four mistakes are commonly made by graduate students when they search for a problem: (1) They select a problem hurriedly without analyzing all of the ramifications of their decision. (2) They procrastinate for months rather than make a systematic search of the literature to locate several problem possibilities. (3) They select a research procedure ("I want to do a correlation study" or . . . "a historical study") before they select a problem. A clear formulation of the problem must be made before an appropriate method of resolving it can be selected. (4) They present a generalized description of their problem rather than the exact dimensions and a clear definition of the terms.

DEVELOPMENT OF A PROBLEM

Many novice investigators have an unrealistic, glamorized conception of research work. The critical tasks of analyzing a problem, refining the statement of the problem, defining the terms, selecting a sample from a population from which to obtain data, and locating or constructing valid and reliable data collection instruments do not intrigue them. They want to leap to the answer stage of problem solving because they are anxious to experience the drama and excitement of collecting information and utilizing sophisticated research tools and instruments. They listen impatiently to advisers who ask: "Have you defined your problem clearly? Do you know what variables are involved? Do you possess the basic skills to conduct the investigation? Have you constructed a sound theoretical framework for this problem?" Without giving these questions serious consideration, they plunge forward headlong, gathering copious notes or setting up elaborate experiments.

Competent research does not consist in playacting with scientific paraphernalia and techniques to produce a senseless stack of statistics, a grab-bag gathering of facts, and a casual collection of glossy generalizations unsubstantiated by acceptable evidence. Solutions to problems are not produced by toying with laboratory tools. Research tools are means to an end; they must be employed purposefully to be of value; and they cannot be used intelligently unless an investigator knows what problem he or she is trying to solve. The analysis of the problem—isolating the variables that are involved and their relationships—may consume more time and generate more difficulties than any other single aspect of an investigator's study. Planning the investigation in advance down to the finest detail is what counts in research;

carrying out the plan—making observations and collecting the data—is largely a mechanical process which requires more persistence than profundity.

Identification of a Problem

Since identifying the exact nature and dimensions of a problem is of major importance in research, an investigator must learn how to recognize and define a problem. How does one locate problems? What conditions give rise to them? John Dewey answered these questions by suggesting that a problem arises out of some felt difficulty (see page 12). Something puzzles or disturbs an individual; a gnawing dissatisfaction nibbles at one's peace of mind until one can locate precisely the source of the trouble and find some means of solving it.

Suppose that late at night the sound of rushing water awakens and alarms you. Having been plunged into a problematic situation, you immediately strain to pinpoint the difficulty. Is the water rushing from the eaves? Is the creek flooding? Has a water pipe burst? What is the precise nature of your problem? Not only household but also scientific problems spring from puzzling experiences. A problem materializes when you sense that something is not right or needs further explanation. Perhaps you find some facts that do not agree with accepted theories or beliefs, note that the results of several investigations are contradictory, detect inconsistencies between your observations and those made by other investigators, or observe something you cannot explain. When you have an inkling that something is wrong or needs to be explained and are anxious to obtain a clearer concept of the factors causing the puzzling or commonplace occurrence, you have established some of the conditions necessary for identifying a problem.

A vague feeling that something is wrong or that some theory is not adequate does not constitute a problem, but these suspicions or doubts indicate an area in which a problem may exist. If, for example, you become disturbed about the amount of time that correcting test papers consumes, you are aware of a problematic situation but have not identified the specific difficulty. To bring the cause of your problem into clearer focus, you may ask several probing questions: "Do I correct tests when I am too tired or experience too many interruptions? Is the form of the test difficult to correct? Would a shorter test serve the purpose equally well?" Until you locate the key to your difficulty, you cannot solve your problem. Recognizing a general problematic situation provides a starting point for an investigation, but before proceeding too far, one must isolate, sharpen, and clarify the pertinent variables and relationships that give rise to the problem.

Analysis of a Problem

Problem analysis in research may be quite complex. Perhaps you will gain a better understanding of the procedures involved if you first examine the analysis of a practical classroom problem made by Miss White, an elementary school teacher (105).

DEVELOPING AN INQUIRY FROM A FELT DIFFICULTY   Miss White's investigation originates from a felt difficulty—as all problems do. She is dissatisfied with the reading progress of her pupils and wants *to solve the reading retardation problem.* But this initial problem statement is vague. Miss White cannot profitably search for a solution until she identifies the dimensions and clarifies the nature of the problem.

COLLECTING INFORMATION THAT MAY RELATE TO THE PROBLEM   To help her locate the specific factors that gave rise to the difficulty, Miss White compiles a list of (1) known and suspected factual items of information and (2) possible explanations that may have a bearing on the problem:

Number of retarded readers

Sex of retarded readers

Hour of day that class is taught

Intelligence of students

Time devoted to reading

Foreign language spoken
  exclusively at home

Broken or unhappy home
  conditions

Children's experiental
  background

Attitude of parents toward reading development of their
  children

Size of textbook print

Amount of vocabulary drill

Speed of reading

Comprehension

Phonics background

Enunciation of teacher

Classroom noise

Dietary problems

Hearing impairment

Visual impairment

Lack of sleep

Class too large for effective
  instruction

Class too heterogeneous for
  effective instruction

Textbook materials not
  sufficiently varied to meet
  different interests

The more known and suspected facts and possible explanations that Miss White can think of, the better are the chances that she will locate the causes of the children's reading difficulty. Teasing out the relevant variables and their relationships will require painstaking care and thought.

DERIVING MEANINGS FROM THE INFORMATION   To squeeze as much meaning as possible out of the listed constituents of the problem, Miss White looks for relationships between facts and facts, explanations and explanations, and facts and explanations. She may inquire whether a relationship exists among hearing impairment, classroom noise, and the teacher's poor enunciation that reveals a key to the difficulty. Facts and explanations that first come to mind may be probed for more detailed information. Upon becoming suspicious that a dietary problem exists, for example, she may ask: Is the real cause a lack of a balanced diet, conditions under which meals are eaten, or improper preparation of the food? Is there empirical evidence available to confirm that a relationship exists between the nature of the breakfast consumed by children and their work capacity?

As she digs more deeply into the problem, Miss White may discover that conditions that first appeared to be important causes of the difficulty are not the specific factors responsible. If the class is taught late in the morning, she may begin to question whether the late hour or some associated factor is responsible for the reading retardation. She may wonder whether the children are restless and uninterested because they do not get enough sleep, do not eat breakfast, or are distracted by the school band which practices outside the classroom during that period. Factors that may seem most important when the analysis first gets under way may merely be clues that lead to the real causes of the difficulty.

SEARCHING FOR FACTS TO CLARIFY THE PROBLEM   After listing the items she thinks might be relevant to the problem and trying to see relationships among them, Miss White searches for facts to determine whether these items are relevant to her problem; whether there are flaws in her reasoning regarding the nature of the problem; and whether there are additional facts, explanations, or relationships that play a determinate role in the reading retardation of her pupils. To obtain the required facts, she observes her pupils while they are reading, studying, and playing; checks their health records, intelligence tests, and reading tests; and studies the information volunteered by pupils, parents, other teachers, and the school nurse. To learn what variables other scholars have found to be related to reading retardation, she examines professional literature and research studies.

EXAMINING ASSUMPTIONS UNDERLYING THE SUGGESTED CONSTITU-ENTS   After Miss White adds new clues to her list of constituent elements and eliminates those items that appear to be irrelevant, she makes a thorough examination of the assumptions underlying the remaining facts, explanations, and relations. Has she jumped to any faulty conclusions? If adopting certain methods of teaching or grouping students seems to provide a logical problem solution, she rigorously examines this assumption: Will vocabulary practice sessions improve reading progress? What kind of practice? How often? How much? Can such practice have adverse effects? Does homogeneous grouping of pupils guarantee greater reading progress than heterogeneous group-ing? Is reading retardation associated with the sex, race, or socioeco-nomic status of pupils? What evidence have researchers produced to support these contentions? Have they found evidence to disprove them? The assumptions underlying Miss White's suggested constituent elements of the problem may be sound, but she must examine them carefully and assemble evidence to support them before proceeding too far with the investigation.

DELINEATING THE DIMENSIONS OF THE PROBLEM   As a result of her investigation, Miss White discovers that ten boys and two girls are not making satisfactory progress. They miss basic sight words, stumble over easy words, call "wrong" words, attack unfamiliar words without confidence, and read word by word; they ignore thought sequences, picture and context clues, and punctuation. They exhibit an indiffer-ence toward reading, they daydream or engage in disruptive activities during reading periods. When someone reads to them, their compre-hension is much better than when they read to themselves. Most of the children come from modest homes in which English is spoken; only two of them have divorced parents. The pupils have little reading material in their homes, and they have not had varied or extensive home, community, travel, and educational experiences. Although some of the students are shy, none of them gives evidence of being emo-tionally disturbed. In mental ability they range from an IQ of 82 to one of 129.

This detailed analysis gives Miss White a clearer picture of the problematic situation. When she discovers that only twelve of the thirty pupils are retarded readers, she can limit further study to them. When facts reveal that some of her "guessed-at" explanations for unsatisfactory reading progress—mental, emotional, and visual conditions—are not the causes of the difficulty, she can eliminate these irrelevant items from the investigation. In the beginning Miss White asked a rather vague question: "Why aren't my pupils making more satisfactory progress in reading?" When she concluded her analysis, she asked a more specific question: "Are twelve children in my class retarded in reading because they lack varied sensory and verbal experiences to help them associate printed symbols with words and ideas?"

SUMMARIZING PROBLEM-ANALYSIS PROCEDURES   The preceding discussion reveals that an investigator engages in many activities when analyzing a problematic situation. The following list summarizes these tasks:

1   Accumulating the facts that might be related to the problem.
2   Settling by observation whether the facts are relevant.
3   Tracing any relationships between facts that might reveal the key to the difficulty.
4   Proposing various explanations (hypotheses) for the cause of the difficulty.
5   Ascertaining through observation and analysis whether these explanations are relevant to the problem.
6   Tracing relationships between explanations that may give an insight into the problem solution.
7   Tracing relationships between facts and explanations.
8   Questioning assumptions underlying the analysis of the problem (see Figure 7.1).

This painstaking probe eliminates irrelevant ideas and forces into view the pertinent facts and explanations involved in the difficulty.

EXAMPLES OF PROBLEM ANALYSIS

Two problems that were undertaken by experienced investigators may give you a clearer comprehension of the problem-identification and problem-analysis aspects of research work.

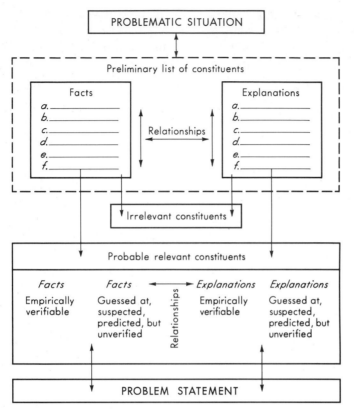

FIGURE 7.1

Schematic analysis of a problem.

Definition of Force

Several centuries ago, Galileo observed a phenomenon that did not seem to conform to the accepted theories of his time (42). When shooting off a projectile, he noticed that its movement did not conform to Aristotle's explanation of motion. By mentally mulling over this projectile phenomenon, Galileo sought to put his finger on the source of the difficulty. He examined the traditional assumptions about what causes motion and finally decided that the difficulty was located not in the flight of the projectile but rather in Aristotle's definition of force.

According to Aristotle, force is that which produces movement; it follows, then, that when force ceases to act on a body, the body will stop moving. Aristotle's definition gives a reasonable explanation of force that holds true in most instances. If you push a box, it moves; when you stop pushing a box, it stops moving. In the case of the projectile, however, the force stops acting the moment the explosion takes place, but the projectile continues to move for some time and distance after the explosion. As Galileo discovered, the projectile phenomenon contradicts Aristotle's definition.

Having identified his difficulty as a need for an all-embracing definition of force, Galileo began to search the facts required to construct a new definition. To analyze the problem, he selected the most elementary example of a force acting on a moving object he could—a ball falling freely under the force of gravitation. While closely observing the ball fall to the floor, he tried to determine what factors might be involved in the relationship between force and motion. Some scientists had concluded previously that temperature, smell, color, and shape of bodies were irrelevant to the problem. The ancient scientists had also assumed that distance and duration of the fall were irrelevant. But Galileo's mathematical, physical, and philosophical background, and his familiarity with the works of certain contemporaries and predecessors, caused him to reject the latter assumption.

After making observations, recalling previous experiences, and searching for the relationships that might be involved in the difficulty, Galileo concluded that there were three factors upon which the fall might depend: (1) the weight of the object, (2) the distance it traveled, and (3) the time required for the fall. His extensive analysis of the problem had enabled him to locate and describe the precise factors that had to be investigated before an acceptable definition of force could be formulated. The next chapter will reveal how Galileo tested each of these factors so as to arrive at an adequate explanation of force.

Assessment of Teacher Effectiveness

Skipping a few centuries, let us turn our attention to a recent analysis of an educational problem (74). The investigator was disturbed about a long-standing educational problem—how to determine the effectiveness of teachers and to predict the degree of success a potential teacher will achieve in a·classroom. To bring the four types of variables and their interrelationships that he decided were related to teacher effectiveness into clear focus, he constructed a paradigm, or model (see Figure 7.2). Study this paradigm as you read the following explanation of it.

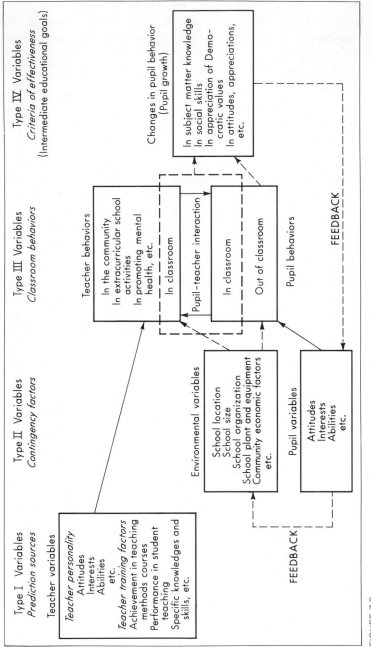

FIGURE 7.2

Generalized schema for research in teacher effectiveness.

Type I variables are composed of an almost inexhaustible number of human characteristics [personality and training factors] on which teachers differ and which can be hypothesized to account, in part, for differences in teacher effectiveness. . . .

Type II variables are contingency factors [school environment and pupil variables] which modify and influence the whole complex of behaviors that enter into the educational process. If Type II variables play a commanding role in the achievement of educational objectives, then we will be required to replicate studies of teacher effectiveness in a great many different situations, and predictions of teacher success from Type I variables will have to be contingent upon Type II variables. . . .

Type III variables, or behaviors [teacher-pupil behavior] . . . are of crucial significance in the process of assessing effective teaching. The classroom provides the focal point wherein the personality and training of the teacher are translated into actions. Likewise school and background influences on pupils determine in part pupils' classroom behavior. It is primarily out of the interaction of these elements that we expect educational goals to be attained. . . .

Type IV variables [pupil growth] are the criteria or standards against which the whole of educational effort must be judged. . . .

The interrelationships among the four types of variables are indicated by connecting lines on Figure 7.2.

In general, solid lines are indicative of direct effects and dotted lines suggest indirect or tangential effects. In such a scheme teacher variables (Type I) and pupil variables (Type II) are direct determinants of teacher behavior and pupil behavior respectively. Environmental variables (Type II) indirectly influence both teacher and pupil behaviors. In the view presented here the complex of pupil-teacher interactions in the classroom is the primary source to which one must look to account for pupil growth.

The investigator in this study (74) also explored the assumptions underlying his conceptual assessment scheme of teacher effectiveness. He recognized that it rested upon at least two fundamental assumptions:

First, there must be some stability in human personality which exerts a consistent governing or modifying effect on a teacher's behavior in the classroom. If the behaviors of a teacher are wholly, or even largely, determined by the environmental and pupil variables operating at any given time, then prediction of behavior seems foredoomed to failure. The second assumption is that the teacher . . . is the primary causative factor in accounting for pupil growth toward the goals of the school. It is on this premise that the whole structure of professional education of teachers is based. Intuitively, we tend to feel that teachers are important, even though we do not yet possess the evidence to show what it is about their behavior that is crucial to children's learning.

The general analysis of the variables involved in teacher effectiveness and the model presented in Figure 7.2 provide a guide for formulating innumerable hypotheses to be tested concerning the relationships among teacher, pupil, and environmental variables in and out of the classroom and teacher effectiveness as measured by changes in pupil behavior in various aspects of growth.

DESCRIPTION AND STATEMENT OF THE PROBLEM

The first draft of a problem statement may be revised several times during the analysis of a problem. While searching the literature, conducting a pilot study, or utilizing models to refine your thinking, you may gain insights into phenomena that make you dissatisfied with your problem statement and motivate you to reformulate it. The problem statement that you place in your final report will rarely be the same one you formulated originally.

Limiting the Scope of the Investigation

If you describe a problem and narrow its boundaries before your imagination has had an ample opportunity to view it from varied vistas, you may overlook the most promising approach to it. You must eventually formulate one or more precisely stated research questions or hypotheses about a particular problem, but you may begin an investigation in a rather fuzzy state of understanding: "I think that A, B, or C [intelligence, physical fitness, supervision] or any combination of them is related to Y [some type of academic or athletic performance or delinquent behavior]." After making a preliminary exploration of the facts and theories relating to this problem area, you may limit the investigation to the relation between A (intelligence) and Y (arithmetic achievement). When you attempt to define these variables, you may encounter problems "Are all the indicants of intelligence related to arithmetic achievement? What indicants of arithmetic achievement am I interested in in this investigation? Which of the indicants of intelligence are related to these indicants of arithmetic achievement? What precise factors am I concerned about in this investigation?"

Like many graduate students, you may initially select a problem that is too broad to be carried out. To trim an investigation to a manageable size, you may have to confine your attention to fewer variables or to a smaller geographical area, sample of subjects, or segment of time. You may break down the original problem you had in

mind into several subquestions. If you are concerned with the effectiveness of programmed learning, you may raise subquestions concerning
the effect of this teaching tool on academic achievement, attitudes of
students, staff morale, etc. Sometimes two or more subquestions are
incorporated in one study, but because of time, cost, or other considerations, you may have to reduce the scope of your investigation. The
subquestions of the original question may provide the basis for separate
studies. Perhaps several studies will have to be conducted to answer
the original generalized question.

Specifying the Nature of the Problem

Problems are not described in general terms. You do not state, "I am
going to examine the facts relating to deviant behavior [or reading
retardation or skill learning]." A research problem is expressed in the
form of a question or statement that focuses on the precise factors that
are to be observed. With the exception of some descriptive and
historical studies, the question identifies the relationship that the
researcher thinks may exist between two or more variables. The
variables are, in turn, so defined that they can be measured; this
narrows the scope of the investigation and clarifies what observations
must be made.

    The statement of the problem sets the stage for the investigation.
The problem question that is raised may be broad in scope and not
directly testable. But a researcher may be able to transform it into a
hypothetical proposition that makes it possible to test whether the
predicted relationship does exist. Suppose, for example, that you think
some relation may exist between body image and self-esteem. You may
define these terms by specifying the operations necessary to measure
them and may formulate your research question and hypothesis as
follows:

Definitions
Body image is the score obtained on a questionnaire that asks one to
   indicate the extent of one's satisfaction with 24 of one's body parts.
Self-esteem is the score obtained on the Janis-Field-Eagley Self-Esteem
   Measure.
Problem question
Is body image related to self-esteem?
Hypothesis
If body image is related to self-esteem, then male and female college
   freshmen with above-average body images will have higher self-

esteem estimates than male and female college freshmen with below-average body images.

The above hypothesis, which omits some of the technical niceties that appear in formal reports, describes the relationship that you predict exists and stipulates what must be observed to test the prediction.

Hypotheses, which are discussed in the following chapter, are one of the most useful tools to use in expressing problems. Some problems, however, such as surveys which describe practices or conditions without concern for their relationships, do not state hypotheses. For studies, including surveys in which relations between variables are a consideration, hypotheses are used to direct the inquiries, although they are not always formally stated. Regardless of the form in which you present a problem, the objective is to present the exact dimensions of the problem in a concrete and explicit statement. You present the background of the study, the theories on which it is based (see Appendix G), the assumptions underlying the statement of the problem, and definitions of the key terms. You state specifically what persons, materials, situations, factors, and causes will and will not be considered. An adequate statement of the problem encompasses the sum total of all the facts, relations, and explanations that the analysis of the problem indicated were relevant. These factors are not listed in an encyclopedic fashion; they are placed in relationship to one another. They are framed in a descriptive statement or question which clearly indicates what information you must obtain to solve the problem and what you must do to interpret the findings. A discussion of how to write the statement of the problem in a research report is given in Chapter 13 (see pages 408–409).

Defining the Terms

Before launching into an investigation and when writing up a research report, an investigator defines rigorously the meaning of the terms used in the statement of the problem and in the hypothesis. The objective in each instance is to write a clear, precise definition that will call up the same core of meaning to all competent workers in the field. Some of the routes that can be taken in defining terms are given below.

DEFINITION BY EXAMPLE   The most direct way to close the gap between a word symbol and sensory experience is to point to it or to introduce a specimen or picture of it. But one cannot define "IQ," "self-concept," and other abstract concepts by pointing to something. Concrete word examples to which a term can be correctly applied give one some understanding of what is meant. A school administrator, for example, may be defined as an official, such as a school superintendent, school principal, or college president. But this denotative type of definition does not identify what characteristics of these examples are related to the concept being defined or indicate the boundaries of the concept's meaning.

DEFINITION BY GENUS AND DIFFERENTIA Identifying the boundaries and stating the "essence of a thing" can be done by indicating its *genus,* the larger class of things in which the referent is included, and then by indicating how it differs from other subclasses of the same genus. To define "full professor," one moves up first to the next larger class, "teacher," and then states the essential *differentia* to eliminate all teachers who are not full professors. One might state, for example, that full professors are teachers of the highest academic rank in institutions of higher education. This definition distinguishes full professors from teachers of lower rank in institutions of higher learning and from teachers in secondary schools and other institutions. Definition by genus and differentia is especially useful in areas where phenomena have been structurally classified and a number of large-class terms have been established whose meanings are not in serious dispute.

DEFINITION BY STIPULATION An initial step that can be taken in defining the terms in a study is to ascertain how the terms (concepts, constructs, properties, variables) are defined in similar research studies or in the specialized pedagogical, statistical, and psychological dictionaries that have been compiled. These definitions can be used as guides, but they cannot be borrowed blindly. A researcher is responsible for stipulating precisely how a concept will be applied in a particular study. A dictionary, for example, may define a gifted underachiever as "a child with high intellectual ability who does not achieve on a level commensurate with his ability." A researcher might stipulate that the gifted underachievers in a particular study were students who had an IQ of 125 or higher and read at least one year below the community grade level. If several investigators conducted studies and their specifications of IQ and reading level differed, it would be difficult to compare and synthesize the results of their studies. One must always be on guard when reading research reports, for the findings may be based on familiar terms that different researchers have defined differently.

Defining an abstract concept, such as "body image" or "social distance," that is not directly observable but rather inferred from behavior is no easy task. An adequate definition lays bare the essential differentiating characteristics of the concept so that through them the term in question is clearly related to the intended referent and distinguished from all other concepts. The differentia can be neither too broad (include other concepts) nor too narrow (exclude some aspects of this concept that are relevant to the study).

The use of commonplace words in a research study can cause as much confusion as abstract concepts. The simpler a term is, the more meanings it may have acquired; consequently, the greater may be the need to define it. Does the term "student" in a study, for example, refer to a nondegree, degree, full time, or graduate student? Does an "unemployed teacher" include a teacher who has lost a job and is looking for work, a teacher who is on strike, a teacher who has lost a job but is not looking for work, or a certified teacher who has never worked?

DEFINITION BY CONSTITUTIVE AND OPERATIONAL ANALYSIS Because research consists of a dynamic interplay between theory on one hand and observable facts on the other, investigators make a distinction between constitutive and operational definitions of terms. A scientific theory of learning, personality, or some other phenomenon consists of a set of constructs that are bound together in a logically unified network of relations that provides an interpretation of what the researcher speculates (infers) exists in reality. A constitutive definition addresses itself to the theoretical aspects of constructs; an operational definition addresses itself to empirical reality—observable aspects of the constructs.

All constructs in a theory must possess constitutive meaning, and a sufficient number of them must be translatable into empirical measurement to ascertain the legitimacy of their existence. Translation is done by operational definitions. Some constructs may not possess direct operational definitions, but they must at least be connected indirectly with observable facts through constructs that do. (See figure 7.3.)

Constitutive definitions, which are placed early in the research report, define constructs by describing how they are linked to other constructs in a set (intelligence is the "product of the interaction of a person's heredity and environment") or by describing their key characteristics (intelligence is the ability "to deal with tasks involving abstractions," "to generalize," "to learn from experience," or "to deal with new situations").

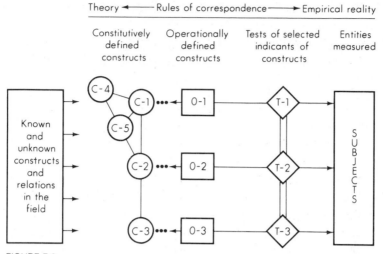

FIGURE 7.3

A schematic representation of a theory: A set of constructs (1–5) and their relations which are constitutively defined (*C*) and linked to observable data by operational definitions (*O*). The operational definitions specify appropriate tests (*T*) that measure selected indicants of the constructs. The results of the tests are correlated to ascertain whether the relations (‖) that the theory predicts would exist do exist in reality. [Adapted from Henry Margenau (70: 85) and W. S. Torgerson (109: 3).]

Operational definitions, which are often placed later in the research report under research procedures, link theoretical constructs with observable indicants of them. They ascribe meaning to constructs by specifying the operations necessary to achieve certain objectives: (1) measured operational definitions specify the operations necessary to measure instances of constructs, and (2) experimental operational definitions specify the operations necessary to manipulate constructs in an experiment to precipitate or prevent their presence. These two types of definitions are discussed in the following paragraphs.

A *measured operational definition* is a rule of correspondence that specifies how to assign numbers to entities to indicate their positions (scale values or scores) on the indicants of the construct. A researcher may say, "The meaning of intelligence (achievement, creativity, or anxiety) in this investigation corresponds to the scores which are obtained on test *X.*" The definition stipulates what to measure, but, of course, evidence of validity and reliability of the test is also supplied. Other examples of constructs and their measured definitions are given below.

Authoritarian: The scores indicating a pattern of responses given by subjects on a battery of questions that tap indicants of this construct.

School achievement: The numbers, 4, 3, 2, 1, and 0 which are assigned to represent grades A, B, C, D, and E, respectively.

Socioeconomic status: The weighted sum of income and job prestige as determined by ratings.

Chest girth: The description of the kind of apparatus used, manner in which it is used, location of body landmarks for measurement, and units of measurement.

An *experimental operational definition* specifies the ways variables are to be manipulated in an experiment, such as how reinforcement is to be achieved. Examples of variables and their experimental operational definitions are given below.

Positive and *negative reinforcement:* Subjects are to be rewarded for specific behavior by statements of approval and penalized by statements of disapproval.

Frustration: Subjects are to be prevented from reaching a desired goal by placing attractive food where it is visible but inaccessible.

Whenever applicable, one uses definitions that have appeared in previous studies, for this procedure makes research comparable. But in many studies one must construct some definitions, and many problems can arise in specifying the procedures to employ in measuring a complex concept, making the indicants correspond with the characteristics in the constitutive definition, and informing the observer or rater precisely what is meant by each of the indicants. If the number of times a child slaps another is specified as a measure of aggression, what should a rater do about a slap of greeting, the slap that athletes give to teammates for a skillful performance, or the slap to keep someone out of danger?

When measurements are made, the question always arises: Did the operational definition produce a valid measurement of the property as constitutively defined? Are what is defined and what is measured the same thing? Operational definitions (rules of correspondence) join together the theoretical and empirical sides of research. Scientific research cannot exist without observations, and observations cannot be carried out without unambiguous, precise instructions on what and how to observe. But the crucial question always is: Does the measuring instrument measure what it is supposed to measure?

Operational definitions of constructs that are close to direct observations, such as height or sex, are virtually coextensive with the constitutive definition they represent. But operational definitions of constructs that are further removed from direct observation, such as anxiety or creativity, stand in a many-to-one relation with the constitutive definition. A perfect indicant of a "true" measure of a complex, abstract construct is rarely found, but some indicants are more relevant and less ambiguous than others. The objective is to find the best possible combination of indicants to represent a construct in a given study. But one must remember that no operational definition taps all the diverse meanings and indicants of a complex construct. The indicants one is instructed to observe are only an approximation of the "true" measure of the construct. The variables a researcher measures are always limited and specific in meaning.

Since different operations may measure similar constructs but not necessarily the same constructs, considerable stress is placed on defining terms in this way. When an investigator defines terms by describing precisely how the phenomenon is measured, the following objectives are accomplished: The gap between term and the experience of direct observation is closed; the phenomenon can be agreed upon and reproduced by others; and the possibility of cumulative research is facilitated.

Examining the Assumptions

Inexperienced investigators often give too little attention to examining the assumptions underlying their problems. In any investigation one reasons: "If *A* holds true—and I assume it does—then *B* occurs." One should examine these assumptions carefully to make certain that they are reasonable. In working with normal subjects, for example, one may assume that they will behave in a rational manner, that no unusual forces are operating that will alter their usual patterns of behavior, that the behavior one is interested in is actually observable, and that the time period selected for observation is adequate and relevant to the problem under consideration. An excellent example of making explicit statements of the basic assumptions underlying a problem is presented in Ryan's study of "teacher behavior" (see Appendix A; for other examples see the study by Butts, page 181, and by Hyram, pages 276–277). Later chapters in this text will discuss the assumptions underlying the use of various research tools, tests, equipment, and statistical techniques. Before collecting any data, an investigator should present all the evidence he can to support his assumptions and should recognize the implications that any questionable assumptions will have on the acceptance and usefulness of his research.

AIDS IN LOCATING AND ANALYZING PROBLEMS

Problems spring from felt difficulties, but one cannot expect to remain idle and aloof waiting for a formal introduction to a difficulty. An impoverished intellect has little opportunity to meet or to recognize difficulties. Problem ideas do not germinate in barren brains but rather in minds enriched by varied experiences and fertile layers of knowledge. Reading extensively in educational and scientific publications will help you prepare an intellectual soil in which ideas are likely to sprout.

Steeping Yourself in the Literature

Promising problem seeds lie dormant in many professional books and periodicals awaiting your discovery. You should form the habit of devoting regular blocks of time to reading topics of interest to you in educational research encyclopedias, handbooks, and review and abstracting journals (see pages 79–82) and in similar publications in related fields. Shift back and forth between macroexamination of a problem area and a microexamination of one or more categories of special interest to you.

Pay particular attention to studies that have tested deductions made from theories. Many researchers, for example, have utilized the reinforcement theory to determine whether different types of reinforcement affect different types of behavior. They have studied how reinforcement, such as comments of approval or disapproval, rewards of candy or money, or feedback to students concerning their performances by teachers, videotapes, TV monitors, or tape recorders, affects their subject matter achievement, motor skill learning, mastery of complex tasks of discrimination and generalization, or interpersonal relations. You may, of course, reverse the theory-searching and problem-finding processes. You may note an interesting relationship that appears to exist between variables and then ask: "What kinds of learning, behavior, communication, or other theories might help me explore this problem? Can I hook this problem into a network of theory and extend the theory or transform it in some way?"

Many graduate students confine themselves to a low level of research because they are not sufficiently informed about learning, personality, or other theories in their field or the theories that can be borrowed from sociology, psychology, political science, or other fields.[1] The time to grow in this respect is the moment you enter the field of research. Indeed, some universities require that problem proposals submitted by Ph.D. degree candidates must be theoretically oriented to be accepted. Theories are invaluable tools, but you must be wary and critical of them as you are of facts: they do not all bear a "scientific seal of approval" and they are not static structures. Utilizing them without first ascertaining their present status in the scientific community is dangerous. Sometimes current reviews of their status are available, such as "Human Problem Solving: The State of the Theory in 1970" (94), "A Theory of American Folklore Reviewed" (32), and "Spence's Theory of Discrimination of Learning: A Re-evaluation" (1).

A thorough review of the research literature in an area of interest will acquaint you with the major theories or points of view, the areas of agreement and disagreement, the types of problems and how they relate to each other, and the findings of the studies and whether they are consistent, contradictory, or inconclusive. You will become acquainted with the concepts, operational definitions, research methods, designs, and data-gathering implements that have been employed in the area and with any problems that have been encountered in using them. You will be warned about unfruitful leads that have been tried, you will be informed about areas in which further research is needed, and you will learn which hypotheses have already been well confirmed and hence in what areas no further replication of research is needed.

Some examples of the suggestions and advice that appear in the literature which might help you locate a problem are given below. In an examination of the links between politics and education, Harman (49) suggested theoretical approaches, such as the system's theory and pressure group theory, that can be used in this area; drew attention to assumptions underlying most existing research which were being challenged; pointed out problems that needed to be examined, such as the horizontal and the vertical links between education and politics on

---

[1]A few examples of the types of books and articles that are available are "Theory Construction for Research on Teaching" by Snow (110), "Administrative Theory" by Griffiths (47), *A Theory of Achievement Motivation* by Atkinson and Feather (3), *Theories of Adolescence* by Muuss (76), *Theories of Child Development* by Baldwin (7), *Theories in Contemporary Psychology* by Marx (71), and *Theories of Learning* by Hilgard and Bower (51).

the various levels of government, the roles of pressure groups in communicating demands to decision makers, and the strategies of implementing particular innovations. In "A Critique of the Research Literature Concerning Pregnant Adolescents," Baizerman *et al.* (6) made explicit and questioned some of the assumptions underlying much of the research, such as the assumption of difference (bad, sick, deviant) and the assumption of homogeneity (failure to allow for individual differences). They suggested that longitudinal studies of girls were needed, beginning before the girls have become sexually active, to discover likenesses and differences among adolescents who do and do not become pregnant. They raised many other relevant research questions and pointed out weaknesses in the methodology of existing studies. Chalfant and Scheffelin (19) summarized both the present status of knowledge in and the future research needs for identifying, assessing, and treating children with central processing disorders arising from minimal brain dysfunction.

As you read the pertinent literature in a given area, you should ask questions such as the following: "Can I repeat a study that was limited in scope (to elementary students in a metropolitan area) to increase the extent to which the findings can be generalized (to include elementary students in rural or suburban schools, high school or college students)? Can I improve on a study that is weak because of the use of imprecisely defined terms, inappropriate statistics for the analysis of the data, inappropriate or unreliable instruments, or faulty methodology? If previous studies have established a relationship between teaching method *A* and performance on task *B,* can I raise additional questions that will make the relationship more precise?"

Contradictory findings that are reported in the literature may alert you to the existence of a problem. If three men study the effect that teachers' praise has on students' achievement and their reports present conflicting results, you may question whether an uncontrolled extraneous factor is producing the difference in the results. You may wonder whether different types of students were used in the studies and may decide to investigate whether pupils who differ in intelligence, socioeconomic status, or other factors react differently to praise.

Exposing Yourself to Professional Stimulation

Placing yourself in a dynamic research environment increases your opportunities for finding and solving problems. Spirited intellectual intercourse in which ideas are presented, explained, analyzed, and challenged is a rich source of inspiration. Graduate courses, seminars, professional meetings—particularly those in which papers are read and criticized—conferences with stimulating professors, lectures by eminent men in education, discussions with fellow research workers, visits to laboratories, and part-time jobs in research centers often give birth to ideas worthy of investigation or provide clues needed for the solution of problems. Engaging in research produces many ideas, for one investigation usually points up other problems that need to be solved.

Examining Everyday Experiences

Since all problems spring from life situations, a practitioner in the field of education is in a favorable position to locate problems. Every day you encounter difficulties with students, equipment, tests, textbooks, guidance, discipline, parents, curriculum, supervision, or administration. Throughout your career, you will experience dissatisfaction with some conditions—wonder how or why they developed—and will notice things or relationships for which you know of no satisfactory explanation. Seize upon these felt difficulties and explore them thoroughly; discover whether they have been or can be solved. An alert mind, sensitively studying classroom situations, serves as an excellent detector of research problems.

Keeping Notes

Keeping systematic notes before and throughout an investigation stimulates critical thinking and leads to the discovery of new ideas. Flashes of insight that identify problems or that marshal facts concerning a problem into a logical chain of evidence may come to you at any time. Fruitful ideas may snap into focus when you are deliberately trying to put tangled thoughts into some meaningful order, or they may pop up unexpectedly while you are talking with friends, listening to a lecture, teaching a class, reading a book, or relaxing at home. These mercurial ideas may produce crucial clues that at the moment appear to be crystal clear and too important to forget. Weeks may pass before you want to use them in your investigation, however, and by that time they may have escaped your memory if you have not made note of them. When a kernel of thought first sprouts in your mind, jot it down immediately and indicate what implications it has for your investigation.

Adopting a Critical Outlook

Problems are neither discovered nor solved by complacent educators who are habitually subservient to traditional authority, smugly satisfied with the status quo, or perpetually parroting pedagogical jargon. Knowledge is advanced by creative minds filled with curiosity. A research worker cannot afford the comforts of conformity. You must experience the difficulties and delights of challenging existing theories and practices. While reading, conversing, teaching, observing, and attending classes, seminars, and professional meetings, you must adopt a critical attitude toward the information, generalizations, assumptions, and procedures you encounter. Question them; challenge their validity; look for deficiencies and contradictions; maintain a healthy skepticism. Keep asking questions: Is it true? Did the investigator interpret the results of the experiment accurately? Is there a better explanation for this phenomenon? Follow Francis Bacon's advice: "Read not to contradict and confute, nor to believe and take for granted . . . but to weigh and consider."

EVALUATION OF A PROBLEM

When you first become aware of a problematic situation, begin to evaluate whether investigating it will be feasible and worthwhile. Whenever you encounter evidence that indicates expending further effort would be imprudent, either drop the problem or refashion it into a more acceptable form. Delaying this evaluation process too long or terminating it too soon may cause you to waste months of valuable time conducting a useless investigation or one that you cannot complete. Problems that are worthy of investigation vary somewhat for classroom teachers, curriculum committees, research staffs of public and private agencies, and graduate students. No matter what problem is being evaluated, however, both personal and social factors must be taken into consideration.

Personal Considerations

Blustering boldly into an investigation is foolhardy if one lacks the necessary qualifications, support, or facilities to complete it. To avoid making such an error, an intelligent investigator explores questions such as the following:

1 Is the problem in line with my goal expectations and the expectations of others?

2 Am I genuinely interested in this problem but free from strong biases?

3 Do I possess or can I acquire the necessary skills, abilities, and background knowledge to study this problem?

4 Do I have access to the tools, equipment, laboratories, and subjects necessary to conduct the investigation?

5 Do I have the time, money, health, and freedom from other responsibilities required to complete it?

6 Can I obtain adequate data?

7 Does the problem meet the scope, significance, and topical requirements of the institution or periodical to which I will submit my report?

8 Can I obtain administrative support, guidance, and cooperation for the conduct of the study?

Since interest is a tremendous stimulus to work in any form of endeavor, you should select a problem that you have a consuming desire to solve. Maintaining the prodigious effort required in research is difficult if you feel that your topic is meaningless and boring. An insatiable curiosity about a subject gives an investigator the extra enthusiasm and drive necessary to withstand the prolonged period of exacting work.

Avoiding a problem may be advisable, however, if you are strongly biased in favor of a particular viewpoint, for you probably will be unable to maintain an objective attitude. Common sense also demands that you work within the framework of the social milieu and your personal potentialities. Before undertaking any study, therefore, you should raise several pertinent questions: "Am I willing to do the background reading and study which will lift me to the level of sophistication that is acceptable to individuals who are knowledgeable in this area? Is the foundation, school administrator, or professor who is sponsoring my work opposed to this problem? Are my advisers capable of offering competent guidance in this area? Are the necessary equipment, subjects, or facilities available?" No matter how enthusiastic you are about a study, these stubborn actualities may prevent you from making any progress. A problem may require, for example, that you read Russian scientific journals, travel to various private libraries for data, obtain access to classified government documents, procure the correspondence of a deceased man from his uncooperative family, possess a knowledge of physiology, or use specialized equipment that is available only at a distant university. If you are unable to do these things, you must face reality and reject the problem—at least for the present.

Social Considerations

Social as well as personal factors must be carefully evaluated when selecting a problem, for a researcher works not only to achieve personal satisfactions but also to advance knowledge for the good of humankind. When evaluating a problem, therefore, questions such as the following must be raised:

1   Will the solution of this problem advance knowledge in the field appreciably without violating the human rights of the people involved in the study?
2   Will the findings be of practical or theoretical value to educators, parents, social workers, or others?
3   What will be the breadth of the application of the findings in terms of range of individuals, years of applicability, and areas of coverage?
4   Will the investigation duplicate work that has been or is being done adequately by someone else?
5   If this topic has been covered, does it need to be extended beyond its present limits?
6   Is the topic sufficiently delimited to permit an exhaustive treatment yet sufficiently significant to warrant investigating it?
7   Will the conclusions of the study be of doubtful value because the tools and techniques available to conduct the inquiry are not adequately refined and sufficiently reliable?
8   Will the study lead to the development of other investigations?

When you become interested in a topic, locate and evaluate all studies relating to it that have been completed or are under way. If this survey reveals that your proposed problem has already been thoroughly explored, you will usually abandon it. You may pursue the problem, however, if you doubt the validity of the conclusions reached by others, discover contradictory findings, believe new evidence or better techniques have been discovered that require a new investigation, or think that there are gaps to fill or extensions to be made in the organized body of educational knowledge.

A more detailed discussion of the social and methodological questions that a research worker evaluates before undertaking an investigation is presented in succeeding chapters. But perhaps some mention should be made here of another evaluative technique that may be employed. After making an extensive analysis of the problem and formulating a plan to carry out the investigation, you may set up a pilot study so that you can see more clearly how the variables in the situation work. During this small-scale study which precedes the main investigation, you will discover whether adequate tools and the re- quired type and number of subjects are available, whether you can obtain the necessary cooperation to carry out the study, and where difficulties may arise in establishing controls and making measure- ments. You will find out where changes should be made in data- collecting methods; in questionnaires or interview schedules; and in directions to subjects, observers, or interviewers. Pilot studies are particularly important when the subjects are children, for the ability to establish rapport with youngsters and convey directions clearly to them cannot be taken for granted. The pilot study helps a research worker evaluate the feasibility of launching into a full-scale investiga- tion.

Approval of Problem

Most graduate schools will require that you submit a research proposal in writing to a faculty committee and a committee for the protection of human subjects before you conduct a study for a master's thesis or a doctoral dissertation. The faculty committee will examine the proposal critically to ascertain whether you have formulated a problem of merit and have properly and adequately delineated the steps that will be followed in collecting and analyzing the data. The human subjects' committee will determine whether the proposed study is ethically defensible (see pages 32–38).

The format of the problem proposal that is required by different graduate schools differs, but the following information is usually requested:[2]

1   Statement of the problem and/or hypotheses and their deduced consequences: expected relationships between and among varia- bles.

---

[2]For a more detailed discussion of these components of a research study see pages 404 and 414.

2 Review of the related literature in which you justify the soundness of your hypothesis by presenting empirical support from the findings of other studies and logical support in arguments based on theories or concepts in the field.

3 Assumptions upon which hypotheses are based.

4 Definitions of terms: give operational definitions for the variables and also define other terms that do not have commonly accepted meanings.

5 Sampling procedures: explain where and how the list of all the units in the population is to be obtained, describe the size and major characteristics of the population, and describe the method to be used in drawing a sample from it.

6 Instrumentation: describe the tools that will be used or constructed to obtain data, defend their appropriateness, demonstrate that the assumptions underlying their proper use will be met, and give reliability and validity data for each instrument.

7 Research procedures

   a. Research design: provide information about the number of groups to be tested; when, where, and under what conditions; how many times; how subjects, observers, test administrators, experimental treatments, equipment, etc., are to be assigned to the groups; types and levels of experimental treatments; number of variables to be manipulated simultaneously; and what controls will be used to ensure obtaining valid and reliable data and to protect the rights of human subjects.

   b. Tabulation of data: how data are to be classified, manipulated, and summarized.

8 Statistical procedures to be employed to analyze data: reasons for choosing the ones selected; level of significance to be used for rejecting any null hypotheses (these topics are discussed later); evidence indicating that the assumptions underlying the use of each statistical procedure employed will be met, such as size of sample, level of measurement scale, number and types (continuous or discrete) of dependent and independent variables.

9 Significance: indicate how the study will make a contribution to knowledge.

The faculty committees that review your proposal may accept it, reject it, or require you to make changes and resubmit it for approval. This stage of research work is somewhat stressful, but it is much less painful than to discover the flaws and weaknesses in an investigation after you have invested considerable time, money, and effort in collecting data that force you to abandon the study or redo much of the work. The quality of your proposal will in a large part determine the quality of your investigation. Nothing you do during the conduct of your study can compensate for the errors you have made in the planning stage. A research proposal should not be looked upon as unnecessary busy work, but rather as an essential road map to guide your intellectual journey into the frontiers of knowledge.

8 SOLUTION OF THE PROBLEM

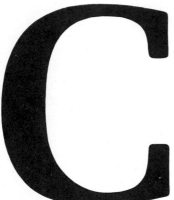reative thought is not a step-by-step process that one can master by following directions in a "how-to-do-it" manual. Successful scientists may appear to pluck problems magically out of the academic atmosphere, but months or years of patient plodding may precede the exciting moment when they describe the precise nature of the particular events or conditions that require explaining. And no blinding flashes of intuition immediately illuminate their minds with brilliant solutions; a long period of arduous intellectual activity may ensue before they evolve adequate explanations.

CONSTRUCTING HYPOTHESES

When attacking problems, educators, chemists, and detectives gather many facts. But they are not interested in "facts and nothing but the facts," for much speculation—bold, imaginative guesswork—is required to solve problems. If undirected observation were the only tool investigators possessed, they might gather data for years without unearthing the particular facts and relationships that are required to solve their problems. To overcome this difficulty, competent investigators structure possible explanations for the puzzling conditions or events that concern them (Dewey's step 3, page 13). These explanations, or hypotheses, are the most useful tools in their "detective kits." A hypothesis suggests where to search most profitably for facts and how to detect relevant relationships between them. Facts must be obtained to solve a problem; facts, however, "never speak for themselves but only *to* someone who has an hypothesis which he wishes to test" (80:123–124).

Nature of Hypotheses

If you begin to analyze a problem—a murder, an airplane crash, or some form of pupil behavior—you may notice that some data are vague or incomplete, that some elements do not appear to be related to other known elements or to fit into any particular order, or that no adequate explanation can be given for some phenomena. You are disturbed and keep asking how you can complete the data, systematize the information, or give some interpretation that will explain the unknown factors. When you reach this agitated mental state, you are standing on the threshold of research. If you can imagine some unknown fact and combine it with observed facts and an existing body of theory to form a reasonable hypothesis, you will take a giant step forward. Leaping beyond the known facts and constructing hypotheses—intelligent guesses that offer possible solutions to the problem—may enable you to push back the frontiers of knowledge.

One uses hypotheses to solve simple as well as complex problems. If the lamp on your desk does not light, you may immediately relate this "known fact" to the following "unknown facts" that you imagine, suspect, or predict may explain the occurrence of this phenomenon: (1) the bulb is burned out, (2) the cord is not plugged into the outlet, or (3) the cord is severed. These hypotheses help you locate and pattern the facts needed to solve the problem. If you put the bulb into another lamp and it lights, you know that hypothesis 1 is not the solution to your problem. After testing the other hypotheses, you may find that hypothesis 3 fits all the evidence and satisfactorily explains why the desk light is out. Hypotheses "are your eyes as you try to approach problems in a scientific manner. Through them you look into the disorder that is a problem and see the possibilities of order" (52:120).

To summarize, a hypothesis specifies the facts (variables, logical constructs) and the relations among them that offer a logical description or explanation of the conditions or events that gave rise to the problem. Some variables or relations in hypotheses are known and others are "invented" to complete and systematize the explanation. By logically relating known facts to intelligent guesses about unknown variables or relations, hypotheses are able to extend and enlarge our knowledge.

Conditions Conducive to Creativity

Hypotheses are calculated guesses, but these guesses are not merely "happy accidents," as some scientists modestly suggest. No precise rules can be given for formulating hypotheses and deducing consequences from them that can be empirically verified, but some conditions are more conducive to their construction than others.

BACKGROUND KNOWLEDGE   A scientist cannot be an isolated rebel who relies on personal observation alone to create fruitful hypotheses. Your work will be hopelessly hampered if you are not thoroughly familiar with established facts, existing hypotheses and theories, and previous research relating to your problem. While manipulating relevant raw materials drawn from these sources, you may locate the key associations or missing data needed to explain puzzling phenomena. Another productive means of creating hypotheses is to examine conceptual schemes developed by the other disciplines and to decide whether they provide insights that would help explain educational phenomena. Kurt Lewin, for example, drew on the concept of force in physics to help explain human behavior.

IMAGINATION   Imagination, the magic catalyst in research, is the product of an adventuresome attitude and an agile intellect. When experienced investigators encounter a problem, they assume that the traditional and obvious explanations for the phenomenon may be inaccurate or inadequate. Stubborn skepticism stimulates them to search for flaws in old theories. To break from traditional thought patterns, they view the puzzling phenomenon from unorthodox positions or fragmentize previous knowledge concerning it and combine the elements into new patterns. To stimulate their imagination, they keep asking questions: What else is like this phenomenon? What can be copied? Does something need to be added, subtracted, enlarged, combined, divided, or rearranged? Can a logical construct be invented that will account for the occurrence of this phenomenon? In many instances a reversal of viewpoint helps them stumble upon the most effective solution for a problem. When strange ideas pop momentarily to the surface of their minds, they do not dismiss them. Any "happy accident" that gives them insight into a situation and kindles a creative flame in their minds is entertained. With intensive concentration, they select, shift, and combine seemingly unalike and previously unconnected known and imaginary facts until they construct a simple, coherent explanation for a phenomenon.

Higher-quality hypotheses are produced if investigators prolong the solution-searching process, separate it from the solution-evaluation process, and delay the solution-selection process. After discovering one possible explanation for a phenomenon, some problem solvers crystallize their thinking and hurry along this promising pathway. After making heavy ego-effort investments in their proposed solution, they are reluctant to start over again or to entertain other solution possibilities which may be better. Because quantity tends to breed quality, experienced investigators first concentrate on piling up alternative hypotheses. Kepler, for example, constructed twelve hypotheses about the satellites of Mars before he stumbled on the correct one. Because critical evaluation and concern about practical considerations depress flights of the imagination, creative people refrain from weighing the merits of each idea as it occurs to them. During the "idea-getting" stage of research, caution is abandoned. Radical ideas are entertained; wild experimental associations are made; risks are taken—they must be taken, for discoveries are not made by jogging along in ruts of past experience. Unconventional thinking is not unconditionally guaranteed to produce problem solutions, but it holds greater promise of advancing knowledge than does clinging credulously to traditional patterns of thought.

ANALOGY   Analogy is an ancient "order-searching" tool that one can use to build bridges from the known to the unknown. When faced with a problem, you may look for a successful previous ordering of nature that might illuminate your present difficulty. Upon spotting some similarity between a new situation and an old one, you may wonder whether the old situation which you know a lot about will provide you with any clues that will help you solve your present problem. You reason that if these two situations have some resemblances in common, they may be analogous in other, as yet unknown, respects.

1   If A (new situation) resembles B (old situation) in regard to X factor,
2   and you know from previous experience that B is related to Y and Z as well as to X,
3   then perhaps A is also related to Y and Z.

Thus, the analogy leads you to clues you might not otherwise stumble upon and hints at hypotheses that you might profitably test.

Analogies are useful but not foolproof tools for finding solutions to problems. If any essential dissimilarity prevails, the analogy is false, as Miss Wilson, an elementary school principal, discovered to her dismay. When the poor attendance at the afternoon PTA meeting disturbed her, she recalled that young matrons had doubled the weekly attendance in her Sunday school class by organizing a nursery to care for members' children. Miss Wilson reasoned that since the PTA and the Sunday school class both had young mothers as members and similar attendance difficulties, the same solution might work in both cases. But Miss Wilson failed to detect an important difference in the two situations: The school children's mothers were career women and could not leave their jobs to attend weekday afternoon meetings even if a nursery were provided. Miss Wilson's experience indicates that problem solvers must be not only exceptionally adept at noting similarities between things but also meticulous about detecting differences between them that might make the analogies false. Despite the danger of mistaking an analogy for evidence, scientists favor using it with caution. They recognize that the reliability of analogical reasoning is restricted, but with proper safeguards it is one of the more helpful means of discovering hypotheses.

OTHER PRACTICES   Research workers find they are more apt to devise hypotheses if they allot sufficient blocks of time—uninterrupted by distractions—to mull over, organize, and reorganize their collected data. After periods of intensive work on a problem, they sometimes abstain temporarily from conscious intellectual effort. In moments of relaxation their subconscious minds may continue to consider the problem and hit upon a useful hypothesis when they least expect it. Dropping a problem periodically permits them to escape from unprofitable ruts of thought they have been following and to return to their labors later with fresh and more objective viewpoints. Conversations with colleagues and authorities from different fields may help them detect errors in their reasoning and may stimulate them to venture up new avenues of thought. Lecturing or writing about the puzzling phenomena may clarify their thinking and force the "key clue" to the surface. Drawing diagrams or constructing models of the factors involved in the problem may also help them break through to a plausible explanation for the phenomena.

Examples of Hypothesis Construction

You engage in hypothesis construction every day when searching for solutions to problems such as "Where did I leave my glasses?" "Why won't my car start?" "Why did so many students fail the last English test?" Perhaps a review of the steps in the scientific method on pages 12–13 and the following illustration will help you recall the mental processes involved in making a constructive attack on a problem.

PERSONAL PROBLEM   If you experience periodically symptoms similar to a cold—dripping nose, watering eyes, annoying sneezes—and yet never develop a cold, the situation is unpleasant and puzzling. You have a problem and want to obtain some explanation for the repeated occurrence of this phenomenon. To initiate the inquiry, you collect empirically verifiable facts about when, where, and how frequently it occurs. At the same time you begin to think of explanations for the phenomenon. From your previous experiences—reading, conversations with friends, observations of people with similar problems—you cull some of the following possible solutions: "Does dust cause it? Do I eat, wear, or become exposed to something that is irritating? Am I allergic to wool or feathers? Do the chemicals I use at work cause it? Do some flowers or plants cause it? Do I have hay fever?" These hypotheses are mere hunches at this stage. They must be analyzed and developed. Empirically verifiable facts must be found to support them.

By examining and reexamining the facts and explanations and tracing relationships between them, you try to determine which hypothesis is in agreement with all the facts in the case and gives a better explanation of the phenomenon than any of the others. If dust causes the phenomenon, you should suffer the most during the spring and fall housecleaning seasons. Since you experience the greatest difficulty in August and December, the dust hypothesis does not stand up under analysis. If chemicals used at work cause it, you should sneeze more at work than at home. But this is not true, for the greatest discomfort occurs during the August and December vacation weeks. Could it be hay fever? The December facts negate this possibility. Could it be a wool allergy? The August facts negate this possibility. Just what is the relationship between August and December? After probing this possibility further and searching for additional facts, you recall that the phenomenon occurs most frequently outdoors in August and indoors in December.

In one magic moment at an August beach party, a reasonable solution springs into your mind. Because the miserable cold symptoms have recurred, the whining questions your daughter Janie keeps asking irritate you. But one of those unwelcome questions suddenly supplies the missing clue that solves your problem. Janie complains, "There are too many old cedar trees around the porch. Why don't we cut them down for our Christmas decorations instead of always taking trees from the clump down by the lake?"

Sitting up—suddenly tingling with excitement—you pounce upon her words. Do they supply the missing link to your puzzle? Cedar trees grow around the cottage where you stay in August; during the Christmas holidays you use them for decorations in your city apartment. Is cedar the cause of your difficulty? This explanation is a more concise and testable hypothesis than the original vague explanation that some plant, dust, chemical, wool, or flower caused your suffering. The hypothesis still has to be tested to determine whether cedar is actually the cause of the difficulty. But you have an informed guess to work on that has a reasonable chance of being the correct answer to the problem.

EDUCATIONAL PROBLEM   If you will recall, Miss White, whom you met in Chapter 7, went through many of the same steps in hypothesis construction. She was disturbed by a problematic situation: her pupils were not making satisfactory progress in reading. With this glimmering of a problem as a prod to action, she made observations and gathered facts to clarify it. Through observing the youngsters, examining their school records, and reviewing the literature in the field, she identified the particular children who were having difficulty and formulated several tentative hypotheses to explain this phenomenon. She asked: "Is there a relationship between the reading retardation of these children and their intelligence, hearing, vision, emotional stability, or sensory experience?" Facts produced by intelligence test scores caused her to dismiss low intelligence as an explanation, and other test scores caused her to dismiss other explanations. She eventually crystallized the following hypothesis, which seemed to agree with all the facts in the case and to offer the most logical explanation of the problem: Twelve third-grade pupils were retarded from one year seven months to two years six months in reading because they lack varied sensory experiences to help them associate printed symbols with words and ideas. To test this hypothesis, Miss White could have exposed six of the retarded readers to varied sensory experiences for six months and then could have administered a reading test to all twelve retarded readers to ascertain whether exposure to sensory experiences was related to reading retardation as her hypothesis had predicted.

TESTING HYPOTHESES

After a hypothesis is evaluated critically for logical consistency and completeness, it remains a mere guess—and possesses little explanatory value—until empirically verifiable evidence is produced to support it. Thus, after formulating a hypothesis, an investigator must (1) deduce its consequences (Dewey's step 4), (2) select or develop tests that will determine through experiments or sense observations whether these consequences actually occur, and (3) carry out these tests (Dewey's step 5), thereby collecting facts that will either support or not support the hypothesis.

Deducing the Consequences

Some hypotheses may be tested directly, but many scientific explanations must be tested indirectly. If one guesses that a noise is caused by rain beating on the roof, one looks outdoors and confirms or rejects this hypothesis by direct observation. If one guesses that Mr. Jones shot Sally Lake, that the world is round rather than flat, or that the professor applying for a job is an impostor, one cannot directly observe these facts or conditions, but one may test them indirectly. After studying the hypotheses to see what they logically imply, one may deduce consequences that must occur if these hypotheses are true. One may reason: If these hypotheses are true, then certain consequences are observable and may be tested directly. In reading research reports, you will find that investigators do not always state the hypothesis in an "if-then" form, but this relationship is understood if not made explicit.

Perhaps a fictitious example will clarify the process of deducing the consequences. Suppose Dean Henry is suspicious of the college training and degree records that Professor Silnatch has included in his application for a job. Since the dean cannot tell whether the man is an impostor merely by looking at him or his application, he proposes the following hypothesis and deduces the consequences that it logically implies:

If job applicant, Professor Stanley Silnatch, received a doctorate from Jones University in 1965,

then (1) Jones University will have a record of awarding him the degree;

then (2) his doctoral project will be listed in *Doctoral Dissertations Accepted by American Universities*;

then (3) he will recall the names of the members of his doctoral dissertation committee;

then (4) his signature will be similar to the one on college records;

then (5) college health records and photographs of student Stanley Silnatch will reveal a number of facts that are characteristic of the job applicant (general height, bone structure, color of eyes, and physical handicaps).

These five consequences may be tested directly. If Dean Henry finds empirically verifiable evidence that agrees or disagrees with these consequences, he indirectly confirms or disconfirms the hypothesis. Thus the deduced consequences of a hypothesis rather than the hypothesis itself are tested in a scientific investigation.

Deducing consequences from hypotheses that can be empirically verified cannot be a hurried or casual procedure. In major research projects the indirect method of attacking problems may lead through extremely intricate and remote channels of reasoning. In any investigation one must check one's reasoning to make certain that the consequences are logically implied by the hypothesis, for there is no point in testing them if they are not. The consequences must also be expressed in clear, precise terms, for testing ambiguously stated ones is a difficult if not an impossible task.

In an investigation researchers may examine facts, formulate a hypothesis or theory that explains a phenomenon, and then test it. Quite commonly, however, they devote their efforts to the deductive elaboration of an existing theory. When a significant theory is proposed, imaginative and disciplined intellectual activity may go on for years with a number of scientists deducing and testing various consequences. Thus, in many investigations researchers do not originate the theory, but rather structure hypothetical statements that are designed to test a specific aspect of a theory.[1] They reason deductively, "If this theory is true, then these consequences [or these facts or this evidence] should be observable." Through the tests they make, they obtain evidence that either strengthens the confirmation of the theory or contradicts it (also see Appendixes C and E). Thus, the thrust of some researchers' efforts is not from fact, to theory, to fact, but rather from theory, to fact, to theory.

Selecting Test Procedures

Having determined what consequences are logically implied by the hypothesis, the researcher next devises a factual situation that will test them. A study by Durkheim (35) may give you an insight into this three-step procedure. (1) He proposed the hypothesis that although the progressive division of labor increases material wealth, it decreases group cohesiveness and hence personal happiness. (2) If this hypothesis were correct, he deduced that the following consequences should be observable: Suicide rates would be (a) higher in nations with greater material wealth, (b) higher in city than in farming areas, (c) higher in some types of occupations than in other types, and (d) higher among religious groups requiring little cohesiveness than in those requiring more cohesiveness. (3) To test whether these deduced consequences were observable, he examined international records on suicides.

Selecting and perfecting suitable testing procedures requires the most careful consideration. A foolish error made when structuring a questionnaire, selecting subjects, controlling experimental conditions, or checking the authenticity of a document may prove to be a fatal flaw in an investigation. If tests do not measure precisely what one wishes to measure, they are of no value. A 100-yard dash, for example, is an invalid test of the maximum running speed of six-year-old children, for it tests endurance rather than speed of youngsters of that age. Nor does an English version of an intelligence test ascertain the IQ of children with little or no command of the language. Before any tests are conducted in an investigation, a rigorous evaluation is made to

---

[1]When reading research literature, you may become confused because some workers refer to the proposed solutions to problems as "theories" and to the deduced consequences of a theory as "hypotheses." Even the present author sometimes resorts to the shorthand statement "One tests the hypothesis," rather than uses the longer but more accurate statement "One tests the deduced consequences of the hypothesis." Whatever language may be used to explain the process, the important thing to keep in mind is that the researcher presents an explanation for certain phenomena, deduces the consequences that must occur if that explanation is accurate, and then conducts tests to determine whether these conditions or events do occur.

ascertain whether they will produce valid, reliable, objective, and suitable data for testing the particular deduced consequences they are supposed to check and whether the selected subjects or data sources are representative of the population that the deduced consequences are supposed to check. In evaluating the testing procedures one may ask: "Will I collect relevant, sufficiently refined, and enough data to test the deduced consequences of each hypothesis? Will the form in which I collect the data enable me to use the statistical procedures needed to answer the questions raised by my problem? Will I be able to make the kinds of generalizations I wish to make with the statistical techniques I intend to use?"

Confirming the Hypothesis

At this point, let us review the problem-solving process. After analyzing a felt difficulty and drafting a specific problem statement, a hypothesis—a proposed solution for the problem—is formulated; subsequently, logical consequences are deduced that should be observable if the hypothesis is to be confirmed. This hypothetical-deductive argument can be stated in an "if-then" form: If hypothesis H_1 is accurate, then the consequences $C_1, C_2, C_3, \ldots, C_n$, should be observable. To test whether these previously unexamined phenomena actually occur in the way H_1 predicts, one conducts appropriate empirical tests. On the basis of the factual evidence obtained from the tests, one draws a conclusion—an inductive inference—about whether the hypothesis is confirmed or disconfirmed (see Figure 8.1).

The success of an investigation rests not only on the problem, hypothesis, deduced observable predictions, tests, evidence, and conclusions, but also on the cogency of the logic with which these elements are connected. The hypothesis must provide a logical expla-

FIGURE 8.1

Representation of the procedure for testing a hypothesis.

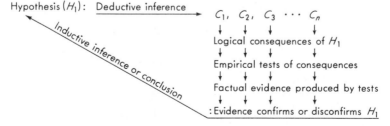

nation for the specific problem that is raised. The deduced consequences must be logically implied by the hypothesis, the test situation must adequately represent the essential factors expressed in the consequence, and the conclusions must be based on the factual evidence collected in the empirical tests.

REQUIREMENTS FOR CONFIRMATION   A hypothesis is not confirmed unless the test results produce evidence that agrees with the consequences implied by the hypothesis. When Dean Henry endeavored to confirm whether the job applicant, Prof. Stanley Silnatch, had been awarded a doctorate degree by Jones University in 1965, he found considerable evidence to support some deduced consequences. The published list of doctoral dissertations indicated that Stanley Silnatch had produced a study in 1965. The Jones University records revealed that in 1965 a doctorate had been awarded to Stanley Silnatch. Dean Henry was almost convinced that his suspicions were unjustified, when he noticed that the student's signature on college records was quite different from the job applicant's signature. This observation puzzled him. When checking the 1965 college health records and photographs, he discovered that Mr. Stanley Silnatch was over 6 feet tall, had blue eyes, and had lost three fingers on his left hand. Obviously the job applicant was an impostor, for he was 5$^{1}/_{2}$ feet tall, had brown eyes, and possessed all his fingers. Dean Henry had discovered evidence that contradicted a deduced consequence; hence, he had definitely rejected his hypothesis. The job applicant was merely masquerading as one of his former classmates who had been an outstanding student at Jones University.

To confirm a hypothesis, the researcher must provide factual evidence that agrees with every consequence logically implied by it. If Dean Henry had claimed that the hypothesis was confirmed merely because a number of facts fitted the theory perfectly, he would have been in error. Whenever *any evidence* produced by a test flatly contradicts one or more consequences and no errors have been made in test procedures, the researcher must abandon or modify his original hypothesis. No matter how much evidence is obtained to support a hypothesis, a single item of contradictory evidence can disprove it.

STRENGTH OF CONFIRMATION   A scientist confirms rather than proves or verifies a hypothesis. The term "prove" carries the connotation of finality and absolute certainty. The term "verify" often appears in research literature, but the word literally means "to prove true," which is not an exact description of what the testing process does. Hypotheses are never *proved* by producing factual evidence that is in harmony with the consequences; they are established only as *possessing a degree of probability.*

You may make the mistake of assuming that you have found the real cause of some phenomenon because you have found empirical evidence that supports one or more consequences of your hypothesis. You may argue as follows:

Major premise

If H_1 is true, then C_1, C_2, C_3 ... will follow.
  (antecedent)   (consequent)

Minor premise

But C_1, C_2, C_3 do follow.
  (empirical evidence affirms the consequent)

Conclusion

Therefore, hypothesis H_1 is true.
  (inferred fact)

This argument does not confirm conclusively that H_1 is true, for it involves the "fallacy of affirming the consequent."

Formal logic rules that if a minor premise affirms the consequent, as it does in this instance, the hypothetical argument is not valid. You may show that C_1, C_2, C_3, supports H_1 or confirms it to some extent, but other hypotheses may also account for these consequences. Moreover, when a wider range of phenomena is examined, some fact related to the problem may turn up that can be explained by a rival hypothesis and not by this hypothesis. You may have argued that low intelligence causes juvenile delinquency, and you may have found empirical evidence that showed that a disproportionate number of children with criminal records obtain low intelligence test scores. But have you proved that low intelligence causes juvenile delinquency? Perhaps low intelligence is associated with juvenile delinquency, but many other factors may also be associated with it. Perhaps low intelligence is merely associated with heredity, early environment, or some other factor or combination of factors which may be the true cause of juvenile delinquency. Perhaps low intelligence is as frequent among law-abiding youths as among juvenile delinquents who come from the same environment.

After conducting an investigation, the conclusion—inductive inference—that is drawn from the empirical evidence may support the hypothesis. The hypothesis, however, is not accepted as being logically fully verified. From the standpoint of formal logic, you cannot prove that exceptions to your hypothesis will never occur. An investigator does not establish an everlasting truth. You cannot state with "absolute certainty" that your hypothesis is the only hypothesis that can explain the phenomenon, but you try to come as close to this goal as possible. The affirmation of one consequence cannot prove a hypothesis is true. The affirmation of several similar consequences makes a hypothesis somewhat more credible. The wider the range of consequences a hypothesis can account for, the fewer is the number of rival hypotheses that can account for the same consequences. Obtaining experimental evidence in a number of widely scattered areas cannot prove that a hypothesis is true either, but testing consequences that embrace many different kinds of implications builds a web of evidence that makes the hypothesis "more probably true."

If little evidence is produced to substantiate the consequences of H_1, the hypothesis is poorly or weakly confirmed. If considerable factual evidence is produced to support several deduced consequences of H_1, the degree of probability that the hypothesis offers a satisfactory explanation approaches greater certainty. But remember, a well-confirmed hypothesis is held only tentatively and provisionally. If the predictions that are made on the basis of H_1 turn out to be correct when empirical evidence is examined, then H_1 has "stood up to trial," but it remains on probation and is subject to modification or abandonment whenever new factual evidence demands it. Empirical support merely confirms, strengthens, or substantiates the hypothesis; it does not *prove* something is absolutely true for all time.

REFORMULATION OR ABANDONMENT OF A HYPOTHESIS Inexperienced research workers often have such an intense desire to confirm their hypothesis that they disregard evidence that will disconfirm it. After formulating the hypothesis "All geniuses exhibit antisocial behavior," they may search eagerly for data concerning drunkenness, dope addiction, riotous living, and immorality among great painters, writers, scientists, and musicians, but they may fail to investigate the lives of Einstein, Pasteur, and other "well-behaved geniuses." Incandescent infatuation with their hypothesis may blind them to its faults and cause them to ignore evidence that may explode it.

Parting with a pet hypothesis is a painful experience for a person who is intellectually impoverished. An imaginative investigator, who can originate a number of alternative solutions, is less reluctant to abandon an untenable hypothesis. The wastebasket of a successful scientist is usually filled with rejected ideas. Einstein observed that ninety-nine out of a hundred of his conclusions were false. Before formulating a fruitful hypothesis, an experienced investigator may explore and discard dozens of hopeless hunches. Darwin once declared that he could not remember ever formulating a hypothesis that he did not modify greatly or abandon. Hypotheses are mere guesses, and the vast majority of them prove to be wrong. Most hypotheses go quickly to their graves, some experience a short life, and only a select few are handed down from generation to generation.

Investigators have no alternative but to abandon or to revise a disconfirmed hypothesis, but they do not abandon a hypothesis merely because finding supporting evidence is difficult. Some scientists have conducted hundreds of tests and endured years of frustration before they were able to produce evidence confirming their hypothesis. Research workers must be capable of judging when they have no choice but to reject a hypothesis and when they should persevere with it. If the tools or techniques needed to obtain confirming evidence have not been devised, they may have to set aside the investigation. If the conditions required to test the hypothesis do not exist, they may have to wait until such conditions do exist. One of the consequences of the theory of relativity could not be tested, for example, until a total eclipse of the sun occurred.

TYPES OF CONFIRMATION   The social sciences encompass many specific subject fields with a wide variety of problems in each area. Each social science problem is distinctive, but most of them fall into two broad categories: (1) problems of fact and (2) problems of value. Each type of problem raises a different kind of question. Many scholars believe that the scientific method cannot deal with problems of value; others argue that it can (77, 101). Some of the difficulties involved can best be understood by reviewing the nature of the problems of fact and value.

1 Problems of fact.   Problems of fact propose questions that ask: What is the actual state of affairs in a given society? These problems raise questions which require the determination of facts. An educator, for example, might propose that the ratio of left-handed to right-handed children who stutter is 3 to 1. To confirm this hypothesis, the educator must find factual evidence in the existing culture that corresponds exactly with it. For the solution of his factual problem, he resorts to the scientific method of inquiry.

2 Problems of value.   Problems of value raise questions that ask: What kind of society should we aim to achieve? Normative social theories answer these problems by defining the ideal society. Different people have different concepts of the social norms at which they aim. The Russians and Americans, for example, do not envisage the same form of ideal social organization. Problems of value differ sharply from problems of fact, for they question what the ideal society ought to be like, not what the facts of the situation are in any given culture. The democratic or Christian ideal, for example, is not realized completely in practice, but this lack of conformity with the theory does not make the theory invalid. Yet this is the conclusion an investigator would have to draw if he confirmed *normative* social theories and *factual* social theories by the same method.

To be valid, a factual theory must be absolutely in accord with the facts in a given society. Since a normative social theory is formulated to change the status of society rather than to coincide completely with the existing facts, an investigator cannot solve problems of value by the same method as problems of fact. Different types of problems require somewhat different methods of solution.

Some scholars argue that some value as well as fact problems may be attacked by the scientific method, but the method of confirmation in the two types of problems differs. To verify factual theories, an investigator checks his theory against the *conditions in society*, and if they agree completely, his theory is confirmed. According to Northrup, an investigator may verify a normative social theory not by checking it against the *facts in society*, now or in the future, but by checking it with the *facts of nature*. For example, American educators believe that a "good" educational system is one that provides for individual differences. This theory, if checked against the facts of society, will not be verified empirically, for many schools do not provide for individual differences. But this theory will be confirmed when checked against the facts of nature, for empirical evidence is available to verify that children differ in capacities.

To solve problems of value, one does not stand aloof from science and the scientific method. Scientific data may help investigators determine which hypotheses regarding *what is* and *what is not* "good" for children are based on observable evidence. The various sciences may supply facts about the likely outcome of courses of action that are based on different value judgments. The most scientifically correct and adequate normative social theory, in the opinion of some scholars, is the one that can care for the widest range of empirically verified facts concerning human beings and nature.

Examples of Testing Hypotheses

Many steps are involved in the process of solving a problem. Perhaps a brief review of two investigations will refocus your attention on the totality of the hypothetical-deductive argument.

GALILEO'S EXPERIMENT   You will recall that Galileo constructed three hypotheses that might offer satisfactory explanations for motion, the phenomenon that he was trying to understand. To determine whether any one of them could be confirmed, he had to deduce and test the consequences of each hypothesis.

Galileo as well as others before him gave consideration to the relationship of weight and the motion or velocity of falling bodies. Thus, he first examined this ancient hypothesis: The velocity with which bodies fall is proportional to the weight of the body. From this hypothesis he could deduce the following consequence: If this hypothesis is true, then when bodies of different weights are dropped simultaneously from the same height, they will reach the earth at different times. Common sense would seem to indicate that the heavier objects would hit the ground before the lighter ones. But Galileo was not willing to accept this explanation merely because it was logical; he insisted upon putting it to an empirical test. In the Tower of Pisa experiment (or if this tale is mythical, some similar test), he discovered that except for differences caused by the resistance of air, objects of different weights fall at the same speed (and in a vacuum they would hit the ground at the same time). Hence, Galileo had disconfirmed the hypothesis that the velocity with which a body falls depends on the weight.

Galileo next examined his second hypothesis: Velocity is proportional to the distance through which the body travels. But he rejected this hypothesis, because he thought he had demonstrated mathematically that one of its consequences presented an impossibility. Thus, he turned to consider his third hypothesis: Velocity is proportional to the length of time during which the body falls. In other words, he proposed that the acceleration, or change in velocity during any unit interval of time, is constant.

Galileo's third hypothesis could not be tested directly. But Galileo deduced that if this hypothesis were true, the distance covered by free-falling bodies would be proportional to the square of the time of their fall. Thus, if a body fell one unit of time and covered one unit of distance, in two units of time it would travel four units of distance, and in three units of time it would cover nine units of distance. If such evidence could be found, it would strengthen his hypothesis that the acceleration of falling bodies is constant.

To obtain empirical evidence that would confirm or disconfirm his hypothesis, Galileo set up an experiment. He placed a metal ball on an inclined plane which allowed the ball to move down freely but relatively slowly, and he observed how many units of time the ball consumed in covering different units of distance. As a result of this experiment, he was able to present empirical evidence that the relation between distance and time is in accord with his hypothesis. Therefore, Galileo's third hypothesis possessed empirical support and provided the basis for a new understanding of motion.

Having acquired a better understanding of motion, Galileo was able to construct a more satisfactory definition of force. According to Galileo's definition, force is not that which produces motion or velocity as Aristotle had described it, but that which produces a change of velocity—acceleration of movement. Thus an object, such as a projectile, experiences continuous acceleration as long as it is being acted upon by force. According to Aristotle's definition, it does not stop moving when the explosion ends; it merely ceases to change velocity. It would continue to move with a constant velocity if the force of gravitation did not draw it toward the earth. By solving the problem that had puzzled him, Galileo was able to present the world with a new, all-embracing definition of force that applied to any motion whatever.

EDUCATIONAL INVESTIGATION If you examine educational research studies, some of the discussion in the reports may be unintelligible to you at the present time. But in many instances, such as in the Balows' study which appears in Appendix G, you can follow the general nature of the arguments that are presented.

The Balows were concerned with the following problem: Is there a significant relationship between lateral dominance and reading achievement in the second grade? Workers in reading clinics had suggested that there might be a relationship between reading disability and left-eye dominance, crossed dominance (opposite eye-hand preference), mixed dominance (mixed-hand preference), and delayed establishment of consistent hand dominance. Although the investigators do not present a formal statement of their hypothetical-deductive argument, they probably reasoned as follows:

If the above deviations from what is accepted as normal ocular and manual dominance are related to reading achievement in the second grade,

then, when second-grade children are classified according to normal, crossed, and mixed dominance, the crossed-dominance and mixed-dominance groups will score significantly below the other group in reading achievement;

then, when second-grade children are classified in terms of strength and direction of hand dominance, the mixed-hand-dominance group will score significantly below the other groups in reading achievement;

then, when second-grade children are classified according to strength and direction of eye dominance, the left-eyed group will score significantly below the other groups in reading achievement;

then, when second-grade children are classified according to time of establishing hand dominance, the group that is late in establishing hand dominance will score significantly below the other groups.

After collecting the empirical evidence that was required to test each deduced consequence and applying appropriate statistical procedures to these data, the investigators examined their findings. Since their data did not conform to the consequences implied by their hypothesis, they concluded that their *research hypothesis* was rejected. They advised other research workers that "lateral dominance does not seem to be a fruitful area for seeking out determiners of individual differences in reading achievement" (8:143).

RESEARCH HYPOTHESIS AND NULL HYPOTHESIS   The type of hypothesis that we have been discussing is often referred to as the *research hypothesis* (H_1), or the *empirical, problem,* or *substantive hypothesis.* The researcher may transform the research hypothesis into a *statistical,* or *null, hypothesis* (H_0). This is done so that tests can be employed that will determine whether the findings are statistically significant or can be attributed to the fact that, by chance, the randomly selected sample of subjects is not representative of the population. Suppose a relation is noted in an investigation between X, a new teaching method, and Y, an improvement in a given skill. Perhaps, by chance, the fifty subjects in the sample that participated in the study were more highly motivated than other members of the population from which they were drawn and this variable rather than the teaching method accounts for their improvement in the skill. Presenting detailed information at this time concerning statistical tools that enable you to determine whether the findings of a study could be expected to occur by chance for a sample of a given size seems to be a premature and imprudent procedure, for many considerations are involved. But the brief discussion that follows will give you some concept of the difference between a research hypothesis and a null hypothesis.

The research hypothesis usually states a relationship between two or more variables that the experimenter predicts will emerge. The null hypothesis (statistical test of no difference) states that no relationship exists between the variables concerned and that any observed relation is only a function of chance.

Research hypothesis
X is related to Y.
Left-eyed children will score significantly below other children in reading achievement.

Null hypothesis
No relationship exists between X and Y.
There is no difference in the reading achievement between left-eyed children and other children.

The null hypothesis does not necessarily reflect the researcher's expectations concerning the outcome of the experiment—indeed, it is usually diametrically opposed to the research hypothesis—but the null hypothesis form is used because it is more suitable for the application of statistical tests. The null hypothesis is usually formulated with the expectation that it will be rejected. If it is rejected, the research hypothesis is accepted. A further discussion of the null hypothesis and a discussion of statistical tests of significance will be presented on pages 509 and 515.

EVALUATING HYPOTHESES

Some hypotheses are more satisfactory than others. But how do you determine whether a hypothesis is worthy of serious consideration? When two hypotheses seem to explain the same facts, how do you decide which is the more desirable? The following criteria may help you make judgments.

Plausibility of Explanation

One of the first questions that a researcher asks is: Does this hypothesis present a relevant and logical possibility? Several criteria are involved in establishing the plausibility of explanations. If two variables are not associated, for example, one cannot cause the other. Blurred vision is a plausible explanation for reading retardation; color of eyes is not. An explanation that *A* causes *B* is not plausible unless you can establish that *A* occurs before or at least simultaneously with *B*. A historian may hypothesize that a certain man was present at a meeting in Paris in 1700 and offer considerable supporting evidence. This hypothesis would be declared implausible, however, if another investigator found well-confirmed evidence that the man was in a distant city the day before and no available means of transportation would have enabled him to travel to Paris in twenty-four hours.

Testability of Explanation

If a hypothesis presents a relevant and logical explanation of phenomena but the variables cannot be defined operationally and the predicted relations among them cannot be tested empirically, it does not constitute a scientific hypothesis. Unless a hypothesis implies consequences that can be checked by observational tests at the present time or in the foreseeable future, it can never pass from the status of a guess to that of a confirmed fact. Some of Freud's theories, for example, are internally consistent, logical arguments, but putting logical propositions to a scientific test that contain constructs, such as "ego strength," "libidinal energy," "repression," or "unconscious" presents a problem. Researchers have not been able to devise and agree on procedures for observing and measuring such variables. Some problems that are of the greatest interest to educators also cannot be attacked, because the variables involved are difficult to define operationally; hence, the hypotheses are not testable.

No hypothesis can be tested if it is embedded with terms that express value judgments, such as "should," "good," and "poor." The problem statement "Consumer education should be a part of the high school curriculum," for example, raises a question of value rather than presents a hypothesis that can be checked by observing conditions that exist in schools. No hypothesis can be tested if the directions for identifying and measuring indicants of the variables are ambiguous. The problem statement "Good pupils' failure to read is due to insufficient practice in the use of phonics," for example, includes vague terms that present problems. Whom, what, and how much would you observe to test this hypothesis? What constitutes "good pupils," "failure," and "insufficient"? The following hypothesis is more precise: "Water temperature does not affect the performance of or the physiological stress (heartbeat and body temperature) on University of California varsity swimmers." This hypothesis provides a satisfactory basis for research because the subjects to be measured are clearly identified, the relationship between the variable water temperature and the other variables (performance, heartbeat, and body temperature) is clearly predicted, and unambiguous instructions about how to measure them (operational definitions) can be given.

Some promising hypotheses are not testable because the evidence or instruments needed to obtain confirming evidence is not available. In many cross-cultural or historical studies, hypotheses cannot be tested because sufficient evidence cannot be located to check the consequences that are deduced from them. Until the development of computers, some hypotheses about complex relationships among the phenomena were not testable because the computations would have required endless effort. No hypothesis can be tested until valid tests can be constructed to measure the variables it predicts are related.

Adequacy of Scope

The most useful hypotheses or theories explain all the facts that are relevant to the phenomena being explained and contradict none of them. In the early stages of development in any field, the hypotheses usually explain some factors but lack the power to explain all factors. With the passage of time, networks of hypotheses evolve and a partially completed patchwork quilt of connected, isolated, complimentary, and conflicting theories may be constructed. Eventually someone may integrate some of these theories or borrow concepts from two or three of them to construct theories that are more extensive in scope.

The scholars who have sought to explain learning, for example, have constructed a number of theories. Each one accounts for some phenomena of learning but ignores factors that other hypotheses explain. The theories form a continuum extending from the stimulus-response theories to cognitive theories, with various combinations of them in the intermediary range that aim at synthesis. The stimulus-response theories are concerned with drill, conditioning, gradual learning by trial and error, reinforcement, emphasis on parts and perceptual elements. The cognitive theories are concerned with flexible patterns adapted to the total situation, problem-solving through insight, emphasis on relation-patterns, and wholes. You will note that these divergent theories differ with respect to their orientation, and there is no substantive overlap between the respective theories. The findings researchers derive from one of the theories would be cumulative, but the findings derived from different theories would have little or no ostensible relevance to each other. The results would be difficult, if not impossible, to combine and reconcile.

In the broader field of child development, several rather comprehensive theories have been developed: the field learning theory of Lewin; the cognitive development theory of Piaget; the psychoanalytical personality development and functioning theory of Freud; the stimulus-response and social-learning theories of Watson, Hull, Miller, Skinner, Dollard, Sears, Bandura, and Walters; the organismic development theory of Werner, and the sociologists' view of child development as one aspect of the family functioning as a social system of Parsons and Bales. The adequacy of all these theories has been questioned. Scholars have criticized the stimulus-and-response theories as being too passive, mechanistic, atomistic, and molecular, and Freud's and Piaget's theories as being too mentalistic and speculative. Psychoanalysts have argued that other theories are superficial and oversimplified and ignore the deeper and more important problems of personality functioning. On the other hand, theorists from different schools of thought have borrowed concepts and have gained useful insights from one another; they have noted some parallels in their theories and have made attempts to integrate some theories.

For the most part the child development theories are complementary rather than contradictory; they rarely make different predictions in the same situation. Each theorist focuses on a given aspect of child behavior to the exclusion of aspects that other theorists regard as fundamental. Although couched in different language, some of the same psychological mechanisms and hypotheses are found in different theories. Baldwin (7) suggests that an eclectic yet integrated theory of child development can be constructed that capitalizes on the hypotheses and concepts in the existing theories, and he makes several concrete recommendations to include in a general integrative theory.

The broader the scope of a theory, the more valuable it is. The more consequences that a hypothesis yields, the greater is its fruitfulness. If H_1 (hypothesis one) explains A and B, H_2 explains A, B, and C, and H_3 explains A, B, C, and D, H_3 is preferable. A hypothesis is of greater value if it establishes a generalization that can be applied in many areas of education or in many fields. As science advances, investigators strive to devise more and more comprehensive concepts to account for phenomena that were previously explained by different, rival, or unrelated theories. In the unified field theory, for example, Einstein attempted to bring gravitation, light, and electricity—all of them manifestations of energy—into one grand formula.

The most satisfactory hypotheses not only explain all the known facts that gave rise to the original problems but also enable scientists to make predictions about as yet unobserved events and relationships. If H_3 explains A, B, C, and D, and also predicts successfully E, F, and G—previously undiscovered phenomena—it will be greatly strengthened. The heliocentric theory, for example, acquired added weight because it enabled scientists to predict the existence of Neptune long before they sighted the planet through a telescope. Whenever predictions projected from a hypothesis are confirmed, the hypothesis gains tremendously in stature.

Usefulness of False Hypotheses

Hypotheses need not be the correct answers to problems to be useful. In almost every inquiry a scholar constructs several hypotheses and hopes that one will provide a satisfactory solution to the problem. By eliminating the false hypotheses one by one, the investigator keeps narrowing the field in which the answer must lie. If two doctors, for example, try to determine why students became ill after a school picnic, they may theorize that the potato salad, cream pie, chicken, or drinking water made them ill. If their tests indicate that the first three items were not responsible, they are on their way to finding that the water was the causative agent. Researchers make a contribution to science even though none of their hypotheses solve a problem. Pointing out lines of inquiry that are unprofitable lightens the task of their successors. The testing of false hypotheses is also of value if it directs the attention of scientists to unsuspected facts or relations that eventually help solve the problem. History is sprinkled with stories of investigators who have stumbled upon clues leading to a successful hypothesis while testing a false one.

Roots in Existing Theories

Science develops by building cumulatively on the existing body of facts and theories. A useful educational hypothesis, therefore, adds something to previously established knowledge by supporting, qualifying, refuting, or enlarging upon existing theories. A hypothesis that is compatible with well-attested theories is in a favorable position to advance science. It does not have to agree with all the established facts but should be consistent with a substantial body of them. Science cannot build sound, well-knit theoretical structures with isolated and conflicting hypotheses. If progress is to be made, new hypotheses must fit into the framework of existing theories and transform them into more perfect explanatory schemes.

Hypotheses that are incompatible with established theories have a low probability of being true; hence, they are regarded with suspicion. Occasionally, however, radical ideas that have little support from what is known about phenomena spark spectacular advances in science. Hypotheses proposed by Newton, Darwin, and Einstein, for example, upset bodies of theory and led to the reorganization of knowledge in their fields. Concepts introduced by Dewey, Thorndike, Köhler, and Lewin revolutionized educational thought. But scientists do not readily relinquish well-established theories. The discoverers of new knowledge rarely discard all older knowledge as they move forward; they usually correct errors in existing theories, extend the coverage of theories, or reconcile conflicting theories. If a new theory explains phenomena previously explained by two or more hypotheses, the new proposal usually receives careful consideration in scientific circles. Hypotheses that overthrow existing theories win support if they eliminate contradictions in the existing ones. Einstein accomplished this feat when he constructed the theory of relativity, which eliminated conflicts in the basic laws of classical mechanics and electrodynamics. In his unified field theory, he attempted to reconcile conflicts in the relativity and quantum theories. Thus even the more revolutionary theories are not completely disassociated from the existing body of knowledge.

Suitability for Intended Purpose

Several hypotheses may explain the same phenomenon, and each may be acceptable. If fifty children lose their lives in a school fire, an architect, pathologist, psychologist, and fire chief may offer different but not necessarily mutually exclusive explanations of the event. Each hypothesis will reflect the past experience, special branch of knowledge, and particular frame of reference of its creator. Obviously, an explanation for the loss of life that satisfies the fire chief will not be the same as that which satisfies the pathologist. But each hypothesis that offers a satisfactory explanation of what it intends to explain is useful for that purpose. The various explanations cannot contradict each other, of course, and they may be mutually supportive. But each hypothesis serves a particular purpose and must be adequate for the purpose it claims to serve.

Simplicity of Explanation

If two hypotheses are capable of explaining the same facts, the simpler one is the better. Simplicity in this instance does not imply ease of comprehension or a low level of significance. Rather, it means that the hypothesis explains the phenomena with the least complex theoretical structure. The theory of relativity, for example, is not easy to comprehend, but it is admired and accepted in part because of its logical compactness. The classic example of simplicity is in the field of astronomy. Both the heliocentric theory and the geocentric theory explain the movements of the sun, moon, and planets. Both theories introduce epicycles to account for the positions of heavenly bodies, but the heliocentric theory introduces fewer epicycles. Because the heliocentric theory offers a less elaborate and less complex explanation, it is more satisfactory. The hypothesis that accounts for all the facts with the fewest independent or special assumptions and complexities is always preferable.

Levels of Explanation

Perhaps the value of hypotheses can best be comprehended by tracing their relationship to facts, theories, and laws. Through inductive and deductive methods of searching for truth, scientists build gradually a hierarchy of knowledge consisting of (1) hypotheses, (2) theories, and (3) laws. Since not everyone employs the same language when referring to these levels of knowledge, students often become confused. In the research literature, for example, the terms "law" and "theory" and the terms "theory" and "hypothesis" are sometimes used interchangeably, and theorizing may refer to the formulation of hypotheses, theories, or laws. The following discussion will distinguish among these levels of knowledge by using the more commonly accepted terminology.

HYPOTHESES AND FACTS   A hypothesis is the first step beyond random suggestions in the direction of scientific truth. In the hierarchy of scientific knowledge, it is the lowest on the scale. This temporary working principle requires testing to determine its worth. If empirical evidence can be found to support the hypothesis, it gains the status of a fact. It retains this status thereafter unless evidence is discovered later to discredit it. Whether or not a hypothesis possesses the status of a fact depends upon the supporting evidence it can secure and hold.

HYPOTHESES AND THEORIES   A theory may contain several logically interrelated hypotheses, and the term "postulate" may be used as a synonym for hypothesis. Hypotheses and theories are alike in that they are both conceptual in nature and in that both seek to explain and to predict phenomena. A theory usually offers a more general or higher-level explanation than a hypothesis. One hypothesis may predict that there is a relationship between *A* and *B*, and other hypotheses may predict that there is a relationship between *C* and *B*, *D* and *B*, and *E* and *B*. A theory may present an underlying principle that will explain or account for all these phenomena. After reading the literature relating to phenomenon *B*, a research worker may ask the question: What common thread runs through these four hypotheses? The researcher may conclude that *X* is present in each instance, and hence is the key factor that is responsible for the occurrence of *B*. Because a theory usually presents a comprehensive conceptual scheme that may involve several related hypotheses and explains diverse phenomena, considerable empirical evidence is needed to support it. This mass of evidence makes the probability of the certainty of a theory greater than that of an isolated, weakly confirmed hypothesis. But no matter how wide a variety of confirming data is obtained, the theory is not established as an absolute truth.

HYPOTHESES AND LAWS   Some hypotheses receive sufficient confirmation to become or lead to the formulation of theories; some lead to the establishment of laws. Laws usually utilize highly abstract concepts, for they offer the most comprehensive type of explanations. A law may be applied to a great number and wide variety of phenomena; a law may explain phenomena that have been explained previously by two or three theories. Because laws are developed and verified by a long, painstaking process, during which they receive extensive empirical confirmation in many areas, they represent the highest level of scientific certainty and are accepted with little question. A law retains its lofty scientific status, however, only as long as it continues to explain every instance which it claims to explain. If new evidence arises that does not conform to its tenets, the law is either reconstructed to conform to the new evidence or abandoned, depending on the nature of the data that are discovered.

IMPORTANCE OF HYPOTHESES

Hypotheses are indispensable research tools, for they build a bridge between the problem and the location of empirical evidence that may solve the problem. A hypothesis provides the map that guides and expedites the exploration of the phenomena under consideration.

Pinpointing of Problems by Hypotheses

Without a hypothesis to guide you, you may waste time making a superficial or generalized attack on a problem. To chisel out a hypothesis, you must examine thoroughly the factual and conceptual elements that appear to be related to a problem, trace their relationships, and isolate and combine the relevant information into an all-encompassing statement. The process of formulating a hypothesis, deducing its consequences, and defining the terms employed clarifies the issues involved in the inquiry and crystallizes the problem for investigation.

Using Hypotheses to Determine the Relevancy of Facts

Scientific knowledge rests not on *the* facts, but on *selected* facts. The selection of facts is a matter of crucial concern in an investigation. Aimlessly collecting a mass of data on a given subject is futile, for the infinity of possibilities prohibits any rational manipulation of them. The strategic facts needed to solve a problem do not automatically label themselves as relevant to it. A hypothesis helps you ascertain what facts to collect and enables you to decide how many facts are required to test its consequences adequately. Without a hypothesis you drift into an unfocused trial-and-error inquiry in which you may become hopelessly confused by a welter of irrelevant facts and may never stumble upon a successful problem solution. A hypothesis directs your efforts into productive channels.

Research Design Indicated by Hypotheses

The hypothesis indicates not only what to look for in an investigation but also how to obtain the data. The hypothetical-deductive argument points up the pertinent issues at stake in a manner that rules out many testing methods as irrelevant. A well-constructed hypothesis suggests what research design or mode of attack will meet its specific demands.

A hypothesis may suggest what subjects, tests, or tools are needed, what operations must be performed, what statistical methods are appropriate, and where to locate the events, facts, or circumstances that it predicts are observable.

Explanations Presented by Hypotheses

Modern scientific inquiry goes beyond the amassing of facts or the describing and classifying of them in accordance with their superficial properties. Rather than merely tabulating symptoms of diseases, characteristics of aggressive behavior, or facts about juvenile crime, a serious research worker seeks to determine the underlying pattern of factors that account for the occurrence of phenomena. To leap across gaps in knowledge, one artfully welds known facts and relationships with imaginative constructs to create provisional explanations for phenomena. These hypotheses—constructed from established facts and flights of fancy—provide the investigator with the most efficient instrument for exploring and explaining the unknown.

The Framework for Conclusions Provided by Hypotheses

If you initiate an investigation with a hypothetical-deductive argument, you have a tailor-made framework available for stating your conclusions. You reason: If H_1 is true, then these facts are observable; empirical tests reveal that these facts are or are not observable; therefore, the conclusion can be drawn that H_1 is confirmed or disconfirmed. A hypothesis provides a framework for interpreting the findings in a sharp and meaningful manner. If a prediction is not hypothesized in advance, the facts do not have a chance to confirm or disconfirm anything. In the "scientific game," as Kerlinger points out (61:24), an investigator bets first and then rolls the dice; he does not roll the dice and then bet; and he cannot change his bet after the data are in.

Further Research Stimulated by Hypotheses

A well-conceived hypothesis not only explains a given phenomenon but also may serve as an intellectual lever by which investigators can pry loose more facts to be fitted into other or more inclusive explanations. A hypothesis is never advanced as a final statement; as Max Weber said, "It asks to be outdated and surpassed." It is our passkey to the unknown, leading us from one problem to another, from modest explanations to more adequate conceptual schemes that successively open up exciting new areas on the frontiers of knowledge.

9 STRATEGY OF EXPERIMENTAL RESEARCH

I f science is to achieve its goal of explaining, predicting, and controlling behavior and events, causal connections among the phenomena in a field must be discovered. By constructing a hypothesis you take an initial step on the road toward making such a discovery. You predict that a relationship—a connection—exists between two or more variables. Then you deduce the consequences that must be observed to test whether such a relationship does exist and select a research design or plan for carrying out the test. The objective is to select the most appropriate and rigorous test available that provides a feasible and ethical way of attacking the problem. Researchers prefer to test hypotheses in a controlled experiment whenever this method can be applied. The controls that are established give them greater assurance than can be attained in nonexperimental studies that the findings concerning the predicted relationships are empirically valid.

NATURE OF EXPERIMENTAL RESEARCH

In experimental research studies, investigators carry out each task that is included in their research proposals (see pages 193–194). The key factor that distinguishes experimental studies from other types of research is that the investigators control the manipulation of X, the experimental variable, to ascertain whether X is related to the occurrence of a particular event, condition, or effect. To manipulate X, the researchers decide what groups will be exposed to the presence or absence of X or various levels of X. In historical and descriptive research, investigators observe evidence relating to an event, but they exercise no direct control over its occurrence because the event has already taken place or for other reasons cannot be manipulated. "Experimention, as distinguished from observation, consists in the deliberate and controlled modification of the conditions determining an event, and in the observation and interpretation of the ensuing changes in the event itself" (112:618–619).

Bases of an Experiment

Because a hypothesis predicts that two or more variables are related, there are always at least two main variables under consideration in an experiment: the *independent variable*, X, which is manipulated purposively, and the *dependent variable*, Y, which is the presumed effect or consequent of the manipulation of the independent variable.

(1) Independent variable   and   (2) dependent variable
       Condition X   *is related to*   *condition Y.*

A hypothesis suggests that an antecedent condition (independent variable) is related to the occurrence of another condition, event, or effect (dependent variable). To test a deduced consequence of a hypothesis, you manipulate the independent variable and control all other variables that might affect the dependent variable. Then you observe and measure what happens to the dependent variable, presumably because of the exposure to the independent variable. The dependent variable is the phenomenon that appears, disappears, or changes as you apply, remove, or vary the independent variable. The values of the dependent variable are presumably dependent upon and vary with the manipulation of the independent variable.

Examples of Experiments

An independent variable may be manipulated or varied in at least two ways: by presence or absence or by different levels of presence. Suppose two botanists predicted that

Sunlight	is related to	plant growth.
X, independent variable		Y, dependent variable

To test this hypothesis they obtain ten plants of the same species, cover each with a bell jar, and place five in a shaded place and the other five in the sunlight. Thus they manipulate the amount of sunlight the plants receive. Their experiment will give them direct empirical evidence that exposure to the sun results in plant growth. The botanists may wish to broaden the experiment by setting out several like plants and shading the bell jars so that various intensities of light fall upon them in order to appraise how much various light conditions affect growth.

In education, experimenters may vary some condition in the students' environment and observe its effect on achievement. They may hypothesize that children will learn to spell better if spaced practice is used rather than massed practice. The independent variable that they manipulate to test this hypothesis is the "spacing of practice." The dependent variable that experiences the effect of this manipulation is spelling mastery. During the experiment, the investigators attempt to keep all conditions the same for two groups of children except that one group studies spelling sixty minutes once a week and the other group has a practice session fifteen minutes a day the first four school days of each week. In other words, all conditions are held constant except the experimental variable—spacing of practice—which is manipulated. Consequently, any difference in the spelling mastery of these two groups at the close of the experiment can be attributed presumably to the manipulation of the independent variable—spacing of practice.

CONTROL OF THE EXPERIMENT

The central idea behind experimental research is control. In a rigorously controlled study, the researcher searches for two types of empirical evidence:

1 Experimental group.

If X, then Y.

If X is administered to the experimental group, then Y occurs.

2 Control group.

If no X, then no Y.

If X is not administered to a control group (which is like the experimental group except for the exposure to X), then Y does not occur.

The no-X aspect of an experiment serves as a control which puts the rigor into the scientific enterprise, for X is a necessary condition for the occurrence of Y only if it is demonstrated that Y does not occur without it.

Experimental strategy is not simple; the investigator does not merely manipulate one variable to see what happens to another variable; an experiment requires *controlled observation.* Eliciting and controlling the expression of the independent variable may involve considerable effort. Identifying and controlling other variables that may affect the dependent variable are equally difficult and important tasks. If the teachers who conducted the spelling experiment did not control the selection of the spelling words, the amount of time devoted to study, and the selection of the subjects, one group of students might have had easier words to spell, a longer total time to study, and a greater spelling mastery before the experiment than the other group. Consequently, at the conclusion of the experiment, the teachers would not know whether the manipulation of the independent variable— spacing of practice—or these other variables were responsible for the difference in the spelling mastery of the two groups.

How does the experimenter determine what variables can affect a dependent variable? Obviously, you do not choose your variables at random or casually; rather, you choose them with extreme care, for such choices are among the crucial ones you must make. Previous experience with the phenomena and a careful analysis of the problem will suggest some clues. An examination of experimental studies in the field will inform you about variables that other scholars have found to influence the dependent variable. Investigators who have studied sensorimotor skill, for example, have found little relationship between intelligence test scores and sensorimotor learning, but they have identified several other variables that are related to such skills: strength, speed, accuracy, endurance, agility, body size, reaction time, steadiness, balance, and control of voluntary movements. To discover whether a new teaching method will influence sensorimotor skill, an experimenter must control the variables that are known to be related to sensorimotor skill, so that their effect will not mask the possible effect of the new teaching method.

Purposes of Control

In an experiment, the investigator seeks to control variables for the following purposes: "(1) to isolate the determiners individually and in combinations; (2) to vary them as magnitudes either singly or in combinations; and (3) to describe quantitatively the extent of their expression and their interacting effects, again, either as single determiners or as combinations of determiners" (13:76).

ACHIEVING ISOLATION   To prevent a factor other than the independent variable from affecting the dependent variable, you may remove the unwanted or interfering variable, or you may either keep constant its effect or equalize its presence in the experimental and control groups.

ACHIEVING CHANGES IN MAGNITUDE   An investigator may strive not only to isolate the independent variable but also to ascertain how much effect it contributes. To achieve this objective, you must be able to vary the magnitude of the experimental variable. In a psychological study, for example, you may make observations for each degree of change in the independent variable—for example, intensity, pitch, or timbre of an auditory stimulus—to determine its effect on the dependent variable. In some studies, of course, you cannot seek this level of control because not enough is known about the independent variable to vary it through finely graded steps. When this condition exists, you investigate whether the presence or absence of a certain factor has any effect and leave it for your successors to study the graduations of effect.

ACHIEVING QUANTITATIVE EVALUATION   The ultimate goal of a researcher is to express the magnitude of the variable in quantitative terms. You want to know not merely that one expression of a variable is larger or smaller than another but precisely how much larger or smaller it is. If two variables are functionally related, you want to state not merely that they are positively or negatively related but rather the specific degree of relationship in terms of some numerical value.

Methods of Control

Researchers have devised a number of procedures to control variables. These procedures fall into three broad categories: (1) physical manipulation, (2) selective manipulation, and (3) statistical manipulation.

PHYSICAL MANIPULATION   Various means of physical manipulation may be employed so as (1) to give all subjects the same exposure to the independent variable or (2) to control nonexperimental variables that affect the dependent variable. A *mechanical means* may be devised: an experimenter may soundproof or lightproof a room or blindfold subjects to screen out unwanted stimuli; employ a tachistoscope to present each subject with a specific number of words, numbers, pictures for brief intervals of duration; or construct a maze to study an ability to learn. *Electrical means* may be employed to effect control: an investigator may utilize constant-speed motors for driving various types of apparatus, such as the memory drum which presents materials through a slot in a machine while the drum revolves at selected speeds. *Surgical means* may be used to exercise control: an experimenter may remove glands from the body of an animal or destroy tissue in certain parts of the brain to determine their effects on behavior. *Pharmacological means*, such as changes of diet, drugs, or gland extracts, can also be used to achieve control.

SELECTIVE MANIPULATION   To make certain that the experimental findings do not merely measure the difference in the ways that the experimental and control subjects are treated, a researcher may endeavor to *hold conditions constant* for the two groups. All treatment sessions, for example, may be held in the same room and at the same time of day. The experimenters may be trained to follow the same procedures, to assume the same attitudes, to give instructions in the same way, and to use the same apparatus when working with all subjects.

Sometimes one cannot hold conditions constant in the experiment; consequently, one resorts to techniques of balancing out, randomizing out, or counterbalancing unwanted variables that may affect dependent variable scores. To equalize or balance out the effect of differences in the abilities of teachers or the sensitivity of apparatus, an experimenter may randomly assign half of the experimental subjects and half of the control subjects to each teacher and to each piece of apparatus. To overcome differences in the subjects, an investigator may pair subjects who are equal in respect to a given characteristic that might affect the dependent variable scores, such as intelligence, and randomly assign one member of each pair to the experimental group and the other member to the control group. The differences in subjects, teachers, and apparatus will affect the dependent variable scores, of course, but they will affect the scores of both groups. Consequently, the investigator can assume that the experimental findings are produced by the independent variable and not by these differences in the groups, teachers, or apparatus.

   Some extraneous variables can be controlled through the selection of materials. Suppose that an experimenter wants to study the amount of time required to memorize materials of different lengths, such as a series of nonsense syllables. Something other than length of materials may affect the time required for learning. If the shorter units of materials are more difficult than the longer units, this condition may affect the amount of time required to master them. To control the unwanted factor of difficulty, the experimenter can select short and long learning units that are comparable in difficulty.

STATISTICAL MANIPULATION   When variables are not amenable to physical or selective manipulation, they may be controlled by statistical techniques. Statistical controls can achieve the same precision as other methods when they are employed to evaluate a variable's effect. Statistical techniques are particularly useful in a situation where multiple variables may be functionally related to a particular effect, as is often the case in education. Suppose that A, B, and C act conjointly on dependent variable Y. If only the relationship between A and Y is obtained, the findings are spurious, for A is partly a product of its interaction with B and C. Thus, some means must be found to hold B and C constant to determine the precise relationship between A and Y. Statistical procedures permit one to do this and thus to approximate the relative importance of the contribution of each variable to Y. Two of the most frequently used statistical procedures for effecting an analysis of multiple-variable situations are the method of partial correlation and the method of the analysis of variance, which will be discussed later in the text.

Types of Factors to Be Controlled

Having briefly examined why and how researchers try to achieve control in an experiment, another question naturally arises: What do they try to control? Before examining arguments concerning this important question, you should become familiar with the symbols that are used in this chapter.

1 Independent variable X. The independent variable, which is often called the treatment, experimental, or antecedent variable, is represented by the symbol X. When various treatments are administered and compared, they are labeled X_1, X_2, etc.

2 Dependent variable Y. The dependent variable, which is often called the "criterion" or "predicted variable," is symbolized by the letter Y.

3 Experimenter E. The person who conducts the investigation or manipulates the experimental conditions is represented by the symbol E, and the plural is Es.

4 Subject S. The symbol for the living organism that is studied, the subject or respondent, is S, and the plural is Ss.

5 Control and experimental groups. The group that is exposed to X is the experimental group. The group that is not exposed to X, or is exposed to another X for comparison purposes, is the control group.

6 Pretest T_1 and posttest T_2. If a pretest T_1 is used in an experiment, it is administered before X is applied. A posttest T_2 is a test that subjects take after X is applied.

7 Mean M. To find the mean of a group (the average score), an experimenter adds the members' test scores and divides the sum by the number of members.

8 Population (universe). A population is a *whole*: all the units (subjects, objects, or events) in a group.

9 Sample. A sample consists of units that are selected from a given population. (Before reading further, master these terms and symbols. What do the symbols X, Y, E, S, T, and M represent?)

When you engage in research, selecting an experimental design is one of the most important decisions that you make.[1] If a design is valid, it will probably yield a truthful result and one that can be interpreted as such. There are two types of validity: internal and external.

INTERNAL VALIDITY When checking the internal validity of a design, you ask: Did the independent variable, X, really produce a change in

---

[1]The author acknowledges his great indebtedness to the work of Campbell (16) and Campbell and Stanley (17). Much of the terminology and conceptual base of the following discussion on experimental design comes from these sources.

the dependent variable, Y? To establish internal validity, you must rule out all plausible alternative hypotheses that might account for the findings in your study. Before claiming that X affected Y, you must make certain that some of the following variables have not produced an effect that can be mistaken for the effect of X.

1 Contemporary history.   Sometimes the Ss experience an event—in or out of the experimental setting—besides the exposure to X that may affect their dependent variable scores. If X is television instruction and the dependent variable is heathful practices of the students, the advent of an epidemic in the community rather than X may cause pupils to change some of their health practices. The simultaneous advent of the epidemic would be said to confound X. (An E uses the term "confound" to indicate that an effect can be attributed to the mixing of two or more variables, and the portion due to each cannot be determined.)

2 Maturation processes.   Biological and psychological processes within the Ss may change during the progress of the experiment, which will affect their responses. The Ss may perform better or worse on T_2 not because of the effect of X but because they are older, more fatigued, or less interested than when they took T_1. Their age, fatigue, or interest would confound the interpretation of the effect of X.

3 Pretesting procedures. T_1 may serve as a learning experience that will cause the Ss to alter their responses on T_2 whether or not X is applied.

4 Measuring instruments.   Changes in the testing instruments, human raters, or interviewers can affect the obtained measurements. If T_2 is more difficult than T_1 or if a different person rates Ss on the rating scales, this factor rather than X can cause the difference in the two scores. Slight fluctuations in mechanical measuring instruments can also cause the difference. If the same person judges the performance of two groups in succession or the same groups before and after the application of X, that person's judgment may vary because he or she becomes more experienced and discriminating or more fatigued and careless.

5 Statistical regression.   In some educational research, particularly in remedial education, groups are selected on the basis of their extreme

scores. When this selection procedure is employed, the effect of what is called "statistical regression" may be mistaken for the effect of X. Suppose that students who do exceptionally poorly or exceptionally well on one test are selected to receive an experimental treatment. The mean (average score) of either of these groups will move toward the mean of the parent population on the second test whether or not X is applied. Suppose that the mean of the population is 75. On the first test, the scores of the top ten Ss range from 82 to 99 and the mean score is 90. The scores of these Ss on the retest will fan out—some will be higher and some will be lower—but the mean of the group will inevitably be lower and closer to the population mean. Similarly, the mean for the lowest ten Ss on the second test will almost inevitably be higher and closer to the population mean.

Upon retesting, low initial means go up toward the population mean and high initial means go down and toward the population mean. Why? Regression toward the mean occurs because of random imperfections in measuring instruments. The less-than-perfect capacity of T_1 and T_2 to measure knowledge will cause a variation of Ss' performances. Pupils are likely to obtain somewhat similar scores on the T_1 and T_2, but their scores are likely to vary within a given range because there is a less-than-perfect correlation between the two tests. The more deviant (extreme) pupils' scores are from the population mean, the more they are likely to vary. Random instability in the population may also account for regression toward the mean. Some subjects may obtain low scores on T_1 because they were upset or careless on that day. On the second test they may have better "luck," feel better, or strive harder to bring themselves up to their natural level. As a result, their higher scores will pull up the mean of their group on the second test.

6 Differential selection of subjects.   If the experimental group is exposed to X, a method of teaching spelling, and the control group is not exposed to X, the T_2 results may reflect a pre-X difference in the two groups rather than the effect of X. Perhaps the experimental group could spell better than the control group before X was applied.

7 Experimental mortality.   If a particular type of S drops out of one group after the experiment is under way, this differential loss may affect the findings of the investigation. Suppose that the low-scoring Ss in the experimental group drop out after taking T_1. The remainder of the experimental group may show a greater gain on T_2 than the control

group, not because of its exposure to X but because the low-scoring Ss are missing.

8 Interaction of selection and maturation, selection and history, etc. When the experimental and control groups have the same T_1 scores, some other differences between them, such as intelligence, motivation, etc., rather than X may cause one of them to get higher T_2 scores. Because of this type of interaction, studies that compare volunteers (self-selected groups) with nonvolunteers must always be questioned. Suppose that an E locates forty children from impoverished homes who are poor readers, and twenty of them volunteer to participate in a cultural enrichment program. The volunteers may improve in reading more without X and benefit more from X than the nonvolunteers, because they are different initially—they are motivated more highly toward self-improvement to begin with.

EXTERNAL VALIDITY   Our discussion thus far has been confined to checking the internal validity of the design. When planning an investigation, you give this task primary consideration, but you are also concerned about external validity—the generalizability or representativeness of the experimental findings. Consequently, you ask: What relevance do the findings concerning the effect of X have beyond the confines of the experiment? To what subject populations, settings, experimental variables, and measurement variables can these findings be generalized?

When checking the design of an experiment, you may ask: Can the findings be generalized to all college students? All students attending Harvard University? All Harvard freshmen? All Harvard freshmen who are enrolled in a particular course? Or must the findings be limited to the particular Harvard freshmen who participated in the experiment? You can strengthen the external validity of your design if you describe the population to which the results will apply *before* you conduct the experiment. If you draw a random sample from this predetermined population (say, Harvard freshmen) and expose the sample to X, you can make the following generalization: The effect that X had on the sample population (fifty Harvard freshmen) will be the same for the population that the sample represents (all Harvard freshmen).

In an investigation you are concerned about the generalizability of your findings not only with respect to an S population but also with respect to settings, independent variables, and measurement variables.

Will the findings be representative of other geographical areas, sizes of schools, times of day, times of year, etc.? Will the findings provide information about situations in which one X, no X, variations of X, or more than one X are present? Will the findings be representative of situations in which one or several types of criteria measurement are used?

The representativeness of the setting that is selected for an experiment will determine how extensively the findings can be applied. If the findings of a study are derived from data that are obtained in a deprived rural area, you cannot claim that they will hold true for wealthy suburban areas. If objective tests are used to measure the effect of a new teaching method, you cannot claim that the same effect would have been observed if essay tests or oral participation had been used as the measuring instruments.

When examining the external validity of a design, you check the following threats to representativeness:

1 Interaction effects of selection biases and X. The characteristics of the Ss who are selected to participate in an experiment determine how extensively the findings can be generalized. A random sample of seventh-grade students from one school will not be representative of all seventh-grade students. The intelligence, socioeconomic status, or some other characteristic of these particular students may cause X to be more effective for them than for other seventh-grade students. If X is a new textbook, it may produce excellent results in the Dort School, where most students have high IQs. But an E cannot generalize that X will produce the same results in all seventh-grade classes, for the textbook may not be equally effective in the Friar School, where most students have low IQs. Similarly, an E cannot generalize the findings for 100 third-grade pupils obtained in one setting (Appalachia), in one time span (late Friday afternoon), by test A (measures speed of reading) to all elementary students in the United States, most of whom are administered other reading tests (that measure comprehension as well as speed), at other testing times, and in other settings.

2 Reactive or interaction effect of pretesting. Giving a pretest may limit the generalizability of the experimental findings. A pretest may increase or decrease the experimental Ss' sensitiveness to X: it may alert them to issues, problems, or events that they might not ordinarily notice. Consequently, these Ss may be no longer representative of the unpretested population from which they came. Suppose that fifty

Harvard freshmen are given a racial attitude test before and after they are exposed to X, a romantic film with a racial prejudice theme. Their responses on T_2 may not reflect the effect of the film as much as the increased sensitivity to racial prejudice that taking T_1 produced. The effect of the film for the experimental Ss may not be representative of its effect for Harvard freshmen who see the romantic film without being pretested.

3 Reactive effects of experimental procedures.   The experimental procedures may also produce effects that limit the generalizability of the experimental findings. If the presence of observers and experimental equipment makes pupils and teachers aware of the fact that they are taking part in an experiment, they may alter their normal behavior.[2] If they alter the very behavior that is being measured, the E cannot claim that the effect of X for the sample population will be the same for Ss who are exposed to X in nonexperimental situations.

4 Multiple-treatment interference.   When the same Ss are exposed repeatedly to two or more Xs, the effects of the previous Xs are not usually erasable; hence, the findings may be generalized only to persons who experience the same sequence of treatments repeatedly. If Ss are exposed to three types of music throughout the day, they may be more productive when marching music is played; but they might not respond in the same way if marching music were played continuously.

DESIGN WITH MINIMAL CONTROL

A research design is to the E what a blueprint is to an architect. If the design is crudely conceived, the flawed product of the investigation will not be worthy of serious consideration. This chapter discusses several basic designs. No one design solves all problems. The nature of the problem dictates which design is the most appropriate for the investigation. In the following discussion, a simple design that provides minimal control is presented. This design will help you understand the advantages of the more rigorously controlled designs that are presented later.

[2]One type of artificial behavior is known as the "Hawthorne effect" from a study in which selected workers were exposed to various improvements in working conditions. With each improvement, their productivity improved; but, contrary to expectations, when each improvement was subsequently eliminated, production continued to increase. Obviously the employees were responding to the prestige and attention they received from participating in the experiment rather than to X.

One-group Pretest-Posttest Design (Design 1)

When this design is employed, the dependent variable is measured before the independent variable is applied or withdrawn and then measured again afterwards. The amount of change, if any, that has taken place is computed.

DESIGN PROCEDURES   To ascertain whether a new teaching method will increase reading speed, for example, an E takes the following steps:

1   Administers T_1 to measure the reading speed of a single group and obtains the mean for the group.[3]
2   Exposes the Ss to X, the new teaching method, for a period of time.
3   Administers T_2 to measure reading speed, and compares T_1 and T_2 means to ascertain what difference, if any, the exposure to X has presumably made.
4   Utilizes a statistical technique, if appropriate, to ascertain whether the difference is statistically significant.

The following is a paradigm for this design:

PRETEST	INDEPENDENT VARIABLE	POSTTEST
T_1 Mean speed of reading for the group: 50 words per minute.	X	T_2 Mean speed of reading for the group: 80 words per minute.

$T_2 - T_1$ or $80 - 50 = 30$ wpm (the difference between the means that is caused presumably by X, the remedial teaching method).

INTERNAL VALIDITY   The pretest in this design provides information that enables an E to ascertain how the Ss performed before the exposure to X and who dropped out of the experiment. If the same Ss take T_1 and T_2, *selection* and *mortality* variables are controlled.[4] But if some Ss drop out of the experiment, are absent from a testing or experimental session, or are replaced by new Ss, these mortality factors rather than X

[3]An alternative technique, which is often preferable, particularly when the groups are small, is to find the difference between the T_1 and T_2 scores for each S and then find the mean of these differences for the group.

[4]The following discussion will be easier to understand if you review periodically the section "Types of Factors to Be Controlled," page 231 and check Table 9.1 on page 280.

may produce the difference in the test results. Consequently, the number and nature of the dropouts must always be checked carefully.

This design has many weaknesses. It does not enable an E to ascertain whether the difference between T_1 and T_2 scores is produced by X or by *history, maturation, pretesting, statistical regression, instrument variables,* or the *interaction of selection and maturation,* etc. If some *Ss* in the reading experiment are fitted with glasses between T_1 and T_2, this history variable rather than X may produce a difference in their scores. A *maturation* factor may also operate: the difference in the *Ss'* scores may be caused by the fact that they are older, more fatigued, less enthusiastic, or more accustomed to school routines when they take T_2 than when they took T_1.

Sometimes the *testing* practice or the motivation that is supplied by T_1 enables *Ss* to do better on T_2. In a weight-control study, a preliminary weigh-in may stimulate *Ss* to lose weight regardless of whether they are exposed to X, a therapeutic program. If *Ss* are asked about their personal practices or attitudes on T_1, they may answer honestly. After thinking about the significance of their replies, they may change their responses on T_2—not because of the effect of X, but because they wish to present themselves more favorably.

If the *Ss* are selected on the basis of extreme scores, *statistical regression* rather than X will almost invariably account for some of the difference in T_1 and T_2 results. Changes in the *measuring instruments* may also cause the differences. Knowledge of how well *Ss* did on T_1 may influence the judgment of the judge who rates them on T_2. This bias can be controlled if T_1 and T_2 are randomly shuffled so that the judge cannot tell which tests were taken first. If the T_1 and T_2 measurements of the dependent variable are taken from different types of records or tests, this difference may produce an effect that is inextricably confounded with the effect of X. Suppose that school accident reports are used to measure the effect of an experimental safety program. If accidents are reported on blank forms before the experiment and on carefully structured forms during the study, more accidents may be reported on the structured forms even though fewer accidents have occurred.

The one-group design does not satisfy the fundamental criteria for experimental methodology and should be used only for preliminary research when the independent variable is likely to produce a drastic effect, for this lessens the influence of extraneous variables; when the interval between T_1 and T_2 is of brief duration, for there is less opportunity for *history* and *maturation* to operate; and when the dependent variable is relatively stable, that is, when it is not apt to change unless a deliberate effort is made to bring about a change.[5]

DESIGNS WITH RIGOROUS CONTROL

During recent decades, educators have been under attack because their experiments were not carefully controlled. As a result, more rigorously controlled designs are now beginning to appear in the literature. No design can be endorsed unconditionally. Satisfying all internal and external validity requirements is almost an unattainable ideal, but competent investigators strive to satisfy as many as possible.

Control Group

To overcome difficulties that Design 1 presents, an E can add a control group. By so doing, the E provides the comparability that is required by science. The control group, which is not exposed to X, strengthens an E's conviction that the independent variable is solely responsible for the change in the dependent variable.

Suppose that Design 1, which requires no control group, is used, and the one group is exposed to X, a new reading method. If the T_2 mean is higher than the T_1 mean, the E wonders: Is this increase in reading ability caused by the new method or by the effects of *maturation, pretesting, history,* etc.?

To eliminate these doubts, suppose that the E assigns Ss to two groups and exposes only one group to X. Both groups will mature about the same amount and will experience the same pretesting practice and contemporary events during the experiment. Consequently, the E can conclude that the difference in their reading improvement is not caused by these factors but presumably only by X, the reading method.

If the Ss are not randomly assigned to the two groups, however, the groups may differ, and these differences may produce effects that may be mistaken for the effect of X. The same thing may occur if the two groups experience different experimental conditions. Suppose the E assigns the more intelligent Ss, the better teacher, the more favorable class hour, and the quieter classroom to the experimental group. These differences between the experimental and control group rather than X, the reading method, may be responsible for the experimental group's

[5]Interaction of selection and maturation, etc., and factors threatening external validity also are present in this design. They are examined more conveniently under other designs later in the chapter.

greater gain in reading achievement. Educators recognized this equivalency problem when they adopted the classical control-group experiment. They emphasized that the success of the experiment rested on one important assumption: *that the experimental and the control groups be equivalent in respect to all factors that may influence the dependent variable except for the exposure to X.*

RANDOM ASSIGNMENT TO GROUPS   While seemingly strange, the best method of attaining experimental equivalency is through the use of simple randomization techniques. Randomization techniques have been recommended previously to select *Ss* from a population so as to obtain a representative sample of *Ss*. *Random sampling* and *random assignment* are two separate steps in an experiment. After a random sample of the population is obtained, these *Ss* are assigned to the experimental and control groups by flipping a coin or some other randomization technique to attain group equivalence. Similarly, teachers, classrooms, equipment, and class periods are randomly assigned to groups. These procedures prevent the *E* from consciously or unconsciously assigning the better ones to the experimental group (see Figure 9.1).

Fortunately, statistical tests of significance[6] are available that enable you to make a judgment about the effect of sampling variations on the findings of an investigation. By chance, for example, the *Ss* assigned at random to the experimental group might be more intelligent than those assigned to the control group. Before conducting an investigation, therefore, you can make a bet about the possibility that the difference between the mean T_2 scores of the experimental and control groups would occur by chance even if no *X* were applied because of the

---

[6]A number of tests of significance are available, such as the *t* test, *F* test, and chi-square test. Each one can be used only if certain assumptions are met in the study. An example of the *F* test will be presented in this text, pages 514 and 530. Statistics books and subsequent courses in statistics will acquaint you with other tests.

FIGURE 9.1

Attainment of experimental equivalency through random sampling and random assignment.

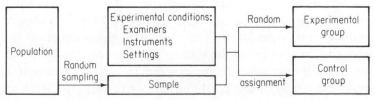

variability of the *Ss* within the groups. You might bet it would occur 1 in 100 times (.01 level of significance), 5 in 100 times (.05 level of significance), or at some other probability level. After obtaining the data, you could apply an appropriate statistical test of significance to ascertain whether the difference between the mean T_2 scores of the groups could be expected to occur by chance for that size sample. If it could not, the *X* presumably caused the difference and is related to the occurrence of *Y*. Perhaps the following example will help you understand this procedure.

Suppose you think that drug 66 will affect the rate at which rats will learn a maze. Before executing your investigation, you transform this problem hypothesis into a null hypothesis: There is no effect of drug 66 on the rate at which rats learn a maze at the .01 level of significance, $p = 0$. (No relation exists between the two variables in the population, $p = 0$.)

After conducting the experiment, you find that the rats who received the drug learned the maze faster than the rats in the control group. The question that must be answered is: Did the drug or did chance sampling variations cause this difference? Perhaps, by chance, the more intelligent rats were assigned to the experimental group and would have outperformed the control group if they had not received the drug. By applying an appropriate test of significance to the data, you can find out whether the difference between the two groups' mean scores would have occurred less than 1 in 100 times on the basis of chance. Tables are available in statistics books that give the values of a test which a sample of a given size must equal or exceed to meet the declared requirement of significance—.01 in your study. If the difference between the means of the experimental and control groups exceeds that which can be attributed to chance, you can reject the null hypothesis and conclude that the evidence supports your problem hypothesis that there is a relationship between drug 66 and the rate at which rats learn a maze.

Randomization procedures do not remove extraneous variables, such as IQ or age, which may affect the dependent variable, nor do they control their presence. These extraneous variables still affect the inquiry, but the laws of chance rather than the personal bias of the *E* now operate. The validity of the assumption that random assignment will result in equivalent groups increases with the number of *Ss* used. The larger the number of *Ss*, the more equivalent or similar the groups will tend to be. If only a few *Ss* are selected, the more intelligent, older, or healthier ones may be assigned by chance to one group. If the groups are small, they are not likely to differ to any great extent, but the probability that differences will occur is greater than if the groups are large.

Statistical tests of significance provide a safeguard against attributing group differences to the effect of X. The probability remains, however, that these group differences may mask the effect of X, particularly if the effect of X is small. To aid in removing this masking effect, analysis of covariance or matching procedures, which are described in the following paragraphs, may be used. If either of these techniques is used to make the experiment more sensitive—to gain statistical precision—it is used in addition to randomization and not as a substitute for randomization. To keep intelligence from masking the effect that a programmed textbook X has on learning, the E may pair Ss who have the same IQ scores and randomly assign the members of each pair to the experimental and control groups. Because this "equating technique" controls only one variable, IQ scores, the E must randomize out other extraneous variables so that they will not differentially affect the comparison groups.

MATCHING WITH RANDOM ASSIGNMENT   Because nature does an excellent job of matching identical twins, they may be used in some experiments in conjunction with random assignment to groups. When a sufficient number of twins is unavailable, matched Ss may be used with validity in investigations but only in conjunction with randomization. The pairs of Ss are matched on their T_1 scores and/or on other variables that are known to have an effect on the dependent variable, such as IQ, age, sex, or socioeconomic background. Then one member of each pair is randomly assigned to the control group and the other member to the experimental group. When matching with randomized assignment is employed, the E has greater assurance that any difference between the T_2 mean scores of the groups can be attributed to X.

Many difficulties may be encountered when matching techniques are employed. Determining which variables affect the dependent variable and which of these should be used as a basis for matching often presents problems. By examining the reports of other investigators who were concerned with the same dependent variable, an E may discover variables that have been demonstrated to affect the dependent variable. But obtaining accurate measurements of some relevant variables, such as emotional status, level of motivation, etc., for matching purposes may be difficult. Not uncommonly, moreover, extensive testing is required before a sufficient number of qualified pairs can be found. Finding enough Ss who are well matched on even two or three variables is difficult.

RANDOM ASSIGNMENT AND ANALYSIS OF COVARIANCE   Because of the difficulties that arise when matching procedures are employed, educators are grateful for the development of procedures that enable them to control variation in the experimental and control groups through an *analysis of covariance*. This statistical tool enables an E to adjust the T_2 mean scores to compensate for a lack of original equivalency between groups that is discovered when T_1 is given or that arises during the experiment.

Suppose we wish to study what effect a method of teaching arithmetic has on arithmetic achievement. If we give an arithmetic test (T_1) to Ss and then, disregarding their pretest scores, assign them at random to the experimental and control groups, we might by chance assign Ss to the experimental group who have higher T_1 scores than the Ss we assign to the control group. These initial differences in arithmetic achievement scores may differentially affect the T_2—postexperimental—arithmetic test scores. The greater achievement of the experimental group on T_2, therefore, may be due not to the teaching method but to a covariate that has not been controlled—in this instance, the superior initial arithmetic ability of the Ss. But through the use of analysis of covariance, we can obtain statistical control over this covariate which affects the dependent variable (T_2) scores and would otherwise be confounded with the independent variable (teaching method).

When analysis of covariance is used, one or more covariates in addition to the dependent variable (arithmetic achievement, in our example) are measured. A covariate is a variable that has not been controlled in the experiment and is believed to affect the dependent variable. Analysis of covariance is not limited to the use of one covariate. In our experiment, for example, both initial arithmetic and intelligence scores could have been selected as covariates. After the covariate and dependent variable scores (T_2) have been obtained, the dependent variable scores (T_2) are adjusted so as to remove the effects of the uncontrolled source of variation represented by the covariate or covariates.

The older matching techniques of equating groups is now being replaced by analysis of covariance because it eliminates the laborious process of testing and discarding numerous Ss in search of matched pairs, and computer programs are now available that reduce the amount of computation effort involved in analysis of covariance. The use of this statistical technique, however, involves certain assumptions that one should have good reason to believe are met before undertaking a covariance analysis. For a more detailed discussion of this statistical technique, consult experimental design textbooks that give the basic formulas and explain how to compute analysis of covariance.

FALLACY OF MATCHING WITHOUT RANDOM ASSIGNMENT   In the past, many educators assumed that the simple (1) matched-pair technique or (2) matched-group technique would attain group equivalency without taking the additional precaution of assigning the Ss at random to groups. But these techniques almost inevitably create internal validity problems; hence, matching alone is not regarded as an acceptable procedure.

1 Matched pairs.   Matching equates groups in a few respects, but human beings vary in a multiplicity of ways. Many other variables beside the matched variables affect the dependent variable, and their effect may be mistaken for the effect of X. Matching closely the Ss in two intact populations, such as two classes or two schools, increases the precision of the method. But it also increases the number of Ss who cannot be matched, particularly the Ss who obtain extremely high or low scores, and ignoring them will limit the population to which the findings of the study may be generalized. An insurmountable difficulty will arise, moreover, because the T_2 means of the residual matched groups will regress toward the means of their respective original populations.[7] The following illustration will reveal how this differential regression toward the mean will almost inevitably "unequate" the residual matched groups.

Suppose that school A has a mean of 100 and school B has a mean of 60, and a sample group with a mean score of 80 is selected from each school population. These two sample groups, a and b, have matching mean scores of 80, but sample a is below the mean of school A, and sample b is above the mean of school B. Upon retesting, matched groups a and b will regress toward the means of their parent populations (see arrows in Figure 9.2). Hence, the mean score of sample a, the experimental group, will tend to rise and the mean score of sample b,

---

[7]You will recall from our previous discussion concerning statistical regression (page 233) that when a group is retested, its T_1 mean will move toward the mean of the parent population whether X is applied or not.

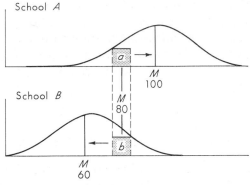

FIGURE 9.2

Illustration of statistical regression: matched samples from dissimilar populations.

the control group, will tend to drop whether X is applied or not. The findings of the study may merely reveal this differential degree of regression rather than any effect that is produced by X.

2 Matched groups   In the older "experiments," without random assignment of Ss, when educators found it difficult to match Ss, they often attempted to *match groups.* Two groups were selected that had about the same average possession of each relevant variable—the same mean scores—and a similar distribution pattern of scores around the mean. If intelligence were the matching variable, the mean IQ of each group was found. If one group had an average of 100 and the other of 110, Ss were shifted until both groups had an average IQ of 105. Since the IQs in one matched group may range widely about the average (80 to 130) and the IQs in the other group may have a narrow range of variation (98 to 115), statistical procedures were also used to ascertain how the scores were distributed. If they differed, Ss were shifted to make them similar.

This matched-group technique did not equate the groups; it merely made them appear superficially equal in a few respects. Regression to the mean would later take its toll. Nonmatched variables could also create problems. If the groups were matched on two variables, such as IQs and skills, and the distributions of the scores about the means were made similar, the Ss could have different combinations of these capacities:

Group A: Low IQs with high skills and high IQs with low skills.
Group B: High IQs with high skills and low IQs with low skills.

If these differences existed, they could affect the conclusions of the study.

The moral of these paragraphs is: Do *not* attempt to match *Ss* or groups without randomizing. Also, do not believe the results of those who do, except under rare circumstances, which are not met in most educational research reports.

Randomized Control-group Pretest-Posttest Design (Design 2)

Because Designs 2, 3, and 4 require the utilization of a control group and random assignment of *Ss* to groups, they control many variables that other designs do not. Consequently, they are the most highly recommended experimental designs.

DESIGN PROCEDURES   When employing Design 2, an *E* takes the following steps:

1   Selects *Ss* from a population by random methods, if possible.
2   Assigns *Ss* to groups and *X* to groups by random methods.
3   Tests the *Ss* on the dependent variable[8] (obtains the T_{1_E} scores for the experimental *Ss* and the T_{1_C} scores for the control *Ss*).
4   Keeps all conditions the same for the groups except for exposing the experimental *Ss*—but not the control *Ss*—to the independent variable for a stipulated time.
5   Tests the *Ss* on the dependent variable (obtains the T_{2_E} scores for the experimental *Ss* and the T_{2_C} scores for the control *Ss*).
6   Finds the difference between the T_1 and T_2 scores for each *S* and the mean of these differences for each group, D_E and D_C.[9]
7   Compares the D_C and D_E[10] to determine whether the application of *X* has presumably caused a change in the experimental group's scores as compared with the control group's scores.
8   Applies an appropriate statistical procedure to ascertain whether the difference in the scores is sufficiently great to be a statistically significant difference or whether it is only a chance occurrence.

---

[8]Sometimes *Ss* are pretested before they are assigned to groups.

[9]If the analysis of covariance technique is employed, the final mean scores are adjusted for pretest differences prior to step 6.

[10]A comparison of D_E—D_C actually reflects the effect of *X* plus any interaction effects of (1) T_1 and *X*, (2) *X* and *U* (uncontrolled events, such as history and maturation), and (3) T_1, *X*, and *U*. Hence D_E—D_C=*X* only if one can assume the effect of these interactions is zero. For this reason, Design 4, a two-group design that includes no T_1, which will be discussed later, is generally best for finding *X* or *X* plus the interaction of *X* and *U*.

Steps 2 to 6 may be depicted as follows:

RANDOMLY ASSIGNED*	PRETEST	TREATMENT	POSTTEST
(R) Experimental Group	T_{1_E}	X	T_{2_E}
(R) Control Group	T_{1_C}		T_{2_C}

D_E = Mean of differences between experimental Ss's pretest and
      posttest scores
D_C = Mean of the differences between the control Ss's pretest and
      posttest scores
Compare D_E and D_C to ascertain effect of X

* In this test, whenever Ss and X are randomly assigned to groups, the (R) placed before the group conveys this information.

This design may be extended to permit the study of two or more variations of the independent variable on a dependent variable. An E may study the effect of different amounts of a drug, different kinds of motivation, or different methods of instruction on performance. To ascertain the effect of teaching long division by two different methods, for example, one group may be exposed to X_a method, a second group to X_b method, and a third group to no X—no long-division instruction.

(R) First group $T_{1_{E_1}}$ X_a $T_{2_{E_1}}$
(R) Second group $T_{1_{E_2}}$ X_b $T_{2_{E_2}}$
(R) Control group T_{1_C} T_{2_C}

If you are merely interested in comparing the effects of two treatments, you may not use the *no-X* control group, but it does give you an added measure of information for fuller interpretive purposes.

INTERNAL VALIDITY   Design 2, generally speaking, controls the potential sources of internal invalidity. The effect of *intersession* developments—extraneous variables that arise between T_1 and T_2—are balanced out by the presence of a randomized control group. The *contemporary historical* events and the changes in the *measuring instruments* that occur between T_1 and T_2 are experienced by all groups; hence, the effects of these variables are equalized and cannot be mistaken in the effect of X.

Additional precautions must be taken, however, to control *intrasession* conditions—differences that the experimental and control groups may experience when they are tested and treated separately. If a measuring instrument becomes less discriminating between the time that two groups take the *same* test, this factor may produce an effect that may be mistaken for the effect of *X*. If only one group takes T_2 in an overheated room late in the day, or is distracted by a troublesome student or the school band during a testing or treatment session, these factors may also affect the results of the experiment. If different teachers are in charge of the groups, differences in their personalities and proficiencies, in the way they administer the instructions, or in their convictions about the value of the treatment may influence the results. Many researchers, for example, make the mistake of selecting superior teachers for their experimental groups.

How does an *E* control intrasession conditions? An *E* tests and treats *Ss* individually or in small groups and randomly assigns *Ss*, times, and places to experimental or control conditions. Contemporary historical events such as newspaper stories, a band practice, or cafeteria odors will affect the *Ss*, but they will affect a few *Ss* or several *Ss* in both groups approximately equally.

To control intrasession instrument differences, an *E* randomly assigns not only *Ss* but also mechanical instruments, teachers, observers, and raters to sessions—to a single session if possible. If a limited number of assistants or pieces of equipment are available, an *E* assigns each one to an equal number of experimental and control sessions. Thus, if two pieces of equipment vary, or if one teacher is more proficient than the other, or if one observer rates higher or lower than other observers, these differences will affect experimental and control groups approximately equally. Ideally, an *E* does not let observers know which *Ss* receive what treatment, for this knowledge might influence their judgments, particularly if the observers believe that one treatment is better than the other.

Differential selection of *Ss* for comparison groups is controlled because the randomization processes practically assure equivalency. If only a few *Ss* are selected, the groups may differ somewhat, but statistical tests of significance provide a safeguard against attributing these groups' differences to the effect of *X*. An analysis of covariance or matching techniques may be employed to aid in removing the effect of group differences that might mask the effect of *X*. These techniques, of course, are used in addition to random assignment.

Maturation and pretesting are controlled by Design 2, for both groups should experience an equal effect of these variables. A comparison of the T_1 and T_2 data that this design provides makes it possible to ascertain whether *differential mortality* has taken place. When *Ss* drop out of an experiment, they may or may not drop out on a random basis.

The *Ss* who fail to attend treatment or testing sessions may differ from those who do; they may be less healthy, less highly motivated, less responsive to the treatment; consequently, their absence may introduce a sampling bias.

Statistical regression is controlled by Design 2. If *Ss* are selected from extreme scorers in the same group and are randomly assigned to groups, statistical regression will take place. But the control group will regress as much as the experimental group. Consequently, the effect of regression cannot be confounded with *X.*

EXTERNAL VALIDITY   The discussion thus far has been concerned with the importance of checking internal validity. The *E* also worries about the external validity of the design—the generalizability or representativeness of the findings concerning the effect of *X.* The *E* asks: Can extraneous variables interact with the experimental treatment and make the *Ss* unrepresentative of the population from which they were selected? Can the claim be made that the effect which *X* had on the *Ss* will be the same for other members of the population who did not participate in the experiment?

When Design 2 is used, giving a pretest (T_1), which is an important part of the design, may limit the generalizability of the experimental findings. Taking a pretest, particularly if it is rather unique or motivating in its effect, may make the *Ss* unrepresentative of the population from which they were drawn. The following example illustrates a problem that may arise because of an *interaction of pretesting and X.* Suppose that forty *Ss* are randomly selected from a population and randomly assigned to experimental and control groups. Both groups are given a pretest, T_1, a racial prejudice attitude scale, and then the experimental group is shown a film designed to change negative racial attitudes and the control group is shown a nature film. Afterwards both groups take T_2 to ascertain whether the film that was presented to change racial prejudice attitudes had that effect. Because the pretest aroused the interest or sensitized the experimental *Ss* to racial prejudice, these *Ss* may be affected more by the exposure to the film than other samples of *Ss* drawn from the same population would be if they had not been pretested. The question that is usually raised when Design 2 is used is: Would the effect of *X* on the experimental *Ss* have been the same if they had not taken a pretest? The T_2 scores of the experimental group may reflect their response not to *X* so much as to the confounding effect of T_1 with that of *X.* Do you see why it may sometimes be imprudent to generalize that the effect of *X* for a pretest sample will be the same for unpretested samples in the population?

When Design 2 is used, an *interaction* of *selection* and *X* may also occur. The cultural background, or some other characteristic of the *Ss* who are selected to participate in an experiment, may make the experimental treatment more effective for them than it would be for students elsewhere. An investigator must be particularly wary if a number of schools or *Ss* are asked to participate before some agree to cooperate. Volunteers are apt to differ from nonvolunteers. If the schools that finally agree to participate are located in a scientific or university center where most parents are college graduates and where superior teachers are employed, an *E* cannot generalize that the findings of the experiment will hold for all schools in the country. Consequently, when designing a study, consideration should be given to reducing the number of *Ss* in a school and to increasing the number and types of schools participating in the experiment. Random selection—or at least a varied selection—of units from the population to which the *E* wishes to generalize, as well as random assignment of *Ss* to groups, is the ideal.

The *interaction* of *X* with other factors, such as *history*, may make it impossible to generalize the findings beyond the specific conditions of the experiment. If an experiment is conducted during a depression, a war, or a catastrophe in the community, these unique events may make *Ss* more responsive to *X* than they might be at other times. If an experiment is replicated in different time and place settings and the hypothesized relations hold up in each instance, generalizations concerning the findings can be made with greater confidence.

The *reactive effects* of *experimental procedures* may hamper generalization. If *Ss* know that they are participating in an experiment, they may not react normally to *X*. Being singled out for special treatment often motivates *Ss* to put forth greater effort. Consequently, they perform better than nonexperimental *Ss* not because of the exposure to *X* but because they want to justify the honor of being selected. Clues concerning the purpose of the experiment or the outcome expectations of the investigator which are provided by test questions, experimental apparatus, or the behavior of the *E* may cause *Ss* to distort their responses to *X*. The *Ss* may try to present themselves as favorably as possible, or they may try to be "good subjects" and help the *E* "prove what he wants to prove." An illustration of the reactive effects of experimental procedures is provided by what happened when college students were given dexedrine in an experiment. The *Ss* who thought they were given dexedrine had typical energizerlike reactions, but the *Ss* who thought they had received a barbituate showed a tendency toward barbituatelike reactions. It is interesting also to note that the percentage of such Ss reponses dropped markedly when the Es knew what drug was being administered.

To minimize the reactive effect of experimental procedures, an effort may be made to keep the Ss and those who administer the treatments or tests unaware of the fact that an experiment is being conducted. This type of control, of course, can be exercised only if approval is obtained from the committee for the protection of human subjects. If Ss cannot be kept ignorant of the experiment, members of both the experimental and the control groups should be made to feel equally singled out. More accurate data will be attained if Ss think they are getting identical treatments or if they are at least unaware of which treatment they are receiving. The less conspicuous the experimental procedures are, the better. If an E can bury T_1 and T_2 in the routine school testing program, can assign Ss at random to groups without making them aware of it, and can have the regular teacher present X as a normal part of the instructional program, the E can make generalizations concerning the findings of the study with greater confidence.

Randomized Solomon Four-group Design (Design 3)

Design 3 overcomes an external-validity weakness which exists in Design 2. The pretest in Design 2 may make the sample of Ss who participate in the experiment more or less sensitive to X than the unpretested members of the population. Consequently, one cannot generalize the experimental findings for the sample to the population.

DESIGN PROCEDURES   To overcome the interaction of pretesting and X, Design 3 adds two unpretested groups (3 and 4) to the two groups in Design 2. One pretested group and one unpretested group receive the experimental treatment.

GROUP	PRETEST	TREATMENT	POSTTEST	DIFFERENCE*
1. (R) Pretested	T_1	X	T_2	$1D = T_1 + X + U + I_{T_1X}$ $+ I_{T_1U} + I_{XU} + I_{T_1XU}$
2. (R) Pretested	T_1		T_2	$2D = T_1 + U + I_{T_1U}$
3. (R) Unpretested		X	T_2	$3D = X + U + I_{XU}$
4. (R) Unpretested			T_2	$4D = U$

*D, the difference between T_1 and T_2 mean scores, represents the sum of the main effects of one or more variables (pretesting T_1, independent variable X, uncontrolled events U, such as maturation and history) and any *interaction effects (Is)* involving the variables.

Design 3 requires that the *Ss* be assigned at random to the four groups.[11] The random assignment of *Ss* makes it possible to assume that the pretest scores for groups 3 and 4 would have been similar to the pretest scores attained by groups 1 and 2. Hence an inferred pretest value is used in groups 3 and 4 which is equal to the mean for all subjects in groups 1 and 2. But since groups 3 and 4 are not pretested, no interaction between X and the effects of T_1 can be reflected in their T_2 scores.

DESIGN VALIDITY The Solomon four-group design enables an E to obtain empirical values for more unknowns than the other designs, but it requires more time, *Ss,* and labor. In the Design 3 paradigm, to the right of each group, is a list of the variables that, acting independently (main effect) and jointly (interaction effect), may contribute to the difference between T_1 and T_2 scores of the group. You will recall that the One-group Pretest-Posttest Design (Design 1) gives minimal control, for the difference (D) between T_1 and T_2 scores is caused by seven unknown quantities: three main (independent) effects and four interaction (joint) effects (see group 1 difference in the Design 3 paradigm). If you employ a one-group design and claim the difference between T_1 and T_2 scores is caused by X, you must assume that the effect of T_1 (the pretest), U (the uncontrolled events), and the four interactions is zero. Six assumptions is a formidable number of guesses. In contrast, with the four-group design (Design 3), all seven quantities appear and any *four* of them can be assessed by assuming values (zero or some reasonable value chosen from other research) for the other three.[12] Hence, the four-group design requires three less assumptions than the one-group design.

By using unpretested as well as pretested experimental and control groups in the four-group design, an E can overcome the interaction of pretesting and X. You will recall that the interaction effect of T_1 and X may limit the generalizability of the experimental findings in a study that uses only two pretested groups. A four-group design enables an E to assess both the *main effects* of T_1, X, and U and the *interaction effect of pretesting and* X (I_{T_1X}). To find these values, the E first examines

[11]Supplementary matching procedures may be used with Designs 3 and 4. If matching is employed in addition to random assignment to groups, the *Ss* are matched on some factor other than the dependent variable. If T_1 and T_2 are reading achievement tests, for example, the matching may be done on IQ scores but not on reading scores.

[12]Ross and Smith (85) have codified eight legitimate sets of assumptions. One may, for example, assess the value of U, X, T_1, I_{T_1}, or U, X, T_1, I_{T_1XU}, or U, X, I_{T_1U}, I_{T_1XU}, or five other sets of four variables by assuming values for the three remaining variables.

group 4, which experienced no pretest and no-X treatment; hence the D, difference, between the T_2 and "inferred" T_1 scores, enables the E to ascertain the main effect of U, the uncontrolled events: $4D = U$. To find the remaining values, the E proceeds as follows (see design paradigm above): $3D - 4D = X$; $2D - 4D = T_1$; $1D - 2D - 3D + 4D = I_{T_1X}$. The four-group design actually amounts to doing the experiment twice (once with pretests and once without). Consequently, if the results of the experiment are consistent (the difference between the T_1 and T_2 scores of the pretested and unpretested groups that received the experimental treatment are both significantly greater than the groups that did not), you can have greater confidence in the findings than if the findings had not been replicated within the study.

Another statistical procedure for this design, reported by Campbell and Stanley (17:195), avoids the use of inferred pretest scores for groups 3 and 4. They point out that because only half the groups are pretested, the asymmetries of the design make an analysis of variance on gain scores inappropriate. They suggest the following alternative analysis using only the *posttest scores*: By comparing the T_2 scores of the X and no-X groups (column means) in Figure 9.3*a*, an E estimates the main effect of X. Then, by comparing the T_2 scores of the pretested and unpretested groups (row means), the E estimates the main effect of pretesting; and from the cell means, the E estimates the interaction of pretesting with X. But Ross and Smith (85:77) point out that this statistical procedure overlooks certain interactions (see Figure 9.3*b*), and hence is valid only when the effect of I_{T_1U}, I_{XU}, I_{T_1XU} are all zero.

Before adding unpretested groups to an investigation, which involves considerable additional work, you should consider carefully whether such action is necessary. The objective is not to introduce numerous controls for the sake of scientific elegance, but rather to

FIGURE 9.3

Illustration of interaction effects. *U* is omitted from example *b* because it is present in all groups and does not distinguish among them.

	X	No X
Pretested	Group 1 T_1, X, I_{T_1X}	Group 2 T_1
Unpretested	Group 3 X	Group 4

(*a*)

	X	No X
Pretested	Group 1 T_1, X, I_{T_1X}, I_{T_1U}, I_{XU}, I_{T_1XU}	Group 2 T_1, I_{T_1U}
Unpretested	Group 3 X, I_{XU}	Group 4

(*b*)

control all *plausible* rival hypotheses. If you use Design 2, with two pretested groups instead of the Solomon four-group design, you should explain satisfactorily in your research report why it is unlikely that pretesting rather than X accounts for your findings. You may argue that pretesting did not sensitize the Ss to the subject matter or to the fact that they were being measured because one or more of several conditions existed; for example, T_1 and T_2 were administered several months apart, the two tests were not identical, the testing was hidden in a normal school testing program, or the pretest consisted of nonsense syllables or some other material that would not be as likely to have a reactive effect as information-type material.

Randomized Control-group Posttest-only Design (Design 4)

Design 4 consists of the last two groups in the Solomon design: the two unpretested groups.

DESIGN PROCEDURES   This design is depicted as follows:

	PRETEST	TREATMENT	POSTTEST
(R) Experimental group		X	T_E
(R) Control group			T_C

As in all rigorously controlled designs, before the application of X the Ss are assigned at random to the experimental and control groups. Why can the E omit the pretest? Because randomization techniques permit the E to declare that at the time of assignment the groups were equal. The probability theory tells the E to what extent the randomly assigned Ss in the two groups might have been expected to differ by chance on T_1, and the test of significance takes account of such chance differences.

After the Ss are assigned at random to groups, the experimental group is exposed to X, such as a film with a racial prejudice theme, and the control group is not. During or after the exposure to X, the two groups are tested for the first time. Their scores are compared to ascertain the effect of X, and an appropriate test of significance is applied to determine whether this difference is greater than might have occurred by chance.

DESIGN VALIDITY   Because a randomized control group is used and no T_1 is given, Design 4 controls—but does not measure—the main effects of *history, maturation,* and *pretesting.* Design 4 is superior to Design 2 because no *interaction effect of pretesting* and X can occur. This feature, plus the fact that the design is less complicated and requires less effort than Designs 2 and 3, makes it worthy of consideration. You do not have to administer T_1, and in many instances you can present X and T_2 simultaneously. Suppose that you want to determine which of two letter formats is superior. If you present two groups of parents with different persuasive appeals for cooperation on questionnaires, you can obtain T_2 data (replies) on the same questionnaires. The number of returned questionnaires with positive responses will indicate which letter had the greater persuasive appeal. Design 4 is particularly useful when pretests are unavailable, inconvenient, or too costly to obtain; when *Ss* anonymity must be kept, and when a pretest may interact with X.

When a limited sample of the population is available for the experiment (when there is some question about the genuine equivalency of the assignment to groups), Design 2 rather than Design 4 should be employed, because the T_1 scores provide an added check on the sameness of the groups. If T_1 scores are available (if they have been accumulated as a routine part of the school testing program), Design 2 rather than Design 4 should be used. The additional T_1 information provided by Design 2 enables you to make some types of analyses that you cannot make without it, and the special statistical tests that are available for Design 2 are more powerful than those that are available for Design 4.

Factorial Analysis of Variance Designs

Our discussion thus far has been confined to classical designs which require that you vary a single X at a time and hold all other conditions constant. Because social and biological phenomena are complex, an educator cannot always fulfill these requirements. If you do fulfill them, you may prevent or ignore the simultaneous functioning of variables with which X interacts in normal situations. Since X may not produce the same effect independently as it does in conjunction with another X, findings concerning a single X may not be too significant.

Suppose that drugs A and B are administered independently, and in each instance a slightly greater healing effect is noted in the experimental group than in the control group. But when drugs A and B are administered together, they produce a much greater healing effect than can be attributed to either drug acting alone. Information about the interaction of the drugs certainly is of much greater significance than information about the independent effect of each drug.

Similar situations can arise in education. If a classical experiment reveals that democratic teachers have a greater effect on pupils' achievement than authoritarian teachers, the experiment has yielded valuable information. But suppose that a factorial design is used to study the effect that different types of teachers X_1 have on students of different levels of intelligence X_2. If the study reveals that democratic teachers have a greater effect on the learning of pupils with high IQs and authoritarian teachers have a greater effect on the learning of pupils with low IQs, this information about the interaction effect of type of teacher and level of intelligence will be even more valuable to educators.

Until relatively recently "the law of the single variable" tended to keep educators from investigating the interaction effects of variables. R. A. Fisher overcame this obstacle when he developed factorial designs and the statistical techniques for their analysis. In a classical design, such as Design 2, the E manipulates and checks the effect of *one independent variable* (a single X or two or more variations of a single X) in each experiment. Experiment 1: What is the effect of X, type of teacher (authoritarian and democratic), on learning achievement? Experiment 2: What is the effect of X, intelligence (low IQ and high IQ), on learning achievement? A factorial design permits the E to manipulate and to check the effects of *two or more variables* (X_1 and X_2) *simultaneously rather than in separate experiments*. A factorial design enables the E to evaluate both the main (independent) effect of each X and the interaction (joint) effect of the two variables. Two separate classical (single-X) designs would reveal the main effect of each X, but they would not reveal the interaction effect of the two Xs.[13]

DESIGN PROCEDURES   Factorial designs of varying degrees of complexity have been developed. They include two or more independent variables, and each one is varied in two or more ways. The simplest factorial design is the 2 by 2 (2 × 2). In this design, the effects of two Xs (factors) are studied, each of which is varied in two ways (two levels or two values).

To illustrate, assume that we are interested in studying the effect of

---

[13]A classical design utilizes a control group unless the E is interested merely in comparing the effects of two variations of X, as was the case in the above example. Similarly, in a factorial design, a control group is not required; but if the E wishes to use a control group, he introduces it as one variation of X, the experimental treatment: effect of X_1, drug A, and effect of no X, no drug A; effect of X_2, drug B, and effect of no X_2, no drug B.

variations in teaching methods X_1 and variations in length of class periods X_2 on learning achievement. The variations of X_1 are lecture and discussion methods. The variations of X_2 are thirty-minute and fifty-minute class periods. (See Figure 9.4.)

Since there are four possible combinations of variables, the Ss are assigned at random, each to one of the four experimental treatment groups. Group 1 is exposed to fifty-minute lecture periods, group 2 to thirty-minute lecture periods, group 3 to fifty-minute discussion periods, and group 4 to thirty-minute discussion periods. (See Figure 9.4.) Note that the Ss in each group do double duty, serving both in the X_1 group (method of teaching) and X_2 group (length of class period).

Six weeks later we measure the learning achievement (dependent variable) of each S, compute the mean score for each of the four groups, and record these scores in the appropriate squares (cells) in Figure 9.4. If the mean score for the fifty-minute lecture group is 59.0, for example, we record that score in the cell bearing the appropriate fifty-minute lecture label.

Since one of our objectives is to compare various combinations of these groups, we also obtain the *mean score for each row*, that is, for the two-lecture method groups (1 and 2) and for the two discussion-method groups (3 and 4), and the *mean score for each column*, that is, for the fifty-minute classes (1 and 3) and for the thirty-minute classes (2 and 4). We place these mean scores beneath the columns or beside the rows of the groups that they represent. If the mean score for the two fifty-minute classes is 70.5, for example, we place that score beneath

FIGURE 9.4

Illustration of a factorial design.

| | | (X_2) Length of class period | | Row | |
		Fifty minutes	Thirty minutes	Means	Differences
(X_1) Method of teaching	Lecture	(1) 59.0	(2) 58.0	58.5	−1.0
	Discussion	(3) 82.0	(4) 84.0	83.0	+2.0
Column	Means:	70.5	71.0	70.75	Grand mean
	Differences:	+23.0	+26.0		−3.0

the column labeled fifty-minute classes.[14] In addition, we find the difference between the mean scores in each column and each row. The difference between the means of the fifty-minute classes, for example, is + 23.0.

DESIGN INFORMATION   Our factorial design produces more information than we could obtain from two classical experiments. Two single-X designs would enable us to answer two questions: What is the main effect of X_1 on the dependent variable? What is the main effect of X_2 on the dependent variable? The data from our 2×2 design enable us to answer three questions:

1. **What is the main (independent) effect of teaching method X_1 on achievement scores?**
    If we compare the mean score of the two lecture groups (58.5)[15] with that of the two discussion groups (83.0), we see that the latter is noticeably higher (see Figure 9.4). Consequently, we suspect that the discussion method has a greater effect on learning achievement than the lecture method.
2. **What is the main effect of length of class X_2 on achievement scores?**
    The mean score for the two groups that had fifty-minute periods (70.5) and the mean score for the two groups that had thirty-minute periods (71.0) is almost identical. Obviously, the length of the class periods had little effect on the dependent variable.
3. **What is the interaction effect, if any, of teaching method and length of class periods on achievement scores?**
    This question forces us to determine whether the joint effect of particular variations of X_1 and X_2 on learning achievement is greater or less than can be attributed to either variable acting alone.
        If there is an interaction, the effect that a teaching method has on learning will differ for thirty- and fifty-minute classes. If the discussion method, for example, is more effective with one length of class than it is with the other, there is an interaction. If there is no interaction, the effect of a teaching method on learning achievement will be the same for both lengths of classes. To summarize: (1) If there *is an interaction*, the effect of one X on the dependent variable *will not be the same* for both variations of the second X. (2) If there *is no interaction*, the effect of one X on the dependent variable *will be the same* for both variations of the other X. Examples of each type are presented in the following paragraphs.

DESIGN DATA REVEAL NO INTERACTION EFFECT   Our data in Figure 9.4 reveal no interaction between X_1 and X_2, for the effect of X_1 on learning achievement is approximately *the same* for both variations of

---

[14] $59.0 + 82.0 = 141; 141 \div 2 = 70.5$
[15] $59.0 + 58.0 = 117; 117 \div 2 = 58.5$

X_2. The mean scores for the lecture method in the two lengths of classes are 59 and 58, and the mean scores for the discussion method are 82 and 84. The lack of interaction may be illustrated graphically if we transfer the scores in Figure 9.4 to Figure 9.5. We note that the groups that were exposed to the discussion method performed better than those exposed to the lecture method.[16] Moreover, we can see that difference A (the difference between the mean scores of the lecture and discussion groups in fifty-minute classes) is practically the same as difference B (the difference between the mean scores of the lecture and discussion groups in thirty-minute classes). Whenever difference A and difference B are the *same*, i.e., when the lines in Figure 9.5 are approximately parallel, it is unlikely that any interaction exists between the variables.

Another way to illustrate the absence of interaction is to compute the differences between the means of the groups. Return to Figure 9.4 and note that the differences between the means of the discussion and lecture groups, which are recorded below the columns, are 23.0 for fifty-minute classes and 26.0 for thirty-minute classes.[17] Since these differences are not far apart, we suspect that there is no interaction present. The same conclusions can be reached by comparing the differences in the other direction (row means); i.e., −1.0 and 2.0 are approximately the same, and no interaction exists.

DESIGN DATA REVEAL AN INTERACTION EFFECT   Our fictitious experiment revealed no interaction effect. But let us alter the data so that they

[16]In most factorial studies, the main effects are probably of the greatest interest to the E. Many times the interactions are not statistically significant. But knowledge of the lack of significance is important, for the E now knows that the discussion method of teaching is effective in and of itself. The importance of the main effects cannot be known, unless the interaction is specifically tested.

[17]$82 - 59 = 23$; $84 - 58 = 26$

FIGURE 9.5

Illustration of a lack of interaction between teaching methods and length of class period.

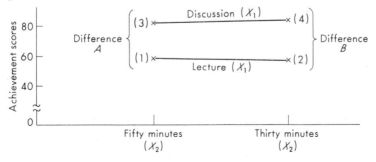

(X_2) Length of class period

		Fifty minutes	Thirty minutes	Row Means	Differences
(X_1) Method of teaching	Lecture	(1) 59.0	(2) 77.0	68.0	+18
	Discussion	(3) 82.0	(4) 66.0	74.0	−16
Column	Means:	70.5	71.5	71.0	Grand mean
	Differences:	+23.0	−11.0		

FIGURE 9.6

New means to illustrate interaction.

will reveal an interaction effect, as illustrated in Figures 9.6 and 9.7. If we examine the main effect of teaching method, the row mean score for the discussion groups (74.0) is higher than the row mean score for the lecture groups (68.0). Hence, the discussion method appears to be somewhat superior. If we examine the interaction effect of teaching method X_1 and length of class period X_2, we note that the discussion method is superior in fifty-minute classes ($82.0 - 59.0 = 23.0$), but it is less effective than the lecture method in thirty-minute classes ($66.0 - 77.0 = -11.0$). Note the interaction effect as it is illustrated graphically in Figure 9.7. The lecture and discussion lines are *not parallel*, as they were in Figure 9.5, for the two methods of teaching do not have the same effect on achievement in fifty-minute and thirty-minute classes. Interaction between the independent variables exists, because the

FIGURE 9.7

Illustration of interaction.

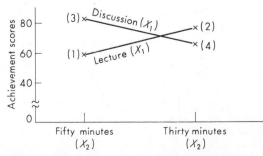

effect of one X on the dependent variable is not the same for both variations of the second X.

DESIGN EXTENSIONS   Factorial designs are not limited to the simple 2 × 2 designs. To these 2 × 2 designs, we may add no-X and other X groups. It is possible to have 2 × 3 designs (two independent variables: one varied in two ways, the other varied in thee ways), 3 × 3, 2 × 2 × 2, etc. Suppose that we add one more X to our previous experiment: X_3 intelligence of the teacher, with two variations of it—high IQ and average IQ. We now have a 2 × 2 × 2 design, which requires eight treatment groups. This design can answer the following seven questions: What is the main (independent) effect on learning achievement of (1) X_1, (2) X_2, and (3) X_3? What is the interaction effect on learning achievement of (4) X_1 and X_2, (5) X_1 and X_3, (6) X_2 and X_3, and (7) X_1, X_2, and X_3?[18]

Factorial designs that are more sophisticated than this 2 × 2 × 2 design can answer an even greater number of questions, but the more complex ones become unwieldy. A 4 × 3 × 2 design, for example, in which X_1 has three variations, X_2 has four variations, and X_3 has two variations, requires twenty-four treatment groups (see Figure 9.8), and a 6 × 5 × 4 × 2 design requires 240 groups.

An important characteristic of factorial designs is that several hypotheses can be tested simultaneously. Factorial designs have released educators from the bondage of classical designs. No longer must they conduct a series of single-X experiments to answer questions about the effect that different Xs may have on learning achievement. Factorial designs permit them to conduct single experiments that will answer more complex questions, such as: What effect does X_1-type

[18]A two-variable interaction X_1 and X_2 is called a first-order interaction; a three-variable interaction X_1, X_2, and X_3 is called a second-order interaction.

FIGURE 9.8

Illustration of a 4 × 3 × 2 design.

(X_1) Method of teaching   (X_3) Sex   (X_2) Length of class period

		30 min	40 min	50 min	60 min
Discussion	Boys				
	Girls				
Lecture	Boys				
	Girls				
Programmed learning	Boys				
	Girls				

teacher have on learning achievement when using X_2-type methods in X_3-length classes with X_4-type students? With these tools in their possession, educators are in a much better position to grapple with phenomena encountered in the field.

Analysis of variance is the statistical technique that is usually applied to factorial designs. To learn how to compute the analysis of variance for the data in Figure 9.4, see Appendix A.4.

DESIGNS WITH PARTIAL CONTROL

The ideal research design is one that provides rigorous experimental control through randomization. If this ideal cannot be realized, you may consider using a quasi-experimental design that incorporates the most control that can be achieved under the existing conditions. If you employ a quasi-experimental design, however, you must know what variables your design may fail to control, and you must carefully consider the likelihood that these variables rather than X may account for the experimental results. The more improbable it is that they do, the more "valid" is the experiment.

Nonrandomized Control-group Pretest-Posttest Design (Design 5)

To achieve equivalent groups, rigorously controlled designs, such as Designs 2, 3, and 4, require that Ss be assigned to comparison groups at random. Employing randomization procedures is not difficult, but upsetting class schedules, getting scattered Ss to participate, and obtaining a sufficiently large sample to ensure that the laws of chance will operate cannot always be done. Under some circumstances, therefore, you may have to use preassembled groups, such as intact classes, for your experimental and control Ss.

DESIGN PROCEDURES   The paradigm for Design 5 is the same as that for Design 2, except for one important difference: The symbol, (R), is omitted to indicate the absence of random assignment to groups. In Design 5, the Ss are not assigned to groups at random. Preassembled groups that are as similar as availability permits are selected and are given pretests. The pretest mean scores and standard deviations[19] of the groups are compared to check their similarity.

[19]Standard deviation means the "spread" or "scatter" of the subjects' scores about the mean.

	PRETEST	TREATMENT	POSTTEST
Experimental group	T_{1_E}	X	T_{2_E}
Control group	T_{1_C}		T_{2_C}

INTERNAL VALIDITY   If similar groups are selected and their similarity is confirmed by the T_1 mean scores and standard deviations, this design controls several potential sources of internal invalidity. The presence of a control group enables you to assume that the main effects of *history*, *pretesting*, *maturation*, and *instrumentation* will not be mistaken for the effect of X, for both the experimental and control groups will experience these effects. Differences that groups experience when tested separately (intrasession history and instrumentation) which were discussed in Design 2 can arise, however, and they should be given serious consideration. The T_1 and T_2 data that are provided by this design make it possible to check whether the two groups differed in mortality.

The main source of internal invalidity for Design 5 is one that has not been discussed previously: it is the fact that an *interaction* of *selection* and *maturation*, an *interaction* of *selection* and *history*, etc., may take place. You may select groups that are similar and that have approximately the same T_1 mean scores; but, in the absence of randomization, the possibility always exists that other differences which distinguish the groups may be mistaken for the effect of X.

A selection-maturation interaction might be mistaken for the effect of X by camp directors, for example, if they used first-year campers for their experimental group and second-year campers for their control group. Suppose that the two groups had similar T_1 mean scores and the first-year experimental group attained a higher T_2 mean than the second-year control group. The superior gain of the first-year group may have been caused not by X but by the fact that the Ss were better adjusted to camp routines when they took T_2 than when they took T_1. Since members of the second-year group had minimal camp-life adjustments to make, their group would not exhibit a similar gain.

If the experimental Ss are self-selected—if they volunteer for exposure to X—and there is no comparable group of volunteers from the same population to serve as a control group, the possibility of a selection-maturation interaction is great. A group of volunteers is almost certain to be more highly motivated than a group of nonvolunteers; consequently, the assumption that the groups will progress uniformly becomes less likely. Suppose that an experimental group is composed of volunteer Ss who scored low on a spelling test, and the control group is composed of nonvolunteers from the same population (low-scoring Ss). If the experimental group exhibits the greater improvement in spelling after being exposed to X, a remedial program, the higher motivation of the volunteers rather than X may account for their greater improvement.

Statistical regression is a source of internal invalidity that can be avoided, but the possibility of its presence should be checked. You will recall that the T_1 mean of a sample group will move toward the population mean on T_2 (see pages 233 and 246). The more deviant (extreme) a sample mean is from the population mean, the *more* it is likely to regress. Perhaps you can grasp this concept better by examining the data on the *left* in Figure 9.9. These data give the means for seven classes in University High School and the population mean, which is 110. Suppose that the class in University High School with the low mean score of 80 on T_1 serves as an experimental group in a remedial program and that the class with the mean score of 120 on T_1 serves as the control group. You will note that the amount and direction of the regression of these two classes will differ. The experimental group regresses upward on T_2 toward the population mean, 110, and may in consequence appear to be making greater progress than the control group, which regresses downward on T_2 toward the population mean, 110. Differential regression may be mistaken for, or may mask the effect of, X.

The mistake of comparing two groups with such dissimilar T_1

FIGURE 9.9

Illustration of statistical regression.

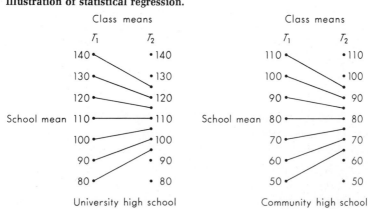

University high school   Community high school

means is not commonly made by researchers. But some educators do make the mistake of assuming that matching on T_1 scores establishes equivalent groups. Comparing matched Ss or matched groups that are *drawn from populations that have different means* is often responsible for introducing a regression effect in this design.

Suppose that Es introduce programmed learning in University High School, which has a school mean of 110, and use Community High School, which has a school mean of 80, for comparison purposes. If they select a class from each school that has a class mean of 90 and compare the progress of these sample groups, the groups will be matched on T_1 means. But the experimental sample in University High School with the mean of 90 is considerably below the mean of its parent population, 110, and the control sample with a mean of 90 in Community High School is above the mean of its parent population, 80, (see Figure 9.9). Since each sample will regress toward the mean of its parent population when retested, the University group will attain a higher mean on T_2 whether or not it is exposed to X. The mean of the University High School sample will regress up, and the mean of the Community High School sample will regress down on T_2. This regression effect in opposite directions might be mistaken for the effect of X.

When utilizing Design 5, every effort to rule out the possibility of differential recruitment of Ss must be made. But Campbell points out that "In this popular design, the frequent effort to 'correct' for the lack of perfect equivalence by matching on pretest scores is *absolutely wrong* . . . as it introduces a regression artifact. Instead, one should live with any initial pretest differences, using analysis of covariance, gain scores, or graphic presentation" (16:7–8).

You will remember that analysis of covariance, which is done after T_2 is given, achieves the same results as matching without discarding or shifting any Ss. The E selects two intact groups, administers the experimental treatment, and then adjusts T_2 means to compensate for the lack of equivalency between the two groups. When the assumptions underlying analysis of covariance can be met, this is the most desirable tool to employ for Design 5.

EXTERNAL VALIDITY   When checking the external validity of this design—the representativeness of the findings—the same problems may arise that are encountered when Design 2 is used. But certain features of this design make it easier to overcome some of these problems.

An *interaction* of *selection* and *X* may occur. Because of particular characteristics of the *Ss* (sex, intelligence, socioeconomic status, etc.), *X* may be more effective for them than for other members of the population to which you wish to generalize. But this problem can be overcome with this design more easily than it can with Design 2. School administrators are often reluctant to disrupt the school schedule to meet the randomization requirements of Design 2, but they may cooperate with you if you are willing to use intact classes for an experiment. Consequently, you can obtain comparison groups for a wide variety of settings with Design 5 more readily than you can with Design 2, which enables you to generalize to a larger subject population.

The *reactive effects of experimental procedures* in Design 5 may also hamper generalization, but they may not be as reactive as those that must be employed when Design 2 is used. Conducting an experiment without the *Ss* being aware of it is easier when intact classes are used for comparison groups than when random samples are taken from classes and are assigned at random to treatment groups.

Counterbalanced Design (Design 6)

When random assignment of *Ss* is not possible and intact classes must be used, Design 6 may be employed to overcome some of the weaknesses in Design 5. This Counterbalanced Design, which is also known as a *rotation, crossover,* or *switchover design,* is most commonly used when a limited number of *Ss* is available, no pretest if given, and more than one variation of *X* is tested.

DESIGN PROCEDURES   In a Counterbalanced Design each group of *Ss* is exposed to each *X* (and, if necessary, no *X* situation) at different times during the experiment. During the first exposure to the experimental treatment, for example, if group A is exposed to treatment X_a and Group B to X_b, the second time group A is exposed to X_b and group B to X_a:

	TIME 1	TIME 2
Group *A*	X_a	X_b
Group *B*	X_b	X_a

If the sums of the X_a and X_b scores of the two groups are compared, $(X_a + X_a$ and $X_b + X_b)$, the difference between the X_a and X_b sums cannot be interpreted as the product of the initial difference between the two groups, for each group affects each X exactly once; nor can the difference be interpreted as the product of the difference between order of testing, for each time of testing affects each X exactly once.

The Latin square arrangement, which is typically employed in counterbalancing, derives its name from an ancient puzzle. The size of the Latin square is determined by the number of experimental treatment levels (Xs). The square always contains the same number of treatment levels, rows, and columns. In each size Latin square, the letters representing the treatments (Xs) may be arranged in the cells in different ways, but they can occur only once in each column and in each row of the square. The number of ways the letters can be arranged and still adhere to the above rule are 2 ways for a 2×2 square, 12 ways for a 3×3 square, and 576 ways for a 4×4 square. Hence, an E should theoretically select a Latin square at random from the population of all possible squares of that dimension.[20] For a 2×2 square, for example, he should choose at random one of the two possible squares:

$a\ b$ $\qquad\qquad$ $b\ a$

$\qquad\quad$ or

$b\ a$ $\qquad\qquad$ $a\ b$

Suppose we use the Latin square counterbalancing technique to determine what effect four styles of type X_a, X_b, X_c, and X_d will have on reading-rate scores. Since there are four experimental treatments, we need four groups of subjects and four experimental sessions. Our 4×4 Latin square, selected at random from the available squares of this size (see Figure 9.10a), will contain three classifications: (1) groups of Ss, the rows; (2) times (order or occasions) of experimental sessions, the columns; and (3) experimental treatments, the cells. Note that in Figure 9.10a, each experimental treatment appears only once in each row and once in each column, a different X (style of type) is presented to each group each time, and each X precedes and follows each other X an equal number of times.

If we turn the Latin square in Figure 9.10a so that the Xs become column heads in Figure 9.10b and record the scores in each cell of Figure 9.10b, we can compute the column mean for each X. Each

---

[20]For a complete discussion of procedures for selecting Latin squares at random, see Fisher and Yates (39).

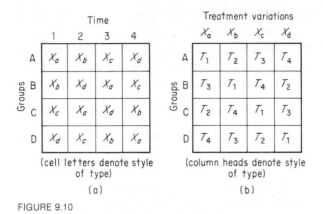

FIGURE 9.10

Two illustrations of the same Counterbalanced Design.

column mean will represent the average reading rate for all groups when exposed to the X represented by the column heading. A comparison of these column mean scores (Figure 9.10b) will reveal what effect the different styles of type had upon reading rate. Assuming that each unit of reading material was equally difficult and there was no carry-over learning from one session to the next, the style of type that received the highest mean reading-rate score is the best one to use.

DESIGN VALIDITY   This design introduces a control that is lacking in Design 5. Because the nonrandomized groups in Design 5 are not equivalent in all respects, some differences in them, such as the superior intelligence of one group, may be mistaken for the effect of X. This Counterbalanced Design rotates or cancels out these initial Ss differences and hence attains a kind of group equation. Because all Xs are administered to all groups (rows) and each time (columns), the sums of scores of the Xs are comparable. The differences in such sums cannot be attributable simply to preexperimental group (row) differences. If one group is more intelligent than the others, each X will profit from this superiority. Similarly, because each time of testing (column) affects each treatment exactly once, the influence of time on treatment will cancel out. If some disturbing event occurs during one of the four times that Ss are exposed to the treatment, each treatment will be exposed to the impact of this event.

The Latin square design offers some control, for the main effect of X (styles of type) will be independent of the main effects of groups and time (and similarly for the main effect of groups and time). This design provides data on main effects, but if interaction effects are present, it may lead one astray. If the highest reading scores are consistently associated with one style of type, X_a, what appears to be a significant main effect of style of type on reading rate, for example, could be an interaction effect between group and time. The four actions of each treatment occur under a unique set of group-time (row-column) combinations; treatment X_a occurs in four different cells from either treatment X_b, X_c, or X_d, and one cannot disentangle the impact of treatment X_a from the unique impact, if any, of its four cells. The four cells may possess no unique impact; if one could interchange the treatments X_a, X_b, X_c, and X_d in the design and get identical results, no interaction would be present. But, if interaction is present, there is little if any way to detect it as can be done in a factorial analysis design.

We have found that group differences that exist before the experiment may not be confounded with X in Design 6 as they may be in Design 5, but those that arise during the experiment may be. All groups, for example, may become more fatigued as an investigation progresses, but in each replication this fatigue factor will affect the mean score of each group and hence of each X. If one group becomes much more fatigued than the others, however, this *selection-maturation interaction* may be confounded with the effect of X. This type of interaction is less likely to occur in this design, however, than in Design 5. In Design 5, if just one group becomes excessively fatigued (selection-maturation interaction) or especially responsive to an extraneous event (selection-history interaction), this interaction effect may be mistaken for the effect of X. In a Counterbalanced Design, this mistake will not be made unless the interaction occurs during several replications—and in a different group each time—or is exceptionally strong on one occasion in one group.

This design presents one very serious problem in education: the effect of an exposure to one X may carry over and be combined with the measurements of the next X. In our previous experiment, for example, the experience of reading small type may enable Ss to read bigger type more rapidly than if they had not read small type beforehand. In a drug experiment, the effect of the first drug may remain in the body; consequently, measurements that are taken after the second drug is administered may represent the effect of both drugs. When the possibility of carry-over effects exists, sufficient time should elapse between replications to permit the effects from the previous treatment to dissipate. In many instances in educational research, however, the assumption that there is no residual or carry-over effect cannot be satisfied. The usefulness of the design, therefore, is limited.

This quasi-experimental design is used when one has little control over the assignment of Ss to groups and must use a few intact existing classes and when it is assumed that all interaction effects are zero. If possible, however, this quasi-experimental design is transformed into a true experiment by assigning each S to each group independently and at random and by replicating the experiment with different Latin squares. If a different and independent random sampling of Ss can be assigned to each cell of the square rather than to each group independently and at random, the problem of repeated measurements and the possibility of carry-over effects can be controlled.

One-group Time-series Design (Design 7)

This design is the same as Design 1 except that several measurements are taken before and after the introduction of X. The paradigm for Design 7 is as follows:

$$T_1 \quad T_2 \quad T_3 \quad T_4 \quad X \quad T_5 \quad T_6 \quad T_7 \quad T_8$$

INTERNAL VALIDITY   Because multiple tests are given over a period of time, a time-series design controls more potential sources of internal invalidity than Design 1. Suppose that eye specialists using standard measuring techniques have appraised a group of Ss periodically over a span of four years, and they have found no appreciable change in the common eye impairment. On the same day all the Ss are given a recently discovered drug X, and within seventy-two hours their vision is normal. There is a possibility that something other than the drug may have caused the improvement in vision, but this possibility is not likely.

When employing Design 7, the justification for concluding that X caused a given effect *depends on the stability of the past performances or measurements*. In Figure 9.11, X may have caused the effect noted between T_4 and T_5 in test series A. But one cannot infer that X caused the increase that appears between T_4 and T_5 in B or C. Maturation rather than X may have caused the increase in B, for example, and random instability may have caused the fluctuation in C.

Multitesting provides this design with a great advantage over Design 1. If there is no appreciable difference in the first four T scores, the difference between the T_4 and T_5 scores is not likely to be caused by *maturation, testing,* or *regression.* Changes in the measuring *instruments* may occur over a period of time, but there is no reason why they should occur between T_4 and T_5 as opposed to earlier tests. If the

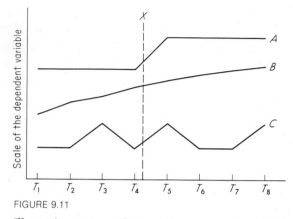

FIGURE 9.11

Illustrative patterns of repeated measurements with the introduction of X.

record-keeping system is changed when X is introduced, however, or the raters know when X is introduced and have strong convictions concerning its potential effect, these changes and biases rather than X may account for the difference between the T_4 and T_5 scores.

    Selection and *mortality* are controlled by this design if the same *Ss* participate in all phases of the experiment. *Contemporary history* variables provide the major internal-invalidity problem: hence, the possibility of their presence must be carefully checked. The difference between T_4 and T_5 scores may not be caused by X, for example, but by the occurrence of an institutional event (dance, examination, etc.), seasonal or weather fluctuations, or cyclical variations (weekends, etc.). Suppose that you check library records for eight weeks to ascertain the effect of X—opening the stacks to all students after the fourth week. You may note a sharp increase in book withdrawals between T_4 and T_5 that is caused by the approach of final examinations rather than by the introduction of X.

EXTERNAL VALIDITY   The extent to which the findings of this design can be generalized depends upon the experimental conditions. An *interaction* of *pretesting* and *X* may occur. If achievement tests or other *Ts* that are commonly used in schools are employed, no problems will arise. Such tests are usually nonreactive, because the population to which one wishes to generalize also experiences them. Unique *Ts*, however, may make the *Ss* differ from the general population from which they came; consequently, the findings may apply only to *Ss* who take these specific pretests.

A *selection-X interaction* may occur when this design is used. An *E* may select *Ss* who have perfect attendance records over an extended period of time, or the repetition of unique *Ts* may cause absenteeism. Data obtained under either of these circumstances might not be representative of the effect of *X* for the general population, for students who have perfect attendance or avoid tests may differ from other students in respect to health, skills, interest in school, or other factors.

Control-group Time-series Design (Design 8)

This design utilizes a control group to overcome one of the weaknesses of Design 7: the failure to control history. If the control group fails to show a gain from T_4 to T_5 and the experimental group shows a gain, then the plausibility of *contemporary history* accounting for the X results is reduced greatly, for both groups have experienced these events. See the following paradigm:

Experimental group	T_{1_E}	T_{2_E}	T_{3_E}	T_{4_E}	X	T_{5_E}	T_{6_E}	T_{7_E} T_{8_E}
Control group	T_{1_C}	T_{2_C}	T_{3_C}	T_{4_C}		T_{5_C}	T_{6_C}	T_{7_C} T_{8_C}

This design is also superior to Design 5, for it controls *selection-maturation interaction* to the extent that, if one group shows a greater rate of gain than the other, this accelerated gain would be revealed in the pre-*X* tests.

The multiple posttests that are employed in Designs 7 and 8 often provide vital information that a single posttest design would not reveal. In some instances, the long- and short-term effects of *Xs* vary not only in quality but also in quantity. Suppose that an experiment is conducted to determine whether children achieve greater mastery of fractions by the "practice" or by the "understand" method. The former may produce greater initial gains, but the latter may produce less forgetting and greater long-term mastery.

EVALUATION OF EXPERIMENTAL RESEARCH

When the experimental method can be used properly to solve problems, it is the most satisfactory means of obtaining reliable knowledge. Knowledge of the past, descriptions of present status, pooled judgments, expert opinions, and hunches of skilled professional workers provide ideas and information that help teachers and administrators make educational decisions. Experimentation puts explanations concerning the relations among educational phenomena to an empirical test. In an experimental study, you manipulate the variables and observe the effect under rigorously controlled conditions. You describe your procedures so that other observers can check your findings under identical conditions. Experimentation serves as a high court of judgment; experimentation refines and sharpens the educational decision-making process.

The following discussion evaluates how well educational research measures up to the experimental standards in the natural sciences, identifies problems that impede progress, and delineates developments that are opening up exciting possibilities.

Formulation of the Problem

The scientific method of research requires a thorough analysis of a problem, the precise formulation of hypotheses, a clear statement of the testable consequences that are logically deduced from them, and a rigorous check on the assumptions and logical arguments underlying the experimental plans. Because these important responsibilities have often been neglected, severe attacks have been made on educational research studies. Griffiths contends, for example, that

> . . . without doubt, the greatest weakness of research in educational administration is the lack of theory. Most studies in educational administration are done at the level of "naked empiricism." By this we mean that the researcher has an idea that a vaguely defined problem needs to be solved. He collects data through a questionnaire, survey, or some other method and attempts to find an answer by "looking at the data." By following this procedure we have amassed tons of data, but have come up with very few answers. The opposite of "naked empiricism" is research based on theory [46:16].

Griffith's criticism of research in educational administration is applicable to many other areas within education.

When experienced researchers conduct experimental investigations, they are less frequently guilty of collecting data aimlessly—without a theoretical orientation—than when they employ other research methods, but the quality of their work varies. Many novices, however, cannot accept the fact that designing an experiment can consume more time than conducting it. To them formulating a hypothesis to test, planning an investigation to the finest detail—carrying out a pilot study—and removing all logical flaws and procedural imperfections before conducting any step of it are unnecessarily burdensome tasks. They do not comprehend that conducting an experiment and writing a scholarly paper are not comparable undertakings. Once an experiment is put into motion, it must be run off exactly as planned; unlike a scholarly paper, an experiment cannot be patched up after it is under way.

STATEMENT OF HYPOTHESES   Hypotheses are the heart of scientific research—the working instruments of scientific reasoning. They are facilitating devices which give the facts obtained by the *E* a chance to confirm or disconfirm whether stipulated relationships among educational phenomena exist. Unfortunately, many *Es* are concerned primarily with experimental designs and statistical procedures and give insufficient attention to the theoretical premises of their investigations. Many research reports are full of statistically significant findings that stand in such isolation of theoretical orientation that they contribute little or nothing to the advancement of science. Science makes great advances through experimental studies, but the experiment itself does not provide the intellectual thrust that pushes back the frontiers of knowledge. The experiment does not initiate discoveries; it tests ideas that are already born. The experimental design and statistical techniques merely check hypotheses that the researcher has developed or has derived from existing theories in the field. Thus, a brilliantly executed experiment is of little value if it tests a poorly conceived hypothesis.

CHAIN OF REASONING   Scientific theories and hypotheses about the nature of things must be tested both logically and empirically. At the beginning of this century, in psychology, "theory ranged far ahead of experiment and made no demand that propositions be testable. Experiment, for its part, was willing to observe any phenomenon, whether or not the data bore on theoretical issues. Today, the majority of experimenters derive their hypotheses explicitly from theoretical premises and try to nail their results into a theoretical structure" (25:674). Sophisticated educational researchers are beginning to take similar steps. They orient their experiments in theoretical propositions that exist in their field or in related fields, and through a chain of deductive reasoning, they set forth a justifiable set of inferences that lead step-by-step through the problem hypothesis to a statistical hypothesis. Once this logical chain of reasoning is forged, they begin to accumulate empirical evidence through experimental procedures. Finally, they utilize the process of inductive reasoning to relate the results of their tests of significance back to the problem hypothesis.

The discussions that appear in many research reports fail to bring this chain of deductive-inductive reasoning into proper focus. The necessity for a problem hypothesis is apparently not recognized, or confusion exists over the function of the problem hypothesis and the statistical hypothesis. The latter statement seems quite plausible, for many *Es* report the statistical, or null, hypothesis as if it were the problem hypothesis. In many studies, the problem hypothesis is not presented in the formal "if-then" form. Readers must restate the problem in this form to check the logic of the arguments. Researchers should make the arguments in their deductive-inductive chain of reasoning explicit in their research reports.

EXAMINATION OF ASSUMPTIONS Experimental studies that are based on false assumptions cannot yield valid results, yet some *Es* fail to examine the assumptions underlying their hypotheses, procedures, and methods of analyzing the results. They assume, for example, that a given test will measure a particular ability of their *Ss* without checking whether there is reliable evidence available to support their assumption. They apply statistical tests without satisfying the assumptions upon which the tests are based. Researchers are obligated to analyze critically the assumptions underlying every phase of their experimental plans, to eliminate those they cannot defend, and to recognize what implications the remaining ones have for the interpretation of their findings.

If assumptions are made manifest and are codified in research reports, they are readily available for critical inspection and cumulative development. Some educators are beginning to include such statements in their studies. To illustrate, one *E* in "An Experiment in Developing Critical Thinking in Children," stipulates that

> . . . In the endeavor to set up criteria for the selection of content material and the development of teaching methods, the following assumptions were posited. . . .

> 1 That thinking is critical when it is essentially logical.
> 2 That logical thinking is no more than the application of the rules of logic to factual data in order to arrive at valid as well as true conclusions. It follows from this assumption that an individual's growth in the ability to do logical thinking must depend upon his acquiring a working knowledge of the basic rules of logic.

3 That children in the upper grades of the elementary school are, in general, mentally capable of acquiring the necessary understanding of logic and a proficiency in the use of its rules.

4 That the most effective way of helping children to acquire the necessary working knowledge of the principles of logic is through direct instruction.

5 That this direct instruction should consist of: *a.* Materials and learning content which embody the principles of logic. *b.* Teaching methods that provide full opportunity for the pupil to discover for himself these principles and to formulate them as generalizations [56].

Observation and Experimentation

Experimental research conforms to the scientific method of acquiring knowledge in that controlled observation is utilized to test hypotheses. But because of the complexity and nonuniformity of human phenomena, "experiment in the social sciences is not possible in the same sense that it is in physics and chemistry where an experiment may be repeated an endless number of times under controlled and practically identical conditions. . . . But it is desirable to approach the methodology of the exact sciences in every way possible, recognizing that in so far as the experimenter falls short of such standards his results are defective" (100:228).

PITFALLS IN EXPERIMENTS   Educational researchers have begun to pay greater attention to the procedures they employ in observing and recording events under study and in analyzing data. But *Es* are fallible human beings who can easily go astray. By becoming sensitized to some of the pitfalls that can lead to misleading experimental results and conclusions, you may avoid them in your own studies.[21]

The directions for carrying out many investigations are too vague to produce reliable results. The *Es* do not write step-by-step detailed instructions for each procedure and do not plan for the various contingencies that may arise with respect to *Ss*, settings, or instruments. As a result, the investigators and their assistants employ somewhat different procedures or standards or make different decisions about how to handle routine and unexpected situations that arise. As a result, they obtain dissimilar data from similar *Ss*. Imprecise descriptions of procedures make it impossible, of course, for other investigators to replicate the studies and check the findings. When procedures are outlined in detail, they are not always carried out the

---

[21]For a more detailed discussion of pitfalls in research see 110:383–404; 84; 81:10–13.

way they are supposed to be. The *Es* or their assistants may consciously or unconsciously misrecord *Ss*' responses and behavior, particularly in the direction of supporting the hypothesis. They may add or delete questions or may give verbal, facial, or bodily cues to *Ss* about expected outcomes or answers. In conducting an experiment, you not only must specify the experimental procedures in detail, but also must adequately train and check all workers to make certain the procedures are carried out properly.

Some *Es* are not as meticulous as they should be about selecting and maintaining the tools that they use to measure the influence of variables, to hold factors constant, to manipulate variables, and to amplify or magnify phenomena. Sometimes they report that the independent variable has produced an effect that has in fact been caused by the improper functioning of the apparatus. Sometimes *Es* do not choose or cannot locate instruments that will produce the required kind and form of data. Sometimes they use tools that are not appropriate for testing the type of *Ss* that participate in an experiment. Quantifying findings also present problems. It is not always possible to construct tools that will make accurate and sufficiently discriminating measurements. When competent observers use crude yardsticks to measure the same phenomenon, they do not always obtain identical measurements.

Some experiments fail because the *Es* require more involvement and effort from *Ss* than can realistically be expected, give instructions that are too complicated, use procedures that are too intellectually demanding or too unfamiliar for *Ss*, or set up overly contrived or unconvincing experimental situations that cause *Ss* to become wary. In experiments designed to change well-established behavior patterns, some *Es* fail to expose the *Ss* to the treatment long enough to effect a change in behavior and fail to administer enough posttests to determine the lasting effects of the treatment. Some *Es* fail to check whether the technique they have employed to manipulate an *X*, such as frustration or anger, has actually produced that effect. Many design and procedural weaknesses can be spotted before launching an investigation, if you conduct carefully conceived pilot tests with representative samples of *Ss*.

If *Es* do not stipulate what procedures will be employed to analyze the data before launching the experiment, the temptation is great to focus on data that support the hypothesis and to ignore or bury negative results. Computation errors and inappropriate analysis of data that are sufficiently great to change the conclusions of a study are not uncommon in research reports, and fudging some data to make the results appear more significant than they are or constructing a hypothesis to account for unexpected findings after the data have been obtained are not unknown.

CONTROL OF THE EXPERIMENT   Physical scientists conduct the majority of their experiments in the laboratory, where they can maintain optimum conditions of control. Whenever possible, educators follow their example. But some problems, such as those concerning crowd behavior, cannot be re-created readily in the laboratory. When phenomena can be reproduced in the laboratory, human beings do not always react to X in the same way as they would in a normal situation. To overcome this, social scientists often test hypotheses in natural settings such as classrooms. They introduce as many controls as possible, but the number of extraneous variables that may affect the dependent variable increases in the nonlaboratory situation.

Because of the complexity of educational phenomena, discovering what variables to control and determining how to control them in any setting is extremely difficult. Educators may not be able to identify all

FIGURE 9.12

Comparison of experimental designs.

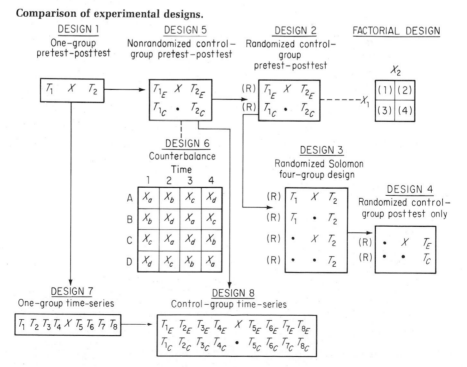

the relevant extraneous variables that may affect the dependent variable. Unlike the physical scientists, they cannot remove many of the variables such as age, IQ, etc., that they do identify; consequently, they resort to a battery of other control techniques.

Educators are acquiring a better understanding of how to control experiments, but because of ethical and administrative considerations they cannot always manipulate human beings and class schedules to meet the requirements of the research designs that are most theoretically desirable. When full experimental control cannot be achieved, they often use quasi-experimental designs that provide partial control. No matter what design researchers use, they must be fully aware of the variables that remain uncontrolled. Table 9.1, which has been adapted from Campbell and Stanley (17), presents a checkoff list for twelve

TABLE 9.1
Factors Jeopardizing the Validity of Experimental Designs

SOURCE OF INVALIDITY	LITTLE CONTROL 1	RIGOROUS CONTROL 2 3 4	PARTIAL CONTROL 5 6 7 8
Internal validity			
Contemporary history†	−	+ + +	+ + − +
Maturation processes	−	+ + +	+ + + +
Pretesting procedures	−	+ + +	+ + + +
Measuring instruments	−	+ + +	+ + ? +
Statistical regression	?	+ + +	? + + +
Differential selection of subjects	+	+ + +	+ + + +
Experimental mortality	+	+ + +	+ + + +
Interaction of selection and maturation, etc.	−	+ + +	− ? + +
External validity			
Interaction of selection and X	−	? ? ?	? ? ? −
Interaction of pretesting and X	−	− + +	− ? − −
Reactive experimental procedures	?	? ? ?	? ? ? ?
Multiple-treatment interference			−

* Names of Designs 1 to 8 are:
1: One-group Pretest-Posttest
2: Randomized Control-group Pretest-Posttest
3: Randomized Solomon Four-group
4: Randomized Control-group Posttest only
5: Nonrandomized Control-group Pretest-Posttest
6: Counterbalanced
7: One-group Time-series
8: Control-group Time-series

† NOTE: A plus symbol indicates control of a factor, a minus indicates lack of control, a question mark suggests there is some source for concern, and a blank indicates that the factor is not relevant.

potential sources of invalidity to help the reader appraise how well certain designs control these factors.

When selecting an experimental design, an *E* encounters many perplexing problems and must make a number of difficult decisions. An ideal experimental design possesses both internal and external validity, but the conditions that are required to achieve each type of validity are often incompatible. The controls that are used to achieve internal validity may limit the representativeness of the findings. *Ss* who take a pretest, for example, or know they are participating in an experiment may no longer be representative of the population from which they were drawn. An *E* wants to select a design that is strong in both internal and external validity. When faced with the dilemma of choosing between them, an *E* must give prior consideration to internal validity.

Generalization and Prediction

Scientists consider that they understand phenomena when they can project findings of a study to other *Ss* and situations. Chemists who apply an experimental stimulus to one pure sample of phenomena in their field can be relatively certain that all like samples will react the same way to the same stimulus under the same conditions. But because of the tremendous variability of people's minds, bodies, attitudes, and backgrounds, educators cannot assume with full confidence that a stimulus which has been applied to one group of *Ss* will produce the same effect when it is applied to another group. Except when dealing with behavior that is practically unmodifiable among human beings, such as reflexes, social scientists cannot project findings from one study to *all human beings.*

SAMPLES OF SUBJECT AND NONSUBJECT POPULATIONS   Overgeneralizing experimental findings is a common error in educational research. The findings of a study in which young men in a Middle Western state teachers' college serve as *Ss* are, at best, applicable to similar males; they are not applicable to "ivy league," premedical, or high school males, or to female college students. Many educators pay too little attention to the external validity of their designs. An *E* cannot be expected to draw a sample that is representative of all children in this country for each experiment. With a little care, however, one can often select *Ss* in a manner that will make ones findings applicable beyond the specific sample that participates in the experiment.

Since generalization is the goal of science, some critics suggest that an E should select representative samples from the nonsubject populations as well as from the S populations to which one wishes to generalize. If the experimental variable that is being manipulated is "anxiety," these critics ask the following questions: Will it be possible to generalize the findings to rural as well as urban settings and to home as well as classroom situations? Will the findings of the study be the same if X is induced by electric shock or by verbal means? Will experimental workers who differ in age, race, sex, social status, physical appearance, dominance, or friendliness obtain different results when testing similar Ss on the same tasks? An interaction can occur between the personal attributes of the E and the personal attributes of the Ss which will determine how the Ss perform when they are exposed to the experimental treatment. If "anxiety" is the variable being manipulated, black students may perform differently for a white E than for a black E. If the findings of the study are to have wide applicability, the experimental design must incorporate a representative sample—or at least a varied sample—of (1) the natural situations in which X is found, (2) the measurement variables, (3) the tasks or learning materials, (4) the methods of administering the experimental treatment, and (5) the Es.

GENERALIZABILITY OF RESEARCH DESIGNS   Classical experimental designs have helped educators gain valuable insights into their phenomena, but the "law of the single variable" has impeded the development of significant generalizations in our field. When one must isolate and vary one X at a time while holding constant the effects of all other variables, the effect that one observes may not be generalizable to nonlaboratory situations. Educational phenomena are usually the product of many variables operating simultaneously in the classroom, and a variable may produce different effects when it interacts with different variables. Educators need to obtain more information about the interaction of variables in the ongoing educational process. This need has been met by the development of factorial designs which make it possible to manipulate samples from a number of populations (Ss, situations, tasks, Es) simultaneously.

Factorial designs are among the most important contributions that have been made to research technique during this century, but they also have limitations. In most instances, only a few variables and levels of variables can be sampled, because obtaining and handling the number of groups that is required for a complex design are too difficult. Restricting the number of variables, of course, limits the representativeness of the research findings.

ACCUMULATION OF RELIABLE KNOWLEDGE At this point it may appear that the search for absolutely certain knowledge eludes the researcher. Indeed it does, and the scientists of tomorrow will fare no better. On the surface, the demand for certainty does not seem an unreasonable request with our modern know-how, but nevertheless, attaining this goal is impossible. Inability to obtain certainty stems from the fact that experimental designs are imperfect; they are not capable of producing evidence that is universally certain. Experimentation produces statements of probability. According to the rules of logic, one is never fully justified in inferring universal statements from single or numerous observations, for any conclusions drawn in this manner may turn out to be false: no matter how many black crows one observes, the conclusion that *all* crows are black is not justified. In short, experimental statements are statistical inferences; they can attain a degree of probability only somewhere along a continuum between truth and falsity.

Certainty cannot be achieved through experimentation, but you should do everything practicable to reduce uncertainty. You should use a design that is technically as good as current knowledge and the given situation permit. You should demonstrate the effect of the phenomena under consideration in as wide a variety of situations as possible and state explicitly the degree of generality to which your hypothesis extends. Your objective is to make the design as valid externally as is feasible without losing internal validity.

Through replication (i.e., conducting additional experiments with other Ss in similar situations), you and other investigators must ascertain how much confidence can be placed in the hypothesis. If the hypothesis is confirmed repeatedly, the probability that it is "true" is greatly strengthened, and this knowledge can become an established part of science. An increase in the generalizability of the original hypothesis can be sought through replicating the experiment with Ss in other settings and situations. Through such replications, educators can build cumulatively toward more comprehensive explanations of phenomena in their field.

10 STRATEGY OF DESCRIPTIVE RESEARCH

efore much progress can be made in any field, scholars must possess descriptions of the phenomena with which they work. Early developments in educational research, therefore, as in other disciplines, have been concerned with making accurate assessments of the incidence, distribution, and relationships of phenomena in the field. To solve problems about children, school administration, curriculum, or the teaching of arithmetic, investigators ask the question: What exists—what is the present status of these phenomena? Determining the nature of prevailing conditions, practices, and attitudes—seeking accurate descriptions of activities, objects, processes, and persons—is their objective. But descriptive research is not confined to routine fact gathering. Identifying and clarifying relationships among variables are the goals of many investigators.

GENERAL OVERVIEW OF DESCRIPTIVE STUDIES

Descriptive data are usually collected by administering questionnaires, interviewing subjects, observing events, or analyzing documentary sources. Descriptive studies range from simple surveys that do little more than ask questions and report answers about the status quo to studies that present explicit statements about the relationships between variables which approach the level of the explanatory hypotheses one finds in experimental research.

In *status descriptive surveys*, investigators do not try to relate one variable to another. They merely search for accurate information about the characteristics of particular subjects (*Ss*), groups, institutions, or situations or about the frequency with which something occurs. In *explanatory descriptive studies,* the investigators are concerned about causality and do seek knowledge about the relationships between variables just as experimenters do. But the strategy involved in experimental and descriptive research differs. Experimenters (*Es*) predict that an independent variable, *X*, is related to or presumably the cause of the occurrence of the dependent variable, *Y*. The *Es* then manipulate *X* in an experiment to ascertain whether empirical evidence confirms that *X* has the predicted effect on *Y*. Two important differences between experimental designs and explanatory descriptive designs must be noted:

1. In explanatory descriptive studies, investigators *do not manipulate X* and then observe what happens to *Y,* as experimenters do. In situations where *X* has already occurred or is not amenable to direct manipulation, investigators must employ a different cause-effect analysis strategy: a descriptive research design. They hypothesize that *X* is presumably the cause of the occurrence of *Y*, and then observe naturally occurring instances of exposure and nonexposure to *X* to determine whether the data confirm their hypothesis.

2. Experimenters employ techniques that control the effect of other relevant variables on *X* before collecting their data; descriptive researchers control the effect of other relevant variables on *X* after collecting their data, usually through statistical techniques.

Writers are not in agreement on how to classify descriptive studies. This text will utilize the following convenient but arbitrarily selected categories: (1) survey studies, (2) interrelationship studies, and (3) developmental studies. These categories are not rigid. Some studies fall exclusively within one of these areas, but others have characteristics of more than one.

SURVEY STUDIES

When trying to solve problems, researchers in educational, governmental, industrial, and political organizations often conduct surveys. They collect detailed descriptions of existing phenomena with the intent of employing the data to justify current conditions and practices or to make more intelligent plans for improving them. Their objective may be not only to ascertain status but also to determine the adequacy of status by comparing it with selected or established standards. Health examination procedures, for example, may be compared with "best practices" as defined by authorities, and children's reading scores may be compared with norms established for specific groups. Educators who wish to improve existing status may survey how others have solved similar problems. Some researchers collect all these types of information.

Surveys may be broad or narrow in scope. They may encompass several countries or may be confined to one nation, region, state, city, school system, or some other unit. Survey data may be gathered from every member of the population (census survey) or from a carefully selected sample (sample survey). The units of analysis are often people, but they may be countries, government agencies, books, teachers' unions, or other units. A given survey may involve more than one unit of analysis. A school survey of a city, for example, may include the following units: school plant, instructional personnel, and pupils. Data may be collected concerning a few or a large number of related variables for each unit. The scope and depth of the study depend primarily on the nature of the problem.

Surveys may be descriptive or explanatory or both. The explanatory surveys are discussed in this chapter under interrelationship and developmental studies. Descriptive surveys are discussed below under several headings. No presumption is made that this classification scheme is universally accepted or that a sharp dividing line separates categories.

School Surveys

A local school district may conduct a survey of an individual school, a particular school level, or all the schools in the district for the purpose of internal or external evaluation or of assessing and projecting needs. These studies are carried out solely by school personnel or cooperatively by school personnel, a visiting team of consultants, and sometimes some lay citizens. These surveys serve a useful practical purpose, but *survey research,* as the term is known to social scientists, is usually more extensive, sophisticated, and rigorously controlled. In *Equality of Educational Opportunity* (23), for example, the investigators reported both differential descriptions and made explanatory analyses using data obtained from 4,000 schools. They employed elaborate statistical procedures to examine the relative effects of both home and school factors on pupil achievement and motivation.

LEVELS OF SURVEYS   Surveys may be conducted on all political levels. In recent years, high-level policymakers have recognized that if they are to make decisions that will synchronize education with technologi-cal and cultural changes and will hasten the attainment of economic, social, and political goals, they must have available a more comprehen-sive and comparable collection of educational data. Consequently, government agencies and educational organizations on the state, na-tional, and international levels have begun to collect educational data more systematically. The Census Bureau and the Office of Education conduct a number of systematic surveys. The *Digest of Educational Statistics,* which is prepared annually, includes data from several governmental sources. On the international level, the United Nations and UNESCO have conducted a number of important educational surveys.

DATA SOUGHT IN SURVEYS   Descriptive researchers may seek infor-mation about one or more of the following categories relating to the educational enterprise, or they may examine intensively specific as-pects of one category.

1 The Setting for Learning   Some investigators gather information about legal acts, regulations, or ordinances from the state to the local level that affect education. Not uncommonly, surveys seek data about school finances, the school plant, and equipment and supplies. Other studies investigate aspects of the social structure in the classroom, home, or community that may influence learning.

2 The Characteristics of Educational Personnel   Many surveys gather information about the backgrounds, responsibilities, and interrelation-ships of teachers, supervisors, administrators, and nonteaching person-nel. Questions may be raised concerning the sex, age, education, health, degrees, socioeconomic background, group memberships, in-

come, and tenure of the personnel surveyed. Numerous surveys focus on the behavior of instructional personnel in the classroom, the department, and the community with the objective of assessing or improving teaching effectiveness. Some studies are concerned with the attitudes of school employees on various questions; the nature and number of the contacts of these employees with colleagues, students, and the community; or the levels of expectation these employees hold for themselves, students, and the school.

3 The Nature of Pupils Acquiring information about the behavior patterns of pupils in classrooms, with peers, at home, and in the community is the purpose of many surveys. Descriptions of pupils' academic achievements, intelligence, aptitudes; of their health, reading, work, or study habits; or of their work, travel, or recreational activities may be sought. Some investigations are concerned with attendance and dropout records, the number and type of physically handicapped or other exceptional students, or the number and nature of disciplinary or delinquency incidents.

4 The Nature of the Educational Process The educational programs, processes, and outcomes may come under scrutiny. Investigators may determine what size the classes are, what is and is not included in the curriculum, and what the time allotments are for activities and for various aspects of each activity. The nature and number of school services, such as health, library, and research may be ascertained.

Community Surveys

Because of the close relationship between the schools and the community, educators often collect data concerning the local setting and particular aspects of life in it. Sometimes they join social scientists in fact-finding projects known as *community surveys, social surveys,* or *field surveys.* These community surveys are closely akin to school surveys; they may contain data concerning the schools, and conversely school surveys may analyze many aspects of the community.

Some community studies focus sharply on a particular condition, such as health services, employment, juvenile delinquency, or housing. Other studies present data concerning a specific segment of society, such as Puerto Ricans, the elderly, or drug addicts. Comprehensive surveys, on the other hand, may seek in-depth information about the government and laws, history and geography, economic and cultural conditions, population composition and trends, and other factors that contribute to the character of the community.

Job Analysis

Sometimes job analysis—a technique borrowed from business and government—is employed to study administrative, teaching, and non-instructional positions. Both administrators and teachers' unions or professional organizations make use of such surveys. In job-analysis investigations, information may be collected about the general duties and responsibilities of workers, the specific activities that they engage in on a job, their status and relationships in the administrative organization, and the nature and type of their facilities. Descriptions of the education, experience, and salaries of workers and the knowledges, health standards, and behavioral traits that they possess also may be sought. The data gathered help investigators describe the current practices and conditions of employment and the competencies and behavioral traits that personnel possess or should possess to carry out their work.

Obtaining an analytical knowledge of job components helps administrators and scholars (1) detect weaknesses, duplications, or inefficiency in the present work procedures, (2) establish uniform classifications for similar work, (3) determine wage or salary schedules for jobs entailing various levels of skill or responsibility, (4) identify the competencies to seek when employing personnel, (5) assign workers to jobs in a manner that will achieve the best utilization of the available manpower, (6) set up training programs and prepare instructional materials for prospective or in-service employees, (7) establish requirements for promotion, (8) make decisions concerning the transfer or retraining of personnel, and (9) develop a theoretical framework for studying administrative functions and structures.

Data for job-analysis studies are obtained from personal observations, authorities or workers in the field, or documents, such as state laws, school district regulations, or court decisions. Obtaining accurate descriptions of a job is difficult. Compiling a list of specific activities performed by a worker gives only a partial picture of what is required for the job. If the qualitative or creative characteristics which are necessary for successful job performance, such as ideals and attitudes, resourcefulness and cooperativeness, dependability and tact, are not appraised, the study will not produce a full job description. But obtaining objective and reliable data concerning these personal characteristics is extremely difficult. A job analysis that gives equal weight to all activities, functions, and personal characteristics associated with a particular position also presents a distorted picture, for each factor does not contribute equally to work performance. Some method of weighing the relative importance of the various job components is needed, but devising an objective method of making such judgments is difficult.

Documentary Analysis

Collecting data can be an arduous task, but sometimes investigators will find that the information they need is available in the data banks of university research centers, government agencies, and school systems. Documents and records may be dull reading to laymen, but researchers often unearth pertinent data or get ideas about relationships that suggest hypotheses they can test from "dredging the data" found in census, birth, accident, crime, library, school, institutional, and personal records. Some of the data, moreover, are collected repeatedly, making possible the analysis of trends over time. Documentary analysis is sometimes referred to as *content, activity,* or *informational* analysis, for it is concerned with the classification, quantification, and comparison of specified characteristics within the content of communication. The communication may be in the form of official records or in any written, printed, verbal, or pictorial form.

TYPES OF ANALYSES A wide variety of documentary surveys are made. Scholars may analyze judicial decisions, state laws, and school board rulings; administrative records and reports; budgets and financial records; and cumulative attendance and health records. University catalogs or bulletins may provide information about curriculum offerings, content of particular courses, entrance or graduation requirements, and tuition. Textbooks, courses of study, or school schedules may help investigators determine what is and is not taught, the grade placement of particular materials, and the amount of time devoted to them. Scholars may also analyze the contents of reference works, newspapers, periodicals, and films. Sometimes they find that personal documents, such as diaries, expense accounts, and letters, provide them with valuable data.

Classroom teachers often complain, "We can't teach everything! What are the most important skills and knowledges that children should attain?" To answer this question, educators have conducted studies to discover what arithmetic processes are most commonly employed in business and social usage, what types of errors are made by pupils in oral and written communication and other subjects, and what facts and generalizations are most frequently used in adult life or in particular professions.

Early documentary research was rather superficial and mechanical. Workers described the surface characteristics of the content and tabulated the frequency of the occurrence of items, but they did not test hypotheses about characteristics, antecedents or causes, and effects of communication. They used convenient categories that did not reveal particularly significant meanings. But many researchers today are "relatively less concerned with the content as such than with content as 'a reflection' of 'deeper' phenomena" (10:123). They may try to ascertain who (source of communication), said what, why (intent or objective of the communicator), how (strategy of communicator), to whom (type of reader, viewer, or listener), or with what effect. The analysis of latent content data (reading between the lines) is used in conjunction with independent behavioral indexes (physiological and psychological processes of the creator or recipient).

In content-analysis studies, researchers may ask questions such as the following: What is the changing character of the content and the communicators' attitudes toward key symbols over time (spot trends, trace developments of a student's or author's work, trace changing attitudes toward social or educational issues)? What is the relationship between the known characteristics of the source (ideologies-values, biases, interests, psychological states) and the content? What are the likenesses and differences in the content of two authors' work, of reports in different media or the same media, of textbooks, educational laws, curriculums in different parts of the country or world? To what extent does the content measure up to certain standards (children's TV programs, adequacy of coverage and bias of publications)? What styles and techniques of persuasion did the communicators use (which in turn may be used to identify an unknown author from content)? How did the communicators adjust content to the age, race, socioeconomic status, geographical location, and other known characteristics of the audience? What inferences can be drawn from the content about the psychological traits of the communicators, about various aspects of the culture, or about cultural change?

When analyzing textbooks, researchers may measure the length of sentences; count the frequency of specific concepts or symbols, of difficult words or of abstract words; check the diversity of words; and count the number of pictures or tables. They may note the amount of space devoted to specific content (31), the omission of specific content, the selectivity of content, the position of items in content, and the number of errors or distortions. From their analysis they may be able to judge the readability of textbooks; determine where, when, and how much is being taught about specific topics; and detect biases and beliefs of the authors about races, women, economic systems, and other factors.

To detect changes in attitudes toward educational issues, investigators may count favorable, unfavorable, and neutral editorials, speeches, articles, and cartoons that have appeared at different points in time. They may analyze on what grounds the positions on the issues were taken, what traits were used to describe personalities, from what source the communications originated, how intensive or emotional the communications were, and what supporting evidence was provided.

In the past two decades researchers have begun to ask questions about more complex themes, such as: How accurately are cultural settings outside of the United States represented in stories found in basal readers (97)? How are minority ethnic groups treated in elementary social studies textbooks? How are the values of country *A* similar to or different from those of countries *B, C,* and *D,* as revealed in the content analysis of handbooks for youth organizations, plays, speeches, or songbooks? What is the relationship between methods of motivation and the achievement of people or a nation as revealed by comparing the frequency of "achievement imagery" in popular literature or in children's readers and the economic development of societies, the number of patents for inventions issued by the government, and other achievement variables. The content of letters from children and their parents has been analyzed for similarity of "wants," "requests," and "demands."

PITFALLS IN DOCUMENTARY RESEARCH   Documentary research is not without pitfalls. Data do not become true reflections of reality through the magic of publication. One must subject each documentary source material to the same rigorous external and internal criticism that a historian does. You will learn about these procedures in the next chapter, but for the time being you might give consideration to the following pitfalls that can be encountered in documentary research. The categories used in available statistical material do not always coincide precisely with the variables the educator wants to investigate.

Sometimes the definitions of the categories are ambiguous, and they may change from one year to the next (black-white, nonwhite-white). The boundaries of some units of analysis (precincts, school districts) can also change; different agencies collecting similar data do not always use exactly the same classification system. The data collected always reflect the orientation, concerns, self-interests, and accuracy standards of the producers of the records, which may not be an accurate reflection of reality or of behavior itself.

Public Opinion Surveys

Rather than formulating school policies on the basis of private hunches, blind guesses, or pressure-group demands, some educational leaders seek knowledge of the public's opinions, attitudes, and preferences. Learning how people feel about school issues before making a policy decision is a prudent practice, but careful consideration must be given to how, when, where, and from whom data are obtained. Information that is elicited from a readily available group will not always reflect the opinion of the rest of the population. Suppose a superintendent passes out questionnaires concerning a school bond issue at all public school PTA meetings. The results of his survey may not correspond with the vote on election day, for PTA members are usually much more interested in obtaining new schools than retired citizens, childless couples, and people who send their children to nonpublic schools. To predict the outcome of an election on a school issue, competent researchers select their subjects with care. They first identify the variables that will affect how individuals vote, such as economic status, religion, and sex. After making these determinations, they evaluate how much weight to give each variable when selecting the sample.

The environment in which a poll is taken may also affect the reliability of the data. Suppose students are asked to express their attitudes toward mathematics. If they do not like their present teacher or have taken a difficult test that day, they may record these reactions rather than their more permanent attitudes toward the subject. Other questions may also arise concerning the reliability of the answers gathered in surveys. If people have given considerable thought to an issue, they may have a definite opinion about it; if they are uninformed concerning the topic, they can make only arbitrary decisions or snap judgments. Measuring the intensity or depth of opinion is also difficult. If two women answer a questionnaire, each may indicate that she is opposed to teaching about the United Nations in the schools, but one of them may easily be convinced to change her opinion and the other may be intensely opposed and adamant in her conviction.

INTERRELATIONSHIPS STUDIES

Some educators do not merely collect facts to obtain an accurate description of existing status; they also endeavor to trace interrelationships between facts that will provide a deeper insight into the phenomena. Several types of these studies will be discussed in this section: case studies, causal-comparative studies, correlation and prediction studies, path-analysis studies, and cross-cultural and comparative studies.

Case Study

A case study is difficult to define because it is not a specific technique but rather a method of organizing data for the purpose of analyzing the life of a social unit. One gathers pertinent data about the present status, past experiences, and environmental forces that contribute to the individuality and behavior of the unit. After analyzing the sequences and interrelationships of these factors, one constructs a comprehensive, integrated picture of the social unit as it functions in society.

Social workers and guidance counselors conduct case studies with the intent of diagnosing a particular condition and recommending therapeutic measures. Their interest is confined to the individual as a unique personality. Research workers, on the other hand, are interested in individuals as representative types. They gather data about a carefully selected sample of subjects with the intent of deriving valid generalizations about the population that the sample represents.

A case study may be made of students, administrators, a teachers' union, or a school. Studies may be made of a subculture, such as an athletic team, a sorority, or a deviant group. Smith and Geoffrey (96) conducted a case study of the complexities of an urban classroom. The ethnographer and the teacher collaborated for a full semester in writing daily reports of their observations and insights, analyzing the data, and developing hypotheses to test.

Investigators may examine the total life cycle of a social unit or focus attention on some specific phase of it. They may make a detailed study of the relationships of teachers with their administrators or with students of different ethnic groups. On the other hand, if investigators want to ascertain what has contributed to the success of teachers, they may investigate almost every aspect of their subjects' lives—their childhood, home, school, work, and social experiences and many of their behavioral traits.

A case analysis is cast within an adequate social framework, and the nature of the case determines the dimensions of the framework. Human beings interact in diverse and dynamic environmental and sociocultural settings; consequently their behavior cannot be understood without examining these varied relationships. To discover what causes youths to commit crimes or to drop out of school, the investigator goes beyond the incidents themselves—the time, place, nature, and immediate cause of the acts. When case studies are confined to a fragment of a human life or an isolated educational setting, they do not usually produce enough data to discover the fundamental cause-effect relationships.

When conducting a case study, investigators saturate themselves in the setting and probe in depth to identify the variables that relate to their problem. They may ask: What number and type of subjects (age, sex, status, etc.) are participants in this social unit? Why are the participants brought together and how do they react to the purpose? How does the physical and sociocultural environment affect the social unit? What cultural continuity or conflict do students experience as they interact with their parents, peers, and teachers? How do the subjects interact with people who differ from them in race, nationality, age, socioeconomic status, or intelligence? Why, when, and with whom does certain behavior occur? Toward whom is the behavior directed and what reaction evolves? What is the frequency and duration of the behavior?

A case study is similar to a survey, but instead of gathering data concerning a few factors from a large number of social units, investigators make an intensive study of a limited number of representative cases. A case study is narrower in scope but more exhaustive and more qualitative in nature than a survey. Because word descriptions reveal a wealth of enlightening information that a quantitative study might not be able to produce, the case study is often used to supplement the survey method. Young claims that "the most meaningful numerical studies in social science are those which are linked with exhaustive case studies describing accurately the interrelationships of factors and of processes" (116:230). Case studies may reveal relevant factors in a given situation that the surveyor can measure quantitatively. Statistical

surveys, on the other hand, may provide a guide for selecting representative subjects for case studies. Thus, the two methods are more or less
interdependent.

A case study may provide insights that will help an investigator
formulate a fruitful hypothesis, for knowledge that a particular condition exists in a unique instance suggests a factor to look for in other
cases. A generalization drawn from a single case or a few casually
selected ones cannot be applied to all cases in a community, country, or
the world, but a negative piece of evidence produced in a single case
will alert investigators to the possibility that they may need to modify a
hypothesis. Case study data also prove useful when the researcher
needs to illustrate statistical findings, for concrete examples drawn
from individual cases may help readers understand statistical generalizations more readily.

Causal-comparative Studies

When scientists want to explain causality—the factors that determine
the occurrence of events or conditions—they prefer to employ the
experimental method. But they cannot always manipulate the presumed cause, X, the independent variable, and observe what happens
to Y, the dependent variable. Investigators cannot assign Ss at random
to a particular race, sex, or social class to equate groups and thereby
control other variables that might contribute to the occurrence of Y.
Ethical considerations prevent them from manipulating crime, violence, accidents, and mental illness. Because of their respect for life,
investigators refrain from conducting experiments that inflict unnecessary pain, hardship, or harm on others or interfere in any way with the
normal growth and development of their Ss.

NATURE OF CAUSAL-COMPARATIVE DESIGNS   When experimental designs cannot be employed, causal-comparative studies may be conducted. In these nonexperimental investigations, which are sometimes
called explanatory descriptive studies or *ex post facto* (after the fact)
studies, the researchers proceed as follows: They hypothesize that X
(cigarette smoking) is related to and presumably a determiner of Y (lung
cancer), but they *do not manipulate X,* the presumed cause, *nor
randomly assign the Ss to groups.* Rather, they locate a group of Ss that
has experienced X (cigarette smoking) in a normal situation and a
control group of Ss that has not. They compare the behavior, performance, or condition (lung tissue) of the two groups to ascertain whether

the exposure to X had the effect predicted by their hypothesis. In a causal-comparative study, the control of all other variables that might cause X is not achieved through the random assignment of Ss to groups, but in a well-designed study some control is achieved through analyzing how certain specified variables other than X affect Y. The following is a paradigm for the causal-comparative design:

GROUPS (NOT RANDOMLY ASSIGNED)	X, INDEPENDENT VARIABLE (NOT MANIPULATED BY INVESTIGATOR)	Y, DEPENDENT VARIABLE
Exposed group (cigarette smokers)	X (cigarette smoking)	T_E (lung cancer)
Control group (nonsmokers)		T_C (no lung cancer)

If researchers think that X may be related to the occurrence of a particular type of emotional disturbance, for example, they cannot justify conducting an experiment in which one group of Ss is deliberately exposed to X to see what happens. But they can test their hypothesis if they select Ss who have already been exposed to X and compare their emotional stability with that of Ss who have not been exposed to X.

DIFFICULTIES ENCOUNTERED   In carrying out a causal-comparative design, investigators can go up many blind alleys in searching for the causes of events that have already occurred. Suppose six debaters went to a tournament and three of them became ill. The debate coach might use John Stuart Mill's method of discovering causal connections (73). According to Mill's Joint Method of Agreement and Difference, if instances of the phenomenon under investigation (ill debaters) had only one circumstance in common (they ate strawberry cream pie) and if the only circumstance in common among the debaters who had not become ill was the absence of the pie, then the strawberry cream pie was the cause or necessary part of the cause of the illness. But life situations are rarely as simple as this.

The ill debaters had undoubtedly had more than one common experience. They may all have taken an aspirin, or have drunk milk, or have been bitten by the same kind of bug. Many things can go together without having a cause and effect relation. The debaters may have become ill not from the common experience of eating the pie but rather from one cause in one instance and another cause in another instance. Mary may have become ill because of overexertion, Bob because of inhaling automobile fumes, and Jean because of overeating. If strawberry cream pie were the cause of the illnesses, perhaps Mary was sicker than the others because of a reaction to the strawberries in addition to the cream filling which had affected Bob and Jean. The occurrence of many educational phenomena are determined not by one variable but rather by the interaction of two or more variables. Often the best an investigator can do is to identify a set of variables that together are usually sufficient to produce a given effect.

Because causal-comparative designs do not incorporate the controls employed in experiments, the results and the interpretation of the data must be treated with care. If researchers obtain data from two existing groups of *Ss,* one that has been exposed to *X* and one that has not, which confirms their hypothesis that *X* is related to the occurrence of *Y,* they cannot be certain whether *X* or some extraneous variable—rival hypothesis—is the real cause of the occurrence of *Y.* Locating existing groups of *Ss* who are similar in all respects except for their exposure to one variable is extremely difficult. The danger always exists that the groups differ in some other way—health, intelligence, home background, previous experience—that will affect the findings of the study.

Suppose that investigators decide to test a hypothesis about the effects of a new health textbook on specific practices of children. If they compare the hygiene habits of students who have read the book with those who have not, the possibility exists that the group that did read the book had better hygiene training in the home than the latter group. Home training rather than the textbook, therefore, may account for the superior health practices of the *Ss.* In an experiment, extraneous variables such as home background can be controlled by assigning *Ss* to groups at random and assigning the experimental treatment to groups at random. But in causal-comparative studies, the *Ss* may "select themselves" into the groups and some difference in the character of these *Ss* other than the experimental treatment may account for the findings of the study. If health were not a required subject, for example, the students who enrolled in the course were probably more interested in health and more highly motivated to improve their health practices than the nonenrollees. The textbook, therefore, might not have the same effect on nonenrollees as it had on the enrollees. The health practices of the two groups may have differed if both groups had read the health text.

THE INTERPRETATION OF CAUSAL-COMPARATIVE DATA   Causal-comparative designs provide a useful method of attacking problems, but certain precautions must be taken when interpreting the data. To meet the criteria required for inferring that X is a cause of Y, you must present data and arguments demonstrating that the following conditions exist:

1   X is related to the occurrence of Y.
2   X preceded Y in time.
3   Plausible alternative explanations for the occurrence of Y have been ruled out.

The first condition is to demonstrate that the two variables vary together in the way specified by the hypothesis. Broken homes could not be a cause of suicide if there were no differences in the suicide rates of youths from broken and unbroken homes. If X is a cause of Y, a change in the first must bring about a change in the second.

After establishing that X is related to Y, you do not immediately claim that this is a causal relationship. You must first give consideration to the time order of the relationship, to the possibility that Y caused X rather than X caused Y. In some studies, the reversed causality argument is obviously unreasonable. Eating candy may cause or lead to tooth decay, but tooth decay cannot cause children to eat candy. Race can be a cause of socioeconomic status, but socioeconomic status cannot cause a person's race. But in some studies the argument of reversed causality is reasonable. It is possible, for example, that excessive absenteeism leads to low academic achievement, but it is also possible that low academic achievement causes excessive absenteeism. Because you do not manipulate X in a causal-comparative study, you often have to supply evidence that Y did not precede X in time, and, hence, could not be the effect of X. In the above instance, for example, you would have to obtain evidence at the beginning of the study indicating that the two groups did not differ on Y, academic achievement, before the one group became excessive absentees.

The third requirement for guarding against drawing an erroneous conclusion about the relationship of X_1 and Y is to control or hold constant any other variables—test variables, X_2, X_3, etc.—that may be related to the occurrence of Y, thereby eliminating their influence on the relationship between X_1 and Y.[1]

Several techniques can be used to control on or hold constant a test variable. Subgroup classification (stratification of the test variable, X_2) is easy to understand and does not involve statistics. In this type of analysis, the data are presented in tables or graphs, usually in percentage and/or frequency form.

Suppose you think that a relationship exists between X_1, education, and the occurrence of Y, tolerance, but you want to control the influence that X_2, age, may have on Y. If you classify the Ss into subgroups that are alike with respect to X_2, age (21–29, 30–39, 40–49, 50–59, 60–69), then X_2, age, is held constant in each subgroup. If the relationship you think exists between X_1 and Y is found consistently in the various age subgroups (if it persists when X_2 is controlled), then the relationship cannot be explained away by differences in X_2, age, and you can be more confident that X_1 is causally related to the occurrence of Y. If the relationship is not found consistently in the various subgroups (if it disappears when X_2 is controlled), then the relationship is explained away by the presence of the test variable, X_2, age.

Stouffer (103) employed the above strategy when he became interested in the underlying forces in our society making for or against a tendency toward growth of tolerance. Through the use of separate bivariate (two-variable) analyses, he ascertained what relationship existed between several variables (level of education, age, where people lived, etc.) and tolerance and how some of these variables were related to one another. His findings for three of these analyses were as follows: A relationship existed between (1) level of education and tolerance: the greater the education, the greater the tolerance (see Table 10.1); (2) age and tolerance: the greater the age, the less the tolerance; and (3) education and age: the greater the age, the less the education. To test the hypothesis that education produced tolerance, he raised the question: Does X_1, education, independent of X_2, age (the test variable), make for Y, tolerance?

To ascertain whether the relation between X_1, level of education, and Y, tolerance, would persist or would disappear when the test variable, X_2, age, was controlled or held constant, a multivariate analysis was made. The total sample was divided into five subgroups based on various values of both X_1, education, and X_2, age. Then the

---

[1] In this discussion, X is now designated as X_1, and the test variables, which are really other independent variables, are designated as X_2, X_3, etc. In some sources, the test variable is designated as T or Z.

several subgroups were described in terms of Y, tolerance. When the relationship between level of education and tolerance was examined within each age group, the better educated in all age groups tested to be more tolerant than the less educated (see Figure 10.1). Hence, Stouffer's original hypothesis that X_1, level of education, was related to and

FIGURE 10.1

A chart. (*From* Communism, Conformity, and Civil Liberties, *1955, p. 93, by S. A. Stouffer. Copyright © 1955 by S. A. Stouffer. Reprinted by permission of Doubleday & Co., Inc.*)

The Older Generation and the Less
Educated Are Less Tolerant of Nonconformists

Percentage distribution on scale of
willingness to tolerate nonconformists

Age	Education	Less tolerant	In-between	More tolerant	N
21 TO 29	College graduates		23	77	60
	Some college		28	69	78
	High school graduates	10	46	44	229
	Some high school	15	53	32	109
	Grade school	17	59	24	46
30 TO 39	College graduates		22	75	96
	Some college	8	36	56	88
	High school graduates	12	46	42	242
	Some high school	15	50	35	154
	Grade school	12	69	19	102
40 TO 49	College graduates	7	29	64	86
	Some college	9	38	53	64
	High school graduates	11	44	45	135
	Some high school	17	49	34	146
	Grade school	23	62	15	184
50 TO 59	College graduates	10	33	57	40
	Some college	14	42	44	48
	High school graduates	19	36	45	64
	Some high school	18	59	23	97
	Grade school	22	59	19	177
60 AND OVER	College graduates	8	61	31	26
	Some college	19	54	27	41
	High school graduates	13	58	29	98
	Some high school	20	65	15	69
	Grade school	27	61	13	283

TABLE 10.1

Relation between Education and Tolerance*†

	PERCENTAGE DISTRIBUTION OF SCORES ON SCALE OF TOLERANCE	
	LESS TOLERANT	MORE TOLERANT
EDUCATION		
College	11% (45)	89% (372)
Noncollege	37% (364)	63% (617)

*The original 5 × 3 table was collapsed into a 2 × 2 table (bivariate) to simplify the presentation of the relations between the education and tolerance variables. The number of Ss is placed within the parentheses.
†Adapted from *Communism, Conformity, and Civil Liberties*, 1955, by S. A. Stouffer. Copyright © 1955 by S. A. Stouffer. Reprinted by permission of Doubleday & Company, Inc.

presumably the cause of Y could not be explained away by age differences in the population, for the Ss in each subgroup were alike on X_2, age.

Now that you have some concept of the principles involved in controlling test variables, you should become familiar with some types of variables that may be examined to obtain a more accurate, precise, and meaningful interpretation of the relationship between variables. The following discussion will acquaint you with extraneous, component, intervening, antecedent, suppressor, and distorter test variables.[2]

1 Extraneous Variables   In the previous example, Stouffer demonstrated with data that the test variable, X_2, did not account for the relationship between X_1 and Y. In some studies, however, X_1 is related to Y but there is no causal link between the variables; the relationship is entirely due to the fact that they are coincidently associated with an extraneous variable, X_2.

Suppose you find that a relationship exists between X_1, age, and Y, book readership: the older the Ss, the less the book readership. Is this a causal relationship or is age merely associated with the extraneous variable, education, which is the cause of book readership? Older people may read less because they are less educated as a group and

[2]The author expresses his indebtedness particularly to the following sources for much of the following discussion and suggests that readers consult them to deepen their understanding of the analysis of relationships: Stephen Cole, *The Sociological Method*, 2d ed., Chicago: Markham, 1976; James A. Davis, *Elementary Survey Analysis*, Englewood Cliffs, N.J.: Prentice-Hall, 1971; Allan G. Johnson, *Social Statistics without Tears*, New York: McGraw-Hill, 1977; and Morris Rosenberg, *The Logic of Survey Analysis*, New York: Basic Books, 1968.

people with less education read less. Suppose you hold X_2, education, constant by stratifying the sample of Ss on level of education (grade school, high school, college) and find that the previous relation between X_1, age, and Y, book readership, disappears. The relationship is not consistently found in the various subgroups, for older people who are well educated may read as much as younger people with the same level of education. By taking the extraneous variable, X_2, education, which is related to both X_1 and Y into account, you avoid making an erroneous interpretation of the relationship between X_1, age, and Y, book readership.

When there is no inherent link, causal connection, between X_1 and Y but both variables are associated with some extraneous variable, these relationships may be represented as follows:

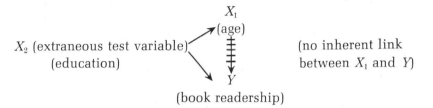

2 Component Variables   Suppose you find that X_1, social class, is related to Y, educational aspirations of parents for their children. Social class is a global variable composed of several subvariables. You may want to know what component of X_1—income level, educational level, occupation, ethnic background, etc.—chiefly accounts for the occurrence of Y. By controlling specific component variables, you may obtain more precise knowledge of what causes the occurrence of Y. Until you know what components of X_1 are of decisive significance, your knowledge of the relationship between X_1 and Y is limited.

3 Intervening Variables   Sometimes you may wish to trace the links in a causal chain. A variable that intervenes in time between X_1 and Y sequence, for example, may give you a better understanding of their relationship. Suppose you find that a relationship exists between X_1, marital status of female teachers, and Y, absenteeism: married female teachers have a higher rate of absenteeism than single female teachers. What aspect of marital status could be determined by absenteeism? Amount of home responsibility is a logical explanation. If you stratify the intervening test variable, X_2, amount of home responsibility (a great deal, little, none), you may find that the relationship between X_1 and Y

disappears and that there is little or no difference in rates of absentee-ism of married and single women who have the same amount of home responsibility. The logical status of the intervening test variable, amount of home responsibility, is clear; it is a consequence of marital status and a determiner of absenteeism, which can be represented as follows:

X_1 ————————→X_2 (intervening variable) ————————→Y
(marital status)   (amount of home responsibility)   (absenteeism)

4 Antecedent Variables In some instances you may gain a better understanding of the relationship between X_1 and Y by tracing the causal sequence one step back to a root cause, X_2. This procedure is diagrammed as follows:

X_2 (antecedent variable) ————————→X_1 ————————→Y
(education)   (level of job)   (income)

Suppose you find that a relationship exists between X_1, level of job, and Y, amount of income: the higher the level of job, the higher the income. What determines the kind of job a person obtains? Amount of education, X_2, is an obvious explanation.

If you stratify the antecedent variable, X_2, to test its influence on the relationship between X_1, job level, and Y, income, you must give evidence that the following conditions exist:

1 All three variables are related: X_1 ————→Y (job—income), X_2 ————→Y (education—income), X_2 ————→X_1 (education—job).
2 When X_2, education, is controlled by stratification (grade school, high school, college), the relationship between X_1, job level, and Y, income, *does not disappear:* the higher the level of job, the higher the income should be on each educational level. The relationship between X_1, job level, and Y, income, should not disappear, for the antecedent variable, X_2, education, does not account for the X_1 and Y relationship; it precedes it in the causal chain. If the relation-ship does disappear, then X_2, education, would be an extraneous variable.
3 When X_1, job level, is controlled by stratification (white collar, blue collar), the relationship between X_2, education, and Y, income, *should disappear; it should not be consistently found in the various*

job level subgroups. Among the people with the same level of X_1, job, those with a higher level of X_2 education, should not consistently have more Y, income, than those with a lower level of X_2, education.

5 Suppressor Variables Suppose you find that there is no relationship between X_1 and Y when you expected there would be one. You may assume that there is no causal link between the variables because the data do not support your hypothesis. But such negative findings may be misleading. Before abandoning your original hypothesis, you should ascertain whether some suppressor variable, X_2, is concealing or reducing the true relationship between X_1 and Y. Sex, for example, is sometimes a suppressor variable. If you hypothesize that X_1, level of occupation (blue collar, white collar), is related to Y, income, the data may reveal that there is no relation between the two variables. When sex is controlled, however, among earners of the same sex there may be some or a substantial relationship between level of occupation and income: the higher the level of occupation, the higher the income. The reason that virtually no difference between levels of occupation and income appeared originally may have been that many more women than men have low-paying white-collar jobs, lowering the overall average for white-collar jobs. Thus, sex acts as a suppressor variable. If sex is not controlled, you get an "unrealistically low" estimate of the relationship between X_1 and Y. If sex is controlled, thereby cancelling out the effect of the sex distribution of employees, the true relationship appears.

6 Distorter Variables The relationship between X_1 and Y may be misinterpreted because a distorter variable makes the relationship appear to be in the wrong direction. A comparison of the average income of residents in some cities and suburbs, for example, may be misleading. The data may cause you to conclude that suburb residents have a higher average income than city residents. But there is usually a large concentration of blacks in cities and of whites in the suburbs. If the distorter variable, race, is controlled, thereby cancelling out the effect of the racial distribution of residents, the true relationship appears: incomes in the city are higher than in the suburbs—on the average—for both blacks and whites. In the original bivariate comparison, the higher average income of the numerous white suburbanites raised the overall suburbanite average above the city average. Controlling the distorter variable, race, reversed the direction of the relation-

ship: city-resident incomes are higher than suburb-resident incomes for both races taken separately. Hence, the correct interpretation of the relation between X_1 and Y is the reverse of that suggested by the original data.

TYPES OF ANALYSIS   Our discussion has focused primarily on a simple form of analysis in which variables are cross-partitioned in order to study the relations between them. Data are presented in terms of frequencies or percentages or both, either in graphs or tables (called contingency or cross-tabulation tables). Because of practical considerations, this method is limited in the number of variables that can be considered simultaneously. Some researchers use more sophisticated statistical forms of analysis in which the same logic is employed as is used in analyzing tables or graphs. In linear regression analysis, which you will become acquainted with in the next section of this chapter, the relationship between variables is usually expressed as a correlation coefficient, r, instead of as a percentage difference. You compute partial correlations to determine whether a relationship is causal. A partial correlation is the relationship between X_1 and Y after the variance due to X_2 has been removed. Path analysis provides another meaningful approach to analyzing causal relations and correlations. A number of other analysis techniques are also available to the researcher.

EXAMPLE OF ANALYSIS   Before leaving the discussion of causal-comparative studies, you may profit from examining questions that researchers might ask when analyzing a specific problem and interpreting the data. To describe accurately and precisely the relationship between *social class and academic achievement,* a combination of some of the following questions might be asked in a series of investigations:

1   Is the direction of the influence of one variable on the other obvious?
2   If there is a mutual interaction, can the dominant direction of the influence be determined?
3   Is social class the factor that influences academic achievement, or is it actually an *extraneous variable,* such as race or residential area?
4   Is the relationship stronger in rural or urban, Northern or Southern, inner-city or suburban areas?
5   Does the relationship remain strong when some *component variables* of social class—income, educational level, or type of

occupation—are controlled but disappear when others are controlled?

6 Is social class responsible for academic achievement, or does social
class produce an intervening variable, such as good or poor self-
concept in students or a culturally biased attitude in teachers, that,
in turn, affects academic achievement?

7 Is a change in social class accompanied by a change in academic
achievement? Does the rate or amount of change differ for children
of different ages, sexes, or social classes?

8 Is the relationship between social class and academic achievement
the same in countries where different degrees of social mobility
exist?

9 If no relationship is revealed by the data, is some *suppressor
variable* operating?

By asking many questions in a causal-comparative study and
testing the effect of many variables on a dependent variable, one can
gradually specify and clarify the nature of the relationships among
variables that directly or indirectly contribute to the occurrence of a
phenomenon. The more empirical evidence that one can present to
buttress one's interpretation of a relationship and eliminate competing
hypotheses, the more confidence can be placed in one's work.

Correlation Studies

To obtain descriptions of phenomena, investigators may employ correlation techniques. In everyday usage "correlation" refers to any kind of
relationship between phenomena; but in statistical analysis, it refers
exclusively to quantifying the magnitude of the relationship between
variables. To gain a better understanding of educational phenomena,
you may ask whether a relationship exists between the performance on
an IQ test and an arithmetic test, secondary school marks and success
in college, or diet and weight control. When you find the magnitude of
the relationship, you may use this information to make decisions and
predictions.

TYPES OF RELATIONSHIPS   Correlation techniques enable you to ascertain the direction and degree of the relationship between variables, that
is, the extent to which two sets of measures from the same *Ss* vary in
unison. Suppose you want to know whether any relationship exists
between the IQ scores and spelling scores of eleven students, and, if so,

what the strength of the relationship is. On the basis of general impressions, you have arrived at the hypothesis that the lower the students' IQ scores, the lower their spelling scores. To test this hypothesis, you record the IQ scores in numerical order—with the lowest at the bottom and the highest at the top—and place each pupil's spelling score beside his or her IQ score (see Figure 10.2). You discover that the pupil with the lowest IQ score obtains the lowest spelling score, the pupil with the second-lowest IQ score obtains the second-lowest spelling score, and the remaining students have the same relative position in one test as the other. The scores on the two tests vary in unison: a given increase (5 points) in one variable (IQ) is accompanied by a consistent increase (5 points) in the other variable (spelling). Hence, a *perfect positive relationship or correlation exists.* In a perfect correlation, the *consistency* rather than the *size* of the increase in the second variable is what is important. For a given increase in IQ score (5 points), the increase in the spelling score could have been consistently 3, 6, or some other number of points.

You will not often find a perfect correlation, for the exact agreement between things is rarely experienced. If the correlation is perfect, however, and you plot simultaneously each *S's* pair of scores on a correlation chart, the points will fall exactly on a straight line as they

FIGURE 10.2

Correlation expressed as agreement between ranks.

Subject	IQ score	Spelling test score
A.	142	97
B.	137	92
C.	132	87
D.	127	82
E.	122	77
F.	117	72
G.	112	67
H.	107	62
I.	102	57
J.	97	52
K.	92	47

do in Figure 10.3. You will note in Figure 10.3 that the two variables are indicated by X and Y. The horizontal scale for the IQ scores increases from the left to the right; the vertical scale for spelling scores increases from the bottom upward. Each point in the chart represents an $S's$ scores; his IQ score can be determined by going above to the X scale and his spelling score by going to the left to the Y scale.

Several relationships can hold between scores on two variables: (1) the direction of the relationship may be negative or positive; (2) the degree of relationship may vary from perfect, to high, to intermediate, to no relationship; and (3) the relationship may be linear or non-linear.

In general, the magnitude of the correlation depends on the extent to which an increase or decrease in one variable is accompanied by an increase or decrease in the other—whether in the same direction (positive) or the opposite direction (negative). A *high positive correlation* exists if the *Ss* who score high (or low) on one variable tend to *score similarly* on the other variable (high IQ—high spelling score; low IQ—low spelling score). With a *high negative correlation,* the reverse is true: the *Ss* who score high (or low) on one variable tend to *score the opposite* on the other (high IQ—low number of accidents; low IQ—high number of accidents). A negative correlation is just as important as a positive correlation. It does not indicate a lack of relationship. A

FIGURE 10.3

Simple correlation chart showing relationship between spelling scores (Y variable) and intelligence test scores (X variable).

X = Intelligence test scores

	90–94	95–99	100–104	105–109	110–114	115–119	120–124	125–129	130–134	135–139	140–144
95–99											•
90–94										•	
85–89									•		
80–84								•			
75–79							•				
70–74						•					
65–69					•						
60–64				•							
55–59			•								
50–54		•									
45–49	•										

Y = Spelling test scores

correlation of −.60 indicates just as strong a relationship as a correlation of +.60.

You would expect to find a perfect (r = 1.00) or high positive correlation between the right and left legs of children. You would expect to find a positive but not a perfect relationship (perhaps r = .786) between the height and weight of children, for tall children tend to weigh more than short children; but some tall children are underweight and some short children are overweight. You would expect to find little or no relationship (r = .00) between the length of legs of children and their algebra test scores, for children who have high algebra scores are just as likely to have long legs as short legs. Correlations range over a scale which extends from a perfect negative correlation (r = − 1.00) to no correlation (r = .00), to a perfect positive correlation (r = 1.00).

From a quick examination of a scattergram you can discern the direction and can obtain some concept of the degree of the relationship between variables. The direction of the pattern of the points (plotted scores) differs for a positive and negative correlation as they do in Figure 10.4, examples *a* and *b*. The degree of the relationship between variables is determined by examining the "scatter" of the points. In a perfect correlation, the points on the scattergram must fall in a straight line as they do in Figure 10.3. In Figure 10.4 note the scatter of points when (*a*) a high degree of correlation, (*b*) an intermediate degree of correlation, and (*c*) no correlation exists.

A scattergram will also indicate whether the relationship between two variables is linear or nonlinear. If a *linear relationship* exists, the points of the scattergram are dispersed around a straight line as they are in Figure 10.4*a* and *b;* that is, the scores on the two tests tend to increase or decrease progressively. In a *curvilinear* or nonlinear relationship the points are dispersed around a curved line as they are in

FIGURE 10.4

Examples of correlations.

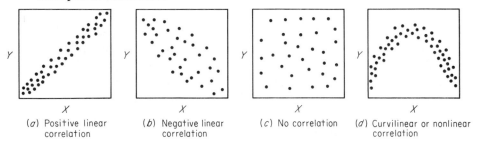

(*a*) Positive linear correlation   (*b*) Negative linear correlation   (*c*) No correlation   (*d*) Curvilinear or nonlinear correlation

Figure 10.4*d*. The linear relationship is most common, but curvilinear relationships are found. A curvilinear relationship will be found, for example, if you correlate performance scores with chronological age over a life-span, for performance increases rapidly, then reaches a plateau, and eventually declines, while age steadily increases. Curvilinear relationships are often found when motivational, physiological, and adjustment measures are correlated with one another or with cognitive measures. *Ss* with low levels of motivation, for example, tend to have poor problem-solving scores, and *Ss* who have higher and higher levels of motivation have better problem-solving scores, but the increase in the scores is not proportional to the increase in motivation.

PEARSON PRODUCT-MOMENT CORRELATION (r)   A number of methods are employed to ascertain the magnitude of the relationship between two sets of measures. If the relationship is linear, which is most commonplace, the Pearson product-moment correlation coefficient, designated r, can be computed. Because this coefficient (r) is probably used most frequently in educational research, you may wish to examine Appendix A.2, which presents the steps in computing it, the assumptions concerning the data underlying the use of it, and alternative methods that may be used when these assumptions cannot be met. You do not compute r, for example, when a curvilinear relationship exists between the variables, for the extent of the relationship will be underestimated. When a curvilinear relationship exists, a correlation ratio or coefficient of nonlinear relationship (η, Greek eta) is computed. The steps involved in computing η can be found in statistics books.

PARTIAL CORRELATION ($r_{12.3}$)   You cannot always confine your attention solely to the variables you are correlating, for the magnitude of r between two variables may be misleading because of their common relationship with a third variable. When this is the case, a more accurate description of the relationship may be obtained through the use of partial correlation ($r_{12.3}$), which eliminates or removes the effect of the third variable.

Age is often a contaminating third variable, for many attributes increase with age from birth to adulthood. If you correlate vocabulary and weight over a wide age range, the correlation will probably be high and positive. Does this mean that the heavier a person is, the larger his vocabulary will be? Obviously, the presence of the third variable, age, makes it appear that this is the case, for as children grow older they weigh more and have larger vocabularies. If the age factor could be eliminated, little or no relationship may be found between vocabulary and weight. The influence of the third variable can be controlled experimentally or statistically: (1) you can keep the age constant by selecting Ss for the study all of whom are the same age, or (2) you can hold the age factor constant through partial correlation. When the common influence, age, has been held constant, that is, it is "partialed out" or eliminated statistically, only the residual relationship between the two variables remains. Because you will often find it difficult to locate Ss for an investigation who have exactly or approximately the same score on the third variable, the partial correlation statistical technique is of particular value to you.

The partial correlation coefficient $(r_{12.3})$ is the net correlation between variables 1 and 2 after their mutual relationship with variable 3 is partialed out. You can also partial out additional variables: $r_{12.34}$ or $r_{12.345}$. The subscripts to the *right* of the decimal point always indicate the variables whose influence is removed.[3] To learn how to calculate partial correlations, see Appendix A.3, where you will learn that the relationship between height and weight in this instance is reduced when the age factor is partialed out from $r = .786$ to $r_{12.3} = .406$.

Partial correlation is a useful statistical tool, but you must be aware of its limitations. A clear-cut interpretation of partial correlations cannot always be made in a meaningful way, for educational tests usually depend upon many contributing factors. When you "partial out" relatively objective components, such as age, height, or school grades, the interpretation is not difficult. But when you partial out IQ scores from the correlation between reading comprehension scores and mathematics ability, a serious interpretation problem arises, for both reading skills and mathematics are functional components in most general intelligence tests.

MULTIPLE CORRELATION $(R_{1.23})$ Perhaps the following summary will help you distinguish between three symbols that are commonly used in correlation studies:

r_{12}: Pearson product-moment correlation is the relationship between two variables (height and weight).

$r_{12.3}$: Partial correlation is the net relation between variables 1 and 2 (height and weight) after variable 3 (age) is partialed out.

[3]Sometimes partial correlations are symbolized by letter subscripts rather than number subscripts.

$R_{1.23}$: Multiple correlation is the relationship between one variable (height) and a team of two or more other variables (weight and age).

In the next section of this chapter you will learn how a correlation coefficient, either r_{12} or $R_{1.23}$, that has been obtained for a sample of Ss can be used in a regression equation to predict the scores of other Ss from the same population. The following discussion will explain why a multiple correlation coefficient, $R_{1.23}$, may enable you to make more accurate predictions than a Pearson product-moment correlation, r_{12}.

A prediction study involves (1) a *predictor variable or variables* which provide information (such as known weight scores) for predicting an event and (2) a predicted or *criterion variable* (such as height) which is the value to be predicted.[4] Suppose you have previously ascertained the magnitude of the relationship between height and weight scores, r_{12}, for a sample of Ss. If you now know the weight of *other Ss from the same population,* you can use this r_{12} data in a regression equation to predict their height. But you can make a more accurate estimate of their height if you know both their weight and age scores and have $R_{1.23}$ data available for the original sample. Because human behavior and the components that contribute to the mastery of knowledge and skills are too complex to base prediction on a single predictor variable, multiple correlation prediction studies are often conducted to improve the accuracy of the prediction.

A multiple correlation ($R_{1.23}$) is concerned with the relationship between a predicted variable (height) and each of the predictor variables (weight and age). But R also takes intercorrelations between predictor variables or joint contributions into consideration. Two predictor variables may each show some relationship with the predicted variable, but their joint influence may be greater than their independent influences. In Appendix A.3, for example, when height and weight are correlated, $r_{12} = .786$, when height and age are correlated, $r_{13} = .852$, but when weight and age are correlated with height, $R_{1.23} = .879$, which is a higher correlation with height than either predictor variable taken separately.

How do you select the predictor variables? The "shotgun" approach, in which you compute a large number of correlations with the hope of finding some variables that will have a high correlation with the predicted variable, is not recommended. A better procedure is to

---

[4]The predictor variable is the independent variable; the predicted variable is the dependent variable.

select predictor variables on a theoretical basis: (1) analyze the skills, aptitudes, and characteristics that relate to whatever phenomena you wish to predict; (2) ascertain what information is available about the phenomena in the literature; and (3) examine educational, psychological, and sociological theories that may suggest hypotheses concerning known or new predictor variables that you can test.

In a multiple correlation, $R_{1.23}$, the subscript 1 to the left of the decimal point is the variable being predicted (height) and subscripts 2 and 3 are the predictor variables (weight and age). More than two promising predictor variables may be added. The most advantageous predictors to add are the ones which show a substantial correlation with the predicted variable but are unrelated to the other predictor variables. But adding a great number of predictor variables will not substantially improve the accuracy of the prediction. If you wish to predict grade-point averages, for example (72:988), a verbal aptitude test (predictor variable) may correlate .56 with grade-point average; the addition of another predictor variable—a quantitative reasoning test— may result in $R_{1.23} = .63$; the addition of a study habits inventory may result in $R_{1.234} = .65$. To add several more predictor variables would probably not increase the multiple correlation to a value in excess of .70 or .71. In most educational situations, little predictive improvement results from using more than four or five predictor variables because of the intercorrelations between these predictors. The computation and interpretation of a multiple correlation and a product-moment correlation are similar. One method of computing a multiple correlation is given in Appendix A.3.

VALUE OF THE KNOWLEDGE OF RELATIONSHIPS   A knowledge about the strength and direction of the relationship between variables is of value when one is dealing with practical, theoretical, or prediction problems.

First let us consider a *practical* teaching problem. Suppose that, from observing typing classes, you have decided that the amount of time spent in glancing away from the copy is inversely related to typing speed. To test this hypothesis, you have all ninth-grade typing students in the Jones School type the same copy. After recording the typing speed of each student and the amount of time spent in glancing away from the copy, you compare the speed scores with the glancing-away time and discover that a high negative correlation exists—that is, the lower the typing speed a student achieves, the more time he spends glancing away from his copy. This correlation suggests, but does not prove conclusively, that time spent in glancing away from the copy is an important factor relating to the speed of typing. The findings of the study suggest that speed of typing may be improved by decreasing the amount of time spent glancing away from the copy.

A knowledge about the degree of relationship between variables is also of value when you are concerned about *theoretical* values. Suppose you want to structure a theory about a factor that determines the differences among individuals in a particular physical ability. You hypothesize the existence of a general trait of manual dexterity and devise different tests of manual operations that would seem to measure the trait, such as punching keys, twisting nuts on bolts, and placing pegs in small holes. If the order of the *Ss'* scores on all of these tests corresponded exactly or closely, then it would appear that the same common abilities, which you call manual dexterity, account for the individual differences on all of them. If, in addition, you find that no relationship exists between the scores on these manual dexterity tests and scores on tests that measure quite different traits, such as mechanical information, you would feel more confident that your tests measure a restricted type of ability and not some general or dissimilar ability.

As you know, a knowledge about the relationship between variables can be used to make *predictions*. You often make predictions on the basis of unverified hunches which may or may not be accurate. A single or multiple correlation coefficient enables you to make a scientific prediction based on a relationship that has been formally determined rather than on a mere guess. Suppose you know the relationship (*r*) that existed between the reading test scores of the girls who entered the ninth grade last year and their freshman grades. If you know the reading test scores of the girls who will enter the ninth grade this year, you can use your correlation data to predict what their freshman grades will be. The following section of this chapter will explain how you do this.

Prediction Studies

Educators may conduct psychological, sociological, or economic prediction studies. They may use the scores that students obtain on certain tests to predict how successful the students will be in particular subjects, curriculums, or fields of specialization. Guilford (48:356–357) conceptualized four types of prediction in psychology and education:

predictions of (1) attributes from other attributes, such as predicting criminality from a knowledge of sex or race; (2) attributes from measurements, such as predicting criminality from known scores on ability tests; (3) measurements from attributes, such as predicting probable test scores from a knowledge of socioeconomic status; and (4) measurements from other measurements, such as predicting achievement test scores from known aptitude test scores. To make predictions, educators may use expectancy tables or regression equations.

EXPECTANCY TABLE   An expectancy table is easy to compute and interpret. If you wish to predict the freshman grade averages of women who will attend your college next year from their college aptitude ratings, proceed as follows: (1) Find the scores on these *two* variables for a *sample* of similar *Ss* (freshman women who attended your college last year) and arrange their scores on a scattergram. (2) Add the frequencies in each row and column of the scattergram and record the row totals at the ends of the rows and the column totals below each column (see Table 10.2). (3) Convert each cell frequency into a percentage of the total *row* frequency by dividing the cell frequency by the total row frequency. In Table 10.2, the bottom row (college aptitude rating 1–10) has a total of 15 frequencies, 9 in the F and 6 in the D grade-average column, and 9 ÷ 15 = .60 and 6 ÷ 15 = .40. Next year, if a woman applicant to your college receives a college aptitude rating score in the range of 1–10, you can use the expectancy table to predict that there is a 60 percent chance that she will receive an F average and a 40 percent chance that she will receive a D average in her freshman year. From Table 10.2, you can inform a woman with a score of between 81 and 90 that she will most likely earn a C average, but she has a 29 percent chance of earning a B average and a 6 percent chance of earning a D average.

Expectancy tables have considerable practical value in educational counseling, but they do not provide as precise a prediction as a regression equation. Because the table is constructed in terms of class intervals, all scores within a given interval are interpreted as having the same predictive value. An examination of Table 10.2 shows that women with the higher aptitude ratings can be expected to obtain the higher grades. You would, however, expect a student with a rating of 79 in the 71–80 interval to obtain a higher grade than a woman with a rating of 71, but the expectancy table does not delineate this precise information.

TABLE 10.2

Scatter Diagram or Expectancy Table for College Aptitude and Freshman Scholarship (Women)*

COLLEGE APTITUDE RATING	FREQUENCY OF EACH GRADE AVERAGE AND PROBABILITY OF GRADE ATTAINMENT					
	F	D	C	B	A	TOTAL
91-100		1 (.02)	23 (.42)	30 (.54)	1 (.02)	55
81-90		3 (.06)	36 (.65)	16 (.29)		55
71-80	3 (.04)	16 (.23)	42 (.59)	10 (.14)		71
61-70	6 (.08)	30 (.41)	36 (.49)	1 (.02)		73
51-60	6 (.08)	41 (.55)	28 (.37)			75
41-50	6 (.10)	36 (.59)	18 (.29)	1 (.02)		61
31-40	18 (.26)	38 (.54)	14 (.20)			70
21-30	8 (.23)	26 (.74)	1 (.03)			35
11-20	9 (.31)	20 (.69)				29
1-10	9 (.60)	6 (.40)				15
Total	65	217	198	58	1	539

* Adapted from John B. Johnston, *The Liberal College in Changing Society*. Century Company, New York, 1930.

REGRESSION EQUATIONS   A regression equation does enable you to predict the most probable value of one variable for each possible value of the other. If you had used a regression equation in the previous problem, you could have made grade predictions for *all* values from 1 to 100 on the aptitude test.

Perhaps you can understand regression equations more easily if you first become familiar with some general prediction concepts. Suppose you had previously depicted on a scattergram the height and weight data for a sample of fifty *Ss* drawn from a population. You now wish to predict the height (*Y'*) of another *S* from that population knowing this *S*'s weight to be 135 pounds. Your best bet would be the mean height of all *Ss* who fall in the 130–139 weight column of the scattergram, which in Figure 10.5 (see below the 130–139 column) is 63.5 inches.[5] Similarly, if you wish to predict a *S*'s weight (*X'*) knowing his height (*Y*) to be 62 inches, your best bet would be the mean weight for all of the subjects who fall in the 62–63 height row, which in Figure

[5]The mean is found by multiplying each frequency (each tally in the 130–139 column) by the midpoint of the row interval in which it falls and dividing the total of these values by the number of frequencies: $1 \times 66.5 + 2 \times 64.5 + 2 \times 62.5 + 1 \times 60.5 = 381.0 \div 6 = 63.50$.

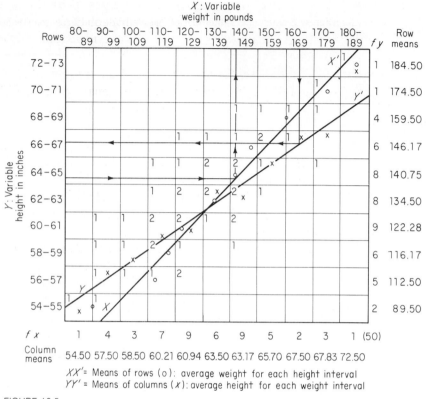

FIGURE 10.5

Graphic representation of the correlation between height and weight of fifty students.

10.5 (see end of 62–63 row) is 134.5 pounds. The predicted variable, X' or Y', is identified by the prime sign ('), which indicates it is a predicted or mean score rather than an obtained score.

One key to prediction, then, is the mean. *A regression line gives you the mean value of one variable for each possible value of the other variable.* Hence, it can be used for prediction. You can roughly locate regression lines by taking the steps given below. If you examine Figure 10.5 as you read the steps and visually check each procedure, you will quickly grasp the principles involved in prediction. Note that the mean of the frequencies in each row and column has been calculated and recorded in the proper place at the end of the row or below the column.

1   Find and mark with a circle (o) the mean of the frequencies in each row (average weight for each height interval). These circles will fall approximately on a straight line.

2 Draw a "best fitting" line through these circles. (The line should balance the number of means (circles) on each side of the line.) *Label this the XX' line: it gives the average weight (X) for each height (Y) interval.*[6]

3 Find and mark with a cross (x) the mean of the frequencies in each column; draw a best-fitting line through the means of the columns. *Label this the YY' line: it gives the average height (Y) for each weight (X) interval.*

4 Use the *XX'* regression line to predict an *X* (weight) score when you locate the *Y* (height) score. If you know that John is 64.5 inches tall, locate his height on the *Y* interval scale, draw a line out to the *XX'* regression line (which gives the *mean weight* of all the sample *Ss* in that height interval), draw a vertical line from this point up to the *X* scale (weight), and read the value.

5 Use the *YY'* regression line to predict a *Y* (height) score when you know the *X* (weight) score. If Jack weighs 165 pounds, locate his position on the *X* scale, draw a line down to the *YY'* regression line (which gives the *mean height* of all sample *Ss* in that weight interval), draw a horizontal line over to the *Y* scale (height), and read the value.

By the above method, you can draw regression lines that look like the best fit, but the predictions you make from them will be rough. By utilizing regression equations, you can locate the two lines that are best fitting in the mathematical sense.[7] In essence, a regression equation gives you the slope of the regression line. The slope describes the amount of increase in the predicted variable (*Y'* or *X'*) for every unit of increase in the predictor variable (*X* or *Y*), such as the number of inches of increase in height to expect for every pound of increase in weight. This information can be used to predict the most probable weight for any given height.

Earlier in our discussion, the statement was made that if you calculate a correlation coefficient, either r_{12} or $R_{1.23}$, for a sample of *Ss*, you can use this information in a regression equation to predict scores of other *Ss* from the same population. A regression equation utilizes (1) the *S's* known score on one variable (*X* or *Y*), and (2) the following

---

[6] The line may not pass through many of the means. If the means were based on a much larger sample of the population, however, they would approximate more exactly a straight line.

[7] These equations, which were worked out by Pearson, are based on the sum of the least squares criterion. A regression line is the one from which the sum of the squared deviations is at a minimum; that is, the sum of the squared distances between the regression line and the points that represent the scores of the sample—the squared errors of prediction—is at a minimum.

correlation data for a sample of similar Ss: (a) the r between their X and Y scores, and (b) the standard deviations, σ_x and σ_y (scatter of their scores around the mean of each variable), and (c) the means, M_X and M_Y.

The regression equations given below look complicated, but Appendix A.3 interprets the symbols and gives a simple explanation of how to calculate them to predict scores.

$$X' = r\frac{\sigma_x}{\sigma_y}(Y - M_Y) + M_X \qquad \text{Used when an } X \text{ score is to be predicted from a given or known } Y \text{ score.}$$

$$Y' = r\frac{\sigma_y}{\sigma_x}(X - M_X) + M_Y \qquad \text{Used when a } Y \text{ score is to be predicted from a given or known } X \text{ score.}$$

The above equations are used for making predictions (such as height) from known scores on a single predictor variable (weight), but educators often make predictions from known scores on two or more predictor variables (weight and age). To learn how to calculate a multiple regression equation, which is a logical extension of single regression and employs the same rationale in making predictions, see Appendix A.3.

STANDARD ERROR OF ESTIMATE (σ_{est}) The predicted (X' or Y') scores that you obtain from calculating a regression equation are the most probable values of one variable that can be obtained from a knowledge of the values of another variable. How accurate are these estimates? The regression lines from which they are predicted represent the means of the rows and the columns. Suppose an S weighs 150 pounds and, through the use of a regression equation, you estimate his height to be 64.88 inches (see Figure 10.6b). This predicted height score (Y') is actually the mean height of the 150-pound Ss in the sample. But the height of the Ss in a sample may cluster on or near the regression line as the five Ss do in Figure 10.6a, or may deviate some distance from the regression line, as they do in Figure 10.6b. The reliability of your prediction, then, depends upon the variability in height of the 150-pound Ss.

The wider the distribution (the deviation or scatter) of scores about a regression line, the larger is the standard error of estimate. Since the standard deviation (σ) is a measure of how spread out a distribution is,

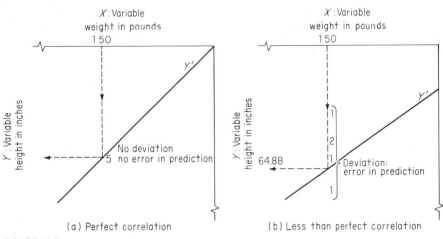

FIGURE 10.6

Deviation from the regression line. In example *b* the second regression line (*X'*) has been omitted, but remember that there are always two regression lines unless the correlation is perfect, as in example *a*.

you can use its size to describe the extent of your errors in prediction.[8] But a series of standard deviations—one for each row or column—is not required, for you can compute one standard error of estimate which averages the errors of prediction for all the rows (and another for all the columns).[9]

The formulas for the standard error of estimate (σ_{est}) are given below.

$$\sigma_{(est\ X)} = \sigma_x \sqrt{1 - r^2}$$ Used in estimating the extent of error in the prediction of *X'* scores.

$$\sigma_{(est\ Y)} = \sigma_y \sqrt{1 - r^2}$$ Used in estimating the extent of error in the prediction of *Y'* scores.

You will note that the size of the standard error of estimate depends on the extent of r (relationship between the X and Y scores) and the extent of σ_x or σ_y (the standard deviation of all the predicted

[8]For an explanation of measures of deviation, see Appendix A.1.

[9]This can be done because, if a Pearson product-moment correlation is calculated, an equal scattering of the scores in the rows and columns is assumed to exist. Hence, for all X scores, the distribution of the corresponding Y scores should be approximately equal in variability and vice versa. This condition, known as homoscedasticity, is discussed in Appendix A.2.

variable scores around their mean score, M_X or M_Y).[10] These symbols may confuse you at the moment, but the following paragraphs of explanation will help you understand them and Appendix A.3 (page 497) explains how to calculate the standard error of estimate.

In general, as the size of the correlation increases, the size of the standard error of estimate decreases. As r approaches 1.00, the standard error of estimate will approach zero. Why?

In a perfect correlation ($r = +1.00$ or -1.00), there is no variation in scores around the regression line (the mean), for all Ss in the sample who have the same score on one variable have an exactly predictable score on the other variable.[11] In Figure 10.6, example a, the five Ss in the sample who weigh 150 pounds are all the same height. Suppose r is perfect and you know that another S from the same population has a score on one variable, X, of 150 pounds. If you predict that this S's score on the other variable, Y, is the mean height of the 150-pound Ss in the sample, your prediction, Y', will be absolutely accurate, for there is no height score in that weight interval in the sample other than the mean height score.

If a correlation is less than perfect, the Ss in the sample who have the same score on one variable have scores that vary on the other variable. In Figure 10.6, example b, the five Ss in the sample (indicated by tallies 1, 2, 1, 1) who weigh 150 pounds have actual heights that deviate from their mean height of 64.88 inches. If another S from the same population has an X score of 150 pounds and you predict the mean Y' score of the sample, 64.88 inches, to be the S's height, your prediction is not absolutely accurate. In a less than perfect correlation, if the r is large and the standard deviation of the predicted variable (σ_y) is small, the amount of error involved in your predictions may be quite small. If the r is low or σ_y is large, or both conditions exist, the prediction you make may be too unreliable to be useful.

What does the standard error of estimate tell you? You know that the predicted score is a mean and the actual score of the S may be above or below that mean. If you calculate the standard error of estimate, you will find within what limits the actual score of the S is likely to fall. Suppose through the use of a regression equation you have predicted a Y' score of 64.88 inches for any individual with an X score of 150 pounds, and you have found that the $\sigma_{(est\ y)}$ is 2.58 inches. If you

---

[10]The predicted score (X' or Y') is a submean and serves as the reference point for the standard error of estimate in the same way that the general mean (M_x or M_y) serves as the reference point for the standard deviation (σ_x or σ_y) of all the X or Y scores.

[11]In a perfect correlation, the means of the columns and rows are the same, hence the regression lines coincide.

assume a normal distribution of scores, then 68 percent of the height scores you predict for 150-pound *Ss* will not miss their actual height by more than plus or minus 2.58 inches.[12] The odds are two in three (68 in 100) that if an individual weighs 150 pounds, his actual height will not fall below 62.30 inches or above 67.46 inches.

Suppose you have predicted an X' score of 161 pounds for *Ss* with a given Y score of 69 inches. If you assume a normal distribution of scores and the $\sigma_{(est\ X)}$ is 14.37 pounds, then approximately 68 percent of your predicted height scores will not miss the *Ss'* actual weight by more than plus or minus 14.37 pounds. The odds are two in three (68 in 100) that if S is 69 inches tall, his weight will not be below 146.62 pounds or above 175.38 pounds. When reporting research which involves the use of regression equations, you should report the standard error of estimate, for the predicted scores will be much less reliable if the $\sigma_{(est\ X)} = 14.50$ than if $\sigma_{(est\ X)} = 5.00$.

In making predictions there are two variables involved, one being the predictor (independent variable) and the other being the predicted (criterion or dependent variable). One can predict Y' values from given X values and X' values from given Y values. One is usually interested in predicting in one direction; however, not both. As a matter of convention, the criterion or predicted variable is usually designated Y and the predictor is designated X.

In summary, there are two regression equations; one is used for predicting an X score from a given or known Y score, and the other is used to predict a Y score from a given or known X score. There are always two regression equations and two regression lines unless the correlation is perfect. When the correlation is perfect, $r = +1.00$ or -1.00. the regression lines coincide, there is no variation in scores around the regression line, the standard error of estimate (σ_{est}) is zero, and there is no error in making a prediction. But two variables are very seldom perfectly related, hence the coefficient of correlation is usually less than 1.00. In general, the greater the value of r plus or minus, the closer together are the regression lines, the smaller is the standard error of estimate, and the more accurate is the prediction.

INTERPRETATION OF CORRELATION AND PREDICTION DATA   If you conduct a correlation or prediction study and find the magnitude of the relationship that exists between variables, you may interpret it with reservations as follows:

---

[12]To make this assumption, check to determine whether the column and row distributions of scores appear to approach a normal curve of distribution. In a normal curve of distribution, 68.26 percent of the scores fall within one standard deviation of either side of the mean.

$r = \pm.00$ to $\pm.20$, negligible relationship
$r = \pm.20$ to $\pm.40$, low relationship
$r = \pm.40$ to $\pm.70$, marked relationship
$r = \pm.70$ to ±1.00, high to very high relationship

The above classification is a useful but tentative guide, for a "high" correlation is not necessarily important and a "low" correlation is not necessarily unimportant. The same size r may be interpreted differently under different conditions. A correlation coefficient is relative and should be interpreted in terms of what variables were correlated, with what instruments, for what sample, under what conditions, and for what purpose, time, and place. The following discussion and Appendix A.4, page 508, will give you some insight into the factors that must be considered in interpreting r.

1 Variables Being Correlated   The maximum correlation that you can expect to obtain is higher between some types of variables than others. In interpreting r, therefore, consideration should be given to the type of variables being correlated. Because previous research studies indicate that the rs between intelligence scores and school grades are usually .40 to .60, an r between these variables must be .70 or better to be considered high. On the other hand, correlations between physical and mental functions are usually quite low, often zero. Hence, an r of .30, although quite low, would be regarded as important for an r between strength test scores and intelligence test scores.

2 Variability of the Subjects   In interpreting r, consideration should be given to the variability of the Ss. If an r is low, the conclusion cannot be drawn that no relationship exists until a check is made of the *range of the Ss' scores on the variables being correlated.* If their scores are restricted in range on either or both of the variables, the r will be rather low. Because the IQ scores of high school and college students usually differ in range, for example, you can expect an r between intelligence and school marks to be lower for college students than for high school students. Likewise, the r between IQ scores and reading test scores will be lower for a single grade than for grades 1 to 12. Perhaps you can grasp this concept more quickly in a graphic presentation. You will recall that the more widely the scores are scattered about the regression line, the lower the r is. In Figure 10.7, note that the narrow range of scores (small square) are widely scattered; hence, the r for that small square is low. The wider range of scores (large square) are less widely scattered; hence, the r for that large square is higher.

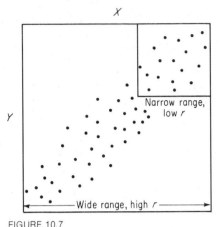

FIGURE 10.7

Correlations for a wide and narrow range of scores.

The value of an *r* can also be misinterpreted if it is spuriously high. Sometimes the *heterogeneity—range or scatter—of the Ss' scores on a third variable* increases the size of *r* quite apart from the true relationship between the two variables being correlated. The failure of the investigator to check the range of the *Ss'* ages or other physical, mental, or cultural characteristics that might affect the size of *r* between two variables is often a source of error in interpreting *r*. As *Ss* grow older, the measures of their weight, height, strength, vocabulary, and other attributes increase. Hence, the correlation between height and weight would be higher for a sample of *Ss* whose ages vary from five to eighteen years than for a sample with age held constant at nine years. Because older *Ss* would be both taller and heavier, the age factor would increase the magnitude of *r* quite apart from any intrinsic relationship between height and weight. With age held constant at nine years, the relationship between height and weight would still be positive, but it would not be spuriously high.

3 Reliability and Validity of the Measuring Instruments   When correlation techniques are employed to judge the reliability and predictive validity of tests or instruments, how high should you expect the correlation to be? You will recall that *a test is reliable* if there is a high correlation between the scores the same *Ss* obtain under similar conditions on the same test or equivalent forms of it. *A test possesses predictive validity* if the correlation is high between the scores the test has predicted the *Ss* will attain and the scores they do obtain.

Experience shows that one can expect a reliability coefficient to be higher (r = .70 to .98) than a validity coefficient (r = .00 to .60). A *reliability coefficient* of .90 for the self-correlation of an intelligence test or equivalent forms of it would not be considered high; an r of .95 would probably be expected. To be sufficiently reliable for discriminating between individuals, a test should have a reliability coefficient of at least .90. However, tests have been found useful with a reliability coefficient in the .80s, and when used in batteries with other tests, with an r as low as .35. Validity rs are usually lower than reliability rs. A *validity coefficient* between the scores on a single aptitude test and an achievement test may be quite low (r = .00 to .60). However, an r between a composite score based on several kinds of predictive test scores and scores on an achievement test may range up to .80.

4 Prediction for an Individual or a Group   From correlation data, a more accurate prediction can be made for the probable performance of a group than of an individual. An actuary in an insurance company cannot tell how long Roger Lee, age eighteen, will live, but from actuarial tables the person can tell quite accurately how many in a group of 10,000 eighteen-year-old *Ss* will live to be thirty, forty, or fifty years of age. Similarly, a rather high r between a battery of tests taken by seniors in the past and their college grades may not aid a guidance counselor in making an accurate prediction of the present seniors' college grades from their high school test scores. A somewhat lower r, however, may enable the counselor to predict with some assurance what percentage of the seniors this year will obtain A, B, C, or D college grades. An r of .40 would not be considered high for predicting the academic achievement of an individual, but an r of .50 would be considered very high for predicting the academic achievement of a group.

5 Correlation and Causation   In concluding this discussion, one point must be reemphasized: prediction does not constitute causation. The coefficient of correlation merely quantifies the extent to which two variables are related or associated; it does not imply that a cause-effect relationship exists. If the relationship between a poor self-concept and low grades is high, a poor self-concept may "cause" low grades or low grades may "cause" a poor self-concept, or both conditions may be "caused" by a third factor such as poor health, poverty, or a broken home. The two variables may be causally related, but this conclusion cannot be drawn from the correlation coefficient alone. Correlation is a necessary but not a sufficient condition for drawing conclusions about

causation. The interpretation of r is subject to all the pitfalls and limitations discussed in the previous section on causal-comparative studies.

Path Analysis

Path analysis is a promising new technique that enables investigators to clarify the nature of the relationships between several variables and to avoid false interpretations. Investigators often pounce on a statistically significant relation between two variables and offer the plausible interpretation that X causes Y, but many other variables may be operating in the situation that offer plausible interpretations for the occurrence of Y. Path analysis forces investigators to formulate a causal model that incorporates all the variables that past research and their own hunches suggest play a role in the drama. The model makes explicit all the relationships between the variables in such a way that the set of interpretations is consistent throughout.

In path analysis, multiple-regression techniques are employed and the data are presented graphically on a *path diagram* that assists in communicating the underlying rationale of the research problem. Basically, path analysis helps establish causal connections and clarify theoretical and empirical relations. This is done by testing alternative hypotheses (independent variables) to determine whether and to what degree they contribute directly or indirectly to the occurrence of the dependent variable.

The assumptions underlying the use of path analysis are that the sets of relationships among the variables are linear (changes in one variable are proportional to changes in another variable), additive (measurable on an interval scale), and asymmetric (causal: the relationship works in one direction only, $X \longrightarrow Y$).

A SIMPLE PATH MODEL   To acquire some understanding of the procedures and principles involved in path analysis, let us examine an example. Figure 10.8 depicts X_1 and X_2 as independent variables that contribute to the occurrence of Y, the dependent variable. Because X_1 and X_2 explain only some of the variance of Y, a hypothetical, residual variable, R_u, is introduced to close the system of analysis. The residual variable combines all the other unspecified variables that explain the remaining variance in Y.[13]

---

[13]Literal rather than numerical subscripts are attached to residual variables to indicate that they are not measured directly.

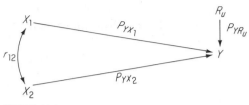

FIGURE 10.8

An example of a causal model represented by a path diagram.

In Figure 10.8, note that a one-way arrow leads from each independent (determining) variable to Y, the variable directly dependent upon it (the relationship works in one direction only, $X \longrightarrow Y$). In the notations for path coefficients (P's), the order of the subscripts is significant; the first subscript denotes a dependent variable, Y, and the second subscript denotes an independent variable, an X. The notation P_{YX_1} represents the partial relationship between Y and X_1 with X_2 held constant, that is, the effect of X_1 on Y independent of the effect of X_2. The notation P_{YX_2} represents the partial relationship between Y and X_2 with X_1 held constant, that is, the effect of X_2 on Y independent of the effect of X_1. These two path coefficients are standardized regression coefficients (beta weights) that indicate the net contribution in standard deviation units of each X on Y.[14]

The path coefficient for the hypothetical residual variable cannot be estimated directly from observed data, but it can be estimated indirectly. The notation P_{YR_u} represents the proportion of the variance in Y that is not explained by the other variables in the system. Therefore, P_{YR_u}, is equivalent to the coefficient of alienation in conventional analysis; it measures the lack of relationship between Y and the other variables in the system.[15]

Finally, note that a curved, two-headed arrow connects the two independent variables X_1 and X_2, and a simple correlation coefficient is added, r_{12}. The curved two-headed arrow indicates that the relationship between the variables r_{12} is not analyzed in causal terms by this particular model.

A MORE COMPLEX MODEL   One advantage of path analysis is that it enables investigators to examine rather extended causal sequences. Eight to ten variables may be included in a causal model. The diagrams

[14]Beta weights in a regression equation provide the number of standard deviations that Y changes for every change of one standard deviation in X.

[15]The coefficient of alienation, unlike r—which measures the presence of relationship between two variables—measures the lack of relationship. Thus, in our example, $P_{YR_u} = \sqrt{1 - R^2}$, where R^2 is the squared multiple correlation coefficient obtained from the multiple correlation of Y on X_1 and X_2.

can become quite complex; obviously, the greater the number of variables within the system, the greater the number of paths on the diagram. Regardless of the number of variables, the principles outlined above remain intact.

In Figure 10.9, let us examine a path diagram representing a model of the socioeconomic life cycle in the Negro population. The model incorporates several variables and includes the numerical values of the path coefficients. Let us begin by reading the data for the Negro population starting at the right of Figure 10.9 with the dependent variable, son's income, and move toward the left, backward in the life cycle. Note that only two independent variables, son's education and son's occupation, have direct paths to the dependent variable, income. Because path coefficients are standardized, their magnitudes can be compared. Note that the son's education has a greater effect on son's income (.21) than the son's occupation (.17) has.

A distinct advantage of the path model, which is not possible in a conventional regression design, is that it allows the investigator to determine whether variables that do not directly (independently) influence the dependent variable have any indirect influence. This estimate is made simply by multiplying the coefficients attached to the connecting paths. For example, son's education influences son's income via the path of son's occupation to the extent of the product of

FIGURE 10.9

**Path diagram representing a model of the socioeconomic life cycle in the Negro, with path coefficients estimated for native men 25 to 64 years old with nonfarm background and in the experienced civilian labor force: March 1962. (*In* On Understanding Poverty: Perspectives from the Social Sciences, *edited by Daniel P. Moynihan, with the assistance of Corinne Saposs Schelling, (C) 1968, 1969 by the American Academy of Arts and Sciences, Basic Books, Inc., Publishers, New York.)*

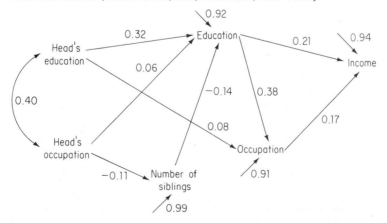

these two paths or (.38)(.17) = .06, which is a very small effect on income.

Let us examine another indirect effect. What effect does the education of the "head" (normally the son's father) have on the son's income? Obviously, in the absence of a single connecting arrow between the two variables, there is no direct effect. But the paths from the father's education to the son's income reveal three indirect effects: first, through the son's education (.32)(.21) = .067; second, through the son's education and son's occupation (.32)(.38)(.17) = .021; and third, through the son's occupation (.08)(.17) = .014. The sum of these three compound paths—.067 plus .021 plus .014—is .102. As you can see, the father's education affects the income the most through the son's education (.067), somewhat through the son's education and occupation (.021), and very little through son's occupation(.014). One interesting revelation is that the Negro father's occupation is not directly related to the son's occupation (no arrow) and has very little effect on the son's income via indirect routings. In a comparable model for the white population, the father's occupation did directly affect the son's occupation. In Figure 10.9, there are four residual variables with arrows coming out of nowhere. Note that the residual arrow with a path to income has a path coefficient of .94, which indicates that the role that unspecified residual variables play in determining income is great. Perhaps in the future some of these variables will be specified, providing a somewhat clearer understanding of the determination of income.

Cross-cultural and Comparative Studies

Cross-cultural and comparative studies, in which comparisons are made of two or more societies, may be conducted for a number of reasons: (1) to increase the range of observations on variables of interest, (2) to determine variations found in variables in different settings, (3) to analyze trends and common problems, and (4) to check the generality of theories and modify them if necessary to account for differences in findings across time and space.

Cross-cultural and comparative studies make an important contribution to our understanding of educational and social phenomena, for they seek to demonstrate whether findings concerning human behavior are valid for all human beings or are limited to one nation or to one culture. These studies increase the range of variability of many variables, which is important; for some educational phenomena vary more among societies than within societies. If the age range of "permissiveness" in child training varies in different cultures, a study of a culture that permits permissiveness only from birth to eighteen months will not tell the whole story. Hence, the researcher cannot develop a universally applicable theory of the effect of permissive child training. Knowledge about some educational phenomena cannot be tested by using data from one country alone, because a single case does not present sufficient variation of the variable to reveal its effect.

The dimension that separates cross-cultural and comparative research, according to Goethals and Whiting (44:441), is the level of theoretical and methodological sophistication. The psychological anthropologists who conduct cross-cultural investigations apply statistical techniques to test hypotheses concerning human behavior that they deduce from theories of cultural evolution, the integration of culture, or the behavioral sciences. But in many comparative education studies statistical tests are not used, and, if the studies are theoretically oriented, they merely test whether hypotheses apply in a more general framework than has previously been demonstrated.

CROSS-CULTURAL STUDIES Behavioral theory has given rise to many cross-cultural studies. Anthropologists have studied the relationship between child-training practices in various cultures and the internalization of moral values (53), the development of guilt (44), and the frequency of occurrence of crime(5). Assuming that the content of folktales reflects the underlying attitudes of people who tell them, investigators have examined the relationship between the content of folktales and aggression (44). Freudian theory has stimulated many investigations. The hypothesis that crime arises partly as a defense against strong feminine identification was tested in a sample of societies with low and high frequency of theft and personal crime (5). The investigators found that as the opportunity for contact with the father decreases, the frequency of both theft and personal crime increases.

COMPARATIVE STUDIES Colorful comparative commentaries on educational practices appeared in early travel reports, but the data were collected in an uncritical and unsystematic manner. With the rise of social science in the late nineteenth century, scholars began to analyze the historical-cultural forces that had shaped education in various countries, but some investigators sought to establish the superiority of a given system and others failed to make explicit comparisons among the nations they described.

Cultural bias is still present today in some comparative education research, and factual and narrative items vastly outnumber statistical analysis and careful explanation. But more causal hypotheses are being tested that provide rational explanations for similarities and differences in educational phenomena in various countries and their relationship with the social order and the environmental matrix within which they have developed. With the development of more sophisticated statistical techniques, the collection of a better quality and greater quantity of statistical data, and the utilization of the theories and tools of other disciplines, the older historical-cultural forces method of obtaining an understanding of education is being supplemented by empirical and quantitative methods. Some of the advanced contemporary work in the field is beginning to move from the descriptive to the explanatory level.

A survey of research in comparative education (12:184–193) reveals that there is no dearth of effort in this field. In selected samples representing various countries, investigators have compared school-church-state relationships; educational reforms; the causes, outcomes, and remedies incident to pupil failure; the accessibility to higher education; plans for the prolongation of compulsory education; and segregation and other forms of discrimination in education. A number of studies have compared educational developments in two or more European, African, Latin American, communist, or capitalist countries. Some studies have compared teacher education programs, educational systems on various levels, and activities of ministries of education in selected countries.

In recent decades studies have been made of the ways education can be affected by and in turn can contribute to economic, political, and social development and change. Investigators have tried to determine whether there are significant statistical relationships between education and social mobility; school enrollments on various levels and economic growth; literacy and gross national product per capita at various stages of economic development. Investigators have compared national expenditure on education and national income, and they have compared indicators of human resource development and economic development.

In an extensive international testing program conducted under the auspices of UNESCO, investigators measured differences in achievement in school subjects in a number of countries and sought explanations for the differences observed (40). Considerable planning was required to carry out this investigation. In the study of achievement in mathematics (55), the test instruments were agreed upon only after they were evaluated, modified, and pretested by local and international specialists. In addition to the mathematics tests, extensive question-naires were employed which permitted the investigators to express a quantitative relationship between achievement scores in mathematics and home, school, and societal variables.

Both UNESCO and the United Nations have published comprehensive comparative studies and an array of statistical data on illiteracy, juvenile delinquency, and education on various levels. In Europe, the Organization for Economic Cooperation and Development has published masses of information and has developed planning models that express in quantitative terms a number of educational-economic relationships within several countries to help national planners predict and control change in their educational systems and achieve their economic and educational goals.

DIFFICULTIES ENCOUNTERED Many difficulties are experienced in cross-cultural and comparative methods of research, but efforts have been made to overcome some of them. The availability, reliability, and comparability of the data present many problems. Some cultures are willing to display publicly behavior that is hidden or taboo in other cultures. The available data may be incomplete or incorrect and may not be described precisely and classified in the same way in all countries. The definition of an elementary teacher in one country may be equivalent to that of a high school graduate in another. Reports about cultures have been written at different times by people with different competencies, interests, and biases.

Weaknesses in communication equivalency are responsible for the errors found in some studies. Investigators must carefully check whether their instruments when used in different countries will actually measure the same phenomena. If they use standardized tests, the directions and test items may not convey the same information to children in all nations. Some concepts are difficult or impossible to translate into another language. If equivalent words are found in two languages, they may have different connotations. Many interviewers and informants do not possess a sufficiently sophisticated command of the language and knowledge of the culture to convey or to grasp fully and clearly the meaning of verbal and nonverbal communication, particularly significant subtle differences in meaning.

In international testing programs, greater confidence can be placed in test results if all test items are checked carefully to ascertain whether they are based on common cultural content and present, for different cultures, as fair a test of achievement as possible. An effort must also be made to establish safeguards that will prevent errors in coding. If this is not done, investigators may unconsciously code in favor of their hypothesis. If they make it a rule to code all doubtful cases against their theory, they will produce as great an error. To cope with this problem, they can have different people code the presence or absence of X and Y, or they may find that ratings of one of the variables are already available in the literature.

Researchers must also exercise caution in selecting informants. Teachers and adults are usually selected as key informants in educational investigations, but their view of what takes place in a classroom may vary greatly from the view of children. To minimize the possibility of collecting biased data, experienced investigators interview and interact extensively with informants of different ages, sexes, social statuses, and subcultures. They pay particular attention to any disagreement among informants' reports and between informants' reports and their own observations.

An investigator can conduct a cross-cultural study by himself if data for his study are already available. But because learning a language, establishing rapport, and developing and validating instruments take considerable time, a single person cannot gather detailed data from several cultures to test hypotheses. To overcome this problem and to increase the comparability of data, research teams, in some instances multinational teams, are trained to collect data in accordance with a strict set of criteria before they go into the field. They are provided with field guides that specify in detail what variables to observe and how to measure them. Considerable attention is also given to selecting the indicants for the variable being studied and to demonstrating that the indicants selected are valid ones. In the *Six Cultures* study (113), for example, teams were trained over a two-year period before going into the field to study the relation of child-rearing practices to personality in India, Kenya, Mexico, Okinawa, the Philippines, and the United States.

Invaluable guides and source materials have been compiled to aid cross-cultural investigators in compiling a bibliography, selecting a sample, and coding data. The Human Relations Area Files which have been established through the cooperative efforts of several universities are composed of ethnographic material on a world sample of some 200 societies. The *Outline of Cultural Materials* (75), produced in conjunction with the files, provides a guide for classifying and coding data. The *Ethnographic Atlas* prepared by G. P. Murdock and others appears cumulatively in each issue of *Ethnology: An International Journal of Cultural and Social Anthropology.* Over 1,000 societies are now listed and over 100 codes are defined. When sufficient data are available, scores are listed for each society on most of these codes.

DEVELOPMENTAL STUDIES

Developmental studies are concerned not only with the existing status and interrelationships of phenomena but also with changes that take place as a function of time. In these studies, investigators describe variables in the course of their development over a period of months or years.

Growth Studies

To teach effectively, one must have knowledge of the nature and rate of changes that take place in human organisms. One must know what interrelated factors affect growth at various stages of development; when various aspects of growth are first observable, spurt forward, remain rather stationary, reach optimal development, and decline; and how the duration, intensity, and timing of an experience in the developmental period affect growth. To obtain such knowledge, researchers conduct a series of systematic cross-sectional or longitudinal observations of *Ss*. They may study one or more aspects of one or more types of growth: physical, social, and/or cognitive.

CROSS-SECTIONAL STUDIES   When conducting a cross-sectional study, researchers make one set of measurements of *different children from each age level.* They might make measurements, for example, of different children from each of four age levels, such as groups of twelve-, thirteen-, fourteen-, and fifteen-year-old *Ss.* They would calculate the averages for the variables for each group and would plot these averages to depict the general growth patterns of each variable for children from, twelve to sixteen years of age. Cross-sectional studies usually include more subjects but describe fewer growth factors than exploratory longitudinal studies. In a cross-sectional study, investigators might record the weight and some length, girth, and breadth measurements of several thousand students from twelve to sixteen years of age. To obtain the "norms" of growth for these phenomena, they would calculate the central tendency of the items measured for each of the four years. Thus, they could state the average weight of children on each age level and the average for each of the other measurements taken.

LONGITUDINAL GROWTH STUDIES   When conducting a longitudinal growth study, rather than making one measurement of different children from each age level, investigators make measurements of the *same children at different age levels.* They might, for example, test and measure the same group of students on a number of variables when they are twelve, thirteen, fourteen, and fifteen years of age and plot their individual growth patterns for these variables during these years. These longitudinal studies can be confirmatory or exploratory in nature.

1 Confirmatory Longitudinal Studies   Although the ideal is not often achieved, the most powerful use of the longitudinal method is a confirmatory study that tests a specific hypothesis deduced from an explicit theory. For example: If X child-rearing practice is employed, then Y behavior can be expected to develop in children in environment P. The current effort to move from purely descriptive studies to a search for predictors of development has led researchers to study the effect of different home and school environments in relation to the child's age, sex, social and emotional development, and interests and achievement. Studies have been made of the effect on development of social stimulation and deprivation (isolation versus varied social interaction); stimulus enrichment and deprivation (verbal, sensory, physical); parental practices and attitudes (permissive and restrictive, affectionate acceptance and cold rejection); separation from the mother or father; social class and ethnic group membership; and various types of motivation.

2 Exploratory Longitudinal Studies The exploratory longitudinal study provides a fruitful source of hypotheses rather than a sensitive method of confirmation. In an exploratory study the researcher usually collects data concerning a number of growth variables, notes relationships among them, and suggests hypotheses that can be tested. Among the many factors studied in the development of "John Sanders" (59), for example, were (1) home, neighborhood, and family background; (2) entry into adolescence; (3) reactions of teachers and classmates; (4) membership in social groups; (5) physical development; (6) motor and mental abilities; (7) interests and attitudes; (8) underlying tendencies—analyses of drive patterns, projective materials, voice records, Rorschach records, and emotional trends; and (9) John as he saw himself and as he judged himself and others.

DIFFICULTIES ENCOUNTERED   Many difficulties are encountered in conducting longitudinal or cross-sectional growth studies. The longitudinal method is the most satisfactory way of studying human development, but the cross-sectional method is less expensive and less time-consuming. A prolonged exploratory longitudinal study is an excellent method of generating testable hypotheses, but it can become unwieldy and nonproductive in the hands of an inexperienced researcher. In a cross-sectional study, data that will provide a rough, general assessment of developmental patterns can be gathered and analyzed in a relatively short time. An analysis of the cross-sectional data may reveal what variables and subpopulations to observe and what specific hypotheses to test in a confirmatory longitudinal study.

The following discussion will examine some sampling, data analysis, and procedural problems that arise in cross-sectional and longitudinal studies and some precautionary measures that can be used to minimize them.

1 Sampling Problems   Cross-sectional studies have a sampling weakness that is not present in longitudinal studies. In a longitudinal study, the researcher can compare each observation of a child with an earlier and later observation of the same child; in a cross-sectional study, the measurements taken of children at each age level may not be comparable because the groups may differ on variables other than age. The *Ss* in the older group may not have had the same early home or historical experiences as those in the younger group. The older *Ss* may exhibit fearful or frugal behavior that is related not necessarily to age but rather to the war or depression they experienced as children. If a cross-sectional study is made of the strength and intelligence of males between fifteen and sixty-five years of age, the *Ss* selected to represent the youngest and oldest age groups may be quite different. The older men are presumably representative of those who at fifteen possessed the physical and intellectual capacity to survive until sixty-five years of age. The fifteen-year-old group undoubtedly contains some boys who will not survive until they are sixty-five years of age.

In cross-sectional studies, researchers cannot remove all the variables other than age in which groups differ, but they can select age-differing groups that are alike as possible in respect to sex, intelligence, socioeconomic status, or any extraneous variable that may significantly affect the growth factor being studied. If a study is being made of subpopulations on each age level, care must also be exercised that the subpopulations do not differ in respect to other relevant variables, such as health.

Longitudinal studies also have sampling weaknesses. The data in these studies are usually obtained from a limited number of Ss, and hence they do not experience the corrective influence of many samples. When Ss are selected from a community with a stable population for the sake of keeping track of them throughout the years of the study, the low mobility of the group introduces a bias that will influence the findings. Longitudinal studies may give accurate measurements for the growth of the individuals studied, but these descriptions are not necessarily representative of less stable populations. Can findings, for example, concerning the growth and development of students in a laboratory school at the University of Michigan be applied directly to children of migrant Mexican laborers?

When researchers utilize the longitudinal method, they face another sampling problem: volunteer and dropout subjects may differ from other members of the population. The parents who cooperate in a long-term research study may employ different child-rearing practices than those who do not volunteer. Obtaining complete data for all Ss over the years may be impossible because some of them may die, become ill, move, or lose interest in participating. The conditions that made the Ss unavailable may have a bearing on the growth patterns being studied, which, of course, cannot be reflected in the last stages of the study results. If strength is measured, for example, the weaker boys may lose interest in the study and "just go through the motions" or even refuse to take the tests after the first few years.

When Ss cannot be easily assigned to subpopulations on the basis of earlier behavior, the longitudinal method is usually used. Researchers can identify and assign sixteen-year-old Ss in a cross-sectional study to subpopulations on the basis of their sex at an earlier age without difficulty, but they cannot identify many characteristics at an earlier age, such as general activity, parental permissiveness, or parental tolerance for aggressiveness. If the researchers wish to study the differential development of high and low early-activity groups, they cannot determine what level of activity older children engaged in in infancy; hence, the best procedure is to identify these subpopulations at an early age and measure them repeatedly in a longitudinal study. In some instances, as an alternative, researchers may conduct a cross-sectional study and collect after-the-fact data from school records or parents, but certain risks are involved. The data that have already been collected by school systems may not be reliable. The records may fail to indicate what tests were used to obtain the scores, and the scores based on different tests may not be comparable. Researchers can interview mothers and check their ability to recall and describe accurately the past behavior of their children by asking: Are the mothers consistent in their reports of their children's past behavior? Are their reports of contemporary events accurate? Do other members of the families confirm their reports? Greater confidence, however, is placed in a longitudinal study than one based on retrospective evaluation of behavior.

2 Data Analysis Problems   Because longitudinal studies usually include a relatively small number of Ss from one locality, they do not give as accurate a picture of the great range of individual differences that exist among children as cross-sectional studies do. But individual variability of growth and development is revealed better in longitudinal than in cross-sectional studies. At best, cross-sectional studies provide approximations about the individuality of growth with time, for they give the average growth status of an age group, which tends to minimize or blot out individual variability. Thus, the growth spurt during adolescence may not be revealed in a cross-sectional study, because the combination of late-maturing and early-maturing Ss tends to smooth out the curve.

3 Procedural Problems   Another complication of the longitudinal method is that the researchers usually cannot make improvements in their techniques as their study develops without disrupting the continuity of the procedures. If they discover a new and better instrument for measuring a particular aptitude after the study has been under way for a year or two and decide to use it, the data they collect with the different tests are not likely to be comparable. Shifts in observational procedures are often necessary because of the absence of a single technique that is applicable across the range of ages. The same instrument cannot be used to discriminate between high and low activity of newborn, five-year-old, and sixteen-year-old children. The researchers cannot assume the equivalence of different procedures, but they can take the precaution of employing two or more procedures that are applicable for a particular age and evaluate the relationships among them.

To prevent the longitudinal study from becoming unwieldy, the researchers can restrict the range of the behavior observed, number of Ss in the sample, or duration of the study. If two teams of workers cooperate in the study, one team can collect data and maintain contact with the *Ss* and the other team can code, summarize, and analyze the data. The concurrent analysis of data may alert the researchers to observations that can profitably be made in the remainder of the study. The two-team approach also reduces the possibility of contamination. If the researchers delay the analysis of their data until the completion of their study, their appraisal of the dependency, aggression, or some other characteristic of the child at an earlier age is apt to be influenced by their knowledge of the child at the conclusion of the study.

Trend Studies

Obtaining social, economic, or political data and analyzing them to identify trends and to predict what is likely to take place in the future is the objective of some descriptive studies. Researchers who engage in this work either repeat the same status study at intervals over a period of years or gather information about past or present events or conditions from documentary sources. After comparing the data—studying the rate and direction of change—they predict the conditions or events that may prevail in the future. This type of study may combine the historical, documentary, and survey techniques.

TYPES OF STUDIES   School authorities often have to determine fiscal needs, when and where to provide new facilities, and whether to expand or contract teacher training and recruitment programs. To obtain data that will help them make decisions, they may conduct or examine studies of birthrate trends, the changing age structure of the population, enrollments in schools of education, the amount and direction of population mobility, home-building in the community, and the age of new residents. School authorities may wish to assess the progress that is being made in various areas or to determine the need for changes in the curriculum, guidance programs, employment practices, working conditions, public relations policies, or the ordering of priorities. To do this, they may examine trend studies that relate to student achievement; changes in the public's attitude toward specific school policies; the health, accident, or police records that relate to youth; the types of available jobs and anticipated job opportunities; the proportion of women and minority groups employed on various levels and in different occupations and professions; and teachers' strikes.

Trend analyses vary widely in scope, purpose, and quality. Some studies examine only a single variable across a period of time and are relatively easy to undertake. Comprehensive studies examine a number of variables that relate to education, a community, or a region and may project developments for a decade or more. The *New York Metropolitan Region Study*, for example, which was conducted under the direction of Raymond Vernon, consisted of nine volumes.

The interaction of two or more variables is examined in some studies. The investigators raise questions such as the following: Do more births, deaths, marriages, and divorces occur in periods of business depression? Do the amount, type, and segment of society involved in juvenile crime fluctuate with the business cycle? As part of a comprehensive economic analysis of countries for a period of 1,100 years, Sorokin (99) mapped the secular trend of the economic well-being for each country as a whole and then broke down the country trends to show the changes in the prosperity ratings for each of the main sectors—the ruling class, clergy, intelligentsia, laboring class—of the class structure.

DIFFICULTIES ENCOUNTERED   Some trends move gradually and cumulatively in a given direction; others fluctuate with some cyclical regularity within the day, month, or year; others fluctuate unpredictably without apparent regularity. Making predictions from social-trend data is a precarious venture because economic conditions, technological advances, wars, personal wants, and other unforeseen events may suddenly modify the anticipated course of events.

Long-range population predictions have usually proved wrong. Malthus foresaw mass starvation because of overpopulation, but he did not foresee the productivity of the Industrial Revolution and agricultural America. With the decrease in immigration and the decline of the birthrate during the Depression years, scholars suggested that the United States should prepare for a leveling-off of the population. But in the 1950s the projections of the Census Bureau on population growth were invalidated almost before their publication because of the unexpected increases in the birthrate. Again pundits prophesy that the worldwide population explosion will bring global misery. Among their predictions is the warning that educational institutions will not be able to cope with expanding enrollments. But new educational techniques and resources may be discovered that will solve this problem. The anticipated increase in enrollments may not be fully realized. Indeed, recent birthrate data for the United States indicate that some forces are already affecting the birthrate. Because of the many unforeseeable factors that may impinge upon social phenomena, trend analyses range considerably in certainty of prediction: most long-range predictions represent mere estimates; short-term predictions possess greater certainty, but sometimes long-term changes actually reverse the short-term direction.

The problem of finding comparable data over a long period of time confronts the investigator in trend studies. Comparing actual salaries over several decades is meaningless because of the changing purchasing power of the dollar. Comparing the actual number of accidents, illnesses, births, votes, or academic degrees in a trend study is of little value because of changes in the size of the population. Likewise, a comparison of the number of people who are married is of little value if the size of the population changes. However, a comparison can be made of the changes in the proportions of people who are married, but if the proportions of people who are of marriageable age steadily increases, age must be controlled. To do this, demographers select a standard year, and the age composition of that year is substituted for the actual age composition of each year. To find the standardized marriage rate for each particular year, they multiply the marriage rate in each category for a given year by the number of persons in that category in the standard year and then take the total of all age categories.

EVALUATION OF DESCRIPTIVE RESEARCH

In some respects, well-designed descriptive studies conform to the scientific method of research, but the complex nature of social science phenomena makes the full realization of this goal unattainable. Sciences develop step by step. Descriptive researchers do the pioneer spadework upon which experimental researchers build; hence the variables in their studies may not be defined operationally with the degree of specificity that they are in experiments, their measuring instruments are often cruder, and many of their data are qualitative rather than quantitative in nature.

Formulation of the Problem

In a descriptive study, the quality of the investigation will depend, in part, on whether the population to be described and the variables on which the description is to be based are clearly defined. This step in research presents problems because educators, unlike physical scientists, have not established universally accepted definitions for the phenomena in their field. Terms such as "maturation," "developmental stage," "aggression," "dependency," or even "learning" may be used quite differently in different theoretical frameworks. In some instances different terms are used to describe the same phenomena and the same term is used to describe different phenomena. The absence in a descriptive study of clearly assigned meanings for terms or any reference to the theoretical framework in which they are used can result in ambiguous communication and erroneous conclusions.

The analysis of phenomena in education is less highly developed than in the physical sciences. Many concepts and classification schemes employed by educators are obvious ones that are not particularly fruitful as principles for yielding and organizing knowledge. Some variables that provide significant clues to the nature of educational phenomena have been isolated and unambiguous, relevant indicants of them have been identified, but such analytical knowledge of many key variables does not exist. A number of methods are available for characterizing individual differences, for example, but student environment, an equally critical domain of inquiry, is commonly described by the crude categories "advantaged and disadvantaged" or "lower-class and middle-class." But some educators have become dissatisfied with the insights that generalized descriptions of educational phenomena and are beginning to isolate and describe more crucial environmental, genetic, and behavioral differences that impede or stimulate human learning and functioning.

To solve a problem, the scientific method requires that researchers formulate hypotheses—provisional explanations of events or conditions—and ascertain whether observable data can be obtained that will support them. Researchers who conduct status descriptive studies do not formulate hypotheses. If the facts they compile are examined, however, they may provide clues that will help workers formulate hypotheses to test in subsequent investigations. Hypotheses are crucial to the interpretation of data in explanatory descriptive studies. Some researchers conduct multistage investigations: They test one hypothesis which generates other hypotheses that, in turn, are tested to eliminate rival hypotheses or to gain a better understanding of the hypothesized relationship. Other investigators incorporate several variables in one design to discover what relationships exist. They ask: Is X_1 related to the occurrence of Y when X_2, X_3, etc., are controlled?

Both of the above procedures are acceptable, but some researchers initiate studies on the basis of vague notions about the phenomena without making a thorough analysis of the dimensions of the problem and formulating any precise hypothesis. When such procedures are employed, only confusion and misunderstandings result. To illustrate the point, let us assume that some investigators collect considerable data on a subject of interest. When they examine the data, they note that a significant relationship exists between X_1 and Y. From among the many plausible explanations for the occurrence of Y, they choose, at will, the interpretation that X_1 causes Y. Such an interpretation possesses a low evidential value, for it is made after the data are in and is supported only by the logical argument that the investigators' interpretation is consistent with their findings. There is no external confirmation that their interpretation is correct. If researchers formulate a hypothesis that incorporates relevant test variables (alternative hypotheses) before the collection of their data, they can later demonstrate with data whether their hypothesis is more plausible than the alternative hypotheses. Thus, their data provide external confirmation for their reasoning processes; their argument does not rest on logic alone. Little confidence can be placed in descriptive studies that do not test hypotheses that incorporate relevant test variables.

Observation and Experimentation

Scientific inquiry requires the presentation of accurate facts that are verified by public tests of common perception. Descriptive data do not measure up to this standard as consistently as the facts of the physical sciences. Some investigators rely on the observations made by others that are reported in questionnaires, interviews, and documentary sources without checking the authenticity and reliability of this secondhand information. Crudely constructed questionnaire and interview schedules and haphazard procedures for coding data are among the commonest flaws in descriptive studies. Some investigators check the data they collect from Ss but make the mistake of assuming that published data carry a guarantee of reliability. They accept at face value information that appears in print or official records which may have been deliberately falsified, include unintentional errors, or reflect the author's biases. Some researchers also forget that data collected from different sources, by different people, by different techniques, or at different times and places may not be comparable. In some instances, variances in data can be controlled by transforming raw data and weighting aggregates so as to provide measures—index numbers—for comparisons across wide spans of space and time. Complex compensated indices are difficult to construct and cannot be used uncritically; but, properly done, they often improve interpretation.

Experimental designs (in which investigators assign *Ss* to groups at random to equalize the groups, manipulate the independent variable, and then observe the results) present the strongest models of scientific proof. When experimental designs cannot or should not be used, descriptive designs offer reasonably useful alternative models. But little confidence can be placed in the findings of descriptive studies unless the investigators examine not only the relationship between the independent and dependent variables but also the effect on that relationship of other relevant variables on which the groups may differ.

By incorporating plausible extraneous, component, antecedent, intervening, suppressor, or distorter variables into a descriptive design, investigators (1) can demonstrate with data whether or not certain rival hypotheses do or do not account for the relationship between the variables that they had predicted existed and (2) can make the circumstances under which the relationship exists more specific. Some investigators fall into the imprudent practice, however, of routinely controlling the same set of test variables (such as age, IQ, and sex) in every investigation. The objective is not to control for control's sake, but rather to make a decision about what variables to control on logical and theoretical grounds. The quality of descriptive studies is determined, in part, by the ability of the investigator to identify the most crucial test variables.

The introduction of relevant test variables enables investigators to approximate some of the controls that are used in experiments, to trace out the nature of the causal relations, and to avoid misinterpreting the findings. But because descriptive researchers do not assign the *Ss* to groups at random to attain group equivalency, they can never be certain that some uncontrolled variable is not the real causal factor.

Greater confidence can be placed in the findings of experimental studies than descriptive investigations, but descriptive explanatory and status surveys contribute to the advancement of knowledge in many ways: by building a foundation of facts upon which explanatory hypotheses can be constructed, by identifying relevant and irrelevant variables, by screening out unpromising hypotheses, by checking the validity of existing theories, by directing attention toward alternative hypotheses which better fit the facts, and by obtaining findings about the relationship between variables in which some confidence can be placed because they persist when other relevant variables are held constant.

Generalization and Prediction

Science seeks to structure broad, imaginative generalizations, hypotheses that explain, predict, or account for the occurrence of events. But many descriptive studies provide for the lowest level of scientific understanding. Many investigators, collect, classify, and correlate data to describe what exists, but they do not fully analyze and explain why phenomena behave as they do. They do not put the relationships they describe to crucial experimental tests. Because many areas within the field of education remain unexplored, a reservoir of information about educational phenomena must be obtained before investigators can sense what is significant. But educators undoubtedly have been too preoccupied with describing variables and relationships between variables. The time has come to move to more sophisticated causal-comparative studies, and, whenever possible, to experimental probes.

Many educators conduct surveys that are limited in scope, life-span, applicability, and lack scientific usefulness. Graduate students often obtain data from nonrandom samples—a cooperative class or a nearby school—to study a problem of interest to them. Administrators often obtain data from their schools or community to help them spot trends, plan for the future, improve or justify an immediate local situation, or interpret problems to the public. These surveys may provide some practical information that aids graduate students and administrators in making decisions about the entities they investigate, but the findings of these studies have limited scientific usefulness. At best, the data obtained may suggest hypotheses that can be tested with random samples of populations in scientific-survey research studies.

Descriptive researchers are beginning to pay more attention to sampling procedures that enable them to generalize their findings beyond the *Ss* or institutions that participate in their studies to a well-defined population. The Stouffer study (see page 300) provides an excellent example of checking the adequacy of random sample procedures for a large sample. Two public polling agencies were selected to draw independently a representative cross section of the American population. Each of the cross sections contained more than 2,400 cases. By using two separate samples, both internal and external checks of the data were made. The agreement between the two groups was quite close. The probability method of sampling that was employed involved selecting a random sample from all counties and metropolitan areas in the United States. Within each of these primary sampling units, urban blocks and rural segments were selected at random, and from these units a random sample of dwellings were obtained. Finally, a random sample of one person from each dwelling was selected. Experienced interviewers from the two agencies obtained data from these selected *Ss*, and no substitutions were permitted.

Graduate students, of course, cannot conduct such extensive descriptive studies, but they can test their hypotheses by obtaining data from a sample selected at random from some well-defined population which will enable them to generalize their findings to that population. If a study is subsequently replicated with other samples from the same population or a number of different populations at different times and places and under different conditions, and the same relationship is found to exist in each sample, the cumulative weight of the evidence increases the confidence that can be placed in the descriptive hypothesis.

Whenever possible, descriptive researchers should observe the niceties of sampling procedures and should replicate their studies; but despite their sincerest efforts, they cannot establish such broad generalizations as do their colleagues in the natural sciences, for they are faced with the "dilemma of uniqueness." Since cultures, communities, students, and schools differ from one another and no culture is absolutely uniform in nature, descriptive data can mirror only particular aspects of specific events or conditions in a given setting. "When social scientists seek generalizations about all human beings, rather than, say, about members of a specific culture or a specific organization, their sample is invariably nonrepresentative. No one has yet studied a representative sample of persons or behaviors from all cultures at all periods" (82:256–257). Chemists can be quite certain that one sample of pure magnesium is substantially like another, but educators can never claim that one child is exactly like all other children.

Educational phenomena involve far too many variables for researchers to spell out detailed laws. One cannot predict human behavior precisely, but neither can one be certain that life consists of random or accidental events, at the level of either organism or collectivities. Descriptions of recurring patterns or regularities of human behavior enable investigators to make some reasonably reliable, limited predictions. Many predictions made by social scientists are more accurate than chance alone would allow. But these forecasts do not possess the universality, precision, or degree of accuracy that predictions do in the natural sciences. They are likely to be stated, "When this happens, this *tends* to occur," or "If this happens, we can expect that to happen in 60 percent of the cases." Evolving universal generalizations that permit highly accurate predictions may be the ideal, but even the physical scientists are less certain today than they once were of their ability to predict in certain areas except in terms of statistical probability.

11 STRATEGY OF HISTORICAL RESEARCH

istorical research has received less attention from educators in recent years than descriptive and experimental research. Why does this gap in research exist? Of what value is historical research in a scientific age? Some people hold that the past is the past, what happened in the past can never be really understood, and future problems and conditions will never be exactly like those that have existed in the past. Other people argue that historical research will enlarge our world of experience, will give us a deeper appreciation of and more adequate insight into our essential nature and uniqueness, and will make us aware of what it means to be human. Knowledge of our heritage will give us a better self-understanding and a better understanding of how the contemporary educational scene was set. History may modify our social, political, and moral parochialism, convince us that individuals and groups can play a vital part in bringing about change, teach us to be more tolerant of others, and make us more patient with our contemporaries when dealing with the complexities of nature and the process of change. A synthesis of the knowledge of the past—the drama of the decisions made and their consequences—may help us make decisions about current problems with greater intelligence and economy of effort. History may not provide us with precise predictive powers, but it can acquaint us with what has been tried before, what kinds of action have been successful and unsuccessful, and can help us appraise alternative courses of action. History seems to tell us that "if men are not masters of their fate, neither are they victims of fate" (24:93).

Obtaining knowledge about the past has always intrigued people, but the purpose and scope of historical writing have changed down through the ages. Most of the early writers sought to achieve literary rather than scientific objectives; they preserved beloved folktales or created stirring epics to entertain or inspire the reader. The ancient Greek scholar Thucydides, however, envisioned history somewhat as a science—a search for truth. Thucydides based his writings on his own observations or the reports of eyewitnesses that he subjected to detailed tests of reliability. For centuries most historians ignored the exacting methods of Thucydides; many of them wrote history to defend or to promote a particular cause, to protect the privilege of a class, or to glorify the state or church rather than to arrive at objective truth. Some historians were disciplined, however, by rigorous critical standards of research, and this practice became more commonplace particularly after the vigorous academic discussions of the historical method that took place about the turn of the century.

Today, historians strive to re-create the past experiences of human-kind in a manner that does no violence to the actual events and conditions of the time. They collect, examine, select, verify, and classify facts in accordance with specific standards, and they endeavor to interpret and present those facts in an exposition that will stand the test of critical examination. Modern historical research is a critical search for truth (62:239–269).

The historical method of investigation may be used not only to ascertain the meaning and reliability of past facts encountered in the subject matter that is commonly referred to as history but also to appraise the past facts encountered in everyday life. When conducting any research, for example, you may employ the critical standards established by historians to help you evaluate previous studies relating to your problem, the tools and procedures utilized by your predecessors, the credibility of the responses given in interviews and questionnaires, and the circumstances that conditioned the results of the previous studies.

When undertaking a historical study, you engage in some activities that are common to all investigations, but the nature of your subject matter presents you with some peculiar problems and requires you to apply some special standards and techniques. In general, you become involved in the following procedures; (1) formulating the problem, (2) collecting source materials, (3) criticizing source materials, (4) formulating hypotheses to explain events or conditions, and (5) interpreting and reporting the findings.

FORMULATING THE PROBLEM

Historical inquiry begins when some event, development, or experience of the past is questioned. You may discover new source materials the meaning of which when interpreted will provide answers about past events; you may question an old interpretation of existing data and devise a new hypothesis that will provide a more satisfactory explanation of past events. Beginning with a rather general, diffused, or even confused notion of the problem, you isolate one by one the crucial points that gave rise to your initial doubts or concern about gaps in knowledge and then formulate a simple, clear, complete description of the problem. Before proceeding further you check whether this problem is answerable by available methods of inquiry and by the available sources of data.

You can investigate individuals, institutions, organizations, laws, curriculums, administrative structures and processes, textbooks, teacher preparation, equipment, facilities, important concepts and ideas that have influenced education, or other educational phenomena during a specific period of time in a given culture—ancient or modern—or in a subculture determined by nationality, color, religion, sex, age, work, or social class. You may confine your study to one era and one sequence of events in a local, national, or regional setting, or you may compare events in different eras, different societies, or different civilizations.

COLLECTING SOURCE MATERIALS

Obtaining the best data available to solve a problem is an initial and important task of a historian. Thus, early in any study, you sift through the vast and varied traces of human activity that testify about past events, and from these you select evidence that is relevant to your problem. Although you may begin your search by examining secondary sources, your ultimate objective is to locate primary sources. Hence, you must be able to distinguish between the two types of source materials and must become adept at locating them.

Primary and Secondary Sources

Since you cannot observe past events for yourself, you endeavor to obtain the "best evidence" available from *primary sources*: (1) the testimony of able eye-and earwitnesses to past events and (2) actual objects used in the past that can be examined directly. The importance of these sources cannot be overemphasized: through these surviving traces of people's thoughts and activities you can gain some understanding of the past; without them you are helpless—"Without them history would be only an empty tale, signifying nothing" (115:185). Primary sources are the basic materials of historical research.

Because you know the worth of firsthand evidence, you make every effort to locate it. But sometimes you find it necessary to consult *secondary sources*: information provided by a person who did not directly observe the event, object, or condition. These summaries appear in encyclopedias, newspapers, periodicals, and other references. Some secondary source materials are actually based on fourth- and fifth-hand information. The more interpretations that come between the past event and the reader, the less trustworthy is the evidence, for the facts may become changed and distorted in transmission.

A rigid classification of source materials is not always possible, for both first- and secondhand information may appear in the same report. A report of a school fire, for example, may describe incidents that the writer observed personally as well as those that other people described to him. In some instances, an item may be classified as either a primary or a secondary source, depending upon how it is used. A general history of education textbook, for example, is many times removed from the original events, and is, therefore, a secondary source. If a scholar is studying how authors organized history of education textbooks and the emphasis they placed on various topics, however, it is a primary source.

A reputable historian obtains evidence from the closest witness to the past events or conditions. A newspaper account of what transpired at an NEA executive meeting should not satisfy you if you can obtain a copy of the official minutes of the meeting. A translation of an educational document should not satisfy you if you can obtain and read the original document. Whenever possible, you should visit an old school building or laboratory rather than study pictures of it. Primary sources are highly prized by a historian. Secondary sources are never trusted completely, but they do serve useful purposes. They may acquaint you with the major theoretical issues in your field and with the work that has been done in an area that you are exploring. They may suggest problem possibilities and working hypotheses and may introduce you to important primary sources. You may use secondary sources to obtain an overview of the problem area, to accumulate background information for your study, and to develop the general setting for your problem. During the investigation, you will alter your problem outline, of course, whenever firsthand information indicates it is imperative to do so.

Records and Remains

For the most part the historian's source materials are *records that have been preserved with the conscious intent of transmitting information.* Diverse types of records of past ideas, conditions, and events are available in written, pictorial, and mechanical forms, for example:

1   Official records.
    Legislative, judicial, or executive documents prepared by federal, state, or local governments, such as constitutions, laws, charters, court proceedings and decisions, tax lists, and vital statistics; the data preserved by churches, such as baptismal, marriage, financial, and board meeting records; the information compiled by federal and state education departments, special commissions, professional organizations, school boards, or administrative authorities, such as the minutes of meetings, reports of committees, administrative orders or directives, annual reports, budgets, class schedules, salary lists, attendance records, accident reports, and athletic records.
2   Personal records.
    Diaries, autobiographies, letters, wills, deeds, contracts, lecture notes, and original drafts of speeches, articles, and books.
3   Oral traditions.
    Myths, folktales, family stories, dances, games, ceremonies, reminiscences by eyewitnesses to events, and recordings.

4 Pictorial records.
   Photographs, movies, microfilms, paintings, coins, and sculpture.
5 Published materials.
   Newspaper, pamphlet, and periodical articles; literary and philosophical works that convey information about education.
6 Mechanical records.
   Tape recordings of interviews and meetings, phonograph records of
   pupils' speech or reading efforts.

In some instances, you do not have to rely on the records, reports, or words of others, for you can actually view or handle objects of the past that have been preserved. *These remains or relics which are handed down from the past without the specific intent of imparting facts or information constitute an unconscious testimony of incidents in the lives of people.* The toys, weapons, and implements found on a burial site, for example, may convey considerable information about the past. Remains sometimes reveal the actual practices and conditions better than official documents. A law may be found, for example, stating it was compulsory for children to remain in school until they were sixteen years of age. But youthful skeletons that are found at isolated working sites where catastrophes occurred and other unpremeditated evidence may reveal that many pupils left school before that age.

Various types of remains a historian might find include the following:

1 Physical remains.
   Buildings, facilities, furniture, equipment, costumes, implements, awards, and skeletal remains
2 Printed materials.
   Textbooks, record blanks, contracts, attendance forms, report cards, and newspaper advertisements
3 Handwritten materials.
   Pupil manuscripts, drawings, and exercises

Since relics and remains are tangible evidence that you can examine personally, they are more trustworthy as sources than records. You can measure, weigh, and describe an ancient instrument found at a school site that was once used to punish children. To interpret what it is and how, when, or why it was used, however, you often must search for clues in reports made by people in the past.

Source materials do not necessarily fall into exclusive categories. An item may be either a record or a relic depending upon the purpose for which it is used and the intention of the producer of the document or relic. A blank form for recording academic studies and achievements, for example, is a remain. But, if someone writes the courses, the grades, credits earned, and the name of the student on it, the form conveys information intentionally; thus, it is a document.

Location of Source Materials

In a preliminary search for historical data, the American Historical Association's *Guide to Historical Literature*, the card catalog, periodical indexes, bibliographies, historical reviews, dissertations, and research journals provide helpful leads. The *Guide to Historical Literature* gives a bibliographical panorama of the best historical literature to the date of publication. This work is divided into general topics, specific eras, and geographical areas.

Useful materials may be located in the local library, but during an investigation the search usually extends to other institutions and to historical depositories. Some individuals and agencies have exerted considerable effort to collect educational records and remains. The types of resources and completeness of the accumulations in the various depositories vary greatly. *A Guide to Archives and Manuscripts in the United States* lists over a thousand historical depositories in fifty states, but it does not include many of those that are specifically related to education.

The Library of Congress, the New York Public Library, and some universities and specialized libraries have valuable collections in particular educational areas. The Museum of the City of New York and similar institutions in other communities possess local educational remains. Some state and local historical societies have museums that contain important remains, newspaper files, and documents. Educational organizations have preserved documents and relics pertinent to their interests; for example, the American Alliance for Health, Physical Education, and Recreation has established a depository at its headquarters in Washington, D.C. A few universities have kept libraries, equipment, and effects of outstanding educators who have served on their staffs. Private citizens and prominent educators have also accumulated exceptional collections, such as the 8,000 old school textbooks that Dr. John Nietz acquired and presented to the University of Pittsburgh.

Not all source materials are collected for the convenience of a researcher. Private probing expeditions may turn up much valuable evidence. Important data may be discovered by talking with "old-timers" in the profession; exploring secondhand stores, bookshops, and attics; visiting school sites, getting permission to examine the correspondence, lecture notes, manuscripts, and files of retired teachers; or studying court, town, church, school, and institutional reports and records.

CRITICIZING SOURCE MATERIALS

In a historical investigation, you do not assume that a remain is genuine or that a record presents an authentic account of past happenings. You examine each one meticulously and attempt to determine how trustworthy it is. Detecting whether a document contains unintentional errors or is a deliberate deception is an essential part of your work. Any investigator who fails to take this precaution is foolhardy, for research based on unreliable sources is labor lost. "In historical studies doubt is the beginning of wisdom" (58:50). To give your readers a credible account of past events, you must subject your source materials to rigorous external and internal criticism.

External Criticism

Through external criticism you check the genuineness and textual integrity of the source material—whether it is what it appears or claims to be—to determine whether it is admissible as evidence. To discover the origins of source materials, you ask many questions: When and where was the document produced? Who was the author or creator? Did the credited author or creator produce it? Is this an original or an accurate copy of the author's work? From what sources were the contents derived and how dependent on them was the author? Questions, questions, questions—you keep asking them until you can ascertain when, where, and by whom a document or relic was produced.

Establishing authorship and the date and place of publication are common tests performed by a historian. Some documents do not carry the name of the writer, conceal his identity with a pseudonym, or present a person as the author who wrote little or none of the work. Educational committees and school administrators, for example, may issue reports that do not clearly identify the writer. Although three committee members may sign a report, only one of them may have written it—or a subordinate of one member may have compiled it. To ascertain the authorship of a superintendent's annual report, a historian may have to investigate several things: Did the superintendent or an assistant write it, or was it a compilation of reports made by various school administrative heads? If the superintendent used other people's materials, did he correct, alter, omit, suppress, or expand parts of their reports?

Enterprising and exacting detective work is often required to establish authorship, trace anonymous and undated documents, ferret out forgeries, discover plagiarism, spot incorrectly identified items, or restore a document to its original form. When sleuthing for clues, you examine items attentively and ask pertinent questions, such as (1) Did pecuniary gain, partisan interests, a desire to perpetrate an amusing hoax, or scholarly, family, community, or national pride cause someone to fabricate the record or remain? (2) Is the explanation of how the source was originally discovered questionable or unsatisfactory? (3) Did this report or story make its first appearance long after the event? (4) Do inconsistencies in the category of time (such as introducing events that belong to a later period in history or claiming a person performed a given act at a given place and time when records reveal the person was elsewhere at that time) indicate the work is spurious? (5) Are the language, style, spelling, handwriting, and printing of the document typical of the author's other work and the period in which it was written? (6) Did the author exhibit ignorance of things that a person of his training and time should have known? (7) Did the writer describe events, things, or places that a person of that period could not have known? (8) Did the donor of letters or papers, a public official, a translator, or anyone else alter a source—intentionally or unintentionally—by copying it incorrectly, adding to it, or deleting passages? (9) Is this an original draft of the author's work or a copy? (10) If it is a copy, is it reproduced in the exact words of the original? (11) If not, can the errors be corrected and the omissions be restored? (12) If it is a copy or bears a very remote date or no date, did the attributed author or a reliable contemporary, preferably several independent contemporaries, ever report that the attributed author wrote such a manuscript? (13) In an undated source of unspecified origin, are there any ideas, theories, customs, outstanding events, names of people or places, fads, fashions, styles of language or print, or kinds of ink or paper that would indicate approximately or precisely where and when it was produced? (14) How much of the source was based on personal observation and how much was derived from other sources? (15) If two or more sources agree in content or form or both, were one or more of the sources original and the others derived? (16) Can the original source or sources from which an author borrowed be detected by checking the publication dates and the agreement in form and content of the sources and by noting, in the derived source, changes in the author's style, unnecessary digressions or repetition that upset the logical order of the discussion, or the mention of details or views that do not coincide with those the author reports elsewhere?

When cross-examining your silent witnesses to determine the genuineness of a document or relic, you will experience greater success if you possess a rich fund of historical and general knowledge. You also need a good "chronological sense," a versatile intellect, good common sense, an intelligent understanding of human behavior, and plenty of patience and persistence. To solve some problems, you may have to be familiar with philology, chemistry, anthropology, archaeology, cartography, numismatics, art, literature, paleography, or various modern and ancient languages. A historian cannot have a knowledge of everything, of course, but you should acquire special training in auxiliary fields that are most closely related to your educational problem. If you are not qualified to undertake certain aspects of textual criticism, you should seek the help of competent experts in the field.

Internal Criticism

After completing the external criticism of a source material, you engage in internal criticism. External criticism is concerned with establishing the time, place, and authorship of the document and restoring the original form and language employed by the author. Internal criticism is concerned with ascertaining the meaning and trustworthiness of the *data within the document*. When checking the content of a source material, you probe for answers to the following questions: (1) What did the author mean by each word and statement? (2) Are the statements that the author made credible? The intent of internal criticism is to determine the conditions under which a document was produced, the validity of the intellectual premises upon which the writer proceeded, and the correct interpretation to be placed upon data.

Determining the meaning of a statement, technical term, or archaic word can be a complicated task requiring considerable knowledge of history, laws, customs, and languages. Many words in older documents do not mean the same thing today that they did in earlier times. Interpreting words and statements in recent publications is a less arduous task, but some words do not convey the same meaning to all people. When English and American writers use the words "football" or "public school," for example, they are not referring to the same thing. Likewise, attitudes, beliefs, and practices that relate to administration, curriculum, educational aims, the nature of the child, sex, religion, social class, race, and dress vary in different cultures and different eras.

Reading documents "through the authors' eyes" is easier if you ask many questions: Do these translations of documents carry the same meaning as the originals? What geographical, school, home, national, racial, or professional environment did these authors experience? What were the level and nature of knowledge in the various disciplines at the time these authors were writing? What was the current level of ethical, aesthetic, and moral standards? What were the burning issues of the day? What were the quality and nature of these authors' relationships with members of their families, friends, and professional associates? How did these authors' early and later economic and social status affect their views? If you can answer such questions and can determine why each author wrote a report, you can interpret the meaning of their reports more accurately.

A wealth of background information will help you determine whether the authors were writing seriously, humorously, ironically, or symbolically and whether they were voicing their real convictions, presenting establishment views for public consumption, mouthing conventional phrases to fill a void or to conceal their own views, or borrowing discriminately from others. Accurate analysis and interpretation of each author's meaning are of paramount importance if you are to detect meaningful relations between data and to re-create a reliable account of past events.

Prudence demands that you remain skeptical of statements made in source materials until you investigate whether the authors were willing and able to tell the truth in each instance. When conducting this probe, you ask some of the following questions: (1) Were the authors accepted as competent observers and reliable reporters by other authorities in this special field? (2) Were their facilities, technical training, and location favorable for observing the conditions they reported? (3) Did emotional stress, age, or health conditions cause them to make faulty observations or inaccurate reports? (4) Did they report on direct observations, hearsay or borrowed source materials? (5) Did they write their reports at the time of observation or weeks or years later? (6) Did they write from detailed notes of observations or from memory? (7) Did they have biases concerning any nation, region, race, religion, person, political party, social or economic group, teaching method, or educational philosophy that influenced their writing? (8) Did anyone finance their research work with the hope of securing a report favorable to a specific cause? (9) Did the authors write under any economic, political, religious, or social condition that might have caused them to ignore, misinterpret, or misrepresent certain facts? (10) Were they motivated to write by malice, vanity, or a desire to justify their acts? (11) Was their objective to win the approval of succeeding generations or to please or antagonize some group? (12) Did the authors distort or embellish the truth to achieve colorful literary effects? (13) Did the authors contradict themselves? (14) Do accounts by other independent, competent observers of different backgrounds agree with the reports of the authors you are evaluating?

Examples of Criticism

Many questions arise when one engages in historical criticism. To give you some insight into typical problems that a researcher encounters, the following discussion presents a case of (1) determining authorship, (2) identifying an unknown manuscript, (3) assessing authenticity, (4) restoring a document, (5) determining an event, (6) ascertaining meaning, (7) finding the correct spelling, and (8) checking origin.

DETERMINING AUTHORSHIP   Sometimes a person will be credited as an author of a work for years and in many reputable references before anyone questions the fact. A book on gymnastics that was used in some early American schools, for example, has the name of Salzmann on the title page. Scholars who traced the origins of this text found that Johann C. F. Guts Muths, a teacher in Salzmann's school, was actually the author of the original book, *Gymnastik fur die Jugend*, which was published in 1793 in Schnepfenthal, Germany. In 1800, an English publisher translated Guts Muths's book and placed Salzmann's name on the title page. A footnote explained that there was no doubt that Salzmann wrote it, for his name was subjoined to the advertisement in which it was announced (66:80). This error of authorship was repeated in the American work of 1802. A comparison of the original Guts Muths edition with the translated versions also reveals that the later editions were altered and condensed.

IDENTIFYING AN UNKNOWN MANUSCRIPT   An interesting story of tracking down the author, time, place, and purpose of a document has been told by Thomas Woody (115:188–189). In the University of Pennsylvania Archives, an old manuscript was found with other original manuscripts relating to the university. It was in relatively good condition, apparently free from alteration and mutilation, but devoid of any external indication of its origin.

After examining the manuscript carefully for clues, Woody was able to formulate the following hypotheses: (1) the document was all or part of an original document or a translated account of the rules and operation of *Pädagogium Regii*, a school established by Francke at Halle, Germany; (2) the appearance of certain awkward expressions suggested that the writer or translator was unfamiliar with the English language; (3) the reference to money in terms of Pennsylvania currency suggested that the author expected the information to be used in that locale; and (4) a reference made to 1726 indicated that the manuscript was probably produced sometime after that date.

To test his hypotheses, Woody turned to the most promising source—the Trustees' Minutes—for supporting evidence. In the minutes, he found that the trustees in 1750–1751 appointed a committee to draw up regulations for the new institution that had been established and placed under their care. The committee, wishing to be better informed about institutional regulations, requested "the Trustees to get a Translation made of a Pamphlet written in the German Language, recommended by the Revd. Mr. Whitefield, containing the Rules and Orders observed by the celebrated . . . School at Hall [Halle]" (115: 189). The minutes stated that the trustees agreed unanimously to the committee's proposal.

Woody suggested that, "from the foregoing, it seems reasonably certain, but the proof is not complete, that the English manuscript *may be the translation* of a document which, presumably, Mr. Whitefield had in his possession" (115:189). This conclusion was also supported by the fact that many of Mr. Whitefield's letters express admiration for the institutions established by Francke. Woody concluded "Further search would probably lead to discovery of the original pamphlet, or a copy of the same, from which this MS. translation was made, and many other matters" (115:189). But his discussion is sufficient to reveal some of the steps and techniques involved in tracing an unknown manuscript.

ASSESSING AUTHENTICITY Historians are curious about whether a document actually is what it claims to be. Hoaxes and intentional falsifications are not common in educational literature, but doubts sometimes arise concerning the validity of a document. This happened in the case of *A Young Girl's Diary* (54), an anonymous work that was claimed to be a genuine and unedited diary of an early adolescent. This book gained wide recognition in psychological circles as a revelation of the beginning of sexual consciousness, its development, and its incorporation into maturer thought patterns.

When a few readers (14) began to suspect that the diary was not the work of an early adolescent, they suggested that it might be a reproduction of childhood experiences by an adult. To support their position they pointed out that the style of writing and the sustained logical thinking were too mature for an eleven- to fourteen-year-old girl. The length of the entries aroused their suspicions, for they thought that writing 2,000 words a day was too taxing a task for a child. The critics held that the continuity, coherence, and clarity of the diary were extraordinary, particularly because it had to be kept secret from an anxious mother and an inquisitive sister. Unexplained allusions and unconnected incidents did not impede the reader's understanding of the passages as would be expected. One did not need editorial notes to explain who characters were, and each incident reported contributed to building the main dramatic theme. Inconsistencies were noted when checking the girl's references to the weather on certain days, visits to places that were nonexistent at the time, and other items (64). Some critics concluded, therefore, that the diary probably was not written by a young girl during the years the events took place.

RESTORING A DOCUMENT   An author's words are not necessarily preserved in print exactly as the person wrote them. *The Autobiography of St. Thérèse of Lisieux* (63), for example, was published after the author's death and became a best seller. When St. Thérèse was canonized, the original script of her autobiography was located and analyzed. In comparing it with the printed work, scholars noted many differences. During the process of restoring the autobiography, they discovered that 7,000 changes had been made in the manuscript!

DETERMINING AN EVENT   In some widely used reference books, Boston University has erroneously been given credit for granting the first bachelor of music degree in 1876. The report of the United States Commissioner of Education for 1873 indicates that such action had been taken by Adrian College, and the Trustees' Minutes of the College dated June, 1873 (36:35), confirm that the degree was conferred on a student that year.

ASCERTAINING MEANING   When people want to settle questions, they may turn to traditional sources of authority for guidance. In recent years, for example, some citizens have urged that sectarian religious instruction be fostered in public schools and that public funds be made available to private and parochial schools. Their opponents claim that such action would violate the principle of the separation of church and state expressed in the First Amendment, which reads: "Congress shall make no law respecting an establishment of religion, or prohibiting the free exercise thereof. . . ." The question raised is: "Does the ban on 'establishment of religion' prohibit 'co-operation' between church and state in education or is greater 'co-operation' than we now have both permissible and desirable? Does 'co-operation' amount to an alliance or fusion of church and state?" (15:xiii). To reach any decision, it is necessary to determine what the principle of separation of church and state means.

Professor Butts tried to discover the authentic meaning of "establishment of religion" by sifting through the available historical evidence. To trace what the term has meant in America from colonial days to the mid-twentieth century, he examined the deliberations and constitutions of colonial, state, and national bodies; the writings of outstanding leaders; and the school laws, legislative acts, and judicial decisions that had a bearing on the problem. Butts's analysis extended over 200 pages, and his conclusions concerning the meaning of the term "separation of church and state" for education were summarized in ten statements (15:209–210). His study reveals the tremendous amount of labor that is sometimes involved in determining what a statement means.

FINDING THE CORRECT SPELLING   Standard works of reference generally possess their quota of mistakes. The *Encyclopaedia Britannica* (11th edition), for instance, referred to the wife of the fourth president of the United States as Dorothy. Some other early encyclopedias referred to her as Dolly or Dorothea. When a group of scholars examined letters from Mrs. Madison to friends, a note to a minister, her will, and her mother's letters, they found evidence which indicated that Mrs. Madison's first was Dolley—not Dolly.

CHECKING ORIGIN   Our national pastime of baseball has also been the subject of historical criticism. Modern literature commonly credits Abner Doubleday as the inventor of the game. The cause of this reputation and the historical criticism of the claim make an intriguing story that reveals how a picture of the past may be distorted.

When baseball became a popular sport in this country at the turn of the century, enthusiastic fans claimed that the game was of American origin. A British-born sportsman, Henry Chadwick, challenged this theory, for he believed the sport was a direct descendant of the English game of "rounders." A. G. Spalding, a popular baseball figure who supported the American theory, complained that he had been fed this "rounders pap" for forty years and refused to swallow the story without substantial proof. He proposed to settle the issue in "some comprehensive and authoritative way, for all time" (50:173) by establishing a commission of six public-spirited men to investigate.

The public was invited to send pertinent information to the commission. Two years later the members accepted the testimony submitted in a letter by Abner Graves, who wrote that his boyhood friend, Abner Doubleday, originated the game. Without any additional supporting evidence, they announced that Doubleday invented and named the game "Base Ball" in 1839 when he marked off a diamond-shaped field and diagramed the location of players at Cooperstown, New York. This report remained unchallenged by most people for years and was copied in a number of textbooks, newspapers, and sports books.

When Henderson examined the evidence, he presented some interesting conclusions (50:170–196). The report was primarily the work of the chairman of the commission, A. G. Mills, who was a military friend of Doubleday. Mills apparently based his findings on a letter written by Abner Graves, for no documents by any other person and no contemporary records were presented to support the Graves story. Henderson points out that when Doubleday supposedly originated the game in Cooperstown, he was actually in West Point and did not return to Cooperstown on leave. After retiring from the army, Doubleday wrote many articles for publicaton but none about baseball, and when he died in 1893, his obituary notice did not mention that he invented the game.

A critical examination of the commission's report revealed many other weaknesses. The name "Base Ball," illustrations of a baseball diamond, and rules of the game that were invented supposedly in 1839 had appeared in print before that time. Although it was claimed that Graves was present when Doubleday traced the first baseball diamond in the dirt, the original Graves letter did not mention this incident. A later letter that appears to have been written by Graves disclosed that he did not know "where the first game was played according to Doubleday's plan." Comparisons of the two Graves letters revealed some inconsistencies, which was not surprising, for the man wrote from memory almost seven decades after the event.

Henderson believes that certain personal factors may have caused members of the commission to accept the report. Because of the pressure of other duties, they probably did not check the facts thoroughly. Perhaps patriotic prejudices also influenced their decision. Some of the men were anxious to prove that baseball was of American rather than British origin. The possibility that General Doubleday, a famous Civil War soldier, invented the great American game must have appealed to them.

General Principles of Criticism

The examples given of historical criticism reveal that researchers make many judgments when evaluating records and relics. Not all the principles of criticism can be fully discussed in this text, but the following suggestions made by Woody will serve as a general guide.

> (1) Do not read into earlier documents the conceptions of later times; (2) do not judge an author ignorant of certain events, necessarily, because he fails to mention them (the argument *ex silentio*), or that they did not occur, for the same reason; (3) underestimating a source is no less an error than overestimating it in the same degree, and there is no more virtue in placing an event too late than in dating it too early by the same number of years or centuries; (4) a single true source may establish the existence of an idea, but other direct, competent, independent witnesses are required to prove the reality of events or objective facts; (5) identical errors prove the dependence of sources on each other, or a common source; (6) if witnesses contradict each other on a certain point, one or the other may be true, but both may be in error; (7) direct, competent, independent witnesses who report the same central fact and also many peripheral matters in a casual

way may be accepted for the points of their agreement; (8) official testimony, oral or written, must be compared with unofficial testimony whenever possible, for neither one nor the other is alone sufficient; (9) a document may provide competent and dependable evidence on certain points, yet carry no weight in respect to others it mentions [115:190].

For a more detailed discussion of external and internal criticism, the reader may consult outstanding authorities in the field (11, 24, 45, 58).

FORMULATING HYPOTHESES

Historians do not aimlessly collect records and relics, subject them to intensive criticism, and then present the mass of facts—names, events, places, and dates—to the public like beads on a string. Unrelated bits of information do not advance knowledge appreciably. Even if scholars group their facts and arrange their groups in a logical order, they produce a narrative that is little more than a series of disconnected and unexplained events. Isolated facts lack meaning; consequently, research workers go beyond the amassing of data or merely description and classification of them in accordance with their superficial properties. Rather than merely placing facts on file, historians, like experimenters, formulate tentative hypotheses that explain the occurrence of events and conditions. They seek the hidden connections, underlying patterns, or general principles that explain or describe the structural interrelations of the phenomena under study. When historians seek to explain how and why events occur, they reach beyond the events themselves—to domains outside of the discipline of history. Psychological, sociological, political science, or economic theories may help them make sense out of their data.

All historians, with the possible exception of compilers of documents and letters, use hypotheses, but the types, levels, and amount of generalization they employ and the rigor with which they examine the conceptual framework of their studies differ. Some historians claim that they are interested merely in concrete events in their singularity; they check the validity and authenticity of facts about past events and arrange them in chronological sequence but do not present hypotheses that explain possible connections between the facts. Their reports relate what happened but do not explain how or why the events occurred in a particular sequence. These historians may not use hypotheses consciously, but nevertheless they have some point of view, value system, or interpretive scheme that helps them determine what facts are significant, how to structure the hierarchy of their significance, what adjectives, adverbs, and verbs to use (great educators acted courageously—weak educators vacillated constantly). Reports based on unexamined assumptions, unstated hypotheses, or unspecified convictions about the nature of human beings, society, the universe, or the causation of historical change may be rather ambiguous. An explicit statement, or at least a systematic awareness of the hypotheses used in determining what facts were significant, clarifies the relationship between the investigator's ideas and the facts the individual reports, and it minimizes the possibility of employing trivial, biased, conflicting, faulty, or archaic hypotheses.

Historians use different types of hypotheses for a variety of purposes. They may use causal-type hypotheses to provide a framework for their entire investigation. (The curriculum became more scientifically oriented for reasons X, Y, and Z.) They may use hypotheses to explain events within that framework. (Factor Y caused Dr. X to take position O.) They may use hypotheses to supply conjectural details that are not supplied directly by the evidence. (Dr. Jackson probably revised the report of his staff members before it was published, for that was his custom.) They may use hypotheses to check out various aspects of their problem, such as authorship, trustworthiness, or interpretation of a source. (X document was not written by Y; X is the correct spelling of Y's name; X meaning is the correct interpretation for term Y at time O.) Historians also use rudimentary generalizations or descriptive concepts to classify people, things, areas, or periods. (Dropouts, textbooks, ghettos, Dark Ages.)

Historians select or construct the hypotheses that are most appropriate for the past events they are investigating and that are rooted in basic assumptions they can accept and defend. The explanations or hypotheses that historians propose lack proof at the time they are constructed. Your duty as a historian is (1) to inform the reader of any assumptions you have made or personal views you hold that may influence the selection of data and (2) to formulate the conceptual and factual elements and relationships in the hypotheses in such a precise and objective manner that their implicatons can be tested.

Upon what sources do historians draw to interpret historical events? The "empathy theory" holds that the best way to understand the past is to get at the purposes in the minds of people in the past through the historian's own intuitive feelings and understandings. The "great man" theory of historical interpretation holds that important events or changes are caused by the presence, absence, or disappearance of forceful historical personalities. The "common man" theory holds that the average person of the age provides the best key to an understanding of past events. Some historians hold that past events can best be explained from a theological view, within the context of the divine plan for creation and from the standpoint of the eternal. Some people hold that while many factors can influence history, in the long run they are all controlled by economics. Some historians claim that laws have played a key role in shaping our development or that wars are crucibles in which opposing convictions are tested and hence give us key insight into the crucial struggles of the past.

In the past, historians had to make certain assumptions about the workings of the human mind and body and the social structure and processes, but in recent years psychologists, sociologists, psychiatrists, economists, anthropologists, geographers, and political scientists have developed an array of hypotheses and analytical techniques, some of which historians can use to gain an insight into the nature of human beings and society. Concepts or theories concerning motivation, social role, self-concept, social mobility, aggression, frustration, and inter-group conflict may be helpful. Theories regarding the physiological or chemical structure of human beings may provide insights. Theories that explain how groups and agencies mold behavior and regulate the distribution of power, how decisions are made, how geographical factors affect political unity, human exertion, health, mobility, and production may be used. Precautions are taken, however, to guard against employing hypotheses, classification schemes, or terms that are based on outdated scientific knowledge.

Historians can also employ statistics to advantage in some problems (4). A qualitative hypothesis which incorporates words such as "significant," "growing," "widespread," "decline" can sometimes be sharpened by the use of the quantitative method. A quantitative hypothesis and statistical presentation of data concerning juvenile delinquency does provide a means of verifying a general statement about juvenile delinquency and helps avoid the pitfall of making generalized statements about large groups of people on the basis of a few illustrated cases. A quantitative hypothesis and statistical data concerning the influx or exodus of nationality or racial groups in a specific area may give insights into the educational problems that arose. The statistical data may make it easier to see differences, likenesses, changes, continuities, and significant relationships that might not otherwise have been detected, as well as exceptions to the hypothesis that indicate the explanation is faulty. If one can determine why the exceptions exist, one may be able to devise an alternative hypothesis that more adequately fits the evidence. Quantitative hypotheses can be of value, but they cannot be employed in many problems, for limited data are available about many past happenings and the sources of the data may be inaccurate, incomplete, based on crude observations, or classified in ambiguous categories. The problem of selective deposit and selective survival of data gives rise to the question of whether one has a representative body of data from which to draw conclusions. Moreover, because only a small part of the data relating to an historical event is used, quantitative hypotheses are limited in outlook and do not tell the whole story.

Historians may study comparable events in other societies or periods of history and borrow a hypothesis. They make an effort, however, to detect any important nuances of difference between the two situations that make the analogy false and, if possible, to modify the hypothesis so that it accounts for this difference.

Locating data and subjecting them to rigorous criticism compose one stage of research; interpreting data is another important step. Many graduate students produce historical studies of little value because they assume that accumulated facts that have been subjected to rigorous internal and external criticism will interpret themselves. A historical study is not merely a "grocery list" of facts; it is an interpretation of the past that is derived at by searching for meaningful relationships between selected, surviving facts. After selecting a problem area, experienced historians engage in some of the following activities to help them formulate hypotheses—guesses about meaningful relationships—that explain what happened in the past, as well as how and why it happened: (1) examine events within the scope of their problems in the full range of their content; (2) steep themselves in knowledge about the educational, religious, social, political, economic, and physical environment and the collective psychology, scientific concepts, and intellectual ideas of the era; (3) ascertain to what extent these forces affected the nature, views, or actions of individuals or groups, and, in turn, what effect the individuals or groups had on these forces; (4) find clues about an individual's self-image; (5) investigate the social role—the attitudes and behavior patterns one was required to exhibit to maintain one's position and status in a given group; (6) search for meaningful interrelationships between events in a person's life, between people, between movements, and between institutions and divisions within them; (7) determine to what extent various activities, institutions, people's views, or other phenomena were the same, how they differed, how they modified or reinforced one another's views or acts, what the contribution of each was, and what their common contributions were; (8) strive to detect changes in individuals, institutions, and ideas that took place over a period of time and the factors that contributed to these changes; (9) remain aware of the fact that beliefs and procedures once established may remain long after the factors that caused their establishment have disappeared; (10) look for frustrations, failures, declines, and defeats as well as fulfillments, successes, and progress; (11) look for causes that are remote as well as near in time or space; (12) remember that unconscious motives, irrational impulses, and emotional factors can determine courses of action as well as rational choices; (13) give consideration to the causal influences of the personalities of great people and the decisions of outstanding leaders; (14) keep in mind that the conspicuousness and influence of a person are not necessarily correlative; (15) remember that some events are in part the product of chance or coincidence; (16) search not only for evidence that B existed and that B caused A's acts but also for data that serve to eliminate the possibility that X, Y, and Z have influenced A's acts, or the nature or extent to which they may have contributed to the acts. Perhaps the best way of gathering a deeper understanding of the process of constructing and testing hypotheses is to examine some concrete examples.

Principle of Separation of Church and State

When Butts undertook the task of determining the meaning of the principle of "establishment of religion," he observed the standards of sound scholarship. In the introduction of the study, he expressed his objective simply:

> This book is an effort to state as clearly, as briefly, and as objectively as possible what the weight of historical evidence means concerning the American principle and practice of separation of church and state.
> ... In the pages that follow, a portion of the available historical evidence is presented in order to help the American people decide whether or not the principle of separation of church and state is an authentic and valid tradition in America [15:5–6].

Because his selection of evidence is necessarily conditioned by his beliefs, Butts frankly states that his work is written

. . . in a framework of values which includes the following assumptions: that religious freedom is a foundation stone of American liberty, that the preservation of the equal rights of religious conscience is a necessity for genuine religious freedom, that the guarantee of religious freedom is an essential function of our constitutional form of government, that public education is a bulwark of our common democratic values, that private education has a legitimate and desirable function to serve in American society, and that "an establishment of religion" (as defined in Chapters 2, 3, and 4) is a threat to religious freedom and to the American tradition of democracy. This all means, by and large, that the historic principle of separation of church and state as defined in 175 years of American history is a desirable tradition to maintain in American education (as outlined in Chapters 5 and 6). These are the working hypotheses upon which the investigation in this book has been undertaken. Whether or not the conclusions reached are justifiable depends in the last analysis upon public judgment [15:xiii–xiv].

Early Roman Education

A study of early Roman education caused Chiappetta to formulate a hypothesis concerning the period, "namely, that the Romans did not accept formal education or use it as a reliable or effective behavior changing device" (20:155). He noted that aside from the writing of Quintilian there were practically no reliable reports on educational practices during this period and there was also a "curious lack of archaeological remains which would indicate the existence of schools in any great number" (20:155). To test his hypothesis, Chiappetta examined "some of the events which occurred, or more importantly, did *not* occur" and reported the following conclusions:

> The scanty evidences indicate that only a small segment of the population attended schools. In general, the sons of the senatorial class became the next senators or patricians, and at no time did the schools become a vehicle for social mobility. . . . Further, while the Romans . . . built not only an empire, but all the appurtenances that go with a complicated society—a language, a priesthood, commercial systems, an architecture, roads, bridges, sanitation systems, armies, navies, *ad infinitum*—at no time do we hear of schools which prepared the Romans to do these outstanding deeds. Apparently there was no institutional educational attempt to prepare people for the vast range of employments required in the constantly enlarged Roman-dominated area. The attempts at secondary and higher education seemed to concentrate on the production of the orator, and . . . the tyranny of the Roman emperors was in the process of becoming so absolute that Rome no longer needed statesmen, educated or not. . . . Finally, the late entry of the state into the support of education seems to indicate that the Romans thought lightly of such matters [20:155–156].

Early New York Schools

Errors may appear in educational literature and be repeated for years before someone challenges them. Around the turn of the century, for example, Andrew S. Draper stated that "all the English schools in the province [New York] from 1700 down to the time of the Declaration of Independence, were maintained by a great religious society . . . called the society for the propagation of the gospel in foreign parts [SPGFP]" [33:29–30]. Other educational historians agreed.

Years later, Professor Seybolt (93), apparently after reading a doctoral dissertation by Kemp (60) on the work of the religious society, began to doubt Draper's generalization. Kemp stated that from 1710 to 1776 the SPGFP supported continuously from five to ten elementary schools in New York. Seybolt got the notion that there were probably many "English Schools" in New York during those years that were not maintained by the religious society. To test his hypothesis, he examined eighteenth-century records and found evidence that there were at least 200 schools not maintained by the SPGFP. Thus, Seybolt had produced facts to refute Draper's generalization and to support his own.

Early American Textbooks

Sister Marie Léonore Fell formulated a hypothesis to guide her study of *The Foundations of Nativism in American Textbooks, 1783–1860.* Previous studies had indicated that considerable opposition to minority groups existed in the United States at this time, but the "contribution of biased text-books to political nativism" remained unknown. She examined more than a thousand reading, history, and geography texts to test the hypothesis that during the formative years of our country the compilers of textbooks "laid the foundations of the anti-Catholic and anti-foreign attitudes, which had their political conclusions in the Nativist movements of the 1830's and 1840's and in the Know-Nothing party of the 1850's" (38:vi). In reporting her findings, she stated that the study "reveals not so much an anti-foreign slant as an anti-Catholic attitude on the part of the compilers of the texts" (38:224).

Origin and Decline of Sports

Because the recreations of people reveal much about the period in which they live, some scholars are interested in tracing the development and decline of sports. After studying various ball games and wondering about their origins, Henderson formulated the hypothesis that "all modern games played with bat and ball descend from one common source: an ancient fertility rite observed by Priest-Kings in the Egypt of the Pyramids" (50:4). To test his hypothesis, he examined the religious ceremonies and folk customs of ancient man and traced the evolution of games played with a ball. Henderson reported finding evidence in rituals, customs, and tombs to support his thesis that the modern bat-and-ball games are vestigial remains of ancient rites.

When Polsky (79:1–30) endeavored to make a serious study of the decline of poolrooms, he found that some of the standard explanations collapsed. He hypothesized that the decline in poolrooms was attributable to the decline in the number of confirmed bachelors. He pointed out that poolrooms, boarding houses, tramp and hobo life, and publications such as the *Police Gazette* had developed in response to the needs of men who had remained unmarried because of economic factors and immigration patterns or who had previously sought refuge from female-dominated society in frontier life. When socioeconomic conditions changed, the bachelor population declined and the number of poolrooms declined. To support his views, Polsky presented evidence that among all males over fifteen, the proportion that was single declined from 42 percent in 1890 to less than 25 percent in 1950, and that the billiard boom started in the 1800s and the decline began in the 1930s.

Polsky refuted the arguments that the cause of the decline of poolrooms could be attributed to the traditional explanations: the opposition of middle-class morality; the rise of mass participation in bowling; the fact that billiards was too difficult a game for many people to learn well; the rise of mass spectator interest in professional sports; and the spread of radios, automobiles, and the movies.

Polsky pointed out that these alternative hypotheses could account for the decline of poolrooms only in a minor way. The opposition to poolrooms had always existed and had been even stronger in periods when poolrooms grew in popularity than during their decline. Pool is a difficult game to learn, but many people enjoy games in which they do not excel, and in the 1850s, billiards superseded bowling in popularity. In the early 1930s Willie Mosconi, an outstanding billards player, could draw 1,500 spectators on a Saturday night while the Chicago Cubs could drawn only 1,200 to a baseball game the next day. At the height of their popularity, poolrooms competed successfully with many popular diversions—vaudeville, dance halls, taverns, and phonographs. It is curious that although pool would be an ideal TV spectator sport, TV has not adopted it.

Two Quantification Studies

D. C. McClelland (68), a psychologist, proposed that the Achievement Motive (*n* Achievement) is a causal factor that accounts for the growth and achievement of societies. To measure the relative prevalence of energetic, enterprising men in a given society, he suggested that investigators score the achievement images found in the literature of the society. One of his students hypothesized that if *n* Achievement were a cause, rather than a result, of the progress in ancient Greece, then *n* Achievement level would be higher during the growth of ancient Greece and would drop during the climax and decline of that civilization. He scored the amount of achievement imagery in works on six subjects by selected authors from each period. Starr (102:12) criticized this quantitative study because he thought the conclusion was known already by subjective means.

Elliott (37) addressed himself to a quantitative view of the American scientists in antebellum society. After making a statistical analysis of three aspects of scientists in society—the occupations of their fathers, their educational backgrounds, and their employment patterns—he further considered the mutual relations of men of science, men of letters, and inventors. Elliott developed the general theme of an intellectual class which in some respects was outside the mainstream of the American people, but had its own internal differentiations.

Quantitative studies demand precision and hard data upon which to base subjective interpretations and provide a means of bringing to light undetected trends in the behavior of people or institutions over time. But statistical data are frequently lacking for some periods of time, classes of people, and types of activities. Quantitative analysis, moreover, does not provide for the impact of ideas, emotions, and other materials of importance to education. Quantification can play an important role in some aspects of educational history and little or no role in other areas of great interest to educators (62:239–269).

REPORTING THE FINDINGS

After completing an investigation, you write a well-organized report of your work. Within the framework of your hypothesis, you pattern your data in some systematic order, such as chronological, topical, or a combination of these. You will also make judgments concerning the amount of emphasis or space to give to various evidence. Considerable information may be collected on relatively minor points in a study and little evidence on more significant events. Reporting everything would produce a distorted picture of the past. Determining which data are most significant and how many facts to include requires a reappraisal of the hypothesis and the study as a whole.

Weaving raw data into a cohesive, well-proportioned, colorful exposition requires painstaking labor. To achieve the twin objectives of maintaining accuracy and interest, you refrain from embellishing a narrative with dramatic flourishes that distort the truth, but you strive for literary excellence. Stretching or supplementing the existing evidence to create a more spirited narrative is not permissible. Fitting the pieces of established evidence into a simple, vivid mosaic that delineates past events dramatically is the difficult but desired ideal. History is life—and it deserves better than a drab description. You cannot sacrifice accuracy for eloquence, but by developing your creative and critical skills you can learn to write lucid, lively, logical accounts without violating the rigorous rules of historical scholarship.

EVALUATING HISTORICAL RESEARCH

Historical research is an exciting and satisfying pursuit, but attaining a proper perspective of its achievements and limitations is important. Some people credit historians with accomplishing more than is possible; others believe they cannot possibly produce scientifically reliable data. The truth probably lies somewhere between these two extreme positions. By reading the following arguments, you may get a better insight into the problem and draw your own conclusions.

Nature of Historical Knowledge

Adulators of historical writing sometimes assume that the researchers present the totality of past actuality. Historians cannot possibly do this; they can give only a fragmentary picture of the past. Historical knowledge is never complete; it is derived from the surviving records of a limited number of events that took place in the past. As Gottschalk points out,

> . . . only a part of what was observed in the past was remembered by those who observed it; only a part of what was remembered was recorded; only a part of what was recorded has survived; only a part of what has survived has come to the historians' attention; only a part of what has come to their attention is credible; only a part of what is credible has been grasped; and only a part of what has been grasped can be expounded or narrated by the historian [45:45].

Because historical knowledge is partial, not total, knowledge of the past, how closely written history represents past actuality is always a matter of conjecture.

Need for Documents

Historical knowledge is no better than the availability of "bits and pieces" of past actuality. Yet the education profession has been negligent about preserving these bits and pieces. Each year important source materials are lost permanently to the human race. Valuable letters, documents, and other materials are discarded from the files of retiring professors; records of embryonic educational organizations are tossed away; old textbooks, school records, and equipment are cleared from attics and storerooms and destroyed. Educators can make an important contribution to the profession by rescuing these primary source materials from oblivion and establishing depositories for their preservation.

Application of the Scientific Method

Some scholars believe that historical researchers can adhere to the same principles and purposes that the physical scientists do. Other scholars contend that history embraces a different kind of subject matter than science and that it therefore requires a different method and interpretation. Scholars from both schools of thought usually agree that the historical method is scientific in some respects, but they do not agree that it is in other respects.

Some scholars, who describe the scientific method as consisting of observation, hypothesis, and experiment, argue that modern historians are scientific in that they (1) examine their source materials critically and (2) formulate hypotheses carefully. But they recognize that historians encounter greater difficulty than physical scientists in applying the scientific method of research. Some of the problems that arise are concerned with (1) critical examination of sources, (2) construction of hypotheses, (3) observation and experimentation, (4) technical terminology, and (5) generalization and prediction.

CRITICAL EXAMINATION OF THE SOURCES Myriads of historical facts are established as scientifically as are facts of the physical sciences. Examining documents and checking the testimony in these sources against one another enable a historian to report the time and place of a particular event with almost the same certainty that a physical scientist reports that mixing two chemicals under given conditions will produce a certain precipitate. But not all facts that interest a historian are concrete, single historical incidents that have been reported by reliable eyewitnesses.

Ascertaining the facts scientifically becomes difficult or impossible for researchers if they cannot locate adequate reports of firsthand observations or if they are interested in causes, motivations, influences, generalizations, or value judgments. After examining available records, for example, researchers can determine whether or not Superintendent Hayes made a particular speech at a certain time or place, but they cannot ascertain with the same assurance that the speech caused 80 percent of the voters to support the school bond issue. Within limits, historical research is scientific, for an investigator's results can be verified by other scholars. But in some instances, investigators cannot isolate and measure pertinent facts.

CONSTRUCTION OF HYPOTHESES   The types of hypotheses and procedures for testing them used by historians usually differ from those that are used by physical scientists. Because their subject matter is more complex than that of the physical scientists, historians experience greater difficulty in ascertaining the causes of events. As you know, scientists hold that an event is dependent upon and conditioned by its causes; that is, certain conditions must exist before an event can take place. Since physical scientists deal with relatively stable elements solely on the physical level, they are able to speak of "the cause"—the precise and exclusive factor or factors that account for an occurrence. When historians attempt to select the probable antecedent conditions that precipitated an event and to test whether one or more of them caused it, they may encounter many obstacles. Some factors that were associated with a past event may be difficult to discern, unmeasurable, or unrecorded; consequently, they are never certain that they are giving consideration to all pertinent antecedent factors. Historical phenomena may have a greater number of antecedents and a more complicated pattern of interaction among them than physical science phenomena.

Since no single cause explains most historical events, investigators resort to multiple hypotheses. They usually present a pluralistic rather than an all-embracing explanation to account for the multidimensional forces from which a historical event springs or establish some hierarchy of causes which indicates their relation to one another. If historians speak of "the cause," they mean "not the only cause but 'the most important cause' . . . among a complex of causal conditions, or the condition which was most decisive to what occurred, or which made the difference between what occurred and what would probably have occurred in its absence" (80:111). Because of the complexity of their subject matter and the limited quantity of their data, historians are unable to draw conclusions about causes that are as conclusive and decisive as those of their colleagues in the physical sciences.

OBSERVATION AND EXPERIMENTATION   Unlike physical scientists, educational historians cannot test their hypotheses by experimentation—controlled observation. They cannot re-create personalities and conditions as they once were for the purpose of further examination and manipulation. Historians cannot set up an experiment in which they control *A*, *B*, and *C*, remove or add *X*, and measure the effect of its presence. Because each past event is unique and cannot be repeated under laboratory conditions, research workers confine their examinations to whatever relevant data are available and attempt to gain a better understanding of them through historical comparisons and hypothetical constructs. They may compare and contrast an event with similar events in the past to detect likenesses and differences. Sometimes they visualize what would have taken place if a particular antecedent event had not occurred and give an answer, "of varying degrees of probability, in terms of approximate regularities observable in other instances" (80:113). But no matter how carefully this work is done, it is not as satisfactory as actual observation.

Since historians cannot personally view the educational practices of hundreds of years ago, they must rely on observations made by others in bygone days and on the examination of relics. Secondhand observations, of course, are not as satisfactory as the direct observations that physical scientists make. But the authenticity and credibility of historical source materials may be checked by subjecting them to intensive external and internal criticism. Ascertaining whether every fact is absolutely true is not possible, for the most reliable witness to an event may have erred in perception or memory. The credibility of relics and testimony is determined in degrees of confidence—from confidence that is approximately certain at one end of the scale to confidence that is mingled with considerable doubt on the other end. Because the reliability of data is dependent on the character, circumstances, and competence of the creators and interpreters, historians are extremely cautious about accepting any artifact or report.

The reliability of historical research reports is determined not only by how critically investigators examine their source materials but also by how well informed they are about the past and present. Historians delineate events of yesteryear in as much detail as surviving evidence permits and in terms of their knowledge about occurrences, peoples, and institutions. Their interpretation of early Greek education, for example, will be conditioned by how much they know about Grecian society, their conceptions of psychology and human behavior, and their familiarity with the present as well as the past. Block points out that "misunderstanding of the present is the inevitable consequence of ignorance of the past. But a man may wear himself out just as fruitlessly in seeking to understand the past, if he is totally ignorant of the present" (11:43). If historians acquire a comprehensive understanding of both the past and the present, they are less likely to ignore, to distort, or to misinterpret important evidence and more likely to produce an accurate account of past events.

TECHNICAL TERMINOLOGY   Many educational terms do not have clearly assigned and commonly understood meanings. When words such as "democracy," "education," "curriculum," "middle class," and "poverty" are used by different workers in the field, they may stand for slightly or radically different things. When Sidney Hook was engaged to make a study of fifty historical terms, such as "chance," "cause," "progress," and "force," he found that "no self-consistent definitions of the fifty historical terms could be based on an analysis and synthesis of the meanings given to them by numerous historians" (80:107). In contrast, the technical terms in the exact sciences, such as "meter," "ampere," "light-year," and "calorie," are instruments of great exactitude. Because a "one-to-one correspondence between symbols and meanings" (65:249) exists, variations due to their use by different physical scientists are kept at a minimum. The absence of a clearly defined technical vocabulary is a distinct weakness in the discipline of educational history, for conceptual vagueness blocks the communication of ideas and information.

GENERALIZATION AND PREDICTION   Some historians dispute whether history can be classified as a science on another basis. Science seeks to generalize. Both scientists and historians may start with propositions about unique events, but the scientist's ultimate objective is to establish broad generalizations—universal laws and theories that will explain many unrelated, singular events or conditions. Scientists strive to establish laws that have precise predictive power.

Historians do not agree on the extent to which they are willing to generalize. Some historians confine themselves to cautious interpretations—hypotheses that explain the causes of a particular temporal sequence. Some historians believe that it is possible to construct hypotheses that are universally applicable at any place or time in the past or future. Philosophers of history search for bold theories—for the fundamental patterns and purposes of history, for the ultimate material or supernatural causes of history that account for the historical process as a whole. The philosophers may view history as an endless series of recurrent birth-growth-decline-death cycles, as a panorama of progress moving step-by-step toward an improvement in human affairs, as a supernaturalistically or naturalistically determined drama moving toward a given end, as an evolutionary process in which human beings pass through recurrent cycles but gradually progress toward a given end, as an intricate pattern of events that consists of some threads of permanency and some threads of instability and change, or as such a complex process that all the varied data of history cannot be stuffed into one all-encompassing explanatory framework.

Gottschalk divides historians into six schools of hypothesis construction: (1) Those who make generalizations only if they are unaware that they are doing so and try to eliminate the ones of which they are aware; (2) those who make generalizations knowingly but intend to limit their generalizations strictly to the exposition of the historical subject matter under investigation and of that subject matter only in its own setting; (3) those who make a deliberate effort to go beyond the historical subject matter in hand in order to indicate its interrelations with antecedent, concurrent, and subsequent events and who thus risk broad interpretative syntheses but still limit their interpretations to interrelated trends; (4) those who with a similar readiness to go beyond the subject matter in hand draw parallels and analogies to it in other times or places of the past, whether or not otherwise interrelated; (5) those who venture propositions about past trends or analogies in such general or abstract terms as to leave the implication, if they do not indeed state explicitly, that their propositions may well be extrapolated to events in the future; and (6) those who propound philosophies that are intended to provide a cosmic understanding of the course of human events past and to come (45:113).

Constructing laws by generalizing about repetitive and common factors relating to past events is entirely outside the province of historical research in the opinion of some historians. They acquire richly detailed knowledge of a particular event or condition that occurred at a specific time and place in the past, and they may trace what preceded and succeeded it. But they are not concerned about what always, typically, or generally happens, about similarities between events, or about repeatable aspects of events. The unique factors associated with a specific occurrence that differentiate it from other events are what interest them. In their opinion, as soon as a fact becomes an instance of a general rule or law, it has lost its identification with the past and therefore is no longer a historical fact. Historians of this school show causal relationships between parts of an event or between the conditions existing before and after it, but they do not seek to generalize about the qualities one occurrence has in common with similar ones. They leave the establishment of generalizations or laws that will predict what will recur under certain conditions to sociologists and psychologists.

Historians with a "particularist passion" are challenged by other scholars who contend that historians must go beyond the description and interpretation of particular events in the past. These scholars are convinced that broad generalizations or laws can be derived from a study of historical facts and that the past should be studied for the lessons it teaches. They believe that historians can discover and formulate the fixed laws that explain human events just as scientists have discovered natural laws that explain phenomena in the physical world.

A more modest role is accepted by most historians. Some believe it is their responsibility to make postdictions about similarities found in *past events*, but that it is not within their power to make predictions about *future events*. Others contend that by drawing historical analogies and tracing historical trends, they may suggest in some instances various possible outcomes "one or more of which may be anticipated with a high degree of probability" (80:139). They provide us with a basis of knowledge for choosing alternative courses of action but do not construct comprehensive generalizations that possess the precise predictive power of laws in the physical sciences. "Historical analogies present us most often with clues to *possible* rather than *probable* behavior, with the ability only to *anticipate* rather than to predict, to take *precautions* rather than to *control*" (45:269).

The possibility that people may someday establish historical laws continues to intrigue many scholars. When critics attack this view as unscientific, they ask whether "it is more scientific to assume that the development of man as a social being has been casual, fortuitious, uncontrolled by law" (90:166–167). But entertaining the idea that historical laws may be constructed does not blind these scholars to the overwhelming difficulties that must be surmounted.

12 PROCESSING OF DATA

The total data collection and data processing procedures should be worked out in detail before any data are collected. Competent investigators determine in advance precisely what data are relevant to their studies and in what forms they should collect their data to facilitate processing and analyzing them. By taking such action, they avoid the disappointment of discovering later that they have collected some ambiguous data or lack vital information. Permission to retest *Ss* or reexamine records to obtain the missing data is not always granted, and the process is time-consuming.

COLLECTION OF DATA

Collecting the data in a form that minimizes the need for recopying or converting scores for data processing is a good habit to establish. Whenever possible, the numbers that are to be used in the calculator or computer analysis of the data should be employed to record data on the data collection instrument: Sex, 1 = male, 2 = female; teaching area, 1

= English, 2 = science, 3 = history; age, 20, 25, 30, 33, etc. years; or 1 = 20–29, 2 = 30–39, 3 = 40–49 years. An investigator should refrain from copying information as it appears in source records—in the form of hours and minutes, for example—if it is to be processed in another form—such as minutes only. If the data are to be analyzed for the two sexes separately, data retrieval time can be reduced by organizing separate files for the sexes.

Investigators should select the simplest, cheapest, and speediest system of data collection that is readily available and meets their needs. Data may be recorded on IBM or handmade answer sheets or on various types of cards. Rather than writing answers directly on questionnaires or test booklets, *Ss* may be instructed to blacken in the appropriate circles on a one-page answer sheet. This technique cuts costs and provides for more rapid and accurate scoring, but it is not recommended for speed tests or for young subjects. The answer sheets can be scored by hand if the number of papers is small and the study is not too complex. More sophisticated investigations can be scored by machines that are made available to the public for a fee. A machine has been developed that can scan each page of questionnaire booklets and record directly on magnetic tape the integrated record for each booklet. This machine eliminates the need for separate answer sheets and the necessity of converting the data on them to a set of IBM cards for computer processing.

Several types of cards are used to record data. On *edge-marked cards*, numbered spaces are positioned around the four edges of the card. Each numbered space is used to record only one type of information, such as space 4 for sex and space 6 for IQ. These edge-marked cards can be sorted quickly into groups, but they are suitable only for studies that involve a small number of variables. On *edge-notched cards,* data are notched into punched holes spaced along the edges of the card. For example, hole number 1 is notched if the subject is male and not notched if the subject is female. By passing a long needle through hole 1, the investigator can lift out the female cards and the notched male cards will be left. The most efficient and rapid way of processing a large volume of data on cards is to prepare *IBM punched cards* for electronic computer processing, which will be explained later in this chapter. On *mark-sense cards, Ss* can mark their answers in the proper space on a card with electrographic pencils. A machine can "read" these marked data, convert them into punched holes on the same card, and record them on another medium or transmit them directly to a computer.

PROCESSING OF DATA

Data processing is the procedure of converting raw data—the nominal, ordinal, interval, or ratio numbers that convey information about some observable aspect of reality—into some form that enables the investigator (1) to summarize the relevant data or (2) to test hypotheses. The data may be converted, for example, into measures of central tendency (means), measures of relationships (correlations), or statistical tests of significance (F ratios, t tests, or chi-squares).

Data may be processed by hand or by calculator if the sample is not large, the variables are limited in number, and the statistical analysis is relatively simple. For a more complex study, a computer analysis is the prudent choice. A computer can save hours of computation time, but an investigator should know how to calculate by hand or by calculator any type of analysis that is to be employed in a study. Firsthand knowledge of various types of statistical analyses gives one sufficient understanding of the logical and mathematical processes involved to select a suitable program for the particular analysis desired, to prepare the data cards and program control cards for the analysis, and to interpret the computer printout.

A computer is an ingenious and versatile machine: it can manipulate symbols that represent information, has the ability to "remember" or "store" these symbols, and can retrieve them later. But a computer is a machine and not a human being. It cannot determine how to solve a problem; it can only follow directions. A computer must be provided with (1) data and (2) a program that gives detailed instructions about what data to process, how to process the data, and how the results are to be shown.

Because a computer does not understand the English language, the instructions must be written in a language or code that the computer can "read." The binary code, which uses only two digits, 1 and 0, is the most commonly used code within computers. Each digit, 1 or 0, is called a bit—short for binary digit. This language is essential, for the electronic parts within a computer can respond only to two states: (1) current on or (2) current off; (1) a switch is opened, or (2) it is closed; (1) a magnetic material is magnetized in one direction or (2) in the other.

How does the binary code differ from the decimal system which you commonly use? The decimal system is based on the power of ten; when you move a digit one space to the left and add a zero, you have increased its worth ten times. The binary system is based on the power of two; when you move a number to the left, you have increased its worth two times.

1,000		100		10	1	← Decimal: successive powers of ten
32	16	8	4	2	1	← Binary: successive powers of two

To count pupils by the binary and decimal systems, you would proceed in the following manner:

Binary		Decimal
00001	one pupil	00001
00010	two pupils	00002
00011	three pupils	00003
00100	four pupils	00004
00101	five pupils	00005
00110	six pupils	00006
00111	seven pupils	00007
01000	eight pupils	00008
01001	nine pupils	00009
01010	ten pupils	00010
1100100	one hundred pupils	00100

One way to convert a binary number to decimal is given below. First you write down the successive powers of two from *right* to *left* to use as a guide, and, on the line below, you match up the binary symbols. In this instance the binary number is 1100100, which converts to the decimal number 100.

64	32	16	8	4	2	1		← Successive powers of two
1	1	0	0	1	0	0		Binary number
64	+32			+4			= 100	Decimal number

A shortcut method for converting binary to decimal consists of doubling and adding. Starting at the *left*, copy the value of the first position, double it, and add the value of the next position; take this sum, double it, etc.

→ 1	1	0	0	1	0	0
1	3	6	12	25	50	100

You must understand the binary code to understand how the computer works, but you no longer have to use the binary code when writing a program—a set of instructions—for the computer. At one time, if you wanted the computer to add something, you might have had to provide the following binary instruction: 1011010111010001. You may now merely use a "shorthand language" for "add," and the computer will automatically translate the symbol into the correct binary instruction. The computer can do this because someone has previously written special assembler and compiler programs that convert the shorthand-language program into the machine's binary language. Today, an investigator can quickly learn enough of a shorthand language, such as FORTRAN, to write a program.

COMPONENTS OF THE COMPUTER

A major computer center consists not of one big machine but rather of a complex of devices connected by cables. In general, the system consists of three major units: (1) an input unit; (2) a central processing unit, which houses the main storage, control, and arithmetic units; and (3) the output unit (see Figure 12.1).

Input Unit

The input unit accepts from human beings or machines the data and instructions needed to solve the problem, and it forwards them to the storage or memory unit. In the beginning, punched cards were used to input information, but now information may be recorded on paper or magnetic tape.

PUNCHED CARDS AND DEVICES FOR HANDLING THEM   Punched cards are of various kinds. One that is commonly used has eighty vertical

FIGURE 12.1

Functional organization of a computer.

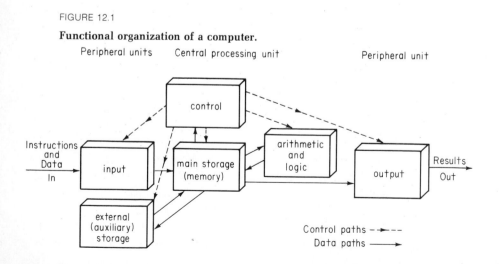

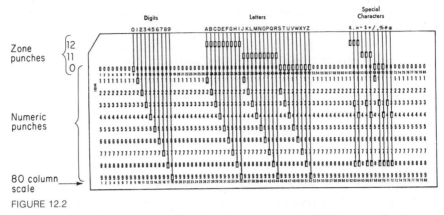

Zone punches 12 11 0

Numeric punches

80 column scale

FIGURE 12.2

The standard computer input Hollerith coded punch card. *(IBM Corporation.)*

columns and twelve horizontal rows. The horizontal rows consist of nine *number rows* and above them three *zone rows*: 0 and punching positions 11 and 12 (see Figure 12.2). In the Hollerith code, one punch in the lower ten rows of a single vertical column can represent any number from 0 to 9. Two punches in a single column—one in a zone row, and one in a number row—can represent a letter in the alphabet. Three punches in a single column can represent certain special characters, such as a period or a plus sign. For example, 12, 3, and 8 are punched in a column to represent a period. Ordinarily data for one *S* goes on one card. Single digit numbers are assigned one column on a card, double digit numbers are assigned two columns, and etc. A single digit entry in an otherwise two-digit field is preceded by 0, to avoid errors.

The data or instructions to be placed on cards are processed by a *keypunch* machine which is operated in much the same manner as a typewriter and is not connected to the computer. The typist presses a key which is labeled with a number, letter, or special character, and the machine records the information on the card, usually in the form of rectangular holes.

Once the data or the program is punched on cards, the deck of cards is placed in the feed hopper of a card reader. On command from the computer, the punched cards move past a sensing mechanism which consists of wire brushes or intense light rays that pass through the holes in the cards and activate electrical signals. The electrical (off-on) impulses go to a buffer, where the information is converted into machine language (0–1) and transmitted to the computer for storage. After a card is read, it is deposited in an output stacker. Some card readers move the cards past two sensing stations; the second station reads the card and checks for errors (see Figure 12.3).

PAPER TAPE AND MAGNETIC TAPE AND DEVICES FOR HANDLING THEM
The paper-tape punching and reading processes used for computer input are similar to those used for cards. The codes that are used for punching the holes that represent the data vary, but a single row across the width of the paper tape represents one character (see Figure 12.4). Magnetic tape, which has magnetized spots that correspond to the holes on punched paper tape, can hold huge quantities of data on a single reel (i.e., the equivalent of seven Bibles). It can be read repeatedly with lightning speed (50 to 100 times faster than paper tape or cards) and can be erased and reused. One inch of magnetic tape may carry 500 to 1,500 rows of magnetic spots in contrast to 10 rows of punched coded holes on paper tape.

Central Processing Unit

The central processing unit, which houses the storage, arithmetic, and control units (see Figure 12.1), receives data and programs from the input unit, executes the mathematical and logical operations it is instructed to carry out, and delivers the results to the output unit.

STORAGE OR MEMORY UNITS   Computer input is stored in various locations. The main storage unit in a computer stores the main program and the data currently in use. The external storage units stores the majority of the data and the auxiliary programs which are read into the main storage unit when needed.

The main storage unit of a computer, which is a warehouse for the data and instructions, is like a block of post-office boxes. Each "box"

FIGURE 12.3

Card reader mechanism. The feed hopper stores cards to be read. Read station 1 senses the presence or absence of holes and counts holes. Read station 2 counts holes again to verify the reading. Output stackers store cards which have been read.

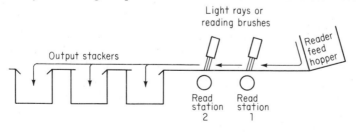

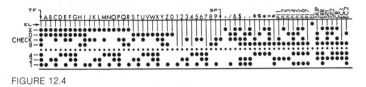

FIGURE 12.4

The code key shown for a full-size paper tape. *(IBM Corporation.)*

has its own identifying number, called an *address*, and each "box" contains one fact or one instruction. A computer is instructed to forward information to and from certain storage locations and to perform certain operations, just as a citizen is instructed on page 1 of an income tax blank to write salary on line 5, write other income (from page 2, Part 2, line 8) on line 6, add lines 5 and 6, place answer on line 7. Perhaps you can gain a better understanding of the computer's address system if you examine the data and instructions for figuring a payroll that are presented in Figure 12.5. You will note that (1) both the instructions (addresses 0–6) and the data (addresses 7–11) are given

FIGURE 12.5

An illustration of the computer's address system.

Address number	Contents of address: program (instructions)	Address number	Contents of address: data
0	Write data contents of address 8 (40 hours)	7	Employee's name (John Jones)
		8	Hours worked (40 hours)
1	Multiply contents of address 9 times address 8 ($3 x 40 hours = $120.)	9	Rate of pay ($3 per hour)
2	Copy previous answer in address 11	10	Health insurance ($1 per week)
3	Subtract contents of address 10 from contents of address 11 ($120-$1 = $119)	11	$120
4	Write pay check for amount of previous answer ($119)		
5	Make out check to contents of address 7 (John Jones)		
6	Load information about next employee into memory locations 7, 8, 9 and 10 (Loading in the new data erases the previous data in the location.)		

addresses and that (2) the address number and the contents of that address are two different things; for example, the contents of address 8 is 40.

The main storage unit may consist of magnetic cores, thin films, plated wires, or other devices. The following description will give you some understanding of how a magnetic core memory system works: Magnetic cores are little "doughnuts" or beads the size of pinheads that are threaded on rectangular frames or grids of wire at the intersections (see Figure 12.6). The grids or frames are stacked on top of one another to make a basic memory unit. Each core can be magnetized in either a clockwise or a counterclockwise direction—one direction for binary 0, and the other direction for binary 1. The vertical and horizontal wires carry the current that magnetizes or demagnetizes selected cores. Diagonal wires "sense" or "read" which cores are magnetized.

FIGURE 12.6

Section of a magnetic core memory plane. *(Honeywell Information Systems.)*

Each column of cores in a memory unit (stack of grids or frames) is connected separately to the computer's control center; hence, it can be activated instantly to store information or to "read out" information. By charging each core in a column in one of two directions, a binary number can be stored that represents one fact or one instruction. Each column of cores is given an address. When the computer is instructed to read a particular address, such as 101 in the example below, it will read each of the cores in address 101. Address 101 in the example below and in Figure 12.7 stores the binary number 1011001, which converts to the decimal number 77.

Cores:	Address 101 Binary	Decimal	Cores:	Address 102 Binary	Decimal	Cores:	Address 103 Binary	Decimal
●	(1)	1	○	(0)		○	(0)	
○	(0)		●	(1)	2	○	(0)	
●	(1)	4	○	(0)		●	(1)	4
●	(1)	8	●	(1)	8	○	(0)	
○	(0)		○	(0)		●	(1)	16
○	(0)		○	(0)		●	(1)	32
●	(1)	64	○	(0)		○	(0)	
		77			10			52

ARITHMETIC OR PROCESSING UNIT   Data from the storage unit are forwarded to the arithmetic unit, which can perform standard arithmetic

FIGURE 12.7

Memory grid showing columns assigned addresses.

Addresses 101 102 103

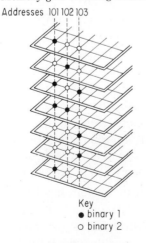

Key
● binary 1
○ binary 2

operations and some logic or decision-making operations, such as comparing or choosing among alternatives. This unit contains a series of electronic logic circuits whose fundamental operation is that of addition. Most computers subtract by adding complements, multiply by making repeated additions, and divide by making repeated subtractions.

CONTROL UNIT   The computer has a control unit in the central processor, and it may also have an external control console which permits the operator to monitor the operation of the computer and to control some of its functions through a special typewriter and various switches and lights.

The control unit in the central processor consists of a complex of registers, switches, and timers and performs a task similar to that of the telephone operator. It controls the pathways through which the electrical pulses that represent data flow from input to output. The control unit brings out, one at a time, the instructions from the program in the storage unit, decodes them, and then sets up whatever circuit pathways and switches are necessary to execute them in the proper unit.

Output Units

An output unit receives data in machine language from the storage unit and translates it into a language a human being or a machine can understand. Output devices are used for intermediate and final output. A card punch, paper-tape punch, or magnetic-tape unit may be attached to a computer to perform an intermediate output operation. The cards or tapes that are produced for output can in turn be used as input for a later computer operation. Some computer equipment, such as printers, graph plotters, and visual display equipment, produces output that can be read or interpreted directly by people.

Over the years, significant improvements have occurred in the output capability of the computer. The earliest equipment possessed a *character printer*, which was capable of printing one character at a time and about ten characters per second. Next came the *line printer*, which printed an entire line at a time, or about 1,500 characters per second. The next development was the *electrostatic line printer*, which operated by means of a cathode-ray tube (CRT) and printed 3,000 lines per minute. More recently, the *page printing system* has been introduced. This high-speed, nonimpact printer is capable of producing 18,000 lines, or about 210 pages, per minute. This printer accepts electrographic paper in roll form and, after printing, cuts it into printed sheets of the required size, then stacks the output reports into trays. The output is then available for immediate distribution to the end user.

INSTRUCTION OF THE COMPUTER

A computer is a magnificient tool, but it can do only what it is instructed to do and nothing more. A computer is useless until a programmer writes a detailed set of instructions that is loaded into its internal storage (memory) unit.

Program Construction

Writing a program is a complex task that involves several steps:

1   Breaking down the problem into a sequence of elementary steps that the computer can perform.
2   Making certain that all the necessary steps are included and have been placed in the proper sequence by writing a *flow chart.* A flow chart shows graphically how all the parts of the program fit logically together. Figure 12.8, for example, shows the sequence of steps in a payroll program. You will note that a rectangular box[1] tells what work is to be done and a diamond-shaped box announces that a decision or choice is to be made, such as "Does this time card show more than 40 hours? No or Yes?"
3   Writing the program—the detailed list of instructions—on a program or coding sheet. A programmer no longer has to write the instructions (commands and storage addresses) in the long strings of 0s and 1s employed in the two-symbol binary code, for simple shorthand-languages, such as FORTRAN, have been developed which employ numbers, letters, English words, and familiar symbols.
4   Punching the shorthand-language program on a deck of cards, one line of coding to each card.
5   Using a special assembly or compiler program developed by a manufacturer to translate the shorthand-language program into the machine language that the computer can read, such as the binary language. An assembler, for example, when loaded into the storage unit of a computer, can (1) read a deck of cards that contains a

---

[1] A standard set of flow-chart symbols can be obtained from American National Standards Institute.

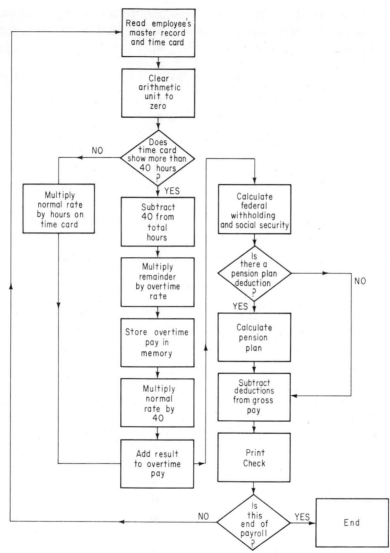

FIGURE 12.8

Flow chart for a payroll. (*Adapted from* You and the Computer, *Schenectady,* N.Y.: Educational Publications, The General Electric Company, 1968, p. 8.)

shorthand-language program, (2) translate these instructions into machine language, (3) assign a storage address for each instruction name and each data name, (4) punch the instruction on a deck of cards in machine language, and (5) print a listing of the program. Hence, the computer is used twice, once to translate (assemble or compile) the shorthand-language program into machine language and once to run the machine-language program to get the results.

6 Debugging the program. This last step consists of various procedures that are followed to eliminate any errors.

The work of programmers has been greatly simplified by the development of the shorthand languages, translators, and libraries of programs and subroutines. Prepared programs and subroutines are now available in the libraries at computer centers for practically all the statistical procedures that graduate students are likely to employ, such as correlations, multiple correlations, *t* tests, and analysis of variance. If a suitable program is found, the investigator need only submit properly punched data and control cards to the computer center in order to have the necessary computations executed.

If you use the services of the computer center, you usually perform the following tasks:

1 Locate a suitable program in the computer library and check its limitations.

2 Read and carry out the instructions in the user's manual that describe how the data may be key-punched and what instruction cards need to be punched to provide the computer with information, such as type of analysis, choice of program, sample size, number of variables, and location of data on the card.

3 Place the instruction and data cards in the proper sequence as specified in the users' manual and deposit it at the computer center.

4 Pick up the printout from the computer center. Look for error messages and correct whatever has caused the problem. If no error messages are found, check the printout of the results to make certain that they make sense. If your data are students' bodily weight scores, and the printout tells you that the mean weight is 15.5, you have erred somewhere—probably misplaced a decimal.

Program Examples

You may never write a program, but you should be able to modify a library program to suit your purpose, to communicate intelligently with a programmer, and to read a program. The following simple explanation of how to write a program in FORTRAN (FORmula TRANslation) and the sample program on page 402 will give you some insight into how a programmer instructs a computer to solve a problem. FORTRAN, the most widely used language for research problems, employs everyday words, such as READ, GO TO, and PRINT, to tell the computer what to do: READ this information, GO TO that instruction, PRINT that outcome.

A FORTRAN program[2] consists of a number of comment, dimension, input and output, format, arithmetic, and control statements; each line of the program is punched onto a separate card. In general, the instructions are written in the sequence in which the computer is to perform the operations.

COMMENT STATEMENTS   A program may begin with the letter C and a comment statement that identifies the program, such as C FORTRAN PROGRAM TO COMPUTE GROSS PAY or C SUM OF N NUMBERS (see sample programs at the end of chapter). Comment statements about other aspects of the program may appear throughout the program. Comment cards are prepared only for the benefit of the human user; they are identified by placing a C punch in the first column of the card, which instructs the computer to ignore the card.

Although an IBM card has 80 columns, FORTRAN instructions are written only in columns 7 through 72. The first column of a FORTRAN card is reserved for a comment statement; columns 2–5 are used for the number of the FORTRAN statement; and column 6, which is rarely used, indicates that the card is a continuation of a FORTRAN statement on the previous card. Columns 73-80, which are reserved for identification, are not processed by the computer.

DIMENSION STATEMENTS   A dimension statement, which is not a part of the operating program, may follow a comment statement:

DIMENSION X (100), B (5,3)

A dimension statement must be provided if the program uses subscripted variables, for a computer must assign a storage address to each value in the set. If the variable X represents only one value, no difficulty arises, because it requires only one address in storage. But in algebraic notation, the subscripted variable X_i designates an array or set of numbers. If X_i designates a set of 100 numbers (the subscript $i = 1, 2, 3, \ldots, 100$), each value of the subscript requires its own address.

---

[2]Note that two decks of punched cards are required for a computer to solve the problem: one deck contains the program or instructions, and the one deck contains the raw data to be processed.

Because the key punch cannot drop a character a half space to indicate a subscript, as a typewriter can, FORTRAN uses parentheses. In the dimension statement above, for example, X(100) instructs the compiler to reserve 100 addresses in storage for X(1), X(2), X(3), . . . X(100); and B(5,3) instructs the computer to reserve 15 storage addresses (five rows and three columns) for the array B. In the dimension statement, the programmer specifies the maximum length of the array of numbers of any use of the program; if all the addresses are not used, no harm is done, but the subscripts on X must never exceed 100.

INPUT AND OUTPUT STATEMENTS   FORTRAN input and output statements consist of a pair of instructions. An input instruction consists of (1) a READ statement and (2) a FORMAT specification statement. An output instruction consists of (1) a WRITE or PRINT statement and (2) a FORMAT specification statement.

READ (5,1) HOURS, RATE   WRITE (6,4) SUM

1 FORMAT (F2.0, F4.3)   4 FORMAT (F15.4)

The word READ, WRITE, or PRINT is followed by two numbers in parentheses and a list of the variables to be processed. The first number in parentheses indicates what input or output device is to be used—for example, the card reader in a READ instruction or the printer or card punch in a WRITE instruction. The second number in parentheses gives the reference number of the FORMAT statement.

In the example above, the "READ (5,1) HOURS, RATE" statement instructs the computer to use 5, the card reader,[3] to read into computer storage the data for hours and rate, which are punched on cards as specified by FORMAT statement 1. The computer then searches through the program for FORMAT statement 1.

FORMAT STATEMENTS   A FORMAT statement identifies the type of data that each variable refers to and specifies how data are punched on IBM cards or how data are to be printed. A FORMAT statement presents the following information:

1   It specifies the exact location and maximum number of columns ("field width") for each variable in the order of their appearance on

---

[3] The numbers employed in computer centers to identify the input and output units vary.

the IBM card, from left to right. In most cases, data for each variable are right justified in a field; hence in a five-column field, the number 28 is punched in columns 4 and 5 of the field. A FORMAT statement uses commas to separate field specifications.

2   A FORMAT statement identifies the type of data (integer, floating-point, etc.) and specifies control with a letter code (I, F, E, etc.).[4]

3   A FORMAT statement specifies the number of digits in the field to the right of the decimal.

"FORMAT (F4.3)," for example, indicates that there is one F-type variable (decimal-type variable) per card, the data have a maximum field width of four columns, and there are three digits to the right of the decimal point.

ARITHMETIC STATEMENTS   In FORTRAN arithmetic statements, which appear in the main body of the program, the following symbols are used: +, for addition; −, for subtraction; *, for multiplication; /, for division; **, for exponentiation (raising to a power). Thus "(X *Y)/Z" means multiply X times Y and divide the product by Z. The symbols used in FORTRAN and algebra are similar except for the equal sign. In FORTRAN, the equal sign means replace or transfer rather than equal. It instructs the computer to replace the value on the left side of the equal sign, =, with the value on the right side of the sign. A = B means transfer the numerical value of storage address B to storage address A. The values to the left and the right of the equal sign are not always equivalent. The statement X = X + 1, for example, does not express equality but rather indicates that the value of X + 1 is to replace the old value of X. The new sum stored in X would then be available for subsequent processing or a subsequent output statement. A number of rules which can be found in programming manuals have been developed for writing arithmetic statements.

---

[4]The codes used to type variables include the following:

I—integer data, which can only be whole numbers.

F—real data, also known as floating-point numbers, which are numbers that contain a decimal point (F-type data may or may not have fractional parts: 8., 10, 200.42).

E—exponential form of real data.

X—skip field. Because every column from first to the rightmost column used on the IBM card must be accounted for in the FORMAT, 4X tells the computer to ignore the contents of the four unused columns between the variables.

CONTROL STATEMENTS Various types of control statements may appear in a FORTRAN program. FORTRAN statements are normally processed sequentially. If the sequence is broken, a transfer of control statement, such as GO TO or IF statement, is written to inform the control unit where the next instruction is to come from. A GO TO statement is used for unconditional branching: "GO TO 6" instructs the computer to branch directly to statement 6. An *If statement* is used for conditional branching; it asks the computer to choose among alternative instructions. The statement IF (X), 2,3 causes the computer to test the numerical value of X and if it is more than a certain value (such as 40 hours), branch to statement 2; if it is less than a certain value (40 hours), branch to statement 3.

If a programmer had to write down every instruction that the computer had to carry out, his work would be tedious and endless. Adding a column of 50 numbers, for example, would require 50 separate instructions and storage addresses—(1) load contents (data) located in storage address 200 into the accumulator, (2) add contents of storage address 201 to the accumulator, (3) add contents of storage address 202 to the accumulator, etc.—until storage address 250 is reached. Fortunately, by writing a *DO statement*, which controls a loop of instructions, the computer can be instructed to do such repetitive work automatically. The DO statement incorporates an instruction for modifying the address of the data to be operated upon through the use of an index register in the control unit. The instruction for adding 50 numbers, for example, can be written as follows:

DO 2 I = 1,N
READ (5,3)X
2 SUM = SUM + X

The statement DO 2 I = 1,N commands the computer to do all the following statements, through statement 2, N times (50 times), setting the index register in the control unit I = 1 the first time and incrementing I by 1 each time until I = 50.[5]

Perhaps you can understand how the instruction and execution cycles are carried out by reading the following example and tracing the steps on Figure 12.9: When the instruction to be executed is moved out of its storage address (address 2, in Figure 12.9), it contains (1) an

[5]Do not confuse I and 1.

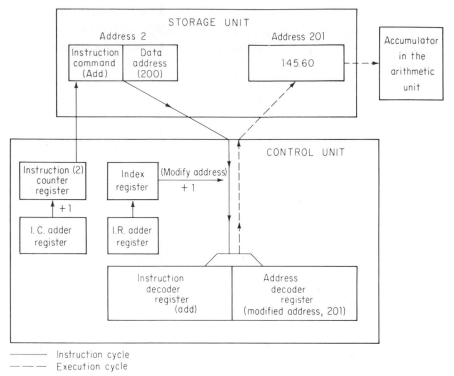

——— Instruction cycle
— — — Execution cycle

FIGURE 12.9

Schematic representation of the control unit.

instruction command (Add)—the operation to be executed—and (2) the storage address (200) of the data that is to be operated upon and any modification of that base address (200) that is to be made by the index register in the control unit. (The modification instruction might command the computer to set the index register, I to 1 for the first loop, increment by 1 each loop and end with I = 50, the last storage address of the data to be operated upon.)

Now let us trace a loop of the instruction. If the base storage address of the data to be operated upon, X, is 200, on the first execution of the loop, this address will be modified by the index register in the control unit to 200 + 1 before it is decoded in the address decoder of the control unit. The control unit will then locate storage address 201 in the main storage unit and transfer the content stored in it, 145.60, to the proper unit (the accumulator in the arithmetic unit). On successive executions of the loop, the index register will modify the storage address containing the data to be operated upon 202 (200 + 2), 203 (200 + 3), etc., until the index register reads I = 50 (I = N). By the completion of the last loop, the contents of the fifty addresses will have been located in the storage unit and transferred to and summed in the accumulator.

SAMPLE FORTRAN PROGRAMS   The following sample FORTRAN program for summing a number of numbers and the accompanying explanation will acquaint you with the general characteristics of a simple program.

PROGRAM	EXPLANATION
Columns on IBM Card 1, 2–5, 6, 7—72	Punch column 1 for a comment; punch statement number in columns 2–5; punch column 6 to indicate it is a continuation card; punch instructions in columns 7–72.
C SUM OF N NUM- BERS	Comment: add a given number of numbers.
READ (5,1)N	Use 5, the card reader, to read into storage, N, the number of numbers to be summed as specified in FORMAT 1.
1 FORMAT (I5)	N will be in the form of I, integers (whole numbers), in a five-column field. Initialize the storage address, which is similar to clearing the accumulator to zero. In this instance the sum is stored temporarily in the accumulator register.
DO 2 I = 1,N	Do all statements below, through 2, N times. Set index register, I, to 1 for the first loop, increment by 1 each loop, and end with I = N.
READ (5,3)X	Use 5, the card reader, to read in X (base address plus contents of index register) as specified by FORMAT 3.
2 SUM = SUM + X	Add X to temporary sum in the accumulator, which initially is set to zero. When index, I, reaches value of N, all the numbers will have been read and summed.
3 FORMAT (F5.0)	The data will be F, floating-point numbers, in a five-column field with no digits to the right of the decimal.
WRITE (6,4) SUM	Use 6, the printer, for output as specified by FORMAT 4.
4 FORMAT (F15.4)	The number will be F, a floating-point value having a maximum of 15 digits with 4 to the right of the decimal.
STOP END	End of program.

A program written by Fox and Wedekind (41) for an IBM-7070 includes IF and GO TO control statements:

**7070 Program to Obtain Estimated Quality Point Averages.
Written in FORTRAN and PEST**[6]

```
***  ESTIMATED QPA, 59, 60, TO 61 ADM OF              5U)
                                                      )PEST
*    COMPILE FORTRAN, PUNCH OBJECT,
       EXECUTE FORTRAN                                )
     Blank Card
C    ESTIMATED QPA, 59, 60 TO 61, L. W. FOX
   1 READ 101, ISEX, ISATV, ISATM, IHSR
     IF(ISEX) 200,200,2
   2 IF(ISEX-12) 3,5,6
   3 JQPA = 7164 + (123*ISATV) + (134*ISATM) +
       (22267*IHSR)
   4 JQPA = (JQPA + 500)/1000
     PUNCH 101, ISEX, ISATV, ISATM, IHSR, JQPA
     GO TO 1
   5 JQPA = -32370 + (102*ISATV) + (188*ISATM) +
       (21958*IHSR)
     GO TO 4
   6 JQPA = 35529 + (247*ISATV) + (75*ISATM) +
       (13058*IHSR)
     GO TO 4
 101 FORMAT 12,38H                                    415,)
 200 END

     Blank Card
     Data
     Card with zero punched in columns 1 and 2
```

Perhaps the following discussion will help you understand the basic FORTRAN statements 1 to 6. In statement 1 the computer reads in terms of the card format listed in 101 (which appears near the end of the set of instructions) the subject's sex and curriculum code, name, SATV score and SATM score (verbal and mathematics scholastic aptitude scores), and IHSR (high school rank). Immediately below is a brief statement—"IF (ISEX) 200,200,2"—which checks for error if the sex-curriculum code is negative or zero. In statement 2 (an IF control statement for conditional branching), the computer branches the data to the appropriate regression equation: statement 3 for liberal arts,

---

[6]Pittsburgh Executive System for Tapes.

males; statement 5 for engineering; or statement 6 for liberal arts, females. In this instance, let us assume the student is liberal arts, male; hence, the data are branched to statement 3. In statement 3 the predicted quality-point average is computed for liberal arts, male. In statement 4 a correction is made for the decimal point: then there is a PUNCH statement which punches a card with the same information as statement 1 plus the predicted quality-point average; an instruction to return to 1 follows. The next student's card is read and the process continues until all cards are processed.

13 WRITING THE RESEARCH REPORT

n investigation begins when a graduate student refines a problem and gets the research proposal approved. The collection and analysis of the data should then be carried out exactly as planned. An investigation culminates with the writing of a research report which transmits the purposes, procedures, and findings of the study to other workers in the field. This chapter provides guidance for the preparation of a research report in a form that is generally approved by members of the scientific community.

FORMAT OF THE REPORT

A rather formal and uniform method of presenting reports has evolved that enables busy members of the profession to locate quickly information that is of interest to them. Most graduate schools and professional journals publish report formats that they expect investigators to follow. These formats differ in details somewhat, but they usually include three main divisions: the preliminaries, the body of the report or text, and the reference matter. Each main division may consist of several sections.

I. Preliminary Materials
    A. Title Page
    B. Approval Sheet (if any)
    C. Preface and Acknowledgments
    D. Table of Contents
    E. List of Tables (if any)
    F. List of Figures (if any)
II. Body of the Report
    A. Introduction
        1. Statement of the Problem
        2. Analysis of Related Studies
        3. Assumptions Underlying the Hypotheses
        4. Statement of Hypotheses
        5. Deduced Consequences
        6. Definition of Terms
    B. Method of Attack
        1. Procedures Employed (designs, sampling, etc.)
        2. Sources of Data
        3. Data-gathering Instruments
    C. Analysis and Interpretation of the Data
        1. Text
        2. Tables (if any, are usually incorporated into the text)
        3. Figures (if any, are usually incorporated into the text)
    D. Summary and Conclusions
        1. Brief Restatement of Problem and Procedures
        2. Findings and Conclusions
III. Reference Materials
    A. Bibliography
    B. Appendix (if any)
    C. Index (if any)
    D. Vita (if required)

Preliminary Materials

Several pages of preliminary material precede the body of a report in a dissertation. The title page, which appears first, contains the following information: (1) title of the study, (2) full name of the candidate and his previous academic background, (3) name of the faculty and institution to which the report is submitted, (4) degree for which the report is presented, (5) year when the degree is to be conferred. These items (see example on page 406) are centered between the margins of the page, and no terminal punctuation is used. The title is typed in capital letters, but usually only the initial letters of principal words are

TITLE OF DISSERTATION

by
Candidate's Full Name

Previous Degrees, Institutions, and Years of Graduation
A. B., University of California, 1971
M. A., University of Wisconsin, 1974

Submitted to the Graduate School of the University
of California in partial fulfillment of the
requirements for the degree of
Doctor of Philosophy

Berkeley, California
1979

capitalized in other items. If the title extends beyond one line, it is double-spaced and placed in an inverted pyramid style. Vague or broad generalizations and ambiguous or unnecessary words are not acceptable in titles. A title should contain key words or phrases that give a clear and concise description of the scope and nature of the report. The key words should make it easy for bibliographers to index the study in the proper category.

If the institution requires an approval sheet, a page of the dissertation allots space for the signatures of the dissertation committee members, and their names are typed below. A preface, if included, usually contains a brief statement of the purpose and scope of the report. In addition, thanks may be expressed to those who gave the writer substantial guidance or assistance, but a long list of effusive acknowledgments is not in good taste.

The table of contents, which occupies a separate page or pages, gives the readers a bird's-eye view of the report and enables them to locate quickly each section of it. The chapter titles are usually typed in capital letters and the subdivision headings in small letters with the initial letter of the principal words capitalized. All titles and headings appear in the exact words and order as they do in the report, and each is followed by the correct page citation. The relationship between main

TABLE OF CONTENTS

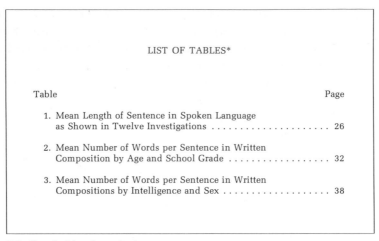

*The list of tables always begins on a new page.

headings and subtopics is shown by proper indention and capitalization. If possible, the headings are confined to one line of space, and parallel grammatical structure is used for the same value of headings. Following the table of contents are separate pages for the list of tables and the list of illustrations. The information for each item in these lists includes (1) number, usually arabic, of the table or figure, (2) exact title, and (3) number of page on which it appears in the body of the report. These preliminary materials are illustrated on the sample pages shown on page 407 and above. A research report that appears in a periodical does not ordinarily present these preliminary materials; the body of the report, moreover, may be condensed, and some sections, unfortunately, may be omitted to save space.

Body of the Report

The kernel of the study, the data and their analyses, follows the preliminary materials. This body of the report contains four logical divisions: (1) an introduction, (2) the method of attack, (3) analysis and interpretation of data, and (4) the summary and conclusions.

INTRODUCTION The first chapter serves as an orientation to the investigation. In the introduction you state and analyze the nature of the problem and review the related studies and theories so as to develop a foundation for your investigation. If the résumé of the literature is lengthy, it may be presented in a separate chapter. The résumé is not a summary of everything you have read nor a chronological list of the most pertinent abstracts that the reader must dissect to discover how they relate to the present problem. Rather, the résumé is a well-integrated discussion of the previous relevant studies and theories which points up the issues involved in this investigation and reveals the importance of the undertaking. Every study that is referred to in the body of the report is incorporated in the résumé. In a logically structured discussion, you bring together the results of the existing research, show how the studies are related, point out areas of agreement and disagreement, and indicate where gaps or weaknesses exist that have given rise to the present study. The significance of the problem, the need for conducting the investigation, and the logical rationale that justifies your hypothesis become evident when the problem is placed in this wider framework of knowledge.

After reviewing the background of the problem and delimiting the precise points of the investigation, you present your hypotheses (the relationship you think exists between variables), the deduced consequences, and the assumptions on which the hypotheses are predicated. You then define the terms that are essential to the study or are used in a restricted or unusual manner. This information gives the reader a clear concept of the scope of the investigation, the precise solution or explanation offered for the problem, and the evidence sought to test it.

METHOD OF ATTACK When describing the procedures employed in the investigation, you give an accurate, detailed description of how the work was done, as well as all the information that the reader needs to judge the validity, adequacy, and suitability of the methods and instruments employed. Your objective is to provide an explanation that will enable the reader to repeat the investigation—reproducing the exact conditions of the original study—to check the findings. This explanation, generally speaking, is rather extensive, and thus is placed in a chapter by itself. Since the findings of a study can be no better than the tools and methods used to solve it, scholars usually examine this section of the report with extreme care.

The kinds of procedural information presented depend on the nature of the study. You may present (1) a definition of the population and an explanation of why this population is relevant for the study; (2) the size of the sample and the rationale for the size; (3) how the sample was selected and the reason for selecting the particular stratifying variables, if they were employed; (4) data (means and standard deviations) that describe characteristics of the subjects that are relevant to the problem, and, if available, comparable data about the population that enable the reader to judge the representativeness of the sample; (5) the number of subjects who declined to participate, dropped out, or did not participate in all parts of the study and why; (6) where, when, and what types of data were collected and by what instruments; (7) the number of times and order in which the instruments were used and the time allotted to each data-collection session; (8) the rationale for selecting the design—the assumptions made, experimental controls established, how subjects and treatments were assigned to groups, and how variables were manipulated; (9) the verbal or written directions, and the briefings and debriefings given the subjects; (10) the characteristics of interviewers or observers and how they were trained; (11) the types of data analyses made, the reasons for choosing the particular statistical procedures employed and the level of significance selected; (12) how the data will be presented; (13) an account of the pilot study; (14) an explanation of any methods that were employed and abandoned because they proved to be inadequate or valueless; and (15) suggestions for improving the procedures in future studies.

Well-known data-gathering instruments and readily available apparatus are described briefly and references are listed to reveal where more detailed discussions may be found. But if new apparatus or instruments or variations of old ones are employed, detailed descriptions and drawings of them and clear explanations of how they were used are given. After describing the investigative instruments, you explain the procedures employed to calibrate those that require it. For any nonstandardized instrument, you obtain independent validity and reliability estimates and, when applicable, report whether they are lower than the estimates in the original study. For standardized instruments, you indicate why the original reliability and validity data obtained during the standardization process apply in this study, or, if you use a sample that differs (severely retarded children) from the samples used in the standardization process (normal children), you obtain independent estimates. Before presenting the results of your findings, you check to make certain that no essential information has been omitted that the reader must possess to follow or to comprehend the rest of the report or to replicate the study.

DATA ANALYSIS AND INTERPRETATION   The data analysis and interpretation may be presented in separate chapters or may be integrated and presented in one or more chapters. These consist of tables and figures which present the data in detail, accompanied by paragraphs of discussion which point out important aspects of the data and indicate whether the hypotheses were confirmed. Because of the wide variety of studies and kinds of data that exist, no specific directions can be given for organizing this section of the report, but the descriptive and inferential aspects of the data are analyzed for each problem hypothesis, null hypothesis, or subproblem in turn. Raw data may be recorded in the most convenient form for collecting; but in the body of the report, data relevant to each hypothesis must be categorized, manipulated, and summarized in ways that reveal the pertinent information required to confirm or disconfirm the hypothesis. In most studies, the raw evidence is subjected to specific statistical treatments, and the values that are obtained, rather than the raw data, are reported in the study. When this procedure is followed, the treatment to which the data were subjected is clearly specified. If formulas or statistical procedures that are not well known were used, reference is made to the fact that they are explained in detail in the appendix.

Statistical information may be presented in many forms. The main forms are sums, ratios, proportions, or percentages; frequency distributions; means and standard deviations or variances that describe the central tendency and the variability of the scores; measures of relation and prediction—coefficients of correlation and standard error of estimates. The levels of significance selected for the tests of significance (t test, F ratio, or chi-square), the degrees of freedom available, and values obtained are reported. For each statistical method used, you present evidence indicating that the assumptions underlying the use of it have been met.

Extracting the meaning from the data is one of the most difficult and delightful phases of an investigation. In the textual discussion of the data, you do not repeat all the detailed information that is in the graphs and tables but rather point out important facts and relationships, make certain generalizations about the data, refrain from making any generalization that 'is not solidly supported by the data, and interpret the data. After drafting an explanation, you examine the data for exceptions, try to account for them, and restate your explanation if necessary. If more than one explanation can be given for a particular aspect of your data, you discuss honestly and thoroughly all explanations—not merely the one you favor; but you are free to marshal all the evidence you can to indicate why you have rejected rival explanations. Your decisions, of course, might be disputed by another investigator.

The fact that a relationship between *A* and *B* exists does not establish that *A* caused *B*, but arguments can be presented that increase the plausibility of a causal relationship. An effort may be made to establish the time priority of *A* through reports of observations or by arguing that the reverse time sequence, *B* caused *A*, must logically be rejected (physical maturity occurs before pregnancy; the order cannot be reversed). Certain logical assumptions may be presented, particularly in historical studies, and then a conclusion made that if these assumptions are true, then *A* contributed to the occurrence of *B*. Other researchers, of course, may challenge these assumptions. When stating the results of the study, careful qualifications are included that stipulate the precise conditions, situations, or limits for which the findings are valid, such as the nature of the population to which the conclusions apply.

In reporting and interpreting the data, you note whether the relationship exists between the independent and dependent variables that must exist to confirm your hypothesis; point out that certain other variables that might have affected the dependent variable were controlled, physically or statistically; and call attention to uncontrolled variables that may have affected the results and discuss their possible implications. The magnitude and the consistency of the relationship under a variety of conditions within the study is examined. If the findings are statistically significant, the size or strength of the relationship required for practical significance is discussed. You make these decisions on the basis of what variables were correlated, for what sample, under what conditions, and for what purpose, time, and place.

In interpreting the data, you once again scrutinize the adequacy and appropriateness of the research design, methods of observation and measurement, and types of analyses for the research problem. You also check whether they all fit together: whether the deduced consequences are logically derived from the hypotheses, whether the design of the experiment is appropriate for testing the hypotheses, whether the instruments actually measure the precise factors that need to be measured, whether the assumptions underlying the data-gathering devices are fully met, etc.

Your main objective in an investigation is to note whether hypothesized relationships are confirmed, but if you note any unpredicted relationships, you report these findings and suggest that they should be substantiated in specifically predicted and tested independent studies. In interpreting the data, you point out not only the size, strength, and consistency of the relationships within the investigation and their significance for your problem but also how consistent or inconsistent your findings are with those of related studies and with the demands and expectations of the theory you have reviewed in the introduction of your report. In this manner, you tie your study into the network of existing scientific information and make your contribution to the advancement of knowledge.

SUMMARY AND CONCLUSIONS   In the summary, you briefly review the procedures, findings, and entire evolvement of the problem. The important points in the study are brought together in the summary, but not all the evidence upon which they are based is repeated. The conclusions are stated precisely and related directly to the hypotheses that were tested; the conclusions reveal whether the conditions that were deduced to be observable if the hypotheses offered an adequate explanation of the phenomena being studied were observable. The conclusions announce whether the findings of the study confirmed or disconfirmed the hypotheses. If the conclusions modify an existing theory, this fact is discussed. If the data have any implications for educational programs or practices, these may be discussed. If the investigation raises or clarifies specific questions that suggest areas for further research, this information is presented tersely. If no further research would appear to be profitable in this area and a new approach to the problem is needed, this suggestion is made.

The summary and conclusion chapter is the most widely read part of a study because it recapitulates the information that has been presented in the previous sections of the report. Most readers scan the summary first to obtain an overview of the problem and to determine the study's usefulness to them. If the study is pertinent to their purposes, they examine the remaining chapters.

In addition to the summary, some institutions require a candidate to submit an abstract of 600 words or less to fulfill requirements for a degree. This abstract may be included in the formal report or may be published subsequently in *Dissertation Abstracts International* or some other source. Some research journals also print a brief abstract in distinctive type at the beginning of each report. An abstract serves not as a substitute for the summary and conclusion chapter but rather as a synopsis, enabling a scholar to judge whether he wishes to read the complete work.

Reference Materials

The bibliography, which will be discussed in detail later in this chapter, follows the main body of the report. An appendix, if included, follows the bibliography. You do not merely dump leftover products of the study in the appendix; rather, you present relevant supporting materials that are too unwieldy to be placed in the body of the dissertation, such as questionnaires, form letters, evaluation sheets, checklists, courses of study, long quotations, raw data, documents, and interview forms. The items in the appendix are grouped, labeled, lettered, and listed in the table of contents. If a study is complex, of major importance, or to be published in book or monograph form, you also prepare an alphabetized index, which follows the appendix. You may be required to submit a brief vita that gives information about your educational background, teaching experience, professional memberships, and previous publications.

STYLE OF WRITING

To avoid making unnecessary, time-consuming revisions of your report, you should study the report format and style manual recommended by your professor or editor. Several style manuals are available to choose from if you are specifically granted the right to select your own (18, 34, 69, 111.) After adopting a style manual, you must adhere to it throughout the report, for switching from one acceptable style of writing to another is not permissible.

Mastering the methods of reporting research is important, for an outstanding scientific investigation is of little value if the findings are not communicated effectively to others. Accomplishing this feat is somewhat different from writing a nontechnical composition. Entertaining, amusing, or persuading the reader is not your objective, nor do you merely discuss your opinions concerning a problem or suggest solutions and argue on the basis of general observations. You present a hypothesis, explain the procedures employed to test it, cite the factual data collected, and announce whether they confirm or disconfirm the hypothesis. A clear, objective, logical presentation and analysis of the evidence rather than an emotionalized argument or diverting descriptions are required in a scientific report.

Organization

Spewing a disordered jumble of raw facts into a report form not only fails to convey information to the reader but also suggests that you have not grasped the significance of your materials. Meaning cannot be derived easily from chaotic masses of isolated items. Data must be grouped and ordered into logical, attractive patterns before they can convey clear messages. Only through arduous intellectual effort can you organize facts so that they deliver the precise ideas you have in mind.

You do not insert a blank sheet of paper in a typewriter and compose a report as you would a family letter. The final draft of a report is the end product of a process that begins in the initial stages of an investigation. When first exploring the literature and pondering upon a potential problem, you notice that certain topics recur and seem to be related to it. If you jot down several of these items, the relationship between a few isolated facts may snap suddenly into focus and enable you to group them under one heading. After scanning several source materials, you can identify some major topics, organize them into a crude outline, and thereafter file your notes under these categories. While refining your hypothesis and doing more reading and more observing, you may note and correct weaknesses in your outline such as gaps that exist, materials that are not in the most logical order, topics that are in poor proportion, or items that need to be combined or omitted. An outline is not a rigid instrument that is constructed accurately in one draft but rather a map that is continuously being improved upon. Even in the most primitive stage of development, an outline serves a useful purpose. With each successive revision, it becomes a more reliable instrument.

What dictates the items and the order in an outline? The report format required by the institution provides the general framework. The hypotheses serve as guides for structuring the specific arguments—the procedures employed, the evidence collected, and the conclusions reached. But within each argument, materials must be ordered in terms of time, place, cause and effect, similarities and contrasts, or some other basis. After all the arguments are structured, they must be placed in a logical order.

An outline also helps you construct chapter titles and section headings. Doing this work carefully is important, for headings give readers an overview of the materials, help them find their way around in the report, and make it easier for them to grasp meanings. Headings cannot accomplish these objectives, of course, unless they are sufficiently specific to suggest the contents of the succeeding paragraphs. When writing headings, you should use the same grammatical structure and style of capitalization for items on the same level.

Right.

Chapter
  I.   Format of the Report
  II. Style of the Report
  III. Typing of the Report

Wrong.

Chapter
  I.   Format of the Report
  II. Style manuals are selected with care
  III. Typing

Language

Words—the writer's communication tools—are selected and ordered to inform the readers about the investigation rather than to impress them with rhetorical flourishes. Encrusting a report with polysyllabic words, technical jargon, involved sentences, and profuse quotations tends to smother the readers' interest. Since a pompous, pedantic presentation blocks rather than increases understanding, you write a simple, straightforward account of what took place in the study and make every effort to prevent misinterpretations from arising. If obscure theories are mentioned in a report, you describe them. If a graph or drawing will make the written discussion easier to understand, you construct one.

A formal rather than a colloquial style is employed when writing research reports. But formal writing need not drain all spontaneity and individuality from ideas and press them into prim, plodding prose passages. A lucid, lively account of an investigation can be produced if you use vivid, varied, and accurate means of expression and prune all hackneyed, extraneous, and vague words from your report. Short sentences are welcomed by readers. Familiar, concrete nouns arouse clearer mental images than planned profundities.

Proportion and Emphasis

To achieve proper proportion and emphasis in a report, you keep revising your outline until you have placed all topics of equal importance on the same level. You refrain from stating main ideas in a few terse sentences and elaborating upon minor points. When revising a report, you delete treasured words and sentences that give too much weight to minor topics and add supporting evidence and illustrations to expand underdeveloped major topics. To avoid burying significant ideas under masses of rhetorical trivia, you place topic sentences where they quickly capture the reader's attention, put key words or phrases at the beginning or end of sentences, and utilize numbers, italics, or warning words to signal that statements are important.

Unity and Clarity

To achieve unity and clarity in your report, you select homogeneous items from your notes, state the ideas in coherent sentences, place these sentences in a logical sequence, and weave them into paragraphs that in turn are logically related. Again and again you examine sentences, paragraphs, and chapters to determine whether like ideas have been placed in juxtaposition and whether one idea leads naturally to the next. After transposing misplaced items, combining similar ideas, culling unnecessary and repetitive materials, and correcting vague or weak reference of pronouns to their antecedents, you check the flow of your manuscript. You may ask: "Have I shown the connection between ideas, so that the readers can easily follow the arguments? Have I used transitional words, sentences, and paragraphs that will alert the readers to changes in the road ahead and lead them gently from point to point?"

Other Style Problems

Many other questions concerning style arise during the writing of a report. This text cannot cover all of them, but the following paragraphs discuss some common ones.

Since a research report is a formal and objective account of an investigation, it is written in the third person. Personal pronouns—"I," "me," "we," "you," "our," and "us"—are not used. Abbreviations are not usually employed *in the textual materials*, but they may be used in footnotes, bibliographies, appendixes, and tables. In dissertations "percent" is spelled out, but some journals permit the use of the symbol % in tables and even in the textual discussion.

Spell out numbers of less than 100, round numbers, ordinals, fractions, and numbers that begin sentences. Among the many exceptions to the above rule are the following: Use numerals in a technical or statistical discussion involving frequent use of numbers, in a group containing both numbers under and numbers over three digits, when a fraction is part of three or more digits, for numbers combined with abbreviations, and for percentages, decimals, and dates. If small and large numbers appear in a series, figures are used for all of them. Although there are some exceptions, numbers of four digits or more usually have commas to point off thousands. The letters or numbers that enumerate items in a paragraph are enclosed in parentheses; either letters or numbers may be used, but not both forms in the same report.

Simplified spelling is not acceptable in research reports. Punctuation conforms to good usage and is consistent. The past tense is used when referring to what the researcher or other investigators have done. The present tense is used when referring the readers to tables that are presently before them and when mentioning general truths and well-established principles. Not all style books present exactly the same rules, but, as has been stated previously, after a style has been selected, it must be followed consistently throughout the report.

CONSTRUCTION OF TABLES AND FIGURES

Tables and figures that are accurately compiled, properly arranged, easily read, and correctly interpreted may convey information more effectively than many paragraphs of written description. Since a large number of graphic procedures have been devised, the following discussion can only point out some general rules governing their construction. More detailed explanations are presented in textbooks devoted to the subject (18, 34, 69, 111).

Tables

When collecting data, you may use the most convenient method of recording information, such as listing pupils' names alphabetically and placing varied information about the pupils in columns bearing the appropriate labels. But you may have to reorder these data later so as to make comparisons on the basis of sex, age, schools, or geographical areas. If possible, of course, you should devise a plan to collect the original data in a tabular form that will force the desired answers into clear focus. Learning how to construct tables in a way that enables you to compare data for different groups to test your hypotheses and plausible alternative hypotheses is of utmost importance. Through the use of a table, you may help readers spot important details, see relationships, get a concise overview of the findings, or grasp the significance of data much more quickly and easily than through many pages of prose explanation.

CONTENT   Simplicity and unity are essential in the construction of tables. A complex table followed by an explanation which extends for several pages may confuse rather than enlighten the reader. While flipping back and forth from pages of discussion to the table, the thread of the argument may be lost. If several comparisons of distinctly different kinds are incorporated in one table, or if like comparisons are separated into many different tables, a reader may become bewildered. A well-constructed table, like a well-written paragraph, consists of several related facts that are integrated to present *one main idea.*

A well-constructed table is self-explanatory; it is complete and sufficiently clear to be understood without reading the textual explanation. Conversely, the textual discussion explains the generalizations that can be derived from the table and the relevancy of the information in a manner that enables the reader to grasp the main ideas without examining the table. In the textual discussion, you refer to the table by number (and page if necessary) rather than by the less specific phrase, "see the following table."

Not all statistical materials are placed in formal tables. A simple statistical statement such as the following may be inserted directly in the body of a paragraph: "Of the 376 children, 120 had received no Salk vaccine shots, 136 had received one, and 120 had received two." A few facts may be organized into an informal pattern and woven into the textual material by an introductory sentence followed by a colon, for example:

The teachers were about evenly divided in their choice of retirement plans:

	Women	Men	Total
Plan *A*	20	19	39
Plan *B*	16	18	34
Total	36	37	73

The table of contents in the dissertation does not list these informally presented statistical statements.

PLACEMENT   A table never precedes but rather follows as closely as possible the first reference to it in the report. A table that will not fit into the remaining space on the page is placed on the next page at the end of the first paragraph. A table that covers more than half a page is usually centered on a page by itself. Long, detailed tables that interrupt the continuity of the discussion may be put in the appendix. If all tables are typed on separate pages, they will not have to be recopied each time the report is revised; when the final draft of the report is assembled, the original tables can be inserted in the proper places.

NUMBERS AND CAPTIONS   All tables are numbered consecutively throughout the report, including those that appear in the appendix. Many styles of constructing tables are acceptable, but consistency of style is required. One style is presented in Figure 13.1. Another acceptable style conforms to the following pattern: The word "table," followed by its number, is placed alone on the first line and the heading or title two lines below it. Both items are typed in full capital letters, arabic numerals are used, and no end punctuation is necessary. A title more than one line long is single-spaced and typed to form an inverted pyramid. An effective heading describes precisely what the table contains; to aid the readers, the key descriptive word is placed near the beginning of the title. In parentheses below the title, information that the readers must possess when they scan the data may be placed such as the unit of measurement (in thousands of dollars) or source of data (1980 Budget of Oakland Public Schools). Sometimes the source is placed just beneath the table, as it is in Figure 13.1.

In tables, the captions (column headings) and stubs (row labels) should be brief yet accurate and complete. Captions should be parallel in grammatical structure; common abbreviations may be used, but other abbreviations are avoided if possible. Long captions may be typed broadside so as to be read up from the bottom of the page. Writers employ different capitalization styles; some capitalize only the initial letter in the first word and proper nouns and adjectives.

To facilitate locating items referred to in the table, the columns may be numbered (sometimes in parentheses) below the column captions (see Figure 13.1). Units of measurement may be given following the column caption or below the horizontal line beneath the caption. Figure columns are aligned on the right, but if decimals are used, the decimals are aligned. When no data are available, the omission is indicated by dots or dashes, or by leaving the space blank, rather than by a zero—which represents a value of zero rather than an omission. Table footnote references are noted by standard typewriter characters (*, **, ***) or by superscript lower-case letters ($_{a,b,c}$). Table footnotes are placed just below the horizontal line at the bottom of the table rather than at the bottom of the page.

SIZE   Tables should be no larger than the pages of the manuscript or publication. Folding tables into the copy is unsatisfactory and should

Table 171.—Funds used in the performance of basic research, applied research, and development: United States, 1970

[in millions of dollars]

Sector	Total	Basic research	Applied research	Development
1	2	3	4	5
Total	$27,250	$3,935	$5,915	$17,400
Federal government	3,650	555	1,275	1,820
Industry	19,250	750	3,550	14,950
Colleges and universities	3,400	2,350	720	330
Other nonprofit institutions	950	280	370	300

NOTE. Data are preliminary estimates.

SOURCE: National Science Foundation, *National Patterns of R&D, Funds and Manpower in the United States, 1953-70*, NSF 69-30.

FIGURE 13.1

A table. (*From the U.S. Department of Health, Education, and Welfare*, Digest of Educational Statistics, *1970 edition.*)

be avoided if possible. If tables will not fit into the normal pages—lengthwise, crosswise, or spread across two facing pages—they may be reduced in size by photocopying them or using smaller print. If a table extends beyond a page in length, the word "table" and the number are repeated, followed by the word "continued," at the top of the succeeding pages (for example, "Table 3—Continued"). The title is omitted on the continued table, but all other captions are repeated. If a table covers two facing pages, the full heading is placed on the top of the first page and only the word "table" and the number, followed by the word "continued," appear on the top of the opposite page.

RULINGS   Rulings or lines are used only if they make the table easier to read. A double or heavy horizontal line may be placed above the column captions, a single one below them, and another below the last row of items in the table. Vertical rules and additional horizontal ones may be added if they break up the data into logical groups or make the arrangement simpler to use. Rulings are not used on the sides of tables.

Figures

Some ideas may be communicated more effectively by figures than by written or tabular presentations. A drawing of a piece of apparatus or a flow chart that traces channels of authority may clarify points that would otherwise require several pages of textual explanation. Presenting data in a graph or chart form may reveal important trends or relationships that a reader might not grasp when examining complex statistical data. Figures do not replace word descriptions, but they may help a researcher explain and interpret complicated instruments and data to the reader.

TYPES   The commonest forms of figures used in reports are line graphs, bar graphs, pie charts, area or volume charts, component or belt charts, pictorial charts, flow charts, maps, diagrams of apparatus, and photographs. A number of reference books explain in detail the methods of presenting these figures, the advantages and disadvantages of utilizing each type, the pitfalls to avoid, and the rules governing their construction (18, 34, 69, 111). The following discussion merely suggests some general rules for constructing figures.

PURPOSE   Figures are not introduced merely to convey simple concepts or to make the report more interesting. A drawing or graph is used only if it snaps important ideas or significant relationships into a sharp focus for the reader more quickly than other means of presentation. Complex, confused, or carelessly prepared figures may be less effective communicators than words. A well-constructed figure weaves a few pertinent related facts together to present one main idea. It is simple and uncluttered with unnecessary details. Concise captions, labels, and legends are placed on the figure to describe the nature of the data and to interpret the information presented.

NUMBER AND CAPTIONS   Illustrative materials are labeled with the word "figure" or "fig." and are numbered consecutively throughout the report with arabic numbers. The word "figure" and its number are usually placed below the illustration. The title for the illustration may be placed either (1) after the figure number, (2) at the top of the illustration, or (3) within the figure. The caption may be typed or lettered in full capital letters and in an inverted pyramid form with no terminal punctuation or as an ordinary sentence in paragraph, underhung, or block form. The advice given previously about the placement of tables in the text and references to them in the written discussion also applies to figures.

ACKNOWLEDGMENT OF INDEBTEDNESS

Research workers acknowledge their indebtedness to other authors not only as a matter of honesty and courtesy but also as a means of confirming their work and indicating the quality and thoroughness of their investigations. To many readers, the footnotes and bibliography in a report, which give clues concerning the related literature in the field, are as important as the textual materials. When writing a doctoral dissertation, therefore, or an article for a professional journal, or a term paper, you should include all the information that readers will need to locate the source materials with a minimum of effort. Sources of all quoted materials and important works that were used in preparing the report must be fully identified in accordance with the style rules that have been designed to transmit such information.

Quotations

Laymen often joke about the array of quotations and footnotes found in research reports, and their barbs are not always unwarranted. Interlarding a report indiscriminately with quotations and footnotes is a cultural affectation that some inexperienced writers assume to conceal shoddy workmanship. Pasting numerous quotations into an authority-laden mosaic does not create an acceptable research report. Strings of these passages reveal that you are little beyond the note-taking stage of your work. A research report is a creative effort—a synthesis of what you have read, observed, thought, and mentally ordered into new patterns—rather than a mere compilation of other people's work. You may use quotations, but use them sparingly and purposively.

ART OF QUOTING If you paraphrase rather than quote materials, your discussion moves more directly and forcefully toward your objective. To credit the original author of an idea that is borrowed but not quoted directly, you place a footnote superscript at the end of the statement and the appropriate documentation in the footnote.

When you cannot rephrase a law, formula, or idea as concisely, accurately, or effectively as the original author has phrased it, you use a direct quotation. Whenever possible, you select a short quotation or strip the chaff from a longer one and plant the kernel in your own sentence. To avoid introducing quotations repeatedly with "Mr. *X* says," you place the introductory phrase within or at the end of the quotation.

MECHANICS OF QUOTING   The rules for presenting short and long direct quotations differ. A short quotation is enclosed in quotation marks, double-spaced, and incorporated in the paragraph. A quotation that appears within a short quotation is enclosed in single quotation marks. The arabic reference numeral to the footnote is typed half a space above and after the phrase or sentence quoted, and after the punctuation mark if it comes at the end of the sentence. Long quotations—four or more typewritten lines—are usually set off in separate single-spaced paragraphs that are indented in their entirety, and no quotation marks are necessary. Quotations within long quotations are set off by full quotation marks. Exceptionally long quotations may be placed in the appendix. A quotation that occurs in a footnote is single-spaced, enclosed in quotation marks, and indented in paragraph style.

In the previous discussion on taking notes (see Chapter 4), the text stressed the importance of checking for accuracy when duplicating quoted material. An explanation was also given of the method writers use to denote omissions in a quotation—ellipses—and to introduce corrections or explanations—brackets. Perhaps mention should be made of some other mechanics. If the first word of a quotation is grammatically linked to what precedes it in the sentence, the word is not capitalized even though it was capitalized in the original sentence. For example: (1) We agree with Dr. Jones that "measurement is essential in research." (2) Dr. Jones stated, "Measurement is essential in research." Questions may also arise concerning the end punctuation in quotations. Only one punctuation mark accompanies the terminal quotation marks: (1) a period or comma is placed inside closing quotation marks, (2) a colon or semicolon is placed outside quotation marks, (3) an interrogation or exclamation point is placed inside if it belongs to the quoted matter and outside if it is a part of the whole sentence.

Footnotes

Footnotes serve various purposes: (1) Some give source references for direct quotations or paraphrased material, (2) some provide cross references to materials appearing in other parts of the report, (3) some indicate sources that contain substantiating evidence, and (4) some explain or elaborate upon a point in the textual discussion. The last type should be kept to a minimum. Many editors insist that if something is important enough to be said, it should be placed in the body of the text.

CITATION OF FOOTNOTES   Several methods for inserting footnotes have been devised. The traditional procedure is to place at the bottom of the page all footnotes for citations appearing on that page. The footnotes are separated from the text by a short line—twenty spaces— drawn from the left margin one space below the written discussion. Beneath this line a double space is left before the first footnote is typed; the footnotes are single-spaced with double spaces between them. Each footnote is indented as in a paragraph and preceded by a superscript numeral that corresponds to the reference numeral used in the textual material. The first word of the footnote follows the reference superscript numeral; no punctuation or space is necessary (see page 426). If the textual material consists of tables, mathematical materials, or formulas, an asterisk or some other nonnumerical symbol is selected to identify a footnote. The writer either numbers footnotes consecutively throughout the report or begins anew on each page or in each chapter, depending upon the institutional requirements.

    If a report is to be published, authors may employ other methods of inserting footnotes to facilitate the work of the typesetter. They may place the footnote immediately following the textual reference on the page and separate this source information from the rest of the paragraph by typing unbroken lines above and below it. To conserve space and to cut printing costs, some publishers prefer to have a coded reference to a source placed immediately after and in alignment with a direct quotation. A bibliographical code similar to the one used in this book, i.e., (12:24–25), may be employed. Many research journals use an author and date of publication code, i.e., Jones, (1970). You will find examples of the latter in Appendix G. If an investigator uses the author-date method, he can omit or add references to a bibliography at any time without renumbering all the entries and making the necessary changes throughout the text. This method of citation is especially applicable for materials that appear in research journals where no quoted materials appear.

ABBREVIATIONS IN FOOTNOTES   To save time and space, full bibliographical information is presented in the footnotes the first time that a reference is made to a source; thereafter, abbreviations are used to identify it. The abbreviation *ibid.* is employed when the succeeding references to a work *immediately* follow the first full citation (see sample footnotes 16 to 18). If references to *other works intervene* between the first and later citations to the same work, the abbreviation *loc. cit.* or *op. cit.* is used. If the reference is to the same page, *loc. cit.* is used; otherwise *op. cit.* and the volume, if necessary, and page number are given (see sample footnotes 20 and 22). The author's last name precedes these abbreviations, but the first name is added if more than one author cited in the report has the same last name. After the second work by the same author is cited, an abbreviated or full title must be given in each subsequent citation to make unmistakably clear which of this author's works is meant (see sample footnote 24). Some writers always use the abbreviated title instead of *op. cit.* and *loc. cit.* The terms *ibid., op. cit.,* and *loc. cit.* are followed by periods to denote that they are abbreviations, and they are underscored in manuscript to indicate italics. The following samples of footnotes illustrate the use of these abbreviations:

[16] Alice W. Heim, "Adaptation to Level of Difficulty in Intelligence Testing," *British Journal of Psychology*, 46 (August 1955), p. 211.

[17] *Ibid.* [same work, same page as above]

[18] *Ibid.,* p. 214. [same work as 16, but page 214]

[19] Robert A. Jackson, "Prediction of the Academic Success of College Freshmen," *Journal of Educational Psychology*, 46 (May 1955), p. 296.

[20] Heim, *loc. cit.* [refers to 16, exactly the same page]

[21] Samuel F. Klugman, "Agreement between Two Tests as Predictors of College Success," *Personnel and Guidance Journal*, 36 (December 1957), p. 255.

[22] Heim, *op. cit.,* 220. [refers to 16, but page 220]

[23] Alice W. Heim, *The Appraisal of Intelligence.* London: Methuen and Co., 1954, p. 169. [second work by Heim is introduced]

[24] Heim, "Adaptation in Intelligence Testing," *op. cit.,* p. 223. [repetition of title indicates which Heim work is meant]

A number of other abbreviations appear in research reports. Many of them are in Latin, although some are now being replaced by English terms. If you are not familiar with these abbreviations, you cannot interpret the footnotes in many source materials and cannot utilize these shorthand devices when writing your report. Thus, in addition to the symbols above, you should master the following common communication symbols:

anon.: anonymous

bk., bks.: book(s)

c. or *ca.*: about (approximate data, *c.* 1245)

cf.: compare (*cf. ante* p. 16, compare above; cf. *supra*, compare any preceding material; cf. *post* p. 26, compare below; cf. *infra*, compare any subsequent material)

ch., chap., chaps.: chapter(s)

col., cols.: column(s)

e.g.: for example

ed., edd.: edition(s)

ed., eds.: editor(s), edited by

et al.: and others (author Jones *et al.* stated)

et seq., et seqq.: and the following (16 *et seq.*, page 16 and the following page)

f.,ff.: and the following page(s) (pp. 3 f., page 3 and the following page; pp. 3 ff., page 3 and the following pages)

i.e.: that is

id., idem: the same as before (the same person)

l., ll.: line(s) (ll. 8–12, lines 8 to 12)

mimeo.: mimeographed

MS, MSS: manuscript(s)

n., nn.: footnote(s) (n. 10, nn. 1–6)

N.B.: please note; mark well

n.d.: no date (given for a publication)

n.n.: no name

n.p.: no place

N.S.: New Series; New Style (of dating, since 1752)

no., nos.: number(s)

O.S.: Old Series; Old Style (of dating, before 1752)

p., pp.: page(s)

passim: here and there (discussed in various places in the work)

pt., pts.: part(s)

q.v. (*quod vide*): which see (used to suggest consulting a work, now replaced by English "see")

rev.: revised, revision

sec., secs.: section(s)

trans.: translator, translated by

viz.: namely

vol., vols.: volume(s)

vs., vss.: verse(s)

Bibliography

The bibliography should give a clear, complete description of the sources that were used when preparing the report. Some bibliographies classify entries under headings such as Books, Periodicals, Newspapers, Reports, Public Documents, and Miscellaneous, but most of them arrange items in a single alphabetized list. The latter method must be adopted and items must be numbered consecutively if, instead of page footnotes, the cross-reference system of citations from the body to the bibliography of the report is used, as is done in this text.

STYLE OF CITING Bibliographical items are usually listed alphabetically by authors' surnames, but a chronological arrangement is used in some studies. When the author's name is not given, the work is listed under the name of the school system, institution, or agency that prepared the report (see Bibliography, 82). When no clue of authorship is available, the work is listed under the first important word of the title (see Bibliography, 69). To make the author's name stand out, the first line of each entry is typed flush with the margin and the remaining lines are indented. Double spacing or single spacing with double spaces between entries is used.

No universally accepted style for constructing a bibliography exists. You adopt one that is approved by your advisor or publisher and use it consistently. The following samples present a simple and workable style:

1 For a book.
   Surname of author, given name or two initials, *Title Taken from Title Page* [underlined]. Edition if more than one, volume if more than one, place of publication; publisher, date on title page or copyright date.
2 For an article.
   Surname of author, given name or two initials, "Title of Article," *Name of Periodical* [underlined]. Volume of periodical (month, day, year), beginning page.

3 For a newspaper.

Name of Paper [underlined], month, day, year, section of paper, page. [If author and title are given, they precede name of paper.]

4 For unpublished materials [speeches, letters, mimeographed materials, etc.].

Surname of author, given name or initials, "Title of Material," nature of material and where it is available or was presented,[1] date.

Sometimes the above bibliographical style is also used for footnotes, except that the regular paragraph indention rather than the underhung style is employed and the exact page of the quotation is given. But most institutions require further changes in footnotes; they stipulate that the author's given name must appear first, and some recommend a different form for the punctuation and placement of items (see page 426). In some institutions, additional information is also required in the bibliography. As the last item in each entry, the total number of pages in the source is listed to give the reader some concept of the comprehensiveness of the work. Brief annotations summarizing the contents, strengths, weaknesses, biases, or unique contributions of sources may also be required. The annotations are single-spaced and separated from the rest of the entry by a double space.

AIDS FOR CITING   If you form the habit early in an investigation of using the same style for like items on your bibliography cards, rechecking each item on every card for accuracy and completeness, and consulting a style manual when uncertain about how to write an entry, you will experience little difficulty in compiling a bibliography for your research report. Different types of bibliographical entries, of course, present different problems. An examination of the bibliography in this text and the following general rules will answer some common questions.

1 When two or more works by the same author are listed, an unbroken line about six spaces in length, followed by a comma, is sometimes substituted for his name after the first entry. The titles of his works are alphabetized under his name. Publications of which he is coauthor follow those of which he is sole author.

[1]For example: Unpublished Ph.D. dissertation, University of California.
Paper read before the annual convention of the Educators' Club, New York City.
Minutes of the Wayne Township Board of Education, Wayne, Michigan.
Letter to the writer from Dr. John Dewey, Teachers College, Columbia University.

2   If a book has two or three authors, the second and third authors'
names are written in the normal order (see Bibliography, 8). If there
are more than three authors, the name of the first is given, followed
by "*et al.*" or "and others" (see Bibliography, 5).

3   An editor or compiler is indicated by placing the proper abbreviation in the parentheses following the name (see Bibliography, 55).

4   When identifying the place of publication, the name of the city is
sufficient if it is well known; otherwise the name of the state or the
complete address is added.

PREPARATION OF THE REPORT

When preparing a report you will adopt the patterns of working that are
most suitable for you. But acquiring some knowledge of how others
have solved common writing, revising, and typing problems may help
you improve your system.

Drafting and Revising the Report

Some parts of a report, such as the review of the literature, may be
written fairly early in an investigation, but most of the writing is done
after the hypotheses have been tested. You collect data and organize
them into tables, graphs, or some other form that brings out relationships. You classify your notes and place them in the order that they
appear in your outline. Then, while examining the data and notes, you
write paragraphs of explanation and interpretation for each section of
the report, compose transitional statements or paragraphs that lead the
reader from one point to the next, and draft the conclusions.

Even at this stage of your work, you may reorder points in the
outline to achieve a more logical presentation or smoother transitions.
Thus, in all but the final copy of a report, you should type each
paragraph on a separate page so that sufficient room is left to make
corrections or revisions. By so doing, you may rewrite materials, add
paragraphs, or shift items from one section of the report to another
without retyping entire pages or chapters of contiguous materials.

Writing is arduous work. The prolonged process of composing,
reordering, adding, deleting, and polishing is taxing. Successful writers
redraft their reports many times before they are satisfied with the
results, and their faculty advisers or editors may make many additional suggestions for improvements. Revising a report usually consumes many more hours than writing the original draft.

A beginner has much to learn before he or she can write effectively. You may make better progress if you form the following work habits:

1 Set aside regular hours for writing and observe your schedule faithfully.
2 Choose an environment that is conducive to work and make certain that the necessary reference books, dictionaries, and files are at hand.
3 To overcome the difficulty of getting started at each writing session, stop writing early each day and spend a few minutes organizing materials and listing the things to do the following day.
4 After working for a few days, set the draft aside and return later to read it critically.
5 Since items in a report do not have to be written in a consecutive order, compose a rough draft of a section whenever sufficient insight into the materials has been gained.
6 Concentrate on communicating information when writing. Do not let minor problems interrupt the flow of thought and block progress—skip over them and return later to find the proper word, devise a deft transition, check a fact, or insert an illustration.
7 When bogged down in a particular paragraph or section of a report, reread the preceding materials and the outline to regain perspective.
8 Ask colleagues to read the report and point out any gaps, weaknesses, or ideas that are not clearly communicated.
9 Allot generous amounts of time for making unhurried, thorough revisions.

Typing the Report

Before typing your report, you should reread the institutional requirements. The style manual usually stipulates that white bond paper of the proper size, type, and weight be used; quite commonly $8^{1}/_{2} \times 11$ inches and a 20-pound-weight stock is required for the first copy and a lighterweight stock for the carbon copies.[2] The style manual gives special directions for the headings, tables, figures, footnotes, quotations, bibliography, and appendix. The regulations for spacing, indention, alignment of numbers, and margins (left $1^{1}/_{2}$ inches, right 1 inch, top and bottom $1^{1}/_{4}$ inches is common) should also be checked. An electric typewriter or Varityper with large (pica) type is usually recommended, and the same one, or at least the same style and size of typeface, should be used throughout the report. A nongreasy, fresh,

[2]Some institutions will accept photocopies of the original copy.

black carbon paper, a medium-inked typewriter ribbon, and clean type characters are necessary to produce a clear, dense copy.

Before typing the final draft of a report, you read the manuscript critically, searching for inaccurate statements, ambiguous passages, omissions, and inconsistencies. After making an exacting examination to locate errors in quotations, footnotes, tables, figures, paragraphing, sentence structure, headings, mathematics, spelling, style, proper names, or bibliography, you mark the copy to provide the typist with the necessary directions for producing a satisfactory typescript. The time spent in checking the above details is well invested, for ultimately you alone—and not the typist, the sponsor, or the publisher—are held responsible for the contents of the report.

A term paper or a master's thesis may be typed personally, but a doctoral dissertation should be prepared by a professional typist who has had considerable experience in doing such work. When the final typed copy of the report is completed, proofreading it with the greatest care is necessary. Proofreading and correcting a page before removing it from the typewriter are a prudent practice. Correction fluid may be used to correct a few errors in a copy, but crossing out and inserting words or sentences and typing over letters are not permissible. If revisions necessitate retyping, care should be taken to equalize the materials which are inserted and deleted so that the last line on the page comes out even. If such care is not taken, one may have to retype the rest of the chapter and renumber the remaining pages of the report.

Every page in a report receives a number. Small Roman numerals are centered at the bottom of all the preliminary pages except the title page, where the number "i" counts as a page but does not appear. Hence, the numbering begins with "ii" on the next page. Arabic numerals are placed on the top right-hand corner of all other pages with the exception of the first one in each new chapter, which is numbered in the center at the bottom.

When typing any draft of an investigation, you should make carbon or Xerox copies. The second copy is valuable if you lose the first one, want to use copies both at home and at the office, or have to refer to the manuscript while your adviser or colleagues are examining the original draft. Filing the duplicate and first copies in separate places gives added protection against loss through fire and other means. Making duplicate copies of the early drafts of a report is a matter of personal choice, but many publishers and all dissertation committees require that at least two copies of the final draft be submitted.

14 EVALUATION AND PUBLICATION OF RESEARCH

ublished research is not necessarily "good research." All publishers reject the poorest studies, but they do not all have equally high standards. In some published studies, generalizations are made that are not supported by the evidence, and flaws are found in methodology, statistical analyses, and the chain of reasoning. To protect readers, such reports should bear the label "Research consumer be wary of contents!"

How can you become a publishable producer of research reports and a selective consumer of the hundreds of studies of varying quality that are published each year? You can prepare yourself by searching for good models and by becoming familiar with the publishing standards and procedures employed by the best-quality journals and book publishers. This chapter will acquaint you with the test of critical scholarship that discriminating investigators and editors who review studies apply to research reports.

EVALUATION

No universally acceptable yardstick has been designed for evaluating a research report, but the following questions provide guides that you can consult before searching the literature and when undertaking various stages of your own investigation.

Title of the Research Project

1 Does the title precisely identify the area of the problem?
2 Is the title clear, concise, and descriptive enough to permit the study to be indexed in its proper category?
3 Are superfluous words such as "a study of" or "an analysis of" and catchy, misleading, and vague phrases avoided?
4 Do nouns serve as the key words in the title?
5 Are the principal words placed at the beginning of the title statement?

Preliminary Materials

1 Does the report contain a title page, approval sheet, preface or acknowledgments, table of contents, list of tables, and list of figures?
2 Are the mechanical features of the above materials in accord with the required style manual?
3 Are all necessary items included in each section and proper headings provided where necessary?
4 Do the captions that appear in the table of contents and list of tables and figures correspond exactly with the captions and page citations they refer to in the text? Are the same grammatical structure and style of capitalization used for captions on the same level?

Description and Statement of the Problem

1 Has a thorough analysis been made of all the facts and explanations that might possibly be related to the problem, and have the relationships between these factors been explored thoroughly?
2 Are the arguments that were used to isolate the pertinent variables, explanations, and relationships logically sound?
3 Does the statement of the problem encompass and agree with all

the relevant facts, explanatory concepts, and relationships that the analysis indicated had a bearing on the problem?

4   Are all the problem elements expressed in an orderly system of relationships?

5   Does the statement of the problem appear early in the study? Is it clearly labeled? Are unnecessary words, such as "the purpose of this study," avoided?

6   Is the problem statement expressed succinctly and unambiguously in a grammatically correct interrogative or declarative sentence?

Scope and Adequacy of the Problem

1   Does the problem meet the scope, significance, and topical requirements of the institution or periodical for which it was prepared?

2   Is the problem sufficiently delimited to permit an exhaustive treatment, yet sufficiently significant to warrant investigating it?

3   Does the problem possess potential value in helping to solve theoretical or practical educational problems?

4   Does the importance of the knowledge to be gained outweigh the level of risks to the subjects?

Review of the Related Literature

1   Has a thorough review been made of all the literature dealing with the variables under investigation?

2   Have previous studies been tapped for relevant methodology and concepts and have they been evaluated to check whether their samples are adequate, their outcomes are measured by reliable and valid instruments, and their conclusions are warranted?

3   Has the background of the earlier studies been developed to show that the existing evidence does not solve the immediate problem adequately?

4   Does the review of the literature merely present studies in a chronological order and force the reader to assimilate the facts and draw conclusions concerning the relationship of the cited studies to the problem? Or does the review bring together pertinent data and theories and weave them into a network of relationships that points up relevant issues, reveals gaps in knowledge, and prepares the way for the logical leap to hypothesis construction?

Statement of Assumptions

1 Are the assumptions on which the hypotheses are predicated made explicit for the critical inspection of the reader?
2 Is the statement of the assumptions and the explanation of the theoretical framework within which the investigator intends to work presented in a logical and inclusive chain of reasoning?
3 Are the assumptions properly labeled, codified, and inserted in the report?

Statement of Hypotheses and Deduced Consequences

1 Are the hypotheses in agreement with all the known facts and compatible with well-attested theories?
2 Do they explain more facts that are relevant to the problem than any rival hypotheses?
3 Are the hypotheses testable?
4 Are the deduced consequences logically implied by the hypotheses?
5 Are the hypotheses and their deduced consequences expressed in clear, precise terms so that they leave no question about the factors to be tested?
6 Are the hypotheses and their deduced consequences clearly labeled and placed early in the report?
7 Will the hypotheses aid in the prediction of facts and relations that were previously unknown?

Definition of Terms

1 Are the important variables and terms defined in clear and unequivocal language?
2 Are the more important constructs (properties, variables) defined in constitutive and operational terms and do the indexes of the constructs correspond with the definitions?
3 In the body of the report, are the terms and constructs used consistently as defined?
4 Is the "definition of terms" section of the report labeled clearly and placed early in the study?

Method of Attack

Since each problem is unique, the means of attacking investigations vary accordingly. The following discussion raises some questions concerning considerations that are common to many problems.

General Considerations

1 Can one collect the quantity and quality of data necessary to investigate the problem? Are the necessary tools, techniques, and subjects or other sources of data available? Does the researcher possess the language, mathematical, and specialized skills necessary to obtain the data?

2 Have controls been established to protect the physical and mental well-being of human subjects and the confidentiality of the data obtained about them?

3 Is an accurate, detailed explanation of the method, techniques, and tools used to test the deduced consequences given early in the report? Are the reasons for choosing them made clear? Is this information brought together in one section of the report and properly labeled? Can another worker replicate the study from a description of the procedures cited in the report?

4 Do the reported procedures adequately and correctly represent the particular indicants, conditions, and relationships of the consequences to be tested?

5 Do these procedures collect the evidence with a minimum of effort or are equally effective but simpler ones available?

6 Will these methods and instruments produce relevant, reliable, valid, and sufficiently refined data to justify the inferences drawn from them?

7 Is it necessary to locate or devise more refined data-gathering techniques in order to obtain deeper insights into the phenomena?

8 Are the assumptions that underlie the use of the data-gathering devices fully met in this study?

9 Have the procedural errors and inadequacies that existed in previous studies been eliminated, the weaknesses of the present study been pointed out, and the procedures that were first employed and then abandoned because they proved worthless been discussed?

10 Does the report describe where and when the data were gathered?

11 Does the report describe precisely the number and kind of subjects, objects, and materials used in the investigation and indicate whether and why any of them did not participate in all parts of the investigation?

12   If a pilot study or pretest was conducted, is an explanation given of the procedures or instruments that were employed and reasons cited for refining the methodology?

13   Are copies of the oral and written directions and the printed forms and questionnaires used in the investigation included in the report?

General Considerations in Descriptive Studies

1   Is the research design adequate, in scope, depth, and precision, to obtain the specific data required to test the hypothesis?

2   Does the design of the study provide for examining not only the relationship between the independent and dependent variables but also the effect on that relationship of other relevant variables on which the groups may differ?

3   Has every possible precaution been taken to establish observational conditions, frame questions, design observation schedules, record data, and check the reliability of witnesses and source materials so as to avoid collecting data that are the product of perceptual errors, faulty memory, deliberate deception, and unconscious bias?

4   Are the specific items the observer is to note when describing a condition, event, or process clearly identified, and is a uniform method provided for recording precise information?

5   Are the standards employed to classify, compare, and quantify the data valid?

6   Are the categories for classifying data unambiguous, appropriate, and capable of bringing out likenesses, differences, or relationships?

7   Does the report admit instances encountered where the elusive quality of descriptive phenomena makes it difficult to obtain and interpret data?

8   Does the study reflect an analysis of surface conditions, or does the investigation probe into the interrelationships or causal relationships?

General Considerations in Historical Studies

1   Is the report based on primary sources? If some secondary sources are used, do they contribute the "less significant" data rather than the crucial evidence for the solution of the problem?

2 Has more than one independent, reliable eyewitness been found to support the alleged facts?

3 Has an investigation been made to check the witnesses' trustworthiness, competence, biases, motives, and position at the time of observation, as well as to check how and when they recorded their observations?

4 Have the source materials been examined critically for authenticity and credibility?

5 Are words and statements from earlier documents correctly interpreted? Is there any evidence to indicate that conceptions of later times have been read into them?

6 When necessary, has advice been sought from experts in auxiliary fields to determine the authenticity of data?

7 Have the sources been assigned to a particular author, time, or place?

General Considerations in Experimental Studies

1 Is the design clearly formulated? Will it answer the questions that the hypothesis raises? Does the design provide the controls required to obtain valid answers?

2 Have all potential sources of threats to internal and external validity been checked carefully?

3 Is the investigator in a position to control the manipulation of the independent variable?

4 Have randomization or other procedures been employed to assign subjects, rooms, teachers, equipment, etc., to groups?

5 Have the number and character of the subjects who refused to participate or dropped out of the experiment been checked carefully?

6 Have the groups in the experiment been stratified into subgroups (sex, IQ, etc.), if pertinent information can be extracted from such data?

7 If a matching or analysis of covariance technique is employed to remove the masking effect of specific variables, do these variables have a known effect on the dependent variable?

8 Have any assumptions underlying the use of statistical techniques been violated?

9 Are the null hypotheses rigorously defined? Are they related to the problem hypotheses?

10 Was the level of significance necessary for the rejection of the null hypothesis specified before the collection and analysis of the data?

Sampling

1 Does the report describe with precision the population that is involved in the study? Does the sample come from this population?

2 Is the method of drawing the sample clearly specified?

3 Do the control and experimental groups come from the same population, and were they selected in the same manner?

4 Were randomization techniques employed to select subjects from the population?

5 If the subjects in the study are self-selected—if they volunteer to participate, to take a class, to take a remedial treatment, to go to college—has consideration been given to the fact they may differ from the groups with which the investigator compares them?

6 Is the sample sufficiently large and drawn in a manner to represent the characteristics of the population?

7 To what subject populations and nonsubject populations (settings, experimenters, teachers, tasks, measurement variables) can the findings be generalized? Has the investigator sampled one universe and generalized to another?

8 Did the pretest, the behavior of the experimenter, or the fact that the subjects knew they were participating in the experiment affect the responsiveness of the subjects to the independent variable and make them unrepresentative of the population from which they came?

Instrumentation

1 Is the investigator familiar with the rules to be observed, the conditions to be met, and the operations to be performed when utilizing the various measures, scales, tests, and instruments?

2 Do the instruments possess the reliability and validity required for the research purpose? Are the instruments and test norms appropriate for the sample of subjects in the study (in regard to age, ability, sex, etc.)?

3 Are the tests appropriate for the time available for administration and conditions under which they are to be administered (size of room or group, abilities of test administrators, scorers, or interpreters)?

4 Do the judges who are to rate the phenomena possess the necessary background and information? Are they predisposed in a given direction concerning the phenomena? Is the basis on which they are to make judgments clearly specified?

5 Are there any items or factors in the testing instruments that might limit the extent or type of the subject's responses?

Questionnaires and Interviews

1 Content of questions.
   a Is each question sharply delineated to elicit the specific responses required as data?
   b Do the questions cover the decisive features of the needed data?
   c Do any questions ask for information that the respondents do not possess?
   d Are more concrete questions required to obtain an accurate description of the respondent's behavior?
   e Are more general questions required to elicit prevailing attitudes or overall facts?
   f Are the questions colored by personal or sponsorship biases, loaded in one direction, or asked at the improper time?
   g Does each question present a sufficient number of alternative answers to permit all respondents to express themselves properly and accurately?

2 Wording of questions.
   a Is each question short and simple and written in unambiguous, understandable, and nontechnical language?
   b Are any questions misleading because of the absence of important alternative choices, poorly constructed alternatives, improper order, or an inadequate frame of reference?
   c Are stereotyped, prestige-carrying, or superlative words and phrases used that bias the response?
   d Are the questions framed so that they annoy, embarrass, or anger the respondents and cause them to falsify their answers?
   e Would a more or less personalized wording of the questions better elicit the desired information?

3 Sequence of questions.
   a Do initial questions "set the stage" for those that follow and aid

in the recall of ideas, or do they make subsequent topics inappropriate and embarrassing?

b Are the questions grouped, ordered, and located so as to arouse interest, to maintain attention, and to avoid resistance?

c Are follow-up questions or "probes" necessary?

4 Form of responses.

a Should the responses be obtained in a form requiring a check, a word or two, a number, or a free answer?

b What is the best type of check question to ask—dichotomous, multiple-choice, or scale?

c Are the directions concise and clear, located next to the point of application, and made easy to follow by the inclusion of properly placed blank spaces, columns, or boxes? Are any illustrations necessary?

d Is the instrument structured to facilitate the tabulation of data?

e Are the multiple-choice responses arranged randomly?

f Was a random sample of nonresponding subjects checked to determine whether their answers differed from those who did respond?

5 Pretesting the instrument.

a Was the questionnaire pretested?

b Was a clear explanation of the purpose of the study and the specific intent of each question given during the pretesting period?

c After redrafting the wording of the proposed instrument, was the reliability of the responses checked?

Collection and Presentation of Data

1 Was a decision made about how to order and break down the data early in the investigation?

2 Are the classification categories sufficiently comprehensive and specific? Are any unnecessary data presented? Is the amount of data collected adequate? Are the methods employed to treat data appropriate?

3 Were the interviewers, observers, or scorers biased because they had access to information about the previous behavior of subjects?

4 Were precautions taken to collect and record data objectively and accurately? Were procedures and results checked for errors made when observing phenomena, making mathematical computations, selecting or carrying out experimental or statistical procedures, or copying quotations, dates, names, or any data?

5 Were source materials examined critically for authenticity and credibility? Are sources given for theories and facts taken from other reports so that the readers can examine them themselves? Are all source materials paraphrased accurately?

6 Are drawings, charts, diagrams, graphs, tables, or photographs used when they can convey ideas most effectively?

7 Do the tables and figures conform to the rules for constructing "good" ones? Do they present the evidence accurately—without distortion or misrepresentation?

8 Are line symbols rather than color variations used to identify lines on a graph if the report is to be reproduced by photographic processes?

9 Does the textual presentation conform to recognized standards of formal English and to the prescribed style and format? Is the discussion unambiguous? Are transitional words, sentences, and paragraphs inserted to clarify the relationship between items?

10 Was the level of statistical significance reported for findings that involved comparisons between groups or relationships between variables?

Analysis and Discussion of Data

1 Is the evidence collected to test each deduced consequence of a hypothesis adequately and logically analyzed?

2 Is the analysis objectively stated and free from mere opinion and personal prejudices?

3 Have broad generalizations been made without sufficient evidence to support them? Are the generalizations carefully qualified?

4 Does the analysis contain any contradictions, inconsistencies, or misleading, vague, or exaggerated statements?

5 Is any evidence omitted or ignored that does not agree with the hypothesis?

6 Is attention called to unpredicted relations as well as the hypothesized relations in the data?

7 Does the research relate the findings to previous research and, if possible, carry the inferences concerning relationships in the data to a higher level of generalization or theory?

8 Are uncontrolled factors that may have affected the results discussed?

9 Have any weaknesses in the data been honestly admitted and discussed?

10   Are statistical significances interpreted properly?

Summary and Conclusions

1   Are the summary and conclusions concisely and precisely stated?
2   Are the conclusions justified by the data gathered?
3   Are the conclusions qualified to show the limits (nature of sample, methods, etc.) within which they apply?
4   Do the summary and conclusions recapitulate the information presented in previous sections of the report, or has the mistake been made of introducing new data?
5   Are the conclusions stated in terms that make them verifiable?
6   Does the researcher state specifically what empirically verifiable evidence has been produced to confirm or disconfirm the hypothesis?
7   Does the researcher make a concluding statement in which he accepts or rejects the hypothesis?
8   Does the study report any new questions that arose and that should be investigated?

Bibliography and Appendix

1   Do the style, content, and arrangement of the bibliography meet the requirements of the readers for whom the report was written?
2   Are all entries in the bibliography placed in the proper order?
3   Does each entry contain all the necessary items of information, and are the items ordered properly, spelled correctly, and punctuated accurately?
4   Is all cumbersome or voluminous supporting material—test forms, raw data, personal communications—located in the appendix? Has any unnecessary material been placed in the appendix?
5   Are the items in the appendix grouped in homogeneous sections with appropriate headings?

Report Format and Style

1   Is the report neat, attractive, and divided into appropriate sections or chapters?
2   Is the report ordered according to the format required by the professor, institution, or periodical?
3   Are concise, descriptive headings used?
4   Is the report free from padding with irrelevant words, phrases,

quotations, statistics, examples, and other data that are not essential for accuracy, clarity, or completeness?
5   Are concrete, familiar words and short, direct sentences used whenever possible?
6   Has an approved style been followed consistently throughout the report? Has a careful check been made of spacings, margins, quotations, footnotes, tables, figures, bibliography, appendixes, headings, abbreviations, capitalization, punctuation, indentions, and the enumeration of items?
7   Are the drawings and graphs prepared in the proper manner to ensure satisfactory reproduction?
8   Are major topics developed insufficiently or are minor ones overexpanded?
9   Does the report require an index?

Abstract

1   Does an abstract accompany the report?
2   Is the abstract prepared in accordance with the institution's or periodical's standards for style and form?
3   Does the abstract cover the principal points: statement of problem, hypotheses, procedures, results, and conclusions?
4   Is the abstract under the maximum number of words in length?

PUBLICATION

After devoting months to an investigation and accepting the assistance of many people, you should observe the academic tradition of publishing your findings. But you cannot get an article printed in a professional journal or book unless you know something about publishers and the procedures involved in preparing manuscripts for them.

Types and Standards of Publishers

Various agencies publish the work of researchers. Professional associations print many studies in an abstract form in their journals every year. Some professional organizations and philanthropic foundations produce monographs of outstanding scientific investigations, and university presses print a few studies of special merit. From time to time, other agencies publish pertinent reports in their area of interest.

Most publishers do not offer remuneration for reports; indeed, some journals require a payment for publication privileges. Because an increasing number of investigations are undertaken each year, journal space is at a premium today. The rising costs of publication, moreover, prohibit the reproduction of many studies in their entirety. One attempt to solve this problem has been made by establishing a private nonprofit organization, the American Documentation Institute (ADI).[1] After depositing the basic data with the ADI, you submit your report to a journal without including the long tables and other items on which your analysis is based. In a footnote to your report, you indicate that a microfilm or photocopy of the complete material may be obtained from the ADI for a nominal fee.

Since the nature, style, and quality of reports accepted by various journals differ, you must evaluate journals to determine which one publishes the type and level of study you have to submit. After selecting a reputable journal, you should become thoroughly familiar with the editor's manuscript criteria. These criteria are usually published in the journal periodically, but if they are not, an examination of a few recent issues will reveal the editor's preferences in regard to the nature, length, and organization of the articles, as well as methods of referencing. To ignore these manuscript requirements is most imprudent. Writing a 1,000-word report for a journal that limits articles to 600 words or neglecting to follow the required organizational pattern can lead only to a rejection slip or a request for drastic revisions.

Preparation for Publication

Writing for publication sometimes requires considerable work in addition to the preparation of the original dissertation. You do not have many prepublication duties if your study is reproduced on microfilm or microcards, which is a common practice. You may have to recast your study somewhat before publishing it—in monograph form, which is sometimes done, or in book form, which is rarely done. If you write an abstract of your study or present your findings in a journal article, you have to compress the contents of your entire report into relatively few pages.

An abstract, for example, may be limited to 600 words. Thus, you must strip the key ideas from your original manuscript—largely from the summary and conclusions—and express them in clear, crisp

[1] Auxiliary Publication Project, Photoduplication Service, Library of Congress, Washington, D.C.

sentences. You also revise your format and style to conform with the publisher's requirements. Preparing a report for a journal involves somewhat similar tasks, but more pages may be devoted to the discussion. Because a doctoral dissertation contains considerable substance, the contents may be divided to produce two or more journal articles of eight to fifteen double-spaced pages in length. Descriptions of master's theses are usually confined to a single journal article a few pages in length.

After pruning and polishing a report to meet the exacting requirements of editors, you number the pages consecutively from start to finish and fasten them together with paper clips. Then you slip them unfolded into an envelope and sometimes, for protection, add a piece of cardboard that is slightly larger than the material—particularly if photographic prints or drawings intended for halftone reproductions are included. After inserting a letter in the envelope which explains that the article is being submitted for possible publication, you mail it to the editors. To protect yourself against loss, you insure the mailed manuscript and place a carbon copy of it in your files.

Before a report is published, you may have to obtain written permission from the copyright holders to use quotations, graphic materials, and speeches. Your letters requesting authorization to reproduce material must identify each item precisely and explain how it is to be employed. Replies to these letters must be kept in the author's or publisher's files for later reference in case questions arise. A copyright may also have to be obtained for the report itself, particularly if it is in book form. This task is usually performed by the publisher, but you may reserve the right to apply to the Register of Copyrights, Library of Congress, and obtain it for yourself.

Reviews and Revisions

When editors receive your manuscript, they may send you a brief note of acknowledgment, but aside from that they do not communicate with you for several weeks. In the interim, qualified specialists serving on the editorial board review the article and decide whether to accept it, reject it, or request that certain revisions be made. A manuscript may be rejected for several reasons: because the work lacks merit, the work is unsuitable for the particular journal, or the publisher has a backlog of articles. A report that is rejected is not necessarily unworthy and may be submitted to another publisher. It is unethical, however, to submit a paper to more than one journal at a time.

A conditionally accepted report is returned to you with suggestions for improvements. The editors may recommend that certain points be expanded or omitted, question the accuracy of statements, point out passages that need clarification, suggest changes in organization and literary form, or note inconsistencies in style. Requests for revisions should challenge rather than discourage the author. Not all the editor's suggestions have to be accepted, but each one should be given serious consideration.

When making changes in the manuscript, the insertions are printed or written legibly. Insertions are never placed in the margin, for the margins are reserved for instructions to the printer. To indicate an insertion, a caret ($\wedge$) is placed at the proper point in the copy and the additional material is written horizontally in the space above—never below—the caret. Long insertions may be typed on small slips of paper and taped to the margin of the copy near the line containing the caret. Material that is to be shifted to another page may be crossed out, retyped, and inserted in the proper place, or the material may be circled and labeled "tr. to p. 16." If the latter is done, the place where it belongs is indicated on page 16 by inserting a caret in the proper place and above it the note, "tr. from p. 5." When material is to be deleted and none added, the unwanted characters are merely crossed out. Revisions of a few sentences in length may be typed on small slips of paper and pasted over deleted materials in the copy.

Galley and Page Proofs

After returning the revised manuscript to the editor, several months may elapse before you receive the galley proofs of your article and the cut dummies (if any) of the engraver's proofs. The galley proofs are long sheets of paper that contain about three normal pages of print and no illustrations or page numbers. You compare the galley proofs with your manuscript and correct any errors. This proofreading task is exacting work that must be done with scrupulous care. You do not merely scan the article to make certain that the copy makes sense. To detect inaccuracies or omissions, you check each character, word, and line. If possible, you follow the galley proof as someone slowly reads aloud from the manuscript. The reader spells out all proper names and technical terms and reads out punctuation marks, italics, paragraph breaks, decimal points, prime marks, and other departures from ordinary type. Particular attention is given to tables, figures, dates, and quotations. Proofreading is done twice if time permits, for the second reading is almost certain to reveal additional errors.

Because a typesetter does not look for corrections in the body of the galley proof unless there is a proofreader's mark in the margin, you must study these standard symbols until you can automatically apply and interpret them. When correcting a galley proof, you communicate your ideas to the editor and typesetter by placing the appropriate symbol in the left or right margin, whichever is nearer the error, and on the same line as the error. When more than one error appears on a line, the corrections are written consecutively from left to right and separated one from another by a slanted line. All notes or queries to the editor or typesetter are circled to indicate that they are not to be set in type. To restore something that has been crossed out, a row of dots is placed under the deleted material, and in the margin the delete sign is crossed out and "stet" (let it stand) is added. When proofreading, the writer utilizes a number of other symbols in much the same manner. Some of the standard symbols are given below.

Insertions, Deletions, Spacing

ℐ//	Delete words or ~~the~~ letters mar~~r~~ked.
the/h	Insert the word or ∧letter in t∧e margin.
#	Insert space between∧words.
⌒	Close up sp⌒ace.

Paragraphing and Punctuation

¶	∧Make new paragraph.
No ¶	No paragraph—run in or on.
⊙	Insert period. (Sixty children participated∧)
∧//	Insert comma. (Smith∧John∧and Valois, Jean)
∨̇ / ∨̇	Insert quotation marks. (Explain the∧mechanism∧of the mind.)
∨	Insert apostrophe. (The teacher∧s equipment was good.)
-/ or =/	Insert hyphen. (ten∧volume encyclopedia)

Type

∧2	Insert inferior figure or letter subscript. (H∧SO$_4$)
2∨	Insert superior figure or letter superscript. (Lee[1] and Ogg∧ conducted studies.)
Caps	SET IN <u>capitals</u>.

Type (cont'd)

Cap	capital letter required.
lc	Use lower-Case letter.
ital.	Set in _italic_ type.
9	Turn a reversed letter.
×	Replace broken type.
lf	Set in (lightface) type.
bf	Set in boldface type.

Position

tr //	Transpose of order words or letters.
⌒	Elevate letters or words. (John ⌐and⌐ Mary)
⌣	Lower letters or words. (John ⌐and⌐ Mary)
ctr	⌐ Center on page or line. ⌐
⌐	Move to right. ⌐
⌐	⌐ Move to left.
//	Align type vertically.
=	Straighten line horizontally. (He gree ted the crow d.)

Miscellaneous

1942 / (?)	Query to author. (In 1952 Hitler delivered the speech.)
stet	Let all words above dots in sentence stand as they are.
(sp)	Spell out. (Tests were given to (20) children.)
⊥	Push down a space that prints.
⌐	Mark off or break; start new line.

   When checking the cut dummies of the engraver's proofs, you make certain that no figure has been placed upside down and that no items have been omitted. In the margin of the galley proof, you indicate near which passage the printer is to place a figure. (For example, you write in the margin of galley 5, "Insert Fig. 2 here" and then jot the number of that galley, "gal. 5," below Fig. 2 in the cut dummy.) Before returning the galley and engraver's proofs to the publisher, you must answer all the typesetter's and editor's queries and supply any missing materials, captions, or credit lines. An editor usually writes a lengthy query on a small colored piece of paper and attaches it to the side of the galley. A brief editorial query is written in the margin of the galley, and a slanted line and circled question mark are placed after the suggested change. To accept a suggested change, you cross out the question mark; to reject it, you cross out the whole query.

Making alterations in the galley proofs other than the correction of printer's errors is extremely expensive. Merely inserting a word may require resetting the type for the rest of the paragraph. Because you may have to pay the charges for these alterations, you should endeavor to submit a perfect manuscript. If changes in the galley proof are necessary, making deletions and additions so that they fill the same amount of space as the original materials will hold costs to a minimum.

After the editor and author have carefully checked the galley proofs, they return them to the typesetter. He corrects all the marked items and then breaks the type into page lengths, inserts the footnotes, places the illustrations where they belong, and adds the chapter titles, running heads, and page numbers. Copies of the page proofs and the dead galley proofs are then sent to the editor, who examines them to determine whether all the errors have been corrected and no new errors have been introduced as a result of the resets or addition of new materials. Journal page proofs are not usually sent to the author for an additional check, but book page proofs are. Some duties, such as inserting the page numbers for cross-reference citations and preparing an index, cannot be performed until you have the page proofs. Upon receiving either the galley or page proofs, you should process them promptly, or you will upset the production schedules of editors and printers.

The rewarding moment comes when you first read your report in print. The publication of a book or article climaxes a prolonged period of cooperative effort on the part of the author, editors, and printers. After an article is submitted, several months may pass before it is published, and a book may be in production for a couple of years. Because many would-be authors do not realize how much work is involved in transforming a manuscript into print, they fail to allot sufficient time for this task. When manuscripts are returned to them, they resent reviewers' criticisms, revise materials reluctantly, or become too discouraged to continue writing. If their articles are accepted, they often do a superficial job of proofreading and disregard the editor's concern about meeting deadlines and printing schedules.

The exacting process of preparing a manuscript for publication may seem burdensome, but these revisions and checks are essential for the production of a worthwhile report. Maintaining a high level of performance in this final stage of your work is of utmost importance, for a carefully conducted investigation may be disregarded by other scholars if the public account of it is poorly prepared. Since you are judged by the quality of your report, you should expend the effort necessary to publish a work that meets the highest standards of scholarship.

APPENDIX A AN EXAMPLE OF CONSTRUCTING A THEORETICAL FRAMEWORK

n the past much research work was devoted to isolated studies. To advance the frontiers of knowledge, strong pleas have been made in recent years for the development of theoretical frameworks or models in various areas of knowledge that will stimulate, guide, and integrate research work. A study made of the characteristics of teachers serves as an example of one attempt to do this.

Over the years, information relative to teacher characteristics has been accumulated in an unsystematic manner with little attention given to building a theory of teacher behavior. Ryans[1] and his associates have taken steps in this direction. He states that his proposals "do not constitute a complete inventory of all assumptions required for a theory of teacher behavior. Nor is any particular claim made at this point for theoretical rigor. But if in the area of teacher behavior there are advantages in resolving and systematizing our thinking, a starting point is necessary regardless of how tentative it may be."

[1]David G. Ryans, *Characteristics of Teachers*, Washington, D.C.: American Council on Education, 1960, pp. 13–26.

To develop a systematic theory, Ryans defined the term "teacher behavior," stated the two major assumptions necessary for a theory of teacher behavior, and listed a number of implications or subassumptions (postulates) relating to each of them. From this theoretical framework he proceeded to make several propositions concerning teacher behavior in general terms that researchers could convert into exact and testable hypothesis form.

Definition

Teacher behavior may be defined simply as the behavior, or activities, of persons as they go about doing whatever is required of teachers, particularly those activities which are concerned with the guidance or direction of the learning of others.

Basic Assumptions and Subassumptions

Assumption I: Teacher behavior is a function of situational factors and characteristics of the individual teacher. In setting out to formulate some theory of teacher behavior, the basic assumption might well be expected to bear resemblance to formulations made for similar purposes in connection with learning theory and personality theory. Indeed, in behavior theory, some expression of faith in the reliability, or consistency, of behavior is required. In the present case the basic assumption may be summarized in the proposition that teacher behavior is a resultant of (*a*) certain situational factors and (*b*) certain organismic conditions, and their interaction—or, simply, that teacher behavior is a function of certain environmental influences and the learned and unlearned characteristics of the individual teacher. . . .

Growing out of the basic assumption that teacher behavior is a function of the conditions under which it occurs are a number of implications or subassumptions, which follow.

Postulate I-A: Teacher behavior is characterized by some degree of consistency. One implication of the basic assumption is that teacher behavior (and social behavior, with which education deals) is characterized by some degree of uniformity; that, as Mill put it: ". . . there are such things in nature as parallel cases, that what happens once will, under sufficient degree of similarity of circumstances, happen again. . . ." We are stating simply that teacher behavior (a particular kind of behavior of a particular teacher) is not haphazard or fortuitous, but instead is consistent, or reliable, and therefore is capable of being predicted.

Postulate I-B: Teacher behavior is characterized by a limited number of responses. Another implication of the basic assumption (and perhaps it is so fundamental to scientific theory that it is unnecessary to state it explicitly with respect to teacher behavior) is expressed by Keynes' Postulate of Limited Independent Qualities, which states that:

". . . objects in a field over which our generalizations extend, do not have an infinite number of independent qualities; . . . their characteristics, however numerous, cohere together in groups of invariable connections, which are finite in number. . . ." Accordingly, the number of responses the individual teacher is capable of making, and the number of stimulus situations and organismic variables that may affect a teacher's behavior, are limited. This assumption is important if we hope to predict teacher behavior. It presents the researcher with a "tolerable" problem.

Postulate I-C: Teacher behavior is always probable rather than certain. All human behavior, characterized as it is by variability rather than by *complete* uniformity or consistency, must always be considered in the light of probability instead of from the standpoint of invariable cause-effect relationships. The error component resulting from such variability will inevitably be present in any assessment that is attempted of either (*a*) situational or stimulus conditions, (*b*) organismic conditions (genetic bases, past experience, motivation), or (*c*) teacher behavior (the dependent variable, or criterion). Behavior can be predicted only with varying degrees of probability.

Postulate I-D: Teacher behavior is a function of personal characteristics of the individual teacher. Teacher behavior is determined in part by the teacher's personal and social characteristics (e.g., in the intellectual, emotional, temperamental, attitudinal, and interest domains), which have their sources in both the genetic (unlearned) and experiential (learned) backgrounds of the individual. Knowledge of such characteristics contributes to prediction, within limits, of teacher behavior.

Postulate I-E: Teacher behavior is a function of general features of the situation in which it takes place. Teacher behavior is determined, in part, by general features of the situation in which it has its setting—features which may be observed to be common to situations of a general class and which, therefore, may be distinguished from the unique features of specific teaching situations. Information about such relevant features assists in the prediction, within limits, of teacher behavior.

Postulate I-F: Teacher behavior is a function of the specific situation in which it takes place. Finally, teacher behavior is determined, in part, by unique features of the particular situation in which it has its setting at a particular time. These features vary from situation to situation and contribute to the aspect of teacher behavior which is, to an extent, unique to the particular situation.

Assumption II: Teacher behavior is observable. When we attempt to study teacher behavior, we also make the assumption that teacher behavior may be identified objectively, either by direct observation or by indirect approaches that provide correlative indices of teacher behaviors. Examples of the indirect approaches are the assessment of pupil behavior, the use of tests of teacher abilities and knowledge, and the use of interviews or inventories to elicit expression of teacher preferences, interests, beliefs, and attitudes.

Several implications of this assumption may be noted here in the form of the following postulates.

Postulate II-A: Teacher behaviors are distinguishable. If teacher behaviors are observable, it follows that those with certain features must be capable of being identified and described so as to be distinguished from other teacher behaviors. Some behaviors have certain characteristics in common which constitute generic or core components that may be abstracted to facilitate (*a*) communication of generalized descriptions of those behaviors, and (*b*) the identification of such behaviors in individual teachers. Teacher behaviors can be distinguished under observation.

Postulate II-B: Teacher behaviors are classifiable qualitatively and quantitatively. A second aspect of the assumption of the observability of teacher behavior is that teacher behaviors are classifiable, both qualitatively and quantitatively. A class, or category, of teacher behaviors is simply a grouping of specific behaviors which have many resemblances to one another and relatively few *important* differences. When we find such behavioral analogues, we take them as an indication that still other resemblances may exist, since resemblances in nature tend to go together in fairly large groups (Postulate of Limited Independent Qualities). When behaviors have been grouped together in the light of their resemblances, it becomes possible to abstract the general class description from the descriptions of specific manifestations and thereby provide the basis for a "concept" of teacher behavior of a certain kind and permit greater common understanding of the behavior.

Teacher behaviors that are similar, that have certain resemblances or common elements, may be classified in the same qualitative category. Within any given category, these behaviors may be further assigned to subclasses, which may be treated quantitatively. This is to say that teacher behaviors are subjectable to measurement—albeit approximate measurement. These quantitative subclasses may be of either of two types: (1) those permitting enumeration, or counting, only, or (2) those characterized by continuity and varying as a metric (exemplified at the lowest level of refinement by ordinal subclasses and at successively more refined levels by equal-interval and equal-ratio subclasses). . . .

Postulate II-C: Teacher behaviors are revealed through overt behavior and also by symptoms or correlates of behavior. Teacher behaviors may be revealed, or may be observed, either (1) by the representative *sampling* of specific teacher acts or behaviors, or (2) by specific signs, or indicators, or *correlates*, of the behavior under consideration.

In sampling behavior, we assume that the performance of the individual during the behavior sample is approximately (and at some level of probability) representative of the larger aspects, or universe, of his behavior. In judging behavior from signs or correlates, it is assumed that a behavior can be inferred or estimated approximately, in probability terms, from observed correlates of that behavior—from phenomena that are known to have been associated with that behavior in the past.

Some Propositions and Hypotheses

From the standpoint of the Teacher Characteristics Study, the foregoing definition and basic assumptions, together with their implications, provide a theoretical framework and starting point from which the researcher might reasonably proceed to propositions regarding teacher behavior—propositions that may be employed as hypotheses and tested against empirical data.

The number of descriptive classifications and specific propositions which might be generated with regard to teacher behavior is almost limitless, although we probably would not be interested in all such hypotheses even if it were possible to assemble them. Some classifications and some hypotheses seem more relevant than others. No doubt many of them could be incorporated in existing research designs and tested to determine their probable acceptability. . . .

Tests of a number of hypotheses about teacher classroom behaviors and other teacher characteristics were attempted by the Teacher Characteristics Study, and a major portion of this volume is given to reporting the data that were collected for these tests. It is not appropriate to list in this chapter—which deals with general theory of teacher behavior and problems related thereto—all the propositions of hypotheses which guided the research of the project. However, to illustrate the kind of propositions which may grow out of the basic assumptions and postulates stated earlier, a few of those to which the staff of the Teacher Characteristics Study gave attention are listed below.

Proposition: General classes of teacher classroom behaviors fall into relatively homogeneous clusters characterized by substantial intercorrelation of behaviors within a cluster. Teacher behavior *in toto* may be described in terms of a limited number of such major clusters of behaviors.

Proposition: The major clusters or families formed by teacher behaviors have the characteristics of *dimensions*. Individual teachers, in their manifestations of a particular behavior pattern, vary along a continuum between two behaviorally describable poles.

Proposition: Reliable estimates of teacher behavior constituting a major cluster (positions along a major dimension) may be obtained through assessments derived from the observations of trained observers.

Proposition: The classroom behavior of a teacher with respect to a major dimension, as represented by assessments made by trained observers, is characterized by substantial stability over considerable periods of time.

Proposition: The extent of intercorrelation among major dimensions of teacher behavior varies for different subpopulations of teachers, such as elementary teachers and secondary teachers.

Proposition: Correlates scales may be developed, using paper-and-pencil responses of teachers as indicators which will permit the indirect estimation of various kinds of teacher characteristics such as social attitudes, educational viewpoints, verbal ability, and emotionality.

Proposition: Teacher characteristics of the type described in the preceding proposition, as revealed by *correlates* in the form of paper-and-pencil responses of teachers to questions about their preferences, activities, and the like, are consistent and stable over substantial periods of time.

Proposition: Different subpopulations of teachers, classified according to grade level and subject matter taught, differ significantly in teacher characteristics.

Proposition: Certain teacher characteristics vary with the age of the teacher.

Proposition: Certain teacher characteristics are correlated with grades or marks earned by the teacher when in college.

Proposition: Certain teacher characteristics are related to the earlier youth activities of the teacher.

For some of these propositions there is considerable evidential support. For others considered by the Teacher Characteristics Study, lack of statistical corroboration or, equally often, absence of adequate controls, indicates that rejection, or at least suspended judgment, is in order. These findings are discussed in later chapters.

APPENDIX B AN EXAMPLE
OF HYPOTHESIS CONSTRUCTION

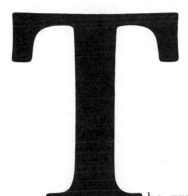he problem of constructing hypotheses often perplexes students, and most examples in the literature are too complex for them to understand. Perhaps the following article,[1] which informally explores a problem area in mental health and proposes several hypotheses, will provide a general understanding of the process. The article is written primarily for classroom teachers and does not present as rigorous an analysis of the problem and as precise statements of the hypotheses as the researcher employs. But it does reveal the types of explorations and explanations that investigators make in the early stages of problem evolvement.

Most classroom teachers are concerned about the mental health of their students for at least two reasons: they know that the level of interpersonal adjustment of the student has an effect on his level of academic learning, and they accept the *health* of the student as being important in its own right. This discussion of group mental health—the mental health of children in the classroom group—is intended especially for the classroom

[1]Allen Menlo, "Mental Health within the Classroom Group," *School of Education Bulletin, University of Michigan*, 31 (May 1960): 121.

teacher. His job is essentially that of a group worker; and as such, he needs to have the understandings and skills essential to hygienic group management.

What follows, then, is an attempt to explore three questions which appear to be basic to an understanding of classroom mental health:

1. What differentiates a mentally healthy from a mentally unhealthy classroom—at least, as far as experience appears to indicate?
2. What kinds of things tend to influence the level of mental health in the classroom—at least, as far as human relations research appears to indicate?
3. What hypotheses, then, can be drawn regarding the management of mental health in the classroom—at least, as far as they sound psychologically reasonable?

Question 1 asks how we can assess the level of mental health in a classroom. Practically, the question asks for an identification of those dimensions along which one must observe in order to evaluate or judge the level of mental health within the classroom group. Four dimensions are suggested.

The amount of acceptance or rejection within the group. This refers to the extent of positive or negative effect in the classroom, or the degree of friendly versus unfriendly atmosphere. This is the kind of thing teachers find out by doing a sociometric study on how much class members like each other, how much they think others like them, how much they like the teacher, how much they think the teacher likes them, and how much the teacher actually likes them. The assumption here is that the predominance of accepting attitudes and behaviors is healthier than the predominance of rejecting ones.

The amount of cooperative action or aggression within the group. This refers to the extent of active or passive movement with or against others, or the degree of helping versus force, threat, coercion, or harm. Teachers find this out when they ask students questions on how much they perceive themselves, other children, and the teacher as either being pushed around or pushing others around. The assumption here is that the predominance of cooperative actions is healthier than the predominance of aggressive actions.

The amount of involvement in or withdrawal from the class process. This refers to the extent of active or passive movement toward or away from others, or the degree of participation versus self-isolation and escape. Teachers assess this when they look for how much children appear to be, or feel they are, a part of the classroom experience. Here the assumption is that the presence of student involvement is healthier than the presence of withdrawal.

The amount of feeling of comfort or anxiety in the class. This refers to the extent of feelings of "at ease" or tension, or the degree of calm versus nervous feelings and behaviors. One way teachers evaluate this is by providing opportunities for students' expressions of happiness or unhappiness with respect to class procedures, other students, the teacher, and the general class situation. The assumption is that a predominance of feelings of comfort is healthier than one of anxiety.

Question 2 calls for a definition of the conditions which may influence a classroom group toward the manifestation of these symptoms. The findings of several studies strongly indicate a causative realtionship between the exposure of human beings to certain conditions and their resultant demonstration of certain behaviors and attitudes consistent with the four sets of symptoms mentioned above. Specifically, these relationships are as follows:

When communication is cut off between people, they tend to develop misperceptions, misunderstanding, and even hostilities regarding and toward each other. When communication is open, people tend to develop realistic perceptions and positive feelings between each other.

When people have a perception of shared objectives, a feeling of cohesiveness, and see each other in a "good light," their contacts tend to produce accepting and mutually supportive attitudes and behaviors toward each other. People's contacts under conditions of uncommon objectives, lack of a spirit of "we-ness," and seeing each other's "poorer" side tend to produce unaccepting, nonsupportive attitudes and behaviors toward each other.

A highly restrictive style of leadership control tends to produce aggressive, scapegoating, and drop-out types of behaviors and attitudes among people. Less restrictive leadership control tends to produce cooperative, noncritical, and stay-in types of behaviors and attitudes.

People tend to get more involved in an experience when they participate in the planning of it, have opportunity to express their feelings about it, hear others' feelings about it, and have some active responsibility in carrying it out. People tend to resist those experiences in which they have no share in the planning, expression of feelings, or responsibility for implementation.

People tend to be attracted toward and feel more involved in activities which they see as having good chances of satisfying their own needs. People tend not to be attracted toward and not feel involved in activities which they see as having a poor chance of satisfying their own needs.

People tend to feel comfortable and secure in situations when they perceive themselves as having value and perceive others as representing friendly forces toward them. People tend to feel uncomfortable and insecure in situations when they perceive themselves as having minimal value and perceive others as representing unfriendly forces toward them.

The answers to the first two questions have described, thus far, the manifestations of healthy versus unhealthy socioemotional dynamics in a classroom group and have indicated the conditions which may be partially or wholly causative to these manifestations.

Question 3 is about the implications of all this for the teacher as a practitioner of hygienic group management. These implications follow in the form of hypotheses which are derived, more or less directly, from the foregoing material. These hypotheses are either partially or wholly untested and will probably remain unsubstantiated until teachers at various levels begin to research them within their own classes and schools. In the absence of experimental evidence, the teacher should find it interesting to test these hypotheses with his own classroom teaching-learning experiences.

Hypothesis A. Teachers who jointly plan classroom procedures and learning activities with their students contribute more to the mental health of students than do teachers who refrain from planning with their students.

Hypothesis B. Teachers who provide their students with opportunities for emotional ventilation and expression of feelings about what goes on in class, their peers, their teacher, and themselves contribute more to the mental health of students than teachers who do not make provisions for this.

Hypothesis C. Teachers who make maximum use of student services for leadership in the classroom contribute more to the mental health of students than teachers who give all or most of the services themselves.

Hypothesis D. Teachers who maintain flexible, uncrowded agenda of activity and subject matter in their classrooms contribute more to the mental health of students than teachers who keep a crowded agenda.

Hypothesis E. Teachers who build motivation to learn by interpersonal cooperation in their classrooms contribute more to the mental health of students than teachers who build motivation by interpersonal competition.

Hypothesis F. Teachers who accept, and help their students accept, a wide range or variation in behavior and attitudes in their classrooms contribute more to the mental health of students than teachers who are, and help their students be, critically evaluative of individual differences in behavior and attitude.

The problem of maintaining good mental health in the classroom is one in which teachers are gaining more understanding and skill. Administrative and supervisory personnel are also becoming more intelligently familiar with the needs and the techniques, and their support, encouragement, and assistance do much to help the teacher accomplish his purposes.

APPENDIX C AN EXAMPLE OF DEDUCING THE CONSEQUENCES

educing the consequences of a hypothesis and discovering whether they are observable through appropriate tests is an important responsibility of the researcher. If factual affirmation can be found for one consequent, a hypothesis gains some support. If factual evidence can be found to support several entailed consequents, the cumulative evidence considerably strengthens the confirmation of the hypothesis. Since students often have difficulty in grasping the process of deducing consequences, the following discussion[1] of Newton's "theory" of the composition of white light may provide a helpful illustration.

Observing the colored spectrum which appears when sunlight is refracted in a crystal, Newton conceived the hypothesis that white light is a mixture of rays differing in refrangibility, and that the different colors of the spectrum correspond to the different degrees of refrangibility. This hy-

[1]W. H. Werkmeister, *An Introduction to Critical Thinking*. Lincoln, Nebraska: Johnsen Publishing Company, 1957, p. 585.

pothesis entailed a number of consequents. We can represent the matter in this way:

If white light is a mixture of rays differing in refrangibility, and *if* the different colors of the spectrum correspond to the different degrees of refrangibility,

then (1) rays of different colors cannot come to a focus at the same distance from the lens (and this explains the "blurred" images seen through earlier telescopes);

then (2) for each color there must be a definite and specific amount of refraction and the refrangibility of every color must be constant;

then (3) mixing in a due proportion all the primary colors should produce white light;

then (4) the rainbow can be explained as the result of refraction;

then (5) the "permanent colors of natural bodies" are the result of the reflection of light rays.

Here we have a hypothesis which entails at least five groups of consequents. If all of them are supported by the facts—and, through a series of ingenious experiments, Newton could show that this is the case—then the hypothesis may be said to be confirmed or verified beyond reasonable doubt.

APPENDIX D AN EXAMPLE OF A PRESENTATION OF A PROBLEM

any students raise questions concerning the logical chain of reasoning that runs through the review of the literature, the theoretical orientation of the problem, and the statement of specific problem hypotheses. These excerpts from a study concerning "Classroom Behavior and Underachievement"[1] may provide some helpful insights.

The low scholastic performance of a substantial number of high-ability students is a continuing concern of parents and educators at all levels. The number of studies that have identified and contrasted the characteristics of the underachiever and the matched achiever is impressive. Shaw and McCuen (1960) concluded that underachievement can be identified in the early elementary-school years and increases with age, and Frankel (1960) found that it continues to increase through the senior high school. Battle (1957), Frankel (1960), Spaulding (1960), and Fink (1962) reported significant differences between achievers and underachievers in values, goals,

[1]Hugh V. Perkins, "Classroom Behavior and Underachievement," *American Educational Research Journal*, 2 (January 1965): 1.

This research was supported by Public Health Service Grant MH 07344-01 and by the General Research Board and the Computer Science Center of the University of Maryland. The author gratefully acknowledges the contribution made to this study by Richard M. Brandt, Arianna Claypool, Angus McDonald, Jr., and Johanna C. Van Looy.

self-concepts, and other psychological factors. Bruner and Caron (1959) and Pierce (1960) found that high and low achievers differ significantly in their patterns of motivation, perceptions, and cognitive structuring, with sex differences so striking that the data for boys and girls were interpreted separately. How family values and training patterns, social class, and ethnic origin influence motivation and performance is discussed by Strodtbeck (1958), Rosen and D'Andrade (1959), Frankel (1960), and Pierce (1960).

The purpose of the present study was to identify those student-behavior, learning-activity, teacher-behavior, and teacher-role variables that are related to a lack of academic achievement among high-ability fifth-grade pupils. The development of instruments for measuring these variables is described in an earlier article (Perkins, 1964).

Rationale and Hypotheses

The rationale of this study is based upon the following propositions drawn from perceptual, developmental, personality, and learning theory: (1) An individual responds to a situation in accordance with the way he perceives it. (2) Areas, events, and activities that have special significance for an individual are those that facilitate or threaten his maintenance and enhancement of self. (3) Behaviors that are reinforced tend to be repeated.

It is reasonable to assume that underachievers and achievers differ in the kinds of behavior they find self-enhancing and reinforcing and therefore differ in behavior. This leads to the general hypothesis that underachievers and achievers differ significantly in the proportion of classroom time spent in certain kinds of behavior and to the following two specific hypotheses:

1 Compared with achievers, underachievers spend a significantly greater proportion of their classroom time (a) intent on work in another academic area (WOA), (b) intent on nonacademic work (WNA), and (c) withdrawing (WDL).

2 Compared with underachievers, achievers spend a significantly greater proportion of their classroom time (a) reading or writing (REWR), (b) highly involved in learning activity (HIAC), and (c) working with peers (SWP).

On the other hand, since human-development theory stresses the need of *every* child to relate himself to significant adults, peers, and the situation, there are certain kinds of behavior in which underachievers and achievers will spend about the same proportions of time. The specific hypothesis is as follows:

3 Underachievers and achievers do not differ significantly in the proportion of classroom time spent (a) listening and watching (LISWAT), (b) interacting with the teacher (SWT), or (c) engaging in friendly nonwork interaction with peers (SF).

Also included in this study is a theory of sex differences leading to the following specific hypothesis:

4 Compared with boys, girls spend more classroom time in language activities (REWR) and in social interaction (SWP, SWT, SF); whereas boys are more highly active (HIAC), more involved in other academic and in nonacademic areas (WOA, WNA), and more withdrawn (WDL).

Finally, group-dynamics theory and studies of teacher interaction lead to the following specific hypothesis:

5 Learning activities, work-oriented student behavior, and the teacher roles and kinds of behavior that facilitate learning are positively and significantly related to academic achievement. Those kinds of teacher and student behavior that are less facilitative of learning are negatively associated with academic achievement.

APPENDIX E AN EXAMPLE OF PSYCHOLOGICAL THEORY

xamples of the development of fairly complex hypotheses stated with some degree of precision are difficult to locate in educational literature. Admittedly, there are some relatively simple statements, but to find more sophisticated presentations, one must turn to other fields. The following illustration from the field of psychology[1] presents a theory of error which includes four postulates. Note the care that has been given to the definition of terms, the statement of the postulates, and the deductions derived from one of them.

Definitions

Error: A response other than that appropriate to the motor set present, where this response is appropriate to other parts of the stimulus complex.

Response: Observable striated muscular behavior by the individual.

Motor set: Bodily orientation for the performance of a given behavior, inferred jointly from the instructions given by the experimenter or subject to himself and the physical orientation of the person. We can to some extent get at it by asking the subject what he intends or intended to do, or

[1]R. B. Ammons, "Errors: Theory and Measurement," Kentucky Symposium: *Learning Theory, Personality Theory, and Clinical Research,* New York: Wiley, 1954, p. 142.

by setting up an objective criterion for determining whether or not the physical orientation would allow the performance of the task.

Appropriate response: The response which the individual says he intends or intended to make and for which he is physically oriented is the appropriate response to the motor set. Appropriate responses to other parts of the stimulus complex are those which would be most frequently made if those parts of the stimulus complex were dominant.

Stimulus complex: Various components which make up the stimulus such as stimuli from motor set, specific drive stimuli, and external stimuli. Any of these can be changed relatively independently, changing the stimulus complex.

Dominance of a component of the stimulus complex: A drive stimulus is more dominant as the drive becomes stronger. When the subject is asked to describe a situation, a particular stimulus component is dominant to the extent that it is mentioned earlier in his description. Frequently, this dominance must be inferred from the past history of the individual. The report may not be accurate from the point of view of the experimenter, as in the case of the individual who has always hated a sibling and now reports that his emotion is one of love and affection, yet behaves as if he hated her. . . .

Drive stimuli: Those stimuli characteristically noted by the human organism in connection with hunger, thirst, sex frustration, fear, anxiety, etc. One could infer the presence of such stimuli in terms of strength of drive.

External stimuli: Environmental energies which affect the receptors of the organism. When the organism is oriented in such a way that the receptor can be affected by the energy and the energy is sufficient to stimulate the receptor, stimulation is normally assumed to take place.

Strength of the response tendency: Latency of the response, physical strength of the response, and probability of the response occurring in the presence of or closely following the presence of a given stimulus complex.

Stimulus similarity: Stimulus complexes are similar to the degree that they contain similar components and are relatively less separated along the various discriminable continua.

Strength of drive: Might be the self-rating of the individual or might be inferred from the past history of the individual with respect to the time since drinking, time since eating, number of times a pleasant or unpleasant consequence has followed a particular stimulus complex, etc. Thus drive stimuli can be associated with primary or secondary drives as conceived of by Hull. Emotions are considered to be drives.

Reward: The satisfaction of some need, goal-object consumption, or avoidance of noxious stimulation. . . .

Postulates

Postulate 1: To any stimulus component or complex, there are a number of possible responses. The strengths of the response tendencies differ. Thus there is present a "strength" hierarchy of responses to any given stimulus component or complex. . . .

Postulate 2: The more similar a stimulus component or complex is to another given stimulus component or complex which has regularly elicited a response in the past, the stronger the response of this kind now elicited by the new stimulus. . . .

Postulate 3: The stronger the drive, the stronger the response.

Postulate 4: The components of a given stimulus complex may in isolation elicit different responses. When the components are combined in the stimulus complex, the greater the dominance of a given component and the greater the strength of a given response tendency associated with it, the more likely the stimulus complex is to elicit this response.

Deductions

Deduction 4*a:* If a response has been regularly elicited under a low drive and is now elicited with a high drive of the same kind present, we will observe an increase in "errors," providing the strongest response tendencies to the motor set and the drive are different and that to the motor set is dominant.

Deduction 4*b:* If a response has been regularly elicited under one drive, and the drive is changed to another without alerting the other stimulus components (especially motor set), there will be more errors, providing the appropriate dominant response to the drive-stimulus component from the original drive was the same as that to the motor set, but that to the new drive stimulus is different from that to the motor set, the motor set staying the same.

Deduction 4*c:* To the extent that a single stimulus component dominates the total stimulus complex, the successive responses given by an individual will be more similar to each other.

Strong emotion leads to stereotypy of responses, as does instruction induced "motor set," and the "same" physical stimulation. In free association, problem areas will be talked about more frequently than other areas. In the case of errors, we find that certain kinds are quite frequent, i.e., certain types of slips of the tongue and certain kinds of accidents in the accident-prone person. These errors shoud indicate the life areas in which the person has problems and thus be of diagnostic value to the clinician.

Deduction 4*d:* Other stimulus conditions being approximately equal, if one arouses a feeling about an error he should get real-life responses associated with a similar set, emotion, or drive more quickly than if no feeling is aroused. . . .

APPENDIX F AN EXAMPLE
OF A MODEL

n recent literature of the behavioral sciences, the term "model" has become quite fashionable.[1] As more and more investigators use the term, it has taken on wider and more varied meanings. In general, it entails finding a structure that enables one to present concepts in such a way that researchers can gain useful insights into their phenomena.

Guilford and Merrifield have constructed a model to organize intellectual factors into a system. They define model as a "set of constructs specified in such a way that their formal connections are evident."[2] They depict the structure of intellect in the form of a three-dimensional rectangular solid as seen below, and carefully define their terms.[3]

[1] May Brodbeck, "The Philosophy of Science and Educational Research," *Review of Educational Research*, 27 (December 1957): 436.

[2] J. P. Guilford and P. R. Merrifield, *The Structure of Intellect Model: Its Uses and Implications.* Reports from the Psychological Laboratory, University of Southern California, 24 (April 1960), p. 13.

[3] *Ibid.*, p. 13.

The constructs in this model are the individual abilities, i.e., the cells in the three-dimensional matrix. The formal connections between the constructs are deducible from the categories with the three variables of classification: operation, content, and product. These three are considered as formally independent, so that no combination of operation, content, and product is logically excluded from the system.

The investigators do not consider the model to be perfect and the positions of the factors in it to be permanently fixed. They expect that additional empirical evidence may lead to some changes. They point out that[4]

A model is used as a theory when connections between its constructs and the empirical world are hypothesized. The acceptance of a theory depends upon the verification of such hypotheses. For the structure-of-intellect model to be supported as theory requires two types of verification. First, previously found factors must be confirmed as distinct from each other, when interpreted in terms of their location in the model. Second, new factors must be hypothesized from the model, and their separate existences verified.

At present the investigators are testing "whether unknown unique abilities that are predicted by the model do in fact exist as distinguishable entities."[5] The model has been used "as a basis for a rough consideration of problems of curriculum in education, in relation to teaching of reading, and as a basis for a systematic orientation with respect to psychological tests."[6]

Definitions   The major concepts are labeled in Figure F.1. We shall begin with the kinds of operations and end with the kinds of products, also defining the parameters themselves.

Operations   Major kinds of intellectual activities or processes; things that the organism does with the raw material of information.[7]

Cognition: Discovery, awareness, rediscovery, or recognition of information in various forms; comprehension or understanding.

Memory: Retention of information in any form.

Divergent production: Generation of information from given information, where the emphasis is upon variety of output from the same source.

Convergent production: Generation of information from given infor-

----

[4] *Ibid.*, p. 13.

[5] *Ibid.*, p. 2.

[6] *Ibid.*, p. 3.

[7] "Information" is defined in a later section of this report as "that which the organism discriminates."

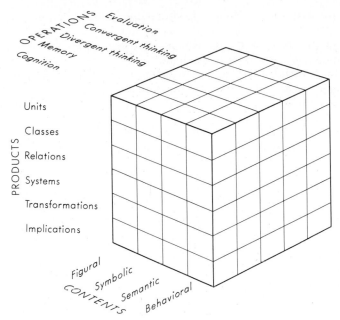

FIGURE F.1

Guilford's structure-of-intellect model.

mation, where the emphasis is upon achieving unique or conventionally accepted or best outcomes.

Evaluation: Reaching decisions or making judgments concerning the goodness (correctness, suitability, adequacy, desirability) of information in terms of criteria of identity, consistency, and goal satisfaction.

Contents   General varieties of information.

Figural content: Information in concrete form, as perceived or as recalled in the form of images. The term "figural" implies some degree of organization or structuring.

Symbolic content: Information in the form of signs, having no significance in and of themselves, such as letters, numbers, musical notations, etc.

Semantic content: Information in the form of meanings to which words commonly become attached, hence most notable in verbal thinking; involved in doing verbal tests, where the things signified by words must be known.

Behavioral content: Information, essentially nonverbal, involved in human interactions, where awareness of the attitudes, needs, desires, intentions, thoughts, etc. of other persons and of ourselves is important.

Products   Results from the organism's processing of information.

Units: Relatively segregated or circumscribed items of information having "thing" character.

Classes: Aggregates of items of information grouped because of their common properties.

Relations: Recognized connections between units of information based upon variables that apply to them.

Systems: Organized or structured aggregates of items of information; complexes or interrelated or interacting parts.

Transformations: Changes in existing or known information or in its use, as in production.

Implications: Extrapolations of information, in the form of expectancies, predictions, antecedents, and consequents.

APPENDIX G AN EXAMPLE
OF A RESEARCH REPORT

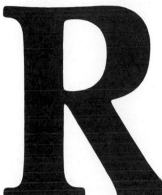esearch reports are written in a formal
style. The division of the contents may vary somewhat, depending on
the nature of the problem and the requirements of the institution or
publisher, but all research reports conform to the same general pattern.[1]
Below is the study which was discussed in Chapter 10.

The relationship of lateral dominance to reading achievement has been the
subject of recurring study for many years. Three important theoretical
formulations have guided much of this research. Dearborn (1931) found
that a preponderance of the children who were referred to a reading clinic
were left-eyed, or lacked ocular and manual dominance, or had mixed
dominance. He believed these conditions to be associated with reading
difficulty because it seems logical that people who have them will tend to
approach a word from the wrong direction.

Monroe (1932) suggested that in moving the eyes to the right, as is
required in reading, the left field of vision is obstructed by the bridge of the
nose, and consequently the development of left-to-right eye movements
may be more difficult for the left-eyed child. She also suggested that a
child who has opposite eye-hand dominance may prefer different direc-

[1]Irving H. Balow and Bruce Balow, "Lateral Dominance and Reading Achievement in the Second
Grade," *American Educational Research Journal*, 1 (May 1964): 139.

tional movements for eye and hand, and therefore find the complex hand-eye coordinations necessary in space perception difficult.

Harris (1957) found mixed hand preference much more common in a clinical group of disabled readers than in the general school population. He suggested that this lack of consistent hand preference may be the result of a special maturational difficulty or slowness.

Balow (1963), working with 302 first-grade children, studied the effect on three measures of reading achievement of these various types and degrees of hand and eye dominance, singly and in interaction: strong, moderate, and mixed hand dominance; normal, crossed, and mixed dominance; and directional confusion. He reasoned that if these characteristics are associated with reading disability, they are also associated with reading achievement in the first grade. Yet, he found no combination of hand dominance and eye dominance, hand-eye dominance and knowledge of right and left, or strength of dominance and knowledge of right and left significantly associated with reading achievement.

The problem considered in this study is whether the dominance anomalies specified by Dearborn, Harris, and Monroe are significantly associated with reading achievement in the second grade.

Procedure

The sample of first-grade children selected by Balow (1963) was retested in the second grade and constituted the sample for this study. The original sample was obtained by listing the first-grade teachers in a middle-class suburb of St. Paul, Minnesota, and assigning a number to each. A table of random numbers was then entered to select 13 teachers. The sample consisted of all children in the classrooms of these 13 randomly selected teachers. Of the original 302 children, 250 were still in the district and completed all the tests. The *Harris Tests of Lateral Dominance* were again administered to those children in the sample who had not established a consistent directional preference in the first grade. Dominance retesting was completed in October and November. The *Gates Advanced Primary Reading Tests* (Word Reading and Paragraph Reading) were administered in February and were used as measures of reading achievement. The IQ scores were secured from the *Lorge-Thorndike Intelligence Tests, Level 1,* which had been administered to these children in the first grade.

Four comparisons were made, all children being utilized in each comparison. The analysis of covariance, with IQ used as a covariate, was used for the tests of significance.

Results

The 250 children were classified according to their hand-eye dominance as follows: normal—those having hand preference and eye preference on the same side of the body; crossed—those having hand preference and eye preference on opposite sides of the body; and mixed—those having mixed hand preference according to the *Harris Tests of Lateral Dominance.* If the views of Dearborn, Harris, and Monroe are valid, the crossed-dominance group and/or the mixed-dominance group should achieve significantly below the normal group in reading achievement.

Table 1 shows the number in each group, the mean raw scores on word reading and paragraph reading, and the mean average grade-equivalent scores on the two tests. Each row of mean scores in Table 1 was tested by the analysis of covariance, with IQ used as an adjusting variable, to determine whether the effect of hand-eye dominance is significant. The largest F ratio (for the word-reading results) was 1.898, which with 2 and 246 degrees of freedom is not significant at the .05 level. The first null hypothesis was therefore accepted. We conclude that in the population of second-grade children of which this sample was representative there is no significant relationship between reading achievement and hand-eye dominance.

To test the second hypothesis, the 250 children were classified according to strength and direction of hand dominance (strong, moderate, or mixed, right or left, as determined by the dominance tests). If mixed dominance, as Harris and Dearborn contend, is an important factor in reading disability, the mixed group in our classification should achieve less than the other two groups. Table 2 shows the number in each group, the mean raw scores on word reading and paragraph reading, and the mean average grade-equivalent scores on the two tests.

Each row of mean scores in Table 2 was tested by the analysis of covariance to determine whether strength of hand dominance or direction of dominance (right or left) is significantly associated with reading achievement. The largest F ratio (.567) was found between adjusted means for the word-reading test and is not significant at the .05 level. The second null hypothesis was accepted. We conclude that in the underlying population neither strength nor direction of hand dominance is significantly associated with reading achievement.

To test the third hypothesis, the children were classified according to strength and direction of eye preference. According to Dearborn and Monroe, the left-eyed child is more likely to have difficulty in learning to read. Table 3 shows the number in each group, the mean raw scores on word reading and paragraph reading, and the mean average grade-equivalent scores for the two tests.

TABLE 1

Mean Scores for Children Classified According to Hand-Eye Dominance

	NORMAL DOMINANCE	CROSSED DOMINANCE	MIXED DOMINANCE
Word reading	31.76	30.08	29.78
Paragraph reading	21.26	20.17	20.96
Average grade equivalent	4.12	3.96	3.98
N	140	87	23

TABLE 2

Mean Scores for Children Classified According to Strength and Direction of Hand Dominance

	STRONG RIGHT	MODERATE RIGHT	MIXED	MODERATE* LEFT
Word reading	31.09	31.06	29.78	31.75
Paragraph reading	20.70	20.74	20.96	22.38
Average grade equivalent	3.99	4.07	3.98	4.25
N	86	125	23	16

*The sample included only two children with strong left dominance. They were included in the moderate left group.

The mean score differences in each row in Table 3 were tested for significance, using the analysis of covariance. The largest F ratio (1.871) was found for the paragraph-reading scores. This value of F is not significant at the .05 level; hence the hypothesis of no difference in achievement between eye-dominance groups was accepted. The data provide no adequate basis for asserting that in the underlying population either strength or direction of eye dominance is significantly associated with reading achievement.

To test the fourth hypothesis, children who had established consistent hand dominance at entrance to first grade were classified in the early-dominance group and those who had not were classified in the late-dominance group. Table 4 shows the number in each classification, the mean raw scores for word reading and paragraph reading, and the mean average grade-equivalent scores. The third column shows the same summary values for the mixed group (who are included in the late-dominance classification). The differences between these groups are smaller than in any of the previous classifications and including the mixed group under late dominance has not appreciably affected the mean scores of that group.

TABLE 3

Mean Scores for Children Classified According to Strength and Direction of Eye Dominance

	STRONG RIGHT	MODERATE RIGHT	MIXED	MODERATE LEFT	STRONG LEFT
Word reading	31.47	29.65	35.47	30.97	29.10
Paragraph reading	21.11	19.39	24.53	20.91	19.76
Average grade equivalent	4.10	3.82	4.54	4.08	3.86
N	114	31	19	35	51

TABLE 4

Mean Scores for Children Classified According to Time of Establishing Hand Dominance

	EARLY DOMINANCE	LATE DOMINANCE	MIXED
Word reading	30.92	31.11	29.78
Paragraph reading	20.79	20.95	20.96
Average grade equivalent	4.04	4.03	3.98
N	151	99	23

The mean scores of the two groups in Table 4 were compared using the analysis of covariance. The largest F ratio (.154) could well have occurred by chance; hence the null hypothesis was accepted. We conclude that establishing consistent hand dominance by the time of entrance into first grade has no significant beneficial effect on reading achievement and failing to establish consistent hand dominance until later has no significant retarding effect on reading achievement.

Discussion and Conclusions

Having the dominant hand and eye on the same side of the body, on opposite sides of the body, or having mixed hand dominance has no significant effect on reading achievement in the second grade. This conclusion adds to the evidence casting doubt upon the validity of the theoretical formulations of Dearborn, Harris, and Monroe when these formulations are extended to randomly selected school children instead of clinic cases of reading disability.

Strength of hand dominance and direction of hand dominance have no significant effect on reading achievement in the second grade.

In this group of 7-year-old children, 9.2 per cent manifested mixed hand dominance. In Harris' group (1957), 18 per cent were classified as mixed hand dominant. Inasmuch as the children in this study average well above the norm in reading achievement, the possibility does exist that in a more nearly average group of children there might be a greater proportion with mixed hand dominance and that mixed hand dominance might be significantly related to reading achievement.

Neither left-eye dominance, mixed eye dominance, nor strength of eye dominance has a significant facilitating or depressing effect on reading achievement in the second grade.

Establishing consistent hand dominance prior to first grade, during the first grade or second-grade years, or not at all, is not significantly related to reading achievement in the second grade.

Lateral dominance does not seem to be a fruitful area for seeking out determiners of individual differences in reading achievement.

References

1 Balow, Irving H. "Lateral Dominance Characteristics and Reading Achievement in the First Grade," *Journal of Psychology* 55: 323–28; April 1963.
2 Dearborn, Walter F. "Ocular and Manual Dominance in Dyslexia." *Psychological Bulletin* 28: 704; November 1931.
3 Harris, Albert J. "Lateral Dominance, Directional Confusion, and Reading Disability," *Journal of Psychology* 44: 283–94; October 1957.
4 Monroe, Marion, *Children Who Cannot Read.* Chicago: University of Chicago Press, 1932. 205 pp.

APPENDIX A.1 STATISTICS:
MEAN AND DEVIATION

ecause a jumbled mass of raw data is confusing and difficult for the eye and mind to grasp, investigators must decide how to organize, reduce, and summarize their data into the most meaningful form. The following statistical techniques will assist them.

FREQUENCY DISTRIBUTION

The entire picture of a set of data is revealed by constructing a frequency distribution table which lists in column X all the possible scores or measures from the highest to the lowest, and, in an adjacent column f, the frequency of the occurrence of each score in the distribution. The pattern of a large number of scores is easier to discern if the total range of scores is grouped into 10 to 20 class intervals, each interval covering the same range of score units. In the chart that follows, for example, the table of ungrouped data on the left, which would be much longer if all of the scores were given, has been reduced to a small table of grouped data on the right with 10 class intervals. The size or width of the *class intervals* is five, $i = 5$.

MEASURES OF CENTRAL TENDENCY

A set of numbers may be made more meaningful by using a single number, such as the average IQ score of a group of students, to indicate the middle of the distribution of scores or the central tendency. The measure of central tendency that is used most frequently is the arithmetic mean. The *mean*,[1] designated as M, is the sum of all the scores (ΣX) divided by the total number of scores (N). For ungrouped data, the formula for the mean is $M = \Sigma X/N$.

Ungrouped Data   Grouped Data

X	f		X	f
109	1	Class interval 105–109	105–109	3
108			100–104	4
107			95–99	7
106	2		90–94	15
105			85–89	20
104	4		80–84	16
103			75–79	10
–	–	Remaining	70–74	6
–	–	78 scores	65–69	4
60	1		60–64	1
N =	86			N = 86

MEASURES OF VARIABILITY

An analysis of the data that goes no further than summarizing a set of scores by describing the mean is inadequate. The mean indicates where the data are clustered, but it does not bring out the variability, spread,

---

[1] In the literature, the mean of a variable (X) is often expressed as $\bar{X}$ (read bar-x) rather than M.

or dispersion of the scores. The most commonly used measures of variability are the variance (σ^2) and standard deviation (σ), but before these measures are explained, you must understand the meaning of deviation.[2] If the mean (M) is 50, no observed score in the distribution need be exactly like the mean. A *deviation,* which is symbolized by x, is the distance between a given score and the mean of the distribution, or x = X − M. The deviation from the mean (x) describes how much in error the mean is as a description of a given score. If the distribution of scores is 62, 60, 58, 42, 40, 38, the mean is 50. If the mean, 50, is subtracted from each raw score, the deviations of the scores from this mean are 12, 10, 8, −8, −10, −12 (see Table A.1).

Calculation of Average Deviation (AD)

The mean is a single number that is used to express the average of the scores in a set. An investigator also needs a single numerical value to express the variability or spread of a set of scores around their central tendency. This value or variability can be obtained by determining the average deviation about the mean. To compute the *average or mean deviation (AD),* an investigator (1) finds the mean of the set of scores, (2) subtracts the mean from each score in the distribution, (3) gets the arithmetic sum of the deviations. (ignores the minus signs), and (4) divides the sum by N (see Table A.1). For ungrouped data,[3] the formula for the average deviation is $AD = \Sigma |(X − M)|/N$, or $AD = \Sigma |x|/N$.

Calculation of Variance (σ^2) and Standard Deviation (σ)

Because the minus signs are ignored in determining the average deviation, the AD cannot be used with the more advanced statistical techniques. Consequently, the measures of variability used by most researchers are the variance (σ^2) and standard deviation (σ). The variance (σ^2) is determined by (1) squaring each of the deviation scores, (2) obtaining the sum, and (3) dividing the sum by N. (See Table A.1.)[4] The squaring eliminates the minus sign, with mathematical propriety, for when two negative numbers are multiplied, the resulting product is a positive number. The variance (σ^2) is much larger than the AD; hence it

---

[2] The symbol σ (sigma) is the Greek equivalent of "small s." In the literature, you will often find σ^2 and σ expressed as s^2 and s and sometimes as d^2 and d.

[3] Bars || enclosing the |(X-M)| indicate that the signs are disregarded in arriving at the sum.

[4] The formula for the variance given here is $\Sigma x^2/N$, for we are concerned only with describing a distribution, but statisticians use N-1 in the denominator of this formula when they are concerned with sampling and inferential statistics.

TABLE A.1

Calculation of the Average Deviation and Standard Deviation

SCORES X	DEVIATIONS FROM MEAN $(x = X - M)$ $x = X - 50$	SQUARED DEVIATIONS x^2
62	12	144
60	10	100
58	8	64
42	−8	64
40	−10	100
38	−12	144
$\Sigma X = 300$	$\Sigma\|x\| = 60$ (ignore	$\Sigma x^2 = 616$
$N = 6$	signs)	
$300 \div 6 = 50$	$60 \div 6 = 10$	$616 \div 6 = 102.66$
M, the mean, is 50.	AD, the average or mean deviation, is 10.	σ^2, the mean of the squared deviation, is 102.66
		σ, the standard deviation (the square root of σ^2, $\sqrt{102.66}$) is 10.14.

is often converted to linear measure by finding the standard deviation. The *standard deviation* (σ) is found by taking the square root of the variance. For ungrouped data, the formula for the standard deviation is $\sigma = \sqrt{\Sigma x^2/N}$.

ASSUMED MEAN METHOD

The methods that have been given to compute M, σ^2, and σ thus far in this chapter differ from the methods statisticians use when they deal with large numbers of grouped scores. The purpose of this text is to give you some concept of the usefulness of statistics rather than to teach you how to compute statistics. A number of elementary textbooks are available that will acquaint you with the rules and various methods of computing statistics. Before the conclusion of this discussion, however, a shortcut method will be presented that does not require the use of a calculator and that can be used to obtain M, σ^2, and σ with grouped data. The formulas look more complicated than those you were given previously, but the arithmetic calculations are much easier.

The Mean by the Assumed Mean Method

In the shortcut method you *assume a mean* in the beginning and then proceed to determine the correction (c) that must be applied to get the actual mean (M).

1   Choosing the assumed mean.

Choose arbitrarily the midpoint value of a class interval, usually near the center of the distribution, for the assumed mean (AM). In Table A.2, the midpoint value chosen for the AM is 37.

2   Coding the deviation scores.

Place in column x' the coded deviations of the midpoint values of the different class intervals. Start by placing a zero opposite the assumed mean; fill in the rest of the column by counting up and down from zero using minus signs for the intervals below zero (see Table A.2). These coded scores are measured from the AM *in units of class interval.*[5] They indicate how many class intervals the midpoint value of a given interval deviates from the AM. (The midpoint of the 35–39 interval, 37, measured from the AM, itself, is zero, and the midpoint of the 40–44 interval, 42, deviates from the AM by one interval, etc.)

3   Decoding the deviation scores and finding the actual mean.

   a.   Fill in the fx' column for each class interval by multiplying the frequency of occurrence of scores by the coded deviation from the assumed mean: $f \times x' = fx'$.

   b.   Obtain c, *the correction in units of class interval* (the mean of the coded deviation values). To do this, find the algebraic sum of the fx' column and divide this sum by N, the number of scores: $c = (\Sigma fx'/N)$ $(c = 25/25 = 1)$.

---

[5]In coding deviations, you actually subtract the assumed mean from the midpoint values of all intervals and proceed to make them smaller by dividing them by the size of the class interval, $x' = (X - AM)/i$. Thus, $(62 - 37)/5 = 5$; $(57 - 37)/5 = 4$; $(52 - 37)/5 = 3$; $(47 - 37)5 = 2$; $(37 - 37)/5 = 0$. In decoding deviations you proceed in reverse; multiply the mean of the coded deviations (c) by the size of the class interval (5) and add the product to the assumed mean (37) to get the actual mean (42), $c \times i + AM = M$.

TABLE A.2

Calculation of the Mean (M), Variance (σ^2), and Standard Deviation (σ) from Coded Grouped Scores

(1) CLASS INTERVALS	(2) MIDPOINT	(3)	(4) CODED DEVIATIONS FROM ASSUMED MEAN	(5)	(6)
	X	f	x'	fx'	fx'^2
60–64	62	1	5	5	25
55–59	57	2	4	8	32
50–54	52	2	3	6	18
45–49	47	4	2	8	16
40–44	42	6	1	6 (+33)	6
35–39	37 (AM)	5	0	0	0
30–34	32	3	−1	−3	3
25–29	27	1	−2	−2	4
20–24	22	1	−3	−3 (−8)	9
		$N = 25$		$\Sigma fx'$ 25	$\Sigma fx'^2$ 113

Size of class
interval $i = 5$

Formula: Mean

$$M = \frac{\Sigma fx'}{N} \times i + AM \text{ or } M = c \times i + AM$$

Computation:

$$M = \frac{25}{25} \times 5 + 37$$

$$M = 42$$

Formula: Variance

$$\sigma^2 = i^2 \left[\frac{\Sigma fx'^2}{N} - \left(\frac{\Sigma fx'}{N}\right)^2 \right]$$

Computation:

$$\sigma^2 = 25 \left[\frac{113}{25} - \left(\frac{25}{25}\right)^2 \right]$$

$$\sigma^2 = 25 [4.52 - (1.00)^2]$$
$$\sigma^2 = 25 \times 3.52 = 88$$
$$\sigma^2 = 88$$

Formula: Standard Deviation

$$\sigma = i \sqrt{\frac{\Sigma fx'^2}{N} - \left(\frac{\Sigma fx'}{N}\right)^2}$$

Computation:

$$\sigma = 5 \sqrt{\frac{113}{25} - \left(\frac{25}{25}\right)^2}$$

$$\sigma = 5 \sqrt{3.52}$$
$$\sigma = 5 \times 1.876 = 9.38$$
or
$$\sigma = \sqrt{\sigma^2} = \sqrt{88} = 9.38$$

c. Obtain ci, *the correction in score units,* by multiplying c by i, the size of the class interval: $ci = c \times i$ (1 × 5 = 5).
d. Obtain the actual mean (M) by adding ci and the assumed mean: $M = ci + AM$ ($M = 5 + 37 = 42$).

Variance and Standard Deviation by the Assumed Mean Method

1 Fill in column fx'^2 by multiplying each x' in column 4 by the corresponding fx' in column 5.[6]
2 Obtain the sum of column 6, $\Sigma fx'^2 = 113$.

[6] $fx'^2 = x' \times fx'$ and you can check the procedure by multiplying $(f) \times (x'^2)$ for each interval.

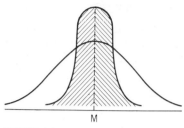

FIGURE A.1*a*

Two distributions with like means but different variability.

3   Substitute this sum (113) for $\Sigma f x'^2$ in the formulas for the variance and standard deviation which are given in Table A.2. In these formulas i = the size of the class interval, which in this instance is 5.

4   Make the necessary computations to obtain the variance ($\sigma^2 = 88$) and the standard deviation ($\sigma = 9.38$).

SUMMARY

Most research problems involve making interpretable comparisons between two or more groups of units at one point in time or between one or more groups of units at two or more points in time. Consequently, an investigator must obtain measures for the two groups that are comparable and must provide information about the ways in which the variables are comparable. The statistical description of the central tendency and variability of a set of scores gives one a sharp perception of the data in a compact form. An investigator who reports the mean should also report the standard deviation or variance, for the mean only informs the reader about one way that two sets of scores are alike. If two groups of students have the same mean IQ of 100, for example, can you assume

FIGURE A.1*b*

Two distributions with like variability but different means.

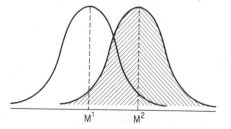

the two groups are alike? Indeed not, for the IQ scores may range from 70 to 120 in Group A and from 95 to 105 in Group B. Obviously, the students in Group B are more homogeneous with respect to IQ than the students in Group A. Figures A.1*a* and A.1*b* illustrate distributions that are alike in one respect but different in other respects. Do these examples help you understand why analyzing the data and solving most research problems would be impossible without computing and reporting both measures of central tendency and measures of variability? A good part of research work consists of comparing variances or standard deviations. To read, design, or do research, one must have a good understanding of various forms of variance. You will be introduced to some of them later in this text.

APPENDIX A.2 STATISTICS: CORRELATION

ur attention thus far has been focused primarily on describing and analyzing the scores on a single variable. But many problems in educational measurement are concerned with the degree to which scores from the same subjects on different variables are related. Hence, you will want to learn how to calculate a correlation coefficient.

THE SELECTION OF A CORRELATION METHOD

In determining the correlation method to employ in a study or how to interpret the findings of a correlation study, you give consideration to several factors: the size of the sample, the distribution of the scores, whether the variables are linearly or curvilinearly related, whether the variables are continuous, dichotomous, or dichotomized, and whether the variables are measured on nominal, ordinal, interval, or ratio scales. The above scales are described on page 109, and the variables are described on page 105.

Assumptions Underlying the Pearson Product-moment Correlation

The Pearson product-moment correlation (r), the most frequently employed method of ascertaining the relationship between two variables, is used when the data fulfill the following assumptions:

1   Linearity of regression is assumed; that is, the paired scores must be distributed in a linear (straight-line) rather than a curvilinear fashion. (Examine Figure A.2a and b.) If r is computed when the variables are curvilinearly related, the extent of the relationship will be underestimated.
2   Homoscedasticity, or homogeneity of variance—an equal scattering of the scores in the rows (and columns) of the scattergram—is assumed. For all Y scores, the distribution of the corresponding X scores should be approximately equal in variability and vice versa. Note the lack of homogeneity of variance in Figure A.2c, where the Y distribution is much less variable for X_1 values than for X_2 values.
3   The distributions of the two variables are assumed to be spread out somewhat symmetrically around a central point. A normal distribution is not required, but the distribution should be unimodal and should not be badly skewed.
4   Both variables are assumed to be continuous (multistep) and to be measured on an interval scale (an ordered scale of equal units) or a ratio scale.

FIGURE A.2

Examples of distributions.

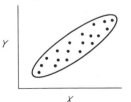
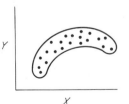

(a) Linear distribution   (b) Curvilinear distribution   (c) Lack of homogenity of variance

5 The sample should be large (more than 30) to obtain the most reliable r.

Other Correlation Methods

When the above assumptions cannot be met, an investigator may use one of the following correlation methods to determine the relationship between variables under the conditions stipulated:

Correlation Ratio (eta or η) determines the relationship between two continuous variables (measured on interval scales) when the data are *curvilinearly* rather than linearly related and the sample is large, such as a physical performance test and chronological age from 7 to 50 years.

Spearman's Rank-difference Correlation Coefficient (rho) determines the relationship between two variables when the scores are arranged into rank orders (measured on ordinal scales) and the sample is small (less than 30), such as 10 girls ranked on leadership and on authoritarianism.

Biserial Correlation Coefficient (r_b) determines the relationship between two rather normally distributed, linearly related, continuous variables, one of which has been dichotomized (reduced to two categories), such as IQ scores (continuous) and mathematics test scores reduced to pass-fail categories.

Point Biserial Correlation Coefficient (r_{pb}) determines the relationship between one continuous variable and one dichotomous (two-category) variable that is not assumed to be continuous and normally distributed, such as spelling test scores (continuous) and sex membership (male-female).

Phi Coefficient (ϕ) determines the relationship between two dichotomous (two category) variables that are assumed to be discrete, such as sex membership (male-female) and residence (on campus–off campus).

Tetrachoric Correlation Coefficient (r_t) determines the relationship between two continuous but dichotomized variables that when continuous are normally distributed and linearly related, such as two tests, each scored pass-fail.

Contingency Coefficient (C) determines the relationship between two variables measured on nominal scales with two or more categories, such as eye color of mothers (brown, blue, hazel) correlated with the handedness of their daughters (left-handed or right-handed).

CALCULATION OF A PEARSON PRODUCT-MOMENT CORRELATION

The Pearson product-moment correlation method, designated r, which is the most commonly employed correlation method, can be computed in different ways. The steps for one procedure, which is used when a calculating machine is not available, are given below. An example of calculating the correlation between the height and weight of 50 subjects is given in Table A.3.

1   The first step is to obtain weight (X) and height (Y) scores for the subjects and to group their scores in pairs.

2   Prepare a two-dimensional frequency table with each distribution, X and Y, labeled and grouped into 10 to 15 class intervals. Place a tally mark in the proper cell in the table for each subject, taking both measurements into consideration. If a subject is 56 inches in height and weighs 95 pounds, place a tally mark in the cell where the 56–57 row and the 90–99 column intersect (see Table A.3).

3   To the right of Table A.3 are six columns in which you will tabulate data about the Y variable, height; below the table are six rows in which you will tabulate data about the X variable, weight.

4   Fill in the frequency (f) scores for each Y interval down column 1 and for each X interval across row 1.

5   In the next three rows and columns, fill in the values necessary to calculate the standard deviation by the assumed mean method.[1] You will recall that you assume a mean in the beginning and later apply a correction (c) to this assumed value (AM) to obtain the actual mean. The prime sign in the coded deviations (x' and y') indicates these deviations are taken from assumed means of the X and Y distributions.

6   Choose arbitrarily an assumed mean at or near the center of the X and of the Y distributions. (Note that the AM, assumed mean, for the weight distribution is taken at 134.5, midpoint of interval 130–139; the assumed mean of the height distribution is taken at 62.5.) In column 2, y', and row 2, x', fill in the coded deviations from the assumed mean by placing a zero opposite the assumed mean, counting up and down from the zero, and using the negative sign where required.

7   Find the algebraic sum of the coded deviation scores by taking the

---

[1]See Appendix A.1, p. 486.

following steps: In column 3, fill in the product of $f \times y'$ for each interval. In row 3, fill in the product of $f \times x'$ for each interval. Obtain the algebraic sum of column 3, $\Sigma fy' = -3$, and of row 3, $\Sigma fx' = -11$. This information about the algebraic sum of the coded deviation scores will be used later to compute c_x and c_y, the corrections in units of interval.

8   Find the sum of the coded deviation scores squared by taking the following steps. In column 4 fill in the product of $f \times y'^2$ or use the simpler procedure of $y' \times fy'$ (that is, multiply the values found in columns 2 and 3). In row 4 fill in the product of $f \times x'^2$ or use the simpler procedure $x' \times fx'$ (multiply the values in rows 2 and 3). Obtain the sum of column 4 and row 4, $\Sigma fy'^2$ and $\Sigma fx'^2$.

9   In column 5 and row 5, you perform a new task: For each person (tally) in a given *height* interval (Y), you find (x'), his coded deviation from the assumed *weight* mean. For each person (tally) in a given *weight* class interval (X) you find (y'), his coded deviation score from the assumed *height* mean. The following instructions require concentration, but they will be easy to follow after you read the example.

    Instruction: To find $\Sigma x'$ values for Y class intervals (column 5) and $\Sigma y'$ values for X class intervals (row 5), multiply the number of tallies in *each cell* of a class interval by its corresponding x' or y'. Sum the products for each class interval and record the answers in column 5 or row 5. Find the sum of all products in column 5, $\Sigma fx'$, and find the sum of all products in row 5, $\Sigma fy'$.

    Example: To calculate $\Sigma x'$ values for column 5 in our height and weight correlation problem, begin with the Y class interval 72–73 inches, which has one tally in one cell. The corresponding x' for that tally, which is found in *row* 2 below the cell, is 5, and $1 \times 5 = 5$, which you record in *column* 5. Having found $\Sigma x'$ (the sum of the deviations from the assumed weight mean) for the 72–73 inches height interval is 5, proceed to make the calculations for the remaining class intervals. When you get to the 68–69 class interval, note that you have tallies in four cells and one tally in each cell. If you multiply each one by its x' value, which is found in *row* 2 below the cell, and sum the products, you will have $1 \times 1 + 1 \times 2 + 1 \times 3 + 1 \times 4 = 10$, which you record in *column* 5. After you have made the calculations for each class interval, sum the products in column 5, and record the $\Sigma fx'$ value, -11, below.

    To find the $\Sigma y'$, in row 5, make the calculations for each class interval, beginning with 80–89 pounds and place the products

TABLE A.3

Calculation of Pearson Product-moment Correlation

X: VARIABLE WEIGHT IN POUNDS

CLASS INTERVALS	80–89	90–99	100–109	110–119	120–129	130–139	140–149
72–73						*(AM)*	
70–71							
68–69							|
66–67					|	|	|
64–65				|	|	||	||
62–63 *(AM)*				|	||	||	||
60–61		|	|	||	||	|	||
58–59		|	|	||	|		|
56–57		|	|	|	||		
54–55	|	|					
(1) f	1	4	3	7	9	6	9
(2) x'	−5	−4	−3	−2	−1	0	1
(3) fx'	−5	−16	−9	−14	−9(−53)	0	9
(4) fx'^2	25	64	27	28	9	0	9
(5) $\Sigma y'$	−4	−10	−6	−8	−7(−35)	3	3
(6) $x'\Sigma y'$	20	40	18	16	7	0	3

Y: VARIABLE HEIGHT IN INCHES

Formula:

$$r = \frac{\dfrac{\Sigma x'y'}{N} - c_x c_y}{\sigma'_x \sigma'_y}$$

Computation:

$$r = \frac{\dfrac{192}{50} - (-.22 \times -.06)}{2.33 \times 2.09}$$

$$= \frac{3.84 - .01}{4.86}$$

$$= \frac{3.83}{4.86}$$

$$= .786$$

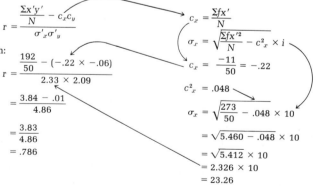

$$c_x = \frac{\Sigma fx'}{N}$$

$$\sigma_x = \sqrt{\frac{\Sigma fx'^2}{N} - c^2_x} \times i$$

$$c_x = \frac{-11}{50} = -.22$$

$$c^2_x = .048$$

$$\sigma_x = \sqrt{\frac{273}{50} - .048} \times 10$$

$$= \sqrt{5.460 - .048} \times 10$$

$$= \sqrt{5.412} \times 10$$

$$= 2.326 \times 10$$

$$= 23.26$$

| | | | | (1) | (2) | (3) | (4) | (5) | (6) |
| | | | | | | | | | |
150–159	160–169	170–179	180–189	f	y'	fy'	fy'^2	$\Sigma x'$	$y'\Sigma x'$
			|	1	5	5	25	5	25
		|		1	4	4	16	4	16
|	|	|		4	3	12	36	10	30
||	|			6	2	12	24	7	14
|		|		8	1	$8^{(41)}$	8	$5^{(31)}$	5
|				8	0	0	0	0	0
				9	−1	−9	9	−11	11
				6	−2	−12	24	−11	22
				5	−3	−15	45	−11	33
				2	−4	$-8^{(-44)}$	32	$-9^{(-42)}$	36
5	2	3	1	50		−3	219	−11	192
2	3	4	5						
10	6	12	$5^{(42)}$	−11					
20	18	48	25	273					
8	5	8	$5^{(32)}$	−3					
16	15	32	25	192					

−11 ——— check ——— $\Sigma fx'$

−3 —check— $\Sigma fy'$

192 ——— check ——— $\Sigma x'y$

$$c_y = \frac{\Sigma fy'}{N}$$

$$\sigma_y = \sqrt{\frac{\Sigma fy'^2}{N} - c_y^2} \times i$$

$$c_y = \frac{-3}{50} = -.06$$

$$c_y^2 = .004$$

$$\sigma_y = \sqrt{\frac{219}{50} - .004} \times 2$$
$$= \sqrt{4.380 - .004} \times 2$$
$$= \sqrt{4.376} \times 2$$

$$= 2.092 \times 2$$
$$= 4.18$$

Subjects:

$N = 50$

Class interval

$Y,i = 2$ inches

$X,i = 10$ pounds

Means:

$$M_X = AM + \frac{\Sigma fx'}{N} \times i$$
$$= 134.5 + \frac{-11}{50} \times 10$$
$$= 134.5 - 2.2$$
$$= 132.30 \text{ pounds}$$

$$M_Y = AM + \frac{\Sigma fy'}{N} \times i$$
$$= 62.5 + \frac{-3}{50} \times 2$$
$$= 62.5 - .12$$
$$= 62.38 \text{ inches}$$

across row 5. When you get to the 130–139-pounds class interval, note that you have tallies in four cells and more than one tally in some of them. If you multiply the number of tallies in each cell by its y' value, which is found in *column* 2, the product will be $1 \times 2 + 2 \times 1 + 2 \times 0 + 1 \times -1 = 3$, which you record in *row* 5. Make the calculations for the remaining class intervals; sum the products in row 5 $\Sigma fy'$, and record the value, -3, at the end of the *row*.

10 To obtain $\Sigma x'y'$, each individual's deviation from the assumed weight mean, x', must be multiplied by his deviation from the assumed height mean, y', and all such products are then summed. Therefore, in column 6, fill in the products of $y' \times \Sigma x'$; that is, multiply the values found in row 2 and row 5. In row 6, fill in the products of $x' \times \Sigma y'$; that is, multiply the values found in row 2 and row 5. Sum the products in column 6 and in row 6, which should be identical, $\Sigma x'y' = 192$. With all six columns filled in, you have accuracy checks on three sums, $\Sigma fy' = -3$, $\Sigma fx' = -11$, $\Sigma x'y' = 192$ (see Table A.3).

11 To calculate r, the correlation coefficient between X and Y, substitute the values you have found in Table A.3 for the symbols in the formula given below the table. Substituting 192 for $\Sigma x'y'$, 50 for the number of scores, N, $-.22$ for cx, $-.06$ for cy, 2.33 for σ'_x, and 2.09 for σ'_y, you will find that r is .786.

12 The computations below Table A.3 give some data that are not needed to compute r but are needed to compute regression equations, which you will study next. In the computations, note particularly the difference between $\sigma'_x = 2.326$ and $\sigma_x = 23.26$ (and similarly σ'_y and σ_y). The following discussion explains why you only obtain σ'_x and σ'_y to compute the r.

Because the deviations are taken from an assumed rather than actual means, the numerator of the r formula requires that you correct $\Sigma x'y'$ by subtracting the product of the two corrections ($cx \times cy$). All product deviations ($x'y''$s) are in interval units. To facilitate computations, the cx, cy, σ'_x, and σ'_y are also left in units of class interval. They are *not* multiplied by units representing i, the step interval (Y, $i = 2$ inches and X, $i = 10$ pounds). But this information is given in Table A.3 because you need to know the standard deviations σ_x or ($\sigma'_x \times 10$) = 23.263 and σy or ($\sigma'y \times 2$) = 4.184 to set up and interpret regression equations which are used in making predictions from the correlation. In the lower right of the table, the two means, M_X and M_Y, are given also, because you will need them in regression equations, which will be discussed in Appendix A.3.

APPENDIX A.3 STATISTICS: PREDICTION

Correlation and prediction are closely related. In Appendix A.2, the correlation between X and Y (height and weight) for a sample of subjects was calculated. If the X scores of other subjects from the same population are known, the correlation data can be used to predict their Y scores. Conversely, if their Y scores are known, the correlation data can be used to predict their X scores. In the following sections, you will utilize what you know about correlation, prediction, and errors in prediction to work out specific prediction problems.

ONE PREDICTOR VARIABLE REGRESSION EQUATIONS AND PREDICTIONS

You will recall that the score form of regression equations are

$$X' = r \frac{\sigma_x}{\sigma_y} (Y - M_Y) + M_X$$ X on Y: Used when an X score is to be predicted from a known Y score.

$$Y' = r \frac{\sigma_y}{\sigma_x} (X - M_X) + M_Y$$ Y on X: Used when a Y score is to be predicted from a known X score.

The symbols used in the above equations are interpreted below.

X' = predicted X score (weight): the mean of the X scores for all persons with a given score.

Y' = predicted Y score (height): the mean of the Y scores for all persons with a given X score.

r = .786, correlation between X and Y.

Y = given or known value of Y (height) from which you are predicting a value of X (weight).

X = given or known value of X from which you are predicting a value of Y.

M_X = 132.30 pounds, mean of X distribution.

M_Y = 62.38 inches, mean of Y distribution.

σ_x = 23.26, standard deviation of X.

σ_y = 4.18, standard deviation of Y.

$r \frac{\sigma_x}{\sigma_y}$, often expressed b_{21}, is the regression coefficient.

$r \frac{\sigma_y}{\sigma_x}$, often expressed b_{12}, is the regression coefficient.

The values given for the symbols above were obtained from the height-weight correlation data that were calculated for a sample of 50 subjects in Appendix A.2, Table A.3. These values provide the primary data needed to calculate regression equations that will enable you to make predictions about the height or weight of other subjects from the same population.

The Prediction of an X Score from a Known Y Score

If you know that Dale's height is 69 inches, you can predict his weight by following the directions and making the corresponding calculations given below.

Directions
1   Select the correct regression equation for predicting weight (X') from a known height score. Substitute the correlation data for the symbols and calculate the regression coefficient, $r = \sigma_x/\sigma_y$, which is sometimes expressed b_{21}. The *regression coefficient gives you the slope of the regression line: it informs you that for every unit in-*

crease in Y (height), an increase of 4.370 pounds in weight can be expected.[1]

2　Substitute Dale's height value for Y in the equation. Calculate X (weight) regression on 69 inches, which informs you that Dale's most probable weight will be 161.23 pounds.

3　To find out how accurate this prediction is, calculate the standard error of estimate of X. You will find that the $\sigma_{(est\ X)}$ is 14.37 pounds. Hence, the odds are that Dale's actual weight will not fall below 146.86 and will not be over 175.60 pounds.

Computation

1　Regression coefficient.

$X' = r\ \dfrac{\sigma_x}{\sigma_y}$	$(Y - M_Y)$	$+ M_X$	Equation[2]
$X' = .786\ \dfrac{23.26}{4.18}$	$(Y - 62.38) + 132.30$		Values substituted for symbols
$X' = 4.370$	$(Y - 62.38) + 132.30$		For every unit increase in Y (height), X' (weight) will increase 4.370 pounds.

2　*X regression on 69 inches.*

$X' = 4.370$	$(69 - 62.38) + 132.30$		Y, known score, 69 inches
$X' = 4.370$	$(6.62)\qquad\ \ + 132.30$		69 inches is 6.62 units from mean height.
			6.62 units × 4.370 =
$X' =$	28.93	$+ 132.30$	28.93 + mean of X, 132.30 =
$X' = 161.23$			Predicted weight, 161.23 pounds

3　Standard error of estimate of an X value.

$$
\begin{aligned}
\sigma_{(est\ X)} &= \sigma_x\ \sqrt{1 - r^2} \\
&= 23.26\ \sqrt{1 - .786^2} \\
&= 23.26\ \sqrt{1 - .618} \\
&= 23.26\ \sqrt{.382} \\
&= 23.26 \times .618 \\
&= 14.37
\end{aligned}
$$

---

[1] The slope of any line is simply the ratio of the distance in a vertical direction to the distance in a horizontal direction.

[2] The translation given below gives you a simple explanation of the equation.

X', weight to be predicted	=	regression coefficient: for every unit increase in height of a specified increase in pounds can be expected	$\begin{pmatrix} \text{subject's} - \text{mean of} \\ \text{known} \qquad \text{sample} \\ \text{height} \qquad \text{heights} \end{pmatrix}$	$+$ mean of sample weights

The Prediction of a Y Score from a Known X Score

If you know that Robert weighs 160 pounds, you can predict his height by following the directions and making the corresponding calculations given below.

Directions

1   Select the correct regression equation for predicting height (Y') from a known weight score. Substitute the correlation data for the symbols and calculate the regression coefficient. The regression coefficient informs you that for every unit increase in X (weight), an increase of .141 inches in Y (height) can be expected.
2   Substitute Robert's weight value for X in the equation and calculate Y (height) regression on 160 pounds, which informs you that Robert's most probable height will be 66.30 inches.
3   To find out how accurate this prediction is, calculate the standard error of estimate of Y. You will find that the $\sigma_{(est\ Y)}$ is 2.58 inches. Hence, you know that the odds are Robert's actual height will not fall below 63.72 or over 68.88 inches.

Computation

1   Regression Coefficient

$$Y' = r\frac{\sigma_y}{\sigma_x} \qquad (X - M_X) \qquad + M_Y \qquad \text{Equation}$$

$$Y' = .786\ \frac{4.18}{23.26} \qquad (X - 132.30) + 62.38 \qquad \text{Values \quad substituted \quad for symbols}$$

$$Y' = .141 \qquad\qquad (X - 132.30) + 62.38 \qquad \text{For every unit increase in}$$

X (weight), Y (height) will increase .141 inches.———┐

2   *Y regression on 160 pounds*

$$Y' = .141 \qquad\qquad (160 - 132.30) + 62.38 \qquad X, \text{ known score, 160 pounds}$$

$$Y' = .141 \qquad\qquad (27.70) \qquad\quad + 62.38 \qquad \text{┌─160 pounds is 27.70 units above mean weight.}$$

$$Y' = \qquad\qquad 3.92 \qquad\qquad + 62.38 \qquad \text{└→27.70} \times .141 = \leftarrow$$

3.92 + mean of Y,

62.38 =

$$Y' = 66.30 \qquad\qquad\qquad\qquad \text{predicted height, 66.30 inches}$$

3   Standard Error of Estimate of a Y value

$$\sigma_{(est\ Y)} = \sigma_y \sqrt{1 - r^2}$$
$$= 4.18 \sqrt{1 - .786^2}$$
$$= 4.18 \sqrt{1 - .618}$$
$$= 4.18 \sqrt{.382}$$
$$= 4.18 \times .618$$
$$= 2.58$$

The Plotting of Regression Lines

In Chapter 10, Figure 10.5, we plotted the two regression lines that roughly fitted the trend of the means of the rows (o's) and means of the columns (x's) on the scattergram. By using regression equations, we can locate the two lines that are "best fitting" in the mathematical sense. Regression lines show graphically the relationship between two variables, weight and height in this instance. These lines intersect where the means of the two variables are located, M_X 132.30 and M_Y 62.38. To plot a regression line for one variable, two points are arbitrarily selected on the other variable, usually one above and one below the mean or the mean and one other point.

To plot the X regression line (mean weight line) in Figure A.3, the two points selected from the Y scores were 69 and 54 inches. When regression equations were calculated for predicting X' (weight) scores from these known Y scores, 69 and 54 inches, the predicted weight scores were 161.23 and 95.68 pounds, respectively. These two points were plotted, and a line was drawn through them to obtain the X regression line.

To plot the Y regression line (mean height line), the two points selected from the X scores were 160 and 100 pounds. When regression equations were calculated for predicting Y' scores from these known X scores, 160 and 100 pounds, the height scores predicted were 66.30 and 57.81 inches, respectively. These two points were plotted, and a line was drawn through them to obtain the Y regression line.

MULTIPLE REGRESSION EQUATIONS AND PREDICTIONS

You may decide that height can be predicted more accurately from weight and age scores than from weight scores alone. In that event, you will calculate a multiple regression equation and use it to make predictions. Let us assume that you have previously calculated the correlation

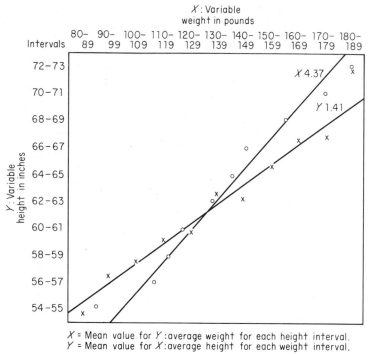

X = Mean value for Y :average weight for each height interval.
Y = Mean value for X :average height for each weight interval.

FIGURE A.3

Illustrating positions of regression lines.

between height and weight (r_{12}), height and age (r_{13}), and weight and age (r_{23}) for a sample of 50 subjects and have obtained the following *primary data:*

Variables	X_1 = height	X_2 = weight	X_3 = age
Mean	$M_1 = 62.38$	$M_2 = 132.30$	$M_3 = 15.22$
Standard deviation	$\sigma_1 = 4.18$	$\sigma_2 = 23.26$	$\sigma_3 = 3.61$
Correlation coefficient	$r_{12} = .786$	$r_{13} = .852$	$r_{23} = .760$

Multiple Regression Equation

You may now use these primary data to obtain certain values that are needed to compute the *score form* of multiple regression equation.

$$X_1' = b_{12.3}X_2 + b_{13.2}X_3 + K$$

The next four sections of this discussion will explain how to find the four values listed below, which must be obtained before you can use the regression equation to make predictions.

1   Partial correlations, $r_{12.3}$, $r_{13.2}$
2   Partial standard deviations, $\sigma_{1.23}$, $\sigma_{2.13}$, $\sigma_{3.12}$
3   Partial regression coefficients, $b_{12.3}$, $b_{13.2}$
4   K, a constant

PARTIAL CORRELATION ($r_{12.3}$, $r_{13.2}$, $r_{23.1}$)   You set up a multiple regression equation by the way of partial correlation. Below, you will find the formulas and computations for ascertaining the relationship between two variables with the influence of the third variable held constant, that is "partialed out," nullified, or removed.

For the r_{12}, r_{13}, r_{23} symbols in the formulas below, you substitute the correlation values given in the primary data above and then make the computations.

1   Formulas.

$$r_{12.3} = \frac{r_{12} - r_{13}r_{23}}{\sqrt{(1 - r^2_{13})(1 - r^2_{23})}} \qquad r_{13.2} = \frac{r_{13} - r_{12}r_{23}}{\sqrt{(1 - r^2_{12})(1 - r^2_{23})}}$$

$$r_{23.1} = \frac{r_{23} - r_{12}r_{13}}{\sqrt{(1 - r^2_{12})(1 - r^2_{13})}}$$

2   Computation.

$$r_{12.3} = \frac{.786 - .852(.760)}{\sqrt{(1 - .852^2)(1 - .760^2)}}$$

$$= \frac{.786 - .648}{\sqrt{(1 - .726)(1 - .578)}}$$

$$= \frac{.138}{\sqrt{(.274)(.422)}}$$

$$= \frac{.138}{\sqrt{.116}}$$

$$= \frac{.138}{.340}$$

$$= .406$$

$$r_{13.2} = \frac{.852 - .786(.760)}{\sqrt{(1 - .786^2)(1 - .760^2)}}$$

$$= \frac{.852 - .597}{\sqrt{(1 - .618)(1 - .578)}}$$

$$= \frac{.255}{\sqrt{(.382)(.422)}}$$

$$= \frac{.255}{\sqrt{.161}}$$

$$= \frac{.255}{.402}$$

$$= .634$$

$$r_{23.1} = \frac{.760 - .786(.852)}{\sqrt{(1 - .786^2)(1 - .852^2)}}$$

$$= \frac{.760 - .670}{\sqrt{(1 - .618)(1 - .726)}}$$

$$= \frac{.090}{\sqrt{(.382)(.274)}}$$

$$= \frac{.090}{\sqrt{.105}}$$

$$= \frac{.090}{.324}$$

$$= .278$$

3   Interpretation.

$r_{12.3}$, the relationship between X_1 (height) and X_2 (weight), with X_3 (age) held constant, is .406.

$r_{13.2}$, the relationship between X_1 (height) and X_3 (age), with X_2 (weight) held constant, is .634.

$r_{23.1}$, the relationship between X_2 (weight) and X_3 (age), with X_1 (height) held constant, is .278.

You will note below that the correlation between height and weight (r_{12}) is reduced when the age factor is held constant; the relationship between height and age (r_{13}) is reduced when the weight factor is held constant; and the relationship between weight and age (r_{23}) is reduced when the height factor is held constant.

r_{12} .786	r_{13} .852	r_{23} .760
$r_{12.3}$ .406	$r_{13.2}$ .634	$r_{23.1}$ .278

PARTIAL STANDARD DEVIATION ($\sigma_{1.23}$, $\sigma_{2.13}$, $\sigma_{3.12}$)   The formulas for partial standard deviations are given below. To compute them you use the partial correlation values ($r_{12.3}$ and $r_{13.2}$) you have just computed and the following values given in the primary data: the standard deviations for the height, weight, and age scores (σ_1, σ_2, σ_3) and the correlation values, r_{12} and r_{23}.

1   Formulas.

$$\sigma_{1.23} = \sigma_1 \sqrt{1 - r^2_{12}} \sqrt{1 - r^2_{13.2}}$$
$$\sigma_{2.13} = \sigma_2 \sqrt{1 - r^2_{23}} \sqrt{1 - r^2_{12.3}}$$
$$\sigma_{3.12} = \sigma_3 \sqrt{1 - r^2_{23}} \sqrt{1 - r^2_{13.2}}$$

2   Computation.

$$
\begin{aligned}
\sigma_{1.23} &= 4.18 \sqrt{1 - .786^2} \sqrt{1 - .634^2} \\
&= 4.18 \sqrt{.382} \sqrt{.598} \\
&= 4.18 \, (.618)(.773) \\
&= 1.996 \\
\sigma_{2.13} &= 23.26 \sqrt{1 - .760^2} \sqrt{1 - .406^2} \\
&= 23.26 \sqrt{.422} \sqrt{.835} \\
&= 23.26 \, (.650)(.914) \\
&= 13.818 \\
\sigma_{3.12} &= 3.61 \sqrt{1 - .760^2} \sqrt{1 - .634^2} \\
&= 3.61 \sqrt{.422} \sqrt{.598} \\
&= 3.61 \, (.650)(.773) \\
&= 1.813
\end{aligned}
$$

3 Interpretation.

$\sigma_{1.23}$, the variability in height when the influence of weight and age is removed, is 1.996 inches.

$\sigma_{2.13}$, the variability in weight when the influence of height and age is removed, is 13.818 pounds.

$\sigma_{3.12}$, the variability in age when the influence of height and weight is removed, is 1.813 years.

Below, you will note that the variability in height (X_1), weight (X_2), and age (X_3) is reduced by approximately one-half when the other two variables are held constant:

$$\sigma_1 = 4.18 \qquad \sigma_2 = 23.26 \qquad \sigma_3 = 3.61$$
$$\sigma_{1.23} = 1.996 \qquad \sigma_{2.13} = 13.818 \qquad \sigma_{3.12} = 1.813$$

PARTIAL REGRESSION COEFFICIENTS ($b_{12.3}$ AND $b_{13.2}$)   To make predictions through the use of a multiple regression equation, you need to know the values of the partial regression coefficients. You will recall that in a simple, *two-variable regression equation*, the regression coefficients give you the slope of the regression lines; they inform you that for every unit of increase in one variable, an increase of a specified amount can be expected in the other variable, and the formulas are

$$b_{12} \text{ or } r\, \frac{\sigma_x}{\sigma_y} \qquad \text{and} \qquad b_{21} \text{ or } r\, \frac{\sigma_y}{\sigma_x}$$

The formulas and computation for partial regression coefficients in a *multiple regression equation*, which serve a similar purpose, are given below.

1 Formulas.

$$b_{12.3} = r_{12.3}\, \frac{\sigma_{1.23}}{\sigma_{2.13}} \qquad \text{and} \qquad b_{13.2} = r_{13.2}\, \frac{\sigma_{1.23}}{\sigma_{3.12}}$$

2 Computation.

$$b_{12.3} = .406\, \frac{1.996}{13.818} \qquad \text{and} \qquad b_{13.2} = .634\, \frac{1.996}{1.813}$$
$$= 0.058 \qquad\qquad\qquad\qquad = 0.697$$

3   Interpretation.

The $b_{12.3}$ value is the multiplying constant or weight for the X_2 values: it tells you that X_1' (the predicted height) increases .058 inch for every unit increase in X_2 (weight) when the effects of X_3 (age) have been nullified or held constant.

The $b_{13.2}$ value is the multiplying constant or weight for the X_3 values: it tells you that X_1' (the predicted height) increases .697 inch for every unit increase in X_3 (age) when the effects of X_2 (weight) have been held constant.

COMPUTATION   You are now ready to calculate the last term in the multiple regression equation, which is K.

1   Formula.

$$K = M_1 \qquad -b_{12.3}\, M_2 \qquad -b_{13.2}\, M_3$$

2   Computation.

$$
\begin{aligned}
K &= 62.38 \qquad -.058(132.30) \qquad -.697(15.22)\\
&= 62.38 \qquad -7.67 \qquad\qquad -10.61\\
&= 62.38 \qquad\qquad\qquad -18.28\\
&= 44.10
\end{aligned}
$$

3   Interpretation.

K, 44.10 is the constant you must add to ensure that the mean of the predictions (X_1') coincides with the mean of the obtained (X_1) values.

Multiple Regression Prediction, Standard Error of Multiple Estimate, and Coefficient of Correlation

You can now use the regression equation data to make predictions, calculate how accurate your predictions are, and ascertain the relationship between the predicted variable and the combined action of the predictor variables.

The regression equation can be used to predict height scores from a knowledge of weight and age scores and weight scores from a knowledge of height and age scores. But because of space limitations, the following example of prediction is confined to an example of predicting height.

PREDICTION OF AN X_1' SCORE FROM KNOWN X_2 AND X_3 SCORES   To predict a subject's height (X_1') when you know his weight is 160 pounds

(X_2) and his age is 16 years (X_3), you substitute these values and those you obtained for $b_{12.3}$, $b_{13.2}$, and K for the symbols in the regression equation and make the calculations indicated.

$$
\begin{aligned}
X_1' = b_{12.3} \qquad & X_2 \quad = b_{13.2} \qquad && X_3 \quad + K \\
= .058 \qquad & (160) + .697 \qquad && (16) + 44.10 \\
= \qquad 9.28 \qquad & \quad + \qquad 11.15 \qquad && \quad + 44.10 \\
= 64.53 \text{ inches} &
\end{aligned}
$$

STANDARD ERROR OF MULTIPLE ESTIMATE   The standard error of multiple estimate indicates approximately how far the subject's predicted score may deviate from his actual or earned score.

1   Formula.
The formula for the standard error of multiple estimate is equal to $\sigma_{1.23}$. Hence, the standard error of multiple estimate is given directly by the partial standard deviation $\sigma_{1.23}$ which you have already computed.

2   Computation.

$$\sigma_{(est\ X_1)} = \sigma_{1.23} = 1.996$$

3   Interpretation.
The standard error of multiple estimate informs you that the chances are two in three that the subject's predicted height score, 64.53 inches, will not miss his actual height score by more than plus or minus 1.996 inches. You can now say, furthermore, that two-thirds of the obtained or actual height (X_1) values will lie within 1.996 inches of the predicted height (X_1') values.

MULTIPLE COEFFICIENT OF CORRELATION   The multiple coefficient of correlation, $R_{1.23}$, informs you to what extent X_1 is related to the combined action of X_2 and X_3. It gives the correlation between the actual, obtained, or earned X_1 scores and the predicted X_1' scores obtained from the best weightings for X_2 and X_3 scores, which are those found for the multiple regression equation.

1   Formula.

$$R_{1.23} = \sqrt{1 - \frac{\sigma^2_{1.23}}{\sigma^2_1}}$$

2 Computation.

$$R_{1.23} = \sqrt{1 - \frac{(1.996)^2}{(4.18)^2}}$$

$$= \sqrt{1 - \frac{3.984}{17.47}}$$

$$= \sqrt{1 - .228}$$
$$= \sqrt{.772}$$
$$= .879$$

3 Interpretation.

You will recall that the correlation between height and weight is r_{12} = .786 and the correlation between height and age is r_{13} = .852. The correlation between height and the combined action of weight and age is $R_{1.23}$ = .879, which is higher than the individual correlations between height and either predictor variable.

INTERPRETATION OF CORRELATION AND PREDICTION DATA

In addition to the factors discussed on pages 323–327, an investigator may give consideration to the following factors when interpreting correlation and prediction data.

Coefficients of Determination, Alienation, and Predictive Efficiency

In addition to the standard error of estimate which has been discussed previously, three other methods may be employed to indicate the goodness of prediction:

Standard error of estimate	$\sigma_x = \sqrt{1 - r^2}$ $\sigma_y = \sqrt{1 - r^2}$	accuracy of prediction
Coefficient of determination	r^2	percentage of perfect relationship
Coefficient of alienation	$k = \sqrt{1 - r^2}$	degree of lack of relationship
Coefficient of predictive efficiency	$E = 1 - \sqrt{1 - r^2}$	r's percent of prediction value better than pure chance

You will note that r^2 rather than r is used in each of the above calculations. A correlation coefficient (r) cannot be interpreted as the percentage of perfect relationship existing between two variables. If $r =$ .50, it is not "half perfect," nor does an r of .60 represent a degree of relationship twice as great as an r of .30. The difference between coefficients of .30 and .40 is not equal to the difference between coefficients of .60 and .70. The coefficient of correlation is an index number, not a measurement on a linear scale of equal units; it cannot be interpreted as a proportion.

A *coefficient of determination* (r^2) overcomes the difficulty discussed above, for when r is interpreted *in terms of variance*, it can be interpreted as a proportion; and when multiplied by 100, as a percentage. A coefficient of determination (r^2) gives the proportion of the total variance of one variable that can be predicted from, attributed to, or explained by the variance in the other variable. If $r = .80$, then $r^2 = .64$. You can move the decimal point over two places $(r^2 \times 100)$ and state that 64 percent of the variance of Y is predictable from the variance of X and vice versa. You know 64 percent of what you need to know to make a perfect prediction of one variable from the other.

The *coefficient of alienation* $(k = \sqrt{1 - r^2})$ is denoted by the letter k. Unlike r, which determined the presence of relationship between two variables, k measures the lack of relationship. The larger the coefficient of alienation, the smaller is the magnitude of the relationship between two variables: when $k = 1.00$, $r = .00$ and when $k = .866$, $r = .50$.

The *coefficient of predictive efficiency* $(E = 1 - \sqrt{1 - r^2}$ or $E = 1 - k)$ is used to find the r's percent of prediction value better than pure chance. Without calculating r, by chance you might make an accurate prediction of height from a knowledge of weight. In Table A.4, which gives the predictive indexes for several values of r, you will note that r must be as high as .50 before the one variable is 13.4 percent better or more efficient than pure chance in predicting the other variable. The correlation must be 0.80 and above in order for the predictive efficiency to be 40 percent or more. The higher the correlation value, the greater is its predictive efficiency.

Statistical Significance of a Correlation Coefficient

In many instances you want to know what the probability is that the value of r in a *sample* could be attributable to chance if the correlation coefficient in the *population, p*, is actually zero.[3] You ask: Is the value

---

[3] The population correlation coefficient is ordinarily symbolized by the Greek letter rho (ρ), but it may be symbolized by r to avoid the confusion that arises because ρ is also used to symbolize Spearman's rank-difference correlation coefficient.

TABLE A.4

Correlations Interpreted in Terms of Their Predictive Efficiency

CORRELATION COEFFICIENT (r)	CHANCES THAT CORRE-LATION IS BETTER THAN PURE GUESS (E)	CALCULATION OF E WHEN r = .50 (E = predictive index)
.10	.005	$r = .50$
.20	.020	$E = 1.00 - \sqrt{1 - r^2}$
.30	.046	$E = 1.00 - \sqrt{1.00 - (.50)^2}$
.40	.083	$E = 1.00 - \sqrt{1.00 - .2500}$
.50	.134	$E = 1.00 - \sqrt{.75}$
.60	.200	$E = 1.00 - .86603$
.70	.286	$E = .134$ or 13.4%
.80	.400	
.90	.564	
.95	.688	
.99	.859	
1.00	1.000 or 100%—a perfect prediction	

of r in the sample attributable to the fact that by chance the sample is made up of a particular type of subjects from the population?

You begin by assuming the null hypothesis: no relationship exists between the two variables in the population, $p = 0$. You also declare at what level of significance (usually .05 or .01) you will reject the null hypothesis and conclude that the population correlation is not zero.

Tables are available in statistics books that give the values of r which a sample of a given size must equal or exceed to meet the declared requirement of significance. Table A.5, informs you that r's as high as those stipulated for the size of the sample could occur by chance (sampling variation) only five times in 100 at the .05 level of significance and one time in 100 at the .01 level.

Suppose you had set the significance level at .05 in advance, then had correlated the height and weight scores of 50 subjects (N = 50) and had found r = .786. You could determine the significance of this r by entering Table A.5 in column 1 with 48 degrees of freedom (the number of pairs of observations in the sample minus 2, 50 − 2 or 48 df). Column 2 would inform you that with 48 df, an r would need to be .279 to be significant at the .05 level; that is, the sample r would have to be .279 or higher in order to reject the hypothesis that the correlation in the population is zero. Since the sample r = .786 is greater than .279, you can

TABLE A.5

**Values of the Correlation Co-
efficient for Different Values
of Significance***

df	P = .05	P = .01
10	.576	.708
30	.349	.449
48	.279	.361
50	.273	.354
70	.232	.302
90	.205	.267
100	.195	.254

*Adapted from R. A. Fisher, *Statis-
tical Methods for Research Workers.* Oliver Boyd, Ltd., Edinburgh,
by permission of author and publishers. The entry "48 *df*" was calculated by means of formula, using
the table of *t*.

reject the null hypothesis, $\rho = 0$, and accept the alternative hypothesis
that a relationship does exist in the population between height and
weight.

You can observe in Table A.5 that the significance of *r* is related to
the size of the sample: small *r*'s may be significant when based on a
large N, whereas large values of *r* may not be significant when based on
a small sample. At the 1 percent level of significance, an *r* of .254 would
be significant for a large sample (*df* 100), but an *r* of .600 would not be
significant for a small sample (*df* 10), for an *r* of .708 is required. Large
r's may occur quite frequently for small samples as a result of sampling
variations, even though no relationship exists between the variables in
the population from which the sample was drawn.

Spurious Correlations

A correlation between two variables is said to be spurious if some factor
other than the two variables being correlated has increased or de-
creased the "true" size of *r*. The fact that the heterogeneity—range—of
the subjects' scores on an extraneous variable, such as age, may do this
was discussed on page 324. Other types of spurious correlations are
discussed below.

A *spurious index correlation* usually results when two indexes having a common variable denominator are correlated with each other. Indexes such as intelligence, educational, and achievement quotients (IQ, EQ, and AQ) are commonly correlated.[4] If you correlate scores on two different IQ tests, r [(MA$_1$/CA)(MA$_2$/CA)], or IQ scores and educational quotients, r [(MA/CA)(EA/CA)], the denominator for both ratios in each correlation is CA, chronological age. If CA were a constant (the same for all students), the division would have no effect on the correlation because the numerators only would be correlated. But if you correlate the scores on two tests of 500 children who differ in chronological age from five to eighteen, the CA varies from student to student, and this fact may appreciably affect the size of r. A similar condition exists when IQs and AQs are correlated, for MA, the common factor, enters into the numerator of one variable and the denominator of the other: r [(MA/CA)(AA/MA)]. The effect is characteristically a negative r between IQ and AQ. The solution in such correlations is to compute r with the spurious element—the extraneous variable—held constant by the technique of partial correlation.

A *spurious correlation between averages* may result if you obtain r's for several subsamples (such as r's between height-weight for each grade 1 through 12) and then average these r's to obtain a population r. Because correlation coefficients are not values on a linear scale of equal units, differences between large r's are greater than differences between small r's. If +r's and −r's are added, they tend to cancel one another out. When the r's to be averaged do not differ in sign, are about the same size, and are not too large, an arithmetic mean may yield a useful result; otherwise it is best not to average the r's or to transform the r's into Fisher's z coefficients and take the arithmetic mean of the z's which, in turn, can be converted into an equivalent r.

Spurious correlations of parts with wholes arise when you correlate subscores with a total score. This is often done to determine how much one test item in a test or one test in a battery contributes to the usefulness of the instrument for discriminating between the performance of individuals. Suppose a test battery consists of three parts, $TB = P_1 + P_2 + P_3$, and you correlate P_1 and TB. Because P_1 is a component of TB, this subtest ordinarily introduces some degree of positive relation-

---

[4] IQ, intelligence quotient, is concerned with mental age or ability in relation to chronological age: (MA/CA) × 100.
EQ, educational quotient, is concerned with educational age or achievement in a number of subjects in relation to average achievement of persons the same age: (EA/CA) × 100.
AQ, achievement quotient, is concerned with achievement age (actual achievement) in relation to mental ability: (AA/MA) × 100.

ship. The greater the relative contribution of P_1 to TB, the greater is this spurious factor. If the positive relationship is very high, regardless of the spuriousness, you might use P_1 rather than the battery of three subtests. You can compare r's between parts and wholes, however, if each part contributes about the same amount of variance to the total or if a part is one of a great many parts, so that its proportion of contribution is relatively small.

APPENDIX A.4 STATISTICS: FACTORIAL ANALYSIS OF VARIANCE

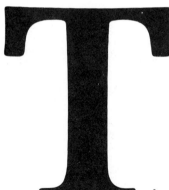

o become familiar with analysis of variance we will use the 2×2 factorial design study presented in Chapter 9 (see Figure 9.4). To study the effect of variations in two independent variables (X_1, teaching methods, and X_2, length of class periods) on a dependent variable (learning achievement), 40 Ss from the same population were assigned at random, each to one of four experimental groups. Six weeks later their learning achievement (dependent variable) was measured.

In analyzing the main effect of each independent variable and their joint effect on learning achievement, we compared means. We noted little difference between the learning achievement mean scores for the 30- and 50-minute class periods (71.0 and 70.5). But because the discussion method mean, 83.0, was greater than the lecture method mean, 58.5, we thought the discussion method of instruction was probably superior for the population of Ss from which our sample was drawn. But we really did not know whether this difference between the means was a real difference produced by the discussion teaching method or merely the result of chance, the chance that the difference was produced by the natural variability of the Ss within the groups, by extraneous variables that may have differentially affected the groups, or by a sample that was not perfectly representative of the population. To obtain such information, we must apply a statistical test to the data. In this instance we will use factorial analysis of variance, because it enables us to test the significance of mean differences between more than two groups in a single test.

The steps below give an overview of the procedures employed in factorial analysis of variance. They may not convey too much meaning to you now, but you can refer to them if you become confused later in the discussion.

1. Structure null hypotheses.
2. Obtain the sums of squares, SS.
3. Obtain the mean squares, which is another term for variance, by dividing each sum of squares by the appropriate degrees of freedom: $SS/df = MS$.
4. Use the mean squares to obtain the F values needed to test the three null hypotheses: $F = $ between MS/within MS.
5. Use a distribution of F table to determine whether the F values obtained are statistically significant for the size of the sample.

NULL HYPOTHESES

Analysis of variance begins with null hypotheses and ends with the calculation of F values (variance ratios) which indicate whether the null hypotheses can or cannot be rejected. Before conducting the experiment, we constructed three precise hypotheses about the population (p) from which our sample of 40 Ss was drawn. Note that we are not exclusively interested in the sample, but that we want to generalize our findings to the population.

1. There is no difference between the effect on learning achievement produced by variations in the method of teaching at the .05 level of significance, $p = 0$.
2. There is no difference between the effect on learning achievement produced by variations in length of class period at the .05 level of significance, $p = 0$.

3 There is no interaction between method of teaching and length of class period at the .05 level of significance, $p = 0$.

BASIC DATA

Before obtaining the F values for our sample, we should examine Tables A.6 and A.7 and familiarize ourselves with the basic data and symbols employed in the study. Table A.6 gives the learning achievement scores of the Ss in each group. Each cell of Table A.7 contains the following data for the specified group:

m = number of observations—scores—in the cell
ΣX = sum of the scores (Xs) in the cell
ΣX^2 = sum of the squared scores (X^2s) in the cell
$\overline{X}$ = the mean of the set of scores in the cell (note that the mean is symbolized by $\overline{X}$ rather than M)

The margins of Table A.7 contain the sum of the values for the rows (teaching methods) and for the columns (length of classes). The new terms mc and mr in the margins are defined below:

mc = number of scores *in a row* found by multiplying number of scores in a cell by number of columns (c), $10 \times 2 = 20$.
mr = number of scores *in a column* found by multiplying number of scores in a cell by number of rows (r), $10 \times 2 = 20$.

TABLE A.6

The Dependent Variable Scores in the Four Groups That Compose the Factorial Design in Figure 9.4

		LENGTH OF CLASS PERIODS (X_2)			
		50 MINUTES		30 MINUTES	
METHODS OF TEACHING (X_1)	LECTURE	79	50	77	49
		39	78	39	68
		59	49	55	53
		55	42	40	47
		68	71	69	83
	DISCUSSION	83	75	99	71
		99	90	95	97
		54	87	61	81
		110	61	111	69
		81	80	76	80

TABLE A.7

Sums and Means for Data of Table A.6

		LENGTH OF CLASS PERIODS (X_2)		TOTALS
		50 MINUTES	30 MINUTES	
METHODS OF TEACHING (X_1)	LECTURE	m = 10 ΣX = 590 ΣX^2 = 36,682 $\bar{X}$ = 59.0	m = 10 ΣX = 580 ΣX^2 = 35,768 $\bar{X}$ = 58.0	mc = 20 ΣX_c = 1170 ΣX^2_c = 72,450 $\bar{X}$ = 58.5
	DISCUSSION	m = 10 ΣX = 820 ΣX^2 = 69,682 $\bar{X}$ = 82.0	m = 10 ΣX = 840 ΣX^2 = 72,816 $\bar{X}$ = 84.0	mc = 20 ΣX_c = 1660 ΣX^2_c = 142,498 $\bar{X}$ = 83.0
TOTALS		mr = 20 ΣX_r = 1410 ΣX^2_r = 106,364 $\bar{X}$ = 70.5	mr = 20 ΣX_r = 1420 ΣX^2_r = 108,584 $\bar{X}$ = 71.0	mrc = 40 $\Sigma\Sigma X_{rc}$ = 2830 $\Sigma\Sigma X^2_{rc}$ = 214,948 $\bar{X}$ = 70.75

The lower right corner of the table contains the values for the total group of 40 Ss. You will note that the $\Sigma\Sigma X_{rc}$ and $\Sigma\Sigma X^2_{rc}$ contain a new symbol, rc. Perhaps the following statement will help you grasp the meaning of rc. The sum of scores in any particular cell, ΣX, is the sum of the scores of a particular combination of methods (r—row) and minutes (c—columns), and hence, is more properly written ΣX_{rc}. Hence, the sum of scores in all cells is written $\Sigma\Sigma X_{rc}$.

SUM OF SQUARES (SS)

Now that we are familiar with the data, we can use analysis of variance to compare the means of the four groups. In our problem we are interested in mean differences rather than variance differences. But a fundamental relationship exists between variances and means; consequently we will analyze variances in a particular way to determine the significance of mean differences.

Variance is a measure of the spread or variation of the scores around the mean; it is a description of the extent to which the scores in a distribution differ from each other. You will recall that the mean, M or $\bar{X}$, is the arithmetic average of a set of scores $\Sigma X/N = \bar{X}$. Variance is determined by finding the deviation of each score from the mean, $X - \bar{X}$, squaring the deviations, $(X - \bar{X})^2$, obtaining the sum of squares,

$\Sigma(X - \overline{X})^2$, and dividing by the number of scores $\Sigma(X - \overline{X})^2/N$ or by the degrees of freedom, df. To obtain the variances in our problem, we must first obtain the sum of squares of various groups of scores. A sum of squares—the sum of all the squared deviations in a distribution about the mean of the distribution or $\Sigma(X - \overline{X})^2$—is referred to by the simple symbol SS[1] in analysis of variance.

The first SS we obtain is the total sum of squares, total SS, which is the sum of the squared deviations of all the scores (40 squared deviations) about the grand mean (the mean of the distribution of all 40 scores). The basic rationale underlying analysis of variance is as follows: The sum of the squared deviations of the scores in the four subgroups (the 40 squared deviations) can be artificially combined into one total group, total SS, and then the total SS can subsequently be partitioned for comparison and analysis into (1) between groups and (2) within groups components in such a way as to permit specification of the relative importance of the component sources. We will see how this is done after we obtain the total SS, between-rows SS, between-columns SS, within-cells SS, and interaction SS. We will in turn use these values to compute the variances.

The within-groups SS, which is sometimes called the sum of squares for error, is free from the influence of treatment effect. Roughly speaking, (1) the within-groups SS (error SS) reflects the extent to which the Ss in each group (cell) vary and (2) the between-group SS (between-rows SS or between-columns SS) reflects the difference between the means of the rows (lecture and discussion methods) or the means of the columns (30-minute and 50-minute class periods). If we expose the Ss in the two rows to different teaching methods or the Ss in the two columns to different lengths of classes, the difference in their scores will consist of (1) the effect of the teaching method or length of class period and (2) the effect of random error—extraneous variables which differentially affect the scores within each group. Hence, to find the "true effect" of an experimental treatment, we must devise a means of separating the effect of random error from the effect of treatment. In analysis of variance we obtain two independent estimates of variance of a single population and place the between-groups variance (error plus treatment) in the numerator and the within-groups variance (error) in the denominator of the F ratio. If the numerator is significantly larger than the denominator, it indicates that the presence of the experimental treatment has produced a "true" difference in the performance scores obtained.

---

[1] Do not confuse SS, sum of squares, with Ss, subjects.

Total Sum of Squares

The total SS is the sum of the squared deviations of all the scores (40) from the *grand mean of all scores*.

1   Formula.

$$\text{Total SS} = \Sigma\Sigma X^2_{rc} - \frac{(\Sigma\Sigma X_{rc})^2}{mrc}$$

2   Interpretation.

Sum the ΣX^2 values for the four groups.

Sum the ΣX values for the four groups, square the sum obtained, and divide by the total number of scores.

3   Computation.

$$
\begin{aligned}
\text{Total SS} &= 36{,}682 + 69{,}682 \\
&\quad + 35{,}768 + 72{,}816 \\
&= 214{,}948 \\
&= 214{,}948 \\
&= 14{,}725.5
\end{aligned}
$$

$$
\begin{aligned}
&- \frac{(590 + 820 + 580 + 840)^2}{10 \times 2 \times 2} \\
&- \frac{(2{,}830)^2}{40} \\
&- \frac{8{,}008{,}900}{40} \quad \text{or } 214{,}948 - 200{,}222.5
\end{aligned}
$$

Between-rows Sum of Squares

The between-rows SS is the sum of the squared deviations in the rows from the *grand mean*. The between-rows SS reflects that part of the total SS that is attributable to the difference between the means of the rows (X_1, the discussion and lecture methods).

1   Formula.[2]

$$\text{Rows SS} = \frac{\Sigma_r(\Sigma_c X_{rc})^2}{mc} - \frac{(\Sigma\Sigma X_{rc})^2}{mrc}$$

---

[2] The $\Sigma_r(\Sigma_c X_{rc})^2/mc$ part of the formula looks complicated, but it breaks down as follows:
ΣX_{rc} Sum of scores in any particular cell.
$(\Sigma_c X_{rc})^2$ Sum the ΣX scores in the columns of each row and square the sums:
590 + 580 = 1,170²
820 + 840 = 1,660²
$\Sigma_r(\Sigma_c X_{rc})^2$ Sum the above row values: 1,170² + 1,660².

2 Interpretation.

Square the ΣX_c values in each — Sum the ΣX values for the four row, obtain the sum, and divide by groups, square the sum obtained, number of scores in the row. and divide by the total number of scores.

3 Computation.

$$\text{Rows SS} = \frac{(1{,}170^2 + 1{,}660^2)}{10 \times 2} - \frac{(590 + 820 + 580 + 840)^2}{10 \times 2 \times 2}$$

$$= \frac{4{,}124{,}500}{20} - \frac{(2{,}830)^2}{40}$$

$$= \frac{4{,}124{,}500}{20} - \frac{8{,}008{,}900}{40}$$

$$= 206{,}225 - 200{,}222.5$$

$$= 6{,}002.5$$

Between-columns Sum of Squares

The between-columns SS is the sum of the squared deviations in the columns from the *grand mean*. The between-columns SS reflects the amount of the total SS that is attributable to the difference between the means of the columns (X_2, the 50-minute and 30-minute class periods).

1 Formula.

$$\text{Columns SS} = \frac{\sum\limits_{c}(\sum\limits_{r}X_{rc})^2}{mr} - \frac{(\sum\sum X_{rc})^2}{mrc}$$

2 Interpretation.

Square the ΣX_r values in each — Sum the ΣX values for the four column and divide by the number groups, square the sum obtained, of scores in the column. and divide by the total number of scores.

3 Computation.

$$\text{Columns SS} = \frac{1{,}410^2 + 1{,}420^2}{10 \times 2} - \frac{(590 + 820 + 580 + 840)^2}{10 \times 2 \times 2}$$

$$= \frac{4{,}004{,}500}{20} - \frac{8{,}008{,}900}{40}$$

$$= 200{,}225 - 200{,}222.5$$

$$= 2.5$$

Within-cells (Groups) Sum of Squares

The within-cells SS is the sum of the squared deviations in the four groups from the *cell means*. The within-cells SS reflects how much of the total SS is attributable to error—the natural variability of the Ss within each group. To calculate the within-cells SS, we use the following formula:

1 Formula.

$$\text{Within-cells SS} = \Sigma\Sigma X^2_{rc} - \frac{\Sigma(\Sigma X_{rc})^2}{m}$$

2 Interpretation.

Sum the ΣX^2 values for the four groups.

Square the ΣX values for the four groups, obtain the sum, and divide by the number of scores in a cell.

3 Computation.

$$
\begin{aligned}
\text{Within-cells SS} \ &= 36{,}682 + 69{,}682 + 35{,}768 & &- \frac{(590^2 + 580^2 + 820^2 + 840^2)}{10} \\
&\quad + 72{,}816 \\
&= 214{,}948 & &- \frac{2{,}062{,}500}{10} \\
&= 214{,}948 & &- 206{,}250 \\
&= 8{,}698
\end{aligned}
$$

Interaction Sum of Squares

The total SS is the sum of its components:

Total SS = between-rows SS + between-columns SS + within-cells SS
           + interaction SS

14,725.5 = 6,002.5   +   2.5   + 8,698 +   22.5
           (error plus (error plus (error) (error plus
           treatment)   treatment)   treatment)

If we know the total SS and three of the other SS values, as we do, calculating the fourth component, interaction, is easy.

To calculate the interaction SS, we sum the between-rows SS, between-column SS, and within-cells SS and then subtract this sum from the total SS. The interaction SS reflects the amount of the total SS that is attributable to the interaction of the two independent variables, methods of teaching and length of classes.

1 Formula.

$$\text{Interaction SS} = \text{total SS} - \left(\begin{array}{c}\text{between-}\\ \text{rows SS}\end{array} + \begin{array}{c}\text{between-}\\ \text{columns SS}\end{array} + \begin{array}{c}\text{within-}\\ \text{cells SS}\end{array}\right)$$

2 Computation.

$$\begin{aligned}\text{Interaction SS} &= 14{,}725.5 - (6{,}002.5 + 2.5 + 8{,}698)\\ &= 14{,}275.5 - 14{,}703\\ &= 22.5\end{aligned}$$

We can now record the five SS we have obtained on an analysis of variance table which we will use to summarize our results (see Table A.8). Note that the four component sums of squares add to equal the total SS.

MEAN SQUARES (*MS*)

We have completed the rather lengthy process of obtaining the sums of squares. The next step is to estimate the *population variance or mean square* for each source of variation: total, columns, rows, interaction, and cells. In many situations the variance of a set of scores is found by dividing the sum of the squared deviations from the mean by the number of scores: $(X - \overline{X})^2/N$. But in the mean square formula, $MS = SS/df$, the denominator of the variance fraction is df rather than N or mrc[3]. This change in the denominator is necessary because the values obtained for the sample are used to make unbiased estimates of corresponding population values. The soundness of these population estimates depends on counting accurately the number of df that go into making them.

Degrees of Freedom

To provide an elementary understanding of df, let us digress briefly from the main theme of the discussion. The question raised by degrees of freedom is: How many pieces of information are free to enter into a distribution before the remainder of the pieces are fixed or restricted by the necessity to produce a certain total? If we know that the sum of two numbers must be 80, we are free to select one number, 20, but the

---

[3] In our problem, mrc, instead of N, is used to represent the total number of observations.

TABLE A.8

Analysis of Variance on Learning Achievement

SOURCE OF VARIATION	SUM OF SQUARES	df	MEAN SQUARE	F
Rows (methods)	6,002.5	1	6,002.5	24,844*
Columns (class periods)	2.5	1	2.5	
Interaction (methods × class periods)	22.5	1	22.5	
Within-cells	8,698	36	241.611	
Total	14,725.5	39		

* Significant beyond .05, or $p < .05$.

second number is fixed; it must be 60 for the sum to be 80. Hence, only one degree of freedom is available—the selection of the first number.

Suppose we conduct an experiment with a sample of 5 subjects from a population of 90 subjects. We add their dependent variable scores, obtain the mean, and compute the deviations from the mean, which we know must add up to zero:

Scores: $3 + 7 + 10 + 15 + 20 = 55 \dfrac{55}{5} = 11$ (mean)

Deviations: $-8 \quad -4 \quad -1 \quad +4 \quad +9 = 0$

Variance is computed from deviations from the mean. This *sample mean* of 11 is to be used as an estimate of the *population mean*. We are free, therefore, to vary *any* four of the five scores and their deviations to make an unbiased estimate of the population variance, mrc $- 1, 5 - 1 = 4$. Below we have selected at random four scores, but the fifth score must be 27 for the estimated mean to be 11, and the fifth deviation must be $+ 16$ for the sum of the deviations to equal zero. One degree of freedom is "used up" or lost when we use the sample mean as an estimate of the population mean.

Scores: $5 + 8 + 9 + 6 + [27] = \dfrac{55}{5} = 11$

Deviations: $-6 \quad -3 \quad -2 \quad -5[+16] = 0$

We must divide the SS by df, 4, rather than mrc, 5, to obtain an unbiased estimate of the population variance.

The rule for determining the number of df available to compute variance is as follows:

$$\left.\begin{array}{l}\text{Number of independent} \\ \text{observations for source of} \\ \text{variance}\end{array} \quad - \quad \begin{array}{l}\text{number of independent para-} \\ \text{meters[4] already estimated in} \\ \text{computing sample variation}\end{array}\right\} = df$$

Total Mean Square (Variance)

In our problem, starting with the largest source of variation, the total sum of squares, the number of df available for making an unbiased estimate of population variance, is the number of independent observations — number of squared deviations in the sample — minus one: $mrc - 1$, $40 - 1 = 39$. One degree of freedom is "used up" (one deviation is fixed) when we use the sample mean as an estimate of the population mean.

$$\text{Total } MS$$
$$= \frac{total\ SS}{df} = \frac{\text{sum of 40 squared deviations from the sample }\sqrt{\text{mean}}}{mrc - 1,\ \text{number of squared deviations in the sample,}}$$
$$\text{minus one that is fixed when the sample}\lfloor\text{mean is used as}$$
$$\text{an estimate of the population mean.}$$

$$\text{Total } MS = \frac{total\ SS}{df} = \frac{14{,}725.5}{40 - 1} = \frac{14{,}725.5}{39} = 377.577$$

Rows Mean Square (Variance)

The number of df available for making an unbiased estimate of the population rows variance is the number of independent observations—the two row means—minus one, $r - 1$, $2 - 1 = 1$. One df is used up when the sample mean is used as an estimate of the population mean.

$$\text{Rows } MS$$
$$= \frac{rows\ SS}{df} = \frac{\text{sum of squared deviations in rows from sample }\sqrt{\text{mean}}}{r - 1,\ \text{number of row means minus one that is fixed when}}$$
$$\text{the sample}\lfloor\text{mean is used as an estimate of the population}$$
$$\text{mean.}$$

$$\text{Rows } MS$$
$$= \frac{rows\ SS}{df} = \frac{6{,}002.5}{r - 1} = \frac{6{,}002.5}{2 - 1} = \frac{6{,}002.5}{1} = 6{,}002.5$$

---

[4] Parameters: a measure computed from all observations of a population.

Columns Mean Square (Variance)

The number of df available for making an unbiased estimate of the population columns variance is the number of column means, minus one, $c - 1$, $2 - 1 = 1$. One of the df is used up when the sample mean is used as an estimate of the population mean.

$$\text{Columns } MS = \frac{\text{columns SS}}{df} = \frac{2.5}{c - 1} = \frac{2.5}{2 - 1} = \frac{2.5}{1} = 2.5$$

Interaction Mean Square (Variance)

The number of df available for making an unbiased estimate of the population interaction (which is a product of $r \times c$) is obtained by multiplying together the df for the main effects $(r - 1)(c - 1)$, $(2 - 1)(2 - 1) = 1$. One degree of freedom is used up when the sample mean is used as an estimate of the population mean.

$$\text{Interaction } MS = \frac{\text{interaction SS}(r \times c)}{df} = \frac{22.5}{(r - 1)(c - 1)}$$
$$= \frac{22.5}{(2 - 1)(2 - 1)} = \frac{22.5}{1} = 22.5$$

Cells Mean Square (Variance)

The number of df available for making an unbiased estimate of the population cells variance is 36, for four deviations are fixed (4 degrees of freedom are lost) because the four sample cell means (parameters) are used as estimates of population cell means $(mrc - rc = 40 - (2)(2) = 36)$.

$$\text{Cells } MS = \frac{\text{within-cells SS}}{df} = \frac{8{,}698}{40 - 4} = \frac{8{,}698}{36} = 241.611$$

We can now record the df and mean square values on the analysis of variance table (see Table A.8). Note that the four component df, $1 + 1 + 1 + 36$, add to equal the total df, 39.

THE F RATIO

The mean squares (variance estimates) are used to calculate the F ratios (variance ratios) by which the tenability of the null hypotheses is assessed. Before determining the F ratios, we should recall that the rationale underlying analysis of variance is as follows: The sum of the squared deviations of the scores in all groups can be artificially combined into a total SS, and the total SS can be partitioned into two components for comparison and analysis: (1) a between-groups component, which is due to any differential experimental treatment effects, and (2) a within-groups component, which results from the extent to which the Ss in each group differ. The between-groups component involves variations of group means about the grand mean of all scores, and the within-groups component involves the variation of scores around the cell means.

The within-groups component is sometimes called the error variance. Within a given group, the Ss experience the same experimental treatment, but because human beings vary, the Ss in each group will not react exactly alike. They will not be equally motivated, and the extraneous variables such as noise, lighting, and other factors may affect them differently. When we expose two groups to different teaching methods, the difference between the two groups' scores will consist of (1) the effect of the teaching method and (2) the effect of error—the natural variability of the Ss within the groups. The within-cells SS is determined by the extent to which the Ss in each group differ; it involves the variation of scores around cell means. If the Ss in one of our four groups were exactly alike and were exposed to the same experimental treatment, they would all get the same learning achievement scores; there would be no variation in their scores about the cell mean; the within-cells variance would be zero. But even in a carefully controlled experiment, the within-cells variance is almost never zero because of the natural variation among Ss and the impossibility of treating them all precisely alike. Hence, in our problem, there is almost certain to be some within-cells (error) variance.

The F ratio for each source of variation is calculated by dividing each between-mean square by the within- or error-mean square. The between- and within-mean squares are compared to ascertain whether the between MS is significantly larger. If it is not, the difference between the groups can be explained simply on the basis of error variance.

$$F = \frac{\text{between-groups mean square}}{\text{within-groups mean square}}$$

The numerator (between MS) of the F ratio contains an estimate of both the treatment variance (if any) and the error variance, while the denominator (within MS) contains only the estimate of the error variance.[5] If there has been no treatment effect, the numerator will contain only the estimate of error variance, for the estimate of the treatment contribution will be zero. Therefore, if we divide the numerator by the denominator, the ratio will be approximately 1.00.[6]

$$F = \frac{\text{error} + \text{treatment}}{\text{error}} = \frac{10 + 0}{10} = 1.00$$

Whenever we obtain an F of 1 or less, we are rather certain that chance (that is, the chance that the error variance introduced by the variability of the Ss within the groups) and chance alone has influenced the dependent variable. Whenever we obtain an F of more than 1, the numerator is larger than the denominator, it exceeds chance expectations, and the likelihood exists that the independent variable (experimental treatment) did cause a change in the dependent variable.

We can now return to our problem and find the F values for each source of variance.

$$F = \frac{\text{between rows } MS}{\text{within-cells } MS} = \frac{6,002.5}{241.611} = 24.844$$

$$F = \frac{\text{between-columns } MS}{\text{within-cells } MS} = \frac{2.5}{241.611} = .01034,$$

$$F = \frac{\text{interaction}}{\text{within-cells } MS} = \frac{22.5}{241.611} = .093124$$

If an F value is 1 or less, an investigator usually does not record it on the analysis of variance table, for he knows the treatment did not have an effect on the dependent variable. Hence we will record only the between-rows F value, 24.844 (see Table A.8).

---

[5] We should be aware of the fact that the correct error term (denominator) for the F ratio is determined by the type of factorial design that is employed in the study: fixed, random, or mixed model. When the fixed model is used as it is in our problem, the correct error term (denominator) for the F ratio is the within-cells mean square. The correct error terms for random and fixed models can be found in statistics books. The definitions of the three models are as follows:

Fixed constant model: the E chooses, in a premeditated manner, the two values for X_1 and X_2; neither types of teaching methods nor length of classes is selected at random.
Random model: the X_1 and X_2 values are selected at random from normally distributed populations.
Mixed model: one independent variable is fixed; one independent variable is random.

[6] The theory of analysis of variance is based on the principle that two estimates of the variance of a single population should be approximately equal. If there has been no treatment effect, theoretically the two estimates of variance will be equal, but sample variances, like sample means, will fluctuate from sample to sample; hence, the variance estimates obtained for a given sample will not necessarily be exactly equal.

INTERPRETATION OF THE RESULTS

Because an F of less than 1 is automatically nonsignificant, we have already concluded that we must accept the null hypotheses that there is no difference between the effect on learning achievement produced by variations of length of class period (columns, $F = .01034$) and there is no interaction between the method of teaching and the length of class period (interaction, $F = .093124$).

Our next task is to ascertain whether the F value we have obtained that is more than 1 (rows, $F = 24.844$) is statistically significant for the size of the sample. Although we assigned Ss at random to groups, by chance the more able students may have been assigned to the discussion group and the less able Ss to the lecture group. Fortunately, statisticians have provided us with a distribution of F table that tells us how large the obtained F values must be to be statistically significant at the .05 and .01 levels. The table informs us that an F value as high as the one it stipulates for the size of our sample could occur by chance (sampling variation) only 5 times in 100 at the .05 level and 1 time in 100 at the .01 level of significance.

Reading a distribution of F table, which, in part, is reproduced on Table A.9 is similar to reading a mileage chart on a road map. Note that the columns are headed by the df associated with the greater mean square (numerator of the F ratio) and the rows are labeled with the df associated with the lesser mean square (the denominator of the F ratio). Turning back to Table A.8, we find that in our problem 1 df is associated with the rows MS (greater mean square), and 36 df are associated with the within MS (lesser mean square). We locate 1 df in the row across the top of the table of F (Table A.9), go down this column to row 36, and read the sum where the column 1 and row 36 intersect: $\frac{4.11}{7.39}$. The upper figure, 4.11, gives the value our obtained F must equal or better for significance at the .05 level, and the lower figure, **7.39**, gives the value at the .01 level.

Our obtained F for rows, 24.844, is more than 4.11, the required F value for significance at the .05 level. We can, therefore, through the magnitude of the F value, reject the null hypothesis that there is no difference between the effect on learning achievement produced by variations of the methods of teaching (rows). We can conclude with confidence that a significant difference does exist between the row

TABLE A.9

The 5 (Roman Type) and 1 (Boldface Type) Percent Points for the Distribution of F*

DEGREES OF FREEDOM (FOR LESSER MEAN SQUARE)	DEGREES OF FREEDOM (FOR GREATER MEAN SQUARE)									
	1	2	3	4	5	6	7	8	9	10
1	161	200	216	225	230	234	237	239	241	242
	4,052	**4,999**	**5,403**	**5,625**	**5,764**	**5,859**	**5,928**	**5,981**	**6,022**	**6,056**
2	18.51	19.00	19.16	19.25	19.30	19.33	19.36	19.37	19.38	19.39
	98.49	**99.00**	**99.17**	**99.25**	**99.30**	**99.33**	**99.34**	**99.36**	**99.38**	**99.40**
3	10.13	9.55	9.28	9.12	9.01	8.94	8.88	8.84	8.81	8.78
	34.12	**30.82**	**29.46**	**28.71**	**28.24**	**27.91**	**27.67**	**27.49**	**27.34**	**27.23**
34	4.13	3.28	2.88	2.65	2.49	2.38	2.30	2.23	2.17	2.12
	7.44	**5.29**	**4.42**	**3.93**	**3.61**	**3.38**	**3.21**	**3.08**	**2.97**	**2.89**
36	4.11	3.26	2.86	2.63	2.48	2.36	2.28	2.21	2.15	2.10
	7.39	**5.25**	**4.38**	**3.89**	**3.58**	**3.35**	**3.18**	**3.04**	**2.94**	**2.86**
38	4.10	3.25	2.85	2.62	2.46	2.35	2.26	2.19	2.14	2.09
	7.35	**5.21**	**4.34**	**3.86**	**3.54**	**3.32**	**3.15**	**3.02**	**2.91**	**2.82**

* Abridged and adapted from G. W. Snedecor, *Statistical Methods*, 5th ed., 1956, Iowa State University Press, Ames, Iowa, by permission of the author and publisher.

means,[7] that is, between the effects on learning achievement produced by the lecture and discussion methods of teaching. To convey this information on the analysis of variance table, we place an asterisk superior to this row F value and indicate the level of significance below the table, $\rho < .05$ (see Table A.8).

Readers of a research report usually focus their attention on the magnitude of the F values attained, for an F value indicates whether a hypothesis can or cannot be rejected at a given level of significance. A statistically significant difference exists between the means of the discussion and lecture methods. This statistical difference, however, is not necessarily of practical significance to educators. They judge the importance and meaningfulness of this difference for their programs by evaluating how large the mean difference is, classroom space available, class size, cost, and other factors.

In closing we should note that theoretically the following assumptions underlying the use of analysis of variance must be satisfied in order to yield information which permits the drawing of valid infer-

[7] The direction of the difference is given by the row means.

ences. These assumptions are as follows: (1) Observations within each group are random samples drawn from a normally distributed population of scores for the variable in question. (2) Variances within the groups are approximately equal. Before the analysis of variance is made, this assumption is usually evaluated by Bartlett's test (or some other test) for homogeneity of variance. (3) Contributions to total variance must be additive. The two estimates of the population variance that are used to obtain the F ratio must be independent of one another.

Although some experiments do not meet the specific characteristics which analysis of variance requires, there is considerable evidence to indicate that the results of the analysis are changed very little by moderate departures from assumptions of normal distributions and equal variances.

BIBLIOGRAPHY

1   Allen, David *et al.,* "Spence's Theory of Discrimination of Learning: A Re-evaluation," *Psychological Record,* 19 (July 1969): 443.

2   Ad hoc Committee on Ethical Standards in Psychological Research, *Ethical Principles in the Conduct of Research with Human Participants.* Washington, D.C.: American Psychological Association, 1973.

3   Atkinson, J. W. and N. T. Feather (eds.), *A Theory of Achievement Motivation.* New York: Wiley, 1966.

4   Aydelotte, William O., "Quantification in History," *American Historical Review,* 71 (April 1966): 803.

5   Bacon, Margaret K. *et al.,* "A Cross-Cultural Study of Correlates of Crime," *Journal of Abnormal and Social Psychology,* 66 (April 1963): 291.

6   Baizerman, Michael *et al.,* "A Critique of the Research Literature Concerning Pregnant Adolescents, 1960–1970," *Journal of Youth and Adolescents,* 3 (March 1974): 61.

7   Baldwin, Alfred L. (ed.), *Theories of Child Development.* New York: Wiley, 1967.

8   Balow, Irving H. and Bruce Balow, "Lateral Dominance and Reading Achievements in the Second Grade," *American Educational Research Journal,* 1 (May 1964): 139.

9   Barker, R. G. and H. F. Wright, *One Boy's Diary: A Specimen Record of Behavior.* New York: Harper, 1951.

10   Berelson, Bernard, *Content Analysis in Communication Research.* New York: Free Press, 1952.

11   Block, Marc, *The Historian's Craft.* New York: Knopf, 1953.

12   Brickman, William W., "Comparative Education," *Encyclopedia of Educational Research.* New York: Macmillan, 1969: 184.

13   Brown, Clarence W. and Edwin E. Ghiselli, *Scientific Method in Psychology.* New York: McGraw-Hill, 1955.

14   Burt, Cyril, "Review: A Young Girl's Diary," *The British Journal of Psychology, Medical Section* 1 (July 1921): 353.

15   Butts, R. Freeman, *The American Tradition in Religion and Education.* Boston: Beacon Press, 1950.

16   Campbell, Donald T., "Quasi-Experimental Design," supported in part by Project C-998, with the Office of Education, U.S. Department of Health, Education and Welfare. Evanston, Ill.: Northwestern University, mimeograph, n.d.

17   Campbell, Donald T. and J. C. Stanley, "Experimental and Quasi-experimental Designs for Research on Teaching," in N. L. Gage (ed.), *Handbook of Research on Teaching.* Chicago: Rand McNally, 1963.

18   Campbell, W. G. and S. V. Ballou, *Form and Style: Thesis, Reports, Term Papers.* Boston: Houghton Mifflin, 1974.

19   Chalfant, James C. and Margaret A. Scheffelin, *Central Processing Dysfunctions in Children, A Review of Research.* National Institute of Neurological Diseases and Stroke, Washington, D.C.: U.S. Department of Health, Education and Welfare, 1970.

20   Chiappetta, Michael, "Historiography and Roman Education," *History of Education Journal,* 4 (Summer 1953): 149.

21   Churchman, C. West and P. Ratoosh, *Measurement: Definitions and Theories.* New York: Wiley, 1959.

22   Cohen, Morris, R. and Ernest Nagel, *An Introduction to Logic and Scientific Method.* New York: Harcourt, Brace & World, 1934.

23   Coleman, J. S., *Equality of Educational Opportunity.* Washington, D.C.: U.S. Goverment Printing Office, 1966.

24   Commager, Henry Steel, *The Study of History.* Columbus, Ohio: Merrill, 1966.

25   Cronbach, Lee J., "The Two Disciplines of Scientific Psychology," *American Psychologist,* 12 (November 1957): 671.

26 Cronbach, Lee J., "Validity," in Chester W. Harris (ed.), *Encyclopedia of Educational Research.* New York: Macmillan, 1960.

27 Cronbach, Lee J. and Paul Meehl, "Construct Validity in Psychological Tests," *Psychological Bulletin,* 52 (1955): 281.

28 Davis, Gordon B., *Computer Data Processing.* New York: McGraw-Hill, 1969.

29 Denzin, Norman K., "Play, Games and Interaction: The Contexts of Childhood Socialization," *Sociological Quarterly,* 16 (Autumn 1975): 458.

30 Dewey, John, *How We Think.* Boston: Heath, 1933.

31 Dimitroff, Lillian, "A Quantitative-Qualitative Analysis of Selected Social Science Generalizations in Social Studies Textbooks in the Intermediate Grades," *Journal of Educational Research,* 55 (November 1961): 135.

32 Dorson, Richard M., "A Theory of American Folklore Reviewed," *Journal of American Folklore,* 82 (July—September 1969): 226.

33 Draper, Andrew S., *Origin and Development of the Common School System of the State of New York.* Syracuse, N.Y.: C. W. Bardeen, 1903.

34 Dugdale, Kathleen, *A Manual of Form for Theses and Term Papers.* Bloomington, Ind.: Indiana University Bookstore, 1967.

35 Durkheim, Emile, *Suicide* (translated by John A. Spaulding and George Simpson). London: Routledge, 1952.

36 Eells, Walter C., "First American Degrees in Music," *History of Education Quarterly,* 1 (March 1961): 35.

37 Elliott, Clark A., "The American Scientist in Antebellum Society: A Quantitative View," *Social Studies of Science,* 5 (1975): 93.

38 Fell, Sister Marie Léonore, *The Foundations of Nativism in American Textbooks, 1783–1860.* Washington, D.C.: Catholic, 1941.

39 Fisher R. A. and F. Yates, *Statistical Tables for Biological, Agricultural, and Medical Research.* Edinburgh: Oliver & Boyd, 1963.

40 Foshay, Arthur W., *et al., Educational Achievements of Thirteen-year-olds in Twelve Countries.* Hamburg: UNESCO Institute for Education, 1962.

41 Fox, Lawrence W. and Carl E. Wedekind, "Studies of Predicted Quality Point Average and Cross Validation Based on the Freshman Classes Entering the University of Pittsburgh in Fall of 1959 and the Fall of 1960." Pittsburgh, Pa.: Office of Institute Planning, University of Pittsburgh, 1961.

42 Galilei, Galileo, *Dialogues Concerning Two New Sciences.* Evanston, Ill.: Northwestern University Press, 1946.

43 Garrett, Henry, *Statistics in Psychology and Education.* New York: McKay, 1966.

44 Goethals, George W. and John W. M. Whiting, "Research Methods: The

Cross-Cultural Method," *Review of Educational Research,* 27 (December 1957): 441.

45 Gottschalk, Louis, *Understanding History.* New York: Knopf, 1956.

46 Griffiths, Daniel E., *Research in Educational Administration.* New York: Bureau of Publications, Teachers College, Columbia University, 1959.

47 Griffiths, D. E., "Administrative Theory," In R. L. Ebel (ed.), *Encyclopedia of Educational Research.* New York: Macmillan, 1969.

48 Guilford, J. P., *Fundamental Statistics in Psychology and Education.* New York: McGraw-Hill, 1965.

49 Harman, Grant, "Continuities and Research Gaps in Politics of Education," *Social Science Quarterly,* 55 (September 1974): 262.

50 Henderson, Robert W., *Ball, Bat and Bishop.* New York: Rockport Press, 1947.

51 Hilgard, Ernest R. and G. H. Bower, *Theories of Learning.* New York: Appleton, Century, Crofts, 1966.

52 Hodnett, Edward, *The Art of Problem Solving.* New York: Harper & Row, 1955.

53 Hollenberg, Eleanor, "Child Training among the Zuni with Special Reference to the Internalization of Moral Values," Doctoral Thesis. Cambridge, Mass.: Harvard University, 1952.

54 Hug-Hellmuth, Hermine (ed.), *A Young Girl's Diary.* New York: Thomas Seltzer, 1923.

55 Husén, Torsten (ed.), *International Study of Achievement in Mathematics: A Comparison of Twelve Countries.* New York: Wiley, 1967.

56 Hyram, George H., "An Experiment in Developing Critical Thinking in Children," *Journal of Experimental Education,* 26 (December 1957): 125.

57 Jackson, Douglas N. and S. Messich, *Problems in Human Assessment.* New York: McGraw-Hill, 1967.

58 Johnson, Allen, *The Historian and Historical Evidence.* New York: Scribner, 1930.

59 Jones, Harold E., *Development in Adolescence.* New York: Appleton-Century-Crofts, 1943.

60 Kemp, William W., "The Support of Schools in Colonial New York by The Society for the Propagation of the Gospel in Foreign Parts," *Contributions to Education,* no. 56. New York: Bureau of Publications, Teachers College, Columbia University, 1913.

61 Kerlinger, Fred N., *Foundations of Behavioral Research.* New York: Holt, 1973.

62 Kerlinger, Fred N. (ed.), *Review of Research in Education.* Itasca, Ill.: F. E. Peacock, 1973.

63   Knox, Ronald (trans.), *The Autobiography of St. Therese of Lisieux.* New York: Kenedy, 1968.

64   Krug, Josef, "Kritische Bemerkungen zu dem Tagebuch eines halbwüchsigen Mädchens," *Zeitschrift für Angewandte Psychologie,* 27 (July 1926): 350.

65   Larrabee, Harold A., *Reliable Knowledge.* Boston: Houghton Mifflin, 1945.

66   Leonard, Fred E. and George B. Affleck, *A Guide to the History of Physical Education,* Philadelphia: Lea & Febiger, 1947.

67   Lohnes, Paul R. and William W. Cooley, *Introduction to Statistical Procedures: With Computer Exercises.* New York: Wiley, 1968.

68   McClelland, D. C., *The Achieving Society.* Princeton, N.J.: Van Nostrand, 1961.

69   *A Manual of Style,* 12th ed. Chicago: University of Chicago Press, 1969.

70   Margenau, Henry, *The Nature of Physical Reality.* New York: McGraw-Hill, 1950.

71   Marx, Melvin, H., *Theories in Contemporary Psychology.* New York: Macmillan, 1963.

72   Michael, William B., "Prediction," *Encyclopedia of Educational Research.* New York: Macmillan, 1969: 982.

73   Mill, John S., *A System of Logic.* New York: Harper, 1846.

74   Mitzel, Harold E., "A Behavioral Approach to the Assessment of Teacher Effectiveness." New York: Office of Research and Evaluation, Division of Teacher Education, mimeograph, 1957.

75   Murdock, George P. *et al., Outline of Cultural Materials.* New Haven, Conn.: Human Relations Area Files, 1965.

76   Muuss, Rolf E., *Theories of Adolescence.* New York: Random House, 1964.

77   Northrop, F. S. C., *The Logic of the Sciences and the Humanities.* New York: Macmillan, 1949.

78   Nunnally, Jum C., *Psychometric Theory.* New York: McGraw-Hill, 1967.

79   Polsky, Ned., *Hustlers, Beats and Others.* Garden City, N. Y.: Anchor, Doubleday, 1969.

80   Report of the Committee on Historiography, *Theory and Practice in Historical Study.* New York: Social Science Research Council, 1946.

81   Richey, Harold W., "Avoidable Failures of Experimental Procedures," *The Journal of Experimental Education,* 45 (Winter 1976): 10.

82   Rose, Arnold M., *Theory and Method in the Social Sciences.* Minneapolis: University of Minnesota Press, 1954.

83   Rosenberg, Morris, *The Logic of Survey Analysis.* New York: Basic Books, 1968.

84   Rosenthal, Robert and R. L. Rosnow, *Artifact in Behavioral Research.* New York: Academic, 1969.

85   Ross, John A., and Perry Smith, "Experimental Designs of the Single-stimulus All-or-nothing Type," *American Sociological Review,* 30 (February 1965): 68.

86   Ruebhausen, Oscar and Orville Brim, Jr., "Privacy and Behavioral Research," *Columbia Law Review,* 65 (May 1965): 1184.

87   Russell, Bertrand, *An Outline of Philosophy.* London: G. Allen, 1927.

88   Salmon, Wesley C., *Logic.* Englewood Cliffs, N. J.: Prentice-Hall, 1963.

89   Scates, Douglas E., "The Conceptual Background of Research," in *The Conceptual Structure of Educational Research,* Chicago: University of Chicago Press, 1942.

90   Schlesinger, A. M., "History," in W. Gee (ed.), *Research in the Social Sciences.* New York: Macmillan, 1929.

91   Searles, Herbert L., *Logic and Scientific Methods.* New York: Ronald, 1948.

92   Sellitz, Claire *et al., Research Methods in Social Relations.* New York: Holt, 1962.

93   Seybolt, Robert F., "The S.P.G. Myth: A Note on Education in Colonial New York," *Journal of Educational Research,* 13 (February 1926): 129.

94   Simon, Herbert A. and Allen Newell, "Human Problem Solving: The State of the Theory in 1970," *American Psychologists,* 26 (February 1971): 145.

95   Sindell, Peter S., "Anthropological Approaches to the Study of Education," *Review of Educational Research,* 39 (December 1969): 593.

96   Smith, Louis M. and William Geoffrey, *The Complexities of an Urban Classroom,* New York: Holt, 1968.

97   Smith, Mildred M., "An Analysis of Stories in Basal Readers with Cultural Settings Outside Continental United States," *Studies in Education 1959,* Thesis Abstract Series, School of Education, Indiana University, 11 (1960): 259.

98   Solomon, Richard L., "An Extension of Control Group Design," *Psychological Bulletin,* 46 (no. 4, 1949): 137.

99   Sorokin, Pitirim A., *Social and Cultural Dynamics,* vol. 3, New York: American Book, 1937.

100   Spahr, Walter E. and Rinehart J. Swenson, *Methods and Status of Scientific Research.* New York: Harper, 1930.

101   Stanley, William O. and B. Othanel Smith, "The Historical, Philosophical, and Social Framework of Education," *Review of Educational Research,* 26 (June 1956): 308.

102   Starr, Chester G., "Reflections Upon the Problem of Generalization," in Louis Gottschalk (ed.), *Generalization in the Writing of History.* Chicago: University of Chicago Press, 1963.

103 Stouffer, Samuel A., *Communism, Conformity, and Civil Liberties.* Garden City, N.Y.: Doubleday, 1955.

104 Subcommittee on Health, of the Committee on Labor and Public Welfare, United States Senate, *Federal Regulations of Human Experimentation, 1975.* Washington D.C.: U.S. Goverment Printing Office, 1975.

105 Taba, Hilda, and Elizabeth Noel, *Action Research,* Washington, D.C.: Association for Supervision and Curriculum Development, 1957.

106 Thorndike, Robert L. (ed.), *Educational Measurement.* Washington, D.C.: American Council on Education, 1971.

107 Thucydides, *The History of the Peloponnesian War* (Translated by H. Dale). London: G. Bell, 1912.

108 Thurstone, L. L. and E. J. Chave, *The Measurement of Attitude.* Chicago: University of Chicago Press, 1929.

109 Torgerson, Warren S., *Theory and Methods of Scaling.* New York: Wiley, 1958.

110 Travers, Robert M. W. (ed.), *Second Handbook of Research on Teaching.* Chicago: Rand McNally, 1973.

111 Turabian, Kate L., *A Manual for Writers of Term Papers, Theses, and Dissertations.* Chicago: University of Chicago Press, 1973.

112 Werkmeister, W. H., *An Introduction to Critical Thinking.* Lincoln, Nebr.: Johnsen Publishing Company, 1948.

113 Whiting, Beatrice (ed.), *Six Cultures: Studies of Child Rearing.* New York: Wiley, 1963.

114 Winchell, Constance M., *Guide to Reference Books,* 8th ed., Chicago: American Library Association, 1968.

115 Woody, Thomas, "Of History and Its Methods," *Journal of Experimental Education,* 15 (March 1947): 175.

116 Young, Pauline V., *Scientific Social Surveys and Research.* Englewood Cliffs, N.J.: Prentice-Hall, 1956.

NAME INDEX

SUBJECT INDEX